Interpreting Fear, Crime, Risk and Unsafety

Interpreting Fear, Crime, Risk and Unsafety

Conceptualisation and measurement

/ ι / οο /

Gabry Vanderveen

Boom Juridische uitgevers
Den Haag
2006

ISBN   90 5454 660 3
NUR   820
www.bju.nl

To Nala, Stip and Dick

Table of contents

Preface...1

1   Introduction: fear and crime 1
   1.1   Background..1
      1.1.1   Six blind men and one elephant 1
      1.1.2   Interdisciplinary approach...3
   1.2   Goal and focus 4
   1.3   Main research questions...6
   1.4   Scientific relevance 6
      1.4.1   Current gaps and debates 7
   1.5   Social relevance 8
   1.6   Structure of this book...17
      1.6.1   Basic terms..17
      1.6.2   Outline 20

2   Overview of concepts and measurement...23
   2.1   Reviewing the literature: concepts and indicators.....................24
      2.1.1   Conceptualisation...28
      2.1.2   Translating concepts: operationalisation 30
      2.1.3   Criteria: validity and reliability 31
   2.2   Data: studies under review 32
   2.3   Findings 35
      2.3.1   Brief overview of general findings..36
      2.3.1.1   Objective, type of knowledge and research questions...............36
      2.3.1.2   Data collection and presentation 37
   2.4   Concepts and theoretical models...38
      2.4.1   Classification of concepts 38
      2.4.2   Theoretical models on causes of 'fear of crime' 41
   2.5   Operationalisations, indicators and items.....................................45
      2.5.1   The cognitive modality: perceptions and estimates....................48
      2.5.1.1   Estimating the magnitude of crime 48
      2.5.1.2   Various comparisons..48
      2.5.1.3   The impact of crime: seriousness of the consequences and vulnerability 50
      2.5.1.4   Perceiving risks..52
      2.5.2   The affective modality: feelings of unsafety, concern and worry..........53
      2.5.2.1   Fear, worry or concern about victimisation................................53
      2.5.2.2   Altruistic fear: fear of others' victimisation 54
      2.5.2.3   Feeling safe at home alone 55
      2.5.2.4   Feeling safe walking alone at night...56
      2.5.3   The conative modality: avoid, protect and prevent 57
      2.5.3.1   Avoiding scary places: behavioural constraints 57
      2.5.3.2   Tear gas and dogs: security measures for protection and defence...........58
   2.6   Appraising the current state of affairs 58
      2.6.1   Problematic conceptualisation and operationalisation................60
   2.7   Do all roads lead to Rome? Consequences of methodological choices....61
      2.7.1   Using a single indicator: Feeling safe when walking alone....................62
      2.7.2   Reliability and validity...64
      2.7.3   Overall evaluation of the current state of affairs 65

3   **Secondary analyses** **69**
    3.1   General method 70
    3.2   Fear of crime in the neighbourhood and shopping area...........................71
        3.2.1   Analysis neighbourhood-items..72
        3.2.2   Analysis shopping area-items..73
        3.2.3   Conclusions..74
    3.3   Perceiving risks..75
        3.3.1   Analysis of five items on perceived risk 75
        3.3.2   Conclusions..77
    3.4   Concern about crimes...78
        3.4.1   Analysis of six items on concern...79
        3.4.2   Conclusions..81
    3.5   General discussion and conclusion..81

4   **Concepts within contexts**...**85**
    4.1   The importance of conceptualisation 86
        4.1.1   Conceptualisation and the social-historical context(s) 87
    4.2   Social constructions 89
        4.2.1   Integration of perspectives 90
    4.3   The meaning(s) of a concept 91
        4.3.1   Analysing meaning 92

5   **Statistics, surveys and attitudinal knowledge**...**95**
    5.1   Statistical opportunities..97
    5.2   Surveying society 100
        5.2.1   Surveys on criminal victimisation and the police.............................100
        5.2.2   Criticism on quantification..105
    5.3   Conclusion: statistics & surveys count...106

6   **The diversity of victimisation** **109**
    6.1   Criminal victimisation..110
        6.1.1   Violence 113
        6.1.2   Gendered victimisation: sexual violence, assault and harassment..........115
        6.1.3   Unpleasant things that happen..120
    6.2   Indirect victimisation and altruistic fear..123
    6.3   Imaginable victimisation 124
    6.4   Images of the victim...127
        6.4.1   Sources of images 129
        6.4.1.1   Stories, rumours and urban myths...130
        6.4.1.2   Crime time on television 134
        6.4.1.3   Crime pictured in motion 135
        6.4.1.4   Crime in print..137
    6.5   The ideal victim 138
        6.5.1   The ideal victim as a role 139
    6.6   Criminal victimisation and the meaning of fear of crime.......................142

7   **Risk (perception)** **147**
    7.1   Risk: a calculated value...149
        7.1.1   Calculus of risk 151
        7.1.2   Signification of risk..153
        7.1.3   Taming of risk: prevention and exposure..156
        7.1.3.1   Exposure, behavioural constraints and victimisation risk 156

7.2	Two regular themes	160
7.2.1	Real risks or irrational fears	160
7.2.2	Increased risk or increased risk awareness	165
7.2.2.1	More and different risks	166
7.2.2.2	More risk consciousness	167
7.2.2.2.1	Demanding safety and the lack of trust	169
7.2.2.3	Issues of safety and ever-present danger	171
7.3	Perceiving hazards	174
7.3.1	Crime as a hazard	175
7.3.2	Typical features of dreaded hazards	177
7.3.3	Crime as (highly) dreaded hazard	180
7.3.3.1	Predictability and cause: attribution of responsibility and blame	182
7.3.3.1.1	Responsibility of institutions: trustworthiness	183
7.3.3.2	Identifiable victims	184
7.3.3.3	Type of consequences: worst case scenarios	186
7.3.3.4	Risk perception and the 'other': unrealistic optimism	186
7.4	Risk and the meaning of fear of crime	188
7.4.1	Analogies between fear of crime and risk perception	190
7.4.1.1	Risk as a feeling	193
8	**More than one 'fear of crime'**	**197**
8.1	Conditions of 'fear of crime'	198
8.2	Fear of crime as political symbol	199
8.2.1	Politics, policy and public opinion	200
8.2.1.1	Vigilantism (eigenrichting)	200
8.2.1.2	Public opinion as feature of a democracy	202
8.2.1.3	Press: 'fear of crime' in the news	203
8.2.2	Law & order: politics of zero tolerance	206
8.2.2.1	Democracy at work	206
8.2.2.2	Fear of crime as social problem	207
8.2.2.3	Concern about crime and drugs: 'fear of crime' politicised	208
8.2.3	The meaning of 'fear of crime'	212
8.3	Fear of crime as psychological construct	213
8.3.1	All kinds of fear	214
8.3.1.1	Fear of crime as propositional attitude	215
8.3.1.2	Fear of crime as personality trait	216
8.3.1.3	Fear of crime as instrument of social control	217
8.3.1.4	Fear of crime as aspect of the quality of life	217
8.3.2	Experiental fear: fear of crime as emotion of danger	218
8.3.3	Propositional and expressed fear	219
8.3.3.1	Fear of crime as fear of strangers	219
8.3.3.2	Fear of crime as infringement of territory	219
8.3.3.3	Fear of crime as part of city life	220
8.4	Meaning of fear	222
9	**Two strategies to improve measurement: continue & start over**	**225**
9.1	Continue or start over: pros and cons	226
9.1.1	Continue	226
9.1.1.1	Pros	226
9.1.1.2	Cons	227
9.1.2	Start over: pros and cons	228
9.1.2.1	Pros	228
9.1.2.2	Cons	228

9.1.3   Two strategies: advantages and disadvantages 229
9.1.3.1   Methodological limitations of the improved measurement instruments. 229
9.1.3.1.1   Respondents 230
9.1.3.1.2   Self-report 230
9.2   Continuation: inventory 232
9.3   Study I: Experiencing safety in the subway 233
9.3.1   Method 234
9.3.1.1   Respondents 234
9.3.1.2   Instrument 234
9.3.1.3   Procedure 235
9.3.2   Analysis and results subway-items 235
9.3.2.1   Multidimensional Scaling 237
9.3.3   Brief discussion of results 239
9.4   Study II: Vignettes 240
9.4.1   Method 240
9.4.1.1   Respondents 240
9.4.1.2   Instrument 240
9.4.1.3   Procedure 242
9.4.2   Analysis and results 242
9.4.2.1   Means 242
9.4.2.2   Three reliable scales 243
9.4.2.3   Latent construct 243
9.4.2.4   Three types of items 246
9.4.2.5   Format of items 248
9.4.3   Brief discussion of results 249
9.5   Study III: The inventory 251
9.5.1   Method 251
9.5.1.1   Respondents 251
9.5.1.2   Instrument 251
9.5.1.3   Procedure 254
9.5.2   General analysis and results of the inventory 255
9.5.2.1   Results of the factor analysis: general relationships 255
9.5.3   Analysis and results three-factor solution 258
9.5.3.1   Retaining three factors 258
9.5.4   Discussion of general results 259
9.6   Deriving an instrument from the inventory 260
9.6.1   Proposal of improved instrument based on traditional instruments 262

10   Starting over: portraying safety, risk and crime 265
10.1   Starting over: measuring meaning, imaging safety 266
10.1.1   Semantic differential 267
10.1.2   The meaning(s) of a concept (again) 268
10.2   Construction of the instrument (semantic differential format) 269
10.2.1   Which concepts? 270
10.2.1.1   Fear 270
10.2.1.2   Crime, rape and violence 270
10.2.1.3   Precautions, protection, defensibility and vulnerability 271
10.2.1.4   Risk and danger 271
10.2.1.5   Safety, unsafety and insecurity 272
10.2.1.6   Accident and natural disaster 272
10.2.1.7   Fault and inattention 273
10.2.1.8   Concern, social concern and concern about others 273

10.2.1.9   Twenty concepts 274
10.2.2   Which adjectives? 276
10.2.2.1   Initial selection...276
10.3   Initial administration 276
10.3.1   Method..276
10.3.1.1   Respondents 276
10.3.1.2   Instrument 277
10.3.1.3   Procedure 278
10.3.1.4   Data...278
10.3.2   Preliminary analyses of the adjectives 278
10.3.2.1   Selection of adjectives: factor analyses....................................279
10.3.2.2   Subsequent analyses of the adjectives.......................................280
10.4   Possible applications: concepts and people..............................281
10.4.1   Concepts..282
10.4.1.1   Grouping the concepts...282
10.4.1.1.1 Results from MDS 282
10.4.1.1.2 Results from HCA..286
10.4.1.1.3 Factor analysis 287
10.4.1.1.4 Interpretation of concepts: results from MDS, HCA and PCA 288
10.4.1.2   Evaluation of concepts..289
10.4.1.3   Profiles of concepts 293
10.4.1.3.1 Fear 293
10.4.1.3.2 Is safety the opposite of unsafety ? 294
10.4.1.3.3 Does risk signify danger?..295
10.4.1.3.4 Is crime just another hazard?..296
10.4.1.3.5 Crime, violence and rape...297
10.4.1.3.6 Comparing the profiles of different groups: gender differences.............298
10.4.2   People..300
10.4.2.1   An attitude scale from the semantic differential instrument.................300
10.4.2.1.1 Comparing Likert-type scales with semantic differential scales 301
10.4.2.1.2 Comparing socio-demographic groups: sex and age 304
10.4.2.1.3 A reduced scale 305
10.5   Portraying safety 308

11   Interpreting fear, crime, risk and safety..311
11.1   Two basic problems: concept and measurement 312
11.1.1   Unclear conceptualisation 312
11.1.2   Defective operationalisation..313
11.2   Improved conceptualisation and operationalisation 313
11.3   Measuring 'fear of crime': guidelines.......................................314
11.3.1   What to do and what not to do in general..................................314
11.3.2   Improved instruments: concepts and their measurement.................316
11.4   Suggestions for future research 319
11.4.1   Start stealing...319
11.4.2   Validity of gender differences..319
11.4.3   Standard of living & wellbeing 320
11.5   Conclusion 320

Appendices..**323**
References **363**
Samenvatting..**421**
Index..**423**
About the author **425**

Preface

'KISS' (Keep It Simple, Stupid), 'Less is more', 'Kill your darlings' and '*In der Beschränkung zeigt sich erst der Meister*'. This acronym and proverbs tell the same thing: it is simplicity we strive for. Some of us succeed: Dick Bruna's ingenious drawings of Miffy (*Nijntje*) are popular across the globe. Also, the stereotypes and schemas that we *all* use are intended to make life simpler and easier. Yet, we do not actually live in the world that Bruna created and our stereotypes or schemas are definitely not always successful; they can cause problems when a dynamic social situation calls for a more advanced conscious interpretation. The balance between the need for simplicity and acknowledging complexity and multi-layeredness is difficult, especially in a constantly changing society within a globalising world.

Balancing between simplicity and complexity has certainly been a challenge for me, in several respects. When I started this research project, 'fear of crime' seemed to me something quite clear and simple, but I know better now. 'Fear of crime' is much more complex; my research has problematised the concept 'fear of crime' and this book is indeed complicating things though it does end with a set of straightforward guidelines. Obviously, neither social phenomena, nor the research process are simple; mine certainly was not. My gratitude to the persons who have stimulated and enabled me to continue my research and finish this book is indescribable. First of all, I would like to thank Dick Hessing and Henk Elffers, my *promotores* who kept believing in the successful completion of this book, even when I did not. I am so saddened that Dick cannot be here today in person. When Dick passed away, Nick Huls kindly agreed to become my *promotor* and together with Henk, he has been of invaluable support to me. Their constructive criticism has not only been *very* clear and essential, but has been inspiring as well and kept me going.

During my time at the Erasmus University, I have met several interesting and special people who have been or still are important to me. I am fortunate that some of them have become my friends and would like to mention Helene, Juan, Miklos, Nadja, Patrick, and Suzan. Since September 2002, I have had the pleasure to work with my enthusiastic and talented colleagues of the Division of Criminology & Penology at Leiden University. I am grateful that they have given me the opportunity to finish this book. My editor, Adriënne Baars-Schuyt, has been of crucial importance in the final phase as well.

Very special thanks go to my family, and papa & mama in particular, who have supported me unconditionally. You, and Tineke & Dick too, have made life easier on me when I needed it the most, sometimes (Kyra!) just by existing or being there. Next to doing research and writing a dissertation, having a relationship, illness, pregnancies and ultimately a gorgeous joyous marvellous daughter certainly complicates things. Nonetheless, together with Robin and Rivka I enjoy the elementary aspects of life. Robin, our relationship has never been a boring routine and I cherish the long-term commitment we share.

1 Introduction: fear and crime

In this introduction, the background, the main goal and focus of the research project will be described, as well as the principal research questions. Also, the project's scientific and social relevance is discussed. This introductory chapter concludes with an introduction of basic terms that are used and with an outline of this book.

1.1 Background

Before one can study the factors that determine or influence the nature and extent of 'fear of crime', two other questions need clarification first. These two questions, on the conceptualisation and operationalisations of 'fear of crime', are addressed in this book.

1.1.1 Six blind men and one elephant

This research project can very well be described by the traditional story of six blind men who encounter an elephant, of which a version is written by for example the American poet John Godfrey Saxe (e.g. Wordfocus n.d.). In short, each man touches a different part of the elephant, which leads to six different conclusions about what the elephant is like. For example, the man who feels the side says the elephant is like a wall, but the man who feels the tusk is convinced the elephant is very like a spear and the man touching the trunk thinks the elephant is like a snake. Each man assumes the whole elephant is like the part he perceives, but by touching only part of the elephant, they fail to see the whole unique creature. The story illustrates how different people can have distinctly different perceptions of the same thing, how limited knowledge of reality can be, or even how truth or reality can be many things. Yet, though the men may be partly right, they are wrong as well. Not only are the men talking about different parts of the elephant, they inadequately believe that by perceiving the one part which they touched, they know the whole elephant. One man alone gives an incomplete description, and their description would probably improve when they would have touched the other parts of the elephant as well; that is, a description that incorporates the different parts, e.g. the trunk, the ear, the tail, as well as how they are joined together into the whole elephant, is a better description and closer to the truth. A complex phenomenon cannot be described or pictured when only one or two parts are studied in isolation, without reference to the context. For example, is the Morale as presented by Saxe true and to what extent is the interpretation influenced when one would know that one of the claimed origins is India, and that the Hindu god Ganesh(a) has an elephant-head and is the god who solves difficulties?

The story of the six blind men is used here to describe the research project. Analogous to the elephant, the concept of so-called 'fear of crime' can be considered a complex phenomenon. Contrary to the elephant, we do not know what the whole picture of 'fear of crime' looks like; of which and of how many parts it is constituted. Yet, during the initial examination of the available

literature it became clear that research on 'fear of crime' is confusing, which begins with the very meaning of the concept. There seem to be several prevailing usages, and some of the disputes that exist in this field may be of the blind-men-and-the-elephant kind, with the debating parties disagreeing on the implicit referents of the terms they use. Also, in many studies the whole complex phenomenon is reduced into one (possible) part in isolation, and conclusions from these studies are gathered much like the blind men's conclusions. In other words, this book is on how the possible conceptual elements of 'fear of crime' have been constructed and how these are usually joined together. The conceptualisation of 'fear of crime' is similar to the question: what does an elephant look like, what characteristics are necessary in order for it to be referred to as 'elephant'. Examples of general questions that will be addressed are:
–   What part(s) of 'fear of crime' can be identified?
–   Is the term 'fear of crime' the most appropriate one?

        But there is more to it. First, several varieties of the blind-men-and-the-elephant story exist; different origins have been put forward and the image of the elephant that sometimes accompanies the printed story has several appearances. Clearly, the whole elephant and the story can be presented in distinct ways, dependent on the time period in which the image was created, the technique and the material that has been used. Is the Japanese engraving from 1818 closer to the truth than Galdone's illustrations in pen and ink that accompany the story in verse by Saxe (Atkinson & Stewart 1998; Saxe & Galdone 1963)? In other words, there is not a single unique (re)presentation of a complex phenomenon; the presentation of reality is related to the characteristics of a time and place and relative to the perceptions of the scientific community as well. Yet, analogous to the different versions and illustrations of the blind-men-and-the-elephant story, the various ways of expression share some common characteristics regarding the notions or concepts to which they refer. Moreover, all the different versions, pictures and drawings are (re)presentations; they are models of reality. A fixed drawing of an elephant, i.e. in a two-dimensional space, represents an elephant that lives alive and well in Africa or Asia. All these drawings are representing reality and share some common features that point out the elephant, yet some of the pictures are said to be more realistic than others. That is, a full colour photograph of an elephant in its natural habitat is said to be more realistic than an abstract drawing or an elephant that is drawn in a cartoon-like manner, yet they all remain models in the sense that they are abstracted from reality. This book is not only on the conceptual elements of the common 'fear of crime' and how these are joined together, but is also concerned with the operationalisation of the phenomenon, on the possible (numerical) representations of 'fear of crime'. The operationalisation and measurement of 'fear of crime' is similar to the question: in what ways can an elephant be presented; what characteristics does the (re)presentation, i.e. the

operationalisation and instrument, need in order for it to be referred to as 'elephant'. Examples of the general questions that will be addressed are:
How are 'fear of crime' and possible parts thereof measured and are these current habits of measurement the most appropriate ones?
- Is the measurement of 'fear of crime' the same as the measurement of a part thereof?
- What can be said about the closeness to the truth, i.e. the validity and reliability, of the measurement of 'fear of crime'?

1.1.2 Interdisciplinary approach

Basically, research on 'fear of crime' is concerned with the experience of safety, threat and danger. 'Fear of crime' boils down to the fear for one's safety. Many different disciplines study safety and security and the perceptions thereof, focusing on different aspects and led by different goals. These disciplines have studied fear and perceptions of threat or the fear for one's safety, and it might be fruitful to aim at incorporating more than a single field of research within a particular discipline, which is argued for by Osgood (1998). His essay, entitled "Interdisciplinary Integration: Building Criminology by Stealing from Our Friends" argues for making a regular practice of academic thievery by keeping our eyes on sister disciplines to see what ideas would be useful to take for ourselves. The other academic specialities that study the topic from a different tradition are methodologically different and encompass a whole other body of assumptions, concepts, and "established facts" (Osgood 1998). The current research project is intended to make use of the different perspectives that are offered by other academic specialities. To use the blind-men-and-the-elephant story once again, though it is difficult or even impossible to get the whole picture of a complex phenomenon, when using different perspectives, a more complete idea will be gained. The six blind men in the poem could have touched all other parts of the elephant as well, and could have used other methods of getting information besides their sense of touch. Yet, even when all six of them would have touched every particular part of the elephant, used all their senses, or even if they were not blind, none of their individual notions of the phenomenon 'elephant' would be exactly equal to one another. Nevertheless, using different perspectives, as well as different methods, has a few advantages. First, more facets of the 'elephant' are considered and thus the total picture of the phenomenon will be more complete. Second, it will be easier to communicate about the phenomenon. The blind men dispute 'loud and long' about their observations, but were not able to talk about the elephant itself. Therefore, the phenomenon 'fear of crime', the 'fear for one's safety' or the 'experience of safety' will be studied from different perspectives. The information acquired will be integrated in order to understand the topic more fully. Using a multi and interdisciplinary paradigm when investigating the experience and interpretation of safety could eventually result in an improved way of communicating on and understanding of the subject.

The overall paradigm is social scientific in nature, that is, this research project uses findings, methods and jargon of especially the fields of criminology and victimology, psychology, sociology and law. Different perspectives are employed; 'fear of crime' is dealt with both as a social construction or a political invention and as the result of a perceived cue from the environment. 'Fear of crime' can be viewed as a cognition based on one's perceptions and appraisals, as an opinion and attitude that is embedded within the social and political context and as an emotion with a clear adaptive function. Likewise, different methods have been employed in the (pilot) studies of this project, varying from observations and interviews to survey research and secondary analysis. Neuropsychological or physiological methods have not been used in the current project itself.

An important issue concerning the use of literature from different disciplines and the use of literature as a source of data (see section 2.2) is the selection of the literature that is referred to in the text. The references that are provided are a selection of the literature that has actually been used and analysed.[1] When in fact selecting the references, I kept an eye on the variety in publication date, type of publication (e.g. report, academic journal article, dataset), and discipline (e.g. gerontology, criminology, psychology, sociology). Besides that, I wanted to include 'classic' works that have been of particular importance. All this implies that other references could have been presented in this book and that the selection of the references that are in fact provided are merely based on my own decisions; somebody else could have made a different selection.

1.2   Goal and focus

In this research the focus is on the safety of humans and (perceived) breaches of this safety by other humans, sometimes referred to as social safety. Therefore, (technical) aspects relating to safety of machines, the natural environment and technology are not of primary interest here, neither are insurances, legal procedures and the safety of or the (perceived) dangers by animals. In that sense, this research project concentrates on 'fear of crime', or rather the fear for one's safety and the experience of safety, which is perceived to be threatened by an expected, perceived or encountered 'dangerous' other person. Throughout this book, 'fear of crime' is put between quotation marks to indicate, as will be shown, that 'fear of crime' is an umbrella concept that embraces all kinds of indicators, and concepts and is not even so much about 'fear' and 'crime'. When the term 'fear of crime' is employed, the familiar, traditional and widely used 'fear of crime' is meant. This traditional 'fear of crime' has been defined as for example the 'sense of personal security in the community' (Conklin 1971) or the 'emotional response to possible violent crime and physical harm' (Covington & Taylor 1991). Chapter 2 will present more of

---

[1]   The database of all kinds of documents was mainly made in Endnote, using different keywords, which enabled searching and categorising of publications. This database will become available (see www.omv.nl for more information).

these conceptualisations, which are further discussed and analysed in the subsequent chapters.

To a certain extent, research on 'fear of crime' so far has failed to produce a cumulative body of knowledge, which might be due to the failing relationship between the theoretical concept and its empirical realisation in the form of its measurement instrument.[2] Osgood (1998) paints the current picture adequately in his plead for interdisciplinary research. Though more complex statistical models have been developed and tested with advanced techniques, some relationships are considered 'established facts' and more variance can be explained, we are still juggling the same set of familiar variables. Thus, the kind of research that follows from these new developments and findings is surely more of the same kind of research that we were already doing. He argues for a specific type of theoretical integration, that ideally leads to new avenues of research, inspires researchers to collect data that they would not otherwise have collected and thereby generate findings about new topics, leads to genuinely new knowledge, and not just refinement of current knowledge. Whether or not the data will support these newly developed theories, based on interdisciplinary integration, is not sure yet. But he continues and states that even if each recent theory proves false, they still will have made important contributions, and this is because the theories have asked new questions of which the answers will be new criminological knowledge, even if the answers were not the ones that were theoretically predicted (Osgood 1998).

The main objective of this project follows from both Osgood's suggestions and a seemingly lack of clear conceptualisation and measurement. In spite of their inevitable value and necessity for both theory as well as measurement, and therefore for policy, some fundamental and basic issues have not received the attention they deserve. The main objective is to contribute to this clear conceptualisation and measurement in order to provide a better understanding of the phenomenon, by analysing, clarifying and improving the conceptualisation and operationalisation of 'fear of crime' and/or aspects thereof. Thus, the main goals of this research project are to:

−   Give an overview of research on the topic and evaluate the current state of affairs by hand focusing on familiar conceptualisations and operationalisations.
−   Connect this field of research with other disciplines that have studied the same or related phenomena and apply different perspectives, by making use of other fields of research and by analysing recurring themes.
−   Develop a more explicit and grounded conceptualisation of what has been called 'fear of crime' and aspects thereof, based on interdisciplinary conceptual analysis in which the socio-political nature of core concepts is taken into account and by analysing the literature.
−   Develop more explicitly grounded operationalisations and propose reliable and more valid measurement instruments, based on two strategies, namely

[2]   In accordance with the finding from De Jong-Gierveld concerning research on loneliness (Gerritsen & De Jong-Gierveld 1995; De Jong-Gierveld 1984).

by improving present instruments and by starting over and developing another instrument.

1.3   Main research questions

The main objective is to contribute to clear conceptualisation and measurement in order to provide a better understanding of the phenomenon, by analysing, clarifying and improving the conceptualisation and operationalisation of 'fear of crime' and/or aspects thereof. Several research questions can be derived from this general objective, unfortunately some restrictions, concerning both number and content, had to be imposed. Therefore, this book is limited to the following main research questions, which will be refined in more specific research questions at the beginning of each chapter:

- What is the current state of affairs, how has 'fear of crime' been investigated and what are the major flaws in this field of research?
- How did the concept, both the term and its meaning, as well as its measurement develop?
- How are core concepts related to one another, traditionally and especially when making use of other disciplines and a multi-perspective conceptual analysis?
- What meanings does 'fear of crime' have?
- What constitutes a measurement instrument that is more founded on a conceptual analysis?

1.4   Scientific relevance

The scientific relevance of this research project is implicated in the objective that is strived for, which is to contribute to the clear conceptualisation and measurement in order to provide a better understanding of the phenomenon. By systematically reviewing what has been done so far, a meta-perspective on the topic is provided. Such a meta-perspective enables the use of findings from other academic specialities that study the same topic, yet sometimes use different names and methods and encompass a whole other body of assumptions and concepts. Thus, part of this research, as well as of its scientific relevance, is actually to inquire the usefulness of academic thievery as suggested by Osgood (1998). The analysis, clarification and improvement of the conceptualisation and operationalisation of 'fear of crime' and/or aspects thereof, could enable the production of a cumulative body of knowledge.

Moreover, as the overview will demonstrate, though more complex statistical models might have been developed and tested with advanced techniques, the same set of familiar questions, (problematic) concepts, variables and indicators prevail. The past developments within this field show new studies that are indeed more of the same kind of research we were already doing. Besides refinement of current knowledge, this project is scientifically relevant because it problematises the current state of affairs and in a sense destabilises the familiar 'fear of crime'. By doing so, other perspectives on current gaps and debates within this field are suggested, which is directly related to the whole issue regarding the nature of 'fear of crime'.

1.4.1 Current gaps and debates

The next chapters will explicitly as well as implicitly elaborate on a few current and ongoing debates, of which the most important ones are briefly pointed out here. Research on 'fear of crime' has been criticised on a number of grounds, especially with respect to conceptualisation and measurement. The field is characterised as being methodologically flawed, and to a certain extent as non-theoretical, non-cumulative and non-comparative, especially because of the conceptual chaos in this field and the use of different labels and indicators. Much attention has been given to epidemiological-like cross-sectional studies in which descriptive socio-demographic categories, e.g. women, elderly, lower socio-economic classes, are applied to explain differences in the level of 'fear of crime'. That is, many studies are concerned with what could be called the prevalence of 'fear of crime' in socio-demographic categories. Quite on the contrary, less is known about the variety in the nature, meaning, relevance and experience of 'fear of crime' in people's personal lives, due to the widespread use of the survey and its data, and because of the relatively little use of qualitative methods like in-depth interviews or focus groups. This implies that not much is known about for example differences between several ethnic groups as far as the nature, meaning, relevance and experience of 'fear of crime' in people's personal lives is concerned, notwithstanding some American research. Because of the typical cross-sectional nature of most (survey) research, not much longitudinal research has been done. Some studies have used a format in which a pre-test as well as a post-test were included, for example when evaluating the effectiveness of an intervention or the consequences of victimisation. Yet, these studies do not provide an understanding of the development of 'fear of crime' during a person's life course. In other words, little is known about the etiological development or (young) children's 'fear of crime'.

Other gaps result from one-dimensional studies in which either environmental characteristics are investigated, or characteristics with respect to the person. Also, little use is made of research for example from social and personality psychology regarding state and trait anxiety and individual differences in the experience of fear, from psychometrics and from research on attitudes or the perception of risk. For the greater part, this can be accounted for by putting the concept into its political and historical context, which is attempted in the chapters 4 to 8. Because of the historical development of the concept 'fear of crime' and its indicators, research has been too narrowly focused. Hopefully, this project, that concerns an extensive process of conceptualisation and research on measurement instruments, can provide a better understanding of the phenomenon by putting it into (a new) perspective. This could very well shed some new light on current and recurring debates, like discussions about the (ir)rationality of fear and the fear-victimisation paradox, the concept and measurement of 'fear of crime', its relationship with perceived risk, and 'fear of crime' as a social construction.

1.5   Social relevance

In this section, the question that is addressed is why this research project, or rather this research topic, is relevant for contemporary Western society. Besides the scientific relevance, which is considered to have intrinsic social value, the topic itself is socially relevant on several grounds. How 'fear of crime' has become a social issue, will be discussed in chapters 5 and 8, but the reasons will be briefly pointed out here.

First and foremost, 'fear of crime' is an extremely salient issue in politics. In 1974, as a result of a discussion concerning the budget of the Dutch Ministry of Justice, a survey was administered to study crime, or rather criminal victimisation, in the Netherlands. The survey included some items on 'fear of crime' as well, asking the public about their opinions on crime and safety. The reasons given for this were in the first place that the government should know whether the public thinks problems concerning crime should have priority. Another reason stated in the report was that public opinion limits the so-called humanisation of the penal system. The authors point to some criminal cases in which the public prosecutors ask for long sentences, referring to the unrest in society. A third reason why the survey had to include items on the experience of safety touched on the danger of being ignorant of certain feelings in the society, which might lead vigilantism, i.e. to situations in which people take the law into their own hands (Cozijn & Van Dijk 1976). Politicians, their campaigns, law & order interventions and all kinds of policy measures pay attention to 'fear of crime' in its broadest sense. This also means that all kinds of information about the public's 'fear of crime' are salient. Several actors, for example politicians and police officers, point to the results concerning 'fear of crime', derived from public opinion polls and surveys. Appeals to public opinion have become central in political discourse, since public opinion provides the ultimate ground of legitimacy for a specific political and legislative agenda (Zaret 2000). In short, public opinion has become a central feature in politics, and appeals to public opinion are central in political discourse. Chapter 5 explores the historical development of acquiring knowledge about opinions and attitudes by and for the government, with the emphasis on polls and surveys concerning crime. 'Fear of crime' receives a lot of attention by state actors and many policy agencies are devoting part of their time and money to the 'reduction' of fear. Therefore, not only a nuanced view on the topic is necessary, the political salience also calls for a rather abstract evaluation of the concept as it is used, together with an evaluation of the measurement instruments that are employed in studies that attempt to check the effectiveness of policy interventions (see Van den Eynde, Veno & Hart 2003).

A second ground why the topic itself is socially relevant, is because it is a (news) media issue. Evidently, the salience in the (news) media is related to the political salience. That is, political parties and several departments for example distribute press releases, and the media are thought to represent and shape 'public opinion' and for example 'fear of crime'. The news media keep the public informed by telling what is going on in the political and social arena, on the other hand the media may express opinions about politics and issues as well. The media select and define issues and social problems and narrow the range of policy options, in other words, the media clearly have a role in establishing or changing the politicians' and policymakers' agendas (Kennamer 1992). In other words, the media may influence politics by paying much attention to particular events or topics, which refers to what has been called the media agenda-setting hypothesis (Tipton 1992). Moreover, besides for example the policymakers, politicians and police officers, the news media too point to the results of public opinion polls and surveys that concern attitudes towards crime and criminal justice, and for example 'fear of crime', or may even conduct polls and surveys themselves.

Overall, 'fear of crime' is very salient in both politics and the media; 'fear of crime' receives a lot of attention, which calls for a nuanced and critical view on the topic. Both arenas, politics and the news media, pay attention to 'fear of crime', but these are not the only ones. Public prosecutors and judges in court also refer to the public's opinions on crime and safety and the social unrest caused by a specific crime, which will be briefly discussed in chapter 8. Knowledge about 'fear of crime', i.e. public concern and attitudes, feelings of safety and so on, is suggested to be important for the judiciary, since for example neglecting public opinion, attitudes and emotions might lead to a society in which people take the law into their own hands (Vanderveen & Elffers 2001).

Moreover, research on 'fear of crime' can be considered socially relevant, since the topic itself appears to be a socially relevant issue, in the sense that opinions, attitudes and concern with respect to crime and deviant behaviour are prominent in social life (see for example I. Taylor 1995).[3] In chapter 7, the concept 'risk' and risk perception is discussed, to examine possible convergent issues with 'fear of crime'. Though crime or the fear thereof is usually not the primary focus in traditional empirical studies on risk perception, every once in a while, the salience of crime for people is unintentionally demonstrated. For example, in a study on perceptions of environmental risk in three communities of El Paso, Texas (USA), crime emerged as a salient hazard (Byrd & VanDerslice 1996). Crime is the hazard that was most often considered a 'high risk' for oneself and one's family and for the whole community, followed by for example the destruction of the ozone layer, illegal dumping of hazardous waste and drugs. Criminal victimisation, and everything associated with it, as one of the most salient hazards in people's everyday lives is also demonstrated in

---

[3] This does not mean that it is the most important concern or worry for all people; see for example Coston (1993) who found that homeless women in New York City worry a lot more about their family's wellbeing, their (poor) health, lack of proper nutrition, and lack of money. Others have argued that the (elderly) 'fear of crime' is overestimated (e.g. Ferraro & LaGrange 1987, 1988; LaGrange, Ferraro, & Supancic 1992; McCoy et al. 1996).

studies that are not concerned with 'fear of crime' or crime in the first place (e.g. Petts, Horlick-Jones & Murdock 2001). A typical example is provided by a study that investigates the preferences of London taxi drivers for driving emissions-free hydrogen fuel cell cars. The taxi drivers who participated in focus groups clearly demonstrated their concern about crime and personal safety. Findings from the focus groups were used to construct a questionnaire. Thereafter, taxi drivers were asked in face-to-face interviews about their preferences and attitudes to several environmental and transport issues, among which concern about crime, along with for example congestion, noise and exposure to air pollution. Interestingly, of all the issues that could have been affecting the taxi drivers in the course of their jobs, traffic congestion raised the most concern for 58%, followed by 'fear of crime', which was the most important issue for nearly a third of the sample (Mourato, Saynor & Hart 2004). Another example of crime as a salient hazard comes from Barer and Johnson (2003). They conducted interviews over an 8-year period with a sample of Whites and Blacks in two cohorts; the younger old people (ages 70–84) and the oldest people (ages 85–103). Few racial differences emerged in worries about one's economic situation (i.e. paying the bills) and both Whites and Blacks complained about deteriorating neighbourhoods and fears for their personal safety; concerns about unsafe, deteriorating neighbourhoods in which crime is common, were prevalent. Respondents of over 85 years said for example: "I would love to go to the park across the street, but you don't dare go out any more", "I don't go out at night with all the dope and too many winos around" and "I'm worried that the house next door will be sold to drug dealers" (Barer & Johnson 2003: 334).

Public opinion polls provide yet another indication of the social relevance of 'fear of crime'. Since 1992, the SCP (Social and Cultural Planning Office of the Netherlands)[4] asks a representative sample of the Dutch population which specific aims are most important for politics to strive for. Respondents arrange a list of aims, and findings from 1992 to 2002 show that a large majority of the respondents think "fighting crime", followed by "maintaining the social order" should be the top priority. This in contrast with, for example, "fighting environmental pollution", of which about half of the respondents in 1992 thought it should be the top priority, which decreased to 24% of the respondents (Becker 2003).[5] Thus, 'fear of crime', that is the large variety in opinions, attitudes and concern with respect to crime is highly salient in social life. The emphasis on (criminal) risks and dangers is often referred to in the literature. Chapter 7 deals with the recurring argument that increased risk awareness is typical for contemporary society. For example, Garland's notions on the 'culture of control' point to an increase of insecurities and 'cultural sensibilities', more

---

[4]   A glossary of abbreviations can be found in appendix A.
[5]   One of the first victim surveys conducted in the 1970s in the Netherlands showed a different picture; half of the respondents thought unemployment was the most important social problem, only 16% mentioned crime (Cozijn & Van Dijk 1976).

concern about crime, a call for 'law & order' and a repressive political reaction (Garland 2001). Friedman (1993) puts it like this:

> Even people who live in quiet suburban enclaves, or rural backwaters, are aware of what they consider the crime problem. They, too, may feel fearful and besieged: safe where they are perhaps, but conscious of a dangerous world beyond their doorsteps. (p. 452)

The whole idea of 'fear of crime' as a political and social issue will be extensively discussed in chapter 8.

Two other grounds of the social relevance refer to (possible) consequences and effects of 'fear of crime'. These consequences are investigated by means of theoretical or conceptual models that explain the effects or consequences of 'fear of crime'.[6] For present purposes, two main groups of models can be distinguished, as schematically presented in Figure 1.1 (see page 12), though in practice they tend to overlap frequently. The first group relates 'fear of crime', like crime, to (aspects of) public health, the quality of life or wellbeing (e.g. Adu-Mireku 2002; Illner 1998; Michalos & Zumbo 2000). Often, a stress-distress perspective is employed; suggesting that 'fear of crime' causes mental distress, which erodes public health (e.g. Garofalo 1981a; Krause 1991; Leather et al. 1997; Linares et al. 2001; Pacione 2003; Ross 2000).[7] The term 'public health' usually refers to the general state of the population's health, both mental and physical, and studies have been done both in a public health context, as well as in the field of environmental psychology and social geography (e.g. Bonaiuto, Fornara & Bonnes 2003). 'Fear of crime', i.e. perceptions of crime, disorder and risk are thought of as environmental stressors, and people adjust their behaviours to cope with it. Since people constrain their daily activity patterns, 'fear of crime' influences the quality of life (Pacione 2003). Constraining one's behaviour might even result in social isolation and exclusion, though this does not necessarily mean that people, like the elderly are all "prisoners in their own homes" because of 'fear of crime' (Lawton & Yaffe 1980; Michalos et al. 2001). In other words, "the portrayals of aging citizens paralyzed with fear behind barricaded doors captures the experience only of a limited segment of elderly America" (McCoy et al. 1996: 201). In turn, social isolation is also thought to increase 'fear of crime' (Gomme 1986; Hartnagel 1979; Toseland 1982). Moreover, research on social indicators of wellbeing and perceptions of life quality incorporates perceived safety. Andrews and Whithey (1976) for example used a top-down strategy to construct a survey. That is, they developed a conceptual model for wellbeing, which distinguishes between different domains of and different criteria for wellbeing. The pilot studies that were employed aimed at finding distinguishable life-domains that would cover most of people's concerns, resulting in a list of domains and a list of criteria. These criteria are the values, standards or goals that are used to judge how one

---

[6] Chapter 2 elaborates on the conceptual models that explain the causes of 'fear of crime'.

[7] Though usually the model is tested with aggregated data, the consequences are conceptually on the individual level.

feels about the life-domains. In their model, safety acts as a criterion for wellbeing. Also, Bramston, Pretty and Chipuer (2002) used an instrument to measure (subjective) quality of life incorporating seven specified life domains. Besides for example material and emotional wellbeing, two other life domains referred to community involvement and safety with respect to crime.[8] Generally, in research on wellbeing or quality of life, there appears to be consensus about (perceived) crime, especially violent crime, or rather the absence thereof as either one of the aspects of wellbeing or as a predictor (see for example Diener 1997; Disch et al. 2000; Ferriss 2001; Michalos 2003; Michalos et al. 2001; Türksever & Atalik 2001).

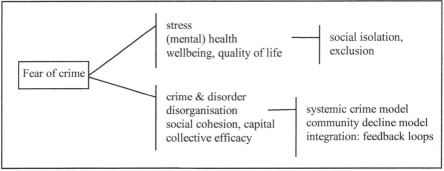

Figure 1.1. Two main classes of models hypothesising consequences of 'fear of crime'.

Though the assumption that 'fear of crime' erodes public (mental) health is rather common, empirical evidence for this relationship is less frequent. Yet, several empirical studies have found significant associations between 'fear of crime', quality of life and health status, suggesting that 'fear of crime' is associated with poorer health and less quality of life (see Green, Gilbertson & Grimsley 2002; Pantazis 2000). For example, Chandola (2001) explains area differences in health by 'fear of crime' in the local area or neighbourhood. 'Fear of crime', as measured by the item "how safe do you feel (or would you feel) walking alone in this area after dark" from the British Crime Survey (BCS), was found to be significantly associated with self-rated health even after adjusting for health behaviours, like for example smoking, and a number of individual and household level socio-economic factors. A version of this general model that relates 'fear of crime' to (aspects of) public health and the quality of life or wellbeing is for example a model in which 'fear of crime' is assumed to cause mental distress and social exclusion or isolation, which affects health. Social exclusion and isolation touch on the social structure and social capital. Chandola (2001: 106) refers to social capital as the explanation of variations in health across geographic localities and suggests that "fear of crime in the local neighborhood may be an indicator of social capital, as to some extent, it measures the breakdown in community trust and networks". Several other

---

[8]   Both community involvement or neighbourhood cohesion and safety were also dimensions in the
      community measures that they used.

empirical studies have used the notion of social capital and feelings of safety in one's neighbourhood as well, incorporating the argument that 'fear of crime' relates to disorder and crime (see Kawachi, Kennedy & Wilkinson 1999).

The second class of models basically suggests that 'fear of crime' contributes to (more) crime, disorder or incivilities, pointing out that attitudes, opinions and emotions can have very 'real' consequences. Versions of this model usually incorporate notions of social (dis)organisation, cohesion, efficacy or social capital and build on Shaw and McKay's theory of community social disorganisation. Social disorganisation theory primarily focuses on the ecological distribution of crime and delinquency, hypothesising that it is due to variation in the capacity of neighbourhoods to constrain its residents from violating norms. This capacity is considered a function of a community's level of social organisation or neighbourhood cohesion, reflected by the size and density of social ties, i.e. local friendship networks, the levels of organisation as well as participation among residents and for example the informal social control of street-corner teenage peer groups (Bursik 2000; Sampson 1988; Sampson & Groves 1989).

As schematically presented in Figure 1.1, this second class of models can be divided in other subclasses of models as well, such as the systemic crime model and the community decline model. Briefly, the systemic crime model focuses on the role of length of residence, neighbourhood or residential stability on social ties and social cohesion within a community. Residential stability promotes social organisation, social cohesion and informal surveillance of the neighbourhood, which reduces street crime. Thus, crime is viewed as a result of social (dis)organisation or residential instability (Bursik 2000; Bursik & Grasmick 1993; Sampson 1988, 1991). 'Fear of crime' is considered a "powerful force in decreasing local community bonds" (Sampson 1991: 51), since it reduces density of friendships and social cohesion and increases anonymity. In other words, 'fear of crime' makes the formation of acquaintanceship and friendship networks more difficult, promoting social disorganisation and eventually crime. Also, crime and deterioration of the neighbourhood will dampen attachment to the community (Taylor 1996b), which leads to the community decline or social disorganisation model. This model focuses on the role of responses to and effects of crime and disorder and merely pictures the other side of the medal. It suggests that crime is a cause since a declining neighbourhood results in increased fear, thus street crime reduces informal surveillance by increasing resident's perception of risk and fear. Serious crimes are linked with heightened 'fear of crime' as well as indications of disorder, the so-called incivilities, and minor misdemeanour offences, decline and decay (Lewis & Maxfield 1980; Lewis & Salem 1986;

Perkins & Taylor 1996).[9] A common hypothesis is that disorder (incivilities) and less serious forms of crime lead to more 'fear of crime', reducing neighbourhood cohesion accordingly, which brings about more serious forms of crime. Typical example is the broken windows-thesis (Wilson & Kelling 1982) that is related to Skogan's work on disorder, incivilities and decline (Skogan 1990a, 1999).[10] Goodstein and Shotland (1980) provide a clear example of the general community decline model by means of their 'crime causes crime' hypothesis. They propose that (street) crime increases fear, which leads community residents to avoid public streets, and consequently, surveillance in public areas decreases, thus increasing street crime. Chapter 2 discusses the main conceptual models that explain the causes of 'fear of crime'; some are discussed here as well, yet in a slightly different perspective, since they touch on the social relevance of 'fear of crime' and research thereof.

Because the direction of many (causal) connections is not clear at all, an integration of these two models, i.e. versions of the systemic crime model and the community decline model, is very well possible and frequently applied (see also section 2.4). The (causal) relationships appear to be recursive and many concepts overlap as schematically presented in Figure 1.2. 'Fear of crime' then, is considered both the cause and the result of crime (e.g. Bursik 2000; Bursik & Grasmick 1993). 'Fear of crime', increased by (street) crime and disorder, leads to physical and psychological withdrawal from community life (Skogan 1990a); residents avoid the public streets in their neighbourhood. The resulting social disorganisation and a decrease of (informal) surveillance in the neighbourhood, that, in turn, increases disorder, incivilities, crime and delinquency rates, again increasing fear, reflects a vicious cycle. The feedback loops frequently stated connect declining social capital and neighbourhood cohesion with more fear, more disorder and rising crime, followed by further disinvestment in social capital, which facilitates more serious criminal offences (Bellair 2000; Goodstein & Shotland 1980; Liska & Warner 1991; Markowitz et al. 2001; Sampson & Raudenbusch 1999; Skogan 1990a). 'Fear of crime' is thought to decrease informal surveillance and the willingness to intervene when community norms are indeed being violated, which in turn leads to increasing resident's perception of risk and fear and higher crime rates (Bellair 2000; Skogan 1990a; Taylor 1996b). The deteriorating conditions lead to the exit of businesses or retail decline (Thomas & Bromley 1996), with accompanying loss of jobs; and residential mobility (Dugan 1999) and thus inducing further change in the composition of people present, often referred to as the "5 pm flight"

---

[9]   Several other publications on this relationship are available (see for example Cohen, Farley & Mason 2003; Covington & Taylor 1991; Crank, Giacomazzi & Heck 2003; Evans & Fletcher 2000; Fisher & Nasar 1995; Nasar, Fisher & Grannis 1993; Perkins, Meeks & Taylor 1992; Perkins et al. 1990; Robinson et al. 2003; Rohe & Burby 1988; Skogan & Maxfield 1981; Taylor 1995; Taylor 1997a, 1997b, 1999; Taylor & Shumaker 1990; Taylor & Covington 1993).

[10]   The broken-windows thesis, the idea that minor offences and signs of disorder will lead to serious crimes and a spiral of decay has been used to support deterrent and order-maintenance policy measures expressed as 'zero tolerance'. For criticism on the broken-windows thesis and the political consequences and implications, see for example Ellickson (1996), Harcourt (1998) and Herbert (2001, 2002).

(Thomas & Bromley 2000) when people leave their offices and go home, the "middle class flight" (Kawachi, Kennedy & Wilkinson 1999) or "white flight" (Liska & Bellair 1995), both referring to the "flight to the suburbs" or "urban flight" by people leaving the (inner-)cities who can choose to do so (see also Luymes 1997).

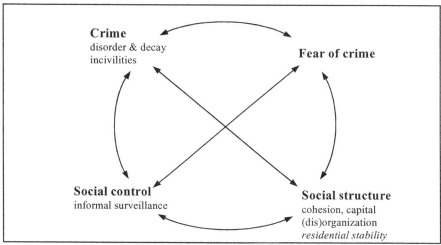

Figure 1.2. Schematic conceptual model of recursive relationships 'fear of crime', crime, aspects of social structure, and informal surveillance.

The notion of neighbourhood or residential stability is present in both the systemic crime model and the community decline model; from a social disorganisation perspective, it influences informal surveillance and in a systemic model, it is a core feature of community attachment. In general, neighbourhoods with strong social ties, high involvement and attachment, or high social capital, have lower levels of 'fear of crime' than other neighbourhoods and higher levels of social control (Ferraro 1995; Lewis & Salem 1986; Skogan & Maxfield 1981). Taylor (1996b) for example, pictures 'fear of crime' as a response to disorder and crime in terms of accommodation, whereas (increased) informal social control is a response to disorder in terms of resistance, which in turn is influenced by neighbourhood stability, attachment and involvement. In other words, informal social ties with neighbours provide a buffer against the fear that is caused by disorder and incivilities such as crime, vandalism, dirt and presence of drugs (Ross & Jang 2000). Overall, an integration of perspectives proposes several feedback-loops between the community decline model and the systemic crime model and suggests multiple reciprocal effects (e.g. Bellair 2000; Markowitz et al. 2001; Taylor 1996b, 1997a, 1997b). For example, the causal relationship that high levels of social capital facilitate the prevention of crime (Kawachi, Kennedy & Wilkinson 1999) is reversed as well; crime also directly affects the levels of social capital in a community, and contributes to the deterioration of social capital, which is partly an explanation of 'fear of crime' (Lindström, Merlo & Östergren 2003). Thus, the basic recursive model comes down to processes in which the mutual relationships between 'fear of crime', social capital or social organisation and crime are reciprocal and interdependent. 'Fear of crime' results in a disorganisation of the community structure, which in turn fuels further crime, and high crime rates deteriorate social capital, social cohesion and the social structure of a community, which induces crime even more (Skogan 1990a).

Models like the systemic crime model, the community decline model and the social disorganisation model are all versions of the second class of models that was distinguished from another major category of models (see Figure 1.1), some of which are also discussed in the overview of the main conceptual models that explain the causes of 'fear of crime' (see section 2.4). The first main class of models relates 'fear of crime' to (aspects of) public health and the quality of life or wellbeing, and refers to possible consequences of 'fear of crime' in terms of mental distress, which erodes public health. The second category touches on the possible consequences of 'fear of crime', since in a recursive model it contributes to (more) crime, disorder or incivilities. Though these two main classes of models are distinguished here, in practice they can overlap (e.g. Adams & Serpe 2000; Bazargan 1994; Ross, Reynolds & Geis 2000). For example, in studies concerning neighbourhood disorder, a part of the community decline model, such an overlap essentially implies that the consequences of neighbourhood disorder for individuals are great and are related to the quality of life (Garofalo & Laub 1978; Lagrange, Ferraro & Supancic 1992). The overlap suggests that neighbourhood disorder reduces individual wellbeing, increases fear, mistrust, isolation and anger, which are all consequences for individuals, yet disorder has its effect on the community as well, by reducing social ties, which further undermines social control and leads to more disorder and crime (Ross & Mirowsky 1999, 2001; Skogan 1990a).

Like the first class of models, versions from the second 'social disorder' class are usually tested with aggregated data, yet the consequences of fear in this latter general model are conceptually on the level of the neighbourhood. Both generalised and simplified models focus on the consequences of 'fear of crime'. The first relates 'fear of crime' to public health and the quality of life; the other suggests 'fear of crime' contributes to (more) crime and disorder. The two models are both abstracted and generalised, that is, they embrace several different specific versions, may overlap and usually employ some notion of social organisation or social capital as well. Empirical research studying these specific versions of the models, provides some evidence for their validity. This, in turn, supports the social relevance of research on 'fear of crime'. That is, if 'fear of crime' actually contributes to poorer health, less wellbeing, more crime and disorder, then it can be considered highly socially relevant. Thus, not only crime, but also 'fear of crime' has real consequences, like Warr (1985: 238) states: "And like criminal victimization itself, the consequences of fear are real, measurable, and potentially severe, both at an individual and social level." Ferraro (1995) makes a similar point by noting that:

many of the problems associated with crime, including fear, are independent of actual victimization [...] because it may lead to decreased social integration, out-migration, restriction of activities, added security costs, and avoidance behaviors. (p. 3)

This research project eventually leads to more explicitly grounded operationalisations. That is, the last chapters discuss the two strategies of continuation and starting over in order to propose reliable and more valid measurement instruments. Policy is made in reference to attitudes of the public; court cases partly depend on what the people feel and think and how people behave. Attitudes play a role in several aspects of the society. The more a government and institutions are (held) responsible, the more the government and these institutions have to deal with the public's attitudes as well. The balance between norms within a democratic constitutional state and civil rights versus the call for law and order and the danger of citizen's taking the law into their own hands is fragile. Paying attention to people's attitudes and public opinion is necessary to check the equilibrium. This holds for Beck's risk society as well as for Garland's (2001) culture of control:

...the new discourse of crime policy consistently invokes an angry public, tired of living in fear, demanding strong measures of punishment and protection. The background affect of policy is now more frequently a collective anger and a righteous demand for retribution than a commitment to a just, socially engineered solution. (p. 10-11).

If knowledge on 'fear of crime' plays such an important role *and* is considered relevant for society and the government, the way this knowledge is acquired deserves a great deal of attention.

1.6   Structure of this book

In order to be as clear as possible, a topic tree is presented at the beginning of each chapter. This introductory chapter presents an outline of this book in the form of such a topic tree in Figure 1.3. The topic tree is intended to give the reader the opportunity to skip particular sections and continue with the next and to provide a guideline of the text's structure. Also, every chapter offers a list of the main conclusions and/or assertions at the end (see Table 1.1). The appendices provide background information, such as a glossary of acronyms and abbreviations (Appendix A).

1.6.1   Basic terms

In this introductory chapter, some basic terms already emerged, most of which will be elaborated on in the following chapters. However, to provide a guideline of these chapters, it is useful to provide some insight in how different terms are interpreted here. Briefly, the terms 'fear of crime', several social cognitive terms and expressions that refer to 'the public' are dealt with. First of all, the concept 'fear of crime' is of importance. This book mainly problematises 'fear of crime' as it is so often (implicitly) conceptualised, measured and used.

To *start* with some notion of what is meant by the familiar or traditional 'fear of crime' in this project, the definition by Ferraro might be presented here, since it is often cited. Ferraro (1995: 4) defines 'fear of crime' as "an emotional response of dread or anxiety to crime or symbols that a person associates with crime". Moreover, Stanko (1994) notes that the many researchers would agree that 'fear of crime' represents individuals' diffuse sense of danger about being physically harmed by criminal violence and is associated with concern about being outside the home, probably in an urban area, alone and potentially vulnerable to personal harm. Several other descriptions of the concept or parts thereof exist, which will be discussed further in chapter 2. Here, the assertion that is stressed concerns the umbrella nature of the concept 'fear of crime'. 'Fear of crime' is an umbrella concept that touches on fear of becoming a victim of crime; the perception of the risk of becoming a victim of crime; feelings of safety; perceptions and responses to the threat of crime and criminal victimisation; worry, concern and anxiety about victimisation and crime, and so on (see sections 2.4 and 2.5). All these perceptions, attitudes, beliefs, worries, concerns, and other social cognitions relate to crime or symbols of crime in the (urban) environment and especially in one's neighbourhood. A few different approaches to 'fear of crime' exist, which will be discussed later, yet, in order to be able to examine the main research question, the notion is used here in its broadest sense.

Second, several terms from social cognition are borrowed, among which are 'perception', 'cognition', 'appraisal', 'attitudes', 'emotions', 'affect' and 'feelings' (e.g. Fiske & Taylor 1984; Forgas 2001). Often, the boundaries between these terms are blurred, and they are used interchangeably; a consensus definition of for example 'emotion' does not exist (Kappas 2002). For now, it is sufficient to note that an emotion is considered a mental state, even when somatic signals participate in this mental experience, with high intensity and high hedonic content (Cabanac 2002). This hedonic content refers to pleasure and pain or displeasure. Both emotions and feelings are usually related to an object, i.e. they are responses to causal-specific stimuli. Feelings are less intense and more fleeting as compared to emotions. Emotions and feelings refer to affect, which is usually conceptualised as positive and/or negative affect, thus implicating an evaluative nature. Also, emotions resemble sequences of events and a continuous interaction; emotions are (cognitive) processes (Frijda 1988; Lazarus 1984, 1991; Schachter & Singer 1962). These processes involve the perception of the situation, the cognitive evaluation or appraisal of this situation, which can focus on the significance of the sensory input as well as on the possible reactions to the situation (Lazarus 1991). Depending on the cognitive appraisal, an internal subjective affective state follows and subsequently the expression of the emotion at a behavioural or physiological level (Frijda 1988). Though perception and cognition do not explicitly refer to valence, cognitive appraisal does incorporate evaluation. An 'attitude' does refer to valence by definition. An attitude can be described as an individual's evaluation of any psychological object, that is the valuation of persons, objects, or ideas (Ajzen &

Fishbein 1980; Fishbein & Ajzen 1975). Attitudes, cognitive appraisals, the valence nature of affect and the "hedonic content" of an emotion all refer to action-oriented mental representations. This means that they specify not just the nature of the object (within a situation), but how to behave toward it as well, for example whether to approach or avoid it (Semin & Smith 2002). A final important notion for now is that all mental or cognitive processes are heavily influenced by characteristics of the social context. Yet, these cognitive processes may be based on implicit, action-oriented representations with an automatic and heuristic style that is used in routine, everyday situations, and on a more explicit, conscious, thoughtful symbolic style of processing that may use language (Smith & DeCoster 2000).

Third, besides 'fear of crime' and social cognitive notions, expressions that refer to 'the public' are employed. Examples are 'public opinion', 'public concern' and 'social unrest', which all refer to some (expressed) common agreement among many individuals within a society, usually operationally defined as the aggregation of individual opinions on public issues (Allport 1937).[11] Therefore, the (aggregated) responses on questions in polls and surveys are of importance. Chapter 5 shows that research on 'fear of crime' can be traced back to the origins of public opinion polls, sketching the political context of 'fear of crime' and its measurement. Public opinion as such is dual in nature; nominally it is a discursive fiction, nonetheless, there are real individuals who participate in debates and public organisations, or who are readers, speakers, politicians and so on (Zaret 2000). Barker (1998) describes public opinion as a body of argument or discussion about (amongst other things) the government, its role and functioning, but not conducted within the limits of governing institutions, e.g. parliament or Senate, nor confined to a governing class (Barker 1998). This body of argument about public issues, and their salience can be derived from for example contents of news media, the letters that were sent to these news media, the amount of participation in demonstrations, petitions that have been offered to politicians, and the foundations of organisations that are primarily concerned with public issues. While 'public opinion' refers to the more immediate, possibly shifting opinions that people hold, usually on current political, economic and (other) social affairs, 'public attitudes and norms' usually refer to longer lasting feelings, viewpoints and perceptions (interpretations, cognitions, ideas), which are more deeply held and less easily changeable. Yet, no absolute difference between public opinion and public attitudes exists (Smoke 1996b).

Most of these basic terms, like 'fear of crime', terms from social cognition and 'public opinion' that were introduced in this chapter will also be used in the following chapters. They were briefly described here to provide some interpretive guideline of these chapters, similar to the outline that follows below.

---

[11] While 'public opinion' can relate to several issues, public concern and social unrest focus on an issue that is negatively valued.

1.6.2 Outline

An outline of this book is presented in the topic tree (Figure 1.3), which shows the parts of this book. The present introduction, that sketches the research project, specifies the main research questions, the goal and focus as well as the scientific and social relevance of this study, is followed by an overview of the current state of affairs as far as conceptualisation and measurement is concerned. In order to give a systematic review of the research on 'fear of crime', the elements of research studies as well as the main criteria are discussed. The findings from the review have been classified by means of a method loosely based on a grounded theory approach, which is briefly discussed as well. Secondary analysis of data that have been used in this field complement this part of the book. Subsequently, the focus is on conceptualisation. Both the findings based on a grounded theory approach as well as ideas from social construction demonstrate the relevance of the social, political and historical context or nature of 'fear of crime'. The meaning of three core concepts, victimisation, risk perception and fear (of crime) are extensively discussed.

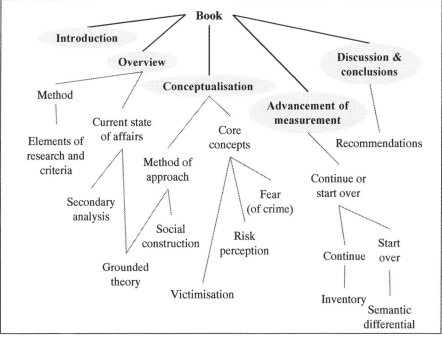

Figure 1.3. Topic tree of this book.

By then, it is evident that research on 'fear of crime' is lacking clear concepts, valid operationalisations and reliable measurement instruments. In the part on the advancement of measurement, two strategies are employed to contribute to the development of appropriate measurement instruments. The first strategy continues with the indicators that have been used so far, which results in the proposal of an instrument that is based on an inventory of these indicators.

The second strategy starts all over from scratch, which results in a proposed instrument that is different in format and content and is based on the semantic differential. In the part that follows, this research project and the two proposed measurement instruments are discussed and the main conclusions as well as some recommendations are presented.

This introductory chapter sketched the background of the research project, which has led to this book. Table 1.1 lists the main assertions of this chapter, regarding the goal and focus, general research questions, and the scientific and social relevance. The next chapter discusses the current state of affairs regarding conceptualisation and operationalisation.

Table 1.1 List of main assertions of Chapter 1.

Topic	Explanation
Background	Six blind-men-and-the-elephant story; conceptualisation and operationalisations of 'fear of crime' needs attention
	'Fear of crime' comes down to fear for one's safety
	Interdisciplinary approach fruitful; other academic specialities study topic from a different perspective
Goal and focus	Safety of humans and (perceived) breaches of this safety by other humans, 'fear of crime'
	Back to basics: conceptualisation and operationalisation, from other perspectives
	Contribute to clear conceptualisation and measurement: - overview and evaluation of current state of conceptualisation and measurement - apply different perspectives (check other disciplines, analyse recurring themes) - develop grounded conceptualisation, conceptual model (contexts of concepts) - develop grounded operationalisations based on two strategies, i.e. improving present instruments and by starting over and developing another instrument
General research questions	- What is the current state of affairs? - How did the concept and its measurement develop? - How are core concepts related? - What meanings does 'fear of crime' have? - What constitutes the measurement instrument?
Scientific relevance	No clarity regarding concept and operationalisation No clarity regarding measurement, validity and reliability of quantitative instruments Hardly any theoretical development or considerations Hardly any progress in knowledge concerning the occurrence, development, influences or correlates
	Thus: contribute to clear conceptualisation and measurement in order to provide a better understanding of the phenomenon; interdisciplinary approach and attention to context necessary
Social relevance	Salient issue in politics, (news) media, social life Possible consequences in terms of distress, health, quality of life Possible consequences in terms of social disorganisation, disorder, crime
	Thus: nuanced, critical and abstract view necessary

2 Overview of concepts and measurement

This second chapter is based on a systematic review of research on 'fear of crime'. While the next chapter presents secondary analyses of data that is typical in research on 'fear of crime', this chapter will sketch the current state of affairs regarding issues of conceptualisation and operationalisation. The review and evaluation of the research indicate what can be soundly gathered from several publications to investigate how 'fear of crime' or aspects thereof have been conceptualised and measured and how well these measurement instruments perform. Table 2.1 lists the elements that were focused on in the various studies under review and which criteria were adopted to evaluate them. Both the elements or key issues that were of interest as well as the criteria are taken from several well-known and basic books on empirical research in the social sciences. Though generally acknowledged, it turns out that the familiarity of elements and criteria has not been a guarantee for research of high quality; seemingly obvious and well-known qualities of research turn out to be not so common after all.

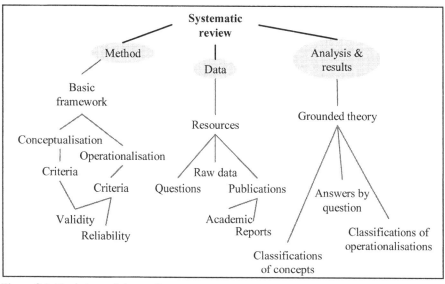

Figure 2.1. Topic tree of chapter 2.

Figure 2.1 presents the contents of this chapter in a topic tree. Following a brief discussion of the elements that were focused on and the criteria that were employed, the four types of sources that provided the 'data', i.e. the studies that were included, are described. The studies concern various aspects of so-called 'fear of crime', the experience and interpretation of safety, fear of victimisation and attitudes on crime. This chapter will pay attention to operationalisation and conceptualisation issues; a summary of the more extensive review is presented in Table 2.4. This chapter subsequently ends with a brief discussion.

2.1   Reviewing the literature: concepts and indicators

A few decades of empirical research on 'fear of crime' or the experience and interpretation of safety in relation to crime is available. The extensive review of research literature focused on different elements within a study and employed specific criteria to evaluate these elements. Both these elements and the criteria are based on a familiar research framework that evidently reflects an empirical approach as developed in the social sciences (see Boudon 1993: 10; Lazarsfeld 1993a, 1993b).[12] The framework was specified in great detail to explicate the elements or issues that were considered relevant when reviewing the available empirical literature, and led to questions that were used as tools to systematically analyse several decades of research. Table 2.1 lists both the elements as well as the criteria that were applied. However, this chapter will not elaborate on all elements of research studies, but will only focus on the question how 'fear of crime' or aspects thereof have been conceptualised and measured and how well these measurement instruments perform.

The underlying presumption here is that research is not done in a (social) vacuum and the research process and thus its outcomes are dependent on the choices the researcher has made, which will be discussed further in the chapters on the key concepts.[13] Thus, reality as extrapolated from research is said to be constructed (Hacking 1999a; MacKenzie 1981), and scientific theories are in a sense social products (Chalmers 1997: 197). For example, the social and political circumstances or environment(s) in which the researcher functions, exert influence(s) on the researcher and the process (see De Groot 1972: 23; Holton 1998; Kuhn 1996; Leahey 1991). This is clearly demonstrated by research on 'fear of crime' and will be elaborated on in chapter 8. The different influences or the interests might even be conflicting (e.g. Coulter et al. 1985) and define the boundaries of the accepted standards, the paradigm or research programme a researcher works in and with.

Moulton (1983) elaborates on the notion that science is never value free by using the concept of paradigm as Kuhn popularised it (1996; see Ball 1984: 27). She states, rather similar to Kuhn (1996: 175) the paradigm is a system:

> of not only generalizations and concepts, but beliefs about the methodology and evaluation of research: about what are good questions to ask, what are proper developments to the theory, what are acceptable research methods. (p. 152)

---

[12]   The framework has been made more explicit by drawing on the works of in particular Blalock (1961, 1968a, 1968b, 1974, 1982), Boesjes-Hommes (1974), Cronbach & Meehl (1955/1968), De Groot (De Groot 1971, 1975; De Groot & Medendorp 1986), Hox (Hox & De Jong-Gierveld 1990; Hox, Mellenbergh & Swanborn 1995; Hox 1997), Lazarsfeld (1968, 1972a, 1972b, 1993), Neale & Liebert (1986), and Verschuren (1994).

[13]   This presumption flows from Weber's emphasis on both the value-bound choices of the researcher and the possibility of value-neutral methods (Burger 1987; Keat & Urry 1975: 196-227).

Table 2.1. Overview of elements and criteria that were of interest in the extensive literature review of the current state of affairs.[14]

Part of research	(element)	Key questions	Criterion	Explanation
Objective		**Why?**		
	Objective	With what purpose?	Congruence	Congruence with other parts
	For whom	Research presented to whom? Research used by whom?	Directiveness	Objective gives direction
Research questions		**What?**		
	Type of knowledge	What type of knowledge?	Congruence	Congruence with objective and all
	Research questions	What (sub)questions?	Directiveness	Research questions give direction
Concepts		**Which?**		
	Concepts	Which concepts?	Congruence	Congruence with theory, conceptualisation and all
			Consistency	Not contradictory
			Parsimony	Theory and model as simple as possible, yet precise and generalisable
			Empirical reference	Delimitation of empirical phenomena
			Theoretical embeddedness	Concepts related to others in theoretical structure

---

[14] Based on literature referred to in footnote 12, and also Berka (1983), Derksen, Korsten & Bertrand (1988), De Groot (1975), Stern & Kalof (1996), Verschuren (1994), Zeller & Carmines (1980); concerning the survey, see Dillman (1991, 1999), Groves (1990), Jenkins & Dillman (1997), and Lyberg et al. (1997). Specific criteria for instruments that use items (i.e. surveys, questionnaires, interviews) were based on especially Converse & Presser (1988), Rossi, Wright & Anderson (1983) and Tanur (1983). Literature on attitude scale construction has been helpful as well (Dillman 1999; Hamblin 1974; Krosnick & Abelson 1997; Krosnick & Fabrigar 1997; Scherpenzeel & Saris 1997; Schuman & Kalton 1985; Schuman & Presser 1981; Upshaw 1968).

Table 2.1 – continued.

Part of research (element)		Key questions	Criterion	Explanation
Theoretical model		Which theoretical model? How are the concepts related?	General desiderata: consistent, complete, general, fruitful, clear, testable	Description or definition of concepts (classification); explanation of concepts and interrelations
Hypotheses		**Which?**		
	Hypotheses	Which hypotheses?	Congruence	Congruence with theory, conceptualisation and all
			Parsimony	Hypotheses as simple as possible, yet precise
			Testability	Test and falsification possible
Operationalisation & measurement		**How?**		
	Operationalisation	How are concepts operationalised?	Construct validity	Congruence with theory and conceptualisation
Instrument (indicators)	Measurement instrument	What instruments are used? How are instruments developed?	Congruence, validity, reliability	
	Item formulation	How is the wording of items?	Proper formulation	Clear, simple, non-suggestive, item reversal etc.
	Scale characteristics	What is the reliability?	Reliability	Little random measurement error; interitem correlations, (exploratory/ confirmatory) factor analyses, multiple indicators, structural equation modelling, scaling model
		What is the validity?	Validity	Little systematic measurement error; content validity, construct validity (convergent & divergent validity), MTMM
	Data collection	How are data collected? What procedure? What method? When? Where?	Congruence, usefulness	

Table 2.1 – continued.

Part of research	(element)	Key questions	Criterion	Explanation
Sample	Participants	**Who?** Who are participants?		
		How are participants sampled?	Congruence	Congruence with objective and all
		In particular studies:	High response rate	Participation or response rate
			Heterogeneous sample	Random sample (of population of interest) with high response rate; representativeness
Data	Nature of data	**What?** What is the nature of the data?	Congruence, usefulness	
	Norms			Means and SDs for subsamples
Analysis	Techniques	**How?** How are data analysed? What technique is used?	Congruence, usefulness, limited violations	
Presentation	Presentation format	**How?** How are results presented? Are results publicly available? What public?	Congruence, usefulness	Not 'lying with graphs'

Keeping this in mind, the general objective behind this chapter can be rephrased as contrasting the paradigm of empirical research on 'fear of crime' with the more general paradigm of empirical research in the social sciences. This general paradigm encompasses a research framework, which in turn comprises the questions that explicate the elements or issues that were considered to be relevant in this review. These key issues are best thought of as the targets of the choices made in the study under review and may be either implicitly or explicitly expressed (see Holton 1998: 215-216). These choices point out certain tasks, "the completion of which is critical to most research endeavors" (Asher 1984: 3). The choices and tasks point to the general parts or elements of the study that were reviewed.

The first and second column in Table 2.1 present the general parts or elements of a study that is of interest for the current review, the third and fourth column propose the questions, used as 'tools', that were asked while reviewing the literature. The next column puts forward the main criteria that were used to evaluate the elements of a particular study. The elements portray the type of choices made in the investigation regarding for example research questions, the collection and analysis of data and touching on issues regarding conceptualisation and operationalisation.[15]

2.1.1   Conceptualisation

Theoretical statements and research questions relating to them are often expressed in terms of "relationships among concepts, abstractions or symbols representing our key theoretical terms" (Asher 1984: 7), which makes the used concepts highly relevant. According to Hempel (1952), *definition* is an important method of concept formation. Hempel and others (e.g. Blalock 1968a, 1968b; Delbeke 1976; Fetzer 1991: 17) state concept formation and theory formation are extremely closely interrelated; they are two aspects of the same procedure. A more inductive data-driven strategy or empirical entry approach (Broers 1994; Dessens & Jansen 1987) reduces observed phenomena to more generalised principles, possibly through a facet design (Canter 1985; Guttman 1954, 1959a; Hox et al. 1995; Shye 1998).[16] Important to note is that either strategy or approach ultimately leads to a study in which some concepts are the focus of attention; in what ways these concepts are constructed is of lesser interest here. Also, in a theoretical model, several concepts may be linked together, although not all of equal importance for that particular project. Relevant concepts for the current project, like 'fear of crime', 'fear of victimisation', 'perception of risk' are sometimes of main interest and explicitly pointed out by the researcher. Other times, the focus of the researcher in a particular study was on another phenomenon, like 'social cohesion', 'quality of life' or 'health', and the concepts relevant here had a less central role within the

[15] The order of the elements in Table 2.1 does not necessarily reflect the chronological order of the steps taken.
[16] Hox (1986: 25-34) describes the empirical-analytical approach that integrates aspects of both the theory-driven strategy and the data-driven strategy. This approach uses the mapping sentence (Guttman 1954) to circumscribe the set of phenomena that is object of the study.

(theoretical) model. In the present review and evaluation of the current state of affairs, concepts in either central or marginal roles were taken into account.

What constitutes 'good conceptualisation' and what criteria can be applied when evaluating the concepts in the literature on 'fear of crime'? As Sorensen (1991: 71) notes, theories and definitions share the same desiderata, attributes that are considered desirable, namely to be "consistent, complete, general, simple, fruitful – and precise". These desiderata and accordingly criteria appear to be quite common. For example, Weber (1949: 76) and others have argued that clear concepts are of great value. However, 'clear' does not necessarily mean 'precise', at least according to Sorensen's (1991) plea for vagueness and 'borderline cases'. His analysis hints at the dynamics of theoretical concepts. Yet, this does not inevitably conflict with the criterion of clarity; the clearer the concepts within a study are the less confusion will arise when the results of that study are discussed, this is a reason why Jones (1984) suggests concept development should take place *before* data are collected. The interdependency of concept formation and other aspects in a research study become clear, since concept formation or development requires some notion of the empirical features of the phenomenon.[17]

Despite its importance, little attention is paid in the (quantitative) methodological literature to guidelines or criteria for the development of theoretical concepts, or research objectives (Hox 1997; Jones 1984; Schwarz 1997). Both Hox and Schwarz suggest this results from the idea that the development of theoretical concepts is placed in the context of discovery, not the context of verification (cf. Popper 1968). Thus, no fixed rules but instead unlimited possibilities characterise the process of conceptualisation. However, it seems useful, as Schwarz (1997) notes, to distinguish between the creative act of theoretical discovery and the logical development of theoretical concepts. He, similar to Hox in the same publication, recommends firstly the elaboration of the *nomological* network of the concept, secondly the definition of subdomains of its meaning and thirdly the identification of appropriate empirical indicators. Lazarsfeld and Barton (1968: 156) say: "One cannot write a handbook on 'how to form fruitful theoretical concepts' in the same way that one writes a handbook on how to sample or how to construct questionnaires." However, according to Lazarsfeld and Barton (1968) the formation of qualitative categories, the classification of social phenomena is an essential action for the researcher to be taken, a viewpoint similar to Glaser and Strauss's grounded theory (Glaser &

---

[17] This necessity is reflected by a fundamental rule that governs definitions according to Schlesinger (1991: 239) that says "the definiendum must not be conceptually prior to the definiens", in which the definiendum is the introduced term or concept and the definiens is an already known group of terms or symbols. This rule means for example that 'music' can be defined by using 'sound' in the definiens, but not the other way around since "sound is conceptually prior to music; a world may abound with sounds where music does not exist, but there is no music where there is no sound. The notion of music is based on the notion of sound, whereas the latter can stand without the former" (Schlesinger 1991: 239).

Strauss 1967; Strauss & Corbin 1994).[18] Jones (1984) argues for more attention to an inventory of concepts used in a particular field. He proposes an interrelatedness criterion, meaning the concepts that are applied in a study should be interrelated. Therefore, he emphasises the use of classifications in this stage of the research process. In a first classification, the classification for general understanding, concepts order "a universe of discourse" (Jones 1984: 53), which enables the researcher to communicate with others about one's understanding of the subject matter. Here, one's objective and the usefulness of concepts related to that objective, are leading. A second classification is more specific than the previous one and arranges the research expectations and possible categories of concepts. This can help when refining the study, although Jones suggests that in exploratory research this might not be possible. The third classification of empirical findings uses concepts that resemble ones in the previous classifications, but other concepts may be modified or introduced. For Jones, the key issue seems to be the closeness of approximation of the empirical findings and the classification of research expectations (Jones 1984: 59).

2.1.2   Translating concepts: operationalisation

Table 2.1 also portrays the type of choices made in the investigation regarding the collection of information or data, how these data are analysed and how results are presented. Concepts that are of interest need to be derived from something that the researcher can get knowledge of; the concepts need to be translated into something that can be perceived or observed, i.e. the operationalisations of the theoretical concepts. The 'restrictive definitions of a conceptual quality in terms of the operations that need to be executed in order to enable the observation of that quality' is indispensable (Delbeke 1976). In a theory-driven approach an abstract concept or the latent construct is translated into an operationalisation, which points to the observable indicator. In a data-driven approach, or empirical entry approach, a more operational definition of theoretical concepts is used (Broers 1994); questionnaires are used as research instruments to define the concepts.

Lazarsfeld (1993a), whose ideas are typically theory-driven, describes four steps of the process of translating concepts into variables. First, an initial creative imagery of the concept "is some vaguely conceived entity that makes the observed relations meaningful" (Lazarsfeld 1993a: 240). The next step is concept specification, which means that the original imagery is divided into components, aspects or dimensions. The next two steps involve the selection of

---

[18]   Lazarsfeld & Barton (1968: 157) propose four requirements; a good classification requires *articulation*, which means the classification should proceed in steps from the general (global groupings) to the specific (detailed categories). A second requirement is *logical correctness*, which means that in an articulate set of categories the categories on each step are exhaustive and mutually exclusive. Next, they emphasise the importance of the *adaptation to the structure of the situation*. Thus, the classification should be based on a comprehensive outline, containing the main elements and processes that are important to distinguish for purposes of understanding, prediction and policy making. The fourth requirement is the *adaptation to the respondent's frame of reference* (Lazarsfeld & Barton 1968: 157; see also Lazarsfeld 1993b).

indicators and finally "to put Humpty Dumpty together again", the formation of indices (Lazarsfeld 1993a). In brief, the actual instrument reflects the operationalisations that have been translated into indicators, yielding observable responses.

2.1.3   Criteria: validity and reliability

In a theory-driven approach, a concept is translated into an operationalisation, which points to the observable indicator. The data-driven or empirical entry approach applies a more operational definition of theoretical concepts (Broers 1994); questionnaires are used as research instruments to define the concepts. Both strategies lead to a study in which some operationalisations are used. The criteria for evaluating the instrument that is used in a study, depend on what procedure is employed to develop a measurement instrument. Therefore, the distinction between the previously mentioned two approaches is relevant: the theoretical (conceptual) and empirical approach, the former of which emphasises the theoretical power, the latter focuses on psychometric appropriateness (Van de Vijver 1998). The theoretical approach begins with the specification of a theory or model and formulates a set of behaviours that are assumed to reflect the underlying theoretical construct. Whether the items are coherent can be studied until empirical data is gathered. Till then, their relatedness is derived from their shared reference to the underlying construct (Van de Vijver 1998). The empirical approach pays much less attention to the development of a theoretical model. The procedure usually starts with collecting a large pool of items, which is refined on the basis of research in large samples. The items that do not perform well according to common criteria like the item-total correlations are excluded. Another common criterion is derived from factor analysis; items measuring the same construct are supposed to have high loadings on the same factor.[19]

Subsequently, the reliability of these items can be calculated. Whether an instrument has been constructed within a theory-driven approach, or a data-driven approach, reliability and validity are the key criteria that have been applied to evaluate the general quality of the measurement strategy, the operationalisations and measurement instruments (Asher 1984: 121; see also for instance Smith 1994; Scherpenzeel 1995; Groves 1987). Table 2.1 considers both reliability and validity as characteristics of a scale (or index). Robinson, Shaver and Wrightsman (1999) present an extensive list of criteria for scales and items that purport to measure political attitudes as well as exemplary and minimal fulfilment thereof, which has been very helpful in the current review. Besides reliability and validity as leading criteria, another key question is to what extent the results and conclusions can be soundly deduced from the analyses and data. This relates to the legitimacy of an explanation as proposed

---

[19]   Guttman (1954, 1959a, 1959b) aimed at combining the strengths of both approaches when he developed facet theory, in which theory and measurement are closely linked. The facet approach offers an opportunity of empirically testing data and integrating the results in a theoretical framework (Canter 1985). Its main critical assumption, based on the principle of contiguity, is that items that are more similar conceptually will be more similar empirically (Brown 1985).

by Outhwaite (1987). A good explanation postulates a mechanism that is capable of explaining the phenomenon of interest, also, on the basis of collected evidence "we have good reason to believe in its existence" and "we cannot think of any equally good alternatives" since possible alternative explanations are eliminated (Outhwaite 1987: 58).

2.2 Data: studies under review

Table 2.1 lists both the elements as well as the criteria that were of interest in the review of the available empirical literature. These elements and criteria led to questions that were used as tools to systematically analyse several decades of research. This section describes the four types of sources that provided the 'data', i.e. the empirical studies that were included in the review.[20] The studies concern various aspects of so-called 'fear of crime', the experience and interpretation of safety, fear of victimisation and attitudes on crime. After the description of the four types of sources, the next part will sketch the current state of affairs regarding conceptualisation and measurement of the bulk of research in this field.

The studies that were examined have been systematically gathered from a number of resources, restricted merely by the language and accessibility.[21] The different sources can be divided into four types and reflect the current questions of interest which are concerned mostly with the conceptualisations and operationalisations used in this field. The first type of source consists of survey and interview questions, which were compiled from several institutions and data archives in the Netherlands, USA and UK. Surveys administered on a regular basis; for example, the large-scale surveys BCS (Hough & Mayhew 1983; Mayhew & Hough 1988), ICVS (Van Dijk 1990, 1994), POLS (Centraal Bureau voor de Statistiek 1998), and the NCVS (Garofalo & Hindelang 1977; Skogan 1990b), as well as the occasional surveys, were usually easily accessible. Often, the interview questions are presented together with percentages of the response categories (e.g. Harris 1969 Urban Crime Survey, no. 1935, see Appendix F: Figure 2.9). Another source for applied operationalisations consists of raw datasets. These datasets were mainly gathered from three organisations, namely NIWI, ICPSR and the IRSS Public Opinion Questionnaire Database and Data Archive. All three organisations provide a searchable archive, which consists of several sources and datasets. For example, the Steinmetz Archive of NIWI contains several datasets from individual studies as well as from national institutes like the SCP and CBS. ICPSR offers many American datasets, like the data used in Skogan and Maxfield's 'Coping with Crime' (1981). The IRSS comprises, among others, the Louis Harris Data Center and the General Social Survey.

---

[20] The four sources of empirical studies have been systematically searched till 2002. The years after that, only the academic sources (e.g. WoS, PsycINFO, Ingenta, JSTOR) have been were systematically searched for relevant articles and books.

[21] Especially reports from institutions and organisations from outside the Netherlands were not always obtainable. The multiple search strategies employed keywords both in Dutch and in English.

Table 2.2. Resources for analysing the current state of affairs, by type.

Survey and interview questions, data in %	
Main sources	SCP, CBS (Statline), WODC, ICPSR[22], NIWI[23], IRSS[24], StatBase, StatCat (Yale), GSS, CASS, BJS, Roper Center, Sourcebook, ABS, UK-Data Archive
Search strategy	Theme, keywords, author
Dutch example	Statline/StatWeb 3.0 [online] (Centraal Bureau voor de Statistiek 2002)
Anglo-Saxon example	Sourcebook of Criminal Justice Statistics (2000). Table 2.86 (p. 161).
Raw survey and interview data	
Main sources	ICPSR, IRSS, NACJD, NIWI, individual researchers in person
Search strategy	Theme, keywords, author
Dutch example	NIPO (1985): NIWI 1069
Anglo-Saxon example	U.S. Dept. of Justice, Bureau of Justice Statistics (1998)
Articles and books	
Main sources	BNSW, Current contents, Francis, Ingenta, IPSA, JSTOR, Medline/PubMed, NCC, Online contents, PiCarta, PsycINFO, Science Direct, Sociological Abstracts, Swetswise, SSRN, SWL, WoS (SCI + SSCI), Wiley InterScience, Women's Resources International (see Appendix A for abbreviations and Appendix B for background information)
Search strategy	Keywords, author, 'snowball'-search
Dutch example	Van der Vijver (1994)
Anglo-Saxon example	Fattah (1993)
Reports	
Main sources	Several websites of (governmental) institutions in UK, USA and Netherlands, GLIN, SOSIG, NCJRS
Search strategy	Institution, theme, keywords, author
Dutch example	Van Dijk & Van Overbeeke (2002)
Anglo-Saxon example	Sarno, Hough & Bulos (1999)

The (empirical) literature; i.e. journal articles and book (sections), function as a third type of source. Many bibliographical databanks, from *Science Direct* to *Ingenta*, were searched, using different keywords, authors and the 'snowball procedure', referring to the use of cross-references. The fourth source consists of non-scientific or non–academic publications, like reports, which were somewhat harder to track down. The websites of (governmental) institutions were used in particular, as well as some bibliographical databanks and again the 'snowball procedure'. In Table 2.2 the different sources are described by type and a Dutch as well as an Anglo-Saxon example are presented. Exploring these four types of sources has led to a database of more than 3,500 studies and publications on various aspects of so-called 'fear of crime', the experience of safety, fear of victimisation and attitudes on crime. It

---

[22] In particular the NACJD.
[23] Especially the Steinmetz Archive.
[24] More specifically, the Public Opinion Poll Question Database and Data Archive of the Odum Institute(University of North Carolina).

would be impracticable to describe all these studies, since the main purpose of this part is to evaluate the research done so far in the light of the conceptualisation and operationalisations of (aspects of) 'fear of crime'. Therefore, the elements and criteria from Table 2.1 have been used as questions to get a systematic overview of the research. The questions lead to possible answers, which were achieved by procedures based on a grounded theory method.

Though interviews and observations are the most common data sources in studies that employ a grounded theory approach, data can actually come from various sources; or in Glaser's (2002b §1-2; 2004 §45) words: "All is data". Merriam (2002) suggests that there are three major sources of data for a qualitative research study, namely interviews, observations, and documents. She argues that

> "The strength of documents as a data source lies with the fact that they already exist in the situation; they do not intrude upon or alter the setting in ways that the presence of the investigator might. Nor are they dependent upon the whims of human beings whose cooperation is essential for collecting data through interviews and observations." (pp. 13)

The data can be technical literature (e.g. professional studies, reports of research and disciplinary writing) as well as non-technical literature (e.g. bibliographies, catalogues, all kinds of archival material), "and even data that have been quantified for other purposes such as census data" (Strauss & Corbin 1990: 18).[25] A nice illustration of the type of data that I gathered and the use of a grounded theory approach to analyse it, is what Anselm Strauss says "the library is like many voices talking to you. All you have to do is listen." (Strauss & Corbin 1990: 55). The data I analysed can be grouped in the four types from Table 2.2 and consists of survey and interview questions, raw survey and interview data and literature. The data were analysed by employing some essential procedures from a grounded theory approach, such as *open coding*, breaking down, examining, comparing, naming and categorising of the studies with respect to the questions derived from the empirical research framework (Glaser & Strauss 1967; Strauss & Corbin 1994). Next, the categories were grouped into more abstract categories, i.e. the main answers to the questions, a process that is referred to as *axial coding* and selective coding (see Heath & Cowley 2004). Besides coding, another feature of this approach is *constant comparison*, that is, the continually sifting and comparison of 'the answers' from several studies, e.g. the specific concepts that were used, in order to form higher order categories, i.e. the main concepts that can be identified (Boeije

---

[25] Though not as common as studies that incorporate data from observations and interviews, there are studies that have used documentary material. For example, Turner (1983) describes a case of grounded theory generation that is based wholly upon analysis of documentary materials. That is, he studied reports of public enquiries set up by the British government following large-scale accidents in the period 1965-1975 (p. 342). He treated the documentary sources like sets of field-notes.

2002).[26] In accordance with general guidelines of grounded theory, notetaking, coding and memoing were overlapping with the collection of more data, that in turn were constantly compared with the patterns that emerged (see Glaser 2002a, especially pp. 2-5). In other words, during the analytical process, possible adaptations of the more tentative 'answers' were constantly checked against the identification of similarities and differences across other data, i.e. the studies under review (Glaser & Strauss 1967).

Usually, both the text and the tables present the main answers to the key questions that were related to the elements and criteria of Table 2.1 and refer to examples of (different) studies, in order to balance between detail and abstraction (cf. Glaser & Strauss 1967: 5).[27] Since not every possible (detailed) answer is mentioned specifically, the results provide a clear more abstract picture of the current state of affairs. However, as an example, Appendix C provides an extensive elaboration of the questions and their answers for one publication by Dull and Wint (1997). The higher order categories of the concepts, the main answers in the present chapter, can be compared and grouped in a similar procedure in even more abstract categories. In this manner, the process can continue until three core categories or concepts are created that are central to 'fear of crime'. These three core concepts are (criminal) victimisation, risk (perception) and fear, which are further discussed in chapters 6, 7 and 8.

2.3   Findings

The focus of this chapter is on what can be soundly gathered from several publications to answer the main question how 'fear of crime' or aspects thereof have been conceptualised and measured, and how well these measurement instruments perform. The studies under review, which concern various aspects of so-called 'fear of crime', the experience of safety, fear of victimisation and attitudes on crime are analysed with the focus on several elements (as presented in Table 2.1). Here, the main aspects of interest are the conceptualisation and operationalisation of aspects of 'fear of crime'; only issues regarding conceptualisation, operationalisation and measurement will be discussed in detail. But first, some general findings regarding the 'general' or 'average' objective, type of knowledge and research questions are briefly described, followed by some notes on the 'general' or 'average' method and procedure of data collection. The next section concentrates on issues regarding conceptualisation and discusses the classification of concepts as well as theoretical models that are derived from the literature. After that, a section on issues regarding operationalisations presents the most frequently used indicators in this field. A summary of all findings can be found in Table 2.4.

---

[26] Throughout the analysis, memos or research notes were recorded. Saturation was achieved; the comparison and addition of more (e.g. recent) studies did not call for another "answer" or category.

[27] The tables in the Appendix provide only one reference as illustration, though this amount could easily be expanded. When selecting the articles that are presented as examples, I kept an eye on the variety in publication date, type of publication (e.g. report, academic journal article), discipline (e.g. gerontology, criminology, psychology) and "national roots" of the research. These factors have been used in the selection of the literature that is referred to in the main text as well.

2.3.1 Brief overview of general findings

2.3.1.1   Objective, type of knowledge and research questions

The question 'why is the study done', when taken narrowly, relates to the research objective or purpose and raises a large variety of answers, since several objectives emerge in studies on 'fear of crime'. A related aspect is *for whom* the study under review is done or who is going to be using the outcomes of the study. Many criminological studies are in some way or another related to the local or national government. Also, many studies on this (and related) topic(s) have been published in academic journals.[28] Many studies aim at describing the phenomenon, and often such descriptive information is intended for the policy making process, which is also the case for studies that intend to describe the development of (the prevalence of) the phenomenon. Outlining a model or theory has been the purpose of several studies as well. Apparently, several theoretical models coexist and some have a bit of an ad hoc character, which will be discussed later.

Though a variety in hypotheses is apparent as well, the one that a particular intervention or measure will (not) have an effect was clearly a separate category. Studies concerned with testing a hypothesis that is concerned with the effectiveness of an intervention (e.g. Bennett 1991; Thompson et al. 2000) are relevant in particular for the policy process (see Vanderveen 2002a). Studies on the effectiveness of measures concern evaluative knowledge, though most publications in the current overview concern descriptive or explanatory knowledge (see Table 2.4).[29]

In an attempt to give a broad overview of the research questions that are involved in the studies under review, Appendix D provides lists of the essential content of a major portion of them. Many publications that are of a quantitative and (pseudo-) epidemiological kind are in some way or another concerned with the prevalence of a phenomenon, like the prevalence of a specific kind of victimisation or attitude. Such publications often have another research question, focusing on the development of the phenomenon over time and using the same survey. Also, several studies provide an answer to the question whether a difference between groups exists and usually relate this possible difference to other correlates. The group classification is based on socio-demographic variables such as sex, ethnicity or socio-economic status. Another common group classification is based on territory; areas are distinguished by means of characteristics like the degree of urbanisation, the postal code, administrative

---

[28] Another public for which publications are designed is the public at large. The general public can buy books that on the one hand focus on *protection*, like "the gift of fear" (Debecker 1997), the "ultimate guide to living safe and smart", written by a "safety chick" (Baty 2003) and a "personal safety guide for women" (Danylewich 2001). Yet, on the other hand, many popular books that are written for the public at large "set the risks in context" (Laudan 1997) and put feelings of fear in *perspective* by pointing out how researchers, statistics, media and politicians construct "our" ideas about danger and risk (see for example Cohl 1997; Furedi 1997; Glassner 1999; Lichter 2001; Murray, Schwartz & Ropeik & Gray 2002; Walsh 1996).

[29] Interpretive knowledge, together with descriptive knowledge, can be found for example in Altheide & Michalowski (1999), James (1997) and Marshall (1995).

divisions or a whole set of socio-demographic characteristic. When countries constitute the areas that are compared, international differences are the key elements of the research question that focuses on an international comparison.

Furthermore, the studies that attempt to answer the question whether differences exist, also aim at describing some relations; that is, they describe characteristics that correlate with characteristics of the different groups. Studies that involve a research question on *relationships* can do this by either centring on mere correlations, or on the consequences of a phenomenon, the causes of a phenomenon and the effects of a phenomenon on another phenomenon or a particular category of people. The phenomenon of interest can be numerous things of course, but in the present field of interest, the most common are for example 'fear of crime' (e.g. Bazargan 1994; Clemente & Kleiman 1976), 'fear of violence' (e.g. Erskine 1974; Mohler 2002), 'victimisation' (e.g. Eijken 1994; Kury & Smartt 2002) and 'feelings of safety' (e.g. Hemenway, Solnick & Azrael 1995; Van der Wurff 1992). This enumeration can easily be expanded with many other terms and concepts, as will be discussed later.

2.3.1.2   Data collection and presentation

As far as data collection is concerned, in this area of research interviews, questionnaires or surveys are used most often, or a combination thereof. Experimental designs are far less often used and usually a questionnaire is used in such a design to test the (quasi-) experimental effect.[30] Another much less common method is observation, both of environmental characteristics and the behaviour of people.[31]

Since many data can be found within the collection of surveys and official (governmental and police) figures, secondary analysis of crime survey data, derived from for example standardised periodical surveys like NCS, GSS, PMB, POLS, BCS or ICVS, is very common in the criminological field of research (Vanderveen 2004; see Appendix A for a glossary of abbreviations). These nation-wide surveys, often conducted by governmental institutions, employ a (random) national sample. Random samples from specific cities or regions are common as well in these kind of studies. Other, non-random and usually less systematic or structured (opportunity) sample techniques are adopted when a specific subpopulation is studied, like victims of a specific crime and tourists and combinations of demographic categories with specific ethnic backgrounds like black elderly. Overall, the technical aspects of the sampling procedures, weights as well as the analytical techniques are very advanced, along with the software enabling these procedures and techniques.

In general, results are presented verbally, in tables, figures and occasionally with geographical maps. Only in studies directly related to policy

---

[30] Although some studies focusing on the perception and cognition of threatening cues have used measurement of reaction time (e.g. Tipples et al. 2002; Yiend & Mathews 2001) and heart rate (e.g. Peasley-Miklus & Vrana 2000).

[31] Mainly when the research question focuses on the role of the media, document or content analysis has been used, either in a more quantitative (e.g. Eschholz 2002; Smith & Wilson 2000) or qualitative way (e.g. Altheide 2000; Cavender 1981).

and governmental, whether on the national or local level, it seems the difference
between 'significant' and 'meaningful' or 'relevant' is sometimes forgotten,
applying graphics that are attempting to illustrate (usually) the change, but could
be regarded just as well as illustrations of 'how to lie with statistics'. A typical
example provides the 'safety index' of Rotterdam, which is constituted of
registered crime and the results from a survey. In May 2003, the local
government published a press release that was warmly welcomed in the media,
with the heading "Rotterdam's safety-formula works" (City of Rotterdam May
25, 2003).[32] The formula works, it was argued, since the 'safety index' changed
from 5.61 to 5.64 on a scale from one to ten (see also Programmabureau Veilig
2002, 2004).

2.4   Concepts and theoretical models

Countless concepts, terms, names and labels are used in the publications
on the experience and interpretation of safety, fear, crime and risk. In Appendix
D a large part of these concepts is presented. One large group of concepts that is
listed consists of simply one word, like safety, fear, danger and risk. Another
major group of concepts is composed of two keywords, like all concepts with
formats as the 'fear of ...', 'feelings of ...', 'experience of ...' and 'perception
of ...', which can be filled in with the concepts that were mentioned, like safety,
danger, crime and more. The different concepts were grouped into more abstract
categories, following a grounded theory procedure (see Glaser & Strauss 1967;
Heath & Cowley 2004; Strauss & Corbin 1990, 1994). The higher order
categories of the concepts, the main answers in the present chapter, can be
compared and grouped in a similar procedure in even more abstract categories.
In this manner, the process can continue until three core categories or concepts
are created that are central to 'fear of crime'. These three core concepts are
(criminal) victimisation, risk (perception) and fear, concepts that which are
further discussed in chapters 6, 7 and 8.

2.4.1   Classification of concepts

Most criteria for concepts, like congruence, parsimony and theoretical
embeddedness, are not met. Much confusion arises from the lack of consistently
applied and definite concepts (Bilsky 1993a; Hale 1996). In order to explain the
relationships between concepts, some classifications have been proposed. Many
classifications of (some of) the different concepts are undoubtedly possible. A
classification can be used when translating the 'imagery' to an empirical
research instrument (Lazarsfeld 1968, 1972a). Such a classification is essential
when doing social scientific research and can even be thought of as inherent to
the whole idea of 'a concept'. Frijda and Elshout (1976) state that within a
cognitive structure, a 'concept' refers to the rules of classification, which leads
to a certain consistency within a concept. A concept has certain different
attributes or stimuli and involves a combination or set of conceptual rules of
these attributes (see De Klerk & Oostlander 1976).

---

[32]   In Dutch: "Rotterdamse veiligheidsaanpak werkt".

A classification, for example as proposed by Lazarsfeld and Barton (1968; Lazarsfeld 1972d), means grouping the concepts from the general (global groupings) to the specific (detailed categories). This is done in such a manner that the categories are exhaustive, mutually exclusive and by comprehensively outlining the main elements and processes that are important to distinguish, in order to understand, prediction or control the phenomenon (Jones 1984; Lazarsfeld & Barton 1968). A classification requires some theoretical notion about the dimensions, which are used to assign the concepts to groups, or some 'underlying trait' (Lazarsfeld 1972a: 20), as well as some observational knowledge (cf. Berka 1983; Lazarsfeld 1972a, 1972c). The notions that are used, as rules, say when an object is part of a certain group.[33]

Table 2.3. Possible classifications.

Dimension		Explanation
Van der Wurff (1990)	Specificity	Specific type of crime – crime in general
	Personal involvement	Personally involved – not personally involved
Bilsky (1993)	Criminal act	Property vs. personal crime
	Costs of victim	Physical, emotional, material (financial)
	Reaction	Affective, cognitive, behavioural
	Offender	Relationship with victim
	Situational context	Indoors vs. outdoors
Ferraro (1995)	Level of reference	General-personal
	Type of perception	Judgments – values – emotions
Vanderveen (1999)	Modality	Cognitive – affective – conative
	Personal involvement	Little – extremely

Some researchers have worked on a classification to order the terminological chaos of 'fear of crime', some of which are presented in Table 2.3. These classifications are concerned with the chaos of operationalisations in particular, and focus on different concepts. For example, Van der Wurff (1990), who observes two dimensions. The first dimension is the specificity of the object (specific-abstract) and the second is personal involvement (involved – not-involved). The fear that is connected to a specific type of crime (e.g. rape) differs from the more abstract concern about crime. When a person is more involved, s/he thinks for example about personally becoming a victim of crime, whereas one could also be worried in general. According to Van der Wurff, the two dimensions are not entirely independent of one another, nor can they always easily be distinguished. The more specific, the more a person is involved, which will lead to fear, whereas less specificity and involvement leads to concern. Although the two dimensions might have been useful in ordering the terminology, Van der Wurff chooses to describe twenty terms, used in research on fear and concern in reference to crime, without associating them with the two dimensions (Van der Wurff 1990). Rather similar to Van der Wurff's dimension 'personal involvement', is Ferraro's dimension 'level of reference' (Ferraro 1995).

---

[33] Therefore, according to Blalock (1968a), classification rules are part of the operational language. The notions on which they are based are part of the theoretical language.

In order to end the confusion over definitions of 'fear of crime', Ferraro (1995; Ferraro & LaGrange 1988) presents a conceptual framework, which defines "various perceptions about crime". As Van der Wurff does, two dimensions are proposed, namely the 'level of reference' and the 'type of perception'. The level of reference is comparable with the dimension of personal involvement suggested by Van der Wurff, it ranges from a general, community-oriented, level to a personal, self-oriented, level. The "type of crime perception" (Ferraro & LaGrange 1988: 279), the second dimension, ranging from cognitive (judgments) to affective (emotions), is comparable to the modes of the reaction as suggested by Bilsky (1993). Ferraro and LaGrange note: "The cognitive dimension on the left end of the continuum encompasses assessments of risk and safety, whereas the affective dimension on the right includes feelings of fear". This means that the dimension is indeed a continuum, that the behavioural mode is excluded, whereas 'values' as a type of perception are included. Here, it remains unclear why Ferraro excludes the behavioural mode entirely, whether the two dimensions are uni or bipolar and what it means that values are conceptualised as concerns, or what these 'values' are conceptually. An example given by Ferraro (1995) of the cell 'personal-value' is 'concern about crime to self'. Another example, of the cell 'personal-emotions' is 'fear for self-victimisation'. According to Ferraro and LaGrange, the "distinction among risks, concerns and emotions" is very relevant and the distinction between fear of victimisation and perceived risk has been fruitful.[34] Bilsky (1993) sketches the 'more or less related manifestations of fear' that are summarised by the term 'fear of crime', describing five analytical dimensions. The concept is refined with regard to the criminal act, the costs incurred by the victim, the modes of reaction, the offender and situational context. These various subconcepts make up the general construct 'fear of crime'. As Bilsky argues, the operationalisations need to be related to these subconcepts in a symmetrical way. The whole concept 'fear of crime' can thus only be measured by using operationalisations of all these subconcepts.

Vanderveen (1999) and Fattah (1993) follow an analytical conception, analogous to the conceptual framework of Fishbein and Ajzen (1975). A distinction is drawn between the cognitive, affective and conative or behavioural modality of the concept 'fear of crime'. The cognitive modality refers to those aspects that touch on processes of perception and interpretation; the affective modality concerns feelings and mood and is evaluative in nature (Fishbein & Ajzen 1975: 11). This affective modality, involving an evaluation, is often referred to as attitude (Fishbein & Ajzen 1975).[35] The conative or behavioural modality touches on intended acts and behaviours.[36] Although the analytical

---

[34] But confusion arises as well when looking at the classification of Ferraro (1995) and Ferraro & LaGrange (1988).

[35] Attitude can be defined as the degree of positive or negative affect associated with some psychological object. Positive affect or feeling is equivalent to a favourable attitude towards the object. Negative affect or feeling is equivalent to an unfavourable attitude towards an object (Edwards 1957: 2).

[36] Fishbein & Ajzen discriminate between intended behaviour (the conative dimension) and use the term 'behavior' to refer to observable, observed overt acts (Fishbein & Ajzen 1975).

distinction between these three modalities is conceptually helpful, in practice it is hardly possible to discriminate between a person's feelings and considerations when studying an emotion.[37] This is also illustrated by Thurstone's (1928) use of the concept of attitude:

> to denote the sum total of a man's inclinations and feelings, prejudice or bias, preconceived notions, ideas, fears, threats, and convictions about any specified topic. Thus, a man's attitude about pacifism means here all that he feels and thinks about peace and war. It is admittedly a subjective and personal affair. (p. 531)[38]

Despite its vagueness, attitude theories can be useful sometimes in research on aspects of 'fear of crime' (e.g. Costelloe et al. 2002; Kuttschreuter & Wiegman 1996, 1997, 1998). Other theoretical models might be useful as well, especially in reference to the criteria of theoretical embeddedness, consistency and generality. However, most studies do not explicitly apply a (theoretical) model within which the concepts are embedded. However, a few theoretical models that attempt to explain 'fear of crime' were introduced and tested in the literature (see Covington & Taylor 1991; Crank, Giacomazzi & Heck 2003; Farrall, Bannister, Ditton & Gilchrist 2000; Taylor & Hale 1986). Also, most research implies a sort of theoretical model, which in a particular research project may only be partly of interest; i.e. just only some hypotheses are implied or introduced. The (implied) models that represent the interrelationships between concepts are briefly discussed subsequently.

2.4.2   Theoretical models on causes of 'fear of crime'[39]

Such models relate concepts to one another in various ways, some manners which touch on the form of the model are presented in Appendix D. The main models, whether implicated or explicitly used, partly or entirely, that attempt to explain the *causes* of 'fear of crime' can be classified in five types; namely the crime-causes-fear-model, the criminal-victimisation-causes-fear-model, the imaginable-victimisation-causes-fear-model, the disorder-causes-fear-model, the tight-social-structure-inhibits-fear-model and the differential-socialisation-causes-different-fear-model. These types are only briefly discussed here.[40] Some of these types have already been described in the introductory chapter, since they touched on the social relevance of 'fear of crime' because of its consequences.

---

[37]   As is also reflected by the classification presented by Ferraro & LaGrange (1988), which will be elaborated on later.

[38]   Early criticism on the vagueness of the attitude-concept reflected the overlap with the concept 'values' and 'opinions' (Bain 1928; Kirkpatrick 1936).

[39]   This section is based on Vanderveen (1998a, 1999, 2002c).

[40]   The models are not mutually exclusive but tend to show overlap in concepts and relations between the concepts; see for example "indirect victimisation", which is of importance both in the victimisation-causes-fear-model and in the imaginable-victimisation-causes-fear-model.

The first type, the crime-causes-fear-model, is probably the oldest and directly relates crime and fear (e.g. Harris 1969; Skogan & Klecka 1977).[41] The basic notion of this model is that crime causes, or is related to, fear.[42] Therefore, variance in crime rates is supposedly reflected by differences in fear.[43] Usually, *crime* is specified as *criminal victimisation* (e.g. Garofalo 1979; Norris & Kaniasty 1994; Silverman & Della-Giustina 2001). This typical model can hold the reciprocal effects or feedback loops of the systemic-crime-model as well as the community-decline-model, saying that informal surveillance of the neighbourhood reduces street crime, but (street) crime reduces informal surveillance by increasing resident's perception of risk and fear.[44] Crime then, is considered both the cause and the result of fear (e.g. Bursik 2000; Bursik & Grasmick 1993). Similar to the process already described in the introductory chapter, fear increases because of (street) crime, residents avoid the public streets in their neighbourhood, resulting in a decrease of (informal) surveillance in the neighbourhood, which in turn will increase crime.[45]

The crime-causes-fear and victimisation-causes-fear-model have been popular, but results from empirical tests have been confusing (e.g. Borooah & Carcach 1997; Gates & Rohe 1987; Skogan & Maxfield 1981). Thus, despite many studies, the relation between victimisation and fear is still ambiguous.[46] This particular model has led to the notion of the so-called fear-victimisation paradox (Chadee 2000; Hale 1996; Vanderveen 1999). In brief, the paradox states that people with the lowest risk on victimisation, exhibit the highest fear, whereas people with a higher risk on victimisation have less fear. Factually, this means that women and the elderly have reported more fear whereas men and younger people end up in the criminal victimisation statistics. Many researchers have criticised the paradox, which has led to several new insights and findings (e.g. Gilchrist et al. 1998; Winkel 1998; Ziegler & Mitchell 2003).

The imaginable-victimisation-causes-fear-model flows from ideas on *indirect* victimisation, the victimisation of others, whether significant others somebody personally knows or a fictional character in a television series (e.g. Chiricos, Padgett & Gertz 2000; Davis, Taylor & Bench 1995). This indirect victimisation can cause fear, which relates to what will be called here *imaginable victimisation*. This means that the sheer *possibility* of victimisation is crucial; just imagining oneself to be a victim of crime is the crucial cause of

---

[41] In 1978 the journal *Victimology* published a special issue on 'fear of crime', which gives a good overview of the past and current issues in the field of research. In that issue for example, Baumer (1978) gives an overview of research in the USA, Gaquin (1978) describes the measurement of 'fear of crime' as an attitude in the National Crime Survey, Hening & Maxfield (1978) discuss measures to reduce fear, Jaycox (1978) concentrates on the elderly and their fear versus risk, Zion (1978) provides a typical example of many studies in this area when describing the reduction of "Crime and Fear of Crime in Downtown Cleveland" and Riger, Gordon & LeBailly (1978) take what could be called a more critical stance in their analysis of the victimisation and fear of women.

[42] See for example Goodstein & Shotland (1980) and more recently Innes & Fielding (2002).

[43] See for example Lawton & Yaffe (1980), Wiltz (1982), Baker et al. (1983) and Evans (2001).

[44] See for example Skogan (1990), Taylor (1996) and Bellair (2000).

[45] See for example Goodstein & Shotland (1980), Liska & Warner (1991) and Markowitz et al. (2001).

[46] See Skogan (1987), Donnelly (1988), Smith & Hill (1991b), Weinrath & Gartrell (1996), Van Wilsem (1997), Weinrath (1999) and Astor et al. (2002).

fear. This typical model stresses the cognitive processes of an individual when explaining 'fear of crime', once again in relationship with known crime rates, and concentrates especially on perceptions of vulnerability and risk (e.g. Wilcox Rountree 1998; Van der Wurff 1992). A number of studies have addressed the question whether some categories of people, like women, perceive a higher risk. Others have related 'fear of crime' to feelings of vulnerability (Killias 1990; Smith & Torstensson 1997). Another notion that has been welcomed, results from findings that the fear of victimisation is mainly caused by the fear of sexual offences and in particular the fear of rape (Ferraro 1995, 1996; Warr 1984, 1987). The question *why* groups of people differ in their feelings of vulnerability, or in the fear of becoming a victim of rape, and the role these differences seem to play, has been a central concern in studies on socialisation processes, which will be outlined later.

The model that concentrates on the idea of imaginable victimisation attempts to explain 'fear of crime' by analysing individual processes. In contrast, the disorder-causes-fear-model and the tight-social-structure-inhibits-fear-model are especially interested in aspects of the neighbourhood (Donnely 1988; Skogan & Maxfield 1981). Crank, Giacomazzi and Heck (2003) distinguish the "disorder/broken windows model" from the "social integration model". Both models and versions thereof have been discussed in chapter 1. The disorder-model, which is very much related to the previously mentioned model that states that crime or neighbourhood decline causes fear, holds that social and physical disorder in the environment are indicators of a lack of control and concern.[47] This in turn leads to more 'fear of crime' or a higher perceived risk to become a victim (Lewis & Salem 1986; Skogan 1990a). Thus, the presence of 'broken windows' and other signs of disorder cause fear (Kelling & Coles 1996; Wilson & Kelling 1982). All kinds of signs of disorder are called *incivilities*, and can be more social and physical in nature.[48] The level of disorder and incivilities have been connected with the social structural aspects of a neighbourhood, that is, a tighter social structure may repel behaviour that leads to incivilities.[49] This typically general model, stating that a tighter social structure inhibits fear, overlaps with the previous crime-causes-fear and disorder-causes-fear models through the concepts of informal surveillance and incivilities (e.g. Bellair 2000; see also section 1.5). Also, the models are based on the social disorganisation theory, which says that the variation in the capacity of neighbourhoods to constrain its residents from violating norms is crucial. This capacity is considered a function of neighbourhood cohesion, reflected by for example the size, density and breadth of network ties (Bursik 2000; Sampson & Groves 1989). An essential concept is collective efficacy, which is the ability to

---

[47] All these models, as well as the Zero Tolerance ideas that are based on it, have been tested and criticised (e.g. Harcourt 1998; Sampson & Raudenbusch 1999; Taylor 1999; see also Van Dijk, Flight & Oppenhuis 2000).

[48] See e.g. Fisher & Nasar (1995), LaGrange, Ferraro & Suspancic (1992), Rohe & Burby (1988) and Sims, Hooper & Peterson 2002.

[49] See e.g. Van Dijk, Flight & Oppenhuis (2000: 16) or Sampson & Raudenbusch (1999).

effectively intervene in neighbourhood problems and to supervise residents to maintain public order.[50]

The tight-social-structure-inhibits-fear-model applies concepts like 'collective efficacy', 'social embeddedness', 'a sense of community', and 'fear of crime' as aspects of the neighbourhood (Martinez, Black & Starr 2002). According to Crank, Giacomazzi and Heck (2003) the "social integration model" suggests an inverse relationship between the social integration within a neighbourhood and the 'fear of crime'. The general idea is that a more tight social structure inhibits fear, whereas anonymity, interpersonal estrangement and distrust are associated with higher levels of fear.[51] The positive connotation of a tight social structure is also reflected by studies on the 'community quality of life' that relate several characteristics of a community, among which are crime and social ties, to the satisfaction of residents (Sirgy & Cornwell 2001, 2002).[52]

The concept 'social integration' bears similarities with concepts like social capital and social cohesion (e.g. De Hart, Maas-De Waal & Roes 2002), and operationalisations of these related concepts have been at least as diverse as operationalisations of 'fear of crime' (see Bursik & Grasmick 1993).[53] Again, the causal relationships between fear and the concepts of social control and cohesion are double-edged (Sampson 1991; Sampson & Raudenbusch 1999).

The last model that is briefly described here has been used to explain differences between men and women on their level of fear. The socialisation-model states that different socialisation of boys and girls results in different levels of fear.[54] Boys are learned to be (or behave) fearless, tough and aggressive, whereas girls are learned to be passive and constrain their behaviour. This leads to a difference in their responses on questions about fear due to social desirability. Men might formulate their responses differently ("sometimes I don't feel at ease", "I'm at my guard then!") than women ("sometimes I do feel unsafe", "I'm scared over there").[55] Maybe women overstate their fear whereas men use understatements to express feelings of fear (see also Pierce & Kirkpatrick 1992). In more general studies on fear, not only do female respondents report more fear (e.g. Croake, Myers & Singh 1987), they show in particular more fear than male respondents in situations that describe men in a

---

[50] See Sampson, Raudenbusch & Earls (1997), Sampson & Raudenbusch (1999) and Gibson et al.(2002).

[51] Conform the notion of guardianship within the routine activities approach (e.g. Lee 2000).

[52] See also Michalos (2003) on the quality of life and local police services, in which two items on "feelings of safety" were used.

[53] Thus, in several studies, 'fear of crime' has been related to the quality and quantity of social ties (e.g. Riger, LeBailly & Gordon 1981; Ross & Jang 2000), trust of neighbours (e.g. Fischer 1981; Walklate 1998a), a sense of community (e.g. Brodsky, O'Campo & Aronson 1999; Zani, Cicognani & Albanesi 2001), feeling part of neighbourhood (Hunter & Baumer 1982), participation in organisations (Austin, Woolever & Baba 1994; Lindström, Merlo & Osterland 2003), number of friends in neighbourhood (Austin, Woolever & Baba 1994; Baba & Austin 1989) and the length of residence (Baba & Austin 1989; Bazargan 1994).

[54] See Dillon, Wolf & Katz (1985), Goodey (1995, 1997), Howard (1984) and Hurwitz & Smithey (1998).

[55] This difference in formulation also appeared in a study of the author on the experience of safety in the subway, in which 250 men and women were interviewed (Vanderveen 1998).

(negative) stereotypical manner; in other words: women are fearful, whereas men are feared (Brody, Lovas & Hay 1995; Warr 1990).

The socialisation-model has been primarily concerned with power relations and the experiences that women (might) have in their daily lives regarding sexual offences and harassment, elaborating on the concept 'victimisation'.[56] Because of the "shadow of sexual assault" (Ferraro 1996), women exhibit more fear than men. Not only legally sanctioned acts like rape are focused on, attention has been given to intrusive behaviour that might be equally offending or threatening as well (Koss et al. 1994; Stanko 1985, 1990). Yet, these behaviours may neither be legally sanctioned, like obscene phone calls (Buck, Chatterson & Paase 1995; Huys 2001; Sheffield 1993) or unwanted sexual attention (Gardner 1995; Johnson & Sacco 1995), nor identified as a *crime* by the 'victim' (e.g. Gavey 1999; Kelly 1987, 1988; Kelly & DeKeseredy 1994; Phillips 1999), but nevertheless have a profound impact. Since sexual assault is "lurking everywhere" (cf. Muris, Luermans, Merkelback & Mayer 2000), women need to be constantly aware of the dangers, thereby socially controlling women's lives (Chan & Rigakos 2002; Clark 1987; Day 1999; Riger & Gordon 1981). Ideas on 'provocative clothing', walking alone at night, giving a ride to a stranger are socially constructed and reinforced (e.g. Liska, Sanchiro & Reed 1988; Yeoh & Yeow 1997). In brief, this model states that women are socialised to be more fearful and to restrict their behaviour (Keane 1998; Riger, Gordon & LeBailly 1978, 1982), whereas men have learned to be fearless and take risks (Devlin 2000; Gordon & Riger 1989; Johnson, Bowker & Cordell 2001; Walklate 1997). Also, these studies elaborate on the victimisation-causes-fear-model, and its variants of indirect victimisation and imaginable victimisation (see chapter 6).

2.5   *Operationalisations, indicators and items*[57]

Since the concept 'fear of crime' is not clear, many operationalisations have been used to measure it, relating it to risk, worry, fear of victimisation and so on. Nonetheless, some items are by far more frequently used than others to measure 'fear of crime' or rather parts of 'fear of crime', which might lead to the conclusion that "there is a surprising consistency in the way fear of crime is measured" (Ferraro & LaGrange 1988). This conclusion is based on the two most frequently used items, namely the NCS-item "feeling safe alone in the neighborhood at night" and the GSS-item "are there any areas around here where you would be afraid to walk at night" (Ferraro & LaGrange 1987).

Despite the importance, in most studies little attention is given to the process of operationalisation. The general and simple picture is that researchers have either used the operationalisations and items as others have done in previous studies, or they have transformed available data into indicators of the concepts of interest. Again, what is known from for example the measurement of attitudes has hardly been applied. Some studies have used a facet theoretical

---

[56] In particular: Stanko (1988a, 1988b), Pain (1997), Acierno (2000) and Felson et al. (2002).
[57] This section is based on Vanderveen (2000).

approach in the process of operationalisation (e.g. Borg & Stauffenbiel 1993; Van der Wurff 1992). The facet design can be used as observation scheme, it is explicitly and exactly stating what observations are to be made, and how, which results in a demarcation of the domain of interest and as a template for the formulation of questionnaire items (Broers 1994). For example, Van Staalduinen (cited in Broers 1994) firstly surveyed the existing research literature about feelings of safety. Then, he derived an underlying facet design from three surveys (see Van der Wurff 1992: 57), that is, he formulated a mapping sentence that resulted in a limited subset of *structuples* (Brown 1985; Guttman & Greenbaum 1998; Levy 1985). These structuples are profiles, drawing one element from each of the facets, thus the total number of structuples is the number of elements of the 1st facet multiplied by the number of elements of the 2nd facet and so on. The mapping sentence specifies three domain facets, facet A is related to time, facet B to place and facet C to a specific situation, of which the 3rd element is further refined (see Figure 2.2). According to Broers (1994), this mapping sentence permits the occurrence of 3x3x3 logically possible observations and a theory should predict that only a subset of these possible observations occur, or should predict the probability of occurrence for different possible observations within the range of specified observations. Continuing Van Staalduinen's study, Van der Wurff (1992) presents the same mapping sentence that he used in his study, but the response range he used ranged from "often" to "never".

| Do you feel safe | a1 during daytime
a2 unspecified
a3 late at night | b1 in your own house
b2 unspecified
b3 in a small alley | |
| c1 when you are in the company of acquaintances?
c2 unspecified
c3 when a group of men ... | c31 rings your doorbell?
c32 approaches you?
c33 is coming towards you? | ⟶ | yes
...
no |

Figure 2.2. Mapping sentence of Van Staalduinen, cited in Broers (1994).

Such a restricting mapping sentence can be useful both to generate survey items since observations are described by the elements of the facets, and to classify several questions that have been used in surveys. However, the mapping sentence of Figure 2.2 and the results derived from its items does not provide an understanding of the relationships with other operationalisations that are frequently used, like the perception of risk.[58] This can be clarified with a so-called conceptual entry approach, for example dimensional or indicator analysis as developed by Lazarsfeld (1968, 1972a, 1993a). This manner is rather similar to content sampling (Fiske 1971; Hox 1997), which requires a large set of items that covers the whole domain and exploratory factor analysis to identify the sets that measure the same construct. In a way, this is done in studies that start with vague concepts and their subdomains, possibly based on exploratory factor

---

[58] Although Van der Wurff (1992: 60) introduces facets that relate to chance or risk, consequences for wellbeing but reduces the number of facets and consequently the number of structuples.

analysis, and create items for the measurement of these subdomains (e.g. Andrews & Whithey 1976; Norris 1997; Wittebrood, Michon & Ter Voert 1997). However, usually the set of items is only administered once, which makes it more difficult to generalise substantive conclusions about the interrelations and nature of the latent concepts.

This is probably the most problematic issue in the current field of research; validity of popular operationalisations is lacking, as is being noted by other researchers as well (e.g. Farrall, Bannister, Ditton & Gilchrist 1997; Ferraro 1995; Ferraro & LaGrange 1988; Gilchrist et al. 1998; Hughes, Marshall & Sherrill 2003; Jeffords 1983). In his discussion about various methods of questionnaire construction, Oosterveld (1996) discriminates between three main methods, which are according to Broers (1994) all examples of a conceptual entry approach because after the construction some sort of validation is necessary. The first method that Oosterveld distinguished is the 'rational intuitive method', meaning that the researcher follows his or her intuition. In this way, face or content validity is established by mere common sense. It seems that this might be a good description of the characteristic method of questionnaire construction in this field of research. The second method is explorative and is similar to a basic content sampling or indicator analyses procedure. This method uses factor analysis or multidimensional scaling for the identification of possible scales. Oosterveld notes that cross-validation is of importance for this method, to test the empirical meaningfulness of scales, that is, to check whether the same scales, factors, clusters or dimensions, are detected in other samples. The deductive method tests a nomological network, in the sense of Cronbach & Meehl (1968). The type of validation central in this method is the construct validity (Oosterveld 1996). When the instrument is a measure of a latent concept, an attribute or quality that is not operationally defined and no definite criterion is available, then the 'nomological net' becomes important. The validation procedure uses analyses of group differences, correlation matrices and factor analyses, studies of internal structure of the instrument and the stability or generalisability (Campbell & Fiske 1959; Cronbach & Meehl 1968). Overall, an evident observation that it is especially construct validity that is lacking, since construct validity touches on the elaboration of theoretical relationships among concepts, the meaning of a concept and the definition of subdomains of its meaning (Schwarz 1997).

The following section elaborates more systematically on the research question *which operationalisations or items are mostly used*. Since in most studies the process of operationalisation was not described, the items that in fact were (usually) presented have been translated into a somewhat more abstract operationalisation. Because of the blurred boundaries between concept, operationalisation and indicators or items (see Lazarsfeld 1972a, 1972c), this procedure did not cause too many problems. Here, the goal is to catalogue these items and give an overview of common operationalisations, which results in the construction of a questionnaire of this inventory (see section 9.5). This questionnaire is used to obtain data from a couple of samples and analysed in order to examine the current state of affairs with respect to the operationalisation of 'fear of crime'. The operationalisations have been systematically gathered from the sources as described in Table 2.2. Despite the variety of the background of the sources, a substantial overlap exists regarding the items or operationalisations used. Thus, constructing an inventory that reflects the most frequently applied items is very well possible. The items derived from the literature, data and reports are grouped and described below according to the previously mentioned distinctions conceptualised by Fishbein and Ajzen (1975). A distinction is drawn between operationalisations tapping respectively the cognitive, affective and conative or behavioural modality of the concept 'fear of crime'.[59]

2.5.1   The cognitive modality: perceptions and estimates

2.5.1.1   Estimating the magnitude of crime

Respondents are asked whether crime has increased, decreased or stayed the same in a certain period. Usually, the item is finished off with a reference to one's own neighbourhood (e.g. Houts & Kassab 1997) or to the nation as a whole. The question in the Gallup Poll, of which the results of the years 1972-2001 are presented in Figure 2.3 is: "Is there more crime in your area than there was a year ago, or less?" Interestingly enough, the two trend lines show that especially since the mid-nineties more (American) respondents think crime has decreased; fewer respondents think crime has increased in their own area. The same conclusion holds for crime in the USA in general, which can be derived from Figure 2.4. This figure depicts answers of respondents to the question "Is there more crime in the U.S than there was a year ago, or less?" from the Gallup Poll. So, the *American* results show a decline in the percentage of people who think crime has increased nationally. However, *Dutch* respondents, who reacted to a similar question that referred to the level of crime in the Netherlands, do not show such a pattern; a large majority of the Dutch respondents thinks crime has increased in the Netherlands.

2.5.1.2   Various comparisons

Similar to the estimation of the magnitude of crime, which asks whether crime has increased, decreased or stayed the same in a certain period, respondents are asked to make other comparisons as well. Sometimes, respondents are asked about their perception of risk, compared to the perceived risk of others, or in other places. This is called the relative risk perception. Other comparisons, not specifically asking about risk but for example on the magnitude of crime or the safety of a neighbourhood, are sometimes touched on as well. A survey by Harris' organisation in 1969 used the question "Generally, would you say that you feel more safe in this neighborhood, less safe or just

---

[59] Many questions about somebody's opinion on crime are asked, which are also used for the measurement of 'fear of crime' or 'concern with crime'; for example the question what the "three greatest problems are" that is responded with 'crime' (e.g. Janson & Ryder 1983; dataset NIWI P1071). This type of questions are not discussed here.

about as safe as you would in most other neighborhoods around here". The British Social Attitudes Survey (ICPSR 3098) asks: "Compared with the rest of Britain, how much crime would you say there is in your area".

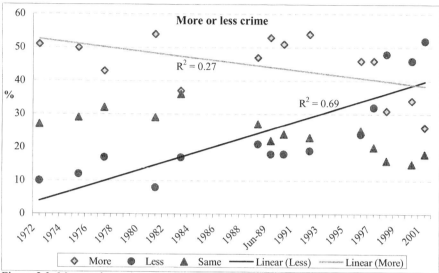

Figure 2.3. More or less crime than a year ago in one's own area, United States, 1972-2001. Source of data: the Sourcebook of criminal justice statistics Online (Maguire & Pastore n.d.), adapted from The Gallup Poll [Online] (Gallup Organization n.d.). Two trend lines are shown, based on a linear relationship. The trend line for 'more crime' has an R^2 of 27%, the 'less crime'-trend line's R^2 is 69%.

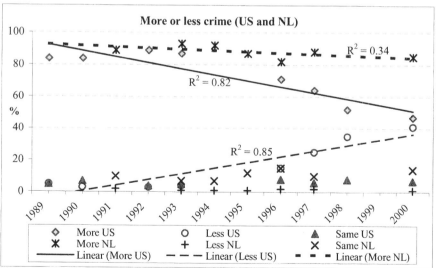

Figure 2.4. More or less crime in the nation than a year ago, United States, 1989-2001 and the Netherlands, 1991-2000. Source of American data: the Sourcebook of criminal justice statistics Online (Maguire & Pastore n.d.), adapted from The Gallup Poll [Online] (Gallup Organization n.d.). Source of Dutch data: SCP, Wittebrood 2001.

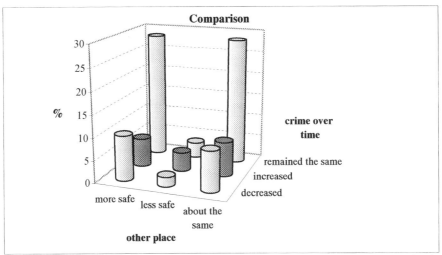

Figure 2.5. Estimation of changes in crime within past two years and how safe is the neighbourhood compared to rest of Atlanta. Source of data: Greenberg (1980/ ICPSR 7951).

In a study on the characteristics of neighbourhoods in Atlanta with a high and low crime rate, several survey questions were asked about neighbourhood problems, avoidance behaviour, worries about crime, security measures and victimisation experiences. Also, questions were asked about "crime in the neighborhood" (ICPSR 7951). One question refers to the previous operationalisation and asks the respondent: "Within the past two years, do you think crime in your neighbourhood has increased, decreased, or remained the same" and another question asks for a comparison: "How safe do you feel your neighborhood is compared to the rest of Atlanta? Would you say it is...more safe, less safe or about the same". As you can see, the responses on these two questions are related in this sample.[60] Most respondents think that crime has not increased or decreased in the past two years and either that their own neighbourhood is the same or more safe compared to the rest of Atlanta.

2.5.1.3   The impact of crime: seriousness of the consequences and vulnerability

Some questions ask directly for a respondent's estimation of the seriousness of the consequences when personally becoming a victim of a specific crime. Other researchers touch on the variance in financial capacity after being victimised. That is, some researchers have included proxies for financial possibilities of coping with the consequences of crime, as a measure of vulnerability (e.g. Pantazis 2000). Overall, these kinds of questions on vulnerability, the estimation of the seriousness of the consequences when victimised are not frequently applied, but some studies have. For example,

---

[60] From the whole sample (N=523) the respondents who did not answer, didn't know or lived less than two years in their current neighbourhood were excluded, resulting in a sample with N=374; $\chi2$ (18.6; df= 4; p < .005).

Lavrakas and Skogan used in their survey on citizen participation and community crime prevention, administered in Chicago in 1979, a series of questions about "how serious these things would be if they happened to you right now in your life" (ICPSR 8086: Lavrakas 1982; Lavrakas & Skogan 1979; Skogan & Maxfield 1981). Respondents were asked about "having a fire in your kitchen", "develop heart trouble", "having a stranger rob you on the street", "having your home burglarized when no one is home" and "having a minor car accident". In Figure 2.6 the percentages of the respondents who thought this would be "not at all serious", "not too serious", "serious" and "very serious" are presented.

The seriousness of the *consequences* of a crime has also been related to the seriousness of the crime itself; since this can be interpreted as "how much harm was done by the offence" (Hoffman & Hardyman 1986: 416). Also, the perceived crime seriousness is said to be "another aspect of people's attitudes towards crime", besides "fear of crime" or "concern" (Kwan et al. 2002). The perceived seriousness of a crime appears to be a function of the perceived consequences, like causing bodily harm or property loss, and of perceived wrongfulness or culpability of the perpetrator (Stylianou 2003; see for example Epperlein & Nienstedt 1989; Hoffman & Hardyman 1986; Monahan 1982). Thus, harmfulness and wrongfulness (Warr 1989) have been the dimensions of interest in research on perceived crime seriousness. In some studies, the perceived seriousness of crime has been examined together with the so-called 'fear of crime' (e.g. Lira & Andradepalos 1993; Smith & Hill 1991a; Vogel & Meeker 2001). For example, Warr and Stafford (1983) related the fear of becoming a victim of different crimes with the perceived risk, which will be discussed below, and the perceived seriousness of the crimes. However, the relation between 'fear of crime' and the perceived crime seriousness seems to be rather unexplored (cf. Stylianou 2003).

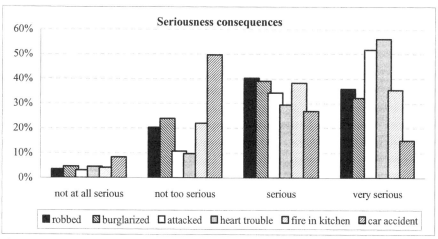

Figure 2.6. Degree of seriousness if something would happen to respondent. Source of data: Lavrakas & Skogan (1979/ ICPSR 8086).

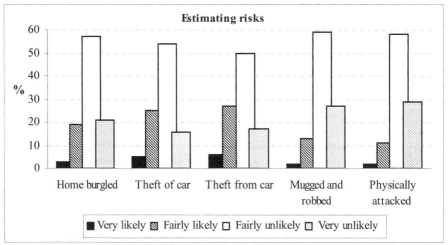

Figure 2.7. British respondents estimate their risk on becoming a victim of a particular crime in the next year. Most persons think it is rather unlikely that they become a victim. Note that the two items regarding theft of and from a car is only posed to respondents who own a car. Source of the data: BCS 2001/02, see Simmons (2002).

Operationalisations that might be related to the "perceived seriousness of the consequences" touch on the *perceived impact of crime* as well. These operationalisations lead to the measurement of perceived vulnerability (e.g. Killias 1990; Killias & Clerici 2000; Madden 1995). For example, Henderson et al. (1997) studied the perceptions of racial injustice in the criminal justice system and used several measures in their analyses, among which a set of four items that intended to measure "experiences with crime". The measure of the variable "vulnerability to crime" was "If you were out walking and someone tried to mug you, do you believe that you would be able to defend yourself without getting hurt, such as by fighting back or by running away from the person attacking you" (Henderson et al. 1997: 461).

2.5.1.4   Perceiving risks

In the contemporary literature, a consensus seems to exist regarding the necessary distinction between fear of victimisation and perception of risk (Ferraro 1995; Lane & Meeker 2003; Wilcox Rountree & Land 1996b). More and more empirical studies use item(s) on the perception of risk, asking respondents how likely they think it is that they themselves become a victim of specific offences. The BCS specifies five different types of offences, as you can see in Figure 2.7 .

2.5.2 The affective modality: feelings of unsafety, concern and worry

2.5.2.1 *Fear, worry or concern about victimisation*

Because of the lack of precision and clarity of the 'fear of crime' concept, Warr (1984) proposed the term 'fear of victimisation'. Whether or not attempting to measure 'fear of crime' or the 'fear of victimisation', questions on the fear of becoming a victim of a specific crime, like burglary or assault, are common as well. The specific formulations of the items touching on this fear of victimisation vary. Sometimes the term 'fear' is used, but 'concern' and 'worry' are common as well.[61] The previously mentioned study of Henderson et al. (1997) used an item to measure "fear of crime" with the formulation: "If you were to go out alone in your neighborhood at night, how afraid would you be that someone might commit a crime against you, such as holding you up or physically attacking you?" The answers ranged from "very afraid" to "not afraid" (Henderson et al. 1997: 461).

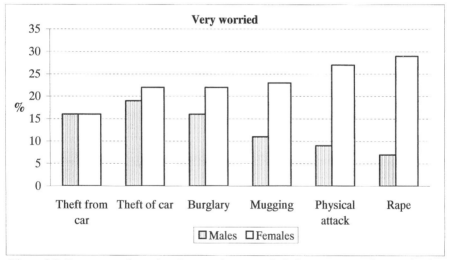

Figure 2.8. Percentage of people who were 'very worried', in response to the question how worried one is about six specific offences. The columns that relate to the items of car crime are percentages of car owners. Data: StatBase dataset ST31908; from BCS 2000, Home Office, England & Wales

As noted before, the terms 'fear', 'worry' and 'concern' are frequently exchanged. So, respondents are sometimes asked about their worries and concern regarding personal victimisation, corresponding with items on fear of victimisation. Formulations like "How worried are you about having your car stolen" are commonly used (Hales & Stratford 1999). The respondent can answer 'very worried', 'fairly worried', 'not very worried' or 'not at all worried'. Also, less specific concerns are sometimes focused on. Items in that

---

[61] The Dutch word that was used in the questionnaire of the inventory, namely 'bezorgdheid', can be translated by both worry and concern.

sphere touch on concern about crime in the community, worry about decline and deterioration. In her study on differences between ethnic groups on 'concern about crime', Walker (1994) differentiates between three aspects of concern, namely 'fear', 'worries' and 'problems'.

In Figure 2.8, the percentage of the respondents who were 'very worried' about being mugged and robbed, and five other victimisation experiences is shown. As you can see, women in comparison with men, report being more worried about for five types of offences. Sixteen percent of both male and female respondents who own a car worry about getting something stolen from their car. Women seem especially worried about a violent confrontation with a perpetrator, according to the relatively high percentages of female respondents who are very worried about physical attack and rape.

2.5.2.2   Altruistic fear: fear of others' victimisation

Besides fear of becoming a victim of crime personally, fear that significant others, like children or spouse, might be harmed is not ignored either (e.g. Kennedy & Silverman 1984; Mesch 2000). Although in the nineties this fear for others was more explicitly formulated as 'altruistic fear' (Warr 1992; Warr & Ellison 2000), asking respondents how fearful they are that somebody they love becomes victimised dates from several decades earlier. Yet, not in the exact same wording, but the central idea seems of the same tenor. A study about crime and 'fear of crime' in commercial areas in 1982 used the item "I worry about the safety of people close to me while they are in the neighborhood" (ICPSR 8167 & ICPSR 2371: McPherson 1978; McPherson, Silloway & Frey 1983; Taylor 1995a, 1995b, 1997a, 1999). Even before that, a survey conducted by Louis Harris' organisation for LIFE Magazine asked several questions about how much concern a respondent feels that a specific thing happens to him/herself or to "someone close to you". The specified offences included "get beaten up", "get robbed on the street" and "sexually assaulted" (Harris 1969 Urban Crime Survey, no. 1935, see Appendix F).

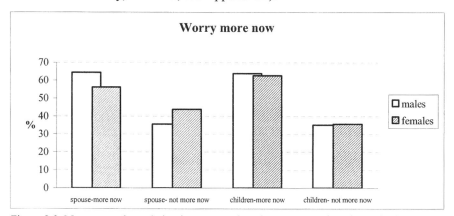

Figure 2.9. Men worry about their wives more when they are away from home in the evening; no difference regarding worry about children. Source of data: Harris 1969 Urban Crime Survey, no. 1935 (see Appendix F).

In the same survey in 1969, several questions were asked about the things people "now do because of their fear of crime". These things were specified and respondents were asked to indicate "because of your concern about crime, it is something you find yourself doing more now than a couple of years ago, or not" (quotes from Harris 1969 Urban Crime Survey, no. 1935, see Appendix F). Two of the specific items touch on worry about one's wife/ husband and children respectively, when they are away from home in the evening. As you can see in Figure 2.9, a large percentage of men and women say they worry about their wife or husband and children more now than a couple of years ago. As far as the worry for one's spouse is concerned, the percentage of men is greater than the percentage of women.[62]

2.5.2.3   Feeling safe at home alone

An internationally well-known item is: "Are you afraid, sometimes when you're home alone at night" and has been asked in many surveys for a long time period (e.g. NIWI 1127), see for example Figure 2.10. Other wording is common as well. For the questionnaire, we reformulated this item into 'how safe do you feel when alone at home at night' and included it in a set of items. For a long time now, an overwhelming majority of the respondents of which the answers are presented in the Figure, report they are 'never' afraid when at home alone at night. In Figure 2.11, the responses towards this item of American participants is depicted, together with another widely used item.

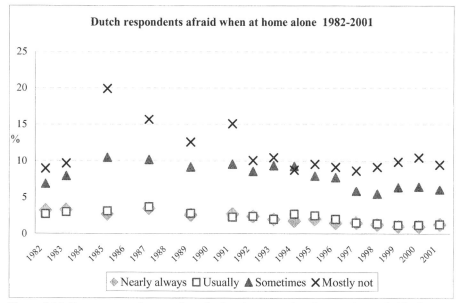

Figure 2.10. Responses to the question whether the respondent is sometimes afraid when at home alone at night. The answer category 'never' that evoked the highest percentage (ranging from 64% to 79%) is omitted. Source of data: Statline (CBS n.d.).

---

[62] This difference is significant; χ^2 (8.3; df=1; p < .005).

2.5.2.4   Feeling safe walking alone at night

Another version of the most frequently used operationalisation (e.g. Garofalo 1979; Hemenway, Solnick & Azrael 1995; Hindelang, Gottfredson & Garofalo 1978; Lewis & Salem 1986; Nikolic-Ristanovic 1995; Skogan & Maxfield 1981) cannot be overlooked. The basic item with the format 'how safe do you feel when walking alone at night?' has several variants. Usually, the respondent may pick out his answer, varying from very safe to very unsafe (see Figure 2.11). The item can be extended by adding a time adjunct (at night or by day), or sometimes a description of the location (in your own neighbourhood, in an unfamiliar neighbourhood). For example, the ICVS uses the item: "How safe do you feel walking alone in your area after dark?" and the Gallup Organization who conducts the polls for the American BJS, uses the item "Is there any area near where you live – that is, within a mile – where you would be afraid to walk alone at night" since 1965.[63]

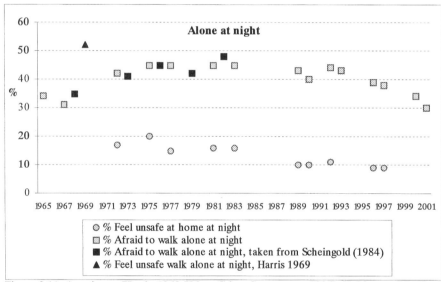

Figure 2.11. Americans (Harris 1969 Urban Crime Survey, no. 1935): Baltimore, Maryland residents) afraid to walk alone at night 1965-2001, compared to percentage feeling unsafe at home at night. Source of the data: Sourcebook of criminal justice statistics Online (Maguire & Pastore n.d.), adapted from The Gallup Poll [Online] (Gallup Organization n.d.), Scheingold (1984) and Harris (Harris 1969 Urban Crime Survey, no. 1935; see Appendix F).

Together with the previously described question "how about when you are at home at night – do you feel safe and secure, or not", the percentage of respondents from a representative sample of the American population who report fear is presented. This operationalisation and the previous one have been

---

[63]   Other surveys use this item or a variant thereof as well. For example, the question "Is there any place - within 3 blocks of your current home - where you are afraid to walk alone at night?", next to several other items of interest, were included in the Seattle-survey (ICPSR 9741: Miethe 1991).

criticised a lot (e.g. Ferraro & LaGrange 1988).[64] Yet, it is still being used in several countries. This is not at all surprising, since the item has a long history, which enables comparability over time, shows variance, which makes it possible to relate its responses with other (demographic) variables, and is parsimonious and extremely cost-effective, since it is usually solely administered in a battery of other items.

2.5.3   The conative modality: avoid, protect and prevent

2.5.3.1   *Avoiding scary places: behavioural constraints*

A common question regarding behaviour modification because of crime or fear thereof touches on the avoidance of certain places because of crime; "How often does it happen that you avoid certain areas in the place you live because of fear of crime" or "Is there an area around your home where you are afraid to walk alone at night?" (e.g. CBS News/ New York Times National Surveys ICPSR 7991; NNSP/IRSS 7901; see Appendix F). In the Dutch PMB, the periodic survey that is commissioned by the police corps and by the Ministries of Justice and the Interior, respondents are asked "does it ever happen that you avoid certain places in your place of residence, because you think they're not safe". Likewise, items on 'not opening the door in the evening or at night, because you think it's not safe', 'leave valuables at home, to prevent theft or robbery on the street' and 'make a detour to avoid unsafe places' are included. Besides these, respondents with children younger than fifteen are also asked the question "does it ever happen that you don't allow your children to go some place, because you think it's not safe". In Figure 2.12 the percentages of the respondents who report that they 'often' do this are presented. According to these figures, fewer respondents avoid places or make a detour during this time. However, an increasing number of people often forbid their children to go somewhere.

The particular behaviour of 'not opening the door at night', only briefly phrased in the PMB, is frequently employed to sketch a more extensive scenario where the respondent finds him/herself alone at home, sometimes about 10 pm but night time anyhow, and unexpectedly hears the doorbell ringing. The respondent is asked to imagine such a situation and tell whether s/he would open the door as usual, would not open the door at all, open the door only when it's somebody s/he knows or when the person at the door makes a reliable

---

[64]   Also, Ferraro & LaGrange (1988) unintentionally illustrate the problem of distinguishing perceptions, cognitions and affect or feelings. They argue that the item "How safe do you feel or would you feel being out alone in your neighborhood at night" asks respondents "to assess their perceived level of personal safety based on a particular scenario-being out alone at night. It does not ask respondents if they are (or would be) afraid in this situation. *Perceptions of* risk and feelings of fear are two distinct reactions to crime." (Ferraro & LaGrange 1988: 280, emphasis of the authors). Here, they suggest that this "feeling safe"-question is an item related to the perception of risk. Also, according to them the question about "any area right around here – that is, within a mile – where you would be afraid to walk alone at night?" asks respondents how afraid they are rather than how safe they think they are while walking alone at night." Thus, they conclude that this latter question can be classified as personal-emotions. All questions on concern, they suggest, are values.

impression. In 1969, Harris already used such a description (Harris 1969 Urban Crime Survey, no. 1935) in a sample of about 1500 residents of Baltimore, US. The question was formulated as "when a stranger rings your doorbell, do you find that, even without meaning to be, you are usually suspicious and uneasy that it might lead to trouble, or don't you usually feel this way". Overall, 50.9% say they "feel usually suspicious and uneasy".

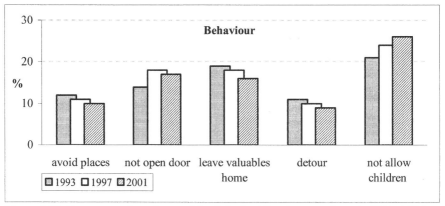

Figure 2.12. Percentages (based on weighted data) of Dutch respondents in 1993, 1997 and 2001 who report that they 'often' exhibit specific behaviour. Source of data: PMB 1993-2001, Ministry of Justice and Ministry of the Interior, see Wittebrood (2001).

2.5.3.2 *Tear gas and dogs: security measures for protection and defence*

From the early surveys on, questions have been asked about all kinds of security measures. For example, researchers used several questions on 'fear of crime', experiences with victimisation and security measures in a survey on neighbourhood structure, commercial centres and (fear of) crime (McPherson 1978; Taylor 1997a, 1999). Respondents were asked: "Do you ever do any of the following to protect yourself from crime while you are in this shopping area?" and after that, items on specific security measures followed (see Figure 2.13). Two items, "avoid the area after dark" and "avoid certain businesses" are behavioural constraints which are focused on risk avoidance; the other items, namely carrying "a weapon of any kind", "tear gas", "a whistle" and "go with another person", "conceal your wallet or don't carry a purse" and "lock the car" relate to the risk management tactics that were mentioned earlier.

2.6 *Appraising the current state of affairs*

A summary of this overview is presented in Table 2.4, which you can find at the end of this chapter. Overall, improvements have been made. The first surveys were primarily concerned with an epidemiological question regarding the prevalence of 'fear of crime'. The relationship between 'fear of crime' and demographic variables was not problematised at first. Later on, other types of research questions were introduced. Besides descriptive knowledge, the aim was to achieve explanatory knowledge. From all these studies more is, at least to some extent, known about the nuances of the differences between groups, precautionary behaviours, the probable crucial role of the fear of rape or sexual assault, the problematic relationship with crime, the relationship with perceived incivilities, control, trust and social cohesion (see also Vanderveen 2002a).

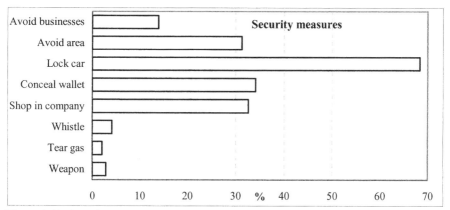

Figure 2.13. Security measures taken by respondents when shopping in Minneapolis. Source of data: ICPSR 2371 & ICPSR 8167.

Moreover, from this overview it becomes clear that the label 'fear of crime' is not a well-defined or specific enough concept to use in empirical studies. Although a misnomer, it is still a very popular name for a diffuse and vague set of phenomena or attributes. As such, it is useful: to situate one's research, study or publication. Yet, the name is not useful to label a latent concept that is going to be measured in a study. Some improvement has been made regarding this aspect as well; the discrimination between 'fear of victimisation' and 'perception of risk', related to different types of crime, seems to be fruitful.

In general, the technical aspects of the sampling procedures, weights as well as the analytical techniques are very advanced, along with the software enabling these procedures and techniques. However, the basic general criteria for measurement instruments (see Table 2.1) are not met, with the possible exception of criteria regarding sampling and formulation. For example, hardly ever does a study provide the means and standard deviations of (sub)groups or Cronbach's alpha, even when more items that purport to measure one thing are applied. When indeed several items are used, a Likert-type scale is assumed, which enables summing up the scores on the separate items to constitute the entire scale. For example, Lewis and Salem (1986) used in their study of neighbourhoods three separate variables with Likert-format to construe a 'fear of crime' variable (Lewis & Salem 1986: 53). Usually these scales are on the ordinal level; it is not exactly known whether the distance between two successive values is the same for every pair of successive values. In their study, respondents were asked in a survey whether four types of crime, namely burglary, robbery, assault and rape, were a problem in the neighbourhood.[65]

---

[65] The scale constructed from these items was called 'concern about victimisation'.

Answer categories were 'almost no problem' ('1'), 'somewhat of a problem' ('2') and 'a big problem' ('3') (Lewis & Salem 1986: 48). Such a (response) scale is exemplary for the ordinal nature of the measurement level, since it is not known whether the distance between 'almost no problem' and 'somewhat of a problem' is the same as the distance between 'somewhat of a problem' and 'a big problem'. Although several assumptions, of the level of measurement and distribution of the data, are usually not discussed in the literature, the application of techniques that assume interval data does not have to be problematic and may lead to the same conclusions. Yet, when nothing is said about the possible violations of assumptions, it becomes difficult to evaluate the persuasiveness of the results.

2.6.1   Problematic conceptualisation and operationalisation

On the whole, the concepts as well as their interrelations appear to be inconsistent, unclear and therefore not very fruitful. Sometimes a concept is used as an explanation of a phenomenon; other times it is an aspect of the same phenomenon, as in the case of the 'perception of risk' and 'fear of crime'. Besides that, the general 'fear of crime' literature does not take (enough) advantage of other disciplines, especially of social, environmental and personality psychology; for example of what has been studied regarding processes of perception and cognition, or about individual differences regarding neuroticism and anxiety. Moreover, much work has been done by Sjöberg (see 1987, 1998a, 1998b, 1999, 2000a, 2000b), Slovic (1999, 2000) and others (e.g. Drottz-Sjöberg 1991; Van der Pligt 1996; Renn & Rohrmann 2000; Ulleberg & Rundmo 2003; Warner 1981; Wildavsky & Dake 1990) on the perception of risk in which 'risk' has been related to recent technologies, (public) health and the environment.[66]

Another issue that emerges from the extensive research overview relates to the negative connotation of the concept 'fear of crime'. In most studies and in the discourse of which they are part, 'fear of crime', whether operationalised as 'the perception of risk' or 'worry about victimisation' or other, is seen as something that is negative, undesirable, as something that calls for interventions, measures and solutions. In most studies, this is not an issue at all, although an older study on "fear of crime in England and Wales" pays some attention to the question whether 'fear of crime' is a problem and whether fear should be reduced or not (Maxfield 1984). As such, it might even be questioned whether crime is in fact an essential feature of what has been measured by all the operationalisations as presented here.

All things considered, it seems necessary to distinguish between different concepts, because the concept and measuring instrument used influence the reported fear of victimisation. The item, and its variants, might measure *part* of the concept, but it definitely cannot be used for generalisations regarding the whole concept. When in fact general conclusions are drawn from this item, it is

---

[66] These studies are not linked to criminology but more to the field of risk management, risk communication and risk assessment.

a good example of an asymmetric relationship between concept and indicator. An asymmetric relationship means that the item, the indicator, represents only a small part of the total concept, or that the item represents a related but distinct concept from the desired concept (Bilsky 1993a; Wittmann 1988).

In a study concerning the psychological determinants of fear, we come across a solid example of the asymmetric relation between concept and indicator. In this study, a measuring instrument called the '*fear of victimisation* index' was used, which asked the respondents to estimate the *likelihood* of becoming victims themselves. In other studies, when respondents are asked about the probability, likelihood or chances of personally becoming a victim, the abstract concept represented by the various operationalisations is called the perception of risk. But the '*fear of victimisation* index', asking respondents about *likelihood* analogous to measuring instruments of the perception of risk, is supposed to measure the concept '*fear of crime*' (Vitelli & Endler 1993). This study, in which concepts were obviously mixed up and unsuitable indicators were used, is not a rare piece of basic methodological flaws. Many differences in results in this field of research might be attributable to weaknesses in the application of different concepts and different operationalisations. A couple of studies tried to overcome the deficiencies, or made them more explicit. For example, Farrall, Bannister, Ditton and Gilchrist (1997) used quantitative as well as qualitative interviews. Respondents were asked how much they worried about burglary, theft, vandalism, robbery and assault. Furthermore, indicators for the perception of risk, concern and behavioural constraints were used. The researchers point to several conceptual problems concerning the measurement of 'fear of crime' (Farrall et al. 1997). Although other authors sometimes do discuss conceptual and methodological problems, they still choose heavily criticised operationalisations, reasoning that others have used them as well, (e.g. Baumer 1985).

As appears from the illustrative figures, several operationalisations or items have been used to measure 'fear of crime' or an aspect of it. In many studies, little attention is given to the process of operationalisation. Besides that, in almost any (quantitative) empirical study, questions that are rather similar to questions that are used in public opinion polls are applied, or, when more items are used, a Likert-type scale is applied. Hardly any studies use other methods, as for example a facet analytic approach, or the semantic differential.

2.7   Do all roads lead to Rome? Consequences of methodological choices

The saying 'All roads lead to Rome' means that it doesn't matter which road you travel, you will end up in the same place anyway, namely Rome. However, travelling one road might lead you through a whole different set of places than another one, leading to a totally different experience of the travel. Also, a specific road might bring you to the southern part of Rome, another to the Western part. Nowadays, it is possible to travel to Rome through the air and many roads have been developed since this saying was introduced.

Similarly, the current field of research has developed and changed. Also, when using this expression as an analogy for research, it would suggest that it does not matter what method you use, the results will be the same. However, this is evidently not the case at all. The concept and its content have consequences for the amount of fear reported by respondents, as well as the way the concept of fear is being measured, which is also reflected by several figures in this chapter. Skogan (1993) emphasises these consequences in a study in which elderly were asked to about 'fear of crime'. The elder respondents report low 'fear of crime' when this fear was conceptualised as 'concern' and measured by asking the respondents to what extent crime is a problem for society. Also, respondents report low 'fear of crime' when asked about their perception of risk: respondents think it is not very likely for them to become a victim of crime. However, using a more behavioural concept of fear, elderly more often constrained or adapted their behaviour for their safety. Respondents of 60 years of age and older more often avoided certain places and persons. Also, they did not walk alone in the street at night as frequent as younger respondent did. The elderly also felt less safe when asked about "the potential for harm that people feel crime holds for them" (Skogan 1993). The importance of clarity of the used concepts and the consequences for the measured phenomenon is also illustrated by studies that discriminate between the perception of risk (the estimation of the probability of becoming a victim) and the fear of personally becoming a victim. Women, for instance, do not think it is very likely that they themselves will be victimised, in spite of their fear of becoming a victim of this crime (Ferraro 1995).

2.7.1.1   *Using a single indicator: Feeling safe when walking alone*

As noted before, one operationalisation is by far the most frequently used, probably mainly because it consists of only one item, which enables researchers and policy makers to cut back on the costs. Although it is unlikely that only one item can function as a reliable and valid indicator for a complex concept, a major advantage of this item lies in fact in its widespread use. Standard questions make comparing patterns in responses possible. However, it can be seriously doubted if this item alone can function as a valid indicator for 'fear of crime' (see Ferraro & LaGrange 1988). Psychometric theory argues that when only a single item is used as an indicator of a concept, it is likely to involve random measurement error, which decreases reliability. The notion that random measurement error will be nullified when multiple indicators are combined into an index results in a criterion of the use of multiple indicators. Another argument for such a criterion is that concepts in social science research are multifaceted or multidimensional. Consequently, only one indicator could never capture the complexity of the concept and important information would be lost (Asher 1984). In other words, conclusions derived from this sole item might be inferior to, or different from, conclusions based on analysis of the data resulting from scales that are more extensive.

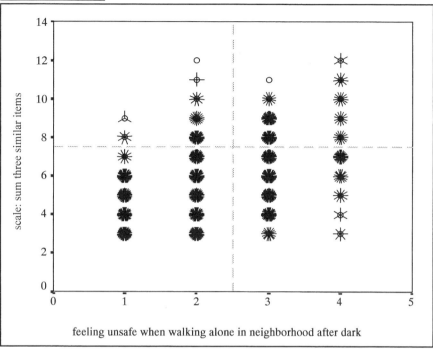

Figure 2.14. Illustration of problem when using a sole item: misclassification of respondents. Source of the data: NSCR (see Appendix F), Wittebrood, Michon & Ter Voert (1997); Wittebrood & Ter Voert (1997).

Figure 2.14 illustrates the problem when only one item is applied.[67] When both the scale and the item would be dichotomised, differentiating between groups of respondents with "low fear" or who are "feeling safe" and those with "high fear" or who are "feeling unsafe" would lead to four groups as is presented in Figure 2.14. Since the scale is made up of three items with an equal number of and similar answer categories, the scale that ranges from 3 to 12 can be dichotomised as well. The group of respondents that is denoted as

---

[67] Another illustration is, unintentionally, provided by for example Chandola (2001: 115), who uses data from the BCS 1996 and suggests that the fear of crime-measure that was used in the study, i.e. the familiar feeling-safe-walking-alone-after-dark, may be criticised, "although there is some evidence that the measure used in this study is associated with worries and anxieties about crime in the local area" (Chandola 2001: 115). This evidence is shown in a figure in which the x-axis reflects the levels of how safe they feel walking alone in their neighbourhood after dark, which was the indicator that was used. Thus, the x-axis portrays the percentage of respondents who belong to the four categories "very safe", "fairly safe", "a bit unsafe" and "very unsafe". The y-axis reflects the percentage of respondents that is "very worried" about a particular crime, namely "burglary", "mugging", "car stolen" and "rape" (Chandola 2001: 115). A perfect correlation between the feeling-safe-item and the four worry-items would show that all people feeling "very safe" are not "very worried" about any of the four crimes. Yet, percentages as derived from the figure, range from roughly 7% (mugging) to approximately 17% (car stolen and rape). On the other hand, such a perfect correlation between the feeling-safe-item and the four worry-items would also show that all people feeling "very unsafe" are "very worried" about any of the four crimes. That is, 100% of the respondents who feel "very unsafe" should be "very worried". Yet, percentages range from roughly 42% (car stolen) to approximately 45% (mugging).

"feeling safe" by both scale and item, together with the group of respondents that is denoted as "feeling unsafe" by both of them, makes up about 80% of all respondents. This means that about 20% of the respondents is not grouped correspondingly. Thus, it becomes clear that the classification of respondents into groups with "low fear" and "high fear" depends on the operationalisation that has been used. Appendix E elaborates on this issue.

2.7.1.2   Reliability and validity

When in fact more items are used, the issues of reliability and validity are hardly accounted for. It seems that face validity or content validity are achieved at the most. This is in part due to the lack of conceptual clarity; how is it possible to investigate construct validity, which is an ongoing process, when the construct itself is unclear and imprecise? Besides that, most studies do not provide from what has been known from psychometric theory, though this flaw does not only appear to exist in this field (see Robinson, Shaver & Wrightsman 1999). A general principle from psychometric theories is that an underlying or latent concept that cannot be directly observed needs an instrument in order to be measured. The items of such an instrument are imperfect, since they are subject to measurement error, but are indicators of one underlying concept. One of the preliminary choices that has to be made is whether the items represent one latent concept, like 'fear of crime', or represent more (interrelated) latent concepts.

Measurement instruments, which are both reliable and valid, enable discussions and analyses about the results. When reliability and/or validity are indistinct, it is hard to discuss the meaning of the results yielded by those (possibly) inadequate instruments. Several contradictory results and conclusions might be a result of features of the instruments used, considering for example the previously described study of Skogan (1993) on 'fear of crime' of elderly. Also, clarity about the reliability and validity of instruments is important for the debate on the so-called fear-victimisation paradox and the inter-individual variety in responses in general. As previously noted, the paradox centres on the finding that according to the figures some groups (e.g. men) become victims more often than others do (e.g. women); whereas the latter groups (women) report more 'fear' (Vanderveen 1999). In the studies in this field of research, the measurement of fear in women is assumed to be the same as the measurement of fear in men. That is, when using a scale for the measurement of fear and the comparison between groups, one assumes that fear and unsafety *means* the same for different subgroups in the sample. A difference between subgroups (e.g. men and women) is expected to represent an *actual* difference on the unobservable concept, but it might as well be a difference on another quality (e.g. social desirability), on which the subgroups vary. Though the instrument is supposed to measure the same abstract concept, it might unintentionally measure some other qualities on which subgroups may differ. Then, the instrument is biased, since it systematically distorts a statistic (Osterlind 1983).

Differences in reported fear could be attributable to a theoretical or conceptual difference in the 'fear of crime', which does not exclude the notion of systematic error. When the measurement procedure itself results in differences between groups and individuals, which cannot be interpreted in actual differences on the construct, the instrument and procedure should be improved.[68] However, when not the instrument and procedure itself appear to result in the difference, a different approach has to be taken. One option is to split up the entire population, doing research on men and women separately. Another option is to study whether a more refined measuring instrument can be developed, for example by including a scale for masculinity and femininity. Also, social desirability might not (only) be located in the measuring instrument, but also function as a latent concept (e.g. socialisation), which is related to 'fear of crime'. Nonetheless, the current state of affairs does not allow such a decision to be made, at least not on sound grounds. Little empirical research is done on the (conceptual) meaning of fear, danger, risk and crime of people and different subgroups.

2.7.3 Overall evaluation of the current state of affairs

This second chapter contains the most relevant findings regarding conceptualisation and operationalisation of a systematic study of a few decades of empirical research on 'fear of crime'. A summary of this study is presented in Table 2.4. The overview of the different operationalisations, and the examples presented in several figures, provides an answer to the question how 'fear of crime' and possible parts thereof are measured. Clearly, these different operationalisations and indicators are related, but not the same. Despite the familiarity of the research framework, the elements and generally acknowledged criteria, seemingly obvious and well-known qualities of research turned out to be not so common. A few relevant matters attract attention and seem to be urgent for the understanding of the whole phenomenon that is labelled 'fear of crime'. These matters boil down to some basic and fundamental questions that arise when overlooking all the publications, namely questions on conceptualisation and operationalisations. The current research project should be regarded as part of an ongoing process, since it does not attempt to be the definite answer on these matters. However, it does attempt to plea for attention to the issues involved, discuss their relevance and contribute to the systematic analysis regarding these issues.

The next chapter presents secondary analyses of data that are typical in research on 'fear of crime' and is in fact a further explanation of the problematic nature of the current habits of measurement in this field. Subsequently, the focus is on conceptualisation, which necessitates a shift of perspective and approach.

---

[68] Like by excluding all words that give opportunities to interpret the items in different ways (e.g. excluding the possibility on a personal confrontation with the perpetrator) and by developing items that appeal less to social desirable notions.

Table 2.4. Summary of review current state of affairs.

Part of research	General picture	Criteria	Notes
Why?			Highly politically relevant; politics and policy provide (financial) resources as well as data; political (and social) contexts influence choices and research questions; findings have political implications
Objective	Descriptive information for policy Explanatory model; evaluation of intervention	Congruence, directiveness	
For whom	Government, related institutions Academic public		
What?			Studies are mainly on an aggregated, sociological level; socio-demographic groups and variables
Type of knowledge	Descriptive, explanatory, evaluative	Congruence, directiveness	
Research questions	Changes over time Difference between groups, areas Relationships with other variables		
Which?			
	Fear of crime, fear of victimisation, feelings of safety	Congruence, parsimony, theoretical embeddedness	Most criteria for concepts not met Lack of consistently applied and definite concepts Little theoretical embeddedness
Concepts	Risk perception, fear of sexual assault, concern/worry about crime/victimisation, reactions to crime, public attitudes/perceptions Some attempts for clarification	General desiderata: consistent, complete, general, fruitful, clear, testable	Little research on the (conceptual) meaning; different subgroups. Distinction between fear of victimisation and perceived risk Umbrella concept, similarity with attitude
Theoretical model	Crime → fear Victimisation → fear Imaginable victimisation → fear Disorder → fear Social structure → fear		Link between crime and fear prevails, whether direct or indirect Crime as in crime, victimisation self and others, imaginable victimisation self and others Salience of sexually connotated victimisation Crime, disorder, social structure on neighbourhood level
Hypotheses	(see theoretical model)		

Table 2.4 – continued.

Part of research	General picture	Criteria	Notes
How?			
	Feeling safe alone-item in periodic surveys		Feeling safe alone-item not supported with (theoretical) argument
	Many studies use data thereof		Little attention is given to the process of operationalisation, some exceptions
Operationalisation	Other operationalisations (see concepts), in one-off studies especially	Construct validity	Concept and operationalisation often not congruent
	Attempts to improve operationalisations/ indicators		Same operationalisations sometimes indicator of concept, other times explanatory variable
			Poor validity of popular operationalisations, some consensus thereof
Data collection	Survey (definitely)	Congruence, usefulness	Large-scale surveys especially useful for comparisons on aggregated level
	Questionnaires, structured interviews		
	Secondary analysis very common		
Who?			
Participants/ sample	Cross-sectional	Congruence	As for the periodic surveys: technical aspects of the sampling procedures, weights as well as the analytical techniques very advanced
	Random (national) sample adolescents & adults		Exclusion in these surveys of specific groups
	Specific groups, in one-time studies especially		
What?			
Nature of the data	Ordinal, quantitative	Congruence, validity, reliability	Findings from psychometric research, theory and measurement of attitudes scarcely applied
Instrument (indicators)	Feeling safe alone-item prevails		Similarity with public opinion research
	Scary areas-item, avoiding areas-item		No studies on differential item functioning; measurement assumed to be the same in different groups
	Cognitive, affective and conative aspects		

Table 2.4 – continued.

Part of research	General picture	Criteria	Notes
How?			
Analysis and presentation	Descriptive and inferential statistics Advanced modelling: multi-level, structural equation	Congruence, usefulness, limited violations	In case of more items: Likert -type scale is assumed Usually, means and standard deviations of (sub)groups or Cronbach's alpha, not presented, but when alpha is available, it usually has value of at least .70 Possible violations of assumptions not always discussed Difference between "significant" and "meaningful" sometimes forgotten, graphics applied accordingly
Overall	Some methodological advancement Knowledge of nuanced differences between groups, precautionary behaviours, salience of rape/ sexual assault, problematic relationship with crime, correlation with perceived incivilities, control, trust and social cohesion Some improvement; discrimination between 'fear of victimisation' and 'perception of risk', related to different types of crime General focus on fear as additional product of crime; 'fear of crime' as social problem; related to public opinion research Comparisons on aggregated, sociological level; socio-demographic groups and variables, related to neighbourhood characteristics Problematic label 'fear of crime', not well-defined or specified concept; points to diffuse and vague set of phenomena or attributes Little use is made of psychometric research, knowledge on (measurement of) attitudes hardly applied		

3 Secondary analyses

This chapter, of which a topic tree is pictured in Figure 3.1, presents secondary analyses of three sets of data that are typical in research on 'fear of crime'. It is in fact a further explanation of the previous chapter, which demonstrated the problematic nature of the current habits of measurement in this field. Secondary analysis of a number of sets of raw data is applied to examine the structure of the items from some datasets, which are briefly sketched in Appendix F. Thus, the two purposes of this short chapter are to illustrate and explain problematic measurement, and to test the measurement models, which have been implicated in previous empirical studies. First, the general method is sketched, followed by a brief description of the four confirmatory factor analyses. The latter two sets of items, one touching on risk perception and the other on concern, are used to show that a model incorporating two latent factors instead of just one might adequately fit the data. This chapter demonstrates the flawed measurement instruments that are used in empirical research on 'fear of crime' by testing the implicated measurement models of four sets of items. The main conclusion from this chapter is that the assumption that these four sets of items measure one latent construct is inappropriate. Therefore, the results cast more doubts on the construct validity. Table 3.8 at the end of this chapter provides an overview of this chapter.

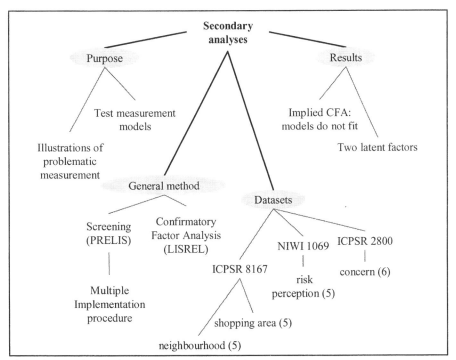

Figure 3.1. Topic tree chapter on secondary analysis.

3.1   General method

Three datasets were selected and analysed in a similar manner. The datasets were chosen because they are typical examples of studies on fear of crime; the raw data was available and the data were used in (academic) publications. Also, these datasets were analysed because more than one item had been used, and the sum of the items were suggested to form a scale of one latent construct, namely 'fear of crime'. Thus, in a sense, they are *not* so much typical examples of research on 'fear of crime', since a large group of studies uses only one item. These are examples of studies that do incorporate more than one item, yet are still flawed regarding the conceptualisation and operationalisation of 'fear of crime'.

The selected datasets were analysed comparably. First, the study, from which the dataset is taken, is sketched. Then the items that were used to measure 'fear of crime' are described, together with the univariate marginal distributions. The data were screened with PRELIS (Jöreskog & Sörbom 1988a), respondents who did not respond at all (to all items), were excluded from further analysis. More respondents used the category "not answered" (NA) or "don't know" (DK), but this does not seem to be a problem (cf. Jöreskog 2001), as long as most respondents do not have any missing values or just one NA/DK-response. Whenever necessary and possible, and no particular patterns could be distinguished, a multiple imputation procedure was applied (see Jöreskog 2001a), that used the responses on the other items to estimate the most likely response on the missing item, which enhanced the effective sample size. Both nonparametric correlations (Spearman's rho and Kendall's tau-b) and parametric correlations gave some indication of the strength of the associations between the items. Next, a procedure similar to Jöreskog (2001b) was followed. Thus, PRELIS was used to estimate the tetrachoric correlations and the asymptotic covariance matrix, since these were needed in the confirmatory factor analysis, conducted by LISREL 8.5, to test the hypothesis that the items represent *one* latent construct.[69] So, one factor, the latent construct, e.g. 'fear of crime' in the neighbourhood' was fixed a priori, and the items correlate with this one factor (see Stevens 1996). In all models error terms were not allowed to correlate; in the case of a two-factor model, the latent factors were allowed to co-vary. As method of estimation, Weighted Least Squares (WLS) was used, again following Jöreskog (2001b; see also Jöreskog & Sörbom 1988b, 1993; Boomsma 1996).[70]

In order to assess to what extent the proposed measurement model does indeed fit the data, indicators of the fit of the model are available (see Boomsma 1995a, 1995b). Since an exact fit is neither expected, nor very realistic (Raykov

---

[69]   This is why a large enough sample (>400, cf. Jöreskog 2001b: 27) is necessary, since the estimation of the asymptotic covariance matrix requires such a sample size.

[70]   Jöreskog (2001b) argues WLS should be used instead of Maximum Likelihood, since the latter assumes multivariate normality, though the absence of normality is not necessarily excluding ML as method (Boomsma & Hoogland 2001). WLS, also known as ADF, Asymptotically Distribution-Free estimator needs a (very) large sample size and a small number of factors in relation to the number of their indicators (Boomsma & Hoogland 2001). As an example; NI/NF = 5 is considerably large.

1998), the Root Mean Square Error of Approximation (RMSEA) as an indicator of close fit is of particular importance. The RMSEA reflects the 'badness-of-fit' of the model while taking the number of degrees of freedom into account. Browne and Cudeck (1992: 239) suggest that RMSEA ≤ .05 indicates a close fit of the model, related to the degrees of freedom. Also, a value ≤ .08 indicates reasonable error of approximation and RMSEA > .1 suggests that the model should not be employed (Browne & Cudeck 1992).[71] An important note is that more than one model can adequately fit the data. Thus, findings from confirmatory factor analysis still need (theoretical) interpretation, since the model needs not to be the only, or optimal, model for the empirical data (Stapleton 1997). Besides that, a model might very well fit a single dataset, but this is no guarantee for an adequate fit in other sets of data; which makes cross-validation even more important, as well as other criteria to select a model (Boomsma 1995: 3).

3.2   Fear of crime in the neighbourhood and shopping area

Two sets of items are examined, which were used in a survey on 'fear of crime', social and physical disorder or incivilities, informal social control and social disorganisation processes in general (see McPherson 1978; Taylor 1995b, 1997a). Each set of five items constituted a scale for 'fear of crime' in the neighbourhood or in the shopping area (ICPSR 8167 & ICPSR 2371: McPherson 1978; McPherson, Silloway & Frey 1983; Taylor 1995a, 1995b, 1997a, 1999). The questionnaire was employed as a telephone survey in a study about crime and 'fear of crime' in commercial areas in 1982. It contains the following introduction:

> We would like to ask you some questions about crime in your neighbourhood. First, here are some statements people have made about crime. For each one, please tell me if you think it's mostly true or mostly false.

Subsequently, respondents were asked to respond to five items; namely "I'm often a little worried that I will be the victim of a crime in my neighbourhood", "I would not be afraid if a stranger stopped me at night in my neighbourhood to ask for directions", "I worry about the safety of people close to me while they are in the neighborhood", "When I have to be away from home for a long time, I worry that someone might try to break in" and finally "When I hear footsteps behind me at night in my neighbourhood, it makes me feel uneasy" (page 4 resident questionnaire; ICPSR 8167 & ICPSR 2371). Specific criteria for surveys and questionnaires that use items were taken from the amply available literature. On the basis of the recommendations of for example Robinson,

---

[71]   Others have suggested that a RMSEA ≤ .08 represents adequate fit and RMSEA ≤ .06 indicates a good model fit (Hu & Bentler 1999). Therefore, the cut-off point is not strictly interpreted. The confidence intervals (not presented here) calculated by LISREL provide another guideline when interpreting the fit of the model. When the confidence interval is entirely above the cutt-of point .05, the model clearly has no close fit. In other cases, close fit would remain tenable (Hancock & Freeman 2001).

Shaver and Wrightsman (1999), some problematic features of these five items immediately come to light. Being a little worried about criminal victimisation, being afraid, worry about other people's safety, worry about burglary and feeling uneasy are all supposed to measure one latent construct. Yet, others have discriminated between these different operationalisations, as discussed in chapter 2. Also, it might not be clear that worry about becoming a victim of a crime does or does not incorporate worry about someone trying to break in. The small number of permitted responses, namely "mostly true", "mostly false", and "refused/ don't know" might cause another possible problem. In their work on effective measurement in surveys Krosnick and Fabrigar (1997) state that more scale points are better, though this should not be overdone.[72] This is because the distortion in the data decreases as the number of the scale points increases, thus validity is improved, yet this improvement is relatively modest beyond five to seven points. Using a very small number of scale points, like in the present two sets of items, does not enhance validity.

3.2.1   Analysis neighbourhood-items

The five items and their variable names are presented in Table 3.1. The responses, "mostly true", "mostly false" and "refused/ don't know", were coded in such a manner that the sum of these variables would be zero if none of the responses indicated any 'fear', and a sum of five would indicate high 'fear'.[73]

Table 3.1. Five items.

Variable name	Description
Worried victim	I'm often a little worried that I will be the victim of a crime in my neighbourhood
Afraid stranger	I would not be afraid if a stranger stopped me at night in my neighbourhood to ask for directions
Worry others	I worry about the safety of people close to me while they are in the neighbourhood
Worry break in	When I have to be away from home for a long time, I worry that someone might try to break in
Footsteps uneasy	When I hear footsteps behind me at night in my neighbourhood, it makes me feel uneasy

The data (N=870) from ICPSR 8167 were screened with PRELIS and a multiple imputation procedure was applied, which enhanced the effective sample size to 869.[74] The nonparametric (Spearman's rho and Kendall's tau-b)

---

[72]   More specifically they say that the optimal number for a bipolar scale consists of seven points and the optimal number for a unipolar scale consists of four to seven points (Krosnick & Fabrigar 1997).

[73]   In other words, "mostly true" was coded 1, except for the second variable, which was formulated negatively.

[74]   From the whole sample (N=870), only one respondent did not respond at all (to all items), this respondent was excluded from any further analysis. Most respondents (795) did not have any missing values or just one NA/DK-response (N=63). From this latter group, 16 times this response was given to the second question (afraid stranger), 25 times to the 'footsteps uneasy'-item and 12 to the 'worry others'-item. The effective sample size (pairwise bivariate) ranges from 819 (afraid stranger-footsteps uneasy) to 852 (worried victim-worry break in).

interitemcorrelations are low to moderate.[75] Table 3.2 presents the univariate marginal distributions before and after the imputation procedure.

The five items were thought to reflect one latent construct, namely 'fear of crime in the neighbourhood'. This model does not fit, neither exactly (χ^2 25.2; df = 5; p = .00), nor approximately (RMSEA = .07). An accompanying test of close fit (RMSEA < .05) has a p-value of .11, which also indicates that the model does not fit.[76]

Table 3.2. Univariate marginal distributions neighbourhood-items.

before imputation	Frequency			Percentage		
Variable	**True**	**False**	**NA/DK**	**True**	**False**	**NA/DK**
Victimnb	323	536	10	37.2	61.7	1.2
Afraidnb	445	401	23	51.2	46.1	2.6
Othersnb	258	596	15	29.7	68.6	1.7
Breaknb	453	409	7	52.1	47.1	0.8
Footnb	466	370	33	53.6	42.6	3.8
after imputation	Frequency			Percentage		
Variable	**True**	**False**		**True**	**False**	
Victimnb	328	541		37.7	62.3	
Afraidnb	458	411		52.7	47.3	
Othersnb	269	600		31.0	69.0	
Breaknb	454	415		52.2	47.8	
Footnb	475	394		54.7	45.3	

3.2.2   Analysis shopping area-items

Similar to the introduction of the set of items on 'fear of crime' in the neighbourhood, this set of items was introduced as follows:

> The next group of questions is about crime in the shopping area. First, here are some statements people have made about crime in commercial areas. For each one, please tell me if you think it's mostly true or mostly false in the case of this shopping area.

Subsequently, respondents were asked to respond to five items, namely: "I'm often a little worried that I will be the victim of a crime in that shopping area", "I would not be afraid if a stranger stopped me at night in the shopping area to ask for directions", "I worry about the safety of people close to me while they are in the shopping area", "Sometimes I worry that my property will be damaged or broken into by people coming from that shopping area" and finally "If I heard footsteps behind me in the shopping area at night, it would make me feel uneasy" (page 8 resident questionnaire; ICPSR 8167 & ICPSR 2371). Similar problematic features of these five items appear; it is not clear to what extent being a little worried about criminal victimisation, not being afraid, worry about other people's safety, worry about damage and break in and feeling uneasy are measuring one latent construct, since other studies have discriminated between

---

[75] The nonparametric correlations range from .20 (afraid-others) to .39.
[76] The estimates are rather low; the standardised solution shows considerable error variances.

these different operationalisations (see sections 2.4 and 2.5). Also, four items clearly refer to the shopping area as the location of danger or threat, whereas one item refers to the "people coming from that shopping area". Again, the permitted responses were "mostly true", "mostly false" and "refused/ don't know". Also, responses were coded in the same way. The data (N=870) were screened with PRELIS and a multiple imputation procedure was applied, which enhanced the effective sample size to 865.[77] Table 3.3 presents the univariate marginal distributions before and after the imputation procedure.

Table 3.3. Univariate marginal distributions shopping area-items.

before imputation	Frequency			Percentage		
Variable	True	False	NA/DK	True	False	NA/DK
Victimsa	95	753	21	10.9	86.7	2.4
Afraidsa	460	370	39	52.9	42.6	4.5
Otherssa	173	671	25	19.9	77.2	2.9
Damagesa	118	731	20	13.6	84.1	2.3
Footsa	393	450	26	45.2	51.8	3.0
after imputation	Frequency			Percentage		
Variable	True	False		True	False	
Victimsa	100	765		11.6	88.4	
Afraidsa	475	390		54.9	45.1	
Otherssa	178	687		20.6	79.4	
Damage	126	739		14.6	85.4	
Footsa	401	464		46.4	53.6	

The model in which the current five items represent one latent construct, i.e. 'fear of crime in the shopping area', was tested. The nonparametric interitemcorrelations are slightly higher.[78] The model (not pictured here) does not fit, neither exactly (χ^2 29.7; df = 5; p = .00), nor approximately (RMSEA = .08; p = .05).

3.2.3 Conclusions

Neither the five items on 'fear of crime' in the neighbourhood, nor the five items with reference to the shopping area, measure one latent construct according to the confirmatory factor analysis. When Hierarchical Cluster Analysis (HCA) of the ten items together is performed, the five items on 'neighbourhood' end up in one cluster, and the five items on 'shopping area' end up in the second cluster. Thus, the items within a set clearly do share some similarities.

---

[77] From the whole sample (N=870), the one respondent who did not respond at all (to all items) was excluded from any further analysis. Most respondents (N=793) did not have any missing values or just one NA/DK-response (N=47). From this latter group, 18 times this response was given to the second question (afraid stranger) and 10 times to the 'footsteps uneasy'-item. The effective sample size (pairwise bivariate) ranges from 816 (afraid stranger-footsteps uneasy) to 837 (worried victim-damage). Note that the pattern of missing values is rather similar to the patterns found for the neighbourhood-items.

[78] The nonparametric correlations range from .12 (afraid-damage) to .46.

3.3 Perceiving risks

The second dataset, i.e. the third set of items, was also analysed to test the measurement model that had been implicated. A representative sample of Dutch residents of 18 years and older (N=1697) were interviewed about attitudes on crime and sanctions, the actual and perceived risk of victimisation. The Dutch survey used five items that touched on the perception of risk. The perceived risk has been compared to the 'actual risk' of victimisation and to several kinds of attitudes regarding punitiveness in relation to crime, delinquents and sanctions (Berghuis & Essers 1986).[79]

As presented in Table 3.4, respondents were asked to estimate the chance of becoming a victim of vandalism, sexual assault, theft of motorcycle or bicycle, physical assault and threat on the street and of a break in (see Appendix F: NIWI 1069). Possible answers ranged from "very small" (1) to "very large" (5). In the original study, the responses were transformed into a scale called "risk perception" that ranged from –5 to +5, indicating low perceived risk and a high perception of risk respectively. Thus, the study used the five items as a scale, implying that the five items represent *one* latent construct.

Table 3.4. Five items; source: dataset NIWI 1069.

Variable name	Description
Vandalism	Deliberate damage or destruction of your possessions
Sexual assault	Assault or rape
Theft	Theft of your bicycle or moped
Threat	Physical assault or threat in the street
Break in	Burglary of your house

3.3.1 Analysis of five items on perceived risk

The multiple imputation procedure in PRELIS enhanced the effective sample size to 1680.[80] Table 3.5 presents the distribution of the data after imputation. Preliminary analysis in SPSS of the data shows that no difference between men and women on the five items can be found.[81] Moreover, the nonparametric (Spearman's rho and Kendall's tau-b) interitemcorrelation as well as Pearson's correlation coefficient are moderate.[82] Reliability analysis of the five items showed a Cronbach's alpha of .78, which is very reasonable.

Similar to the previous procedures, LISREL and WLS as method of estimation was used to test the model in which the five items together represent a latent construct, i.e. 'perception of risk'. Contrary to what is expected on basis of the literature, the model is not fitting, since RMSEA = .08 and the test of

---

[79] The authors found that neither the actual, nor the perceived risk had a relation with punitiveness (Berghuis & Essers 1986: 161).
[80] The number of missing values per variable varies from 30 to 41 and 96% of the respondents did not have any missing values on these items.
[81] Indicated by the chi-squares in the crosstabs-procedure.
[82] For example, Pearson's r = .35, p = .000 for the items 'sexual assault' and 'break in'. The pair 'threat' – 'break in' has the highest correlation, r = .51, p = .000. The nonparametric correlations are also in that range of magnitude.

close fit (RMSEA < .05) has a p-value of .00.[83] The standardised solution shows considerable error variance (see Figure 3.2).[84]

Table 3.5. Univariate marginal distributions after imputation.

Variable	Frequency (%)				
	Very small	Small	Not small, not large	Large	Very large
Vandalism	191 (11.4)	492 (29.3)	483 (28.8)	387 (23.0)	127 (7.6)
Sexual assault	545 (32.4)	564 (33.6)	412 (24.5)	126 (7.5)	33 (2.0)
Theft	210 (12.5)	327 (19.5)	423 (25.2)	477 (28.4)	243 (14.5)
Threat	186 (11.1)	569 (33.9)	553 (32.9)	303 (18.0)	69 (4.1)
Break in	111 (6.6)	401 (23.9)	616 (36.7)	436 (26.0)	116 (6.9)

This set of items is analysed further in order to explore whether another measurement model does fit the data adequately. Some studies on fear of victimisation have suggested making a distinction between offences that are more related to one's possessions or property and offences that are more directly related to one's own body and physical health (Bilsky 1993; Warr 1984, 1985; see also Kearon & Leach 2000). Accordingly, the latent construct might not be 'risk perception', but rather 'risk perception related to property' (rp prop) and 'risk perception related to personal harm' (rp pers). Thus, the items on vandalism, break-in and theft were fixed to be related to 'rp prop', and the items on threat and sexual assault to 'rp pers' (see Figure 3.3). This model has been tested, using WLS and results suggest the badness-of-fit is less high, but still considerable (RMSEA= .06, p = .19). Yet, this model seems to have a better, though still not very good, fit.[85] Moreover, a common recommendation is to have at least three indicators per latent factor, since two indicators per latent factor usually show much larger standard errors and are less reliable (Marsh et al. 1998).

Findings from HCA and PROXSCAL suggest that the items on vandalism, break-in and threat are most similar, and the item on sexual assault is not similar at all to the other items. Another measurement model can be derived from research on the relative severity or perceived seriousness of crime. As noted in the discussion of the different operationalisations, two aspects appear to be of importance when categorising crimes in terms of their seriousness, namely their harmfulness and wrongfulness (Hoffman & Hardyman 1986; Stylianou 2003; Warr 1989). Harmfulness refers to the perceived seriousness of the consequences, whereas wrongfulness is related to a negative evaluation of the behaviour and offence in itself, because it is a 'bad' thing to do. Maybe, the latent construct is not so much the perception of risk, but rather the perception of serious, harmful or wrongful risk. Then, only the most 'threatening', harmful or

---

[83] When the model does not fit approximately, a perfect fit is not possible (χ^2 59.8, df = 5, p = .00).

[84] The lack of fit is not caused by the method of estimation used (WLS). The regularly employed method ML (Maximum Likelihood) that does not use the asymptotic covariance matrix and assumes multivariate normality did not enhance the fit ((χ^2 117.9, df = 5, p = .0; RMSEA = .12, p = .00).

[85] The confidence interval for the RMSEA is (.04; .08), obviously embracing the cut-off point (.05).

wrongful crimes, that is, the more serious offences, might represent one construct. Since theft of a bicycle or moped is, at least in the Netherlands, generally considered a less serious crime compared to sexual assault, threat and burglary (e.g. Carlson & Williams 1993; Van Dijk & Van Kesteren 1996; Van Kesteren, Mayhew & Nieuwbeerta 2000; Kwan, Ip & Kwan 2000), this item is excluded from the model. Thus, the new hypothetical model proposes that the four items on the perception of risk to become a victim of sexual assault, threat, vandalism and burglary are indicators of 'rp pers' and 'rp prop' respectively (Figure 3.3). Though the RMSEA (RMSEA = .04, p = .59) suggests this model fits, the confidence interval (.0; .08) of the fit is not good.[86] Moreover, as was mentioned previously, a general recommendation is to have more than three indicators per latent variable.

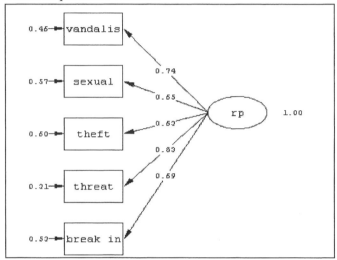

Figure 3.2. Standardised solution, five items do not represent one construct.

3.3.2   Conclusions

Though the interitemcorrelations were moderate and Cronbach's alpha sufficient, this set of data does not support the model that pictures the five items as representing one latent construct. Moreover, the model that distinguished between perceived risk related to property crime and personal crime did not fit either. However, when the item that points to the least serious crime (theft of a bicycle or moped) is omitted, the remaining four items might moderately fit a model with two latent factors. The perception of risk to become a victim of sexual assault and threat are indicators of the risk perception concerning personal harm; the items on vandalism and burglary are indicators of risk perception concerning one's property.

---

[86]   Omitting the theft-item and only including the items on the perception of risk to become a victim of sexual assault, threat, vandalism and burglary as indicators of on latent factor 'rp', suggests a bad fit as well (RMSEA= .07, p = .14).

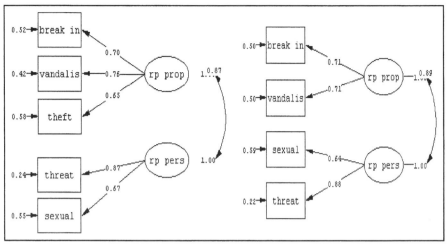

Figure 3.3. Standardised solution, two latent constructs. In the model on the right the theft-item has been omitted.

3.4   Concern about crimes

In a survey that was developed to evaluate initiatives of community policing, six items were used that referred to concern about a specific crime. The survey was conducted in 1996 and 1997; using telephone interviews and two times a random sample of 300 residents (ICPSR 2800: McCoy 1997). Besides the six items on concern, questions were asked about the police and activities undertaken. Also, a familiar item was used (see section 2.5 and 2.6), namely "How serious a problem do you think crime is in your neighbourhood compared to other neighbourhoods in the U.S." Two other questions were posed about changes in personal safety in the US and the neighbourhood following the format: "In the United States as a whole, do you think that personal safety is changing?" with permitted responses "becoming safer", "not changing" and "becoming less safe". Respondents were also asked "To what extent has fear of crime caused you to change your activities". Table 3.6 presents the six items on concern, answer categories range from "great concern" (1) to "no concern" (3). The interviewer introduced the items: "each of the following statements indicate the degree of concern you have that the problem might happen in your neighbourhood."

When looking at the wording of the items, some remarks can be made, which are complementary to the discussion in chapter 2. Firstly, four items use the phrase "try to", which suggests an attempt, while the two remaining items about a break in and damage of house or property do not use this phrase. Since the items were used to construct a scale of 'fear of crime', similar wording might be more appropriate. Besides that, the phrase could easily have been excluded from the four items that use it, or could have been included in the other two items.[87] Secondly, in a few items, more questions are asked, which might

---

[87] It is not clear whether this difference in wording is intentional.

not be a problem for the item 'damage', but becomes more problematic in the case of the (attempted) stealing and damaging of the car. Most obvious however is the problem in the last item. This item asks more than one question; about concern regarding an attempted sexual attack both directed at him/herself and at a significant other. Moreover, the phrase "while you are outside" might refer to the respondent being sexually harassed when s/he is out, to the significant other who is attacked sexually when the respondent him/herself is outside, which implies nothing about the location of the other and consequently leads to the possibility of multiple interpretations.

Table 3.6. Six items; source: ICPSR 2800 (McCoy 1997).

Variable	Description
Rob	Someone will try to rob you or steal something from you
Attack	Someone will try to attack you while you are outside
Break in	Someone will break into your home
Car	Someone will try to steal or damage your car
Damage	Someone will damage or vandalise your house or property
Sexual	Someone will try to attack you, or someone you care about sexually while you are outside

3.4.1 Analysis of six items on concern

The data were screened with PRELIS (Jöreskog & Sörbom 1988a). Only the car-item had two missing values, the other items had none. The distribution of the data is presented in Table 3.7. Polychoric correlations as well as the asymptotic covariance matrix were estimated to apply in further analysis. Preliminary analysis in SPSS of the six relevant items revealed that on two items (attack and sexual) a significant difference between male (N=250) and female (N=350) respondents exists.[88] These items touch on a direct personal confrontation with a perpetrator.

Table 3.7. Univariate marginal distributions.

	Frequency (%)		
Variable	Great concern	Some concern	No concern
Rob	215 (35.8)	257 (42.8)	128 (21.3)
Attack	140 (23.3)	147 (24.5)	313 (52.2)
Break in	205 (34.2)	306 (51.0)	89 (14.8)
Car	171 (28.6)	245 (41.0)	182 (30.4)
Damage	184 (30.7)	260 (43.3)	156 (26.0)
Sexual	146 (24.3)	162 (27.0)	292 (48.7)

The nonparametric (Spearman's rho and Kendall's tau-b) interitemcorrelation as well as Pearson's correlation coefficient are moderately

---

[88] Both 'attack' (χ^2 12.8; df = 2; p = .002) and 'sexual' (χ^2 15.1; df = 2; p = .001) are significant, but not the item 'rob', though this item implies a personal confrontation as well.

high.[89] Though an interval level of measurement cannot be assumed since only three scale points are applied, calculating Cronbach's alpha gives a value of .88, which is very good.[90] The whole sample is considered large enough (N=600) to apply LISREL to test the hypothesis that the six items represent one latent construct, 'concern'. Results from the confirmatory factor analysis show this particular model is not fitting the data (RMSEA = .11).[91]

Similar to the previously discussed model regarding the five items on perceived risk, this model that has been tested proposed two latent constructs, namely 'concern related to property' (cprop) and 'concern related to personal harm' ('cpers'). Thus, the items 'car', 'damage', 'rob' and 'break in' were fixed to be related to 'cprop', and the items 'attack' and 'sexual' to 'cpers'. This model has been tested, using WLS and does not fit either (RMSEA= .09, p = .01).[92] Subsequently, another theoretical plausible model was tested. Two items directly refer to property crime (car and damage); two others touch on a personal confrontation (attack and sexual) whereas the remaining items (rob and break in) refer to a *possible* confrontation, suggesting a mix between a threat of property and one's physical wellbeing. This model was tested as well, but results indicate a bad fit (RMSEA= .1; p = .00).

Findings from HCA and PROXSCAL suggest that the two items 'attack' and 'sexual' are very similar, just as the items 'rob and break in'. The two items (car and damage) that directly refer to property crime are less similar. This indicates that a model that only includes the items that imply the possibility of a personal confrontation with the perpetrator, combined with the emphasis on either a person's physical wellbeing or property might be well-fitted. This model and its standardised estimates is presented in Figure 3.4 and seems to fit the data better than the previous models (RMSEA= .0; p = .78), yet the confidence interval (.0; .09) contains the value of .05, indicating that "not close fit is still tenable" (Hancock & Freeman 2001).[93] Another corresponding model, in which the items 'rob' and 'break in' have been replaced by the other items, fits the data very well (RMSEA= .0; p = .96).[94] These items, 'car' and 'damage', may be more typical examples of crime that is directly concerned with one's property, though the HCA findings suggested less similarity between these two items.

---

[89] For example, the lowest correlation (Kendall's tau-b = .46, p = .000, Spearman's rho = .50 Pearson's r = .45, all p = .000) for the items 'car' and 'break in'. Most interitemcorrelations are higher, the items 'attack' and 'sexual' show the highest Kendall's tau-b = .71, Spearman's rho = .75, Pearson's r = .77 (all highly significant, p = .000).

[90] Standardised item alpha is .89.

[91] The test of close fit (RMSEA< .05) has p-value of .00.

[92] Since the item on robbery might also be interpreted as an offence with a personal (physical) confrontation with the perpetrator, a model was tested with this particular item loading on both latent variables. This model did not fit (RMSEA= .09; p = .008).

[93] The simpler model in which the items on car and damage were excluded and the four remaining items are indicators of one latent construct, has a very bad fit (RMSEA= .16; p = .00).

[94] This is the only model that showed a good fit. The confidence interval (.0; .04) lies entirely below the .05-value.

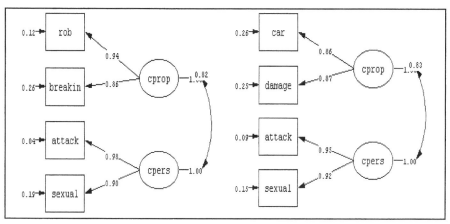

Figure 3.4. Standardised estimates of model on concern-items.

3.4.2   Conclusions

The six items that refer to concern are problematic, which might be the result of a lack of specific wording. Multiple interpretations are possible. The conclusion derived from the confirmatory factor analysis show that the six items do not represent one latent construct, like 'concern' or 'fear of crime'. The model that included all six items and distinguished between concern related to property crime and personal crime did not fit either. The model that only includes the items that touch on a possible personal confrontation with the perpetrator is more or less fitting the data, at least in a model containing two latent constructs. Also, the confidence interval for the RMSEA of this model suggests that a "not close fit" might still be tenable. This particular model contains the two items 'rob' and 'break in' that are indicators of concern regarding one's property; as well as the two items 'attack' and 'sexual', which refer to concern regarding one's body. The model in which the items 'rob' and 'break in' are replaced with the items 'car' and 'damage' is the only model in this chapter that fits the data. However, it is theoretically not clear why this is so.

3.5   *General discussion and conclusion*

The datasets that were analysed in this chapter were selected because they are typical examples of studies on 'fear of crime'. At least, they are examples of studies that incorporate more than one item. The set of items that were invented, were suggested to form a scale of one latent construct. However, confirmatory factor analyses show this is not the case. None of the models that embraced all items, which were all assumed to measure one latent construct, did fit the data. Two sets of items, on risk perception and concern, were examined to explore whether another measurement model would adequately fit the data. The proposed models were based on theoretical inferences. The findings suggest that models with two latent constructs, one referring to property, the other one to physical integrity, while omitting the items that touch on less serious crimes, might provide a more adequate fit. Yet, these models contain only two indicators per latent factor, which might possibly mean poorer reliability, larger standard errors, smaller power, and a flattered fit (Hancock & Freeman 2001; Marsh et al. 1998).

Table 3.8. List of main assertions Chapter 3.

Topic	Explanation
Purpose	Further explanation of problematic nature of the current habits of measurement
	Illustrate and demonstrate problematic measurement
	Test implicated measurement models
Research questions	Do the items measure one latent construct, as implicated?
	How well do other substantively grounded measurement models perform?
Data	Three datasets; four sets of items: typical examples of studies that use more than one item to measure one latent construct
	ICPSR 8167 (five neighbourhood-items, five shopping area-items)
	NIWI 1069 (five risk perception-items)
	ICPSR 2800 (six concern-items)
	See Appendix F for a brief sketch of characteristics of the datasets
Method in general	Screening with PRELIS; multiple imputation procedure for missing values
	Items loading on one latent factor, no correlating error terms
	Confirmatory factor analysis by LISREL, employing WLS
	RMSEA ≤ .05 indicates good fit; RMSEA > .1 model absolutely rejected
Results	Bad fit: all models that were implicated in the literature, namely:
	All neighbourhood-items, one latent construct
	All shopping area-items, one latent construct
	All risk perception-items, one latent construct
	All concern-items, one latent construct
	All concern-items, two latent constructs (property & person)
	Possible close fit:
	All risk perception-items, two latent constructs (property & person)
	Four risk perception-items (excl. theft), two latent constructs (property & person)
	Four concern-items (excl. car & damage), two latent constructs (property & person)
	Good fit:
	Four concern-items (excl. rob & break in), two latent constructs (property & person)
Conclusions	Demonstration of flawed measurement instruments
	Items do not measure one latent construct, as implicated
	Measurement model with two latent factors, more adequately fit the data
	These two factors relate to one's property and to one's body
	These two factors possibly relate to more serious crimes
	Construct validity doubtful

In general, this chapter demonstrates the flawed measurement instruments that are used in 'fear of crime' research. Table 3.8 summarises the main issues that were discussed in this chapter. The main conclusion is that the items do not measure one latent construct, though this has been implicated in these particular studies. A measurement model with two latent factors might more adequately fit the data and these two factors relate to one's property and to one's body, as well as to more serious crimes. Overall, the construct validity of 'fear of crime' measurement instruments is extremely doubtful. This is in part due to the unclear conceptualisation of the construct itself. The previous chapter contained a systematic study of empirical research on 'fear of crime' and gave an overview of the many different operationalisations of 'fear of crime' or parts thereof. The relevance of issues on conceptualisation and operationalisations became very clear. This chapter illustrates this relevance by demonstrating that current measurement instruments are flawed. The secondary analyses of data, typical in research on 'fear of crime', explain the problematic nature not only of the current habits of measurement, but also of the construct itself. Therefore, the next part of this book focuses on the construct 'fear of crime'.

When dealing with matters of conceptualisation, a shift of perspective and approach is necessary. How is one to make sense of the meaning of several terms that are used? For example, the concepts (terms) that have been employed in the studies that provided the data, which have been used in the secondary analyses, were: 'perceptions of crime', 'responses to disorder', 'fear of crime', 'perceived incivilities', 'fear and worry', 'perceived risk', 'responses to crime such as perceived risk and fear of crime', 'concerns for personal safety', 'concern' (ICPSR 8167), 'opinions on crime', 'societal reactions to crime', 'actual or perceived risk of victimisation', 'attitudes', 'estimations of risk' (NIWI 1069; Berghuis & Essers 1985), 'primary concern', 'crime seriousness', 'concern about crime', 'public attitudes', 'fear of crime', and 'personal safety' (ICPSR 2800: McCoy 1997). How are these concepts theoretically related to one another? Appendix D contains a list of concepts, which all have been employed in research. The strategy that was used to analyse several studies from the four types of sources, led to the extensive list of concepts presented. Evidently, these different concepts do not occur equally frequently; they have been grouped and categorised employing a constant comparative method (cf. Glaser 2002a: 2-5). This strategy enabled the grouping of these concepts into higher order categories and even more abstract categories. The three core categories or concepts that emerged to be central to 'fear of crime' are (criminal) victimisation, risk (perception) and fear. In order to be able to focus on the conceptualisation of 'fear of crime', the meaning of victimisation and of risk are discussed in chapters 6 and 7. Subsequently, the meaning of 'fear of crime' is discussed in chapter 8. But first, the shift of perspective and approach that is required will be dealt with in the next chapter, and chapter 5 discusses the very basic grounds on which the meaning, and its development, of the three core concepts (criminal) victimisation, risk (perception) and 'fear of crime' is based.

4 Concepts within contexts

This chapter will explain the perspective and approach that will be used in the following chapters on conceptualisation. The previous chapters already demonstrated that the concept 'fear of crime' is not clear at all and that many operationalisations have been used to measure it. 'Fear of crime' has frequently been related to risk, worry, fear of victimisation and so on, but substantive conclusions about the interrelations and nature of these different concepts, pointing to the validity of the popular operationalisations, have been lacking. The strategy that was used to analyse several studies from four types of sources, led to the extensive list of concepts such as presented. The systematic collection of concepts, operationalisations and items that are mostly used, demonstrated the blurred boundaries between these matters (see Lazarsfeld 1972a, 1972c). The secondary analyses showed that the items that are used are flawed and hence provide another illustration of problematic measurement. Overall, the construct validity of 'fear of crime' measurement instruments is extremely doubtful; both conceptualisation and operationalisations of the construct itself are problematic.

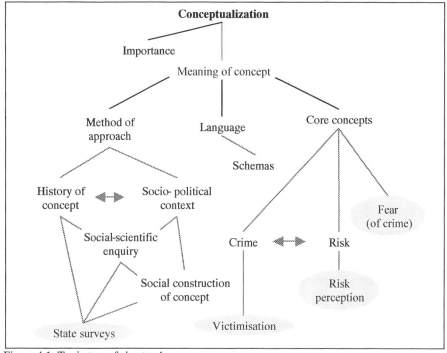

Figure 4.1. Topic tree of chapter 4.

Evidently, the different concepts do not occur equally frequently in research. By means of a strategy based on a grounded theory approach, several concepts were constantly compared and grouped into higher order categories. The three core categories or concepts that emerged most clearly and that appear to be central to 'fear of crime' are (criminal) victimisation, risk (perception) and fear, which will be discussed in chapters 6, 7 and 8. The underlying question in these chapters is what certain concepts mean with respect to their social context. When and why did the concept 'fear of crime' become an issue in research, politics and the media? When did 'fear of crime' become a social problem? Why is 'fear of crime' measured the way it is currently? How is one to make sense of the meaning of several terms that are used? How are these concepts theoretically related to one another?

This chapter explains the perspective and approach that will be used in the three chapters on conceptualisation. An outline of this chapter is pictured in Figure 4.1. The objective is to explain the method of approach, by which means the meanings of concepts are analysed. An understanding of a concept can be derived from its history; the social and political context or scene in which the concept has and still is being used. Such a history, the social and political aspects of the development of its meaning requires a broad perspective and attention for the background or scene in which the concept is employed. This perspective, which implies the relevance of social and political circumstances in order to understand the meaning and relationships of concepts, is a key idea in research on so-called 'social construction' (see Liebrucks 2001). Briefly, this chapter explains what is meant by the social construction of a concept, e.g. 'fear of crime'. Subsequently, the analysis of 'meaning' is discussed. First, however, the importance of conceptualisation is dealt with.

4.1 The importance of conceptualisation

Theoretical concepts are dynamic and require elaboration on their meaning (Rozeboom 1962/1971: 339). The terms conceptualisation or concept formation are used here to refer to the process of carefully defining concepts or constructs-as-intended (cf. De Groot 1975). Concept formation is the process that establishes the meaning of a construct (or concept) by discussing the nomological network and by defining the most important subdomains (Hox 1997). A concept then, reflecting a phenomenon, gets incorporated into the theoretical frame and is structured by a set of assumptions and presuppositions about its nature (Garfinkel 1981: 12).[95]

Conceptualisation is considered to be crucial (Blalock 1982). At least, it is considered crucial in a theory-driven research strategy, the top-down process in which the concepts and its operationalisations are derived from theory (Hox

---

[95] Since concepts themselves are the result of theoretical choices and the translation of a concept into something that is observable is dependent on theory as well, the empirical data resulting from such an operationalisation are inevitably theory-laden; in that sense facts have ideological aspects (Feyerabend 1970: 52). If observations (empirical data) are theory-laden, comparing rival theories is still possible, namely "when theory-laden but disconfirming observations are possible" (Jones 1978: 90). On the incommensurability thesis, the problem of comparing theories and their empirical claims when there is no universal or shared observation language (since these observations are theory-laden) see for example Sankey (2000), on the problem of theory-neutrality of observations see for example Keat & Urry (1975: 50-54). Butts (1966) analyses Feyerabend's account of the absence of a standard observation language.

1986, 1997).[96] In such a hypothetical-deductive or conceptual entry approach, the next step is finding empirical indicators for each concept or each subdomain (Hox 1997).[97] Conceptualisation implies clarity about the meaning of a concept and conceptualisation is considered the core task of the theory (Hempel 1952), thus allowing the specification of the phenomenon in a model from which hypotheses are derived (cf. Bezembinder & Roskam; Delbeke 1976; De Groot 1972). Concept formation and theory formation are extremely closely interrelated; they are two aspects of the same procedure (Fetzer 1991: 17; Hempel 1952).[98] For example, the basic types of concept formation result in different types of concepts; like a classificatory concept that implies mutually exclusive categories, or a comparative or quantitative concept (Hempel 1952). Thus, defining[99] the concepts can be thought of as part of the theory (Delbeke 1976) and is expressed in the 'language of theory' (Blalock 1968a, 1982) or L_T, the theoretical language that constitutes the language of science together with L_O, the language of observation (Carnap 1968; Psillos 2000).[100] According to Boesjes-Hommes (1974) the three layers of a theory are the propositions, the hypotheses and the operationalisations, which all require some notion of the concepts adopted. In sum; conceptualisation lies at the core of theory construction and development.

4.1.1 Conceptualisation and the social-historical context(s)

Since concepts are dynamic and extremely closely related to theory, the dependency on the social-historical context of the meaning and interpretation of concepts is almost self-evident. Knowledge of the social-historical context is necessary for understanding the meaning of the concept and for providing an

---

[96] This in contrast with a data-driven (inductive or bottom-up) approach (see Hox 1997; Hox & De Jong-Gierveld 1990).

[97] However, a common presumption is that the theoretical concept has a surplus meaning; the operationalisations and empirical indicators cannot cover the whole theoretical concept (e.g. Boesjes-Hommes 1974; Hox 1997; Rozeboom 1962/1971). Especially 'disposition terms' are considered to have a surplus meaning; therefore, they can only partially be defined and operationalised (Carnap 1936, 1937).

[98] Considering concept formation as important in the light of theory is also reflected in for example Outhwaite (1983). In his analysis of positivist, hermeneutic and rationalist or realist accounts of concept formation in the social sciences, Outhwaite explicitly relates concept formation to the role of description and explanation (e.g. Outhwaite 1983: 11).

[99] Strictly speaking, 'definition' and 'definability' are not the correct terms to denote the specification of the concepts in the (social scientific) publications that were reviewed, since they do not meet the formal requirements of common theories of definition (see Rantala 1991). A more proper term would come from the theory of identifiability, which holds that the interpretation of a concept is not based on the theory alone, but is determined by the theory together with a number of auxiliary empirical results or observations (Hintikka 1991: 161). The concept then is identifiable on the basis of some model that is based on the theory (Hintikka 1991). Here, the term 'definition' and related terms are used rather loosely and stand for the more or less explicit specification of (the meaning or interpretation of) a concept.

[100] Here, the notion of these languages is used to refer to a difference in level of abstraction since the triad concept-operationalisation-indicator is useful for present analytical purposes. It is not said here that the distinction between the components of the triad are clear-cut or that observable and unobservable entities can be distinctly distinguished (see Spector 1966a, 1966b; see also Gilman 1992; Keat & Urry 1975: 18-22; Outhwaite 1983: 9). See also Putnam (1962/1971) for the rationale of the analytic-synthetic distinction.

answer to some of the main research questions that were described in the introductory chapter, e.g. when and why did the concept 'fear of crime' become an issue in research, politics and the media. The importance of social and political ideas and circumstances for the research on 'fear of crime' has already been noted. This is mainly because politicians, policy makers and activists or the whole diversity of political and social contexts are influencing the ideas about what is to be considered worthwhile to investigate and are acting on the suggested explanations and theory. Accordingly, since political and social contexts may change over time, the social phenomena that are considered *relevant* for researchers to investigate may vary. The selection of the object to study is related to what Weber has called "value-relevance", which relates to the cultural significance of a phenomenon (Weber 1949; see Burger 1987; Keat & Urry 1975: 196-199). Weber (1949) points out that the objects of study are apparently perceived as meaningful to us; they are "worthy of being known" (Weber 1949: 72; see also Turner & Factor 1984).[101] The current field of interest is a perfect example of the notion that research is not done in a (social) vacuum but instead depends heavily on choices, values and priorities, on the social and political circumstances or environment(s) in which the researcher functions (see De Groot 1972: 23; Holton 1998; Kuhn 1996; Leahey 1991).[102]

Garfinkel (1981) argues that the objective, the research questions and the concepts are interdependent. He states not only that a change in the explanatory frame(s) coincides with a shift in the question being asked, but also that an explanation always implies an implicit question. Moreover, every social phenomenon makes a multiplicity of questions possible, each of which make different explanations and different concepts possible. This means that the concepts used are highly relevant, because they provide further insight in the questions, explanations and objectives that accompany the concept(s).

In brief, the concepts that are employed, the research questions that are investigated, the explanations that are offered, reciprocally reflect the social and political background. Therefore, by examining the social and political context, the meaning of the concepts is clarified. In other words, an understanding of a concept can be derived from its history; the social and political context or scene in which the concept has and still is being used. Such a history, the social and political aspects of the development of its meaning requires a broad perspective and attention for the background or scene in which the concept is employed. To acknowledge the relevance of social and political circumstances in the research of 'fear of crime' in order to understand the meaning and relationships of concepts is very common in research endeavours that are frequently labelled as 'social construction'.

---

[101] Many disputes arise from this relation. Researchers within the (radical) feminist tradition or critical criminology attempt to resist the so-called mainstream, dominant, establishment or traditional criminology and social science that are considered to represent the dominant values of the social and political context (see for example Inhorn & Whittle 2001; Sauvageau 1999; Sprague 1997; Young 1997).

[102] However, this is not contradictory to either the empirical research framework nor does it necessarily lead to relativism (see Sauvageau 1999; Sokal & Bricmont 1999).

4.2   Social constructions

Reality as extrapolated from research is constructed (Hacking 1999a; MacKenzie 1981), scientific theories are social products (Chalmers 1997: 197) and "fear of crime is a social construct". To describe a concept like 'fear of crime' and related issues of validity, the work on social construction, and especially the work of Hacking (1983, 1999b, 2000), is helpful.[103] Elaborating on his work on the 'sociology of concept formation', Hacking (2000) suggests the notion of 'social construction' is liberating, since something (X) and its meanings are not inevitable, but rather a product of historical events and social forces. This is not to say that since this something (e.g. child abuse in Hacking 1988) is socially constructed, persons are not suffering from it, nor does indicating that X is a social construction help them. Because of the hereto related "great fear of relativism", Hacking recommends to ask *what's the point* that something is socially constructed. He proposes two major underlying aims in studies that incorporate the idea of social construction, namely the raising of consciousness and to criticise inevitability, the status quo. These aims can be achieved in three different ways, which Hacking presents in the form of three theses of the social construction of X. The first thesis states that X need not have existed, nor need to be at all as it is. X, its existence or character as it is at present, is not determined by the nature of things, it is not inevitable. X has been brought into existence and is shaped by the social context, namely by social events, forces and history. This social context could well have been different, which would have brought about another type of X. The second thesis claims that X is quite bad as it is and the third maintains that we (i.e. society, people) would be much better off if X were done away with, or when X would be at least radically transformed (Hacking 2000; see also Denner 1992).[104]

All three theses and the very notion of 'social construction' share a general precondition for social construction theses. This precondition holds that in the present state of affairs, X is taken for granted, X is unchanging and X appears to be inevitable.[105] For example, Clark's book on sexual assault within the social context of 18th and 19th century England, which will be discussed further in chapter 6, starts with "It seems to be a fact of life that the fear of rape imposes a curfew on our movements; a fact that if we stay at home we will be safe, but if we venture out alone we face the strange rapist in the dark alley." (Clark 1987: 1). By investigating the social and historical context, she concludes that sexual violence is real, but that rape used as warning is a historical creation. She argues that the protection that is offered by the warning or the myth, in exchange for obedience is illusory, more danger exists in one's home than on dark streets and rapists are male acquaintances, friends as well as strangers.

---

[103] Social construction or social constructivism *per se* is meta-theoretical in nature, but could for example be considered a rhetorical approach (cf. Coogan 2002).

[104] Similarly, Risse and Wiener (1999: 776) discriminate between "diverse constructivist approaches" and a variety of "constructivist positions" (see also Danziger 1997; Gergen 1985, 1997; Greer 1997).

[105] Hacking (2000) notes that essentialism (e.g. race is essential for someone's identity) is the strongest form of the precondition, of inevitability.

Therefore, her analysis of 'rape as a warning' seems to be an example of the third thesis that Hacking distinguishes, i.e. 'rape as a warning' is quite bad as it is and we, or more specifically: women, would be much better off if 'rape as a warning' were done away with. An example of the first thesis is Green's study (1997), which describes a "history of accidents" and traces the contemporary concept of accident back to history by investigating how it was called, i.e. classified and conceptualised then. The main question concerns the essential characteristics to be labelled as such in a certain period, the conditions that made the current classifications possible and thus when it became possible to speak of accidents.

Here, the proposition is discussed that the concept 'fear of crime', and the categorisation, classification and ideas related to this concept (e.g. "men have less fear of crime") are socially constructed, which means that this concept refers to a network of social relations and that it is employed to serve certain ends. The concept 'fear of crime' does not exist in a vacuum, but inhabits a social setting which Hacking (2000) calls the matrix. Within this matrix the idea and concept 'fear of crime' is formed. Thus, the social construction of 'fear of crime' refers to the idea of 'fear of crime' (in its matrix) that is meant by those who employ this concept, how 'fear of crime' is a result of historical events and social processes, how 'fear of crime' became an issue or even a problem.[106] This does *not* mean that what is named 'fear of crime' cannot be a 'real' social problem.

4.2.1   Integration of perspectives[107]

To suggest that something is socially constructed, is not to say that it is non-existent, not a problem or that it should not be influenced or measured. Scientific research findings are socially constructed in the sense that social processes influence the factual results and how they are used to provide support for a theory (Sargent 1997). Other studies have developed a more integrative approach as well, for example combining an evolutionary psychological perspective with a social construction theory (see also Funder 1995; Geary 1995, 1996; Glassman 1996). Although differences on ontological and epistemological issues do exist, the different perspectives share features as well (e.g. Annells 1996; Borsboom, Mellenbergh & Van Heerden 2003; Jasanoff 1998; Rychlak 1993; Yanchar & Slife 1997).[108] The interdisciplinary framework on which this research project is based, applies social construction similar to the first thesis or way that is described by Hacking (2000). It is posed that 'fear of crime', its meaning(s) and related issues, are a product of historical, cultural and social

---

[106] Hacking also notes that "the social construction of X" might relate to the consequences of being so classified (as X), how individual persons and their own experiences are changed by being so classified and how this process of reification functions, like for example Seccombe, James & Battle Walters 1998 on the social construction of the welfare mothers. This is not the type of social construction that is meant here.

[107] Here, the word 'perspective' could easily be changed into 'paradigm', since what is meant here is the way of doing research in the broadest sense (Moulton 1983: 152).

[108] For example, most perspectives are committed to explanation, though the language used might be one of understanding and interpretation (Risse & Wiener 1999).

circumstances or contexts. Other contexts would have brought about another type of 'fear of crime', its meaning (or name) would have been different then. Basically, the current framework supposes that perception, (learned) interpretation and social interactions in which these interpretations are learned are most relevant when studying the meaning(s) of a concept.

4.3 The meaning(s) of a concept

The meaning(s) of a concept are conveyed by language (symbols, signs) used by individuals or for example by mass media, narratives, (urban) myths, institutions and their politics and policy measures.[109] This, in turn, continuously shapes or constructs the context in which we again perceive, interpret and give meaning to our everyday lives. In other words, meanings are "born twice", because meanings are considered products of both individual cognition and of the social and cultural context (Shore 1991, 1996). Meanings are both established in culture (communal, shared communal life, meaning of some expression or act), and yet idiosyncratic meanings are the meanings for an individual in a specific situation (Shore 1996). This interdependent reconstruction makes a question about meaning both a cognition and a culture or context question.

The link between culture and individual cognition has been analysed thoroughly by Shore (1996). He refers to cultural models as part of cultural knowledge. Such a cultural model is a cognitive schema that is intersubjectively shared by a cultural group. These schemas coordinate groups of individuals, are property of communities, and are socially mediated forms of knowledge. Furthermore, Shore distinguishes such cultural schemas from personal mental models, which contain personal associations with words, one's personal history and for example one's home and its location and the mental (geographical) map thereof. A mental model, mental representation or schema is part of the stock of shared cognitive resources and can be externalised as shared institutions as well as internalised by individuals, who are thus guided by social norms and are in this respect socially constrained. A schema is usually simple; it functions as a simplification of the world, it refers to an ideal type, or prototype. Schemas are mental models in the sense that they are the product of continual social production of publicly available forms. They are an externalisation in social world of particular models of experiences (Shore 1996). Schemas are an important research subject in social cognition (Fiske & Taylor 1984). The cognitive structures, 'shortcuts', organise knowledge and guide the selection (attention), interpretation and organisation (encoding), and recollection (retrieval) of new information; they provide the tools for making sense, for everyday understanding. Schemas enable us to make sense of social reality, of experience and of information, by simplifying, structuring and providing meaning, they help clarify or disambiguate an otherwise confusing situation (e.g. Axelrod 1973; Correll et al. 2002). For present purposes, the notion of schemas is applied to serve as a general thread in these chapters on

---

[109] See for a brief overview of a narrative approach with respect to the cultural context Howard (1991).

conceptualisation of risk, victimisation and crime to refer to the general interpersonally shared meaning of concepts with respect to their social context.

4.3.1   Analysing meaning

In these chapters on conceptualisation, the concept 'fear of crime' is analysed. Though the label 'fear of crime' might be unproblematic and obvious at first sight, the review of the past decades of research shows that its conceptualisation is far more complicated and not at all trivial. In order to rediscover some of the clues to how 'fear of crime' has come to be self-evident, universal and necessary in the late 20th century the past research has been examined already. In particular the classification of concepts and/or operationalisations is of importance here, since the manner in which is a concept is handled in the literature, conveys some of its meaning. Questions that will be addressed are: How did it become possible to talk about 'fear of crime', what constitutes 'fear of crime', how did 'fear of crime' become an issue in politics, why is 'fear of crime' measured the way it is, how did it become a social problem and more in general: what does the concept 'fear of crime' mean? These questions are examined by unravelling three core concepts related to 'fear of crime': victimisation, risk and fear respectively. This analysis of the meaning of this family of concepts provides insights that are used in a discussion of the re-definition of 'fear of crime' (see Pawlowski 1980). The unravelling of the core concepts is done thoroughly; undertaking the procedure of conceptualisation by means of what Green (1997) calls a sociological or social-scientific enquiry. Similar to Green (1997), the question that is asked here is: How did the concept become an inevitable part of the universe in the late 20th century, how have concepts been reified "*as if* they were something other than human products" (Berger & Luckman 1966: 89). In the next two chapters, the emergence of the concept in Western thought is examined, by diving into two discourses, the discourses on victimisation and on risk.

The discourse of 'victimisation' is of importance, since crime and more specifically, criminal victimisation lies in the centre of the whole notion of 'fear of crime'. In the discussion of 'fear of crime', what is meant by 'crime', what is meant by (criminal) victimisation? Three types of victimisation represent three different approaches to the concept 'victimisation': criminal victimisation, indirect victimisation and imaginable victimisation. Whatever type of victimisation, attributions of deservedness, responsibility or culpability to the victim are of major importance in the interpretation and meaning of the concept 'victimisation'. These attributions are moulded by the social context, by popular images that arise from various sources, and are related to characteristics of the victim, in particular gender. The popular images, or schemas, that focus on the typical (or prototypical) victim, offender and crime are re-created by several sources, among which the media. Several times, the victimisation discourse points to another discourse, just as the discourse on 'fear of crime' in general. Risk appears to be a core concept as well. The discourse of 'risk' is twofold, a more theoretical debate on the concept risk in Western societies, and an empirical area of research on the perception of risk. It will become clear that research on 'fear of crime' shows remarkable similarities with another field of research named 'risk perception'. Though one would not consider the two fields to be that similar to one another, careful examination shows that themes, questions and social context are comparable, but findings derived from several studies on risk perception seem to be applicable to 'fear of crime'. These two discourses, on victimisation and on risk, provide a better understanding of the meaning of the concept 'fear of crime'. The concept as it is understood in Western society can be marked by a sort of consensus about the threat of crime, criminals, in particular for so-called ideal victims. Another general feature is that 'fear of crime' is problematic and the (local) government, police and other institutions should *fight* 'fear of crime' or at least try to do so. As has already become clear, the idea is that 'fear of crime' can be measured. The effects of (governmental) interventions, the state of affairs can be measured by means of large-scale surveys. It will become clear that the concept implies moral beliefs, about who is to be protected and who is not, about who can become a real victim and who cannot and about who is rightly fearful and who is not. Subsequently, these insights are used in a discussion of the re-definition of 'fear of crime'. This re-definition can be thought of as the proposal of a cognitive structure, within which a 'concept' refers to the rules of classification (Frijda & Elshout 1976). These rules lead to a certain consistency within a concept since the essential attributes or stimuli and combination or conceptual rules of these attributes become clearer.

Before the discourses on victimisation and risk will be analysed, the antecedents of these discourses and of the concept itself needs to be dealt with briefly. These antecedents have made the concept appear as an inevitable one; a history of 'fear of crime' starts with its birth. Or maybe even with its (grand) parents. Without statistics, surveys and the (governmental) need for knowledge on attitudes and opinions, the concept 'fear of crime' would not have been born. Also, the same developments have led to the interest in the empirical research of 'risk perception'.

Table 4.1 lists the issues that were presented in this chapter, which attempted to explain the perspective and approach that has been used in the next chapters on conceptualisation. From the previous chapters, it became clear that the construct validity of 'fear of crime' measurement instruments is extremely doubtful and both conceptualisation and operationalisations of the construct itself are problematic. Therefore, three core concepts that appear to be central to 'fear of crime', namely (criminal) victimisation, risk (perception) and fear, are unravelled thoroughly in chapters 6, 7 and 8. The underlying question in these chapters is what these concepts mean with respect to their social context. In order to get a better understanding of the nature and meaning of the relevant concepts involved, a broader perspective is necessary. Such an approach shows similarities with a so-called 'social construction' perspective, in which a history of the concept 'fear of crime', on the social and political circumstances are central. The meaning of concepts is assumed to be conveyed by language,

language employed by individuals, mass media, in (urban) myths, politics, and policy. Meaning can be gathered from discourses, using the notion of schemas; (intersubjectively shared) simplifications that are used to make sense of social reality. This perspective puts personal cognition into a social context.

Table 4.1. List of main assertions Chapter 4.

Topic	Explanation
Purpose	Explain the perspective and approach that has been used in the next chapters on conceptualisation
Research questions	Why is conceptualisation important? What kind of approach has been taken in this part on conceptualisation? How can "meaning" be analysed?
Method of approach	History of concept & relevance of social and political context Social construction (not conflicting with (quantitative) empirical research) Social-scientific enquiry; discourses Meaning conveyed by language Language from individuals, mass media, (urban) myths, politics, policy Reconstruction of meaning: cognition in context Schemas: (intersubjectively shared) simplification, make sense of social reality
Information on meaning	Language from individuals, literature, mass media, (urban) myths, politics, policy
Why these three concepts	Core concepts; victimisation, risk and fear Based on findings from overview (based on grounded theory approach)
Closing	Antecedents of 'fear of crime': statistics and surveys by governments

5 Statistics, surveys and attitudinal knowledge

In this part on conceptualisation, three core concepts, namely risk (perception), (criminal) victimisation and fear (of crime) are unravelled thoroughly in chapters 6, 7 and 8. The previous chapter described the method of approach regarding conceptualisation and stated that an understanding of a concept can be derived from its history; the social and political context or scene in which the concept has and still is being used. Such a history, the social and political aspects of the development of its meaning requires a broad perspective and attention for the background or scene in which the concept is employed. Also, the meaning of concepts is assumed to be conveyed by language, language employed by individuals, the mass media, in (urban) myths, politics, and policy. During the research process, it became clear that the discourses on victimisation, risk perception and 'fear of crime' shared similar roots or antecedents, which have led to the current paradigm, i.e. the habits of conceptualisation and measurement. These antecedents have made the concept appear as an inevitable one; and therefore the roots of 'fear of crime' are of importance. Without statistics, surveys and the (governmental) need for knowledge on attitudes and opinions, the concept 'fear of crime' would not have been born. Also, the same developments have led to the interest in the empirical research of 'risk perception'.

When looking at the huge amount of surveys performed, it seems that government, institutions and researchers have little doubt about the necessity of survey research in the field of safety, fear, crime and risk. The concept 'fear of crime' is politically loaded, as will be discussed in depth in chapter 8. The necessity and existence of acquiring knowledge about opinions and attitudes is unquestioned or even evident. But when did people or more specifically, the government, start to obtain knowledge about misfortunes like accidents or deaths by certain causes. What about attitudes regarding these misfortunes? Some questions have been addressed in a previous paper (Vanderveen 2002c); like the question whether or not knowledge about people's attitudes, feelings of safety and the like are of importance, and the question whether or not knowledge about actual unwanted incidents, events or misfortunes, like criminal victimisations is not enough. The main conclusion of that paper was that knowledge about people's attitudes, feelings of safety, opinions about unwanted incidents, like criminal victimisations, and the like are of importance to the State, government and society.[110] More in general, attitudinal knowledge is considered societally significant, especially when it is crime-related (e.g. Chevigny 2003; Wiles, Simmons & Pease 2003). The term 'attitudinal knowledge' was used to point to knowledge about attitudes, ideas, desires, feelings et cetera of people in a certain region.

---

[110] State was defined as an institution, of which in the modern times part of it constitutes the government but in earlier times it could be the King, that exercises sovereign power within a strictly bounded (geographical) area, in which people live (Vanderveen 2002c).

This chapter, outlined in the topic tree in Figure 5.1, is primarily concerned with the history of surveys on 'fear of crime'. The main purpose is to explain how 'fear of crime' is primarily related to statistics and surveys by governments and to stress the political uses of surveys, yet to challenge the global criticism of surveys. Questions that are addressed are for example related to the history of 'fear of crime' items, the dependency of the whole notion of 'fear of crime' on crime surveys, which were in turn a reaction to criminal statistics. First, the historical roots of crime statistics are briefly pointed out, which demonstrate the pervasive instrumental role these statistical developments already played. Politics, i.e. governments and institutions, were extremely interested in statistics and statistical analysis of social phenomena. The major idea was to 'count & control', or to 'explain and tame'. Criticism regarding the reliability of these (crime) statistics became more apparent, and issues regarding the dark number, together with achievements in polling and sampling, led to the development of the crime victim survey. Several aspects of society were surveyed, among which were all kinds of opinions and attitudes, which is described in the second section. These early crime victim surveys, as well as surveys on living conditions, often contained the familiar 'feeling safe alone after dark'-item, which became internationally known. Other countries besides the United States conducted several victim surveys as well. The most common surveys that were (and still are) administered in the Netherlands are briefly described. After that, some observations regarding criticism on the use of surveys and quantification in general are noted. The conclusion of this chapter states that statistics and surveys are conditions for the concept 'fear of crime' and despite several flaws and criticism, surveys and their resulting statistics play a major, and often instrumental, role. This will be discussed in chapter 8 more extensively. Table 5.1 briefly summarises this chapter.

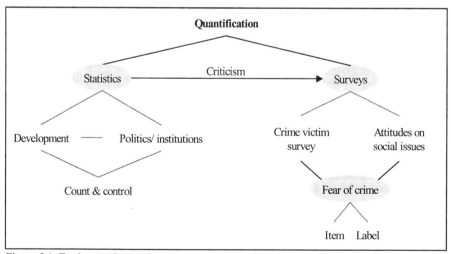

Figure 5.1. Topic tree chapter 5.

5.1 Statistical opportunities

Originating from a long development in history, in the early nineteenth century the possibilities of using statistics expanded rapidly (Hacking 1975b; Pearson 1978; Van der Vlis & Heemstra 1989).[111] From the 15th and 16th centuries on, the state becomes gradually *governmentalised*. That is, the government started to govern on the basis of rational calculations, technical analyses, procedures and tactics (Foucault 1991). Categorising and counting social phenomena in the formation of knowledge about society began to form the basis of discussion as well as policy decisions of institutions (Duncan 1984; Porter 1996).[112] Better yet, the statistics were introduced as pure, incontrovertible facts and became eagerly welcomed by the Napoleonic state and Britain (Emsley 1999). When in the 1660s a book on the 'London Bills of Mortality' was published, the statistical study of social problems began (Cullen 1975; David 1998; Pearson 1978).[113] This is described by Cullen (1975) as a science of society tied to the notion of quantification of social phenomena, and Hacking (1975b: 102) denotes 'statistics' as the systematic study of quantitative facts about the State.[114] The use of statistics expanded rapidly, printed numbers became increasingly important, which also eroded determinism and instead increased the awareness of possibilities of social control (Deflem 1997; Hacking 1990). Quantifications were used to justify specific interventions (Hacking 1990; H. Taylor 1998b). Figure 5.2 pictures this process schematically.

In the nineteenth century, social scientists began to analyse the aggregated data, starting with Quetelet who published criminal or 'moral' statistics in 1827 (Beirne 1987; Salas & Surette 1984; Stigler 1986; H. Taylor 1998a). In 1810, the British Home Office began publishing crime statistics, since 1830s on a regular basis. Examples from the British Home Office can be found in the National Archives with numerous documents from the Public Record Office archives, such as hand-written figures from the Home Office that show a comparison of the amounts of various crimes, like murder, burglary and robbery, in 1880 with the annual averages for 1875 to 1879 (HO45/10424 R19175), and an even earlier example that compares the number of criminal offenders in 1826 with 1825 (HO44/17 f.1).[115]

---

[111] Along with the development of statistics, several techniques to analyse the numbers expanded as well, going 'beyond' frequencies and percentages (e.g. Van Bemmelen 1958; Koren 1918), for example by applying Pearson's correlation (e.g. Macdonell 1902; McCormick 1945). The development of these techniques and their historical background are not described here.

[112] Also, from the seventeenth century on, new concepts and techniques were developed in the study of the "combination of observations" (Stigler 1986: 11), like probability, induction, statistical inference and likelihood tests, which enabled the "measurement of uncertainty" (Bernstein 1998; David 1998; Hacking 1964, 1971, 1975a, 1975b). These concepts have been of particular importance regarding the concept 'risk', which will be discussed later.

[113] Several reprints of Bills of Mortality from the eighteenth century can be found in Glass (1973). The London Bill of Mortality from 1665 can also be found in David (1998: 101).

[114] In the seventeenth century, the statistician Conring already argued that the State must have the facts on which decisions can be based and act rationally (Salas & Surette 1984).

[115] These examples can be found on http://learningcurve.pro.gov.uk/candp/crime/g07/g07cs2.htm.

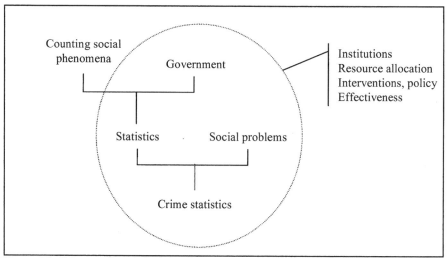

Figure 5.2. Schema of statistical development regarding 'counting and controlling' social issues.

According to Cullen, the national crime statistics were born out of the issue of capital punishment, which during that time was topic of campaign and debate (Cullen 1975: 13). He describes the role of governmental departments and committees in the use and publication of social statistics in period 1832-1852, as well as the development of private statistical societies, like the Statistical Society of London in 1834, which is now called the Royal Statistical Society (Hacking 1975b; Koren 1918).[116] Cullen has little doubt about the political nature of statistics and refers to "improvement by numbers" (page 149).[117] With urbanisation, not industrialisation, as a leading motive, the statistical movement was concerned with the moral effects of urbanisation on the working class. Statistics were used to provide support for public health reforms and education, in particular to fight poverty (Wohl 1983). For example, Florence Nightingale had very much faith in the value of statistics and quantification as a means to reveal higher laws of anticontagionism in order to fight disease and illness (David 1998; Freedgood 2000). Freedgood, in her account of the Victorian notion of risk, explores the 'count and control' ideas in the Victorian Era. She concludes that the increasing ability of bureaucracy (institutions) to collect large numbers meant that reassuring regularities could be discovered and published. Counting, i.e. the numbers as well as the theory,

---

[116] Australia, Austria, Belgium, Canada, Denmark, France, Germany, Great Britain as well as Ireland and Scotland, Hungary, India, the Netherlands, Norway, Russia, Sweden and the United States all established departments, or bureaus, of statistics that started publishing 'moral', 'criminal' or 'judicial' statistics in the nineteenth century (Koren 1918).

[117] The political nature of statistics is also illustrated by several "letters to the legislator", from 1753 on, in which the 'medical, moral and political' advantages of numerical knowledge on the population is presented (in Glass 1973). Van Bochove (1999) claims the number of household surveys increased rapidly not only because of the funds that became available, but also because the government needed more information on social phenomena.

would "explain and tame the apparent disorder of so much of British society" (Freedgood 2000: 69). The principles and regularities derived from statistics make social problems manageable and knowable (Foucault 1991; see also Lee 1999).

The political nature of statistics appears from the figures on crime as well. In many countries, the emergence of official crime statistics in the nineteenth century made the construction of national 'pictures of crime' possible, enabling to view this picture or phenomenon as a national problem requiring a national solution (Emsley 1999). For the United States, the picture was related to the State-region (Cummings 1918; Deflem 1997; Gettemy 1918). Since the States of the USA all have sovereign jurisdictions of crime control, without one particular body of criminal law, institution or procedure that relates to the United States as a whole, many difficulties arise in drawing together *national* statistics on crime and correction. Although from 1850 to 1890 the Bureau of the Census collected statistics on prisoners in connection with each decennial Census of Population, it was not before 1926 that the Bureau of the Census made the first nationwide collection of criminal data (U.S. Bureau of the Census 1997). The second nationwide collection of crime figures began in 1930. This time, the Federal Bureau of Investigation collected summary reports from many police departments on serious offences known to the police, as well as arrests made by the police (U.S. Bureau of the Census 1997).[118]

In the Netherlands, the Central Bureau of Statistics (Centraal Bureau voor de Statistiek – CBS) began collecting official police figures on crime, in addition to census data on the Dutch population they already collected (Maarseveen, Gircour & Schreijnders 1999; Verrijn Stuart 1918). In 1939, Kempe and Vermaat published a study in which criminal statistics, derived from police figures, of two provinces were presented, together with factors supposed to correlate or cause crime, like church visits, illegitimate children, the use of alcohol, living circumstances, police capacity and also issues concerning surveillance due to impassable roads (Kempe & Vermaat 1939). Van Bemmelen (1958) used official crime statistics from the CBS as well, while briefly describing the 'dark number' issue (Van Bemmelen 1958: 41-43, 250-253).

Thus, since the nineteenth century, statistics on crime, accidents etc. were collected to check whether (in line with popular belief) crime was increasing or how crime changed (Deflem 1997; Godfrey 2003; Robinson 1933; Wilkins 1980). Besides that, people analysed and interpreted the statistics by not only showing regularities from year to year, but also by explaining these patterns with other variables, like Quetelet and Gatrell had done earlier (Beirne 1987; Emsly 1999; Stigler 1986). For example, Wichman used crime statistics to show that education and the social situation in general were important in explaining increasing crime rates. Also, she noted that crime increased during crisis periods, like World War I (Van Bochove 1999). The crime figures were

---

[118] See for more information the National Archive of Criminal Justice Data [NACJD] as well as the CD-ROM of the U.S. Bureau of the Census; especially Series H952-1170 on crime and correction and Series H971-986 that provide data on homicides and suicides from 1900 till 1970.

used for controlling costs and the general finances as well (Emsly 1999). Consequently, the police and special institutions got the task to provide statistical knowledge, like the number of murders and thefts within a certain region. Obviously, these statistics increasingly became political instruments (Best 2001; Chevigny 2003; Morris 2001; Porter 1996; H.Taylor 1998a, 1998b), as Haggerty (2001) notes: several micropolitical considerations influence decisions regarding the studies that are conducted, the agencies that control the official figures, the way the measures are standardised and how statistical facts are communicated to the public.

In sum, as pictured in Figure 5.2, the governments in Western societies took an interest in the counting of social phenomena, and statistics on all kinds of social issues were used to make an argument, to justify specific interventions and to increase the general awareness of possibilities of social control. Statistical analyses have become more and more technically advanced and more common. Institutions, governmental departments and committees were concerned with 'counting and controlling' and with 'explaining and taming'. Statistical regularities were used to develop interventions, make policy and allocate resources, for example concerning crime.

5.2   Surveying society

O'Muircheartaigh (1997) describes the history of the sample survey and its error sources in the Anglo-Saxon world. He notes that the survey as a source of information became established in the 1940s and 1950s and three sectors in society in particular used the survey as a tool, namely the government, the academic community and business. These three sectors have developed their own distinct frameworks and terminologies, based on different disciplines like statistics, sociology and experimental psychology. Thus, three lines in the historical development of survey research can be distinguished; firstly the governmental and therefore official statistics, secondly academic or social research and finally the strand of commercial, advertising or market research (O'Muircheartaigh 1997). Likert, in a reprint from a 1951-article, elaborates on the sample survey as a tool of research and policy information (Likert 1968). He proposes various origins, like the polls, which aroused much public interest in their results, consumer market research and methodological origins in mathematical statistics and the field of attitude measurement. According to Likert, the sample interview survey would have a great future, in which he was right; public opinion research creates a totally different perspective of phenomena (Osborne & Rose 1999). Although it took sometime before the increasing criticism regarding the reliability of the official crime statistics was met by making a *victim survey* (Decker 1977; Inciardi & McBride 1976; Vanderveen 2001), see Figure 5.3.

5.2.1   Surveys on criminal victimisation and the police

The victim survey consists of a questionnaire that is administered to a sample of the population, asking questions on personal victimisation experiences of several offences like theft and burglary. Although mainly concerned with evading the dark number of official (police) figures and enhancing comparative analysis of official figures and survey rates (e.g. Cantor & Lynch 2000; Decker 1977; Ernst Eck & Riccio 1979; Gardner 1994; Hindelang 1974; Maltz 1975; Marenin 1997; Menard & Covey 1988), it paved the road for the idea that not only the people's victimhood could be measured, but their ideas and feelings regarding crime as well (see Figure 5.3).

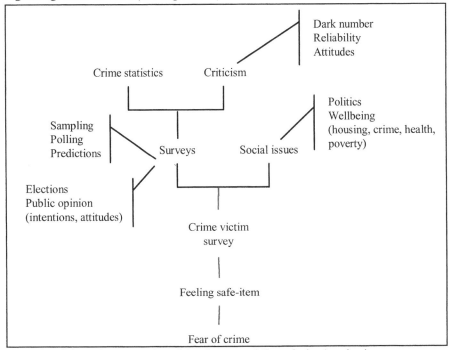

Figure 5.3. Schematic presentation of development of 'fear of crime'-notion in surveys.

In the 1960s, public opinion surveys administered in the United States began asking about crime and related themes (Harris 1969). For example, the Harris Poll in 1964 asked whether "juvenile delinquency and crime" were a problem or not (Harris 1964 in Appendix F), the Harris Poll in 1969 asked respondents whether they "keep a weapon or instrument of protection by your bed when you go to sleep" and the famous items on the stranger who rings the doorbell and how safe they felt when they walked in their neighbourhood during the day. Two more items were added regarding their "worry about wife or husband when they are away from home in the evening" and "worry about children when they are away from home in the evening" (Harris 1969 Urban Crime Survey, no. 1935, see Appendix F). In 1967, the National Opinion Research Center (NORC) conducted the first nationwide study of victimisation in the United States.[119] This survey asked people from 10,000 households about criminal victimisation over the twelve months prior to the interview (Hindelang

---

[119] This survey was conducted for a governmental commission on Law Enforcement and the Administration of Justice (Hindelang 1974).

1974). Moreover, more surveys were administered in the United States, which were (partly) aiming at the measurement of experiences and the *fear* of criminal victimisation. Around 1970, the focus of the study of crime extended to the impact of crime on the victim, the costs of crime and losses of the victim.[120] In 1973, Miller focused his attention on 'fear of crime' of victims and of those aware of the risk on victimisation (Miller 1973). In that year, the National Crime Survey, after some years of preparation, was developed further.[121] Changes in attitudes and habits could be derived from "attitude data", because, as Gignilliat (1977) suggests:

> Knowledge of citizen reactions to crimes is particularly useful in planning programs, such as treating victims during the investigation of a crime or during a subsequent rehabilitation period. Fear related to the use of public utilities, entertainment, and migration could also be investigated. (p. 186)

The 'attitude data' consisted of the responses on questions about the "change in frequency of crime in neighborhood", "change in frequency of crime in U.S.", whether crime had an "effect on activities of people in neighborhood", "effect on activities of people in general", "effect on activities of respondent" and an "effect on travel to areas of city during day" or during the night. Also, questions were asked on the "perceived safety in neighborhood", compared to other neighbourhoods, during the day and during the night (Gignilliat 1977). Not only crime was seen as a social problem, 'fear of crime' itself became a problem for the community as well and became a research subject in itself (e.g. Block 1971; Erskine 1974; Flango 1979; Garofalo & Laub 1978; Skogan & Klecka 1977).

In the Netherlands, where the sample survey was introduced after the Second World War (Van Bochove 1999), it was not until 1973 that the first criminal victimisation survey was carried out, which was to a certain extent copied from the American victim surveys. Respondents were asked not only about their experiences with crime, but also about safety measures and reactions to crime (Fiselier 1978). Again, this survey mainly aimed for a more reliable estimation of the occurrence of crime, by surpassing the police statistics and thus avoiding the 'dark number' issue (figure 5.3). Besides that, Fiselier acknowledged the possibilities of the victim survey for research on for example the costs of victimisation. Moreover, he noted that crime can be viewed as a

---

[120] Kempe (1967) notes in his book that provides an introduction to criminology that not much literature is available on the victim or on victimology. In this book, which is an adaptation of Bonger's introduction from 1932, Kempe refers to classic works as for example Von Hentig's *The Criminal and his Victim* (1948). In Kempe's book, no reference is made to systematic study of public opinion or of attitudes regarding crime or sanctions, other than two studies on "delinquent situations" (Kempe 1967: 34-35).

[121] The surveys were part of the National Crime Panel (NCP) Program, which is sponsored by the Law Enforcement Assistance Administration. The political background of the survey is clear again, as Gignilliat (1977: 183) notes: "NCP's goal is to help criminal justice agencies improve their effectiveness by providing a new source of detailed information about the victims of crimes, numbers and types of crimes reported and not reported to police, and uniform measures of selected types of crimes".

social problem, which causes that crime does not only pertains to victims of crime, but instead that everybody has to do with crime (Fiselier 1978).

The Ministry of Justice and its research department, WODC, found the victimisation experiences relevant and conducted a few surveys from 1974 till 1979 (e.g. Buikhuisen 1975; Vanderveen 2001, 2004). These surveys asked about victimisation and reporting to the police, in order to estimate the extent of crime. Specific crimes and particular groups of people, based on demographic variables, like sex, age and residence, were distinguished from one another, which ended in a "victimological risk analysis" (Van Dijk & Steinmetz 1979). In these surveys, no items related to 'fear of crime' were included, unlike the survey that aimed at gauging the opinions and feelings of the population on the issue of crime (Cozijn & Van Dijk 1976: 1).[122] In the report, four legitimisations are noted, to explain why the study of these opinions and feelings is relevant. First, the authors claim that it is important for the government to know what priority the problem of crime should have, at least according to the public. Second, the public opinion determines the boundaries of the reform of penal and criminal justice. Next, by studying opinions and feelings, the government can observe trends, so as to prevent vigilantism.[123] A final legitimisation concerns wellbeing, which can be affected by feelings of fear and behavioural constraints (Cozijn & Van Dijk 1976).

The contents of the survey, which were conducted with a representative sample, are very similar to the American surveys. Questions referred for example to thoughts about crime, has the likelihood of becoming a victim increased the past two years, feeling safe at home and in the street, avoiding places because of fear of becoming attacked or robbed and preventive measures that were taken.[124] Another survey from that time paid attention to the public's opinion as well, in relation to police and the tasks of the police. For example, one item stated that "when there wouldn't be police, you wouldn't feel safe" (Junger-Tas 1978). So in the 70s, some surveys were conducted that were quite similar to the American victim surveys, yet no attention was paid to 'fear of crime' on a regular basis. This changed in 1981, when the ESM, a survey of crime victims, was administered annually till 1985 and bi-annually from 1985 till 1993 (see Beukenhorst 1992; Centraal Bureau voor de Statistiek 1991). Thus, responses on the question "Are you afraid when you're at home alone at

---

[122] Again, the survey had definite political origins. When the Dutch Lower House (Tweede Kamer) discussed the Budget of the Ministry of Justice for the year 1974, a working group for the prevention of crime (Stuurgroep Preventie Criminaliteit) was established. The survey was conducted at the request of this working group.

[123] Cozijn & Van Dijk (1976) use the Dutch term 'eigenrichting', which refers to the situation that somebody takes the law into his/her own hands.

[124] Also, statements like "when walking in the neighbourhood, you have to look around you, since you never know who you come across" (als je een straatje om gaat moet je altijd goed om je heen kijken. Je weet maar nooit wie je tegenkomt), "one used to be able to walk in the neighbourhood, but nowadays, that's not possible anymore" (vroeger kon je wel 's avonds een straatje om gaan, maar tegenwoordig kan dat niet meer), and "before you go to sleep, you have to check whether all doors and windows are closed and shut" (voor je slapen gaat moet je eerst zorgvuldig kijken of alle deuren en ramen goed gesloten zijn).

night" are available since 1982 from the CBS.[125] The ESM was transformed into the ERV, the survey of legal protection and safety, which in turn changed into the POLS.[126] This latter survey, POLS, still exists and the CBS provides data and analyses derived from this survey (Centraal Bureau voor de Statistiek 1998, 2002; Huys 1997).

Next to POLS, a major source of statistical data is the PMB, which was introduced in 1990 and has been administered bi-annually since 1993 and commissioned by the Home Office, the Ministry of Justice and the police divisions (e.g. Huls et al. 2001; Huys 2001; Maas- De Waal 2002a, 2002b; Sociaal Cultureel Planbureau 2000). Familiar items, on avoiding places because of crime, not opening the door at night and forbidding children to go to a particular place, are included. In brief, the Dutch surveys, analogous to the developments in the USA, gradually focused their attention to the experience of safety as well, as well as on victimisation experiences.

Following this tradition, the linking of personal victimisation incidents with the experience and interpretation of safety, the British Crime Survey (BCS) was for the first time conducted in 1982. The BCS is very similar to the victim surveys as applied in Scotland (SCS), Australia (ACSS), the United States (NCVS), Canada (GSS) and the Netherlands (Hough 1986; Hough & Mayhew 1983). The International Crime Victim Survey (ICVS) was developed in the late eighties and has been used four times now, in 1989, 1992, 1996 and 2000 (Van Dijk & Mayhew 1992; Van Dijk, Mayhew & Killias 1990; Van Kesteren, Mayhew & Nieuwbeerta 2000; Mayhew & Van Dijk 1997). Over time, more countries are involved and the latest ICVS has been administered in more than fifty countries all over the world, which makes the amount of data on criminal victimisation and aspects regarding the experience of personal safety overwhelming. The 'feeling safe when walking alone'-item is included, as well as an item on the perceived risk of becoming a victim of burglary (Vanderveen 2002b).

In sum, Likert was right when he predicted a great future for the survey. Since the development of the victim survey, something which could not have happened without the previous developments in statistics and probability theory, numerous surveys on the local, national and international level (e.g. in the UK, USA, Canada, the Netherlands). These surveys are used in policy making (e.g. see Grogger & Weatherford 1995; Vanderveen 2002a), financial decisions and international comparisons. Victim surveys have proven to be important instruments in politics and cutting costs (Baer & Chambliss 1997; Body-Gendrot 2001; Kuttschreuter & Wiegman 1998; Rodgers & Thorson 2001). Though the victim surveys were originally developed to counter criticism concerning the reliability of (crime) statistics, i.e. dark number issues, the surveys contained questions on attitudes regarding crime as well. As such, the development of the

---

[125] Translated from the Dutch: "Bent u wel eens bang als u 's avonds alleen thuis bent".
[126] In 1993, both the ESM and ERV were used, and the ERV was also used in 1995 and 1997. A major difference between these two surveys is that the ERV incorporates several questions related to problems with the law, i.e. criminal law as well as civil law (Beukenhorst et al. 1993).

crime victim survey since the 1960s is a result of the developments in public opinion and election polling, technical advancement in sampling techniques and an overall increasing interest in intentions and attitudes of the general public and of consumers (in market research). From this period on, the item 'feeling safe after dark' has been used (figure 5.3). This item, and related items on 'worry' and 'stranger ringing the doorbell', soon became known as relating to 'fear of crime'. The item came first, the concept appeared on the stage later.

5.2.2   Criticism on quantification

Together with the increasing development and use of statistics, criticism rose. The crime victim survey was developed to counter much of this criticism, and with its increasing (international) use, criticism regarding the surveys also rose. Yet, given the prevalence of quantification, public opinion and its measurement have become extremely relevant, in spite of legitimate criticism of polls and surveys, even if opinions and attitudes do not reflect the 'real' or 'objective' world (Vanderveen 2002c). An example is given by Pride (2002), who says the public evaluation of schools and education is distorted by focusing on critical events (e.g. school shootings) rather than performance trends, since these kind of events get massive attention of competing politicians and commentators.

Moreover, the contemporary identification of survey research and public opinion is criticised (e.g. Sanders 1999). The "trust in numbers" (Porter 1996) and "doctrine of quantification" in the social sciences is widespread, and "the desire to formulate some indicator measures, on any basis, is almost irresistible" (Holton 1998: 203). Statistics are used instrumentally; Best (2001) notes that people who present statistics have a reason for doing so; they want *something*, just like the media who repeat the statistics in their publications. Especially in social science statistics "can become weapons in political struggles over social problems and social policy" (Best 2001: 10).[127] Criticism regarding quantification and the so-called administrative criminology (Lupton & Tulloch 1999) in general has also been widely discussed in several studies concerned with so-called interpretive knowledge (see Bryman 1984; Edwards 1990), which is in particular related to studies within a framework that is more 'feminist' (see Flavin 2001; Walklate 1995).[128] Of course, several scholars within the mainstream quantitative tradition have identified (methodological as well as conceptual) flaws regarding the use of surveys (e.g. Duncan 2000; Gottfredson & Hindelang 1977; Hox & Jansen 1995; Skogan 1975). Moreover, criticism regarding the use of police statistics in criminological research had already been expressed in the nineteenth century, the dark number issue for example had

---

[127] During the review of the available literature, I came across examples of how to 'lie with statistics' (Huff 1969; Morris 2001).

[128] Studies in these frameworks have taken a particular stance regarding the question which social phenomena are relevant for researchers to investigate, how this phenomenon should be studied and what should be done with the results of the research. In particular, whether social research should be used to induce social change (see Denner 1992; Dobash & Dobash 1988; Greenwood & Levin 2000; Pini 2002).

already been raised in 1836 (Salas & Surette 1984).[129] In 1915, Bowley (cited in O'Muircheartaigh 1997) wrote about 'The Nature and Purpose of the Measurement of Social Phenomena' and states "In conclusion, we ought to realise that measurement is a means to an end; it is only the childish mind that delights in numbers for their own sake."

5.3   Conclusion: statistics & surveys count

Fear, crime and social deviance have been considered problems throughout history, on which the next chapters will elaborate as well. Using large-scale surveys and the information deduced from these in politics, public opinion and policies, has been a relatively new phenomenon. Criminological statistics developed within a general social statistics system (Salas & Surette 1984). When these statistical possibilities became known, researchers and governmental institutions have not only used statistics to understand social phenomena but mainly to prove their point and use it as a tool in policy and for decisions in financial matters, like cutting back costs. The notion of the *crime victim survey* was developed as a reply to criticism regarding the reliability of official (police) figures and the call for more attention to victims. At first, the victim surveys were not primarily focused on acquiring attitudinal knowledge, but rather on improving the estimation of the crime rate. Yet, the interest in and the measurement of intentions and attitudes increased rapidly. From first surveys related to crime or for example housing, the item 'feeling safe after dark' has been used (figure 5.3). This item, and related items on 'worry' and 'stranger ringing the doorbell', soon became known as relating to 'fear of crime'. Clearly, the item came first, the concept appeared on the stage later.

This development is not solely an American characteristic, but a feature that has become common in many western and non-western societies (see Lee 1999). The first Dutch crime victim surveys are based on the earlier American crime victim surveys and the different variants on national and local level have been copied ever since. Concluding; without a doubt, statistics and surveys are conditions for the concept 'fear of crime' and despite several flaws and criticism, surveys and their resulting statistics play a major, and often instrumental, role in contemporary society. Also, the internationally famous items, some of which are used in almost every survey, were originally intended and/or used as a sort of public opinion poll-question. The label, let alone the theoretical concept, 'fear of crime' was invented later. Neither a systematic theory-driven (hypothetical-deductive) approach, nor a systematic data-driven (inductive) approach has been used to develop the concept and its operationalisations. Rather, the concept derived its meaning from the items that were used from the beginning. The context and the use of these items indicate that they merely resemble items used in public opinion polls, implying that the meaning of the concept 'fear of crime' refers to the problematic consequences of crime for everyday life as felt and perceived by the general public.

---

[129] Several historical debates concerning the use of numbers, statistics and techniques can be found in Stigler (1999).

Table 5.1. List of main assertions Chapter 5.

Topic	Explanation
Purpose	Explain how 'fear of crime' is primarily related to statistics and surveys by governments Stress the political uses of surveys, yet challenge the global criticism of surveys
Research questions	How can the history of fear of crime surveys be described? How were the concept and the familiar items developed? To what extent has the notion of 'fear of crime' been dependent on crime surveys? Within this context, what does 'fear of crime' mean?
Main notions	Since 1960s, attitudinal knowledge on crime is being surveyed Crime statistics and victim surveys have been conducted by governments and their institutions Governmental interest based on notion of controlling social phenomena Instrumental purposes; interventions, allocation of resources Criticism on statistics & development of sampling and polling led to victim survey Main purpose of victim survey: provide reliable crime figures Included questions on attitudes, intentions regarding crime; 'feeling safe', 'ringing doorbell' Item was first, the label (concept) later International cross-fertilisation; reproduction of 'fear of crime' items Criticism on quantification, surveys did not decrease use or interest Crime statistics and victim surveys still instrumental tools (international, national, local level)
Conclusion	Crime statistics and victim surveys conditions for concept 'fear of crime' Well-known items at first intended/ used as public opinion poll question Later, theoretical concept 'fear of crime' invented Despite several flaws and criticism, surveys and statistics play a major, and often instrumental, role Meaning of concept 'fear of crime': problematic consequences of crime for everyday life as felt and perceived by the general public

6 The diversity of victimisation

In the centre of the whole notion of 'fear of crime' lies the concept of crime and more specifically, criminal victimisation. In the discussion of 'fear of crime', what is meant by 'crime', what is meant by (criminal) victimisation? How are these concepts related to one another? The concepts of 'crime' and 'victimisation' are necessary in order to be able to think about the idea of something like 'fear of crime'. Before a 'fear of crime' can even be brought to existence, something like crime is a prerequisite. Here, the aim is not to describe what crime is, nor to present 'the social construction of crime'. In this chapter, the popular ideas about crime, victimisation and criminal victimisation are explored with emphasis on gender differences and with respect to the main question on the meaning of certain concepts in their social context.

In chapter 2, the 'criminal victimisation causes fear'-model, and its variants involving indirect victimisation and imaginable victimisation, were briefly described. These persistent models connect crime, or (criminal) victimisation, directly to fear. The 'criminal victimisation causes fear'-model has led to the notion of the so-called fear-victimisation paradox, suggesting that people who are victimised the least, are the most fearful (see Lindquist & Duke 1982; Vanderveen 1999). Not only has criticism regarding this paradox concentrated on the measurement of *victimisation risks* (see chapter 7); criticism is also directly related to the concept of (criminal) victimisation. Often, the critics argue for a broader conceptualisation, by pointing out the possibility of indirect victimisation and other forms of victimisation. Apparently, the concept 'victimisation' is less clear than it seems at first sight. The discussion of the development of the victim survey and the measurement of 'fear of crime' demonstrated the habits of directly relating 'fear of crime' to crime and criminal victimisation. How has this been done and what role does crime and victimisation play?

This chapter consists of three basic parts; the first stresses the diversity of victimisation by explaining the wide variety of different interpretations (see the topic tree in Figure 6.1). Thus, different types of victimisation are described, which are all different approaches to the *concept* 'victimisation'. The first approach focuses on the nature of the victimisation; which can vary from burglary to violent assault and all kinds of sexual victimisation. Though in research on 'fear of crime' the nature of victimisation is often restricted to a few forms of criminal victimisation, other experiences might be at least as unpleasant; it is the interpretation of the event and its consequences that matters here. Another approach focuses on the person who is victimised. This can be the person him/herself, somebody's spouse or children or another person one knows. The victim might also be someone else who is not known to the person, but whose victimisation is seen in the street or subway. The victim might even be someone whose victimisation is not seen in real life and with whom the person has no relationship, but instead in a movie, or pictured in a newspaper article. This relates to the third approach to victimisation as a possibly occurring event, which is especially relevant in the context of 'fear of crime'. This imaginable victimisation is also salient in reference to the images of victims in several (indirect) sources. Apparently, victimisation is not an unequivocal term, not even when specified as criminal victimisation. In this first part of this chapter, it will become clear that the different interpretations of victimisation are connected with attributions, notions of responsibility and culpability. These attributions and notions stem from social and cultural context(s) that provide images on the typical victim, offender and crime (see Melossi 2000). These typical images are (re)created by several sources of information and these are discussed in the second part of this chapter. This second part demonstrates the commonness of the typical images in stories, television programmes, movies and newspaper articles. Finally, the third part discusses the notion of the 'ideal victim', which is based on the typical images as well as on social cognitive understandings.

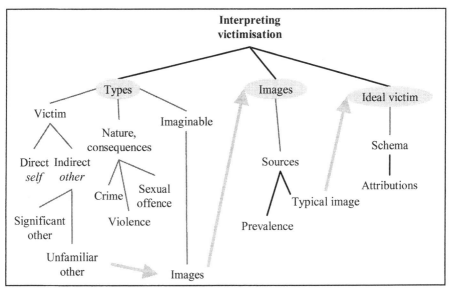

Figure 6.1. Topic tree of chapter on victimisation discourse.

6.1 Criminal victimisation

The first approach to make sense of the variety in victimisation focuses on the nature of the victimisation; which can vary from burglary to violent assault and all kinds of sexual victimisation. Such an approach concentrates on the question: the victimisation of what? The overview of concepts and operationalisations (chapter 2) showed that research on 'fear of crime' often restricts the nature of victimisation to a few forms of criminal victimisation, like burglary, robbery and assault. It is the law that defines these forms of victimisation. However, other experiences that might be at least as unpleasant are sometimes included, like obscene phone calls (Buck, Chatterson & Paase 1995; Huys 2001; Sheffield 1993). Even when one would define 'crime' by the limits of the law and legal code, it is clear that when the law is changing, the concept 'crime' is changing as well. Especially sexually connotated behaviours, sexual harassment and violence, may be (de)criminalised as a result of social and legal change, see for example Roberts and Mohr (1994), Carrington and Watson (1996) and Stevens (2002). Also, the public's willingness to criminalise acts that are perceived as domestic abuse strengthened from 1987 to 1997 and is becoming increasingly favourable for the victim (Johnson & Sigler 2000). Sometimes, the societal disapproval of behaviours is leading to legal sanctioning (cf. D'Anjou 2000; Sherman 2000), thus constituting a 'crime' even when applying a narrow interpretation, for example in the case of stalking (e.g. Groenhuijsen 1998; Saunders 1998).

Stalking has been a relatively recent legally defined crime, which is not to say that the phenomenon itself is recent (e.g. Baas 1998; Budd & Mattinson 2000). Fisher, Cullen and Turner (2002: 275) defined 'stalking' as "the same person exhibiting repeated pursuit behavior that seemed obsessive and made the respondent afraid or concerned for her safety".[130] In their survey, women in college were asked about their experience with stalking.[131] They find that a substantial minority of women will experience stalking and are more at-risk for sexual victimisation. More than 80% was not reported to police, because of varying motivations, like "not serious enough to report", because it wasn't clear that stalking was a crime or that harm was intended; despite that they were concerned or feared for their own safety. The authors elaborate on the "seriousness" of stalking and of a crime in general. They argue that this is a dynamic concept; assessments of seriousness are not only tied to what occurs in a stalking incident, but also to whether the larger social and cultural context defines stalking as a "crime" and whether the local campus "raises consciousness" about this form of victimisation (Fisher, Cullen & Turner 2002). Moreover, they argue, that the stalking experience was not "serious enough to report to the police" does not mean that the incident was not serious or that the stalking experience has not otherwise been consequential (e.g. Kamphuis & Emmelkamp 2001). The dynamics of the concept are also illustrated by new forms; lately 'stalking' has also been linked with the Internet: cyberstalking (Ashcroft 2001; Meloy 1998). Whatever type of stalking, before it was legally sanctioned in a nation's criminal law, its consequences might have been equally

---

[130] Though both men and women can experience stalking, often stalking has been connected with violence against women especially (Walker & Meloy 1998; White et al. 2000). The majority of stalking victims are women, being stalked by men who either want to re-establish or initiate a relationship (Hall 1998). Also, see for example the study "Violence and Threats of Violence Against Women and Men in the United States, 1994-1996" (ICPSR 2566: Tjaden & Thoennes 1998a, 1998b, 1998c, 2000a, 2000b), that aimed at providing "reliable estimates of the prevalence and incidence of various forms of violence against women, including rape, physical assault, and stalking". Also, the "Longitudinal Study of Violence Against Women: Victimization & Perpetration Among College Students in a State-Supported University in the United States, 1990-5" (ICPSR 3212: Humphrey & White 2000; White & Smith 2001a, 2001b) that focuses on physical and sexual violence against young women.

[131] A screening question was used, namely "since school began in the Fall of 1996, has anyone – from a stranger to an ex-boyfriend – repeatedly followed you, watched you, phoned, written, e-mailed, or communicated with you in other ways in a way that seemed obsessive and made you afraid or concerned for your safety?" Fisher, Cullen & Turner (2002).

serious. On the other hand, even though 'stalking' might be legally sanctioned, whether or not it is considered a crime worthwhile telling the police is dependent on other factors than just the pure legal definition. Notwithstanding one's concern or fear for one's own safety, it might not be clear that stalking is a crime or that harm was 'really' intended. In brief, whether the victim and the larger social and cultural context define concrete series of events that would meet the criteria for legal definitions of 'stalking' actually as a "crime", depends on other factors. Thus, 'crime' and 'criminal victimisation' is not as clear-cut as might seem at first sight, similar to interpretations of other (criminal) victimisation events, like for example rape.

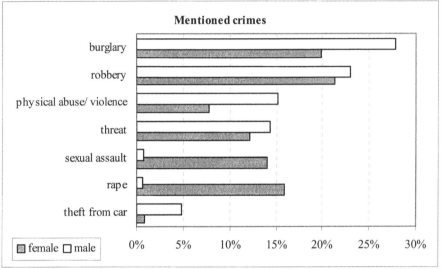

Figure 6.2. Typical example of most often mentioned crimes. Source of data: NIWI 1127 (Appendix F).

So, what kind of crime, defined by law, is thought of when talking about 'fear of crime'? What type of crime is feared the most? According to Pelser, Louw and Ntuli (2000), who studied 'fear of crime' in South Africa's rural areas, people fear the crimes that they are most likely to experience, like burglary and stock theft, as well as those with the most serious consequences (e.g. murder). A similar conclusion can be derived from results of a survey in Dar es Salaam (Robertshaw, Louw & Mtani 2001), and in Durban and Cape Town (Shaw & Louw 1998). Respondents said they feared a break-in and mugging the most, which both are the most prevalent crimes in Dar es Salaam. Robertshaw et al. (2001) asked respondents in Durban, what they feared the most about crime and grouped their answers in four categories, namely the loss of life, sexual violence, physical injury and loss of property. Thus, the first three groups, which were the most common expressed, all touch on a personal, violent, confrontation with a perpetrator. A similar survey in Cape Town (Camerer et al. 1998) asked what respondents feared the most, ranging from loss of life, physical injury, loss of property, sexual violence, and sexual intimidation (in this order of magnitude), showed similar results.

The popular image of crime in the context of 'fear of crime' in the *Western* world concentrates especially on (random) violence that might occur in the public sphere (Heath & Gilbert 1996).[132] One of the first victim surveys in the Netherlands asked respondents whether they ever thought about becoming a victim of crime, and if yes, what kind of crime. The main crimes that were mentioned were sexual assault, robbery and physical abuse (Van Dijk & Steinmetz 1979). The ICVS contains the item on the perception of risk on *burglary*, which is also included in other victim surveys, like the Dutch POLS. As advocated by for example Ferraro (1995), surveys that primarily focus on attitudinal knowledge with respect to crime often incorporate more than just one offence (e.g. NIWI 1069; ICPSR 2800). Figure 6.2 presents a typical example of the most common offences that are mentioned by fe/male respondents (NIWI 1127). The majority of the 2230 male respondents, about 60% could not answer the question which specific crime he is most fearful of, whereas 44% of the 2894 female respondents did not mention a specific crime. Respondents could specify two offences, the most common ones, which are presented in the figure, are burglary and robbery for both men and women. Physical abuse/ violence and threat are often mentioned as well, but females far more often referred to sexual violence, namely rape and sexual assault, which is very similar to other studies, like findings from the BCS (e.g. Mirrlees-Black & Allen 1998). In contrast, only some men referred to these specific offences, yet mentioned theft from a car more often than women did. The general picture expresses the focus on (violent) personal confrontation with the offender and on (random) *violence* that might occur in the public sphere.

6.1.1   Violence

Violence, however, might seem a self-evident concept, but appears to be more problematic than it first seems. The interpretation of a (violent) incident depends on characteristics of the various circumstances, of the victim and of the perpetrator; different scenarios generate different meanings as is shown in for example May's study. May (1999) used in-depth interviews (narratives) with relatives of people who had been convicted of murder to study how 'murder' is understood in everyday life, i.e. how 'murder' is socially constructed by the relatives. The interviews contained explanations of what had happened and how they were interpreted. One group of relatives defined the killing as manslaughter, whereas another group agreed with the verdict that the killing was in fact a murder. May (1999) relates their definitions of what happened to particular criteria regarding the concepts 'victimisation' and 'culpability'. Similar dimensions, namely concern, violence, commonness, and intentionality,

---

[132] Whether these popular images are (theoretically) viewed as "means of communicating and preserving history, shared myths, cultural symbols, and ideological messages" or as a "marketing strategy: it has become violence, pure, simple, and isolated from its mass ideological significance" (cf. Lynch & Krzycki 1998) is of less significance here.

are underlying the implicit cognitive representations of crime (Forgas 1980). These four dimensions that appeared in a multidimensional scaling analysis were important, and categories such as offences against persons, property, or public order appeared clearly in the cognitive space as well (Forgas 1980). Richardson and May (1999) studied how interpersonal violence is defined within the social context, e.g. when violence is 'tolerated' or 'rejected'. They suggest that understandings of violence are both gendered and sexualised, which means that specific characteristics of the victim, like sex and sexual orientation, as well as the context in which the violence occurs, influences how the violence is interpreted. These characteristics influence notions of deservedness, since blame and responsibility are attributed to both victim and perpetrator, i.e. when a victim is regarded 'undeserved' or 'innocent' in contrast with a 'deserving' or 'just' victim.

Moreover, the public-private distinction is of importance in the interpretation of violence. Though this distinction and the interrelationship between the public and the private is complex, the traditional ideal holds that the private sphere refers to the home, domesticity, care and safety, whereas the public sphere is traditionally more related to violence and crime (Richardson & May 1999).[133] Yet, even within this traditional view, certain places are labelled as less safe than others, sometimes depending on the time of day. This is reflected for example by the avoidance of dimly lit spaces, not going to places known as 'dangerous', or not using public transport at night. People who "do not follow exactly the rules for precaution" are implicitly held responsible for things possibly happening to them (Green, Hebron & Woodward 1987: 89; Stanko 1990: 49). Thus, temporal (day vs. night) and spatial markers shape the context of the violence and attributions of 'deservedness' and culpability even further.

These attributions are also present in notions of the 'ideal victim', which is "a person or a category of individuals who – when hit by crime – most readily are given the complete and legitimate status of being a victim" (Christie 1986: 18). Lamb (1999b) refers to the convincing victim, the culturally approved victim that reinforces ideas about women being the weaker sex, needing protection and special services. Christie (1986) notes five characteristics that are of importance: the victim is weak, carries out a respectable project, being somewhere where s/he can not possibly be blamed for being, the offender is big and bad, and the offender is unknown and in no personal relationship to the victim. In other words, the victim is and does nothing that can be viewed as violating the social norms concerning appropriate conduct for women. Christie emphasises that the ideal victim is weak compared to the unrelated offender and has made a reasonable effort in protecting herself against becoming a victim. In summary, he concludes that the ideal victim is most often an innocent woman, doing a good job, somewhere where she is supposed to do it, who unfortunately meets the ideal offender, a strong, evil, dangerous man coming from far away,

---

[133] Moreover, everything that is (not) done in the private sphere might be viewed as one's own personal business, that should be free from interference of others, the government or the police (e.g. Wöstmann & Van de Bunt 1987).

he is "a human being close to not being one" (Christie 1986: 26). As appears
clearly from Christie's analysis, the attribution processes are gendered; women
are more likely than men to be blamed for "being in the 'wrong' place at the
'wrong' time" (Richardson & May 1999: 313), but might be more 'ideal
victims' as well (Christie 1986).[134] Previously, the salience of sexual crimes in
particular was noted. Therefore, sexual victimisation will be explored in the next
section.

6.1.2   Gendered victimisation: sexual violence, assault and harassment

The notions of deservedness or culpability, the attribution of blame and
responsibility to both victim and perpetrator, turn out to be especially relevant in
the interpretation of sexual violence (e.g. Shalhoub-Kevorkian 1999; Shotland &
Goodstein 1983). Koski (2002) extensively describes his analysis of the social
context of jury decision-making in highly ambiguous criminal cases and uses the
story model that stems from research on social cognition. This model suggests
that the "entire juror decision process is a matter of creating a plausible account
– a "story"– of the crime, assimilating the presented facts to that story, and
arriving at a judgment consistent with it" (Olsen-Fulero & Fulero 1997: 415).
Koski employs three different consent-defence rape trials, in which both a
victim's consent and her credibility is at issue, but in which the sexual act itself
is undisputed. Though according to a black letter approach to the law, the focus
of the jury is on conduct, intentions and culpability of the perpetrator, in practice
the jury's attention is primarily focused on the behaviour, motives and
blameworthiness of the victim that may have contributed to what has happened
(Koski 2002). This is also illustrated by Scutt's account of legal decisions in the
case of rape of prostitutes and other 'incredible women' (Scutt 1992).[135]

Previously, the interpretation of violence was discussed with reference
to the public-private distinction. The traditional perspective, that amounts to the
private sphere, i.e. the home as safe and the public sphere, i.e. outside the home
as dangerous, evokes more and more criticism, especially since child abuse,
sexual violence and violence or abuse within the family is neglected (e.g. Flavin
2001; Scutt 1986). Nevertheless, the stereotypical images or archetypes derived
from this traditional perspective are ubiquitous (see Eschholz & Bufkin 2001;
Lamb 1999b). The implicit rules for precaution reciprocally act on the notions of
ideal, innocent victims and a just, deserving victim; all moulding the context of
violence and victimisation, refining the attributions of 'deservedness' and
culpability. As noted before, the attribution processes are gendered, the rules for
precaution are (in part) different for men and women, which is emphasised in
incidents of rape. The extent to which a perceiver attributes responsibility to an

---

[134] This is reflected in the two stock media images of women, archetypes like virgin vs. vamp are
portrayed in the media (Cavender, Bond-Maupin & Jurik 1999; Eschholz & Bufkin 2001; Gordon &
Riger 1989; Hedley 2002).
[135] For example, one judge decided "rape was likely to cause women working as prostitutes less
psychological harm than other women" (Scutt 1992: 451-454).

assailant and a victim depends mostly on the perceiver's sex and his/her acceptance of 'rape myths', which are "descriptive or prescriptive beliefs about rape…about its causes, context, consequences, perpetrators, victims and their interaction" (Bohner, cited in Abrams et al. 2003: 111). Men and people who accept rape myths are more likely to blame the victim and attribute responsibility to the victim's behaviour and perceive a particular incident less likely as a rape (e.g. Morry & Winkler 2001; Weisz & Earls 1995).[136] Rape myths are thought of as general stereotypic beliefs that exonerate the perpetrator and blame the victim of sexual violence (e.g. Bohner 2001; Lonsway & Fitzgerald 1995; Morry & Winkler 2001; Viki & Abrams 2002).[137] These rape myths and attitudes to rape in general are subject of several empirical studies on social cognition (e.g. Bohner et al. 1998; Jimenez & Abreu 2003), which will be discussed later to provide an overall framework.

The gendered attribution processes are also presumed by the socialisation-model or gender role socialisation model, briefly described in chapter 2, that explains the differences between men and women on their level of fear by proposing that differential socialisation is causing gendered notions of 'victim' and 'victimisation'. Authors who adopt this model often argue that these notions socially control women's lives, since women need to be constantly aware of the dangers outside the home and follow the rules for precaution, which usually implies limiting and restricting one's activities and behaviours. The traditional perspective identifies strangers and deviants, thus men in the public sphere, as rapists, "which enables other men to extort submission from women in exchange for protection" (Clark 1987: 1). The perspective is connected with ideas about masculine and feminine roles and scripts, some of which are denoted with 'rape myths' (Brownmiller 1975), like the 'date rape' that is not considered to really be a rape. Milburn, Mather and Conrad (2000) explicate such a script by connecting it with legitimacy:

> For, if a woman has consented to a situation where sexual relations could occur (i.e., a date), then she has implicitly consented to sexual relations because it is only at the initial stage, when solicitation of a date occurs, that a woman may legitimately refuse. (p. 646)

However, the work of for example Phillips (1999, 2000) shows that 'victimisation' is not straightforward unwanted behaviour and daily harassment. She investigated young women's accounts of women's experiences of relationships and sexualities, i.e. hetero-relationality. These daily experiences often related to complex paradoxes and contradictions. Contradictory feelings were very common in the women's reflections. For example, men in the public sphere, e.g. in a café, on the street making comments about a woman's body, her

---

[136] Sex is also an important correlate of the acceptance of 'rape myths' (e.g. Jimenez & Abreu 2003; Morry & Winkler 2001).

[137] Abrams et al. (2003) present the full description of rape myths, as defined by Bohner, which directly refers to the cultural function they serve: "descriptive or prescriptive beliefs about rape (i.e. about its causes, context, consequences, perpetrators, victims and their interaction) that serve to deny, trivialise or justify sexual violence exerted by men against women".

attire, mood etc. does *not* always and only feel terrible, it might feel as a 'compliment' as well. Phillips concludes that the accounts are filled with confusing and contradictory emotions and can best be described as 'flirting with danger', playing around where the boundaries or lines are, and play around the edge, which might make these women feel powerful. In most descriptions of incidents, whether described as entirely frightening or entirely fun, elements of danger as well as excitement emerged and were usually interwoven. The mixed feelings, i.e. a sense of pleasure and of potential danger, of power and of powerlessness, of flattery and humiliation, reflect the coexistence of pleasure and danger. Phillips points out that the women are feeling acknowledged because of comments and whistles on the street, as an affirmation of their adult womanhood, yet are simultaneously feeling degraded in the context of unequalised power and having fear for serious repercussions, being aware of not getting in too much trouble and not letting it go too far (Phillips 2000: 99). In the interviews, notions referring to the 'ideal victim' and related stereotypes from the traditional perspective appear frequently, like the warnings the women receive that involve usually "crazy-looking strangers", not the "normal-looking" men or people. For example, Phillips reports on an interview with a girl who had asked a nice, respectable boy to walk her home, yet later forces himself on her:

> It never occurred to me that he might be the one who was dangerous, because all the warnings I had gotten were about strangers who leap out at you from the bushes or lure you into their cars or something. (p. 55)

The traditional perspective itself is a result of the social-historical context as well. Clark (1987) goes back to England in the late 18th and early 19th century, the period 1770-1845 in which British society changed dramatically because of the Industrial Revolution and the rise of Victorianism. She collected more than 1000 cases of sexual assault from various sources, like newspapers, police and court records or transcripts, as well as petitions from an archive of a London charitable institution that took in illegitimate children of unmarried mothers and tells the circumstances. In that time, both country and city women faced the danger of rape everywhere, and from every kind of man. Public space in the late 18th century was seen as dangerous for everyone and rape incidents excited little public outcry. Newspapers concentrated on highway robberies of gentlemen and did not use rape as warnings to women to behave, since they hardly reported on rapes at all. Novels of that time did express a constant fear of rape, but the incidents portrayed in these novels often took place within the home, by somebody known. Thus, in the late 18th century, women did not enjoy freedom from the fear of rape, yet incidents of rape were not used to warn women to stay out of public space. The use of rape as a warning, the myth of the safe home and dangerous streets, the warning that "rapists punish women who stray from the proper place" only became prevalent in the early 19th century and is present in popular images till today (Brownmiller 1975).[138] According to Clark, the warning stems from middle-class efforts to control the activities of working women in public space, e.g. factories, linked with an increasing stress on sexual purity as measure of woman's worth. In the 19th century women were safe only when they stay at home, which is referred to as the traditional perspective here. In summary, Clark (1987) connects the public-private distinction, or the ideology of separate spheres, to the use of rape and sexual assault as a warning for women to stay away from the public sphere and thus to notions of responsibility and the culpability of the victim. She argues that the protection the myth offers in exchange for obedience is illusory; more danger exists in one's own home than on dark streets; rapists are male acquaintances, friends as well all strangers. Thus, though the fear of rape is real, the illusion of safety is false.

The 'gendered' victimisation is reflected by results from studies on 'fear of crime', which suggest that 'fear of crime', or the 'fear of victimisation' is caused by the fear of sexual offences and in particular the fear of rape (Warr 1984); the "shadow of sexual assault" (Ferraro 1996) reaches far. A typical example is presented by the findings from a victimisation survey among residents in Cape Town (Camerer et al. 1998). The survey asked of which crime the respondent was most scared, varying from burglary, murder to rape, and the results clearly indicate that women are far more fearful of rape occurring in their areas (30.9 %) than men (4.5%). However, when asked about the aspects that the respondent fears the most, similarities exist, both women and men feared the loss of life, followed by physical injury the most, though for women this was almost matched to their fear of sexual violence.

Several authors argue that the term 'victimisation' is too strictly interpreted when it is directly derived from criminal law. Other behaviours, like obscene phone calls (Buck, Chatterson & Paase 1995; Huys 2001; Sheffield 1993), unwanted sexual attention (Gardner 1995; Johnson & Sacco 1995 Koss et al. 1994; Stanko 1985, 1988a, 1990) and flashing (McNeill 1987) could, according to several authors, be defined as sexual violence as well.[139] Moreover, some behaviours that are in fact criminalised in a legal sense might not be identified as a *crime* by the 'victim', as in the case of stalking, flashing or rape. The hundred women that were interviewed by McNeill together recalled 233 incidents of flashing, usually total strangers and sometimes masturbating, of which 14 were reported to the police (McNeill 1987). Kelly (1987, 1988)

---

[138] For example, Yanich (2001) shows that television news provides the message that the city is a dangerous place. The popular images flowing from the traditional perspective, teach people "what crimes to fear, where and when to be afraid, who is dangerous and who is safe" (Madriz 1997b: 343). Similar to Clark (1987), others have argued that the whole discourse on 'fear of crime' is a source of informal social control of women since they severely limit women's daily activities (e.g. Madriz 1997a, 1997b). Green, Hebron & Woodward (1987) also conclude that the social control over women's leisure activities is normal, i.e. is unexceptional and part of normal, everyday life, and this control is generally seen as natural and legitimate.

[139] These behaviours of unwelcome male attention are not only connected with 'fear of crime', but with feelings of irritation, anger, disgust, shame or guilt as well (e.g. Ensink & Van Buuren 1987; Green, Hebron & Woodward 1987: 88; McNeill 1987).

interviewed several women on forms of sexual violence and found that the factors of importance in defining 'pressurised sex' as rape were that a stranger was involved, it happened outside and at night, that physical force was used and that the woman (physically) resisted. Though the women that were interviewed did usually not define incidents with boyfriends and acquaintances that involved 'pressurised sex and coerced consent' as 'rape', many women made explicit links between pressurised or coerced sex and rape (see Kelly 1987: 57). This provides an illustration of the 'continuum of violence', concerning pressure, threat, coercion and force (Green, Hebron & Woodward 1987; Kelly 1987). Also, within an explanatory framework on gender-role socialisation, the finding that women who had been raped by an acquaintance as opposed to a stranger are less likely to define an incident as 'rape' (e.g. Koss 1985) provides an illustration of a 'rape myth' (Burt 1980; Lonsway & Fitzgerald 1995) or, which will become clear later, a *schema*. These studies also show a resistance to the label 'rape' and 'rape victim'. Gavey (1999) asked women whether they had been raped, and later whether they had had any experiences that matched behavioural descriptions of rape. The women who are not self-proclaimed victims, are considered to be raped nonetheless, according to Roiphe (1994) because the researcher uses operational definitions, i.e. certain behavioural descriptives.[140] The concept 'victimisation' is even problematised further by Phillips (1999, 2000) who presents several descriptions of incidents: "it was violent and hurtful and really scary. But I don't think I could ever call it rape. Let's just say that things went badly" (Phillips 2000: 149).

By analysing in-depth interviews with women, Kelly (1987, 1988) suggests that (sexual) violence is more a matter of a continuum of incidence, with everyday forms of abuse on the one end of the continuum, and rape and incest at the other end. The continuum of experience indicates pleasure and danger are not mutually exclusive, but are the desirable and undesirable ends of the continuum. These common forms of sexual harassment are coped with in various ways, like ignoring them, not defining them as abusive at the time it happens, or forgetting them (Kelly 1987). The interviews conducted by Kelly,[141] as well as the work of Stanko (especially 1985, 1990) and others, generally illustrate the omnipresence of the threat or fear of violence in women's everyday lives, as is widely analysed in for example Wise and Stanley (1987) and is reflected in the very first lines of Clark's (1987) book on sexual assault within the social context of 18th and 19th century England:

> All women know the paralyzing fear of walking down a dark street at night, hearing mysterious footsteps clicking behind, wondering whether the night out was worth these moments of terror . ..the dread that strikes us when we hear that a woman has been raped in our neighbourhood . . .

---

[140] This points to a complex feminist discussion on the label of 'victim' vs. 'survivor' (see Atmore 1999; Lamb 1999b; Rock 1998; Roiphe 1994; Römkens & Dijkstra 1996), which can be interpreted as a resistance to the stereotypes of both the 'ideal victim' and 'survivor'.

[141] For example: "It's something that happens so much – you just experience it in the street all the time, its almost a background of what going out of doors seems to mean." (Kelly 1987: 53).

the sudden resolve to be more cautious, not to accept the offers of dubious men to walk us home, or not to go out at night at all. (p. 1)

The measurement of 'fear of crime' in women is assumed the same as the measurement of fear in men. That is, when using a scale for the measurement of fear and the comparison between groups, one assumes that fear and unsafety means the same for different subgroups in the sample. However, according to some studies on this topic, on the one hand men tend to report less fear due to social desirability, on the other hand it appears that women have a different 'complex of fear'. For example, rape is perceived to be a possible consequence of another offence that might involve personal interaction, like robbery or burglary. So, fear of rape influences the fear of becoming a victim of other offences, in particular personal offences that might result in a personal confrontation. By making a distinction between different offences, women appeared to have more fear of rape than of murder (Ferraro 1995). When the fear of rape is controlled for, men are more fearful than women to become a victim of murder (Ferraro 1996). This calls for discriminating between offences that incorporate the probability of a personal confrontation with the perpetrator and offences, which exclude such a confrontation. The offences, which might result in a personal confrontation, are associated with the possibility of assault and rape (Warr 1984). Women, more than men, tend to link or associate this type of offences with others. These offences are perceived to happen contemporaneously (Warr 1985) and this elicits (more) fear. This becomes clear in McNeill's (1987: 101) study on flashing as well; the women she interviewed indicated they made a "fairly realistic personal assessment of the possible danger to herself in that situation" or as one respondent said: "you wonder what he is going to do next" (McNeill 1987: 102). Warr states that both the perceived seriousness of the consequences and the *perceptually contemporaneous offenses,* create a *differential sensitivity to risk* (Warr 1984, 1987). This means that the same perception of risk might lead to different levels of fear; the relationship between fear and perceived risk is different for men and women. Again, this reasoning is related to another typical model, the model that states that imaginable victimisation causes fear. However, 'rape' is only one of the experiences that are connected with sexual victimisation and harassment (e.g. Stanko 1995).

6.1.3   Unpleasant things that happen

Two studies illustrate and confirm the notion that the term 'victimisation' might have been too strictly interpreted; people perceive other behaviours as intrusive as well, though these might not constitute a crime. In the subway study (Appendix F; Vanderveen 1998b, 1998c) people in the subway of Rotterdam were asked whether something nasty or unpleasant had happened to themselves and whether they had seen something unpleasant happening to somebody else in the subway (see Figure 6.3).[142] These two questions were meant to inquire the direct and indirect victimisation of respondents without limiting the concept 'victimisation' to the offences in the scope of criminal law. Moreover, since the method of field-coding was used, all responses were possible and classified by the interviewer. The majority of the respondents indicates that nothing happened to them (81.9%), nor that they had seen something nasty happening to somebody else (63.5%). Most affirmative answers on the 'indirect victimisation'-question were classified as 'physical violence', like seeing somebody being stabbed. The affirmative responses to the question whether something nasty had ever happened to the respondent personally, referred to being approached, bothered or harassed. Mostly women responded with reference to "being approached".[143] The category 'other' embraces various things, like "a man got a heart attack", "I got stuck between the doors" and "being delayed". Also, reference was made to the presence of drug addicts or the use of drugs, like "a junkie with a needle" or "joints".

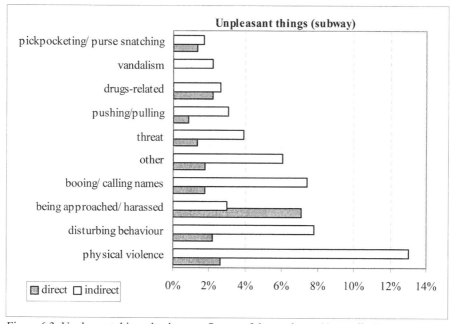

Figure 6.3. Unpleasant things that happen. Source of data: subway (Appendix F).

Similar questions were asked in the study that used vignettes (valid N=228; Appendix F), in which students of three different departments received a paper-and-pencil questionnaire. They were asked whether something nasty or

[142] The original Dutch wording was: "Heeft u wel eens in de metro gezien dat iemand anders iets vervelends overkwam" and "Is u zelf wel eens iets vervelends overkomen in de metro". These questions were asked at the end of the questionnaire.

[143] Men and women did not differ in their personal victimisation of pickpocketing or purse snatching, vandalism, threat or physical violence, but this might be due to low victimisation rates overall and the small sample (N=230).

unpleasant had happened to themselves and whether they had seen something unpleasant happening to somebody else in the subway.[144] More than one response could be chosen, but the questionnaire listed the alternatives, so the recalling of certain incidents was probably enhanced by the presentation of several options.[145]

Figure 6.4 presents the percentages of different types of incidents, with regard to the total number of incidents that were indicated by the male or female respondent on the two questions. On the question whether they had seen something happening to somebody else, about 20% (19.9% of the male and 21.8% of the female responses) indicated they had never seen something happening, a slightly smaller group of incidents related to "booing/ calling names" and incidents that touch on "pushing/pulling" were perceived as well. Many more responses to the question whether something happened to the respondent personally were negative, though more male respondents denied this. Both male and female responses indicated that being approached or harassed is rather common, which contains both remarks on "begging" and (sexual) "harassment". The category 'various' embraces various things, like "keeping the doors closed", "putting feet on the bench" and "chewing gum". Drugs-related disturbing behaviour incorporated for example "smoking joints", "using drugs" and "a drunken man who vomited right in front of me", whereas other types of disturbing behaviour are for example "being stared and laughed at", "an exhibitionist/ flasher" and "men in the subway who are standing or leaning against you".

The results of the four items regarding something 'unpleasant that happens' show that many respondents who responded affirmatively point to some sort of threatening behaviour. Calling names, being approached or harassed, physical violence and other disturbing behaviour are recalled (subway) or indicated (vignette) most often. During the interviews in the subway, many respondents touched on behaviours that were considered intrusive, though they did not all constitute a (serious) crime. Important to note however, is that the large majority of respondents in both studies did not mention anything.

---

[144] The original Dutch wording was: "Heb je wel eens in de metro gezien dat iemand anders iets vervelends overkwam" and "Is jou zelf wel eens iets vervelends overkomen in de metro". Similar to the interviews in the subway-study, the questions were asked at the end.

[145] Possible responses to the "somebody else"-question were: "disturbing behaviour, like...", "booing/ calling names", "pushing/pulling", "pickpocketing/ purse snatching", "vandalism", "threat", "physical violence", which was specified further by "fight, abuse, harassment/ assault" ('handtastelijkheden'), "other, namely...", "no" and "don't know/ do not want to answer". Possible responses to the question whether something happened to respondent personally: "harassed or bothered" ('benaderd worden'), "booing/ calling names", "pushing/ pulling", "pickpocketing/ purse snatching", "vandalism", "threat", "physical violence", which was specified further by "fight, abuse, harassment/ assault" ('handtastelijkheden'), "other, namely...", "never been a victim" and "don't know/ do not want to answer". The responses that were written down, when alternatives "disturbing behaviour, like..." and/or "other, namely..." were chosen, have been categorised into existing groups and in three general classes, consisting of responses that referred to drugs, alcohol and addicts (drugs-related), being bothered or approached, including answers that indicated 'begging' (bother) and a diverse category of answers but that nevertheless all relate to disturbing interpersonal behaviour (other).

In brief, even when the variety of different interpretations of criminal victimisation alone is considered, 'fear of crime' refers to a complex social phenomenon. This first approach to the *concept* 'victimisation' is common, and is sometimes complemented by another approach. The second approach focuses on the person who is victimised. This can be the person him/herself, somebody's spouse or children or another person one knows, and is called indirect victimisation.

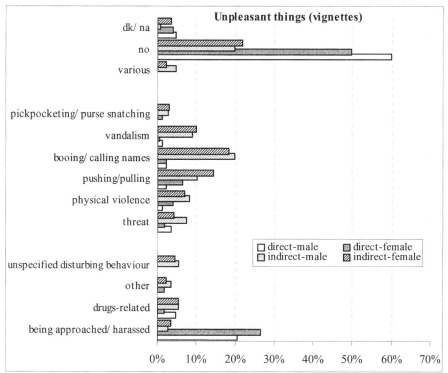

Figure 6.4. Indirect or direct 'victimisation' of incidents, with regard to the total number of incidents that were indicated by fe/male respondents. Source of data: vignette (Appendix F).

6.2   Indirect victimisation and altruistic fear

The basic model that directly relates crime to fear can be refined further by proposing that not only personal victimisation but also the victimisation of others can cause fear (see Box, Hale & Andrews 1988). Though the Harris Poll of 1969 already asked about victimisation of people "whom you personally know" and whether this person was close to the respondent, more systematic analysis has been relatively recent. Research on this so-called vicarious (e.g. David, Nias & Phil 1979; Langworthy & Whitehead 1986; Vitelli & Endler 1993; Ziegler & Mitchell 2003), indirect or secondary[146] victimisation (e.g.

---

[146] Note that the term 'secondary victimisation' is also used to refer to the psychological harm that might be caused by criminal justice procedures, like criminal or judicial proceedings (e.g. Habel & Schneider 2001; Orth 2002; Winkel & Steenstra 1987).

Covington & Taylor 1991; Lane & Meeker 2003) shows that indirect victimisation is related to higher levels of fear (Crank, Giacomazzi & Heck 2003; Ferraro 1996), especially for females (Davis, Taylor & Bench 1995). Several studies have investigated the consequences of this 'witnessing of crimes' on 'fear of crime', in a real life context (e.g. Levine & Wachs 1986b; Melville & Brinton Lykes 1992; Williams, Singh & Singh 1994), and through several media, like newspapers (e.g. Heath 1984; Koomen, Visser & Stapel 2000; Liska & Baccaglini 1990) and television (Chiricos, Eschholz & Gertz 1997; Chiricos, Padgett & Gertz 2000; Doob & Macdonald 1979; Romer, Jamieson & Aday 2003). Some studies indicate that more exposure to news and stories on crime in the media, contributes to higher levels of 'fear of crime' (Baker et al. 1983; Warr 1980, 1982), but the processes are not entirely clear (e.g. Heath & Gilbert 1996; Heath & Petraitis 1987) and newspapers for example, vary in their coverage and mode of presentation, which is of influence as well (e.g. Williams & Dickinson 1993). This indirect victimisation is a concept that is also used in a cognitive model on the individual level, the imaginable-victimisation-causes-fear model. Both models, which were briefly discussed in chapter 2, employ images of crime and its victims.

6.3   *Imaginable victimisation*

Indirect victimisation, the victimisation of others, whether significant others somebody personally knows or a fictional character in a television series can cause fear, overlaps with *imaginable victimisation*, which might be considered as another mode of indirect victimisation. This sort of victimisation is primarily based on the possibility of victimisation. The notion that imaginable victimisation causes fear is illustrated in research on intra-individual processes (cognitive) processes in which perceptions of vulnerability and risk, as well as social psychological models of perception and cognition, like the social comparison theory (Buunk & Mussweiler 2001; Festinger 1954).

One of the essences of the social comparison approach is that persons acquire knowledge about (crime) victims, similar to indirect victimisation. Whether this knowledge is accurate, real or true is of minor or no importance. Neither is important whether the victim really exists, is a fictional character, somebody who is actually (privately) known, or whether the victim is simply somebody in the news or a public figure. What is fundamental is that knowledge about others, in this case about others who have been victims, is perceived and processed and the way(s) that this is done, accounts for 'fear of crime'. Two aspects with two possibilities each make up four general ways of social comparison that are distinguished (e.g. Buunk et al. 2001; Van der Zee, Bakker & Buunk 2001). The first aspect relates to the status of the comparative other, whether s/he is doing worse or better, which refers to the social comparison orientation or the direction of social comparison (Buunk, Van der Zee & Van Yperen 2001; Michinov & Michinov 2001). When a person compares him/herself to a comparative other who has come of well on the comparison dimension, this is called upward social comparison, whereas downward social comparison refers to a comparative other who is in a worse shape. The second aspect relates to the identification or contrast of the person with the comparative other. Thus, the four ways of social comparison are downward identification, downward contrast, upward identification and upward contrast.

Accordingly, somebody who is reading a local newspaper and reads about a situation in which somebody was victimised with severe consequences, and perceives this person to be in a worse shape than her/himself, may either identify or contrast with the character in the newspaper. Identification, which is more likely to happen when the character and his or her behaviours are very similar to the reader, will lead to the idea that something like that might happen to the reader her/himself as well, which seems to be connected with a higher perceived risk or vulnerability.[147] Supposedly, this would lead to an increase in negative affect, like fear, and distress. Research on the influence of stories of indirect victimisation in the media shows that 'fear of crime' is higher when the identification or identifiability is greater (Vrij & Winkel 1990).[148] However, when the reader is able to contrast him/herself, this will lead to the idea that "this could never happen to me", resulting in relief: "I have much better locks on my door". This is nicely pictured in Madriz (1997b: 350) who describes a discussion within a focus group of Latina teenagers about fear and victimisation. They made remarks like: "White women are more victims because they do not know how to fight" and "We do, we know how to take care of ourselves". Moreover, in their study of the relationship between newspaper coverage of crime and 'fear of crime', Liska and Baccaglini (1990) suggests that people who read about crime that did not take place in their own neighbourhood, but in other neighbourhoods or cities may make them feel "safe by comparison" (Liska & Baccaglini 1990: 372). A similar conclusion can be derived from the study of Smith and Wilson (2000), who found that the proximity of a story (local vs. non-local crime) had influenced children's responses. The children who were told that the incidents took place locally were more frightened and perceive themselves personally vulnerable, in contrast to the children who were told that the stories took place in a distant city (Smith & Wilson 2000).

The social comparison mode of downward contrast in combination with attribution processes (see Rohlman 2001) might also result in 'blaming the victim', statements about "should" and "should not". This refers to assertions

---

[147] When selecting and deciding which criminal incidents to cover in the news, reporters even indicate they "considered the kinds of people who were most likely to read the newspaper" (Pritchard & Hughes 1997: 62). One reporter for example said: "it is important that we give something to our readers that they can relate to as opposed to something that does not affect them", and another reporter said: "if the reader could say 'that could have been me that was killed,' then that has more news value" (Pritchard & Hughes 1997: 63). The importance of the personal identity of the victim in the decision process to 'make crime news' refers to what Katz (1987: 52) has called "a symbolic challenge to collective identity".

[148] This can also explain why reading newspapers that provide more details of the incident and the victim, like 'sensational crime' reports, presumably inducing downward identification, is related to more 'fear of crime' (e.g. Williams & Dickinson 1993). See also section 7.3 on the so-called 'identifiable victim effect', the death (or victimisation) of a particular person invokes far more reactions than statistical victims and receives extraordinary attention (Small & Loewenstein 2003).

like "She should never have parked her expensive car there, everybody knows it gets stolen then" and "He shouldn't have provoked him like that, he should have known when to shut up". Again, popular images that reinforce a picture of the 'ideal victim' are of importance here. In the interviews of Madriz (1997a, 1997b), many (female) respondents made remarks that implied ideas of this 'ideal victim' and expressed a blaming attitude towards non-ideal victims, like women who do not follow a certain dress code; these women "look for it" and "are inviting trouble" (Madriz 1997b: 351).[149] Upward identification is linked with assertions like "I would have beaten the crap out of that guy as well", which requires a sense of control. Upward contrast, e.g. "I could never have defended myself like that", seems to be more related to perceived vulnerability and a lack of control (see Table 6.1).

Table 6.1. Social comparison processes.

Manner	Status of comparative other – social comparison orientation	
	better: upward	worse: downward
Identification	I can do that as well or even better! *sense of control*	That might happen to me too.... *perceived vulnerability*
Contrast	I can never make it like s/he did... *lack of control; perceived vulnerability*	That would never happen to me! *contrast with victim; blaming the victim*

Perceived vulnerability refers to the subjective assessment of one's own capabilities to hold one's own, be able to cope with the situation without getting things out of hand (Killias 1990).[150] Van der Wurff (1992) identifies the 'comparison of power' as an important factor of influence on fear, which refers to the assessment of one's own capabilities to stand up to a threat. Besides the 'comparison of power', 'target' refers to the extent to which one beliefs to be an attractive victim. Both factors are connected with the perceived vulnerability, since one can feel vulnerable because one thinks the threat is too great to cope with, or because one is a very attractive target, or even both. Vulnerability and the perception of risk are probably interrelated (e.g. Ferraro 1995; Smith & Torstensson 1997). Also, the four ways of social comparison, i.e. downward identification, downward contrast, upward identification and upward contrast, are interrelated. Again, in Madriz (1997b: 350) an illustration is found of both downward identification as well as downward contrast, expressed by 15-year-

---

[149] An elderly white woman also expresses a good example of 'blaming': "Especially in these days women use these tights, showing everything. And then they complain if men look or grab them or if they tell them something they don't want to hear." (Madriz 1997b: 351).

[150] This may touch on one's physical capabilities, but also on one's financial situation and is, as previously noted, related to the perceived seriousness of the consequences. For example, Africans in Durban, South Africa, far more often said their main fear was loss of property than Whites and Asians did, which reflects the seriousness of the consequences due to financial vulnerability: "For those who cannot afford insurance and are less able to replace stolen goods – particularly if it is the car used to get to work – the impact of such a property crime is much higher than for the wealthy." (Robertshaw et al. 2001).

old Jody: "I think the size has a lot to do with it. Tiny women, like me, are more likely to be victims". This is clearly an example of downward identification, but she goes on: "Especially tiny women who walk around looking as if they are totally out of it" (Madriz 1997b: 350). This is an example of downward contrast; Jody firstly points out her and other 'tiny women's' vulnerability because of her own size, but is able to contrast herself with part of these other women.

How people come to differ in their feelings of vulnerability, or in the fear of becoming a victim of rape, has also been examined in studies on socialisation processes. The social context and especially the media might be of influence on perceived vulnerability as well (Heath, Kavanagh & Thompson 2001). All kinds of sources provide the social context and the material and ideological constraints that act on individuals. Several sources are reinforcing; they are the results of and further shape the shared assumptions of appropriate behaviour for people and victims and set the limits of appropriate behaviour (e.g. Green, Hebron & Woodward 1987). Also, as Madriz (1997a, 1997b) notes, the 'popular images', reflected in everyday narratives, are affecting people's lives in various ways; leisure and other (professional) activities are restricted, people are taught "what crimes to fear, where and when to be afraid, who is dangerous and who is safe" (Madriz 1997b: 343).

6.4   Images of the victim

Legal definitions of crime and violence change and may leave out all kinds of behaviour that can be experienced as crime or violence, while on the other hand such legal definitions may include acts that are less experienced and defined as crime. That means, of importance are the "popular images about what is criminal, who is more likely to commit a crime and who is more likely to become a victim, what are the connections between criminals and victims, where and when is a crime more likely to occur, and what are the best ways to control or prevent crime" (Madriz 1997b: 342). These typical images are quite stereotypical regarding the 'ideal victim' as innocent, helpless, respectable, i.e. not violating social norms, and average, or the 'typical criminal' as a stranger, non-White and/or immigrant, monstrous, cruel and evil. The images are very well reflected in notions of what has been called *random violence* (Anderson, Grandison & Dyson 1996; Best 1999).[151] The stereotypical images within the traditional perspective are learned and shaped in various ways, for example by movies, newspapers and television (Barak 1994; Kania 1998; Milburn, Mather and Conrad 2000; Pritchard & Hughes 1997).[152] Films, whether drama or documentary, are said to "convey an ideological message concerning crime and criminals" and consequently, on victims as well (Cavender 1981: 431). Whether

---

[151] In the Netherlands, the term indicating random violence is 'zinloos geweld' (pointless violence), which has been employed since the late 1990s (e.g. TK 1997-1998, 1; Ministry of Justice 1998, TK 1997-1998 25907, 1; Beke, De Haan & Terlouw 2001; Van Oudenhoven, Pieper & Engelfriet 2001: 134; Vanderveen 2001a; WODC 1999).

[152] Therefore, the stereotypical notions and accompanying attributions are results of the cultural context as well (e.g. Morris & Peng 1994) and seem to correlate with restrictive beliefs about the social roles and rights of women (Ramasubramanian & Oliver 2003; Shalhoub-Kevorkian 1999).

this 'ideological message' had been the news or filmmaker's intent or not, is not of relevance here.[153] Of importance is that ideas and images about (social) reality are heavily influenced by media portrayal (e.g. Funkhouser 1973; Hamlin 1988; Heath 1984), the media may even contribute to a 'moral panic' (Burns & Crawford 1999; Lowry, Nio & Leitner 2003).[154] Since most research indicates that violent crime, especially in public space, is being overrepresented in the media, varying from (local) newspaper, television news to movies and novels, the stereotypical or popular images of crime, criminals and victims are hardly surprising.[155] An overall conclusion is that the media misrepresent crime (e.g. Lowry, Nio & Leitner 2003; Rodgers & Thorston 2001). The main distortion is usually the disproportionate attention given to violent crimes such as murder, homicide, robbery, whereas crimes concerned with property, like theft, are far less focused on (e.g. Dominick 1973; Kuttschreuter 1990; Marsh 1991; O'Connell 1999; Sheley & Ashkins 1981). Not only the type of crime, but characteristics of the victim, defendant and place are related to the coverage as well (Chiricos & Eschholz 2002; Paulsen 2002). Homicide incidents involving white, female and young victims (like children) and multiple victims are covered more than those involving non-white, male, older and single victims (Chermak 1998; Dixon & Linz 2000; Pritchard & Hughes 1997; Sorenson, Manz & Berk 1998).

The influence of these stereotypical images is persistent; as is being reflected by ballads, stories and literature for a long time, often conveying moral messages (Luger 1989; Pearson 1983).[156] The stereotypical images are also reflected by the old 'horror stories', narratives about one's own personal 'worst

---

[153] In a different context, yet related because of the role of the media in shaping perceptions of safety, Weiner (1986) has little doubt about the intent of some organisations in 'orchestrating the media' and using the press to inform the public and to 'keep the story alive'. Media coverage escalated in the case of toxic shock syndrome caused by tampons, a notable public health threat, but a very rare one. The media however, reported in a scientific or factual manner but possible disaster stories, i.e. interviews with disaster or disease victims were common as well. Weiner (1986) observes a clear "distinction between dramatic deaths and statistical ones" (Weiner 1986: 157).

[154] Also, governmental institutions react on publications in the media by developing communication procedures and protocols and employing public information officers as 'crime news gatekeepers' (Body Gendrot 2001; Surette 2001; Surette & Richard 1995). In Amsterdam, the Netherlands, a special protocol has been developed that should be used when minors are suspected to be involved in sexual offences, to prevent escalation of social unrest (Pollmann 1997).

[155] The relation between media portrayal and the popular images of crime has been studied widely. An often-cited study on crime coverage in the news is from Davis (1952), who concludes that official crime rates and crime news coverage are unrelated and popular ideas about crime reflect presentations of the news papers better than the crime rates (Davis 1952). Jones (1976) analysed the coverage of local crime incidents in two St. Louis newspapers between 1969 and 1972 and findings indicated that trends in crime rate are unrelated to the attention given in the press, yet type of crime as well the location of the incident influenced the amount of coverage. For example, crime against persons, like murder, rape and robbery received much more attention than crimes concerning property, like burglary and car theft (Jones 1976). Information on the overrepresentation of crime in the media till the 1970s can be found in Gordon & Heath (1981), Garofalo (1981b), Greene & Bynum (1982). Other overviews are provided by Katz (1987), The relationship with 'fear of crime' is further discussed in studies of Lane & Meeker (2003), Romer, Jamieson & Aday (2003)

[156] Yet, some media sources are not or less in accordance with the traditional stereotypic images of the criminal, the victim and the detective; e.g. the detective television series 'Cagney & Lacey' or crime fiction of Paretsky or Wilson (Decure 1989, 1993; Rowland 2001).

nightmare'. In Madriz's (1997b) study, a respondent called Sandra tells the following, which is exemplary:

> My biggest fear is to be randomly taken away and my body to be found in a forest or in a ditch, you know, and have my family saying: "I thought she just went to the store, but she never returned." You know … that is really scary. I mean, the very thought that any time I am walking anywhere, and some lunatic can take control of you and kill you and end your life like that. And, many times they rape and torture you before killing you … That is the worst. (p. 347).

6.4.1   Sources of images

The focus on crime and violence has a long-standing tradition, the 'pleasurable fascination with crime' is evident, (e.g. Katz 1987: 57), along with responses of censorship and a general public outcry against shows, movies, photographs, comics and books containing images and/or descriptions of violence, crime and horror.[157] The fascination with crime has been explained by referring to cultural anxieties (e.g. Sparks 1992) or because it enables people to handle their fears (Schubart 1995; Wachs 1988). For example, narrators can use humour in several ways, to comment on a concern, "as a way to make light of their own and others' misfortunes, and to distance themselves from the trauma of the experience" (Wachs 1988: 5). Also, the stories from various sources provide information about cultural and social rules for living; they provide an explanatory framework of how to make sense of (urban) everyday life; in that regard, Altheide (1997, 2002) for example notes that the format that is used by the news media is a version of a morality play. The (American) comics published in the 1940s and 1950s offer another example of how information about cultural and social rules for living is presented; a comic series like 'crime detective' featured "The only sure thing about crime is PUNISHMENT!!" on the cover, as well as: "This magazine is dedicated to the prevention of crime. We hope that within these pages the youth of America will learn to know crime for what it is: a sad, black, dead-end road of fools and tears." One comic series was called 'CRIME does not pay' and an issue in 1947 had "dedicated to the eradication of crime!" on the cover. The series 'Thrilling Crime Cases' and 'Law Against Crime' featured "The law will win" and "Law always wins" respectively (see Ellis & Highsmith 2000).

Here, the major sources are discussed; (oral) narratives like stories, rumours, urban myths and urban legends, news and infotainment on television, movies and printed material like newspapers and books. The image provided by these sources is rather similar to traditional, stereotypical notions of what has been called the 'ideal victim'.

---

[157] These responses have produced yet another research question; the cultivation hypothesis that focuses on the influence of these descriptions of violence, crime and horror on fear as well as on violent and criminal behaviour (see for example Chiricos, Eschholz & Gertz 1997; Chiricos, Padgett & Gertz 2000; Felson 1996; Greene & Bynum 1982; Guo, Zhu & Chen 2001; Mastro & Robinson 2000; Perse, Ferguson & McLeod 1994; Romer, Jamieson & Aday 2003).

6.4.1.1   Stories, rumours and urban myths

An important source of images of crimes and victims, as discussed previously, is interpersonal communication; the stories, rumours, myths and legends in contemporary society, all narratives part of (urban) folklore and the communication infrastructure (Matei, Ball-Rokeach & Qiu 2001). This urban folklore depends on "a shared set of culturally determined traits, assumptions, and expectations" (Wachs 1988: x). These traits, that are the characteristics common to the stories, refer to "population density, heterogeneity, alienation, anonymity, bystander apathy and invasion of privacy" and often involve aspects of criminal victimisation (Wachs 1988: x-xi). The purpose of the stories is to address human predicaments by showing how people act in times of crisis and dangers; they provide models for the reconstruction of everyday experience (Wachs 1988: 32). The narratives may or may not be 'true' or 'real', they may refer to a friend's victimisation experience, to one's own personal experience with criminal victimisation or to a rumour about what happened to a 'distant acquaintance of a cousin of a friend', but they are convincing because many aspects are recognisable.[158] Wachs (1988) collected narratives, or 'crime-victim stories' as she calls them, on victimisation with reference to mugging (89), murder (18) and rape (13). All these stories, competing for being the most horrible, incredible and unpredictable, were narrated as true accounts, in a dramatic style. As far as the representation of the victim is concerned, the ideal victim and offender emerge again; the criminal is anonymous, "a stranger lurking in a dark alleyway ready to pounce on an innocent victim" (Wachs 1988: 17).

Moreover, the offender in the narratives takes the victim by surprise, appears almost out of nowhere and this all takes place in common settings in the midst of ongoing urban activity and mostly in (semi) public places where entrapment is easy. An everyday situation is reversed; a benign moment turns into a scene of unexpected danger, touching on 'fated victimisation' and bystander apathy. The innocent, frightened and vulnerable victims often die a senseless and meaningless death or are needlessly harmed, the victimisation incident is often violent and shocking and the motives for the crime are often unknown.[159] The victims have little change of defending themselves, but are pictured as somebody who should have been suspicious, but was not, and paid the consequences. Therefore, as Wachs notes, the stories stress *street smarts*; the importance of being on one's guard, being aware of the environment, follow one's intuition and being suspicious as part of sensible urban behaviour, since it

---

[158] Wachs (1988: 55-60) found a couple of newspaper accounts of collected crime-victim stories.
[159] This is often the narrative in rape and murder stories. Another character that frequently comes on the stage in robbery stories is the clever victim, accompanied by the trickster offender.

increases the ability to act in the case of danger.[160] The stories have an important function in warning people, and especially women, about dangers and threats and telling them how to protect themselves in cases of danger and "imparting knowledge about appropriate urbanite street behavior", in order to be able to 'survive' in the city. Thus, "the crime-victim narrative is a testimonial to urban resilience" (Wachs 1988: 12). They validate and justify institutions, beliefs and attitudes and are means of applying social pressure, of exercising social control. The particularly frightening stories about urban violence serve as cautionary tales (Wachs 1988: 61).

The stories that Wachs collected were a mixture of accounts of personal victimisation, victimisation of an acquaintance, and other stories related to rumours and adaptations of so-called urban legends. A rumour does not involve narratives of one's own personal victimisation or the victimisation of a friend, but instead refers to a story without any clear author, containing information without a definite origin and whose truth is always in question (Castaneda 2000), and might have many variations on the same theme. The rumour is very much related to the so-called modern urban legend, that appeals to generic and universal fears, which are associated with modernity, circulate widely and contain traditional plots (Wachs 1988). Crime legends, as subcategory of urban legends are 'apocryphal tales' about modernity and urbanism (Donovan 2002: 190). They lack empirical evidence, documentation and direct testimony as well, and therefore they are thought to resemble myth or folklore.[161]

According to Donovan, rather similar to Wachs (1988: xv, 35), the crime legends are a sort of social practices that not only reflect "diffuse anxieties about risk and fear", but serve "several interlocutory purposes: warning, revelation of the raconteur's fear and revulsion; the solicitation of the same in hearers; and a frontal assault on scepticism itself" (Donovan 2002):

> Crime legends, as social practices, have both aggressive and solidaristic features. They are aggressive in the sense that believers wish to disrupt the hearers' sense of safety or confidence in the protection currently provided by both 'official guardians' (state powers), and 'official' sources of warning about crime threats (mass media). Yet they are also solidaristic in the sense that the crime legend is offered by individuals as a warning and a gesture of protection; an attempt to mend a collective bond. (p. 190).

---

[160] Street smarts are propagated by American city councils and police departments and portray the popular images of crime as well. For example the Philadelphia police department (http://www.ppdonline.org/ppd4_personal_street.htm, July 18 2003): "Wherever you are – on the street, in an office building or shopping mall, driving, waiting for a bus or subway – stay alert and tuned in to your surroundings", "Trust your instincts. If something or someone makes you uneasy, avoid the person or leave", "Stick to well-travelled streets. Avoid shortcuts through wooded areas, parking lots, or alleys" and "Avoid parking in isolated areas. Be especially alert in lots and underground parking garages". The popular image of the offender as a stranger instead of an acquaintance is reflected by for example: "Have to work late? Make sure there are others in the building, and ask someone – a colleague or security guard – to walk you to your car or transit stop".

[161] However, these legends are contemporary, make informal claims to be news, and usually do not make reference to supernatural themes or heroic historical figures (Donovan 2002).

Donovan (2002) concentrates on three of these persisting 'crime legends' by investigating messages and stories that circulated on the Internet. The three stories were on the market in snuff films, i.e. films and videotapes of real murders, usually sex-related murders, circulate in underground social networks and markets, and on the kidnapping of children from public restrooms in theme parks, like Disney Land, and shopping malls. The third 'crime legend' on the theft of organs in order to use for transplantation, has been investigated by Castaneda (2000) as well. All three legends that were examined in their various forms by Donovan (2002) and Castaneda (2000), pictured women and children as the predominant victims, though men might get their body parts stolen too in the stories. Donovan (2002) found that an evidential basis for the legends was not of importance for the 'believers', but rather that the legends are used to cope with generalised, diffuse fear or insecurity. According to her, the legends:

> express fears of a kind of post-modern social drift. This sense of drift centres around loss of authority in a double sense: civil society is depicted as having lost all power to protect, that is, its informal guardianship powers; and, at the same time, the world is seen as one in which *information* about danger and safety can no longer be reliably evaluated or deemed authoritative. (p. 190).

Thus, Donovan (2002: 209) argues "Authority, in both the sense of *authoritative knowledge* and in the sense of *law and order*, is under strain in and around crime legends." This is very similar to the supposed decrease of trust in authorities as proposed by Beck and others who employ the 'risk society' (e.g. Adam, Beck & Van Loon 2000; Beck 1992, 1999; Ericson 1994). For example, Sjöberg (1987) refers in his foreword to a major change in all Western industrial societies that is a "new element of public anxiety about hazards, which threatens to erode the confidence and trust that people place in the most powerful institutions". Also, Franklin (1998b) points to the "conflicting information from experts and politicians, whom we can no longer trust to keep us informed".

Authoritative knowledge and its trustworthiness are also relevant in Katz's study. Katz (2003) and Manning (2001) adopt the term 'myth' in their studies. According to Katz (2003), the story that youth gangs have plagued Los Angeles and interventions of the police have worsened the situation, is expressed in major metropolitan newspapers and by political and community leaders. Also, the stories circulate among people, as is nicely illustrated by a resident from the neighbourhood 'Delhi', south of LA, presented in Lane (2002):

> It's neighborhood news, you know. It's neighborhood news. People tell you, oh, so-and-so got shot. Oh, did you hear about this guy in this barrio getting shot? So-and-so did it. It's just, it cycles. People know where it's coming from and they go, "Oh, okay, these gangs are warring, you better not be around there or they are going to come after you." Basically, in Santa Ana, there are some gangs that get along, you know, but with Delhi, Delhi has very few allies, but it has a lot of enemies. (p. 459).

The metropolitan crime myth as pictured for New York resembles the LA portrait not at all, since media and political leaders have attributed crime to 'a diffuse culture of chaos', instead of gangs, and the police and mayor have been extremely successful in the reducing crime. For Katz, the contrast between the divergent portraits on the one hand, and the similarity of the histories in criminal violence and police activity on the other hand, makes an analysis of these metropolitan crime myths necessary. He employs the term 'myth' to express that the ideas, which are not necessarily false, cannot be established as true or false. Also, a myth 'resonates deeply' because it provides a sort of solution for immediate existential concerns and can have very real consequences for the distribution of power in society. In the analysis of the divergent portraits of LA and New York, he addresses how crime and law enforcement are differently interpreted and he analyses the (historical) patterns of crime and law enforcement. The crime stories of LA that circulate are cantered on the gang as reason for crime and victimisation, and have a general format like "Martha Naverette....became the 100th victim of street-gang violence in greater Los Angeles during 1991" (Katz 2003). The sheer notion that victimisation was 'gang-related' provides explanatory attributions, i.e. images why the incident happened, like 'revenge' or territorial fights.[162] These images and the 'fear of gangs' is also illustrated and further explored in a study of Lane (2002), "in Santa Ana, California, a primarily White and Latino city just south of Los Angeles that has struggled with social disorganisation and gang crime for decades" (Lane 2002: 438).

Stories of New York centre on chaos, similar to frontier violence in the 'Wild West'; the randomness, wildness and senselessness of crime and victimisation (Katz 2003). To examine the patterns of crime and law enforcement in New York and LA, Katz uses demographic statistics of people that were arrested for homicide as well as homicide counts and arrest counts by year and age. These patterns show that a substantial drop in homicides can be seen in both cities; yet, only New York has the image of an exceptional decrease of crime, caused by good police management. However, this image is a result of biased views and use of crime statistics, like presenting raw homicide numbers instead of percentages and applying a 'favourable' time span to illustrate the drop. Thus, he concludes that the patterns of crime and law enforcement in New York and LA cannot explain the differences in interpretations, but differences of the institutional and social context can. The different immigration experiences of the two cities, also reflected in Lane (2002; Lane & Meeker 2000), the structure of the criminal justice systems in LA and New York, which is also proposed by Manning (2001), and the concerns of metropolitan crime news are of major influence in the establishment of the metropolitan crime myths.

---

[162] A woman in Lane's study expresses an example of such explanatory attribution: "They have to kill somebody– to be in a gang and to make them powerful. . . . They kill for nothing." (Lane 2002: 458).

6.4.1.2   Crime time on television
The long-standing tradition of the focus on crime and violence is equally evident for television broadcasts. Newman (1990) discusses the presence of violence and images of criminal justice and law & order in television detectives, which have been broadcasted on prime-time early on,[163] as well as in other television shows, in advertisements, music lyrics, comic books and movies. As Surette and Otto (2002) observe, news and entertainment cannot be clearly distinguished anymore, boundaries are blurred, which is reflected by the term *infotainment* (Surette & Otto 2002). Three types of infotainment are common in contemporary (American) society, the first type being news and newsmagazines, the second reality-based crime shows, like Cops, and the third co-opted courtroom dramas and media trials (Craig 2003; Surette 1989; Surette & Otto 2002). For example, a violent incident can be presented as news with "story lines, plot and character development, victims, villains, and dramatic endings" (Surette & Otto 2002: 445). Gilliam and Iyengar (2000) also found that (local) news stories follow a 'narrative script' that contains two essential elements, namely that the crime is violent and the perpetrator is a non-white male.[164] Only a few studies have recently compared the incidence of violence or crime by sex, and results are not conclusive. In general, the overwhelming majority of offenders as presented in the news media seem to be men, whereas women are slightly more frequently pictured as victims, though others found that men are (Chiricos, Eschholz & Gertz 1997).

Similar to the true crime genre in the literature, reality-based crime shows are on television, like COPS, Real Stories of the Highway Patrol, and America's Most Wanted (see Eschholz et al. 2002). They typically employ dramatisations of actual crimes, police narratives and interviews or actual video footage (Surette & Otto 2002). Episodes from the first season, the 1988-1989 and the 15th, 1995-1996 seasons of the program 'America's Most Wanted' were compared to examine how female victims were portrayed (Cavender, Bond-Maupin & Jurik 1999). Again, a distorted picture emerges; 84% of the offences that were presented in the 1st season contained violent personal crimes, like (attempted) murder, molestation, robbery and rape, and this had increased to 98% in the 15th season. The majority of victims, in both seasons, was white and strangers are overrepresented as assailants. Also, the crimes were described as brutal and savage. The general image of the female victim that is offered by the program is the victim as worthy, sympathetic and innocent, and a less flattering image, i.e. a victim that is perceived as violating social norms, suggests that the victim is partially to blame (Cavender, Bond-Maupin & Jurik 1999), which

---

[163] Some examples provided by Newman (1990) are Kojak, Columbo, Miami Vice, Cagney & Lacey and Hill Street Blues.

[164] More Anglo-Saxon studies have examined the relationship between crime and race in television news and infotainment. Though some studies found that non-whites were overrepresented as perpetrators (e.g. Skogan & Maxfield 1981), others did not. A content analysis of entertainment shows that were broadcasted during a week in 1972, reveals that TV crimes are generally violent, and both offenders and victims are male and white (Dominick 1973). Chiricos & Eschholz (2002) found that non-Whites more often appear as suspects and not as victims.

points to the stereotypical image of the innocent victim again. Interestingly enough, the contents of the narratives in Wachs (1988) and Cavender, Bond-Maupin and Jurik (1999) are strikingly similar, though the sources of the narratives are different.

6.4.1.3 Crime pictured in motion

Crime in films has a long history as well (Rafter 2000). Movies illustrate the long-standing tradition of the focus on crime and violence, as diverse as the movies on organised crime (the Mafia), police, detective, courtroom, or prison films. These films often provide an (implicit) explanation of crime and express a point of view why somebody has become a victim. Hollywood films play a major role in the representation of for example organised crime, e.g. in Russia (Rawlinson 1998) and criminal trials (Rafter 2001). Also, crime movies are thought to raise social, economical and political issues.[165] Moreover, the movies reflect ideas of crime and justice, the conflict between these and hence, of good and evil (Rafter 2000).

The pervasiveness of crime in films is well depicted in a study of Allen, Livingstone and Reiner (1997). They applied a content analysis of 1440 films, a random sample from films that were released in Britain during 1945-1991, aimed at providing a reliable indication of trends in crime content (Allen, Livingstone & Reiner 1997). Though the researchers found that the percentage of crime films that were released each year and the proportion of crime content in all films together have been fairly constant, the representation of crime changed. This became apparent in the comparison of crime content within different genres. Some genres declined (e.g. the Western) whereas films in other genres increased (e.g. fantasy films), but more importantly, the prominence of crime within a genre changed. That is, now only 38% of all the films with crime content central to the narrative are crime films (as a genre), whereas, 62% of the films with a central crime content are classified into other genres, like 'adventure', 'fantasy' and 'drama'. Since crime content is more evenly spread across different genres, it is less clear from knowing just the genre of a film whether it will contain crime, thus the predictability of whether or not a film will contain crime is reduced, which decreases the opportunity for people to see a film without crime (Allen, Livingstone & Reiner 1997).

How are crime and the victim portrayed in these numerous movies? In general, archetypes of 'good' and 'bad' characters both use violence and are victimised. Yet, how the victim and the victimisation incident are presented, varies. For example, Eschholz & Bufkin (2001) utilised a content analysis of

---

[165] And the movies themselves raise issues as well, which is reflected by ratings and research on the relationship between violence and the movies, as well as the attitudes thereof. For example, the Texas Crime Poll (Criminal Justice Center 1998) asked about the relationship between crime and violence on television and in the movies and the rate of crime in society both in the 1978 survey and in the 1998 survey. The number of Texan respondents who think there is a direct relationship between depiction of crime and violence and the actual crime rate has increased a lot. The two questions were formulated as: "Do you think that crime and violence shown on television/ movies have caused a large increase in the crime rate, caused a moderate increase in the crime rate, caused very little increase in the crime rate, or had no effect on the crime rate?"

movies and searched for patterns in the portrayal of those who use violence and their victims in the 50 most popular movies that were released in 1996 in the USA.[166] A common theme pictured duels in which good confronts evil and the main characters both use violence to reach their goals. They made a distinction between sex (men vs. women) and gender of a movie character, which touches on power, femininity and masculinity.[167] They found that sex was not related to the use of violence in the movies or to victimisation of violence, yet archetypes involving gender, i.e. masculinity and femininity, was significantly related to both violent offending and victimisation. Masculinity is highly correlated with committing violent acts as well as with becoming a victim of violence in movies. The authors propose that both high and low femininity are associated with victimisation, the first because of the notion of the 'ideal victim', the archetype of the virgin, the latter because of the archetype of the 'bad girl' or the 'vamp' who gets what she deserves (Hedley 2002; Phillips 2000). Indeed, results indicated that femininity was not associated with victimisation and the victimisation of 'good', i.e. feminine, women generally demonstrates the inherent vulnerability of the female condition. Their victimisation is not only recognised and legitimised, they are 'ideal victims'; their need for male protection is emphasised as well. The 'bad' woman, i.e. not-feminine or masculine, who does not behave in accordance with the boundaries of 'good behaviour' is 'punished' with violent victimisation (Eschholz & Bufkin 2001), yet both hero and heroine use violence. This is not necessarily the case in other cultures; a content analysis of popular Hindi films released in India from 1997 until 1999 (Ramasubramanian & Oliver 2003) reveals that the films show female characters as victims of sexual violence, and male characters as the perpetrators of sexual violence. Moderate sexual violence, both by the hero and the villain, was portrayed as fun and a normal expression of romantic love, but severe sexual violence, i.e. rape or eroticised murder, was depicted as criminal and was committed more often by the 'villain'. Moderate sexual violence, i.e. all other forms, that was committed by the hero of the movie, was rewarding in some cases, since it ultimately resulted in the victim and the hero becoming romantically involved. Regarding (sexual) violence, men, not women, only used this and victims were mostly women.

In summary, crime, violence and victimisation are common themes in movies of diverse genres. Violence and crime are primarily related to men and masculinity. Characters that use violence are (violently) victimised as well, but only feminine characters and non-masculine women in general are portrayed like 'ideal victims'; they were not to blame. The movies as source of crime and victim stories generally provide an (implicit) explanation of crime and the

[166] Thus, the sample consisted of various movies like 'The English Patient', '101 Dalmatians', 'Twister' and 'Mission Impossible' (see Eschholz & Bufkin 2001: 671-672), which were movies released in Britain and the Netherlands as well.
[167] In brief, masculinity is more related to being competitive, athletic and strong and femininity with nurturing, caring and being romantic (Eschholz & Bufkin 2001; Goodey 1997; Levant 1996). Masculinity and femininity correlate with sex, yet the difference between men and women is much larger for femininity scores than for masculinity scores.

reasons why somebody has become a victim that is in accordance with a traditional perspective regarding appropriate behaviour derived from social roles and scripts.

6.4.1.4   Crime in print

Another important source of images of victims and victimisation incidents is printed material, i.e. newspapers, magazines, (non-)fiction books and comics (e.g. Clarke 2001; Ellis & Highsmith 2000; Newman 1990). Here, only the newspaper as a source of images is discussed. Again, the pervasiveness of crime is obvious, and the portrayal of victims in the newspapers is rather stereotypic, which has been noted previously. The early newspapers already helped to "construct crime as the social equivalent of sin", but most of all, they provided entertainment (Surette & Otto 2002). Peelo and Soothill (2000) discuss the role of newspapers in the reproduction of social order; they analyse the newspaper accounts of a murder trial throughout July 1992, in which two sisters were convicted for the murder. In their study, the newspapers are 'agents of conformity' and construct public narratives that establish what is and what is not generally acceptable behaviour surrounding a crime, since the newspapers "communicate to the crowd strong clues about what behaviour (beyond the murder itself) and which people are perceived as morally unacceptable" (Peelo & Soothill 2000: 138). Again, morality and the media are connected; the media draw the boundaries of acceptable morality, of who is and who is not acceptable to the public and deviant behaviour itself is a perfect means of ensuring social order and control since the boundaries are sharpened. Peelo and Soothill (2000) give the following example:

> The Taylor sisters' trial is, in this sense, a case study of a public narrative in the form of a fairy story about solving crime masquerading as justice; it subtly (and sometimes not so subtly) transmutes from being about a brutal murder into a tale about sexual morality. And when we look at the reporting of the Taylor sisters' trial, it soon becomes clear, indeed, that it is a lifestyle which is found guilty: it is a trial about an affair between the victim's husband, John Shaughnessy, and the accused, Michelle Taylor; and with that an inherent judgement of appropriate womanhood. (p. 138).

Pritchard and Hughes (1997) are interested in the newsworthiness of homicides, they applied content analysis of 560 news items about the homicides published in Milwaukee's two newspapers and also interviewed five reporters who covered these homicides. These interviews focused on how the reporters learned about homicides, their sources of information, and on decisions regarding the newsworthiness of the homicides; i.e. the length of their stories, and what kinds of homicides were considered to have higher news value. The reporters consider homicides especially newsworthy if the victims were children, or defenceless, vulnerable victims who were not engaging in risky activities; all exemplary for 'victim innocence' and similar to notions of the 'ideal victim'. Pritchard and Hughes (1997) state that the murders of certain victims, e.g. children, women, are culturally deviant, and thus especially newsworthy. Chermak (1998) found that the number of victims involved was the most important predictor of story salience, i.e. the amount of space and attention that an incident received in the newspaper. Yet, a certain number of victims are not enough to become a salient story in newspapers, characteristics of the context is of relevance as well. In a case of 'corporate crime' or 'corporate violence' newspapers appear to use different frames or narratives. Though 25 people were killed in a fire at a chicken-processing plant and the defendant pleaded guilty to manslaughter, a content analysis of the newspaper coverage of this particular incident showed that the newspapers initially focused on the safety regulations and paid far less attention to the criminal trial and convictions (Wright, Cullen & Blankenship 1995).

In summary, though newspapers vary in their coverage and mode of presentation (Koomen, Visser & Stapel 2000; Williams & Dickinson 1993), newspapers all misrepresent crime as other media do; they give disproportionate attention to violent crimes and to crimes involving 'ideal victims' (Marsh 1991; Paulsen 2002; Sorenson, Manz & Berk 1998). The newspaper's sensational crime coverage is also apparent in for example Hong Kong and in Guangzhou, a city on the Chinese mainland (Guo, Zhu & Chen 2001).[168]

6.5   The ideal victim

This chapter focused on a central concept within the field of 'fear of crime', namely victimisation with emphasis on gender differences. As a rule, 'fear of crime' has been directly related to crime and (criminal) victimisation, yet the abstract concepts of 'crime' and 'victimisation' appear to display only a partial overlap; on the one hand, 'crime' embraces more than is thought of when interpreting 'victimisation', on the other hand 'victimisation' incorporates more than just legal defined criminal offences. A few concluding observations are put forward here. First, 'crime' and 'criminal victimisation' are not similar, and 'criminal victimisation' is a far more problematic concept than it seems at first sight. As for the discussion of 'fear of crime', 'crime' appears to touch primarily on violent, personal confrontations with an offender, or to offences that have serious consequences and are relatively likely to happen. Whether these violent confrontations actually take place (or have taken place) is of lesser importance; it is the notion of imaginable victimisation that is of relevance. Obviously, neither 'crime' nor 'victimisation' is gender neutral. The imaginable possibility to be the victim of sexual violence is entirely different for men and women and appears to be salient in women's everyday life, not in men's.

A second observation regarding the concept 'victimisation' in the context of 'fear of crime' relates to the dynamics of the concept. 'Victimisation' is, even within a black letter law approach, not a static concept; it is a diffuse, dynamic concept that is connected with attributions of responsibility and culpability of the victim. Depending on characteristics of the incident, the offender and the victim, these attributions are induced, making some persons

---

[168] Findings also indicated the resemblance of newspaper contents and interpersonal communication in their portrayal of crime (Guo, Zhu & Chen 2001).

'more victim' than others, that is, some victims are in conformance with 'the ideal victim' and others are clearly not. This is highlighted in the case of rape in particular, and in cases of sexual violence in general (see also Wesely & Gaarder 2004).

The attributions of responsibility stem from social and cultural context(s), that provide images on the typical victim, offender and crime, which leads to the third observation; the imagery of crime, violence, victimisation and criminal justice in general in popular culture is highly pervasive (Newman 1990). Sources of information provide several varieties of narratives regarding crime, violence and victimisation. Crime and victimisation in the broadest sense are popular, as illustrated by the contents of oral narratives, like stories, rumours, urban myths, urban legends, by the topics of television news, infotainment series and shows, by themes in the movies and by the subject matters of newspapers and other printed material. All these sources reflect and generate social values, providing (part of) the social context in which typical images are (re)created.

Fourth, the images that are portrayed in all kinds of sources are generally similar; crime, the criminal and the victim are depicted in rather comparable ways, in spite of a small portion of exceptions. Popular images usually are in accordance with notions of the 'ideal victim'. They (re)establish rather stereotypic notions and provide information of 'rules for precaution', e.g. which places are 'wrong' at specific times. Again, neither these rules and notions, nor the images themselves are gender neutral, quite the contrary. The attributions of deservedness, responsibility or culpability to the victim are of major importance in the interpretation of victimisation, by the victim him/herself, by the offender(s) and by others, are highly related to sex and gender (see Berns 2001).

6.5.1   The ideal victim as a role

The notion of the 'ideal victim' and related attributions of deservedness and culpability originate from a (traditional) perspective on appropriate behaviour and roles. Attributions of responsibility to victims of rape have been a popular research topic in social psychology (Jimenez & Abreu 2003), or more specifically: in social cognition. Social cognition is the main paradigm in social psychology that studies how mental processes such as attention, memory, interpretation and so on, shape our social judgments and social behaviour and has been studied extensively.[169] Besides attribution processes, stereotypes and schemas in general are major topics in social cognition research and provide an explanatory model of the 'ideal victim' and related attributions of deservedness and culpability.

Schemas are cognitive structures, 'shortcuts', that organise knowledge and guide the selection (attention), interpretation and organisation (encoding), and recollection (retrieval) of new information; they provide the tools for making sense, for everyday understanding. Schemas enable us to make sense of

---

[169] Many overviews are available, e.g. Fiske and Taylor (1984), Forgas (2000, 2001) and Kunda (1999).

social reality, of experience and of information, by simplifying, structuring and providing meaning, they help clarify or disambiguate an otherwise confusing situation (Correll et al. 2002). A few different types of schemas can be distinguished, among which two are of relevance here, namely the role schema and the event schema. The role schema, or stereotype, provides information about social categories, e.g. gender or ethnicity, and about which behaviour is appropriate for a person belonging to that social category. Another type of schemas is a script or social episode, which is an event schema, which provides information about an event, a situation that enables people to recognise the typical ways in which a sequence of actions tends to unfold and are affective in character (Forgas 1981a). The 'ideal victim', defined by Christie (1986: 18) as "a person or a category of individuals who – when hit by crime – most readily are given the complete and legitimate status of being a victim" is such a role schema and very much related to the event schema or script of the victimisation incident. Another script embraces the so-called 'rape myths', which were previously defined as descriptive or prescriptive beliefs about rape, its causes, context, consequences, perpetrators, victims and their interaction.

Schemas provide the typical images of a type of person or a type of incident; they embrace the characteristics that are perceived to be essential for the particular type or label (see Table 2.4). The 'ideal victim' and her victimisation are in accordance with a social script, fitting within a cognitive schema. An ideal victim is a victim that behaves according to a specific social role and any role inconsistencies make the victim less ideal. In other words, people tend to discredit information that is inconsistent with the schema, give it less weight or reinterpret the information in schema-consistent terms, i.e. making the victim less ideal and attributing responsibility. The women in Phillips (1999, 2000) used similar strategies for coping with incidents and for "controlling the damage" by construct explanations that were consistent with stereotypical notions of the 'ideal victim'. She notices throughout the interviews a 'marked discrepancy' in the naming and forming of attributions in abstract or political assertions about female victimisation and their assessments and attributions for their own painful experiences. The women were uncomfortable in seeing themselves as victims and gave several reasons why their own experiences cannot be labelled as abuse, for example by attributing responsibility to themselves ("I should have known better" or "if only I hadn't" and "I really should have been more careful") or in different naming ("for her it was rape, for me it was just complicated"). Phillips observes different strategies; one type indicated the refusal of being a victim by transforming meanings and attributions, like the attribution of responsibility to themselves, or for example, "Maybe my no wasn't no enough". By taking responsibility and reinterpreting the incident, the women tried to make sense of their experiences. Others indicated a notion that mature, well-adjusted women aren't victims ("I'd like to think I had enough strength") or reflecting the need of a just world ("I couldn't imagine that happening to me"). Another strategy was replacing male responsibility with their own personal responsibility, e.g. "he hurt me" becomes

"I *let* him hurt me" and "he forced me" becomes "I should have stopped him" (emphasis Phillips 2000: 176). According to Phillips the women "found a sense of psychological safety in maintaining that they were not powerless beings who had been unjustly acted on, but that they were instead responsible for their own fate, however damaging" (Phillips 2000: 178; see also Miller 2002). Especially incidents of acquaintance rape, when victims had trusted their assailants, this self-blame is common (McEwan, De Man & Simpson-Housley 2002).

Schemas are learned in various ways, which makes them dependent on the social and cultural context in which they are formed and makes social cognition *social* (Forgas 1981b), but individual differences in content and use of schemas exist as well; people may interpret the same situation in very different ways. People differ in their use of schemas and might have different ones because of for example varying previous experience. Depending on the situation, i.e. the perceived information and the importance, a certain schema is triggered. Previous experience and cues from the social and physical environment are of importance, but the structure of the schema itself is also relevant; what is most salient, what sticks out. Therefore, the appearance of a person is most important. Broad social categories relating to sex (male vs. female) and ethnicity (white vs. non-white; Caucasian vs. Asian vs. African-American) are extremely salient.[170]

Table 6.2. Essential characteristics of role & event schema.

Essential characteristics ideal victim/ ideal victimisation	
Victim	Weak, vulnerable, innocent
Offender	Evil, cruel and bad
Activities victim	Respectable (e.g. going to school, getting groceries for sick friend)
Relationship	Stranger, unknown offender, no relationship victim-offender
Incident	Physical force/ violence, deliberately Victim protests and resists (physically) Offender is brutal, cruel, violent Random & senseless (random violence) or specific selection (e.g. series of eroticised murder)
Protection	Victim has made a reasonable effort in protecting him/herself
Location	Somewhere where s/he can not possibly be blamed for being, somewhere s/he was supposed to be (e.g. home)
Time	Somewhere where s/he can not possibly be blamed for being at that particular time, somewhere s/he was supposed to be at that time (e.g. during the day)

The 'ideal victim' and the 'rape myths' are schemas that provide expectancies of appropriate behaviour and roles. The label 'victim' is a product of social relations, culture and language and different groups might compete over the exact definition of a label (Lamb 1999a). The related attributions of responsibility are in accordance with these schemas. Since the category 'sex' is

---

[170] For example, it would be hard to remember ever having talked to someone of whom one couldn't recall later whether the person had been a male or female.

extremely salient, and schemas for men and women differ to varying degree, the findings from the studies presented in this chapter come as no surprise. Nurius (2000) describes two familiar situations:

> Imagine two situations: One is of a party where people one's age– some of whom are friends and acquaintances– are partying (talking, drinking, laughing, flirting, dancing). Another is of a lone woman walking through an empty parking garage at night. In which situation are most women likely to feel alert to potential threat? To search for and prepare for threat? To question whether they can control the situation? And in which is a woman actually at greater risk? (p. 64)

Nurius (2000) presents these two situations in her social-cognitive account of women's levels of perceived personal risk with respect to acquaintance sexual aggression in contrast to their levels of perceived risk involving stranger sexual assault and their subsequent efforts to protect themselves. In the case of sexual violence involving a stranger "women are reflecting an agentic response to perceived threat; that is, active efforts to reduce exposure to risk and to increase women's capacity to protect themselves" (Nurius 2000: 64). Women perceive their risk on becoming a victim of sexual violence involving an acquaintance very differently, rather consistent with familiar schemas, and act accordingly.

6.6   Criminal victimisation and the meaning of fear of crime

So far, the diversity of victimisation was stressed by explaining the wide variety of different interpretations and focusing on the nature of victimisation. Table 6.4 at the end of this chapter lists the main assertions. The conclusions that can be derived from this chapter regarding the concept 'fear of crime' all refer to the inaccuracy and invalidity of the historically developed common interpretation of 'fear of crime'. This common interpretation is slightly adapted over time, but even the earliest interpretations are still common, whereas the popularity of the more 'advanced' interpretations still seems to suffer from a lack of familiarity or attractiveness.

A given interpretation or conceptualisation of 'fear of crime' is connected with a specific hypothesis. For example, the earliest common interpretation, which still abounds in the literature, essentially comes down to 'fear of crime is about or has to do with crime'. This earliest interpretation of the meaning of 'fear of crime' is written down in the first column of Table 6.3. Hypotheses that are linked with this interpretation are variants of the basic hypothesis that when there is more crime, there is more 'fear of crime', and less crime implicates less 'fear of crime'. Thus, in countries, cities, or neighbourhoods with more crime, more 'fear of crime' should be reported. In addition, crime and 'fear of crime' should correlate longitudinally. These hypotheses have been and are still being tested numerous times, which has not led to a clear unambiguous conclusion. A common adaptation of this basic and oldest hypothesis, is that not crime itself, but it is criminal *victimisation* that influences 'fear of crime'. Thus, people who have been victimised should have a higher 'fear of crime'. In addition, the demographic groups that contain more victims, should report more 'fear of crime' compared to the demographic groups embracing fewer victims. In this argument, the victims are victims of particular types of crimes. That is, crime is restricted to a few typical examples of offences in the public sphere. The so-called fear-victimisation paradox fits this line of reasoning perfectly and critics of this paradox have adjusted the meaning of 'fear of crime' again, suggesting it is not so much crime in the public sphere that is of importance, but rather crime in the private sphere (see Table 6.3).

Table 6.3. Interpretations of meaning 'fear of crime' in relation to victimisation.

Common interpretation	Common adaptation
Fear of crime has to do with crime	Crime in 'fear of crime' has to do with victimisation
Crime in 'fear of crime' relates to crime or criminal victimisation by a stranger in the public sphere, though this has not always been explicitly operationalised	Crime in 'fear of crime' relates to crime or criminal victimisation by an acquaintance, household or family member ('hidden violence')
Crime in 'fear of crime' relates to crime or criminal victimisation, in which crime is legally defined	Crime in 'fear of crime' relates not only to crime or criminal victimisation such as legally defined, but to behaviours that are (currently) not legally sanctioned as well; thus 'fear of crime' is (also) related to the problematic consequences of crime for everyday life as felt and perceived by the general public
Crime in 'fear of crime' relates to crime or criminal victimisation	Crime in 'fear of crime' relates to crime or criminal victimisation that involves a (possible) personal and violent confrontation with offender
Crime in 'fear of crime' relates to crime or criminal victimisation that involves a (possible) personal and violent confrontation with offender	Crime in 'fear of crime' relates to crime or criminal victimisation that involves a (possible) personal and sexually violent confrontation with offender and thus relates primarily to sexual violence, rape, and/ or assault ('shadow of sexual assault'; perceptually contemporaneous offences)
Less common interpretations	**Explanation**
Crime in 'fear of crime' relates to an ideal type of crime that is typical and highly gendered	Crime nor victimisation is self-evident, but subject to typical images of crime, victims and offenders, and connected processes of attributions of culpability and deservedness, in which gender is an important factor
These typical images are schemas
Crime in 'fear of crime' relates to crime and victimisation of significant others	Indirect, vicarious or secondary victimisation refers to the victimisation of others
'Fear of crime' has to do with imaginable victimisation	Imaginable victimisation of one personally or of significant others
The social comparison mode of downward identification (with a victim) affects 'fear of crime'

In the previous chapter on victim statistics and surveys, the main purpose of victim surveys has been noted, which mainly was to provide reliable crime figures. For that purpose, particular crimes are specified (e.g. burglary, robbery) and respondents are asked whether or not they have become a victim of that particular crime. Consequently, in research on 'fear of crime', the nature of victimisation is often restricted to these few forms of criminal victimisation. Such a research strategy has evoked criticism, arguing that victimisation defined as such is too narrow. Other victim surveys focused on more forms of criminal victimisation, for example by concentrating on violence within a household instead of random violence by an unknown stranger in the public sphere. In addition, other studies attempted to show that experiencing not-legally defined victimisation might be at least as unpleasant (see Quinn 2002). Apparently, the common meaning of the concept 'fear of crime' touches primarily on a (violent) personal confrontation with a perpetrator in the public sphere with serious consequences. This confrontation, as well as the possible consequences, are highly gendered in the sense that interpretations of victimisation is different for women and men; victimisation, and consequently the fear of victimisation, seems to have a different meaning or connotation for women than for men (cf. Stanko 1987: 127).

Even in the case of a violent confrontation in the public sphere, it might still not be interpreted as 'crime'. Clearly, victimisation is not at all unequivocal; the interpretation of the event as well as its consequences is of importance. Irrespective of the approach to victimisation, whether concentrating on criminal victimisation, indirect victimisation and imaginable victimisation, apparently attributions of deservedness, responsibility or culpability to the victim are of major importance in the interpretation of victimisation. This is so even in the case of what seems to be a simple legally defined offence like a break-in. These attributions are moulded by the social context, by popular images that arise from various sources, and are related to characteristics of the victim. In the case of a break-in, the 'seriousness' of the victimisation and whether or not the victim is *acknowledged* as a victim depends on what was taken, how much it was worth, the quality of the security measures that were taken by the victim, whether a personal confrontation has occurred or would have been likely, whether the burglar was a total stranger and all other aspects that are embraced by the schema of the ideal victim.

The previous chapter concluded that the concept 'fear of crime' derived its meaning from the items that were used from the beginning, which were items that resemble the items that had been and still are being used in public opinion polls. These items all refer to the problematic consequences of crime, that is, crime by strangers and on the street; when away from home in the evening; in the neighbourhood after dark; and thus avoiding places in the public sphere. Even the items that refer to 'fear of crime' when a person is in one's home (are you afraid when you're at home alone at night; keep a weapon or instrument of protection by your bed when you go to sleep; stranger who rings the doorbell) refer to the home as a safe place, a safety that might be violated by a stranger from outside. In such a context, 'fear of crime' can only be interpreted as limited to the public sphere and a threatening stranger from the outside. Unfortunately, such an interpretation disregards the problematic nature of the concepts crime, (criminal) victimisation and 'fear of crime'. Consequently, such a narrow interpretation of the meaning of 'fear of crime' will lead to invalid inferences.

Table 6.4. List of main assertions Chapter 6.

Topic	Explanation
Purpose	Demonstrate the enormous diversity of 'victimisation', depending on nature of victimisation, person of the victim and the relationship with victim Demonstrates commonness of typical images in various sources Explain how certain interpretations of 'victimisation' and 'fear of crime' are connected
Research questions	How can the concept (criminal) victimisation be interpreted? What types of victimisation exist? To what extent has the notion of 'victimisation' been dependent on crime surveys? Within this context, what does 'fear of crime' mean?
Main notions	Main purpose of victim survey: provide reliable crime figures, but only for specific crimes in the public sphere Criticism on interpretations of victimisation: often too narrow and too juridical Victimisation not unequivocal; three different approaches to concept 'victimisation' 1st approach focuses on nature of victimisation: varying from the specific crimes that are usually included in the victim survey, to experience with behaviours that are not legally sanctioned 2nd approach focuses on person who is victimised; direct and indirect (secondary) victimisation 3rd approach views victimisation as possibly occurring event, the imaginable victimisation
	Interpretation of event and its consequences of importance, even in case of legally defined criminal victimisation, and different for men and women Attributions of deservedness, responsibility or culpability to the victim of major importance in interpretation of victimisation, which reflect ideal types of victim & perpetrator (irrespective of approach to concept victimisation)
	Sources (narratives, television, news media, movies, detective novels etc.) within social and cultural environment (re)create typical images (ideal types); commonness & pervasiveness of these typical images Ideal types as schemas, provide information on appropriate behaviour and attributions of deservedness, responsibility or culpability These attributions, images and ideal types are highly gendered
Conclusion	Meaning of concept 'victimisation': three different approaches to concept demonstrate diversity; narrowing down the concept victimisation to legally sanctioned behaviour neglects too much
	Meaning of concept 'fear of crime': depending on approach to concept victimisation, common interpretations not accurate Common interpretation has longest history, but lacks validity. Though slightly adapted over time, even the earliest interpretations are still common, whereas the popularity of the more 'advanced' interpretations still seem to suffer from a lack of familiarity or attractiveness

Evidently, 'fear of crime' is a complex concept when the supposedly core of 'fear of crime', i.e. crime, is problematic. Crime, criminal victimisation and victimisation are interpreted in a variety of ways in this respect. The meaning of 'fear of crime', that is, how the concept usually is interpreted, is based on a particular interpretation of crime and victimisation. In spite of criticism and some adjustments, the core elements of the earliest interpretations of 'fear of crime' are still the most common, pervasive and therefore influential. That is, crime is restricted to a few typical examples of offences in the public sphere. Consequently, such a narrow interpretation of the meaning of 'fear of crime' will lead to invalid inferences. Nonetheless, when the complexity and dynamics of the concepts crime and (criminal) victimisation is taken into account, part of the problematic nature and meaning of 'fear of crime' is acknowledged.

This chapter, which main assertions are presented in Table 6.4, demonstrated the diversity of victimisation by explaining the wide variety of different interpretations and focusing on the nature of victimisation. The most important conclusion that can be derived from this chapter regarding the concept 'fear of crime' is that the historically developed common interpretation of 'fear of crime' and its derivations are inaccurate and invalid in the context of the diversity of victimisation. The label 'fear of crime' is not specific enough and highlights 'crime', while 'crime' has only a little to do with it.

Besides 'crime' and 'victimisation', another core concept 'fear of crime' is 'risk' and the perception thereof. In order to get a further understanding of the meaning of 'fear of crime', 'risk' and 'risk perception' will be analysed in the next chapter.

7 Risk (perception)

The questions that are of importance in the chapters four to eight touch on the meaning of concepts with respect to their social context. Issues like when and why did the concept 'fear of crime' become an issue in research, politics and the media or when did 'fear of crime' become a social problem can only be addressed when elaborating on the social context. These issues are relevant in order to gain an understanding of how particular concepts are embedded and what they mean, since the concept 'fear of crime', its meaning(s) and related issues, are a product of historical, cultural and social circumstances or contexts. The concept 'risk' is salient in the context in which 'fear of crime' is perceived and interpreted. For example, frequent issues involving 'fear of crime' refer to the difference between actual risk vs. perceived risk or anxiety in a 'risk society'. Also, the debate on the fear-victimisation paradox centres on the risk of becoming a victim of crime. In this chapter the main focus is on the concept 'risk' and risk perception and how 'risk' has been interpreted. It will become clear that 'risk' as a concept is as complex as the concept 'victimisation' and 'risk' is connected with attributions of responsibility and blame as well (Douglas 1992; see chapter 6). Likewise, notions of 'risk' are not neutral, but highly gendered (Chan & Rigakos 2002).

Much research has been done on (perceived) risk, like studies on risk perceptions involving for example AIDS, nuclear power and waste and industrial accidents, as well as analyses regarding the role and function of risk in society and responses to risk.[171] Different disciplines, e.g. epidemiology, engineering, sociology and psychology conduct research on risk.[172] Unfortunately, cross-fertilisation between these disciplines and (criminological) research on 'fear of crime' has not been facilitated well, which makes it difficult to systematise and integrate theory and empirical findings (see Hayes 1992). For

---

[171] See for example publications by the Royal Society (Warner 1981; 1992), most work by Sjöberg (e.g. 1987, 2000a, 2002a), Drottz-Sjöberg (1991), Slovic (e.g. 1980, 1987, 2000), Fischhoff et al. (1978, 1982; Fischhoff 1995), Renn & Rohrmann (2000), Johnson & Covello (1987), and Margolis (1996) that focus primarily on environmental, industrial or technological risks and aspects of risk communication, risk assessment and risk management.

[172] Though these different disciplines are partly overlapping and boundaries are not that rigid, the points of interest differ. Obviously, epidemiological studies are mainly concerned with perceived risk and behavioural correlates, for example regarding HIV and intravenous drug use (e.g. Connors 1992) or condom use (e.g. Nitz et al. 1997). Psychological research is interested in the relationship between perception of and attitudes towards risks and behavioural implications as well (e.g. Ellen et al. 2002), next to cognitive processes and biases (e.g. Kelaher & Ross 1992) or personality aspects such as 'sensation seeking' (e.g. Hampson et al. 2001; Hansen & Breivik 2001) and 'locus of control' (e.g. Crisp & Barber 1995). Another stream of research analyses perceived risks regarding accidents, for example road accidents (e.g. Jonah 1986; Ulleberg & Rundmo 2003) or accidents in industrial settings (e.g. Mearns & Flin 1995). Criminology has mainly focused on the risk and correlates of "becoming criminal"(e.g. Baron & Hartnagel 2002) and "becoming a victim" (e.g. Gottfredson 1984). Both streams of research identify so-called high-risk groups within the population that are "at risk" (e.g. Lindquist & Duke 1982) by means of factors that aim to predict or explain either criminal behaviour or victimisation, or both. Moreover, a few studies pay attention to the perceived risks of getting caught or arrested in the context of decision making regarding criminal behaviour (e.g. Fried & Repucci 2001).

example, Sjöberg (1987) refers in his foreword to the change in all Western industrial societies. This change is a "new element of public anxiety about hazards, which threatens to erode the confidence and trust that people place in the most powerful institutions" and has resulted, among other things, in the study of hazards as a set of related phenomena. Yet, the index does not contain an entry for 'crime'. However, in this chapter an attempt is made to distil relevant cross-disciplinary themes and findings from several disciplines, for example from the work of Sjöberg, Slovic and others on perceived risk.

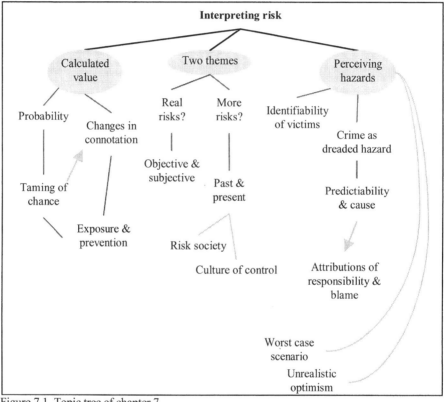

Figure 7.1. Topic tree of chapter 7.

Important aspects surrounding the concept 'risk' will be discussed, beginning with the mathematical element, i.e. the notion of possibility, chance, probability instead of fate and a determined outcome, and subsequently the nature of this outcome. Changes over time in thinking and talking about risk, i.e. risk language or risk talk, shifts attention to the notion of exposure as the idea that action now can influence probability or the consequences without changing the value or desirability of the outcome. Though much more could and will probably be written about risk, only two recurring themes will be discussed here. These themes are of particular relevance for present purposes, namely the theme of the reality and (ir)rationality of risk perceptions with respect to fear, and the theme of discontinuity, i.e. the difference between risks in the past and in 'contemporary' society. In the last part, the perception of risk with respect to crime, victimisation and fear is dealt with.

7.1   Risk: a calculated value

Current researchers in the field of risk agree on the multidimensional nature of risk and the interdependency of risk and risk perception. Most authors point to the social and institutional aspects of the concept, which affirm the idea that risk is a social construction. Social and cultural influences on risk (perception) are connected with how risks are selected, how people in modern society come to take certain risks and not others (Douglas 1986), the sensibility to threat is subject to the cultural context (Bankoff 2001; Lianos & Douglas 2000). Garland (2003) provides some key aspects of 'risk', all of which demonstrate the profoundly interactive and social nature of risk that is generally agreed upon across disciplines. First, risks are conditional; they are calculated and assessed by someone for a specific purpose. A risk is always a risk of something, for someone, is usually estimated with respect to a certain exposure and is calculated using specific instruments of measurement and expressed in specific units. Second, risks are reactive; the identification of uncertain future events is intrinsically limited, future events can be predicted on the basis of past experience and risks respond to the attitudes and actions that people adopt towards it. Third, risks are continually calculated and compensated in everyday life. People have the tendency to adjust their behaviour in response to changing perceptions of risk, which is usually called 'risk compensation'. When perceived risks alter, levels of vigilance and exposure do so too. This again demonstrates the dynamically interactive and reactive nature of risk. The fourth key aspect is that risks are interactive on a social level; not only do people adjust their behaviour in response to the changing perception of hazards in their environment, but different individuals have different comfort levels in the face of particular risks and particular kinds of risks. That is, everybody has a specific 'risk thermostat' (Adams 1995), and since these 'risk thermostats' may be different, different actors may take different risks. Moreover, the risks somebody runs depend on the actions of others and the risks they take. In summary, for Garland (2003) 'risk' is above all interactive and social in nature.

Briefly, researchers agree on the multidimensional and social nature of risk. The whole concept 'risk', how it is (re)created, measured, represented, communicated, perceived, reacted on and interpreted is dependent on the interaction with social and cultural aspects (e.g. Halfmann 1999, see Slovic 1999 and Tansey 2004a). Risk is multidimensional in nature, not the simple product of probability and consequences, which is also mirrored by several operationalised definitions of risk (Hayes 1992). Even the mathematical assessment of risk flows from social and institutional assumptions and processes, thus calculated risk is socially constructed as well (cf. Bankoff 2001; Warner 1992). Risk is not 'objective', but produced, negotiated and manipulated within social interaction, for example, sometimes taking specific risks is socially legitimated (Douglas 1986; Green 1997). For instance, *risk assessment* as defined by Warner (1992) involves both risk estimation, which includes identification of outcomes, estimated magnitude of associated consequences and estimation of probabilities of these outcomes, and risk evaluation, which is a complex process of determining significance, value of identified hazards and estimated risks to those concerned with or affected by the decision, including study of risk perception and taking the trade-off between perceived risk and perceived benefits into account (Warner 1992).

Numerous expressions and (operationalised) definitions of risk can be found (Viscusi, Hakes & Carlin 1997).[173] Despite that, it seems that most researchers in the field of risk would agree that the concept 'risk' involves at least two elements: first, the element of possibility, chance or probability, that is an outcome that is not certain or determined. This refers to the mathematical assessment of risk. The second element of risk is related to the consequences of the possibility and especially whether these consequences are desired or not.[174] Thus, this element contains the notion of value. It is not only the second element that implies a value and therefore a dependency on the social-cultural context; the first element is nested within this context as well. After all, the choice which specific outcomes are used in a mathematical assessment depends on the context; the context provides a framework for the cultural significance of a phenomenon (Weber 1949), for the salience of 'terrible' events and which risks are "worthy of being known" (Keat & Urry 1975: 196-199; Weber 1949: 72). As Hacking unravels the term 'possible' or 'possibility' (Hacking 1967a, 1967b, 1975a), he not only notes that a necessary condition for the logically possible is what "might have been", but also: "A terrible dog is not terribly doggy but a dog that is terrible in the way dogs can be. Likewise, a terrible possibility is not

---

[173] Crossland et al. (1992) offer some expressions of risk, among which "individual risk" that is usually presented as a mortality rate, e.g. number of deaths per unit time. Next, the Fatal Accident Rate, which is directly related for exposure, for example the number of deaths per unit measure of activity. Also, the loss of life expectancy, from various hazards, for example smoking. Slovic (1998) presents several different ways of expressing mortality risks concerning a toxical source, like deaths per million people in the population, deaths per million people within x miles of the source of exposure, deaths per unit of concentration, deaths per facility, deaths per ton of air toxic released, deaths per ton of air toxic absorbed by people, deaths per ton of chemical produced, deaths per million dollars of product produced and the loss of life expectancy associated with exposure to the hazard. Common epidemiological quantifications expressing the probability that a disease will occur in a defined population over a specified period of time are the incidence rate, also-called the absolute risk (number of people that develop the disease during a specific time period divided by number of people at risk for developing the disease in same period) and mortality rate (the number of people whose death is caused by particular disease divided by number of people at risk of dying from this disease in a specific time period). Relative risk, or risk ratio, is the incidence rate for persons exposed to a factor, e.g. smoking, divided by the incidence rate for those not exposed, i.e. non-smoking. Thus, a relative risk equal to one means that the risk in both populations, e.g. smoking and non-smoking, is equal. A relative risk greater than one means that the risk for exposed persons is greater than for non-exposed persons, yet this does not demonstrate causality. A relative risk less than one means that the risk in the exposed population is less and might imply that the exposure is protective. Vlek and Keren, cited in Pidgeon et al. (1992) also provide a list of formal definitions of risk.

[174] For example, Cox et al. (1992) show how risk can graphically be represented by plotting the frequency of specific events against the consequences, often referred to as the number of fatalities. A low frequency (probability) and a low number of fatalities makes up a "negligible" risk, whereas a high frequency and high number of fatalities entails an "intolerable" risk.

terribly possible but a possibility that is terrible in the way possibilities can be."
(Hacking 1967a: 163). What is considered to be a terrible possibility is
dependent on the context and not a mere calculation, 'risk' is subject to one's
ideas about the 'ideal society', a utopian vision of society (Douglas &
Wildavsky 1983; Halfmann 1999). In other words, 'the language of risk'
contains ideological dimensions (Hayes 1992), a risk is not a neutral prediction
about the future (Lianos & Douglas 2000). Neither is the discursive framework
within which disasters, hazards, risks and dangers are presented, neutral, as
Bankoff (2001) argues.[175]

7.1.1   Calculus of risk

The first important element of risk is possibility, chance or probability,
that is an outcome that is not certain, determined or a matter of fate. In the first
place this refers to the mathematical assessment of risk. All quantitative as well
as many qualitative assessments of risk are framed in terms of the language of
chance, likelihood and/or probability (Adams 1995). Questions of risks have
been effectively transposed into questions of probability, a mathematical
concept. Probabilities and probability assessments can only be derived from
studies of collectives and collectivities and make statements about collectives
(Prior, Glasner and McNally 2000), and therefore risk is situated in the context
of statistical development.

As noted by for example Hacking (1975b, 1990) and David (1998), the
modern world is a world without a place for chance or misfortune (Green 1997;
Luhmann 1993).[176] However, the calculus of risk in the Western world, designs
for minimising loss and guaranteeing profit and a risk discourse, is at least as old
as the mid-17th century and has always been used to serve specific interests; it
has always been a political project (Rigakos & Hadden 2001). Mathematicians
in the late seventeenth century were interested in games of chance implying a
priori independent equiprobable outcomes, e.g. playing cards and tossing coins,
and chance became calculable. The word 'risk' referred to the probability of an
event occurring combined with the magnitude of losses *or gains*, a neutral
connotation that developed over time into a negative connotation (Douglas
1986, 1992, 1993; Douglas & Wildavsky 1983). A little later, it became clear
that not everything took an equiprobable form, e.g. life and death, illustrated by
the Bills of Mortality (Hacking 1975b; Wohl 1983). The application of
probability to legal problems and the 1st textbook on probability by Huygens
demonstrate the emerging ideas about probability, shifts in scientific thoughts
and emergent concepts of evidence and deduction, all in the second half of the
17th century (Hacking 1975b). As the modern notion of probability became
possible, the science of statistics could emerge as the study of quantitative facts
about the state and its population. This eventuated in a new 19th century theory

---

[175] Bankoff (2001) convincingly argues that the Western academic discourse on disasters reflects cultural
    values that reflect a particular world view, in which the World is divided in *us* (the West) and *them*
    (everywhere else, but the equatorial zone in particular).
[176] This is reflected by the Dutch motto 'pech moet weg'.

of probability that did not focus on the singular, unique, particular and individual, but on properties of the collective. Before, data about births and deaths were seen as 'signs' of the plague, and not as data that could be examined in the way as evidence, from which conclusions could be drawn (Hacking 1975b: 106). Briefly described in chapter 5, the study of large numbers, frequency theory and statistics, provided the general epidemic model as proposed by for example Quetelet. Probability indicates 'frequency in the long run' (Hacking 1964). Probability belongs to the series, not to the individual events; probability is a property of a collective, of populations rather than of singular individuals (Prior, Glasner & McNally 2000). Looking for patterns in the data became possible, as well as predictability on a magnified scale. Attempts were made to calculate the risk of various kinds of death in an "objective" way, i.e. exact chance of death from various causes based on empirical evidence and untainted by the subjective fears people have of these different causes and chances (Green 1997). Chance became a pattern, a *hazard* was not "an unpredictable danger, but a calculable "risk", which could be understood and mapped, if not yet manipulated and managed" (Green 1997: 65; see also Alexander 2002; Luhmann 1993).[177]

This argument is similar to those that are used by supporters of a 'risk society', in which knowledge of risk is used to control danger. As Ericson and Haggerty (1997) in their foreword of 'Policing the risk society', contemporary society is a society that has shifted towards the "provision of security through surveillance technologies designed to identify, predict, and manage risks." Yet, the history of risk management is much older than 'contemporary society' (Rigakos & Hadden 2001). In the 17th century already "penology, sovereignty and insurance are often overlapping issues that find their rationality in economic concerns about the protection of property and the construction of a quintessential bourgeois state." (Rigakos & Hadden 2001: 75; Deflem 1997). The ideas of 'improvement by numbers' and that 'counting is controlling' are not something that was invented recently; as is briefly pointed out in chapter 5. Quite the contrary, as soon as statistical measurement became possible, statistical probability has been used for several political or ideological purposes (see Cullen 1975; Douglas 1993; Wohl 1983).

Indeed, the late 20th century has a growing risk assessment industry, which attempts to objectify situations through measuring the probability of the risk that these situations are leading to an accident as well as the extent of damage likely to be caused by the possible accident (Green 1997). Risks however, are not always calculated in the same manner; sometimes statistics of identified casualties are available, or some evidence might be there, but

---

[177] The words 'chance' and 'hazard' are linked; Hacking (1975b: 6) notes that "hazard", of Arabic origin, is the old word for chance. Contemporary definitions of 'hazard' or 'risk' are undoubtedly related to danger or undesirable outcomes (Douglas 1992; Luhmann 1993). For example the definition offered by Lee (1981), a hazard or risk refers to a situation or activity involving events whose consequences are undesirable to some unknown degree and whose future occurrence is uncertain. Also, Giddens (1998) attempts to distinguish risk from hazard or danger, yet 'risk' remains to refer to the chance of avoiding an unwanted outcome.

connection between suspect cause and injury cannot be traced, or the expert gives an estimation of probabilities of events that have not yet happened (Crossland et al. 1992). When information on casualties is available, like crime and victimisation statistics, then risk could be calculated *in retrospect*. This is the sort of risk estimation that is proffered in the criminological or victimological field, but it is not the same as knowing what has caused the event, i.e. the victimisation, to happen. Next to different calculation methods, risk can be expressed in several ways as well (Cox et al. 1992), for example in the format of a mortality rate, e.g. the number of deaths due to murder per year (see note 173).

In sum, an important element of the concept 'risk' is possibility, chance or probability, that is an uncertain outcome. Some early 'risk analysts' and statisticians who worked with the concept assumed that collective and reliable sense of security could be achieved by this statistical knowledge; facts and figures would banish panic (Freedgood 2000). Danger would be located and quarantined in reassuringly predictable circumstances and would therefore reliably produce psychic security (Freedgood 2000). Apparently, this is far more difficult. Modern cosmologies, as Freedgood labels them, continue to locate and thereby contain risk, they are strategies that provide large-scale consolation and reassurance, "structures of containment that attempt to offer totalizing explanations of a part of the world" (Freedgood 2000: 2). Engaging in, representing and theorising risk are always cosmological projects. That is, these projects are always aimed (symbolically or materially) at increasing safety, reducing danger and the hope is always for ever-greater security. The cultural productions of risk are always working to create a safe paradise (Freedgood 2000). Risk signifies a violation of that paradise.

7.1.2   Signification of risk

Though previously 'risk' referred to the probability of an event occurring combined with the magnitude of losses *or gains*, the neutral connotation changed over time into a negative connotation: risk is associated only with losses, negative or unwanted outcomes (Douglas 1986; Douglas & Wildavsky 1983).[178] This is also demonstrated by Green (1997), who employs 'risk' and 'misfortune' in an analysis of the question how some misfortunes have become classified specifically as 'accidents' in the late twentieth century. Though the word 'accident' covers a seemingly infinite range of possible misfortunes that will happen and have to be expected from time to time, misfortunes which might be universal, but the ways of classifying, understanding and managing them are not. Therefore, she examines the social construction of accidents and some of her findings are briefly discussed here, since her argument is convincing for the context of crime as well. Green (1997) notices that the word 'accident' is used in every day life in two rather different ways; the first way refers to certain kinds of outcome, e.g. as synonym for injury

---

[178] Yet, a study by Lupton & Tulloch (2002) shows that some people noted that risk may have both a positive or negative outcome and the danger that is associated with risk can have positive aspects.

or damage. Accident is used as a moral term as well, referring to causal sequence and a lack of cause, to an unmotivated event which was unpredictable, without culpability. In everyday life, the 'ideal accident' is blameless. However, accident is more complex than that; it does not only refer to necessarily blameless events. Indeed, an accident can have been unforeseen, but sometimes it is said that people did (not) deserve the accident. Moreover, an accident is not necessarily unambiguously unpredictable, since it is said that the "accident was waiting to happen". Why are some misfortunes labelled as accidents? Green's purpose is to rediscover some of the clues to how 'accident' has come to be "self-evident, universal and necessary" in everyday talk in the late 20th century. Accidents had been interpreted as a given, research has been primarily concerned with how it is caused or how people react to it. She examines the emergence of the concept in Western thought and the rules when an accident is labelled as such, and notes that two conditions, consensus about rationality or the emergence of modern rational explanatory systems and the emergence of probabilistic thinking, made it possible to have an accident. Medicine, a key discourse on accidents and disasters, shows some dramatic transformations in how 'accidents' are classified, discussed and managed; epidemiological patterns and predictability emerge. Statistical patterns and correlates on an aggregated level identify social, environmental, psychological and biological risk factors.

These patterns and their correlates have led to ideas on for example accident proneness (Cameron 1975; McKenna 1983). Apparently, some subgroups turn out to be more prone than others, have a potential susceptibility to accidents, are more 'at risk' and a discourse of 'risk' and 'disaster' emerges (Bankoff 2001; Green 1997). As such, risk is not a danger or a hazard; risk relates to a decision "without which the loss could not have occurred" (Luhmann 1993: 16). Green (1997) concludes that the late 20th century embraces the challenge of predicting the unpredictable, the *random* accident has become *preventable* accident. Ideally, in the 20th century, accidents should no longer happen, they should be prevented. Accidents transform from random misfortunes, only understood in aggregate, into preventable misfortunes. Prevention became booming business, the prevention of crime and victimisation alike. This led to the professionalisation of prevention, as well as to the need for 'expert voice' and a general proliferation of risk. The predictable is preventable, and experts and information are needed in order to correct public misconceptions, as well as surveillance in order to manage risks: the 'risk society' should be policed (e.g. Ericson & Haggerty 1997) and modern cosmologies locate risks and aim at increasing safety and reducing danger (Freedgood 2000).

So, a central notion in the current discourse is that the accident should not happen, but should be prevented from happening. Green (1997) wonders what this means for the victim who potentially suffers from an accident. Ideally, rationality does not imply blame, victims of an accident in the current discourse of risk management may not be seen as malicious, yet, they are in a sense culpable, in their ignorance; like the victim of a crime who is not 'streetwise' is seen as more responsible (see chapter 6; Douglas 1992). Victimisation, whether of crime or a road accident, entails similar processes of attributions of blame and responsibility. Individuals are constructed as responsible for the surveillance and management of their own risk environment. Risk is no longer a neutral term for calculating probabilities, rather, it signifies danger and is associated with hazards. Risk has a definite negative connotation. For instance, Warner (1992) defines risk as the probability, in statistical sense, that a particular adverse event, i.e. an occurrence that produces harm, occurs during a stated period of time, or results from a particular challenge. A hazard is specified as a source of danger, that has the potential for adverse consequences, or for a situation that in particular circumstances could lead to harm or damage. Additionally, harm refers to loss to a human being (or to human population) and damage to loss of inherent quality suffered by an entity (physical and biological). All these terms clearly have negative connotations; danger, risk, loss and harm are to be prevented or avoided. The dominant Western discursive framework within which disasters, hazards, risks and dangers are presented, attributes disasters to natural forces and "denies the wider historical and social dimensions of hazard and focuses attention largely on technocratic solutions" (Bankoff 2001: 24). The general conviction is established that governments and societies do have the opportunity and possibility to avoid or ameliorate disasters, if only they would apply the appropriate technocratic measures and had the adequate knowledge and preparedness. Consequently, since governments and societies did have the opportunity to reduce risks and prevent or ameliorate disasters, they are blamed if they fail to do so (Bankoff 2001).

In general, risk is mostly associated with unwanted outcomes, representing for example a physical danger or financial losses. Yet, a study by Lupton and Tulloch (2002) shows that some people noted that risk has or may have both a positive or negative outcome. Moreover, the danger that is associated with risk can have positive aspects, as a participant in their study expresses: "It can mean adventure, challenge, being open to possibilities" (Lupton & Tulloch 2002: 324). So risk is not purely negative for everybody, which is in accordance with the psychological literature on adventure, risk, thrill or sensation seeking (e.g. Aluja-Fabregat & Torrubia-Beltri 1998; Franken, Gibson & Rowland 1992; Hansen & Breivik 2001; Slanger & Rudestam 1997). Renn (2004) identifies a few characteristics of this risk-as-a-personal-thrill, namely the voluntary involvement, personal control of and ability to influence the particular risk, a limited period of exposure to the risk situation, the possibility of preparation and practice and social recognition for overcoming the risk (Renn 2004: 407). Renn (2004) describes different notions of risk perception. Besides risk as a personal thrill or as a test of strength and as a game of chance, he distinguishes between the idea of risk as fate, as a fatal threat or as an early warning indicator. Especially these last two conceptions of risk are of importance for current purposes.

7.1.3   Taming of risk: prevention and exposure

Now chance has been tamed (Hacking 1990) and the random has become predictable, prevention and risks have become big business, as is illustrated by the insurance industry and private security (Furedi 1997), and by the policy relevance of risk as well (Margolis 1996). Over the past 30 years, the application of techniques and methods for the formal analysis of 'risk' in the literature on health and health care became widespread and spheres of literature have emerged in which 'risk' is the primary focus of concern, among which are Health Risk Appraisal and Risk Analysis/Assessment/ Management. These analyses of risk "are typically undertaken to reduce, modify or anticipate the extent or nature of uncertainty in decision-making processes" (Hayes 1992: 401).[179]

Prevention strategies include enforcement, education and engineering. Adams (1995) argues that these strategies are limited, because they do not take into account the way in which human behaviour changes in response to reduced risk. He proposes a *risk thermostat*, which is some sort of psychological mechanism that sets the level of risk with which an individual feels comfortable (Adams 1995). If the environment is made safer, for example because of enforcement of using a seat belt, then individuals increase the amount of risk they face, by driving faster. Behavioural modifications will compensate for (changes in) risk, like communicating vessels. Thus, when the environment is made safer, by prevention strategies, this will lead to more risky behaviour or risk may be redistributed to the most vulnerable members of the society. Similarly, the 'thermostat' implies that when cars have an airbag, people will drive more 'risky', less careful, than when the airbag would have been replaced by a spike (Adams 1995). Despite the utility of preventative action might not be proven, they still have value as talismans, as rituals appealing to the rationality of risks and its management (Freedgood 2000). By reducing the dangers in our environment, we construct ourselves as competent risk managers and individuals are constructed as responsible for the surveillance and management of their own risk environment. One of the strategies to manage the dangers in the surrounding environment is to decrease the exposure. Whenever appropriate, risk must refer to "an exposure to hazard specified in terms of amount or intensity, time of starting or duration" (Warner 1992: 3). This means that all risks are conditional, though these conditions are often implied by the context rather than explicitly stated.

7.1.3.1   *Exposure, behavioural constraints and victimisation risk*

Researchers who have criticised the so-called fear-victimisation paradox have focused on the measurement of *victimisation risks* especially (see chapter 6). Other criticism is directly related to the concept of (criminal) victimisation and argues for a broader conceptualisation by pointing out the possibility of indirect victimisation and other forms of victimisation. The

---

[179] Yet, the translation of patterns or generalisations based on aggregate data to preventive measures or strategies of an individual is rather misleading (Green 1997: 104).

criticism that concentrates on the measurement of risk argues that the victimisation risks are not properly established. This is because of the distortion of police statistics, since they suffer from dark number issues. For example, research on acts of violence by family members and acquaintances (e.g. Bell 1985; Van Hightower, Gorton & Demoss 2000; Skogan 1976) and on sexual violence (e.g. Frenken 1997; Vogel & Himelein 1995) showed that women are much more likely to be victimised than always had been assumed on the basis of official statistics (see Acierno 2000; Felson et al. 2002; Pain 1997; Stanko 1988a, 1988b), but this has not been conclusive evidence to 'solve' the paradox (see for example Bilsky & Wetzels 1997 vs. Smith & Torstensson 1997). Others dispute the idea that the 'risk of becoming a victim' can be derived from criminal victimisation statistics alone. The fundamental assumption of the fear-victimisation paradox is that information about the occurrence of victimisation (for example victimisation surveys, police data) can be used as information about the *risk* on victimisation (Cohen, Kaufman & Gottfredson 1985; Vanderveen 1998a, 1999). Risk (on unwanted outcomes) can be defined as the number of unwanted outcomes (accidents, criminal offences) divided by the extent of *exposure*, analogous to the definition of risk used in safety management and risk analysis (Saunders and Wheeler 1991). So, in accordance with this definition of risk, the risk on victimisation cannot be derived only from information about the number of unwanted outcomes, that is the number of victimisation incidents. Risk on victimisation can only be deduced from information about victimisation *and* the extent of exposure to risk (see Cohen, Kaufman & Gottfredson 1985).

This notion of exposure is a basic presumption in 'lifestyle' or 'routine activities' approach of victimisation (e.g. Finkelhor & Asdigian 1996; Garofalo 1986; Hindelang, Gottfredson & Garofalo 1978), related to the criminal opportunity theory (see Miethe & Meier 1990).[180] Lifestyle or routine activity theory argues that people who have lifestyles or routines that are characterised by four key factors are more likely to be victimised than people who do not lead such lifestyles or have such routines (Cohen & Felson 1979; Garofalo 1986). Such lifestyle or routines have factors that firstly place individuals in close physical proximity to motivated offenders; secondly, frequently place individuals in risky or deviant situations that expose them to crime; expose individuals as attractive targets to offenders and lack capable guardianship to

---

[180] Miethe & Meier (1990: 244) refer to exposure when talking about the "convergence in time and space of motivated offenders, suitable targets, and the absence of guardianship". Though these aspects can be related to variables on both the individual and the aggregate level (see Cohen, Kluegel & Land 1981; Lee 2000; Sampson, Morenoff & Gannon-Rowley 2002; Smith & Jarjoura 1989), the focus here is on the individual behaviours.

deter the offenders (see Fisher, Cullen & Turner 2002; Miethe & Meier 1994).[181] Thus, besides exposure, other key concepts in such an approach are proximity to offenders, target attractiveness and guardianship (Cohen, Kluegel & Land 1981; Miethe & Meier 1990). Persons can become victims when they are exposed to motivated offenders, are suitable or attractive targets and guardianship is absent. The routine activities approach holds that differences in 'lifestyle' explain the differences in (probability of) victimisation (e.g. Mesch 2000; Rountree & Land 1996a). How 'lifestyle' is specified, operationalised and measured varies from demographic proxies, like marital status and employment (e.g. Massey & McKean 1985; Wittebrood & Nieuwbeerta 2000) to nature and frequency of out-of-the-house activities, like the major daytime activity and frequency of night time activity (Lee 2000; Miethe, Stafford & Long 1987).

Overall, it seems that people who are less fearful, tend to have a lifestyle that exposes them more to offenders whereas people with higher fear tend to employ less 'risky' activities (e.g. Norris & Kaniasty 1992; Stafford & Galle 1984).[182] Also, people who are more fearful seem to expose themselves less to possible offenders by *refraining from* certain behaviours as walking alone at night, giving a ride to a stranger, walking in scary neighbourhoods (e.g. Keane 1998; Liska, Sanchiro & Reed 1988). Such avoidance tactics are primarily taken to decrease one's exposure by trying to avoid situations that are related to a highly perceived risk of criminal behaviour. Besides these risk-avoidance behaviours, 'risk management tactics' are ways of dealing with these situations when avoidance is not desirable or possible.[183] In terms of the routine activities approach, people can take more precautions to become a less attractive victim, for example by not wearing 'provocative' clothes, jogging in the company of the dog, leaving the lights on while absent, fixing reliable locks on doors or having a watchdog (e.g. Luxenburg et al. 1994; Williams, Singh & Singh 1994; Yeoh & Yeow 1997). Also, people attempt to influence the level of

---

[181] Fisher, Cullen & Turner (2002) used the lifestyle-routine activity approach in their study on stalking victimisation in a sample of college women; the key factors were specified for the college situation. Proximity to motivated offenders was related to the frequency of social and recreational activities, several situations where a large number of male students is present, the housing on campus, the social events and so on. Exposure to crime was related to the presence of bars, parties and availability of alcohol and illegal drugs. Target attractiveness in the case of stalking was linked with the age of the students (young women) and the notion that there is usually a relationship between stalker and woman being stalked, together with the students; i.e. women who regularly date. The authors discuss the mixed results on the fourth key factor; capable guardianship. They hypothesise that a woman living alone lacks capable guardianship that is needed to deter a stalker.

[182] Within this approach, it comes as no surprise that deviant, delinquent or criminal activities are quite highly correlated with victimisation rates and thus that offenders and victims are often members of the same group (e.g. Jensen & Brownfield 1986; Sampson & Lauritsen 1990; Zhang, Welte & Wieczorek; 2001). However, within the group with a deviant lifestyle, interindividual differences exist and people within this group with more fear of victimisation, take more precautionary measures (McCorkle 1992). See also Walklate (1997) who notes that risk seeking behaviour has received far less attention in 'fear of crime' research than risk avoidance.

[183] Cobb (1976) notes that avoidance and management tactics are not mutually exclusive; yet, in general, avoidance tactics refer to adaptive (passive) behaviour that changes one's routine activities to improve the "person-environment fit". Risk management behaviour refers to the (active) "manipulation of the environment" (Cobb 1976: 311).

guardianship, for example, by going out with another person and telephoning a friend before returning home (Johnson-Dalzine, Dalzine & Martin-Stanley 1996) or carrying a mobile phone (Chapman & Schofield 1998). The latter overlaps with the *extra* actions that people perform for security reasons in order to protect oneself and thus to lessen the seriousness of the consequences of victimisation. A typical example is carrying weapons, for example holding a bunch of keys in one's hand, a tin of hairspray for protective reasons (e.g. Kleck 1996; Riger, Gordon & LeBailly 1982; Simon, Crosby & Dahlberg 1999).

With this research in mind, discussants of the fear-victimisation paradox state that it is a logical consequence; since all these sorts of avoidance and security behaviours (or measures) influence the extent of exposure to risks, and people who feel more fearful apply more of these behaviours. In particular, women tend to use more so-called precautionary tactics than men (e.g. Devlin 2000; Gordon & Riger 1989; Johnson, Bowker & Cordell 2001). Thus, it is argued that women in general have a reduced exposure to risk and when this reduced exposure and the use of security and avoidance behaviours would be taken into account, the paradox is less clear. Indeed, studies that have investigated the exposure to risk show that the higher the fear, the less exposure to risk (e.g. Mesch 2000). Others conclude that a *correspondence* exists between fear and victimisation instead of a paradox (Levine & Wachs 1986b) or that when exposure to risk is allowed for, women have a higher 'risk' on victimisation than men (Balkin 1979; Gottfredson 1984) or similar victimisation rates (Jensen & Brownfield 1986).

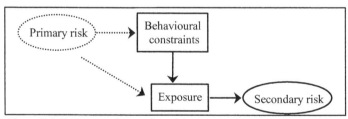

Figure 7.2. Primary and secondary risk.

Figure 7.2 illustrates the former line of reasoning. The primary risk is the risk on victimisation when no measures whatsoever are being taken and thus when exposure would be maximal. In an empirical way, this is the risk when security measures, avoidance strategies and so forth are taken into account. However, the operationalisation of the primary risk is very difficult, since the primary risk is in a sense hypothetical. The secondary risk is the risk in which the use of measures has been processed and is connected with the prevalence of victimisation. The secondary risk is composed of the primary risk, influenced by the extent of exposure. This is the 'risk of becoming a victim' in the case that is has been derived from criminal victimisation statistics, which does not allow for the extent of exposure, for the variety of measures being taken to minimise or avoid the risk on victimisation. The so-called fear-victimisation paradox concerns an inference about the primary risk, based on statistics and data, which touch on the secondary risk. In other words, the fear of victimisation concerns the primary risk; the (prevalence of) victimisation itself concerns the secondary risk.[184]

7.2   Two regular themes

The current cross-disciplinary endeavour to gain relevant themes and findings from several disciplines, two themes come to light that have striking similarities across disciplines, among which the criminological or victimological field. Moreover, these themes are of particular relevance for present purposes, since they reveal various comments on different conceptualisations of risk, victimisation and fear. First, the theme of the reality and (ir)rationality of risk perceptions is discussed, which resembles many of the discussions involving the fear-victimisation paradox. Subsequently, the theme of discontinuity, i.e. the difference between risks in the past and in 'contemporary' society is dealt with.

7.2.1   Real risks or irrational fears

One of the themes that resurfaces in innumerable studies, no matter what discipline, touches on the reality and (ir)rationality of risk perceptions (see Lupton & Tulloch 1999). Not only the entire notion of the fear-victimisation paradox, but numerous other studies as well, whether mainly empirical or theoretical, stem from a distinction between 'objective' and 'subjective' risk. Many studies connect the 'real', 'actual' or 'objective' risk, i.e. risk calculated from statistics by the experts, to the 'unreal', 'perceived' or 'subjective' risk of the public (Thompson 1990). A common method of empirical approach is the study of experts' perceived risks in comparison with the public's perceptions (e.g. Fischhoff, Slovic & Lichtenstein 1982). When exaggerating a little, two major streams of research have developed; the first supposes a gap between the expert view of risk, i.e. the 'objective' risk and the public's perceptions (see Slovic 1992, 2000), whereas the second argues that there is no gap (see Sjöberg 1998, 2002a). Nonetheless, both streams incorporate the recurring subject of the (ir)rationality of these public perceptions (Douglas 1986), often combined with the (ir)rationality of fear or 'legitimate' fear, that is fear proportionately related to the calculated risk. Obviously, the manner in which the subject is dealt with, varies.

Margolis (1996) identifies three main headings that capture the accounts that aim to explain the expert/lay conflicts. The first suggests that the controversy is not so much about risk, but rather about *ideology*, power and responsibility and about what ends public policy is going to serve (e.g. Corburn 2002); risk perceptions reflect basic values (Pidgeon 1998). For instance, Lee (1981) notices the emphasis on the *rationality* of the calculation of the future likelihood of a hazardous event as predicted from its frequency per unit of past

---

[184] However, the relationship between 'routine activities' and the 'fear of crime' is not clear; it has been found that people who use several measures, become more fearful. For example, avoiding certain places can reduce the secondary risk, but can also increase the fear of victimisation (Liska, Sanchiro et al. 1988).

time, or by aggregating the influence of the variables that determine it, whereas in contrast, the public's perception is often called 'irrational'. Lee (1981), however, claims that in assessments of seriousness, only the public can judge, since social and moral values are the ultimate criteria (cf. Woollacot 1998). Thus, the two risk assessments, based on 'objective', scientific measurement or on personal, individual perception, are different, but complementary forms of rationality; the public's perception of risk is just another form of risk assessment; it is not the future likelihood of a hazardous event that is predicted from its frequency per unit of past time, or by aggregating the influence of the variables that determine it, rather the risk perception is an assessments of seriousness, which relates to social and moral values (Lee 1981).

The second heading that Margolis (1996) distinguishes states the problem is a loss of *trust* in the institutions, e.g. government, police, that seek to assure the public that danger is under control. The loss of trust is a common explanation, yet disbelief might cause distrust as much as distrust might cause disbelief. Besides, this is an illustration of the confusion between what is the cause of a perceived risk and what is a consequence of a perceived risk (Margolis 1996). Also, the role of trust seems to be quite limited, not trust, but beliefs that there are clear limits to how much science and experts know and that there are many unknown effects of technology appear to be strongly related to perceived risk (Sjöberg 2001b).

The third heading of the accounts that attempt to explain the expert/lay conflicts is called the *rival rationalities* view (Margolis 1996: 21). This holds that the public is concerned with a far broader sense of danger, including many dimensions and not just the number of expected fatalities. This is related to the major stream of research that was pointed out previously; though not identified by Margolis, this group of accounts argues that the difference is not a difference at all: the experts' do not employ such a simple structure in which risk equals probability multiplied by the consequences (Rowe & Wright 2001; Sjöberg 2001a, 2002a). Indeed, experts often see risks *in their own field of expertise* as smaller than the public does, but that does not imply that their risk perception is also driven by other factors (Sjöberg 2002a; Wright, Bolger & Rowe 2002). Structural properties of the risk judgments appear to be similar and the level difference between experts and the public might largely be explained in terms of attitude. This again implies an ideological component; when an attitude or an activity is of considerable importance to a person, s/he will have corresponding perceptions on the hazard (Sjöberg 2001a, 2002a). Moreover, the label of 'expert' does not mean that that s/he is able to make more valid judgments than non-experts, since many task and measurement factors can enhance or degrade the relative validity of expert versus non-expert judgment (Wright 2002). According to Pidgeon (1998) the sharp distinction between assessment of 'objective' 'correct' risk and probabilities by experts, and subjective biased evaluations by laypeople can, in its strongest form, be found in the literature of the 1970s and early 1980s, but this distinction is not tenable anymore (see Pidgeon et al. 1992; Slovic 1998). Yet, the theme itself remains persistently present, rather similar to the persistency of comments on the fear-victimisation paradox.

Scholars within the tradition of the 'risk society' have been concerned with the reality and (ir)rationality of risks and their perceptions as well. They note that risks are real; risk rationalities make life real, give confidence in taking action and bring imagined futures to the present. Risk logic is based on fears of threats and dangers, therefore they function as standards set by science and the law as orderly accounts of danger (Ericson & Haggerty 1997: 89). Van Loon (2000) wants to get rid of the whole distinction between 'real' and 'imaginary' risks, he proposes to call all risks *virtual* risks. Risks always imply uncertainty, and talking about real risks and perceived risks is ridiculous, since the *virtuality* of risks is all we can deal with, risk is a becoming-real, a virtuality. (Van Loon 2000).[185] The virtuality of risks and the unclear distinction between 'objective' and 'subjective' risk is also emphasised by Beck (2000), who gives an account of the sociological concepts of risk and the 'risk society'. First, he notes that risk per se is not the same as destruction, rather it characterises the peculiar intermediate state between security and destruction, where the *perception* of threatening risks determines thought and action. Thus, risks are a type of real virtuality; cultural perception and definition constitutes risk in a "no-longer-but-yet" format, i.e. no longer trust and security, but not yet destruction and disaster. Risks are real and constructed at the same time; they are real because of the impacts, and constructed because they stem from perception, which is always and necessarily contextual and locally constituted. Moreover, the concept 'risk' reverses the relationship of past, present and future, since a threatening future functions as a parameter for current action. Discussing risk means discussing something that has not happened yet, something that is not the case, but *could* happen if nothing is done. Beck points out that both factual and value statement risk statements are neither pure factual claims nor exclusively value claims (cf. Jasanoff 1998). As factual mathematical calculations, risks are both directly and indirectly related to cultural definitions and standards of a tolerable or intolerable life, the question is always how we want to live, which is expressed by the notion of a mathematicised morality.

The theme of the reality and (ir)rationality of risk perceptions turns up everywhere, just like comparisons between 'actual' crime rates and 'fear of crime' do in criminologically oriented (policy) publications. When the conclusion refers to irrationality, reasons are offered to explain this irrationality, an important reason being the influence of the media. For example, Weiner (1986) points to the "distinction between dramatic deaths and statistical ones" as a consequence of TSS, i.e. toxic shock syndrome caused by the use of tampons (see note 153). When TSS is compared with other diseases and causes of death, TSS turns out to be a notable public health threat, but a very rare one. Weiner (1986) argues that the "escalation of media coverage" was of primary influence:

---

[185] Maybe it is because of this reasoning that the terms 'risk' and 'risk perception' are often used interchangeably, as synonyms (e.g. Adam & Van Loon 2000).

In only four months, TSS went from a virtually unknown disease to the cause of a multimillion dollar recall. The case of TSS is an extreme but revealing example of the pressures that shape perceptions of the safety of consumer products. (p. 141)

Similar case studies in Sapolsky (1986a) of the power of public opinion, misrepresentation of product risks and societal distortions are explicitly connected with more knowledge about product fears in order to understanding the confusion that appears to exist about what is *truly* dangerous and what is not, since too often we either dismiss risks or are prisoners of them (Sapolsky 1986b, 1986c). All these case studies refer to *distorted* perceptions and describe the manipulation of the public's opinion, anxiety and concerns by the media, industries and organisations made possible by the absence of conclusive, uncontested and univocal scientific evidence (e.g. Sapolsky 1986b).[186]

The role of the media has been studied further, in particular by means of a model concerning risk communication in general, namely the social amplification of risk framework (SARF) or social amplification model (e.g. Kasperson et al. 1988; McComas 2003; Renn et al. 1992; Williams, Brown, Greenberg & Kahn 1999). The model presents various processes that lead particular hazards or events to become a focus of social and political concern and activity (amplification), though experts regard these hazards and events as presenting a relatively low statistical risk. The model describes the processes of attenuation, referring to the comparatively little public attention that other hazards receive, while these are potentially more serious (Petts, Horlick-Jones & Murdock 2001). Empirical investigations of the social amplification-model are relatively rare, which has partly to do with several factors that can not be easily controlled by the researcher. Hence, changes in risk perception are difficult to attribute to an increases and/or decreases in the media. However, some empirical work does support the model, e.g. in the sense that risk perceptions involving

---

[186] Levine (1986) analyses the diet-heart disease hypothesis, which suggests first a relationship between the level of cholesterol in the blood and the development of atherosclerosis and coronary heart disease, and second that the level of cholesterol in the blood, is influenced by the amount of (dietary) cholesterol and saturated fats that is eaten. She describes chronologically how these ideas affected politics, science and consumption of cheese and meats of different origin (e.g. poultry vs. beef), the consumption of butter, margarine and eggs, as well as regulation and politics and reactions from the food industry, in the form of both defences and new products. Segal (1986) focuses on the issue of salt and hypertension. Hypertension is considered to be a risk factor for cardiovascular disease, kidney disease and stroke. Sodium is considered to be one of several factors in developing hypertension. Recommendations by medical and scientific organisations, food safety regulations because of governmental pressure, opinion polls are all exemplary for the "politics of salt". According to Segal (1986: 83) "Attempts to modify public attitudes toward salt typify the rising public anxiety of consumer products. Growing public interest in nutrition intersects with product worries and with regulatory efforts regarding health and safety." Another case study that notes the distorted perception and manipulation of the public's opinion, concerns and consumer behaviour investigates the role of the FDA, the Food and Drug Administration (Cummings 1986). The FDA declared saccharin to be a carcinogen and initiated proceedings to eliminate the use of artificial sweeteners in consumer products., yet since the extent of the actual risks remain uncertain, the interests of the sugar industry, the diet industry and concerns of the public are major factors. In other words: "With an indeterminate scientific base for regulation, the role of non-scientific factors has assumed decisive importance in policymaking." (Cummings 1986: 119).

genetically modified foods did increase in line with expectations (Frewer, Miles & Marsh 2002). Also, media coverage may amplify the public's interest in an issue, the media do not create this issue; 'a good story' is one in which both the interests of the public and the media reinforce each other. (Bennett 1999, cited in Chartier & Gabler 2001). In other words, the media can only amplify or attenuate risk if they capture or resonate with an existing public mood (Petts, Horlick-Jones & Murdock 2001).

The similarity across disciplines of the research topics and findings is remarkable once again. The theme of the reality and (ir)rationality of risk perceptions resembles many of the discussions and explanations involving the fear-victimisation paradox. Research on 'fear of crime' has for example focused on the media as a source of information as well and is used as an explanation of 'fear of crime' by means of *indirect victimisation* (see chapter 6). Furthermore, the role of the media in the distortion of perceptions because of the misrepresentation of 'reality' and 'actual risks' is an issue within the field of 'fear of crime' research as well. Many findings from risk perception studies that focus on environmental, technological or industrial risks resemble findings from criminological oriented studies. In part this tells something about how institutions and people work. For instance, both criminological research as well as 'traditional' risk perception research have consistently identified some key factors which account for the 'distorted' picture represented by the media. The newsworthiness of events, whether this event is a homicide, a train accident or a power fallout, correlates with these factors (see chapter 6). News is selected in particular when questions of blame are involved, when a party can be identified upon which to place blame (cf. Douglas 1992; Bennett 1999, cited in Chartier & Gabler 2001). Moral outrage, which refers to fear, anger and the assignation of blame, is a very important trigger for a story to take off in the media (Sandman 1994). Bennett (in Chartier & Gabler 2001) suggests blame is the single most important trigger, though he proposes other factors as well, among which are alleged secrets and attempted cover-ups, the presence of identifiable heroes, villains as well as victims, links with existing high-profile issues or personalities, stories with a strong visual impact, like pictures of suffering and, which comes at no surprise within the present context, links to sex and/or crime. These factors mirror the features of newsworthiness with respect to crime (see chapter 6). In Sandman's words (1994), the mass media are in the outrage business.

In summary, to some extent a cross-disciplinary consensus exists regarding the reality and (ir)rationality of risk and its perceptions, a theme that clearly has received exceptional attention. In general, most researchers would agree with the following observations. First, risk, how it is conceptualised, measured, calculated, portrayed and the reaction it evokes, is dependent on the context and on value judgments.[187] This is linked with a second observation on which consensus exists: risk does have a 'quantitative' as well as a 'qualitative' side. Quantitative features embrace risk that is calculated according to an operationalisation, a formal definition that incorporates (a form of) statistical probability, that is based on limited knowledge, and some interobservable measure of consequences, like the number of deaths. Evidently, on a sublevel and frequently less obvious, these quantitative features involve value judgments and decisions, which can be contested. So, at least the operationalisation, the formal definition(s), the fabrication of the statistics, in a sense everything that states *how* the risk is calculated, can be disputed. Qualitative features not only deal with value judgments and decisions that precede the quantitative features of one exclusively specified risk, but with all value judgments of numerous more quantitatively defined risks. Moreover, the qualitative features concern attitudes, values, perceptions and so on of the hazard *itself* and the possible or imaginable *consequences* of what might happen, which will be discussed later. Relating to the previous remarks, pointers like 'real', 'actual' and 'rational' or 'objective' versus 'unreal', 'perceived', 'irrational' or 'subjective' are somewhat misleading. Slovic (1998a) states:

> risk does not exist "out there", independent of our minds and cultures, waiting to be measured. Instead, human beings have invented the concept risk to help them understand and cope with the dangers and uncertainties of life. Although these dangers are real, there is no such thing as "real risk" or "objective risk". (p. 74)

The theme on the reality and (ir)rationality of risk perceptions, on the distinction between 'real', 'actual' or 'objective' risk and 'unreal', 'perceived' or 'subjective' risk, is one of the two themes that shows up in several different disciplines and in the empirical studies within these disciplines. Another regularly recurring theme that is relevant here is the theme of *discontinuity*. The idea that risks in the past are different from risks in the present, in content and/or in extent.

7.2.2   Increased risk or increased risk awareness

Next to the (ir)rationality of risk perceptions linked to the (ir)rationality of fear, another recurrent theme in risk literature is *discontinuity*, i.e. the difference between risks, dangers and hazards in the past and in present 'contemporary' society. Contemporary society is typified by the construct of a no-risk society (Aharoni 1981), a culture of fear (Furedi 1997; Glassner 1999), a commercial risk-averse culture (Douglas 1992) or as the famous risk society (Adam, Beck & Van Loon 2000; Beck 1992, 1999; Franklin 1998a). Have risks increased or is it just a matter of a risk consciousness, an increased risk

---

[187] It is argued here that most researchers would agree with such a 'contextualist' approach (Horlick-Jones 1998; Slovic 1999; Wakefield & Elliott 2000), also by researchers from "extremes" that Renn (1998) observes and simplifies by means of the labels 'realist' versus 'constructivist' approaches. The research questions and purposes, that likely mirror the researchers' interests, are different for these approaches, but this should not be exaggerated (see Royal Society 1992; Sjöberg 1998a).

awareness? Some authors (implicitly) note that more or at least *different* risks are present in contemporary society, while others suggest just the risk consciousness or awareness has increased, or that risk is less tolerated. Again, these debates involve issues that relate to the previous theme of 'real' risks and 'constructed' risks. For instance, Garland (2003) argues it is not that we are facing more, or more dangerous risks, rather, the point is that there is more risk reduction, regulation and management. Garland (2003) too employs a narrative of discontinuity and refers to the objective measure of danger:

> If we live in a 'risk society' it is not in the sense of one that is more dangerous than before by any objective measure. If we live in a 'risk society' it is because we are more democratically engaged, more reflexively rational and more prone to distrust in our engagement with the phenomenon than were previous generations. (p. 32).

One thing is clear though, 'risk' is a popular concept (e.g. Burger 1993; Hayes 1992; Lianos & Douglas 2000). Yet, the frequent cross-disciplinary adoption of the term 'risk' does not (necessarily) equal a rise in risks or dangers, nor in risk consciousness. For instance, when the number of (medical) articles with the term risk(s) in the title and/or abstract would be employed as an operationalisation of the presence of 'actual' risks, the conclusion could only be that risks have rapidly increased during the period 1967-1991, a rise that resembles an epidemic (Skolbekken 1995).[188] Skolbekken (1995) suggests the rise of articles on risk is a result of developments in science & technology that have changed beliefs about the locus of control. Similar to the notion that chance has been tamed in the light of probability statistics; beliefs about the locus of control changed from factors outside to factors inside human control. Moreover, an increased focus on risk management and health promotion, as well as developments in computer technology, have also contributed to the 'risk epidemic' in articles.

7.2.2.1 More and different risks

Authors employing the concept of a 'risk society' hold that current society is different from past society, a narrative of discontinuity prevails (Scott 2000). Besides the cultural importance of universal value of survival, the present political salience of risk comes from the attribution of dangers to producers and guarantors of the social order and the suspicion that producers and guarantors may well be identical actors. Also, the nature of risk is said to have changed (e.g. Franklin 1998b); there is a distinction between 'old' risks and 'new' risks. Risks, i.e. the 'new' risks, are man-made hybrids (Beck 1998), the clear distinction between nature and culture is lost. Risks are produced as consequence of scientific and political efforts to control or minimise them, they are manufactured uncertainties, inescapable, unknown and barely calculable

---

[188] An alternative hypothesis, proposing that changes in terminology can explain the increasing number, is not supported convincingly; as comparisons of the developments in the number of terms as risk, hazard, danger, and uncertainty have shown (Skolbekken 1995).

(Beck 1998). The manufactured uncertainties express both control and lack of control; the attempts to control risk turn into a broadening of uncertainties and dangers. Also, manufactured uncertainties exhibit a synthesis of both knowledge and unawareness. That is, more and better knowledge is becoming the source of new risks, yet risks consist of unawareness, i.e. non-knowledge or potential knowledge. This refers to a risk trap (Beck 2000). Deciding in a context of uncertainty features a threatening sphere of possibilities and risks only suggest what should not be done, not what should be done. Again, the mathematicised morality comes to the surface, the cultural definitions and standards of a tolerable or intolerable life. Woollacott (1998) notes that the world might be more safe than in previous times, but nuclear breakdowns and global warming and other (possible) disasters that we ourselves have manufactured are different from the risks in the past, moreover we have higher expectations of control and are far more responsible for the dangers we face than in the past. The central insight of the risk society is that industrial societies both manufacture and must control risk, which is a major concern of the government. In this process of risk management, the public punishes overcaution as well as a lack of caution; that is, public opinion is veering between greed and fear (Woollacott 1998).

Similarly, Parish (2001) states that "conspiracy theorising", conspiracies have caught the public imagination more than ever. In line with Beck's (2000) accounts, she asserts that expert knowledge is uncertain, leading to an erosion of trust in experts and invisible victims appear everywhere. The insecurity of the global economy accompanies an increased uncertainty in every day life. The traditional conspiracy has the function to provide neat explanations, it is a type of meta-narrative. Conspiracy theorising is a way of assembling possibilities and information, rather than recovering a truth. Truth is not hidden, waiting to be discovered; truth is a matter of interpretation instead of discovery and conspiracies fill the gap because real explanations are lacking (Parish 2001; Parker 2001). Conspiracy theories provide a sense of agency, which is the more desired in an "age of anxiety" and in a culture that wants to or even must explain everything (Parker 2001).

Furedi's (1997) critique regarding Beck's ideas concerns the narrow focus on dangers that are posed by technology and science, anxieties about risks today are not so much reactions towards a particular incident or technology, neither do they reflect real scale and intensity of the danger. Rather, the reaction to dangers and events has varied according to the mood that prevailed in society at that time; technology is of importance as for the nature of the threat and how the risks or dangers can be dealt with. A narrow interpretation fails to consider the changing perception of dangers. (Furedi 1997). Just like Beck, he observes a change, an increase; only not a change in risks, but rather in risk consciousness.

7.2.2.2 More risk consciousness

Furedi (1997) notes a contemporary "worship of safety" and the fear of taking risks. Risk consciousness has led to an explosion of risks, illustrated by for example the precautionary principle, that is institutionalising caution. Risk seems to refer to the probability of damage, illness, injury, death, or other misfortune associated with a hazard and a hazard is a threat to people and what they value. Risk equals danger and the intrinsic riskiness of virtually every type of human activity is highlighted. Being at risk is not about what you do, but about who you are, similar to Ericson and Haggerty (1997) when they write about "making up people". Further, it seems that everything is dangerous, doomsday scenarios prevail and the scale of threat is heavily exaggerated, e.g. a ruling culture of abuse and a whole world of risky strangers. The entire political spectrum share a common consciousness of risk and a consensus that we live in an increasingly dangerous world. All this has led Furedi to conclude that an explosion of risks has arisen and panic is created as a legitimate way of educating people, e.g. law & order campaigns: "unhappily, the use of fear has become a widely accepted device for the promotion of a variety of good causes." (Furedi 1997: 25). He argues that the constant amplification of danger in virtually every sphere of social life must be symptomatic of some underlying problem. Thus, since a consensus exists on (an increase of) risk consciousness, the question he examines is where this consensus comes from and attempts to explain why concerns about risks are salient and the explosion of risks so apparent. The media might amplify or attenuate risk consciousness, but they do not cause society's sense of risk. By emphasising the unnatural and technological foundation for risk concern, like Beck and others do, the social influences of such perceptions are continually underestimated (Furedi 1997).

Furedi continues and says that risks do not transcend society, hazards affect people in relation to their power and influence and risks are situated in their social and historical specificity. Whether or not the perception of risk is real or not does not concern him, what matters is why something is considered to be a problem. Society selects its own problems, the process of problematisation is very important, which is a rather similar point that has been made by Douglas (1986; Douglas & Wildavsky 1983). According to Furedi, this process of problematisation has no direct relationship to the experiences it refers to, i.e. activities that are labelled "sexual harassment" have been present throughout history, yet have only been identified as problem in recent history. Thus, the historical and social context are extremely relevant for an increase in risk consciousness. The main reason for contemporary consensus regarding risks and the salience of risks is that today's insecurity, which on itself is of all times, has created an intense consciousness of risk because of the changing relationship between society and the individual. Issues involved that Furedi points out are fragmentation, reinforced by a lack of consensus about what society's values should be and regarding elementary norms, individuation, changes in labour market, weakening of social institutions. Moreover, the emphasis on issues of health, crime and personal security shapes a peculiarly individuated concern with survival. Individuation engenders isolation, which in turn enhances feelings of vulnerability and of insecurity. Social roles are continually subject to modification, what is right and wrong is unclear, and then people are entitled to feel unsure about the future. According to Furedi (1997), the most important consequence of these social processes is a diminished sense of control or an erosion of trust:

> what was once routine, is now troublesome, confusion about appropriate forms of behavior has always existed, but nowadays such confusions are expressed through a highly charged moral climate of risks........The insecurity inherent in an existence where little can be taken for granted is evident. However, such insecurity does not automatically transform itself into a consciousness of risk. That transformation has been mediated through the experience of disenchantment with humanity. The coincidence of the process of individuation with a mood of social pessimism helps to produce a sense of cynicism regarding the merit of social engagement. This lack of belief in the problem-solving ability of human beings helps to heighten the sense of vulnerability. It is this convergence of insecurity with the sense that we have run out of answers that makes society feel that it is entitled to panic. (p. 69-70).

Douglas and Wildavsky (1983) state that there is not so much an increase in 'real' risks but rather in perceived risks, since powerful actors have claimed that real dangers have been increased. Their argument is not on the reality of dangers, which "are only too horrible real, in both cases, modern and premodern" (Douglas 1993: 8), but on how dangers and risks are politicised.[189] Though for example Giddens (1990: 16, 43) claims that modernity is characterised by an unprecedented acceptance of permanence of risk, attitudes towards risk in modernity might be distinguished from past attitudes "more by its strategies of containment than by a new acceptance of the inevitability of risk" (Freedgood 2000: 2), similar to Garland (2003). However, the increasing public awareness of the 'true' extent and limitations of scientific ignorance and uncertainty as part of a 'postmodern' condition does not conflict with Beck's risk society (Durant 1998).

7.2.2.2.1 Demanding safety and the lack of trust

The public wants a safe society, which does not seem a recent demand in social history. Headlines in the newspaper claim that crime is increasing, and other dangers are present as well. Contemporary society is said to be driven by institutional demands for knowledge of risk (Ericson & Haggerty 1997). Garland (2000, 2001) suggests that crime rates, rising since the 1960s, together with insecurities and 'cultural sensibilities' which accompany social changes as well as economical recession, have caused more concern about crime, a call for 'law & order' and a repressive political reaction. According to Garland (2001):

> people increasingly demand to know about the risks to which they are exposed by the criminal justice system and are increasingly impatient

---

[189] This politicisation of dangers is in effect different from group to group, the four main groups that Douglas & Wildavsky (1983; Douglas 1992) contrast with one another, i.e. egalitarians, individualists, hierarchists, and fatalists, are supposedly different in choosing what to fear and what kind of risk taking is favoured (Dake & Wildavsky 1993).

when that system fails to control 'dangerous' individuals who are within
its reach. (p. 155).

Garland's notions on the 'culture of control' seems to be applicable to the
Netherlands as well. Polls, newspaper articles and political debates show Dutch
citizens and politicians appearing to be in favour of CCTV and registering DNA
as well as sexual offenders (Elffers 2000; Vanderveen 2001). The attacks in the
USA on September 11th 2001 as well as the murder on the popular politician
Pim Fortuyn one week before the elections in 2002 greatly contributed to the
idea that the world is not a safe place anymore; it is not as safe as it used to be.
The 'culture of control' seems to be extensively present in our (industrial) 'risk
society'. Also, by acknowledging that society lacks solutions, a culture of
uncertainty is consolidated (Furedi 1997). Others have also challenged the 'risk
society' in the sense of being exposed to more, or more serious dangers (Garland
2003). Garland hints at his 'culture of control' when he suggests that if
contemporary society is indeed a risk society, "it is because we have come to be
more conscious of the risks that we run and more intensely engaged in attempts
to identify, measure and manage them." (Garland 2003: 22).

Many assertions that touch on a 'risk society', an increasing risk
consciousness and a decrease in risk tolerance point out again that trust or
credibility is a key concept. The only way to face a risky future, is a high-trust
democracy (Coote 1998: 131). In a risk society, the experts' infallibility is no
longer trusted; experts and politicians provide conflicting information, and they
can no longer trust to keep the people informed (Franklin 1998b). The issue of
trust is highlighted in Freudenburg's (1993) concept of recreancy, which refers
to the loss of faith in institutions or the failure of institutional actors to carry out
their responsibilities as socially expected, yet fail "to fulfil the obligations or
merit the trust" (Freudenburg 1993: 917). These institutions, or individual
actors, are failing in socially expected obligations (see Clarke & Short 1993).
Trust is also a frequent issue in the (empirical) literature on the perception of
environment or technological risks (e.g. Slovic, Layman & Flynn 1991). In that
respect, trust is related to the regulator's abilities to protect and to attributions of
responsibility and blame. Consequently, risks are a powerful symbol in politics,
policy and communication thereof (Margolis 1996). For instance, Irwin, Allan
and Welsh (2000) pinpointed several discursive strategies that have been utilised
in newspaper articles, which helped to normalise the "perilous uncertainties of
nuclear risk". Some examples of these interrelated discursive strategies concern
the use of credible, *trustworthy* sources, i.e. sources that are restricted to official
sources accredited with expert status.

In general, the major aim of many 'risk communication systems' is to
enhance the institutional credibility (e.g. Johnson & Slovic 1995). These risk
communication systems are the primary focus of Ericson and Haggerty (1997)
when they discuss policing in a 'risk society' in which knowledge of risk, which
refers to external danger, is used to control this danger. They argue that *policing*
is best understood in terms of a model of risk communication and the system for
communicating risk, its rules, formats and technologies, is part of the social

mechanisms of these systems create profiles of human populations and their risks to ascertain what is and is not probable for those populations: "Collective fear and foreboding underpin the value system of an unsafe society, perpetuate insecurity, and feed incessant demands for more knowledge of risk." (Ericson & Haggerty 1997: 6).

7.2.2.3   Issues of safety and ever-present danger

Those who advocate or apply ideas of the *risk society* say risk consciousness reflects real risks, the nature of risk has changed (e.g. Adam & Van Loon 2000; Franklin 1998b), implying that dangers in contemporary society are almost entirely different from the dangers, hazards and risks in earlier societies.[190] Risks nowadays are characterised as risks that are not apolitical *anymore*, have *become* inescapable and incalculable, within the context of a *loss* of the clear distinction between nature and culture (Beck 1998). The class society, dreaming of a world without scarcity, has turned into a risk society, with utopian projects aiming at the elimination of risk (Scott 2000). Clearly, we would not deny here that to some extent society has changed or that *other* risks have left or appeared on the stage, which is reflected in for example the study of (the perceptions of) hazards as a set of related phenomena (Drottz-Sjöberg 1991; Johnson & Covello 1987; Renn & Rohrmann 2000; Sjöberg 1987; Warner 1981). Often, these (perceived) risks or possible new hazards originate from the historical development of technological innovation, the so-called 'manufactured risks' (Giddens 1998), or new consumer products (Sapolsky 1986, 1993). Certainly, the ILOVEYOU-virus may be defined as an "invisible risk" and "hidden threat" (Knight 2001), that was not existing before computers were.

Yet, when taking a helicopter view, it becomes evident that violence and danger as well as perceptions and attitudes of safety are from all times; "when identities shift and boundaries fail, danger and safety begin to appear in all the wrong places" (Freedgood 2000: 9). The debate and discourse on misfortunes, threats, risks, accidents, disasters and dangers is everlasting (see Green 1997; Figure 7.3). Also, every time in history has its own dangers and anxieties, although these anxieties appear to show a remarkable stability (Pearson 1983). Moreover, in conformance with Pearson (1983), it seems that on every point in time, people have said that it's (becoming) more violent, unsafe and dangerous *nowadays* than it used to be. People have always referred back to some earlier era in which violence, danger and crime was not common at all,

---

[190] For example, risks in the risk society are portrayed as being invisible and unknown, like BSE, HIV, and nuclear radiation. Yet, risks we *now* apparently perceive as 'visible', 'calculable' and more or less 'known', like contagious diseases were at the time a major source of concern or even terror, not only for the population, but for governmental institutions as well. Examples directly relating to public health are the "the Black Death" in the 14th century in Europe and the "Great Plague" in London, 1644-5, both examples of bubonic plague; the Cholera outbreaks in 19th century Britain, or the flu epidemic in the USA after WWI. Other 'invisible' threatening dangers, or perceived as such in history, with far-reaching (personal as well as societal) consequences were communism (viz. the Red Scare, McCarthyism). Most of these risks and dangers were considered to be 'invisible' and 'unknown' yet disastrous at that time.

which is illustrated by the typical article in Figure 7.4. Pearson demonstrates that every time period, at least in Britain, has similar fears and scenes of disorder, the stability of the complaints and accusations is remarkable and centre on social alterations, nostalgia and an emphasis on boys, like 'hooligans' and 'artful dodgers'.[191] Fears and the "vocabularies of reaction" are constant (Pearson 1983: 128). But where can this stable time, with hardly any violence, with a sense of solidarity, a feeling of security, be historically located? Or put more simply: when was this? Has there ever been a time in which for example women were actually free to walk the streets at night without the possibility of sexual violence, harassment or molestation?[192]

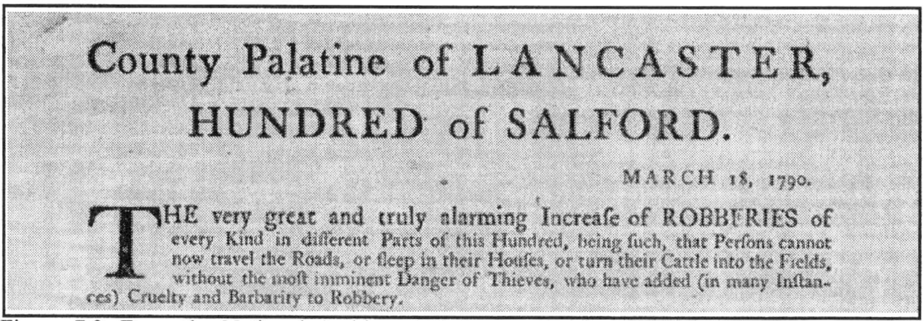

County Palatine of LANCASTER,
HUNDRED of SALFORD.

MARCH 18, 1790.

THE very great and truly alarming Increafe of ROBBERIES of every Kind in different Parts of this Hundred, being fuch, that Perfons cannot now travel the Roads, or fleep in their Houfes, or turn their Cattle into the Fields, without the moft imminent Danger of Thieves, who have added (in many Inftances) Cruelty and Barbarity to Robbery.

Figure 7.3. From the National Archives UK (source number DL41/1163), shows a notice calling a meeting in Salford (1790) to deal with the "increase of robberies". During the meeting, it was agreed to raise money in order to set up a system of local police.

Pearson explores history and demonstrates it cannot have been in the 1950s, when a delegate at the 78th annual conference of the Tory Party says: "our wives and mothers, if they are left alone in the house at night, are frightened to open their doors" (Pearson 1983: 13). Neither does the history of the 1920s and 1930s justify the "cosy nostalgia that is now cloaked around the pre-war years." Pearson (1983) mainly concludes:

> Nevertheless, what is most notable is the remarkable stability of the complaints and accusations that were arranged around the criminal question, providing firm lines of continuity between pre-war and post-war Britain. Then, as now, fears of national decline and cultural adulteration were much in evidence, and it was a cause for great concern that the nation's youth were slipping away from the standards of their forebears. (p. 48).

Earlier in British history, similar to historical processes in for example the Netherlands, USA and Germany, from 1890s till WWI, several social changes and circumstances, such as the Boer war, the industrial advance, the

---

[191] See also McGrath (1984) who describes youngsters in mining town Bodie (USA) in the early 1880s who engendered concern about their delinquent activities; they were hanging on the streets, smoking and gambling, using obscene language or exhibited bad habits. They committed some petty thefts and burglaries indeed, but hardly any violent crimes. Their delinquent activities consisted almost entirely of "youthful pranks and malicious mischief" (McGrath 1984: 164).

[192] As is suggested by rallies or marches with the slogan "reclaim the night" or "take back the night".

movement for women's emancipation, music halls, early moving-pictures, changing relations between working class and middle class were "sending ripples of anxiety through British society..."(Pearson 1983: 61). The bicycle craze of the 1890s led to excitement, sensationalised and ridiculised in the newspapers that also reported on deaths, injuries and 'hit-and-run' cyclists; "cycling was at the center of a number of social panics. It was feared that the push-bike was a health hazard..." (Pearson 1983: 66). Pearson explores history even further, describing concerns about racial degeneration, hooliganism and becoming a victim of garotting. He cannot find the golden ages, the time when people were safe and felt at ease. Instead, he exhibits "a seamless tapestry of fears and complaints about the present" while reference is made to the past as a haven of tranquility. For example, the Times of 7 November 1862 notes: "Our streets are actually not as safe as they were in the days of our grandfathers. We have slipped back to a state of affairs which would be intolerable even in Naples."

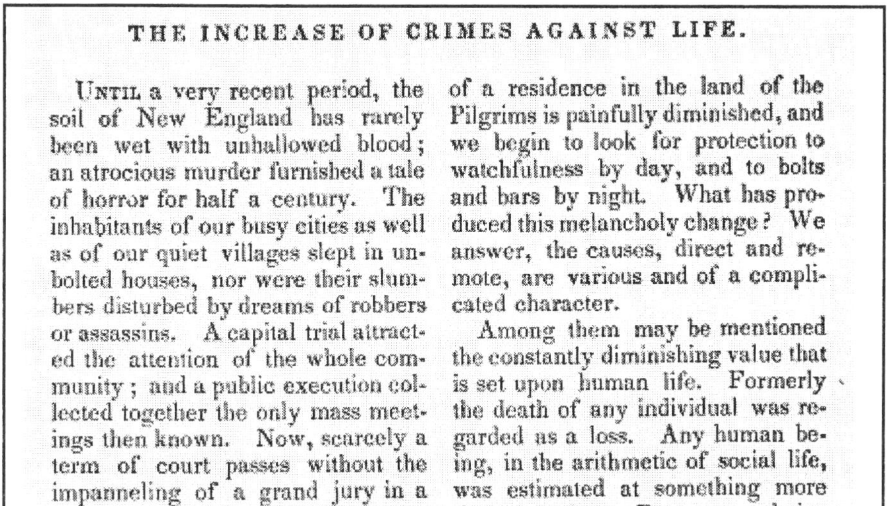

THE INCREASE OF CRIMES AGAINST LIFE.

UNTIL a very recent period, the soil of New England has rarely been wet with unhallowed blood; an atrocious murder furnished a tale of horror for half a century. The inhabitants of our busy cities as well as of our quiet villages slept in unbolted houses, nor were their slumbers disturbed by dreams of robbers or assassins. A capital trial attracted the attention of the whole community; and a public execution collected together the only mass meetings then known. Now, scarcely a term of court passes without the impanneling of a grand jury in a case of life and death. The youngest judge on the bench in Connecticut has already tried three cases of murder. That feeling of security which constituted one great charm of a residence in the land of the Pilgrims is painfully diminished, and we begin to look for protection to watchfulness by day, and to bolts and bars by night. What has produced this melancholy change? We answer, the causes, direct and remote, are various and of a complicated character.

Among them may be mentioned the constantly diminishing value that is set upon human life. Formerly the death of any individual was regarded as a loss. Any human being, in the arithmetic of social life, was estimated at something more than a cypher. But as population increases, individuality is lost. It is scarcely in the power of the warmest benevolence to shed a tear at the death of one of the myriads

Figure 7.4. Beginning of the article 'The Increase of Crimes against Life', in the New Englander and Yale review, Volume 2, Issue 7, 346-350, July 1844.

According to Pearson, "The safety of the night is not a 'thing of the past': it is a prospect for the future" (Pearson 1983: 235). Social alterations have always been accompanied by fears of the New, the Different, the Young and the Deviant. This does not mean that present-day fears, violence, crime or the call for 'law & order' are denied or not real, but rather that they are not novel. In other words, the fears and dangers of the past were *at that time* as real as *present* fears are in contemporary social reality and functioning as strong social and political forces. Also, it is very likely that dangers and fears will always play a role in society, as will social deviance (cf. Box 1975).

Modern, current or contemporary society does not have the exclusive right to dangers, nor to attitudes towards dangers, whether they are referred to as risks or risk perceptions or not. Naming something a 'risk' or a 'danger' and coping with it are not social activities characterising solely the 'present'. Cosmological projects of engaging in, representing and theorising risk, have always been aimed at increasing safety and reducing danger (Freedgood 2000). Attitudes towards risk in modernity might be distinguished from past attitudes "more by its strategies of containment than by a new acceptance of the inevitability of risk" (Freedgood 2000: 2). For instance, mid-Victorian anticontagionist theories of disease transmission already attempted to eliminate the possibility that things might go wrong, and provided strategies that promise to predict and locate risk, and thereby eradicate it. Freedgood demonstrates how 'dangers' or 'risks' were dealt with; namely by the construction of a safe England in a dangerous world, by defining and precisely locating risk, e.g. in the home, in Africa, in the Alps, and then by eradicating it, e.g. by means of statistics (notion of count-and-control), cleanliness and geographical maps (see also Bankoff 2001). Risks could then be avoided altogether, or engaged voluntarily. Risks were resolved geographically or voluntarily confronted, which made it possible to re-describe an engagement with danger or risk as a special kind of pleasure, as in the case of ballooning (Freedgood 2000).

In sum, there does not seem to be a contrast between the 'premodern' need for a universe that is inherently orderly and the 'modern' acceptance of danger and contingency as irremovable facets of an uncertain world after all. Violence and dangers as well as (accompanying) perceptions, feelings and attitudes on danger and safety are from all times. There is no time in history that can be said to be completely safe for all, neither is there a time in history, which was, at that time, perceived as completely safe. Furthermore, all eras have their discourses on threats and dangers, and ways of expressing anxieties. Part of the current discourse, that is to say the scientific discourse on risk, contains the ideas and findings of the academic enquiry and empirical studies on the perception of risks and hazards. This branch of research will be discussed in the next section.

7.3   Perceiving hazards

The qualitative features of the concept 'risk' concern attitudes, values, perceptions and so on of the hazard *itself* and the possible or imaginable *consequences* of what might happen. Research on these qualitative features within the field of risk perception is of relevance in the present discussion of the concept 'fear of crime'. Many studies in that particular field are interested in the perception of hazards, of sources of danger, though this has been referred to as "risk perception". Since crime might be considered to be just another one of those hazards, the findings from studies on the perception of hazards might be applicable here (see also Taylor & Shumaker 1990).

7.3.1   Crime as a hazard

The research topic that has been called 'fear of crime' in the criminological field can be considered to be a small part of the research topic that is named "risk perception" in the field of disaster, accident, error and risk analysis; the similarities manifest themselves clearly. Exemplary are for instance the two recurring themes that were discussed previously, on the reality and (ir)rationality of perceptions and fear and on discontinuity, contrasting the risks and dangers in the past and present. Moreover, research on 'fear of crime' and on 'risk perception', as well as research on disasters share conceptual and methodological confusion. Not only the conceptual labels of 'fear of crime' and 'risk perception' and 'disasters' themselves can be criticised, the operationalisations of the concepts are rather confusing. For instance, rather similar to the term held equal within the 'fear of crime' field, 'risk perception' is often held the same as "reaction to risk" or "concern with risk" (e.g. Elliott et al. 1999; Grobe, Douthitt & Zepeda 1999a; Petts, Horlick-Jones & Murdock 2001; Pilisuk, Parks & Hawkes 1987). Also, disputes about the approach that should be taken emerge in both fields; a qualitative, theoretical and constructionist approach is often contrasted with a quantitative and empirical approach instead of offering a pragmatic and integrative approach.

Besides these similarities between the topics 'fear of crime' in criminological studies and 'risk perception' in the field of accident, error and risk analysis, another indication that findings from the latter field could be applied to crime or social threats and dangers as well, is that crime or specific offences are sometimes used as one of the hazards in studies on the perception of hazards or risks. Crime, then, is just another hazard. For example, Douglas and Wildavsky (1983), who claim that contemporary society exhibits only an increase in *perceived* risks, partly because people have claimed that there is an increase in real *dangers*, distinguish between three generic areas of risks, primarily based on the nature of the source of the risk, namely socio-political risks, economic risks and natural risks. Crime belongs to the socio-political risks and has been connected with a hierarchical-institutional culture (Lash 2000; Slovic 1999; Tansey 2004a). Empirical studies have also considered crime along with other hazards, Weinstein (1989) for example reviews the influence of personal experience on self-protective behaviour. He focuses for example on the effects of car accidents on seat belt use, myocardial infarction on smoking behaviour, as well as on the effects of criminal victimisation on crime prevention. Slovic, Fischhoff and Lichtenstein (1980) asked their respondents to estimate the frequency of causes of death, among which murder along with for example car accidents and stroke. In a study on perceptions of environmental risk in three communities of El Paso, Texas (USA), crime emerged as a salient hazard (Byrd & VanDerslice 1996). Crime was one of the twenty hazards that were mentioned and to which respondents could answer how high the risk for oneself and one's family was, or for the community. Crime is the hazard that was most often considered a 'high risk' for oneself and one's family and for the whole community, followed by for example the destruction of the ozone layer, illegal dumping of hazardous waste and drugs. In this study, crime is considered to be one of the many (environmental) hazards, similar to Taylor & Shumaker (1990) who discuss the similarities between local crime rates and natural hazards. Likewise, a specific criminal offence, namely mugging, was included in a list of 13 'risk issues', such as sunbathing, nuclear power, terrorism and alcoholic drinks, that respondents rated on their 'riskiness' with respect to risk attributes like involuntary exposure, severity and unfairness (Langford et al. 1999; Marris, O'Riordan & Langford 1996).

Moreover, crime and several other (natural) hazards have been regarded as particular characteristics of a neighbourhood or area, which have an effect on health. The incidence of diseases and particular causes of death may reflect environmental conditions as well as the behavioural patterns and other personal characteristics of the local population. Epidemiological studies have investigated many environmental features and their relationship with health, features that are not limited to physical variables of the environment, like air pollution, but social variables are studied as well. For example, Sooman & Macintyre (1995) investigated the relationship between several features of different neighbourhoods, among which 'fear of crime' and 'incivilities' and self-reported health. 'Fear of crime' has also been used as *explanation* in area differences in health (Ellaway & Macintyre 1998; Jones & Duncan 1995). Chandola (2001) for example found that the association between 'fear of crime' and self-reported health remained, even after adjusting for health-related behavioural characteristics and several socio-economic variables. Aneshensel & Sucoff (1996) examined the relationship between threatening conditions in a neighbourhood and mental health. The presence of these threatening conditions is indicated by the perception of what they call "ambient hazards", like crime, violence, drug use, and graffiti, named *incivilities* in the 'fear of crime' literature. Adolescents in neighbourhoods with a low socio-economic status perceive more of these ambient hazards than do adolescents in neighbourhoods with high socio-economic status. Moreover, when the neighbourhood is perceived as threatening, i.e. more hazards are perceived, symptoms of depression, anxiety, oppositional defiant disorder, and conduct disorder are more common (Aneshensel & Sucoff 1996).

Others have pointed to the shared common causes or social origins of crime and ill health, like poverty. Like Kawachi, Kennedy and Wilkinson (1999) who state that crime is a social mirror, a mirror of the quality of the social environment. Accordingly, they use crime as an indicator of wellbeing in a model that represents the influence of the social environment on public health, since the level of crime in their model is influenced by the degree of relative deprivation, i.e. income inequality, in a community and of social cohesiveness or social capital, which is related to fear of crime. Their findings show that crime rates of homicide, assault, robbery and burglary were consistently related to relative deprivation and low social capital, and that areas with high crime rates have higher overall mortality rates. They conclude that the same social environmental factors that are related to area differences in crime are related to area differences in health as well (Kawachi, Kennedy & Wilkinson 1999). In other words, studies being primarily concerned with public health, have regarded crime as well as 'fear of crime' as an environmental feature affecting health and thus as a public health issue, similar to other hazards.

In sum, research on 'fear of crime' and 'risk perception' clearly show resemblance. The research on 'risk perception' in the field of accident, error and risk analysis sometimes includes crime or specific offences as one of the hazards. When crime is viewed as just another hazard, findings from studies on 'risk perception' are of interest here. Therefore, this part will focus on some general results from these studies, which is useful in the understanding of the concept 'fear of crime'. First, attributes or characteristics of the risk, or rather of the hazard, will be briefly described, which are all related to the amount of concern and 'outrage' it invokes. Many of these characteristics pop up again, though in a slightly different manner, when discussing some major findings that can be found in research on perceiving hazards. Similar to victimisation, the matter of cause, the attribution of responsibility and blame is of great importance, as is the type of consequence and the characteristics of the victim(s). As noted previously, the perception of risk and the whole notion of risk is intertwined with the presence (or imagined presence) of other human agents whom may be considered responsible for dangers; risk perception and blame are inseparable (Alexander 2002; Bernstein 1998; Douglas & Wildavsky 1983). Risk is not a matter of a pre-determined path to the future or a matter of fate; choices can be made and who is to blame for the consequences of these choices is the question (Lash 2000). In empirical studies, blame has been connected with risks that are human based, voluntarily taken, controllable and predictable, which will be elaborated on below. Other findings from research on 'risk perception' that are of interest for our current purposes demonstrate for example unrealistic optimism or the optimistic bias as a relatively stable trait of a person. These relevant studies will be discussed in the next section.

7.3.2   Typical features of dreaded hazards

A hazard refers to a situation or activity involving events whose consequences are undesirable to some unknown degree and whose future occurrence is uncertain (Lee 1981), like (criminal) victimisation. In other words, a hazard is a source of danger, and incorporates the potential for adverse consequences, i.e. harm or damage (Warner 1992). Thus, neither hazard nor danger is the same as risk (Luhmann 1993: 21-28); *formally* defined risk holds the (statistical) probability that a particular adverse event occurs during a stated period of time, or that results from a particular challenge and preferably refers to an exposure to hazard specified in terms of amount or intensity, time of starting or duration (Warner 1992). Yet, perceived risks, dangers or hazards show something that has been called *probability neglect* (Sunstein 2003). Probability neglect expresses the focus on the hazard, the bad outcome itself, while being inattentive to the (un)likelihood that the bad outcome will occur. In other words, the intensity of affective reactions, the strength of emotions, towards a danger or hazard does not greatly vary even with large differences in the likelihood of harm (Sunstein 2003). This is shown by several studies employing a so-called *psychometric paradigm* as well.

Table 7.1. Relevant risk and hazard characteristics affecting outrage or concern. Adapted from: Covello, Sandman and Slovic (1988: 54), frequently cited, for example in Margolis (1996: 28).

Characteristics	Outrage / concern >	Outrage / concern <
Hazard		
Catastrophic potential	Fatalities and injuries grouped in time and space	Fatalities and injuries random
Origin	Human based (on purpose)	Nature based (by accident)
Familiarity	Unfamiliar	Familiar
Predictability		
Uncertainty	Risks uncertain	Risks certain
Controllability	Uncontrollable (inescapable)	Controllable
Victim & behaviour		
Voluntariness of exposure	Involuntary	Voluntary
Children	Children at specific risk	Children not at specific risk
Victim identity	Identifiable victims	Statistical or anonymously abstract
Consequences		
Dread effects	Dreaded	Not dreaded
Reversibility	Irreversible	Reversible
Context		
Trust in responsible institutions	Lack of trust	Trust
Media attention	Much attention	Little attention

The work of Fischhoff, Slovic and others on perceived risk is often referred to as the psychometric paradigm and has been very influential (e.g. Fischhoff et al. 1978; Grobe, Douthitt & Zepeda 1999; Jasanoff 1998; Langford et al. 1999; Sjöberg 2002a). The studies have produced 'cognitive maps' of hazards and identified factors or *risk attributes* that explain the perception of these different hazards. The basic research method in these studies on the assessment of risk perception or rather hazard perception is a questionnaire that presents a list of (possible) hazards to a sample of respondents (Lee 1981). Thereafter, the respondents are asked to scale the hazards in order and magnitude of severity, or are asked to evaluate each hazard on a set of characteristics that are offered. Usually factor analyses or multidimensional scaling procedures are applied, leading to a number of dimensions that have been frequently replicated, which are of particular interest here. Typically, the hazards are related to industry or technology, like 'asbestos', 'pesticides' and 'nuclear power' or are more environmental in nature, like 'flood' and 'tornado' (Fischhoff et al. 1978; Royal Society 1992; Slovic 2000; Slovic, Fischhoff &

Lichtenstein 1979, 1981).[193] Like Sunstein's (2003) notion of *probability neglect*, Slovic, Lichtenstein and Fischhoff (1984) demonstrate that any model of societal impact, i.e. public distress and social and political turmoil, of fatal accidents that is based on a function of N fatalities is inadequate. Instead, the societal impact is mostly related by what it signifies and portends, since the accident is a warning signal for society of future trouble. Accidents, hazards and risks have signal value, which is related to catastrophic potential, uncertainty or what is called dread, fright values or outrage factors (Slovic 1987).[194]

So, perceptions of risk are based on much more than just the probability of occurrence and the outcome of an event. Several aspects are shown to influence risk perceptions, the attitudes and judgments about hazards or the signal value, which is one of the characterisation of risk. Researchers, who studied perceived risk concerning for example nuclear power and consumer products, have identified a distinct set of risk characteristics that are related to risk perceptions and reactions to the source of the risk (see Chilton et al. 2002; Covello, Sandman & Slovic 1988). For example, the familiarity with the hazard and the catastrophe size, i.e. the seriousness of the hazard derived from the potential size of a single catastrophe, affect the public's perception. Whether the risk is voluntary or involuntary, and subject to one's own control and is escapable, is important as well and may be especially of influence on attribution processes and the perceived locus of control and blame. Many of these characteristics are described as 'fright', 'outrage', or 'dread' factors, which have been identified in several empirical studies (e.g. Byrd & VanDerslice 1996; Lupton & Tulloch 2002; Sandman 1994; Sjöberg 2002a; Slovic 1992). These characteristics in particular are related to or supposed to influence public concern, worry and perceptions of risks, dangers and hazards and influence the acceptability of the hazard. Fright, outrage and dread factors are mostly applied when touching on for example concern, alarm, anxiety, anger, resentment and fear (e.g. Grobe, Douthitt, Zepeda 1999; Sunstein 1997). In other words, risks that are perceived as involuntary, industrial, unfair, memorable, and dreaded evoke more concern and more extreme reactions that risks that are voluntary, natural, fair, familiar, not memorable, and not dreaded. Though the characteristics, of which the most relevant ones for present purposes are listed in Table 7.1, seem to be categorical at first sight, they are more a matter of degree and not an all-or-nothing matter (Sunstein 1997).

---

[193] Similar to sociological theories of risk, like the work of Douglas (e.g. 1986, 1992) and Beck (e.g. 1992, 1998, 2000).

[194] Much more can be said about the psychometric model and other models within this line of research, see for example the review of Boholm (1998) of cross-national risk perception studies, Renn's review (1998) of risk research in general and the article of Wåhlberg (2001) concerning the three main models in empirical risk perception research. Furthermore, criticism of Sjöberg on the psychometric model (1999, 2000a, 2000b, 2002b) deserves more attention than is possible here. The empirical tests of cultural theory as developed by Douglas & Wildavsky (1983) is beyond the scope of this book and current purposes, but see for example Brenot, Bonnefous & Marris (1998), Marris, Langford & O'Riordan (1998), Sjöberg (1998a, 2003) and Tansey (2004a, 2004b).

7.3.3 Crime as (highly) dreaded hazard

Empirical studies on 'risk perception' have identified a set of somewhat interrelated characteristics, presented in Table 7.1, that are particularly related to or supposed to influence public concern, anxiety, worry and perceptions of risks and hazards. Also, crime is one of the most salient hazards in people's everyday lives, as is for example demonstrated by Byrd and VanDerslice (1996) and by Petts, Horlick-Jones and Murdock (2001). Consequently, when crime is considered a hazard similar to the hazards that are mostly concentrated on in 'risk perception' research, then the typical features of a much-dreaded hazard, the fright, dread or outrage factors, must be applicable to crime. Indeed, the dread characteristics or the so-called outrage factors seem to be operative as far as typical crime is considered. That is, these characteristics are mostly related to the typical popular images of crime and violence, which have been discussed in chapter 6, and comprise (random) violence in the public sphere, rape, and other violent acts that involve a personal confrontation between offender and victim. These are the most salient (criminal) victimisation experiences in the discussion of people's 'fear of crime', and are most frequently portrayed in the media as well. Interestingly, in the context of crime, the outrage characteristics are very much related to the stereotypical images of victim and offender, i.e. the particular role and event schema of the ideal victim and victimisation, and the accompanying attribution processes.

As for the hazard characteristics, i.e. catastrophic potential, origin and familiarity, obviously the fear of for example spiders or heights is of little relevance here, since our current primary interest is on behaviour that is human in origin.[195] Though both victim and hazard are human, frequently the hazard/offender/criminal is contrasted with the victim, as became clear in the discussion about stereotypical images of the offender and victim. The ideal offender is almost like a wild beast, he is "a human being close to not being one" (Christie 1986: 26). Yet, the origin of the hazard remains human; thinking about situations in which the victim is being attacked by a human or by a lion appeals to different notions, and evokes (partly) different attitudes and attributes regarding blame of both victim and attacker. What is meant by the labels 'human based' and 'nature based', also in the field of risk perception, is a matter of purpose and intent; the origin of the hazard being human means that, at least potentially, harm was done on purpose or intentionally. The origin of the hazard being based in what is viewed as nature means that nobody could do anything to prevent it from happening; it was an accident. In other words, the labels seem to represent Nature's impartiality and Man's inhumanity (cf. Alexander 2002). Obviously, there is a large grey area that comprises hazards that are thought of as being both human and nature based, to varying extent; accidents have in part become preventable misfortunes (Green 1997), which again makes a human responsible for the misfortune to happen (see Alexander 2002). This

---

[195] Yet, fear in general and of other objects might be of interest when discussing the individual differences in fear and the function of fear (see chapter 8).

characteristic is in that sense not a categorical all-or-nothing matter, but rather a matter of degree. Again, attributions of blame are related to human responsibility. The hazard feature that refers to familiarity resembles the discussion on schemas of ideal victims and victimisation (see chapter 6). The salient, popular image of the typical offender and victim is that the offender was unknown to the victim; the victim and offender do not have a relationship (see Table 6.2). In general, the more familiar victim and offender are, the less the victim is an 'ideal victim', and the less public outrage. This is in conformance with the schema about the ideal victim, which provides expectancies of appropriate behaviour, roles and matching attributions of responsibility.

The catastrophic potential of crime in general, when compared with other hazards, may be rather average. This characteristic is used in the risk perception literature to point towards the grouping of fatalities or injuries at a particular time and place and is therefore much related to the *identifiability* of victims. In other words, the hazard is not chronic and leading to a number of deaths over a particular *period* of time, but catastrophic, disastrous and directly leading to (numerous) deaths or irremediable injuries at the same time (Fischhoff et al. 1978).[196] Typical examples of catastrophes or disasters are explosions and fires, earthquakes, the sinking of a ship, plane crashes or a nuclear reactor meltdown, but war and bomb explosions are labelled disaster or catastrophe as well (Rundmo & Sjöberg 1996; Tansel 1995).[197] This means that the hazard characteristic of catastrophic potential merely indicates the bad outcome, the grouping of deaths or injuries, and does not refer to attributions of blame (Shaluf, Ahmadun & Mat Said 2003).[198] For instance, a terrorist attack or

---

[196] For example, Leger (1991: 180) studies mining accidents in South Africa and operationalises 'disaster' by defining it as six or more lives lost in one incident.

[197] Exemplary for a disaster is the event in which toxic gas leaked from a chemical plant in Bhopal (India, 1984). Concrete events in the Western world that are named disaster or catastrophe are for example the sinking of the Titanic in 1912, the Hindenburg zeppelin in 1937, the collision of the KLM and PanAm Boeing's (Tenerife 1977), the 'crowd catastrophe' in the Heysel Stadium (Belgium 1985), the explosion of the space shuttle Challenger (USA, 1986), the P&O ferry the Herald of Free Enterprise that left Zeebrugge to Dover but capsized and sank (Belgium, 1987), the bomb explosion of a PanAm airplane near Lockerbie (Scotland 1988), the crash of an ElAl Boeing in the Bijlmer block of flats (Netherlands, 1992), the sinking of the passenger ferry Estonia in 1994, the fire at a party in a discotheque in Gothenburg (Sweden, 1998), the fire and explosion in Enschede (Netherlands, 2000), the fire in a cafe in Volendam (Netherlands, 2001), the crash of a plane at an airshow (Ukrain, 2002) and the explosion of the space shuttle Columbia (USA, 2003). A concrete "manmade disaster" that has been extensively discussed in the risk perception and accident analysis literature is the nuclear disaster in Chernobyl (Soviet Union, 1986), see for example Drottz-Sjöberg and Sjöberg (1990) and Havenaar et al. (2003). Other natural catastrophes are investigated in this respect as well, like hurricanes (e.g. Riad, Norris & Ruback 1999), volcanic eruptions (e.g. Johnston et al. 1999) or landslides (e.g. DeChano & Butler 2001). Part of the so-called manmade disasters are also referred to as technological, socio-technical or industrial disasters, similar to 'industrial', 'technological' or 'manufactured' risk (Brittkov & Sergeev 1998; Giddens 1998; Shaluf, Ahmadun & Mat Said 2003; Woollacott 1998).

[198] Also, there is no universally accepted definition of disaster or catastrophe, the same events can be called 'incident', 'accident' or 'tragedy', dependent on who is using the term (Quarantelli 2001; Shaluf, Ahmadun & Mat Said 2003). Nonetheless, the (large) bad outcome is a central feature in all terms, and the disaster or catastrophe may be further refined as something that happens relatively sudden and disrupts a community (Quarantelli 2001).

war can be named a catastrophe or disaster (e.g. Jones 2002; Sunstein 2003). Moreover, when a disaster or catastrophe has happened, rumours or narratives referring to causes and blame are common (e.g. Jones 2002; Stallings 1994) and the temptation to moralise is hard to resist (Alexander 2002: 6).[199]

The catastrophic potential of the popular image of crime is typically sudden and dramatic and in that sense catastrophic. The number of victims that are identified is of influence on media coverage and probably on outrage (see chapter 6). Yet, the popular image of a crime with only one victim, like the imaginable victimisation of oneself, has some degree of catastrophic potential, since the consequences of these crimes (e.g. violent attack, murder, rape) are irremediable or perceived as such. On the other hand, the catastrophic potential is less applicable to crime as far as randomness is concerned. As noted before, the perceived randomness of violence seems to mirror the uncontrollability and unpredictability of becoming a victim and enhances the possibility of identification with the victim, which is something that induces public concern or outrage.

7.3.3.1   Predictability and cause: attribution of responsibility and blame

The uncertainty, uncontrollability and unpredictability of such incidents of random violence is exemplary for typical victimisation incidents and very much related to notions of deservedness, blame and responsibility as discussed in the chapter on victimisation. Table 6.2 presented the essential characteristics of the event schema of victimisation and identifies both randomness, i.e. unpredictable and unpreventable, and specific selection victim as features of such a schema. Also, the more predictable a victimisation incident is, the more it is seen as preventable and hence the less 'undeserved' or 'innocent' and the more 'deserving' or 'just' the victim is (see chapter 6). Blameworthiness of the victim is also related to three hazard characteristics that relate to the victim and his/her behaviour. When the exposure to the risk, here: of criminal victimisation, is involuntary, public outrage is higher than in the case of victimisation when the exposure had been voluntary. But again, voluntariness is a matter of degree and not an all-or-nothing matter and it seems that voluntariness has to do with the (extremely) high costs of avoidance of the risk altogether (Sunstein 1997). The less the victim is perceived to have contributed to the victimisation, like young children and in the case of totally involuntary exposure, the larger the public outrage. Again, public outrage is in accordance with attributions of blame to the victim: when the victim is seen as contributing to the incident, public outrage is lower. Recall the schema of the 'ideal victim' that presents the victim as weak, as doing something that is respectable, is somewhere where s/he can not possibly be blamed for being, i.e. the costs of avoiding the risk would be extremely high, and makes a reasonable effort to protect him/herself. This schema is consistent with the findings from the empirical risk perception

---

[199] Likewise, research attempts to reconstruct what happened and identify causes, sometimes referred to as "lesson-seeking" (e.g. Cassutto & Tarnow 2003) and resulting in for example compensation payments (Beach 1990).

literature on the outrage factors, yet differently framed. Moreover, the purpose for which the risk is incurred may seem to be "involuntarily" run when this purpose is respectable, adequate or laudable, whereas the risk is perceived as more voluntarily run when the purpose is not approved of or when the risk itself is a part of the benefit of the activity, as in the case of sky-diving, unsafe sex or dating (see Sunstein 1997). So (perceived) voluntariness is much related to questions of the purpose for which the risk is incurred, the costs of avoiding the risks and blameworthiness of the victim. A sequence of events and circumstances resulting in a victimisation of which the victim is perceived as at least partly responsible for, is also perceived as more predictable, having relatively low costs of avoiding or minimising the risk on victimisation and accordingly end up with a victim that is perceived to have taken the risk voluntarily. Instead, a victimisation with quite similar consequences, e.g. the death or rape of a person, and the blameworthiness of the victim is perceived much differently when the sequence of events and the circumstances are considered unpredictable and the victim took no chances at all. Again, this is similar to the schema of the 'ideal victim'. Moreover, gender is highly important in the interpretation of the events and circumstances or the purpose for which the risk is incurred; the blameworthiness of the victim and his/her behaviour is different for men and women (Chan & Rigakos 2002). Similar patterns were discerned in the review on the concept 'victimisation' (chapter 6).

7.3.3.1.1   *Responsibility of institutions: trustworthiness*

Not only victims can be blamed for their own victimisation, obviously institutions who are supposed to be responsible for the protection of people, like the police or the government, can be blamed too. In this way, empirical findings on risk perception have identified trust in responsible institutions as another important risk characteristic that influences public outrage or concern (Table 7.1). While outrage and blame go hand in hand, trustworthiness and blameworthiness almost seem to be communicating vessels; more trustworthy implies less blame, while lesser trustworthiness comes down to more blame, at least as far as individual victimisation incidents are concerned. Recall for instance the elaboration of the victimisation concept, that described the narratives or 'crime-victim stories' that Wachs (1988) collected. These stories refer to individual victimisation experiences, namely mugging, murder and rape, and the stories all stress *street smarts*. They highlight the importance of being on one's guard, trust one's intuition and being suspicious. The victims that were presented in the narratives had little change of defending themselves, yet, they are pictured as somebody who should have been suspicious, but was not, and paid the consequences for *trusting*. Again, trustworthiness (of the offender) and blameworthiness (of the victim) are communicating vessels; a victim who "should not have trusted" is more blameworthy.[200]

---

[200] Also, as has been pointed out in chapter 6, with rape incidents in which the victim had trusted the assailant, self-blame is more common as well.

The field of risk perception focuses on a different mechanism on a more institutional level, which concentrates on the perceived obligations of these institutions. Previously, Freudenburg's (1993) concept of recreancy was introduced, which refers to the loss of faith in institutions or the failure of institutional actors to carry out their responsibilities as socially expected, yet fail "to fulfil the obligations or merit the trust" (Freudenburg 1993: 917). Because of the increasing dependency and reliance on expert's judgments, the public will view science increasingly unable to explain and handle the threats that scientific and technological development creates. These institutions, or individual actors, are failing in socially expected obligations (see Clarke & Short 1993). Trustworthiness, together with responsibility, has been discussed in relation to politics, authoritative knowledge (see chapter 6; Donovan 2002; Franklin 1998b) and decision and policy making. The concept of trust is thought to provide the basic cement of contemporary society (McDonell 1997: 823) and facilitates "the only way to face a risky future" (Coote 1998: 131). Here, the loss of faith in individuals and institutions in whom (it is implied) we would have trusted in former times goes hand in hand with trustworthiness: trust is directly related to the regulator's abilities to protect and attributions of responsibility and blame. When the responsible individuals and (governmental) institutions refuse the perceived duty of care, public distrust is the consequence; the institutions cannot be counted on. Thus, trust seems to refer to matters of competence and confidence (Siegrist, Earle & Gutscher 2003). Moreover, the lack of trust in responsible institutions, and the fallibility of experts and public bodies, have been used as explanation both in the field of criminology and of risk perception (e.g. Adams, Rohe & Arcury 2005; Das & Teng 2004). Garland's (2000, 2001) culture of control for instance deals with the concern about crime, the call for 'law & order' and repressive political reactions. In his view, expectations are raised, while trust has decreased (Garland 2003). Also, the distrust people have in many of the individuals, industries, and institutions that are responsible for (environmental) risk management is linked to the idea that risks are unacceptably high (Slovic 1998, 1999). The authors who typify contemporary society as a no-risk society (Aharoni 1981), a culture of fear (Furedi 1997; Glassner 1999), a risk society (Ericson & Haggerty 1997) or a culture of control (Garland 2001) all illuminate the erosion of trust in experts, the lack of trust in the government's or police's abilities to protect, and the demands for protection, safety or compensation. Also, trust or confidence might be an important explanatory construct for societal concerns (Sjöberg 1998a).

In sum, outrage and blame go hand in hand when institutions are failing in their socially expected obligations; the trust of the public is betrayed. An institutional actor that betrays this trust, will be blamed for the unwanted consequences, for example in the case of a technological accident. Thus, institutional failure, a breach of trust, is directly linked with blame.

7.3.3.2   Identifiable victims

One of the characteristics that has been identified in empirical research on risk perception refers to the *identifiability* of the victims. Being one of the so-called outrage factors, identifiability evokes public concern or outrage. Again, this outrage factor or dread characteristic seems to be applicable to crime as well, insofar as is known from empirical research on typical crime and images in the media of victims thereof. The notion of *imaginable victimisation* was used to refer to the imaginable possibility to be the victim of a (specific) crime, which can for example be triggered when perceiving another (fictional or actual) victim. As research on the influence of information about victims shows, identifiability as well as possibilities of identification with the victim(s) varies according to characteristics of the contents and presentation of that information. Thus, information can provide more vivid details of the incident and the victim, like 'sensational crime' reports and dramatic narratives do. There is a clear "distinction between dramatic deaths and statistical ones" (Weiner 1986: 157) and in the risk perception literature, this has been called the 'identifiable victim effect'. The identifiable victim effect refers to the death (or victimisation) of a particular person that invokes far more reactions, i.e. outrage, than statistical victims and receives extraordinary attention as well (Small & Loewenstein 2003).

The so-called statistical victims, which are anonymously, abstract and have not yet been identified, and identifiable victims evoke very different reactions. The 'identifiable victim effect' holds that *specific* victims draw extraordinary attention (and resources), but it is often difficult to draw attention to (and raise money for) interventions that would help prevent people from becoming victims in the first place (Small & Loewenstein 2003). A specific victim, as Schelling noted in 1968 (cited in Small & Loewenstein 2003), a particular person invokes: "anxiety and sentiment, guilt and awe, responsibility and religion, [but]. . . most of this awesomeness disappears when we deal with statistical death." Identifiable victims are not only more vivid, they are *certain*, whereas statistical victims are probabilistic (Jenni & Loewenstein 1997). Besides that, since an event already has occurred, the interpretation or evaluation of the identified victim promotes the saliency of attributions of blame and responsibility. Another explanation of the identifiable victim effect is directly related to the size of the reference group, or rather the proportion of victims within the reference group they are part of. When the number of victims is spread across a large reference group, e.g. a whole population, these victims are less identifiable and this will evoke less (extreme) feelings. People generally are more concerned about the victims or the risks that are concentrated within a specific geographic region or within a limited population than about those that are dispersed. One specific victim becomes his or her own reference group and hence, extremely salient in the perception and interpretation (Jenni & Loewenstein 1997). In other words; the distribution is of importance (Slovic, Fischhoff & Lichtenstein 1980). Jenni and Loewenstein (2003) give an example to clarify how an identifiable victim represents the highest concentrated distribution:

> if 120 people are likely to die in a plane crash this year, these are only
> 120 people out *of the millions who fly*. Once a plane carrying 120

passengers crashes with all aboard lost, however, these are 120 fatalities out of the 120 *on board the plane.* (p. 238; emphasis in original).

The more identifiable a victim, the more outrage (Table 7.1). Once again, this particular characteristic or outrage factor is mostly related to the typical popular images of crime and violence. These images concern incidents that have high 'news value' and dramatic aspects and which are the most salient (criminal) victimisation experiences in the discussion of people's 'fear of crime'. The schema of the 'ideal crime' and the 'ideal victim' is not concerned with statistics on the number of children that suffer from abuse or figures on domestic violence.

7.3.3.3   Type of consequences: worst case scenarios

The popular image of crime is generally one that happens suddenly with a dramatic impact, and is in that sense catastrophic. Also, the typical image of crimes when only one victim is involved, like the imaginable victimisation of oneself, are those crimes that generally renders the consequences as irremediable, like in the case of violence, murder and rape (see chapter 6). The irremediability and irreversibility makes these crimes perfect examples of a dreaded hazard: "it will never be the same again". Due to the (perceived) seriousness of the consequences, these crimes are catastrophic for an individual and his/her family. Hazards that incorporate the *possibility* of great damage, and physical damage especially, suffering and fatalities, will evoke concern and outrage (Slovic, Lichtenstein & Fischhoff 1984). People perceive the risk of hazards in the light of the worst case scenario, the severity of the consequences (Sjöberg 1999, 2000a; Sjöberg & Drottz-Sjöberg 1991), which naturally can be different according to perceived vulnerability.

The type and scale of the *worst case scenario* that is *possible,* however improbable, is a chief characteristic of relevance. Even though statistically the risks are low, *"you just don't want to be that statistic"*, as an participant in the study of Petts, Horlick-Jones and Murdock (2001: 43) puts it. Sunstein (1997) argues that people neglect probability and focus primarily on elements of the worst case scenario; people are especially concerned about and want to avoid so-called bad deaths, those deaths that are especially dreaded, uncontrollable, involuntarily incurred, and inequitably distributed (Sunstein 1997). The typical images of crime that have been discussed in chapter 6 feature the dread characteristics as proposed by research in the field of risk perception remarkably.

7.3.3.4   Risk perception and the 'other': unrealistic optimism

The worst case scenario that is possible is reflected in popular images of dangers, hazards, of which crime is only one. This worst case scenario usually incorporates the qualities that lead to outrage and concern the most and conceptually refers to qualities of a general and even abstract situation. Though worst case scenarios are important in people's thinking and reasoning about risks and hazards, this is not to say that they actually think that they themselves have a high risk of ending up in that worst situation. On the contrary, average (i.e. 'healthy') people think that they are at (much) less risk than other average people; they are unrealistically optimistic (Taylor 1989; Weinstein & Klein 1996). This bias revolves around the contrast between oneself and others and people vary on the extent to which they demonstrate this self-serving bias.

Joffe (1999) examines the two major human responses to risk, both templates of the 'not me – others' response. First, she distinguishes 'the other is to blame', or 'that I am in danger is other people's fault' linked to attribution processes which have been discussed previously. The second template of the 'not me – others' response is simply 'not me', 'others are more likely than I am to be in this danger', or 'it won't happen to me'. The latter 'not me' is connected with unrealistic optimism. Unrealistic optimism, also known as optimistic bias or optimistic illusion is a classical common and robust finding in numerous studies on social cognition and on risk perception, regardless of discipline (Weinstein 1980).[201] Though people do know the existence of particular risks, and for example read about car accidents or see them, "the victims are *other* people" (Slovic, Fischhoff & Lichtenstein 1978: 282). Unrealistic optimism refers to the finding that individuals often think of themselves as being less at risk than others, especially when the comparative other(s) is or are typical member(s) of a larger group. That is, a typical member of a larger group is generally judged to be at higher risk than the typical member of a smaller group (Price 2001), a group size effect which is in conformance with the identifiable victim effect. Of importance is that the optimistic bias can be manifested in different ways, ranging from an underestimation of the absolute susceptibility to biased expectations concerning the relative likelihood of negative events in one's own life compared to others (Thornton, Gibbons & Gerrard 2002).

Unrealistic optimism is a self-serving or self-enhancing bias that implies that the majority thinks they are less risky, more capable and more skilful than the others, i.e. the majority thinks "it couldn't happen to me". The bias contributes to an "illusion of unique invulnerability" with regard to personal risk on victimisation (Perloff & Fetzer 1986). In general, studies from the last decades indicate firstly that views of oneself as generally more favourable than others prevail. Secondly, greater risks are accepted if some kind of control is experienced in a situation, which leads to a third important general finding that has been demonstrated, namely that inter and intraindividual differences exist. The more an individual feels he or she controls the exposure, the hazard or the consequences, the more optimistically biased the individual will be. Thus, people differ in their psychological predisposition, notwithstanding that risk and hazard perceptions as psychological constructs are formed in a societal context, and hence are relative, reactive, and dynamic in nature, and people in general show unrealistic optimism as a form of self-enhancement (Williams et al. 1999).

---

[201] The optimistic bias has been investigated especially because of its supposed relationship with behaviour modification, safety measures and prevention (e.g. Svenson, Fischhoff & MacGregor 1985). For instance, several studies on seatbelt use, driving safety and car accidents demonstrated the bias, specified as the tendency to judge oneself as safer and more skilful than the average driver, with a smaller risk of getting involved and injured in an accident.

Interindividual differences exist; some people tend to be more 'optimistic' concerning the risks they run, whereas others are more 'pessimistic', but in particular: some people feel more in control than others (McKenna 1993). Especially dispositional fear and anger are important determinants of perceived risk. That is, fearful people systematically make pessimistic risk assessments and favour risk-free options over potentially more rewarding but uncertain options, whereas angry people make optimistic risk assessments, that is they systematically perceive less risk and make risk-seeking choices (Lerner & Keltner 2001). These interindividual differences overlap with intergroup differences, for example concerning sex. A common finding is for instance that females perceive greater risk than males, both for personal risks and for the average person's risks. This difference seems to reflect men's experiencing greater anger, leading to greater optimism (Fischhoff et al. 2003). Though not uncommon among personality theorists, the suggestion that individual differences in specific emotions or stable traits consistently shape how the individual perceives the social environment is rather infrequent among researchers studying 'fear of crime'. In contrast, research on risk perception has given considerably more attention to intraindividual stable factors. The next section presents more dissimilarities and similarities between research on 'fear of crime' and on 'risk perception', which might be helpful for further understanding of the meaning of 'fear of crime'.

7.4   Risk and the meaning of fear of crime

As suggested before, three core concepts are central to 'fear of crime', namely (criminal) victimisation, risk (perception) and fear (of crime). The current chapter discussed risk and the perception of risk. The previous chapter on victimisation demonstrated the complex meaning of 'fear of crime' and argued that this meaning is problematic, since the supposedly core of 'fear of crime', i.e. crime, is in itself problematic. The diversity of victimisation was described by explaining the wide variety of different interpretations and focusing on the nature of victimisation. Chapter 5 described the importance of statistics and surveys and mainly suggested that the concept 'fear of crime' derived its meaning from the items that were used from the beginning, which were items that resemble the items that had been and still are being used in public opinion polls. In brief, the conclusions derived from the previous chapters regarding the concept 'fear of crime' all refer to the inaccuracy and invalidity of the historically developed common interpretation of 'fear of crime'.

The metaconclusion of the *current* chapter on risk and risk perception basically comes down to a call for research using a multidisciplinary and ideally interdisciplinary lens. This chapter, of which the main assertions are presented in Table 7.3 described and analysed research on risk and risk perception. Through an interdisciplinary lens, I attempted to explore the concept 'risk', a concept that is salient within the discursive framework on 'fear of crime'. This salience has been demonstrated by pointing out the similarities between research on risk perception and on fear of crime, which is more systematically explicated below. Conceptually, 'risk', or at least the outcome, and 'victimisation' share the connectedness with attributions of responsibility and blame, quite similar to the notions of the ideal victim as discussed previously. Furthermore, whether the source of danger, or the hazard, is technological or social in nature does not seem to matter for these attribution processes: even in the case of an industrial accident, blaming is essential. In general, becoming a crime victim is an outcome that is similar to other unwanted outcomes in risk (perception) research, except for the scale on which the number of possible or imaginable victims could be situated. In that sense, research on risks of terrorism or the perception of the risk of becoming a victim of a terrorist attack exemplarily bridges the field of risk perception on the one side and the field of 'fear of crime' on the other side.

In recent publications, terrorism has been included in the list of possible hazards to be investigated. In November 2001 data was derived from an American panel, a nationally representative sample, of Americans.[202] Subsequent analyses of these data focused on risk perceptions in the aftermath of September 11th. Respondents judged the probability that within the next twelve months they themselves and the average American would experience specific "risky events or precautionary actions" (Lerner, Gonzalez, Small & Fischhoff 2003: 145), of which five were terror-related (being hurt in a terror attack, having trouble sleeping because of the situation with terror, travelling less than usual, screening mail carefully for suspicious items and taking antibiotics against anthrax) and three other events (getting the flu, being the victim of a violent crime other than terror and dying from any cause). These three other events are called "routine" risks (Lerner et al. 2003: 145). This is a good example of 'crime' viewed as a hazard, analogous to other hazards in risk perception research, and 'becoming a victim of a violent crime' as a risk of which the probability can be estimated.

The concept 'risk' embraces facets as *possibility* and uncertainty, i.e. no determined outcome, *value*, i.e. outcomes or consequences that are desired or not, *exposure* and the notion that *action* now can influence the probability or consequences in the future, while exposure and behavioural adaptations do not change the value of (possible) consequences. The concept, its measurement, portrayal and the reaction it evokes, is dependent on the context and on value judgments. In addition, risk is about *control* and *policing* (Beck 1992; Ericson & Haggerty 1997). Historically, probability and risk have been used for political purposes, all the more since "risk represents a discursive technique which implies faith in the *controllability* of social phenomena" (Hier 2003: 14; cf. Beck 1992; Douglas 1992; Hollway & Jefferson 1997; Reddy 1996). Decisions on *controlling*, in terms of avoiding and preventing hazards, are personal and individual as well as societal and political. While 'objective' probabilistic computations can serve as actuarial tools and as a basis for the political decision process, the acceptability of a risk and the degree of protection are still a matter

---

[202] See the publications of Lerner, Gonzalez, Small & Fischhoff (2003) and Fischhoff, Gonzalez, Small & Lerner (2003).

of political choice and priorities (Vrijling, Van Hengel & Houben 1998). The same holds for the prevention or control of crime and supposedly related fears. In general, all these facets of the risk concept apply to the 'fear of crime' concept as well, which will be elaborated on in the next chapter.

Thus, risk is salient within the context of fear of crime, similar attribution processes are found and 'crime' is viewed as a hazard, analogous to other hazards in risk perception research, and 'becoming a victim of a violent crime' is a risk of which the probability can be estimated. Besides this, there are other reasons for acknowledging the research on risk. As discussed in this chapter, two themes are recurring in the literature on both risk and its perception, and on fear of crime. First, the theme of the reality and rationality of risks versus the irrationality of fears. This theme embraces the plentiful work on the difference between actual risk and perceived risk or accompanying anxieties. Within the research on 'fear of crime', work on the fear-victimisation paradox is exemplary in that sense. The second repeating theme is discontinuity; the contrast between past and present. The narrative of discontinuity contains the difference between risks, dangers and hazards in the past and in present 'contemporary' society, which might touch on an increase in risks or in risk awareness or on a difference in the nature of the risks. Overall, an important conclusion from this chapter is that research on risk perception resembles research on 'fear of crime' in many ways. This could very well eventually lead to applications and generalisations from one field to another. At the least researchers should make an effort to integrate findings and set up new research based on this integration of different perspectives. A first attempt is presented below, which anticipates the next chapter about the 'fear of crime' concept.

7.4.1   Analogies between fear of crime and risk perception

When overlooking this chapter, the salience of 'risk' and research on the perception thereof is obvious, which is why the metaconclusion of this chapter is a plead for multi or interdisciplinary research that attempts to integrate findings on risk perception and fear of crime. Table 7.2 lists the preliminary findings to do so, and summarises the analogies between research on 'fear of crime' and research on risk perception. Though the disciplines in which research on risk perception and 'fear of crime' are different, the methodological roots are essentially the same. Again, statistics, the development of survey methods and the advancement of polling have provided the methodological basis of both (see chapter 5). The underlying idea of both research areas is that the public's opinion matters, especially to the government and (semi-) governmental institutions. Researchers are asked for specific studies, and write reports that are used in policy and the decision making process.

In the field of fear of crime, fear is generally viewed as undesirable, this is a little more complicated in the whole field of risk perception research. Regarding risk perceptions concerning technological and industrial risks, a high risk perception is viewed as undesirable. This chapter elaborated on these risks and their perceptions in particular. Yet, it might be important to note that in medicine and general research on issues on public health, campaigns attempt to heighten the public's perception of risk, for example as for smoking and condom use. The studies that were of interest in this chapter do not see outrage, worry and concern as desirable aspects, but do generally acknowledge the importance of the public's perception. Therefore, trust appears to be a key issue (see Cvetkovich et al. 2002; Siegrist & Cvetkovich 2000; Sjöberg 2001b; Viklund 2003). As a consequence, in risk perception research, public participation into both risk assessment and risk decision making and the democracy of the decision process in order to both increase the legitimacy and the public acceptance of the resulting decisions (Slovic 1999). *Trust* has been included in research on fear of crime, especially trust in the police and trusting one's neighbours, as a possible influencing factor (e.g. Bazargan 1994; Ohlemacher 2001; Walklate 1998a, 1998b). The major (implicit) desirable aspect that is essential in 'fear of crime' research, is that people feel safe. Table 7.2 presents the two recurring themes that have been discussed, as well as two other important topics that are similar, namely the role of the media and methodological issues on measuring perceptions. Though in both fields the media is thought of as important factor, the discursive frameworks are different.

As Hill (2001) suggests, research on risk employs the social amplification model, which was discussed previously, whereas criminologists deal with moral panics and the effects of media violence. She analyses the social amplification of physical and moral risks of media violence, taking the James Bulger case as example. By applicating the social amplification of risk model to media violence, media violence is, at least symbolically, considered an environmental hazard or environmental risk. Similar to other risks, non-governmental organisations, professional groups and other direct action groups, such as anti-violence campaign groups, use arguments from several scientific, moral and environmental discourses to plead for the control and regulation of media risks (Hill 2001). Overall, Hill's study is a successful integration of risk perception and 'fear of crime' research. Furthermore, the study confirms the analogies and similarities between these fields.

Some other examples of correspondence refer firstly to the typical images of crime that have been discussed in chapter 6. These typical images feature the dread characteristics as proposed by research in the field of risk perception remarkably. Second, the perceived seriousness of a crime as a function of both harmfulness and wrongfulness (Warr 1989) is also in accordance with ideas and findings from the risk perception literature. A next example of the similarity is the empirical finding that the same groups, distinguished on the basis of demographic categories, show higher levels on 'fear of crime' and 'risk perception'. In other words, women, parents, non-Whites and elderly show more concern (Palmer 2003). Next, operationalisations of 'fear of crime' are sometimes quite similar to operationalisations of risk perception in the literature on risk perception. For example, Grobe, Douthitt & Zepeda (1999a, 1999b) operationalise 'risk perception' as 'expressing a concern level', more specifically as expressing concern over both future and immediate health risks. In an earlier study, 'perceived future risk' was operationalised as 'expressed concern there would be future discovery of ill-health effects' (Grobe & Douthitt 1995). As discussed in chapter 2, *concern* is a well-known operationalisation of 'fear of crime' as well, and the literature on 'fear of crime' contains the *perception of the risk* of becoming a victim of a specific crime is not disregarded (e.g. Kanan & Pruitt 2002; Smith & Torstensson 1997; Wilcox Rountree 1998). Wilcox Rountree and Land (1996b) argue that while fear and risk, considered as two types of 'fear' share some specific predictors, they nevertheless are conceptually and empirically distinct dimensions of fear of crime. The correspondence is underlined even more by the 'risk as feelings' perspective, which is discussed next and anticipates the next chapter about the 'fear of crime' concept.

Table 7.2 Analogies between research on 'fear of crime' and research on risk perception.

Characteristics	Risk Perception	Fear of Crime
Background		
Discipline or field	Accident & error-analysis, engineering, industrial, technological and medical disciplines social psychology	Criminology, victimology, sociology, social geography and public health
Methodological roots	Statistics, surveys and public opinion polls	Idem
Context	Technological, industrial, environmental context	Urban, social, criminal context
General purpose	Provide information on public opinion Description, explanation	Idem
Political and policy context; relationship with policy	Environmental & technological innovations and initiatives, safety & security	Crime, criminal law & order, public safety, public wellbeing, living conditions
	Support for these initiatives; risk management & risk communication; marketing	Support for measures regarding crime prevention, punishment and other 'law & order' -initiatives
Examples		
Work with (mainly) empirical orientation	Marris et al. (1997) O'Connor, Bord & Fisher (1999) Siegrist, Keller & Kiers (2005) Sjöberg (2002b)	Adu-Mireku (2002) Clemente (1977) StJohn & Healdmoore (1995) Wilcox Rountree (1998)
Work with (mainly) theoretical orientation	Bickerstaff (2004) Hier (2003)	Smith (1984) Maruna, Matravers & King (2004)
Main subject		
Unwanted outcome	Hazards: nuclear waste, tornados, gene technology etcetera	Social threats: crime, (sexual) violence, incivilities and nuisances
Undesirable aspects	Outrage, concern, worry	Fear, concern, worry,
Desirable aspects	Trust	Feeling safe

Table 7.2 – continued.

Recurring themes		
Reality of risks vs. irrationality of fears	Real, actual, objective risks vs. perceived risks and subjective judgments	Idem
	Statistics vs. perceptions	Idem
	Lay people vs. experts	Fear-victimisation paradox
Discontinuity in risks	Increase in risks	Idem
	Decrease in trust	Idem
	Increase in risk consciousness, risk awareness	Increase in fear of crime
	Risk society	Idem (culture of control)
	Different risks	Increase in violence of crimes
Other similar topics		
Role of the media	Social amplification of risk	Moral panic, media violence
Methodological issues: measurement of perception	Psychometric model	

7.4.1.1 Risk as a feeling

The risk-as-feelings hypothesis, situated in research on judgment and decision making, highlights the role of affect experienced at the moment of decision making and considers emotions as important informational inputs (Loewenstein et al. 2001). Within such a perspective, fear is an affective determinant of perceived risk (Lerner & Keltner 2001). Albeit fear and anxiety have been acknowledged as important coping mechanism in the assessment of risk earlier (Lee 1981), the 'risk as feelings'-perspective is more recent (Lerner & Keltner 2000, 2001; Loewenstein et al. 2001). According to Slovic et al. (2004), the 'risk as feelings' was already present in the early studies employing the so-called psychometric approach to risk perception (Fischhoff et al., 1978; Slovic, 1987). The major findings from these studies were discussed previously in this chapter and showed the importance of *dread*, which has been associated with for example voluntariness and controllability and other *outrage* factors (see Sandman 1994). Dread as the major determinant of the public's risk perception and the acceptance of risks and hazards provides early evidence of the 'risk as feelings' hypothesis (Slovic et al. 2004).

Loewenstein et al. (2001) take advantage of the distinction within modern cognitive psychology between two qualitatively different modes of information processing when they postulate their 'risk as feelings' hypothesis. The first mode of information processing is characterised by rule-based processing, which requires effort and conscious appraisal of information. The other mode is characterised by associative processing, which is more spontaneous, automatic and intuitive, which operates by principles of similarity and temporal contiguity and which is not easily accessible to consciousness (see Epstein et al. 1992; Sloman 1996). Briefly, the risk-as-feelings hypothesis states that responses to risky situations are twofold, corresponding with the dual processing theory. Loewenstein et al. (2001) describe the risk-as-feelings hypothesis as follows:

responses to risky situations (including decision making) result in part from direct (i.e., not cortically mediated) emotional influences, including feelings such as worry, fear, dread, or anxiety. People are assumed to evaluate risky alternatives at a cognitive level, as in traditional models, based largely on the probability and desirability of associated consequences. Such cognitive evaluations have affective consequences, and feeling states also exert a reciprocal influence on cognitive evaluations. At the same time, however, feeling states are postulated to respond to factors, such as the immediacy of a risk, that do not enter into cognitive evaluations of the risk and also respond to probabilities and outcome values in a fashion that is different from the way in which these variables enter into cognitive evaluations. Because their determinants are different, emotional reactions to risks can diverge from cognitive evaluations of the same risks. (p. 270).

A person's behaviour in such a risky situation is then the result from the interplay between the two responses. For Loewenstein et al., the possibility that the two responses are (often) conflicting is of importance. The focus of the risk-as-feelings hypothesis is not on the complementary role of the two modes of information processing, rather, the focus is on the possibility that the two modes result in *diverging* reactions or responses. The risk-as-feelings hypothesis directly connects 'risk' with 'fear'. Lerner & Keltner (2000, 2001) link fear, as well as anger, and risk even more explicitly in their studies on the influence of emotions on judgment. Their work on emotion-related appraisal tendencies is of particular importance in the current analysis of the concepts 'risk perception' and 'fear of crime'. The next chapter will elaborate on their work in order to enhance further understanding of the 'fear of crime' concept. The main assertions of this chapter are presented in Table 7.3.

Table 7.3. List of main assertions Chapter 7.

Topic	Explanation
Purpose	Demonstrate the salience of 'risk' with regard to 'fear of crime'
	Explain how 'risk', just as 'victimisation', is connected with attributions of responsibility and blame
	Attempt to distil relevant cross-disciplinary themes and findings
	Show the (dis)similarities between research on risk perception and on fear of crime
Research questions	How can the concept risk and risk perception be interpreted?
	What themes are of importance in work on risk and risk perception?
	How is risk perception investigated and what are the main findings?
	In what way can research on risk perception contribute to the understanding of 'fear of crime'?

Table 7.3– continued.

Main notions	Risk can best be interpreted as a calculated value; multidimensional Risk and risk perception not independent of social context Risks are conditional, reactive, compensated for and interactive on social level Two essential elements: uncertainty and (nature of) an outcome Historical changes: calculation of probability and nature of possible outcomes: changes in meaning and connotation 'risk' Nowadays: risk mostly associated with unwanted outcomes; risk should be tamed Taming of risk by taking measures and altering behaviour: influencing exposure
	Two regular themes across disciplines; 1ˢᵗ theme: reality of risks vs. irrationality of fears 2ⁿᵈ theme: discontinuity in risks; risks now vs. risks then
	Research on risk perception: similarities research fear of crime Familiar historical roots: statistics and survey Many concepts in common (e.g. concern, worry, anxiety, seriousness of consequences, risk, perception) Crime as perceived hazard: crime itself as well as its imaginable consequences Typical features of dreaded hazards: outrage Attribution of responsibility and blame linked with predictability and causality
Conclusion	Meaning of concept 'risk': risk as a feeling corresponding with 'fear of crime' Meaning of concept 'fear of crime': when using a multi and/or interdisciplinary lens 'fear of crime' and risk perception can be viewed as parts of same complex Integration of research desirable

8 More than one 'fear of crime'

The previous chapters discussed victimisation and risk, two of the three core concepts that appeared to be central to 'fear of crime', at least to the discourse concerning 'fear of crime'. The main question behind these chapters is what certain concepts mean with respect to their social context. Issues like when and why did the concept 'fear of crime' become an issue in research, politics and the media or when did 'fear of crime' become a social problem can only be addressed when elaborating on the social context. These issues are relevant in order to gain an understanding of how particular concepts are embedded and what they mean, since the concept 'fear of crime', its meaning(s) and related issues, are considered a product of historical, cultural and social circumstances.

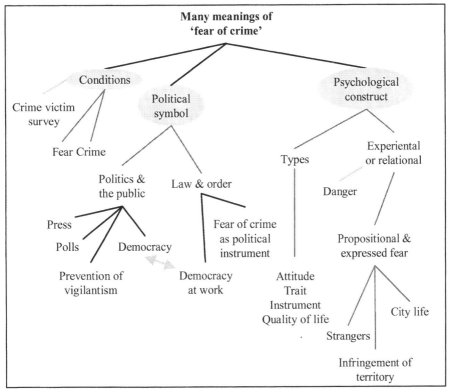

Figure 8.1. Topic tree chapter 8.

In the past decades, in which *fear of crime* as a concept has grown in popularity and familiarity, the component of *fear* has been unquestioned and has hardly been problematised. This chapter concentrates on 'fear of crime' and is divided into three parts, beginning with the conditions of something like 'fear of crime' as you can see in the topic tree in Figure 8.1. Next, 'fear of crime' is analysed as a political symbol. In this respect, public opinion polling and the use of the results are of major importance. Subsequently, the focus is on 'fear of crime' as a psychological construct; i.e. 'fear of crime' is analysed in the light of personality traits, emotions and attitudes. The main argument of this chapter is that something seemingly simple as 'fear of crime' has many meanings. The meaning of 'fear of crime' is contingent and contextual, and as this chapter shows, highly dependent on the perspective one takes.

8.1   Conditions of 'fear of crime'

The concept 'fear of crime' has frequently been related to risk perception, worry, concern, fear of victimisation and so on. The strategy that was used to analyse several studies from four types of sources, led to an extensive list (see chapter 2). Evidently, the different concepts do not occur equally frequently in research. Several concepts were grouped into higher order categories, a procedure that continued until three core categories or concepts are created that appear to be central to 'fear of crime'. The first and second concepts, i.e. (criminal) victimisation and risk (perception), were discussed in chapters 6 and 7. Much attention was paid to the concept's history; the social and political context in which the concept has and still is being used, which is essential from a social construction point of view. Following Hacking (2000), I would say that 'fear of crime' and its meanings are not inevitable, but rather a product of historical events and social forces. In other words, 'fear of crime' need not have existed, or need not be at all as it is; 'fear of crime' is neither determined by the nature of things, nor is it inevitable. 'Fear of crime' has been brought into existence and is shaped by and therefore dependent on the social context. This social context could well have been different, which would have brought about another 'type of fear of crime'.

In general, this is similar to Lee's (1999) contention regarding the contingent nature of both 'fear of crime' research and the 'fear of crime' concept; in other words, 'fear of crime' is not a pre-discursive social fact. He sketches the history of the discourse of 'fear of crime' and carries out a genealogical analysis in which the role of the government is of primary interest. His analysis follows the shifts, (dis)continuities and alignments of the governmental discourse regarding statistics and regulation, the popular and political discourse (the law & order debates) and the criminological and social scientific discourse. His Foucauldian genealogy illustrates how particular practices and ideas concerning 'fear of crime' became doable and thinkable and concentrates on power and the processes and practices of government in particular. Lee (1999) says:

> Genealogy, therefore, makes it possible to observe how 'fear of crime' research becomes entangled in a web of governmental strategies and techniques that have as their object the regulation of individuals, in this case the regulation of *fearing subjects*. (p. 472)

Lee (1999) too notes statistics and surveys as the primary conditions of 'fear of crime' as we know it. First and foremost, the crime victim survey has certainly been crucial for the very beginning of 'fear of crime'. The history of the crime victim survey has been extensively discussed in chapter 5, placing the victim survey in a tradition of (crime) statistics, instrumental uses and governmental interests (see Deflem 1997; Lee 1999). In other words, 'fear of crime' could only begin to exist because statistics and surveys existed and the idea of the crime victim survey developed, and obviously because something like 'crime' and 'victimisation' existed. Apart from statistics and surveys, a general interest, for whatever reason, in the public's opinion (or even in the public's fear) and issues of wellbeing is a condition for 'fear of crime' as well. In addition, another condition relates to the whole idea that the public would *have* ideas, opinions, and feelings regarding the issues involved. That is, the idea that the very first and familiar items 'feeling safe walking alone after dark' or 'being at home alone at night' would evoke responses from the public, would be appealing in a certain way. Apparently, these items are deemed as tapping the fear that people have. In other words, another condition is the idea that people fear or have fear.

The two basic conditions of 'fear of crime', that it concerns fear and crime, are assumptions, which are not always met. The broad umbrella concept 'fear of crime' embraces many more or less distinct concepts, varying from the perception of the risk of becoming a victim of a burglary to concern that something will happen to the children, from the fear that becoming a victim of rape evokes to the alarm that was installed. Chapter 2 has discussed these different issues extensively. Furthermore, 'fear of crime' is not (only) about crime in the strict legal sense. 'Fear of crime' is about social norms, incivilities, trust, and control. These two basis conditions are mere assumptions, which have hindered the conceptual and theoretical development within this field of research. Apparently, it is very hard, even for criminologists, to dismiss the idea that firstly 'fear of crime' has everything or something to do with crime. This has resulted in numerous studies on the so-called fear-victimisation paradox and examinations of the relationship between 'fear of crime' and the 'actual' crime rate. Secondly, most research has focused on the fear that is supposedly connected to crime. The idea that not fear, but for example anger is of much greater relevance in people's lives, appears to be hardly received.[203] Anger, often simultaneously with fear and sadness has been studied as emotional responses, evoked by a (violent) victimisation experience (e.g. Greenberg & Beach 2004; Herek, Gillis & Cogan 1999; Moscarello 1991). Far less common is research on anger analogue to research on 'fear of crime'; anger, just like, worry, concern or fear, connected to the mere idea of victimisation or crime. Some rare studies however, indicate that anger might be at least as relevant (Ditton et al. 1999; Ensink & Van Buuren 1987; Phillips & Smith 2004).

8.2   *Fear of crime as political symbol*

In this section, it becomes clear that 'fear of crime' is a political symbol. Its historical roots, which are similar to other statistics and surveys on

---

[203] Ensink & Van Buuren's (1987) research is an interesting example of a study that did focus on anger as well as fear; their publication led to a heated debate with Junger & Van der Heijden (1987a, 1987b) on methodological issues (see Ensink 1987; Vanderveen 1999).

social issues, provide the argument of its instrumental role (see Haggerty 2001; Lee 1999).[204] 'Fear of crime' can be seen as an aspect of public opinion, which is highlighted by the instrumental role and features of its measurement. The public's opinions are in constant interaction; not only with politics and policy. The press, i.e. the news media, is incorporated in the dynamic interplay between several actors as well, just as actors within the judiciary are. A brief intermezzo sketches the role of the public's opinions in the courtroom and highlights the notion of vigilantism and people taking the law into their own hands. Occasionally, jurisprudential cases appeal to public opinion and the possibility of people taking the law into their own hands when they are not satisfied with the court's decision. Much more common are appeals to public opinion by politicians and policy makers, often to legitimise a policy measure. These policy measures are mostly connected to a political agenda concerned with 'law & order' and 'zero tolerance'. This will be elaborated on in order to show how 'fear of crime' is politicised and what 'fear of crime' means in such a context.

8.2.1   Politics, policy and public opinion

The introductory chapter addressed the question why 'fear of crime' is relevant for contemporary society. Several reasons were put forward, of which the first and foremost is that 'fear of crime' clearly is a noticeable issue in politics. Because the entire political discourse pays attention to 'fear of crime' in its broadest sense, all kinds of information about the public's 'fear of crime' are salient. Besides politicians and police officers, several other actors point to results concerning 'fear of crime' that are derived from public opinion polls and surveys. For example, judges and public prosecutors often refer to the public opinions and attitudes in court, when giving reasons for a sanction, which will be briefly elaborated on next.

8.2.1.1   Vigilantism (eigenrichting)

In an exploratory study, published legal proceedings of criminal cases in the Netherlands were analysed to see to what extent the judiciary explicitly refers to public opinion (Vanderveen & Elffers 2001).[205] About forty criminal cases were read thoroughly, drawing comparisons between different cases. The

---

[204] Haggerty's analysis of the production and publication of official criminal justice statistics by a national statistical agency (i.e. the Canadian Centre for Justice Statistics) provides overwhelming evidence of the instrumental uses of statistics, by showing the 'micropolitical considerations' of the many agencies involved in the production of official statistics about crime and criminal justice. For example, he describes the influences on the decisions regarding the studies that are done, the institutions that control the official data, the counting rules and the standardisation procedures (Haggerty 2001).

[205] Dutch jurisprudence can be found at a few places. In the current exploration, the "Jurisprudence Online" has been used, which is a data source for legal professionals one can subscribe to. It consists among other things of all published criminal law cases since 1965. In this data source, we searched the archives using Dutch equivalents of keywords like *eigenrichting*, social unrest, feeling(s) of unsafety, public opinion, as well as all combination of words like fear, alarm, and concern together with terms like community and society. Similar keywords were used when searching the official publications of the Dutch parliament and government.

material was sorted out and could be arranged in three useful groups.[206] The first group consisted of cases in which the feelings of the public, such as feelings of unsafety, social unrest and shock, were considered explicitly, mostly when motivating the sentence. In the cases of the second group, the judiciary explicitly referred to (the influence of) public opinion. On the one hand, the forming of the public opinion towards the trial was pointed to, on the other hand the pressure of the public opinion was considered. The third group held cases in which the social shock, unrest and discontent is linked with (the danger of) the public taking the law into their own hands. For example cases concerned with defendants who had taken the law into their own hands, or cases that amounted to the court's assertion that shock, unrest and discontent doesn't justify taking the law into one's own hands.

The jurisprudence illustrates how public opinion influences the prosecution directly. When a criminal act by a certain defendant causes a lot of turmoil, it appears to be necessary to prosecute, and ask for a more severe sentence. Otherwise, the constitutional state might be jeopardised by situations in which the people take the law into their own hands. Alternately, the interaction between the judge, prosecution and the defence, and how this interaction is portrayed in the media, influences how the public perceives the trial. In some cases, the judge motivated the verdict by referring to the feelings of the public, for example to minimise vigilantism and people taking the law into their own hands (or in Dutch: *eigenrichting*), though the claim of the public did not seem to be crucial for the verdict. In general, though politicians, prosecution and judges deliberate about the feelings and opinions of the public, they also strongly resist extra-judicial, extralegal manners of 'self-help justice', i.e. vigilantism (Vanderveen 2002c; Vanderveen & Elffers 2001).

Vigilantism is repeatedly linked with the notion that the processes of law appear inadequate (see Brown 1977; DelaRoche 1996; Johnston 1996).[207] The literature on vigilantism directly connects 'do-it-yourself-justice', extralegal and self-help crime control to people's trust in the State and the State's just power to protect them. When people would feel that the State, government, the (legal) institutions or the police aren't trying hard enough, this essential trust is subverted, confidence in the criminal justice system is lacking (e.g. Rosen 2001). Extralegal initiatives viewed in such a way are merely methods to cope with ineffective criminal law enforcement or a bad functioning criminal justice system in general (Little & Sheffield 1983). In other words, a general explanation for vigilantism is the dissatisfaction of people with the performance of the State (and its institutions); the formal system is perceived as ineffective

---

[206] A fourth group was not considered further, namely the group in which the more legal technicalities acted as the subject matter (Vanderveen & Elffers 2001).

[207] Johnston (1996, 2001) describes vigilantism as 'autonomous citizenship', i.e. as a social movement of which the participants voluntarily engage in planning and premeditation and use violence (force) or the threat thereof. According to Johnston (2001: 968), vigilantism "arises when an established order is under threat from the transgression, the potential transgression or the imputed transgression of institutionalised norms". In addition, similar to "other forms of policing" vigilantism attempts to offer guarantees of security to the own participants and others (Johnston 2001: 968).

and irrelevant (Ingalls 1988). For example, in a study on interpersonal violence in the Georgia-South Carolina region, the use of violence (and firearms) to ambush adversaries, is directly connected with the lost legitimacy of legal institutions (e.g. Roth 2002).[208]

Against this background of vigilantism, the argument that was used during the introduction phase of the crime victim survey in the Netherlands makes sense; knowledge about public concern and feelings of safety were said to be important for the judiciary, since neglecting public opinion, attitudes and emotions could lead to a society in which people take the law into their own hands (Cozijn & Van Dijk 1976). People's feelings, the public's opinions and concerns, 'fear of crime' are apparently topics that are not neglected in court by the judiciary. So besides politicians and police officers, judges and public prosecutors refer to the public opinions and attitudes as well. The literature that will be outlined in the next paragraph section suggests that this is an important feature of a democracy, which forms the basis of the so-called 'democracy-at-work' thesis. This thesis suggests that harsher legislation and punitive measures were primarily taken because of an increasing public concern with the rising crime rates and is discussed later.

8.2.1.2   Public opinion as feature of a democracy

Appeals to public opinion have become central in political discourse, since the public's opinion provides the ultimate ground of legitimacy for a specific political and legislative agenda (Zaret 2000). The importance of the public's opinions, attitudes and perspectives is evident within a democratic system (Citrin & Muste 1999; Ferguson 2000). Authors like for example Ippolito, Walker and Kolson (1976) claim that a distinguished feature of democratic politics is the assumption that political leaders should be sincerely interested in what the public thinks. Smoke (1996b) states that the importance of the public's perspectives on issues of foreign and security affairs is evident, even in countries that are not democracies, because what the public feels constitutes "primary facts of a certain political kind about that country" (Smoke 1996b: 24). Since democracies offer ways to people to ensure that their government pays attention to their opinions, the importance of the public's perspective is even greater in democratic countries and countries in the process of becoming democratic. It is very well possible that views of the public conflict with ideas of government and experts. Nonetheless, Smoke (1996b) insists that the government cannot neglect the public's opinions. A reaction is necessary, "if only to try to reshape the public's opinion" (Smoke 1996b: 24). In short, the public's opinions have become a central feature in politics, and appeals to public opinion are central in political discourse.

---

[208] According to a majority of mental health professionals, recent technology (Internet) has raised the danger of vigilantism as well (Malesky & Keim 2001). Most respondents in this study think that public access to sex offender registries through publication on the Internet will lead to cases of vigilantism.

One of the frequently employed ways to get knowledge of the public's opinion is the public opinion poll, or the survey.[209] Chapter 5 explored the historical development of acquiring knowledge about opinions and attitudes by and for the government, with the emphasis on polls and surveys concerning crime. Statistics, surveys and the (governmental) need for knowledge on attitudes and opinions brought about the concept 'fear of crime' as an inevitable one. The chapter described a history of surveys on 'fear of crime' and showed how 'fear of crime' is primarily related to (crime) statistics and (crime victim) surveys, administered by governmental institutions. The pervasive instrumental role that the (crime) statistics and crime surveys played, including the items on 'fear of crime' became clear; statistics are thought to enable politicians and policy makers to 'count & control', or to 'explain and tame'. In other words, statistics and surveys are conditions for the concept 'fear of crime' and despite several flaws and criticism, surveys and their resulting statistics play a major, and often instrumental, role.

The instrumental role is for example reflected by the attention that 'fear of crime' receives from state actors or (semi-)governmental institutions. Several policy agencies are devoting part of their time and money to the "reduction" of fear, leading to many policy measures and practical implementations that, in some cases, subsequently are evaluated in studies that attempt to check the effectiveness of policy interventions. Elsewhere, I have described a number of these policy measures, which in general led to the conclusion that these measures do not lead to unequivocal changes in 'fear of crime' (Vanderveen 2002a). Nonetheless, this does not keep numerous governmental institutions, local, regional or national, from similar or other implementations.

8.2.1.3   Press: 'fear of crime' in the news

Besides the importance of 'fear of crime' within political discourse, 'fear of crime' as well as crime is a prominent (news) media issue. Evidently, the salience in the (news) media is related to the political salience (Altheide 1997, 1999, 2002, 2003). That is, political parties and various departments for example distribute press releases, which is represented by an arrow from politics to press in Figure 8.2. The active role of politicians is nothing new; Barker (1998) suggests that contemporaries in 18th century England were convinced that the press was influential. She explores the press's relationship with politics and readers, and analyses how newspapers from that time represented and helped shape 'public opinion'. This is one side of the press; to keep the public informed by telling what is going on in the political arena. On the other hand, the media are expressing opinions about politics and issues as well and therefore shape public opinion or involve the public, for example by using the pronoun "we", when referring to its readers (Farge 1995). Other examples can be found in American newspapers from the early 20th century; in several cases of vigilantism, and lynchings, the popular press has made comments.

---

[209] This contemporary identification of survey research and public opinion, however, is criticised (e.g. Sanders 1999).

Encouragement or approval of newspapers of hangings was common (e.g. McGrath 1984: 243). In other cases, newspapers have objected to vigilantism and lynchings. For example, an article on the 'Omaha riot' (1919) stated that the excuse that lynching is "the only efficacious remedy for certain crimes" should not be tolerated by the people or by the government.

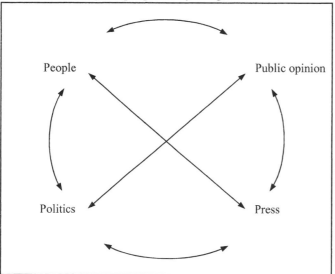

Figure 8.2. Feedback loops between politics, press (news media), people and public opinion.

Before statistical methods became known and widely employed, information about unrest in society was derived from narratives of eyewitnesses of (violent) conflicts, articles and illustrations in the (popular) press, official messages as well as rumours.[210] Also, the more academic literature was used as a source of information and might be intended to persuade people.[211] From whichever source, this information in turn, could lead to direct institutional State intervention or in alterations and amendments to the law (e.g. see Katajala 1999). In the nineteenth century, several ways of representing crime existed. Statistics as well as novels (e.g. the 'Artful Dodger', the young pickpocket in Charles Dickens' *Oliver Twist* appeared on the stage in 1837-1839) and the (popular) press portrayed 'crime' and the 'criminal', each source with its own agenda (Emsly 1999). Overall, the press is thought to act on the readers and viewers (people), public opinion and on politics (see Figure 8.2); the press is shaping public opinion.[212] This is the argument of Ericson, Baranek & Chan (1991), who state that the news media are an agency of policing, like the law-

---

[210] Despite the immense popularity of reporting statistics and survey results, which emerged in the nineteenth century, narratives are still very persuasive and frequently used (see chapter 6; Donovan 2002; Girling, Loader & Sparks 1998; Mastro & Robinson 2000).

[211] For example, Hobbes' works *Leviathan* and *De Cive* were supposed to be persuasive (Sorrell 1990) and thus meant to be informative and influential.

[212] Sometimes the news media not only point to the results of public opinion polls and surveys, but conduct polling themselves, which can be seen as 'making' public opinion.

enforcement agencies are.[213] By reporting on law-enforcement and the criminal justice system, the media are not just mirrors of the agreed social moralities, of a society or the public's opinions, they are actively reproducing the social and moral order (Ericson, Baranek and Chan 1991). Since this order, the social moralities and values are not static, the active reproduction of the social order by the news media depends on an interaction between the media and the readers, or at least part thereof (Peelo & Soothill 2000).[214]

The press is shaping public opinion, or even reproducing the social norms within a society. That means that on the other hand, the press is viewed as representative of the public as well, by reflecting the public's opinion. For example, newspaper editors in 18th century England were presumed to represent "the voice of the people" (Barker 1998). This is another view on the relationships between press, public opinion and politics and refers to what has been called the media agenda-setting hypothesis (Tipton 1992). The press or news media select and define issues and social problems and narrow the range of policy options, in other words, the media clearly have a role in establishing or changing the politicians' and policymakers' agendas (Kennamer 1992). Politicians and policymakers in turn might be forced to respond to the issues being covered by the media. In this way, the mass media contribute to setting the political agenda (Altheide 1997, 2002, 2003). Burke (1998), in his analysis of the socio-political context of 'zero tolerance', says:

> The media – in particular, television – is central to the post-modern political agenda in New York City. It is a primary means by which politicians get across the message to the general public that they are doing something. But it is not a one-way syncopatic relationship. Public servants and politicians in New York City are constantly challenged and brought to account by the media as incidents happen and develop. The public expect – and get – speedy action.

The public servants, politicians and policymakers are forced to respond to the issues being covered by the mass media. On the other hand, these same politicians and policymakers use the news media as surrogates for public opinion, especially in the absence of polls and based on the idea that the mass media have some insight into the public mind (Kennamer 1992).

---

[213] A similar argument can be derived from Osborne & Rose (1999). They suggest that the social sciences, helped by the development of the representative sample, have created opinioned persons and an opinionated society. In other words, the social sciences have created a new phenomenon; a new way of describing and acting, which in turn has several consequences. Thus, researchers might be agencies of policing as well. Not only the social phenomena that are considered relevant for (and by) researchers to investigate are dependent on the social and political environments, the political and social contexts are acting on the suggested explanations and theory as well, and accordingly may change over time (e.g. Flanagan 1987; Jenkins 1989; Lianos 2000).

[214] A clear illustration of such an interactions are letters, sent by readers to newspapers. Dupre & Mackey (2001) analysed these letters in order to assess crime salience in people's everyday lives. Their findings implicate that crime and justice issues might be less important than other concerns.

8.2.2   Law & order: politics of zero tolerance

The instrumental role of crime statistics and crime victim surveys is clear, including the use of statistics on 'fear of crime' in the news media. 'Fear of crime' is a political symbol, it has become a reference to a set of social problems and accompanying solutions. 'Fear of crime' as symbol is primarily used to set a specific public agenda, one that is concerned with crime control and what has been called 'law & order' and 'zero tolerance'. Harris (1969) gives a detailed outline of the growing calls for tougher action in terms of policing, disciplining and punishing criminals, a discourse and political agenda that uses 'fear of crime' to a large extent. For example, crime and 'fear of crime' are said to be a "public malady", for which politicians should "seek its cure" (in Harris 1969: 17-18).[215] In this section, the symbolic uses are discussed further. The work of Beckett and Scheingold will be elaborated on in particular, since their analyses provide a general frame of the relationship between fear, crime and (punitive) politics.

Contemporary Western, at least Anglo-Saxon, societies seem to show an increasing punitiveness and emphasis on crime control (Beckett 1997; Beckett & Sasson 2000; Garland 2000, 2001; Newburn 2002).[216] Newburn (2002) analyses the USA as a direct source of the law & order policies, and suggest 'zero tolerance' is probably the best known example of imported crime control in the UK (Newburn 2002). He notes that it is not only policies that are transferred across the Atlantic, but more so "elements of terminology, ideas and ideologies" that are often "phrases that have both powerful symbolic value and also act as an incitement to law and order" (Newburn 2002: 174). These phrases are exemplary for symbolic politics, e.g. 'three strikes and you're out', 'war on crime', 'war on drugs' and more recently the 'war on terrorism' as well as the metaphor of 'broken windows' introduced by Wilson & Kelling (1982, Burke 1998).[217] Language and symbols are important in politics and policing, especially when crime, risk and safety are involved. 'Fear of crime' is such a powerful phrase as well, and can be used perfectly as a symbol in politics, of which several studies provide evidence (see Altheide 1997, 2002; Altheide & Michalowski 1999; Beckett 1997; Chevigny 2003; Gore 2004; Schlesinger, Tumber & Murdock 1991; Sparks 1992).[218]

8.2.2.1   Democracy at work

Beckett (1997; Beckett & Sasson 2000) observes increases in the levels of crime in the USA, the costs of the criminal justice system, as well as an

---

[215] Harris (1969) published one of the first books on 'fear of crime' and discusses the history, i.e. its alterations and modifications, of a piece of legislation called *The Omnibus Crime Control and Safe Streets Act 1968* through Congress and into law.

[216] This development is strengthened by the events in the USA on September 11, 2001, the series of bombings in trains in Madrid (March 11, 2004) and in the Netherlands by the murder on politician Pim Fortuyn (May 6, 2002) and on filmmaker Theo van Gogh (November 2, 2004).

[217] The 'war on drugs, crime or terrorism' is reflected by the Dutch '*strijd* tegen drugs, criminaliteit of terrorisme'.

[218] A whole issue of *Social Research* (2004, vol. 71, issue 4) provides evidence for the political and instrumental uses of fear in American politics.

increase in the public support for punitive policies and incarceration rates. The 'democracy-at-work' thesis explains these increases and holds that an increasing public concern with the rising crime rates and insufficient punishment forced politicians and policy makers to respond through harsher legislation (Scheingold 1984). In other words, the thesis explains the adoption of law & order policies by the increasing threat of criminal victimisation and the engendered anxiety or 'fear of crime' (Beckett 1997; Beckett & Sasson 2000). Figure 8.3 presents the 'democracy-at-work' thesis, the mainstream interpretation of politicisation of crime adapted from Scheingold (1984: 50). The thesis suggests that an increase in crime rates results in more victimisation and higher levels of fear, leading to punitive political demands on which politics react with law & order policies. This sequence fits the idea that appeals to public opinion provide the ultimate ground of legitimacy for a specific political and legislative agenda (Zaret 2000).[219]

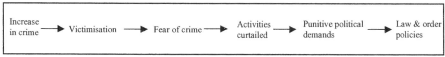

Figure 8.3. Schematical presentation of the 'democracy-at-work' thesis, adapted from Scheingold (1984: 50).

Beckett (1997) admits this 'democracy-at-work' thesis is intuitively appealing, but claims that when it is closer examined, the thesis does not hold. Law & order policies show no consistent association with crime figures but are only loosely related. Also, a more close examination of popular attitudes shows that they are not simply punitive, but more complex and equivocal in nature, even in the midst of campaign of law & order. Beckett concludes that public beliefs do not provide clear and unambiguous support for current criminal justice policies. She suggests that social problems are socially constructed and especially crime-related issues are socially and politically constructed, since "they acquire their meaning through interpretive, representational and political processes" (Beckett 1997: 5). This means that the socio-historical context, public discourse and popular sentiment, which are related in complex ways, are of importance when studying how law & order politics have become popular, and how 'fear of crime' became a social problem.[220]

8.2.2.2   Fear of crime as social problem

These law & order politics are directly linked to the notion of 'fear of crime' as a social problem or issue. Has 'fear of crime' always been an issue in politics and policy and how exactly did 'fear of crime' become an issue in

---

[219] For example, the appeals to opinion polls regarding the toughness of the courts. Gaubatz (1995) discusses the apparent consensus regarding what should be done about crime. Ten polls, from 1982 to 1991, show that about 80% of the respondents think that the courts aren't harsh enough with criminals.

[220] Beckett (1997) refers to the constructionist perspective, proposing that reality is not known directly, but comprehended through frames that select, order and interpret this reality (see also Beckett & Sasson 2000: 6-7).

politics and did it become a social problem? In the discussion of the historical development of statistics and survey practice, it was noted that in the 1970s, not only crime was seen as a social problem, but 'fear of crime' itself became a problem as well (Harris 1969).[221] In the late seventies, 'fear of crime' became a research subject in itself (e.g. Block 1971; Erskine 1974; Flango 1979; Garofalo & Laub 1978; Skogan & Klecka 1977). Likert (1968) was truly right when he foresaw a great future for the survey. When the crime victim survey was introduced in the Netherlands, the idea that crime can be viewed as a social problem became acknowledged, which causes crime not only to pertain to victims of crime, but instead that everybody has to do with crime (Fiselier 1978). Also, measures to decrease 'fear of crime' were taken and evaluated (e.g. Hening & Maxfield 1978; Zion 1978). A typical example is the Hartford Project in Connecticut, which was aimed at the reduction of crime, like burglary and robbery, and the fear of those particular crimes. Five victimisation surveys that were administered in 1973, 1975, 1976, 1977 and 1979 were used to analyse the effect of several implemented measures and to evaluate the project (Fowler 1979, 1982).

    More large-scale surveys were administered, which enabled the connection of the experience of safety with other variables of interest (e.g. housing and community life in the Harris 1975 Housing and Health Care Survey, see Appendix F) and research on fear within the framework of theoretical traditions. The research project of Lewis and Salem (1986) is a classic example by linking safety to the social control perspective. Between 1975 and 1980 they collected data on the fear of criminal victimisation and neighbourhood characteristics, pointing out that fear of criminal victimisation can be primarily traced back to the lack of control people feel they have over their (social) environment. Hartnagel (1979) studied the relationship between 'fear of crime' and social-environmental aspects of the neighbourhood, like cohesion and social activities. In 1977, about 340 interviews with residents of Edmonton (Canada) were conducted. In these interviews, one item asked about their "perception of crime" and two items measured 'fear of crime'.[222] At about the same time, yet another 'war on crime' began, accompanied by the 'war on drugs' from the 1980s on.

8.2.2.3   Concern about crime and drugs: 'fear of crime' politicised

    Beckett and Sasson (2000) examine the historical and cultural context related to the question how and why crime-related issues were constructed as problems of insufficient punishment and control in respect of two particular periods. During these two periods, concern about crime, during 1964–1974, and concern regarding drugs, 1985–1992, became more salient. Yet, these concerns

---

[221] This leads some researchers to conclude that "there was no 'fear' of crime in Britain until it was discovered in 1982" (Ditton et al. 1998: 10; cited in Pain, Williams & Hudson 2000).

[222] The item on the perception of crime asked how much of a change there had been in violent crime in the city during the past five years. The two items on 'fear of crime' referred to the degree of personal safety the respondent felt in their own neighbourhood and the safety of the city as a whole (Hartnagel 1979: 181).

were related to prior initiatives in politics and policy, not the other way around: public concern did not cause political initiatives. Beckett and Sasson (2000) describe how crime and drugs became a major issue in American politics since the 'crime issue' first emerged on the political scene during the 1964 presidential campaign, together with 'fear of crime' and an increasing concern about crime in general.[223] At least, this concern became salient within a specific context. 'Fear of crime' is used as a symbol in order to set the public agenda (see Harris 1969). According to Beckett, the political elites, who have focused on crime and drug use and framed them as consequence of insufficient punishment and control, provide or shape the definitions of popular attitudes about crime and drugs, among which 'fear of crime'. Anxiety about social change and a pervasive sense of insecurity are sentiments that can be channelled partly by scapegoating the underclass (Beckett 1997).

Scheingold (1984) makes a similar point when discussing the 'myth of punishment', which provides reassurance that something immediate and direct can be done about the source of our anxiety. Crime is used as a symbol and refers to the politicisation of crime, which began in the mid-1960s when crime became a salient political issue. According to Scheingold, concern about crime reflects concerns that transcend crime as such: "Calls for law and order were, then, integrally linked to an unsettling sense of rapid and unwelcome social change as well as to the crime rate." (Scheingold 1984: xi). In other words, 'fear of crime' is symptomatic of even greater fears. Like Beckett, he notes an increase of public anxieties about social order, e.g. protests against racial injustice, poverty, war in Vietnam, which is channelled by the symbol of crime or rather the fear of crime. Scheingold states that politicians are served by 'fear of crime' and crime as a symbol; if one takes a get-tough stand, then crime is a good issue when campaigning. Also, 'fear of crime' works out well for law enforcement officials, the result of public concern is frequently that more resources are directed to agencies of criminal process. Besides these two groups, private security organisations profit from 'fear of crime' as well, as do organisations arguing for the necessity of legal firearms ownership (Łoś 2002; McDowall & Loftin 1983).

How private security organisations profit from the symbolic nature of 'fear of crime' is well illustrated by a study of Walsh and Donovan (1989), who explored attitudes toward safety within a community that employs a private police department. That is, they asked respondents familiar questions like 'How safe do you feel being out alone at night in Starrett City', 'How safe do you feel being out alone during the day in Starrett City' and 'How safe do you feel at home during the day'. Also, eight items measured perceptions of Starrett City and "what their lifestyle would be like without the private police department". A large majority of the respondents, "indicated that Starrett City would no longer be a safe place to live", "thought crime would increase" and "indicated that

---

[223] Since, then, all American presidents have included the 'crime problem' on their political agenda (Oliver 2002, 2003). Before 1964, other American presidents have addressed crime in their State of the Unions (see Oliver 2002).

without their security department robberies would increase" (Walsh & Donovan 1989: 193). The authors market private security even more explicitly when they say:

> As native New Yorkers these individuals knew that their residential complex would be an inviting target for predatory criminals without the protection provided by the private security officers. (p. 194)

The private security industry, law enforcement institutions, politics and the press all comment on levels of fear of crime, which are generally denoted as being high or too high. According to Scheingold (1984), increases in 'fear of crime' since 1965 are not as dramatic as sometimes pictured by politicians and he presents the familiar figures that show a rapid increase from the mid-1960s and a levelling off in the mid-1970s.[224] Moreover, when respondents are asked what the most important issue is that is facing the USA and respondents can answer freely, i.e. an open choice is used, then 'crime' is not often mentioned from 1968 to 1974. When a forced choice is applied, crime seems much more consistently important for Americans. Responses to the poll question whether too much or too little money is spend on several problems do not show an enormous increase. The respondents who indicated "too little" money is spent on "halting the rising crime rate" rose from 64% in 1973 to 69 % in 1980 (Scheingold 1984). Overall, he suggests that it is not 'fear of crime' itself that has increased; it is the political salience of crime and 'fear of crime' that increased much more. In other words, crime as well as 'fear of crime' is politicised.

The 'democracy-at-work' thesis claims that the politicisation of crime reflects the demands forced on political leaders by the public. Harris (1969) observes:

> The fear of crime, more than the fact of it, guaranteed that some kind of action would be taken, for the public demand had to be met. (p.17)

These demands are thought to originate from an increasing crime rate and more people becoming a victim, which supposedly increased fear that led the public to demand the politicians to do something about it.[225] Scheingold (1984) asserts that the punitive law & order values are in harmony with pervasive cultural themes and satisfy a personal need. No overt or covert conspiracies with the

---

[224] Besides Scheingold (1984), others have suggested that levels of 'fear of crime' are overestimated as well (e.g. Farrall et al. 1997: 676; Farrall & Gadd 2004).

[225] Scheingold (1984) discusses another possible explanation of the politicisation of crime next to the 'democracy at work thesis'; i.e. a Marxist interpretation of the finding that 'fear of crime' outpaces actual victimisation and that the public focus is disproportionately on violent crimes. This is because the ruling elites have the will and ways to make the public as fearful and vindictive as needed to divert the attention from the failing of capitalism, reflected by for example poverty, to anxiety about crime. The interpretation poses that crime is politicised by the ruling classes in order to legitimate repression of political opponents. Scheingold argues that both the 'democracy at work thesis' and the Marxist interpretation are one-sided. Besides that, the mainstream 'democracy at work thesis' is too simple since it cannot explain that people who are not victimised are fearful anyway, i.e. it cannot explain the fear-victimisation paradox. According to Scheingold, the opposite conclusion, a Marxist interpretation of politicisation of crime seems to have a somewhat better fit with available data but overstates the conspiratorial and manipulative elements of politicisation of crime.

media are needed to 'deceive' the public. Scheingold instead advocates a cultural perspective; the politicisation of crime is an interactive process that combines elements of both responsiveness to the public, as well as elements of manipulation, e.g. through the media. Politicians simply take advantage of the opportunities provided by the public's state of mind in their election campaigns (see for example Marion 1997). Scheingold suggests that 'fear of crime' is more the product of the rather distorted public images of crime than of crime per se. He advances the increased crime rate, the increase in media attention to crime, or both as starting points. These increases lead to more personal victimisation and vicarious (indirect) victimisation and, following the (indirect) victimisation-causes-fear-model described in chapter 2, this causes an increase of fear, according to Scheingold (1984). Since this fear can trigger either punitive or non-punitive reactions of the public, it is up to the politicians who can capitalise on and contribute to the public emotions by promising punitive and/or non-punitive solutions to the crime problem. The Republican Richard Nixon, who later became president of the USA, issued his first policy position paper titled 'Toward Freedom from Fear' (Harris 1969). Harris, in his analysis of the political uses of 'fear of crime' notes:

> The proper response to crime, according to Mr. Nixon, lay not in cleaning up the slums, where it was bred, but in locking up more malefactors. "If the conviction rate were doubled in this country", he explained, "it would do more to eliminate crime in the future than a quadrupling of the funds for any governmental war on poverty." (p. 73-74)

Scheingold (1984) continues his argument by pointing to the myth of crime and punishment, a myth that dramatizes the conflict between good and evil: bad people make this a dangerous world.[226] America's fascination with violence represents the projection of insecurities; crime and punishment provide the symbols that are used in order to unconsciously release the tensions of insecurities. These insecurities, e.g. worry about marriage, career, children, are compounded in perception of social crisis. The myth of crime and punishment is particularly compelling when people "are most frightened by crime and extremely anxious about other threats to our way of life or our peace of mind" (Scheingold 1984: 75).

So, the initial precondition of a politics of law & order is a public perception that crime threatens the social order, although other threats to society and other personal insecurities are relevant as well. All this paves the road for 'campaigning on crime', on the one hand depicting appealing portrayals of crime, less abstract and more direct, and arousing anxieties, on the other hand providing a solution to the problem, namely more punitive crime control measures. The famous 'broken windows thesis' of Wilson and Kelling (1982)

---

[226] The myth is especially pervasively present in American culture and it resonates well with contemporary insecurities; the myth is culturally well founded and sustained by the easy identification with the vigilante tradition and a belief in individual responsibility. These two themes enable the notion of swift, certain and severe punishment for those who violate society's rules.

also contributed to the idea that deterrence measures and especially the strict control of minor offences, or incivilities, would reduce fear and crime (see Burke 1998; Harcourt 1998; Herbert 2001).[227] Scheingold (1984) sees crime and the 'fear' thereof as typical cultural symbols for focusing the more general concerns about unwelcome changes in society (Scheingold 1984). In other words, Scheingold still acknowledges the notion that the public's fears and opinions are perceived or picked up by politicians. Oliver (2002) shows in a study on the impact of presidential rhetoric on crime over the public's concern for crime being "the most important problem facing the nation", as measured by the Gallup Poll. The findings show that the more attention the American presidents give to crime policy in their State of the Union Addresses, the more respondents become aware of crime as an important issue in their lives, thus shaping their opinion of crime as being one of the "most important problems facing the nation" (Oliver 2002).[228]

8.2.3   The meaning of 'fear of crime'

When 'fear of crime' is analysed as a political symbol, the meaning of 'fear of crime' depends on what is symbolises. Its meaning can be derived from its uses and from the actors who use 'fear of crime' accordingly. So how is 'fear of crime' politicised or used? Generally, 'fear of crime' has been used as argument in favour of a politics of law & order and 'zero tolerance' (Lee 2001). A reduction in fear, derived from surveys and public opinion polls, is often used to indicate that a policy measure has worked well, or that a trend is clear.[229] The instrumental uses of statistics and surveys, including the ones on 'fear of crime' is well expressed by Best (2001), who suggests that people who present statistics have a reason for doing so; they want something just like the media who repeat the statistics in their publications. Especially in the social sciences, statistics "can become weapons in political struggles over social problems and social

---

[227] Exemplary of this strict control, in the sense of aggressive patrol and large numbers of arrest, occurred in New York City, where Mayor Rudolph Guiliani clearly has taken political advantage of reductions in crime (Herbert 2001).

[228] In his analysis of the Gallup Poll Series, the problem of 'crime' included juvenile delinquency, narcotics, drugs, crime, law enforcement, drug addiction, law & order, alcohol, lawlessness, drugs, and drug abuse. All these categories were totalled, giving an aggregate percentage that indicates 'public opinion of crime' (Oliver 2002).

[229] See for example the *Jaarrapport Politie 2003* (BZK 2004) which shows trends in victimisation rate and a version of the familiar 'feeling safe' item. The trends are graphically presented, to indicate that fear is reduced.

policy" (Best 2001: 10). Altering the scales of the axis is just one of the few tricks to make it possible to 'lie with statistics' (Huff 1969; Morris 2001).[230]

When 'fear of crime' reflects power structures depending on gender, class, race and ability, then 'fear of crime' boils down to people's needs (Stanko 1994). Stanko (1994, 1995) suggests that it is unlikely that women's fear is reduced unless all women's needs are addressed, i.e. good lighting, good transport, adequate child care, decent education, safe houses and safe relationships. In this perspective, a lack of autonomy and freedom from sexual danger are conditions of 'fear of crime' (see Stanko 1994, 1995). Most frequently, 'fear of crime' functions as a totally different political symbol. Policy measures that attempt to reduce fear are not presented as reflections of the politician's or government's worry that their image as public protectors is being undermined, as is suggested by Hanmer and Stanko (1985), quite the contrary. These policy measures are proffered as guarantees of security, as "assurance that an established order will prevail", similar to vigilantism and "like any other form of policing" (Johnston 2001: 968–969). In this perspective, 'fear of crime' and the related public opinion polls are viewed as demands for more punitive or repressive actions (e.g. ICPSR 8100 in Appendix F). A higher 'fear of crime' means that more actions should be taken, whereas a lower 'fear of crime' means that the policy measures have worked indeed and should be sustained, increased or toughened. In other words, 'fear' is the legitimation of surveillance, punishment and punitive laws (Altheide 2002). Altheide (2003: 53) concludes his article on the discourse of fear in the mass media in relation to terrorism as follows: "Fear is perceived as crime and terrorism, while police and military forces are symbolically joined as protectors."

8.3 Fear of crime as psychological construct

In this section, the focus is on 'fear of crime' as a psychological construct. 'Fear of crime' has been applied as if it were a personality trait, an emotion or an attitude. Many theories of fear exist; this section clearly does not have the goal to discuss these theories (see Cabanac 2002). Several theories

---

[230] See the classic book on the graphic presentation of numerical data by Tufte (1983), see also Cleveland (1993). Jacoby (1998) seems to maintain one basic criterion for the visualisation of (multivariate) data, which is that the graphics should not be "misleading" (Jacoby 1998: 4), which appears to be Huff's (1969) criterion as well. The review of the available literature on the experience of crime and safety indicated that especially in studies directly related to policy and government, whether on the national or local level, it seems the difference between "significant" and "meaningful" or "relevant" is sometimes forgotten, applying graphics that are attempting to illustrate (usually) the change, but could be regarded just as well as illustrations of "how to lie with statistics". A typical example is provided by the 'safety index' of Rotterdam that has been discussed in chapter 2. The 'safety index' changed from 5.61 to 5.64 on a scale from one to ten, which led the local government and media to conclude that the Rotterdam approach to policing is definitely working (see also Programmabureau Veilig 2002, 2004).

touch on different kinds of fear.[231] Fear, it is asserted here, is an emotion that can be learned, communicated and has a function, with an object that can be real, perceived, as well as constructed.

When an emotion term like *fear* is structurally analysed, by means of for example factor analysis, usually two or three dimensions are found, which appear to be essentially invariant across several languages (e.g. Fontaine, Poortinga, Setiadi & Markam 2002). The first dimension concerns evaluation or valence; i.e. the emotion terms can be categorised on a pleasant/ positive – unpleasant/ negative dimension. The other dimensions are activation (active – passive), dominance (strong – weak) or arousal (high – low).[232] In the study of the cognitive structure of emotion terms of Fontaine et al. (2002) with a Dutch and Indonesian sample, fear is characterised by its position on the first dimension, fear being a negative instead of positive emotion term, and by the second dominance or potency dimension, which separates anger (e.g. 'hate') terms from the fear and sadness terms (e.g. 'fear'). The third dimension that was found in both samples, related to arousal or activation, which distinguishes between sadness terms (e.g. compassion) on the one hand, and fear (e.g. 'panic') and anger terms (e.g. 'fury') on the other hand (Fontaine et al. 2002). Overall, several terms that are related to fear can be grouped together, based on three dimensions. This grouping concerns primarily the connotative meaning of the fear terms; the varieties of fear that play the leading part in several theories are distinct, at least in some respect.

8.3.1   All kinds of fear

Fischer (1991) observes four key aspects of a Western layman's view of emotions, namely corporality, irrationality, involuntarity and animality. Corporality refers to the conviction that emotions are inextricably bound up with the physical and that emotions can be identified by bodily changes. Cannon (1914) for example noticed that these bodily changes are not subject to voluntary action. Irrationality concerns the distinction between passion and reason, incorporating the idea that impulses are far away from rational reflection, are lacking logic, purpose and well-considered judgment (see Frank 1988). This aspect is evident in debates on subjective and objective risk, on the rationality of 'fear of crime' and the discrepancy with 'real' crime rates and on the fear-victimisation paradox, which was discussed in chapters 2, 7 and 8. The third aspect that Fischer considers typical for the Western layman's view of emotions concerns involuntarity; lacking control over one's emotions, which can be seen in expressions such as "being overwhelmed by emotions". Finally,

---

[231] First, *strategic* fear, e.g. studies that take an evolutionary approach and point out the function of fear; *physiological* fear, focusing mainly on biological and physiological changes; *motivational* fear, primarily related to action and action tendencies; *learned* fear, based on learning theories and for example concentrating on socialisation; and finally *political* fear, which is the type of fear that is central to some examinations of social construction.

[232] The three dimensions Evaluation, Potency and Activation are well-known dimensions in the connotative meaning of words and will be discussed further in chapter 10 (see Osgood, Suci & Tannenbaum 1978).

animality, which is suggesting that emotions are connected with primitive or childish behaviour. These last two aspects are primarily related to experiental fear, one of the three basic types of fear as distinguished by Gordon (1980) and Davis (1987). *Experiental fear* refers to the experience or (emotional) state of fear and is marked by the well-known bodily changes and physiological characteristics like sweating and a rapid heartbeat. This is the state of fear (Gordon 1980). In other words, *experiental fear* is actually *being afraid*. The other two types of fear are relational in nature. *Propositional fear*, which means fearing that something is or will be the case, is called relational since it is related to that 'something'. The third type of fear is *reactive fear*, which means being afraid of or frightened by something, it is fear as a result of something and therefore relational as well (Davis 1987).[233]

8.3.1.1   Fear of crime as propositional attitude

Davis (1987) explains these three types of fear, by noting that experiental fear is expressed by 'afraid', whereas propositional fear is expressed as 'afraid that' or 'afraid to', which is usually followed by an action or behaviour, i.e. a verb phrase VP. In general, 'S is afraid to VP' is a reduction of 'S is afraid that if he does VP then something undesirable will result.' Thus, somebody who is afraid to walk in a certain area at night may be certain that s/he will never do that, yet if s/he does and actually would walk in that particular area then something undesirable will happen. Being 'afraid of' is often reducible to 'afraid that' or 'afraid to' and thus can be propositional fear. Following Davis's example, 'being afraid of crime' can be the simple transformation of 'being afraid of becoming a victim of crime'. Yet, 'being afraid of the group of boys hanging around in the neighbourhood' might mean that somebody is afraid that the group of boys will harm him/her. According to Davis (1987), it might also mean that somebody actually experiences fear as a result, somebody might be frightened by the group of boys, which implicates a reaction to the group of boys with fear (reactive fear). In most studies about 'fear of crime', it is not so much the experiental fear (an experiental state) or the reactive fear, rather it is the propositional fear that is investigated. In terms of Davis (1987), 'fear of crime' often is a propositional attitude.

A related distinction is made by Jackson (2004). He argues for a broader attention to 'fear of crime'; researchers should not only focus on the experienced fear, but on 'fear of crime' as a symbol as well. This latter 'fear of crime' is called expressed fear, which refers to the broader social concerns that share social meaning with crime, such as social change and disorder (Jackson 2004), or the violation of social norms (Gabriel & Greve 2003). In addition, specific crimes, the so-called *signal crimes*, are highly relevant for this type of fear. Innes and Fielding (2002) specify *signal crimes* and *signal events* as "an incident that is disproportionately influential in terms of causing a person or

---

[233] The psychoanalytic tradition distinguishes between fear (the German 'Furcht') that has a definite object, and anxiety ('Angst'), which is not related to a conscious object (see Bamber 1979). In general, fear refers to an immediate threat, a specific localised danger, while anxiety is an anticipated subjective danger.

persons to perceive themselves to be at risk in some sense." (5.2) The incident is interpreted as a warning signal that something is wrong or lacking and this signal influences how people construct beliefs concerning other potential dangers and beliefs (Innes & Fielding 2002). People are not actually being afraid, in the sense of experiencing fear with all the bodily changes involved, it is expressed fear that is of concern here. This expressed fear bears similarities with the relational fears, i.e. the propositional and reactive fear of Davis (1987).

Such a distinction between experienced and expressed fear clarifies the many different conceptualisations and operationalisations of the umbrella concept 'fear of crime'. In most research, the expressed (or relational) fear is subject of inquiry. For example, studies that focus on one's own fear of becoming a victim of crime are interested in propositional fear, the fear that this victimisation *will* become the case one day. Studies that utilise indicators of feelings of safety, worry, concern and anxiety about victimisation and crime such as discussed in chapter 2; all these perceptions, attitudes, beliefs, worries, concerns, and other social cognitions relate to crime or symbols thereof crime in the (urban) environment and especially in one's neighbourhood. These studies are basically concerned with the expressed 'fear of crime', or at least a small part thereof.

8.3.1.2   Fear of crime as personality trait

Only a few studies have implied that 'fear of crime' might be a relatively stable trait of someone's personality, similar to satisfaction with life, neuroticism or anxiety. Vitelli and Endler (1993) found that perceived competence and trait anxiety accounted for a significant proportion of the observed variance in reported 'fear of crime'. A more recent article applies the psychological notion of state/trait to the fear of personally becoming a victim of crime (Gabriel & Greve 2003). 'Fear of crime' might be situational (state) or dispositional (trait). Situational 'fear of crime' is a transitory state that varies within a person according to the situation at hand. Dispositional 'fear of crime' – the tendency to experience 'fear of crime' in certain situations and the tendency to react fearfully– is a relatively stable trait, and varies between people. People with such a dispositional 'fear of crime' will have more frequently 'experiental fear'. Gabriel and Greve (2003) say dispositional 'fear of crime' is one of the factors that influences the situational 'fear of crime'. Factors that are correlated with either the dispositional or the situational 'fear of crime' are traits as well; for example emotional wellbeing and one's sense of control, which is related to subjective assessment of one's own capabilities to hold one's own, and being able to cope with the situation without getting things out of hands, i.e. perception of vulnerability and defensibility (Coston & Finkenauer, 1993; Gibbs, Puzzanchera, Hanrahan & Giever 1998; Hollander 2001; Hughes, Marshall & Sherrill 2003). In this perspective, 'fear of crime' is a personality trait. This is in clear contrast with the next perspective, that views 'fear of crime' as a reflection of society's power relations.

8.3.1.3   Fear of crime as instrument of social control

Several authors point to the use of 'fear of crime' as an instrument of social control. Individual choices are restrained by a framework of material and ideological constraints, which embraces, among other things, shared assumptions about appropriate behaviour. These shared assumptions set the limits of appropriate (feminine, street-wise, street-smart et cetera) behaviour (Green, Hebron & Woodward 1987). As discussed elsewhere, when a person did not behave according to the appropriate rules, this has consequences for his or her culpability when s/he becomes a victim. Women especially are seen as particularly culpable if they are unescorted in public places after dark (Green, Hebron & Woodward 1987).[234]

Feminist criminologists stress the political and social structures that underlie the (gendered) patterns in 'fear of crime'. That is, groups that supposedly have less power, i.e. women, the poor, ethnic minorities, homosexuals, report more fear. This fear is considered both a product of and it reinforces their social positions (Koskela & Pain 2000; Stanko 1990, 1999). Fear is normalised, avoidance and precautionary tactics are part of ordinary life (Day 1995; Stanko 1993, 1994). Green, Hebron and Woodward (1987) also conclude that the social control over women's leisure activities is normal, i.e. unexceptional and part of normal, everyday life, and this control is generally seen as natural and legitimate (see Hanmer & Maynard 1987).

In this perspective, 'fear of crime' is an instrument of social control (Clark 1987; Riger & Gordon 1981). Madriz's findings (1997a, 1997b), which were discussed before, demonstrate several examples of this controlling feature. Many respondents pointed to ideas of an 'ideal victim' and expressed a blaming attitude towards non-ideal victims, i.e. victims who had not behaved appropriately and had not violated social norms. An example of inappropriate behaviour is not following a certain dress code. Popular (stereotypical) images of crime and victims affect people's lives in various ways; leisure and other (professional) activities are restricted, people are taught "what crimes to fear, where and when to be afraid, who is dangerous and who is safe" (Madriz 1997b: 343). The stories on crime and victimisation that Wachs (1988) collected often function as cautionary tales, they apply social pressure, reinforce and exercise social control.

8.3.1.4   Fear of crime as aspect of the quality of life

The introductory chapter elaborated on the relation between 'fear of crime' and 'quality of life' or 'wellbeing'. The main argument that is relevant here, states that research on 'fear of crime' is socially relevant when 'fear of crime' has (possible) consequences for the quality of life (Warr 1985). The first category incorporates several studies that basically relate 'fear of crime', similar to crime itself, to (aspects of) public health, the quality of life or wellbeing. A

---

[234] Some women in the interviews explicitly indicated that they did not like to walk alone after dark: "I do it, but I think your nerves are always on edge . . . I've known of so many women that have been attacked."; "That fear is always there." (Green, Hebron & Woodward 1987: 89).

general assumption is that perceptions of safety, i.e. low 'fear of crime', low crime rates are important ingredients of positive quality of life (e.g. Mulvey 2002).[235] This main class of models related 'fear of crime' to (aspects of) public health and the quality of life or wellbeing, and refers to possible consequences of 'fear of crime' in terms of mental distress, which erodes public health.[236] 'Fear of crime', similar to crime, disorder, and other hazards, is viewed as environmental stressor, and people adjust their behaviours to cope with it. In general, there seems to be evidence that 'fear of crime' does contribute to, or at least is related to, poorer health, less wellbeing and less life satisfaction, possibly 'fear of crime' causes mental distress, which erodes public health (see for example Hanson et al. 2000; Krause 1996; Wandersman & Nation 1998).

Apparently, a consensus exists in research on wellbeing, public health or quality of life, about 'fear of crime' and (perceived) crime, especially violent crime, or rather the absence thereof as being either one of the aspects of wellbeing or as a predictor. This becomes clear in studies on social indicators of wellbeing and perceptions of life quality that incorporate perceived safety or the familiar items on 'feeling safe' (e.g. Michalos 2003, 2004). In an American textbook, freedom from fear is contrasted with violence: "Violence results in *human destruction* and is, therefore, a *contradiction* to American values of well-being and freedom from fear." (Lauer & Lauer 2004: 125).

8.3.2   Experiental fear: fear of crime as emotion of danger

Following Frijda (1988), fear, whether elicited in an animal or in a human beings, can be viewed as action tendencies that are functional adaptations to dangerous situations. These action tendencies are rooted in the evolutionary history of humans (see Darwin & Ekman 1998). Fear functions to quickly prepare one to behaviourally respond to danger (Rosen & Schulkin 1998: 327). The experience of fear does not need to be conscious, although it can be; research in this field indicates that fear can be generated rather automatically and unconsciously, just like the appraisal of stimuli as dangerous (Öhman & Soares 1994).

Fear is a central motive state of action tendencies, an emotional state during the expectation of or encounter with danger (Rosen & Schulkin 1998). In the case of a perceived danger, threat or aversive situation, an adaptive fear response is elicited. The fear responses such as changes in heart rate and blood pressure, as well as increased vigilance, are functionally adaptive responses elicited during danger to facilitate appropriate defensive responses that can reduce injury (e.g., escape and avoidance). The increased vigilance suggests *readiness*; a readiness to respond to danger, threat or aversive situations. In other words, when danger is imminent, fear can motivate defensive behaviours such as fight or flight. (Rosen & Schulkin 1998). Fear enables a rapid and energetic

---

[235] This is also reflected by the mapping sentence that Van der Wurff (1992) developed to measure 'fear of crime' or more specifically, 'feelings of safety'. One of the facets that is included in the mapping sentence is related to the consequences for wellbeing.

[236] The other class of models that was distinguished in chapter 1 incorporates the notion of 'fear of crime' having consequences for the extent of crime, disorder and incivilities.

response to imminent threat or danger (Poulton & Menzies 2002). In brief, this perspective suggests that fear and anxious apprehension are emotional responses to danger or threat and motivate the individual to relieve the negative emotional state.

8.3.3   Propositional and expressed fear

Next to experiental fear, i.e. the state of being fearful or afraid, Davis's (1987) distinction was used to explain that 'fear of crime' is primarily propositional fear, i.e. 'fear of crime' is a propositional attitude. In addition, Jackson's (2004) distinction between experienced fear, which is similar to Davis's experiental fear, and expressed fear, in which 'fear of crime' represents a much broader phenomenon than the mere 'feeling safe when walking alone at night'. 'Fear of crime' has to do with crime, especially with signal crimes (Innes & Fielding 2002), but it has much more to do with broader social concerns and personal anxieties than acknowledged in the bulk of research so far.

8.3.3.1   Fear of crime as fear of strangers

In the (empirical) literature, 'fear of crime' frequently comes down to a 'fear of strangers', a fear of the unknown. Fear of strangers seems widespread and is already present in young children, especially the fear of male strangers. The fear of strangers is about Freud's notions of the *unheimlich* and the uncanny (Wilton 1998). The stranger's otherness and the visibility thereof mirrors Douglas's (1978) notion of dirt as 'matter out of place', as something anomalous or inappropriate in a given context, the stranger's otherness is inappropriate and threatens the 'purity' of for example rural space (Little, Panelli & Kraack 2005). When it is easier for someone to be identified as a stranger, as someone who does not belong, as someone 'out of place', the fear of this stranger is reinforced (Valentine 1997).

8.3.3.2   Fear of crime as infringement of territory

Within environmental psychology, researchers have been concerned with 'fear of crime', a sense of safety and security within an environmental context (see Evans & Garling 1991; Gifford 1987; Taylor & Harrell 1996). For example, in a study on instruments that measure quality of the relationship that inhabitants have with their urban neighbourhoods, 'security and tolerance' was found in factor analysis as an independent dimension (Bonaiuto, Fornara & Bonnes 2003). The items that loaded on this factor were for example 'late in the evening there is the risk of dangerous encounters', 'it is not risky to go around late evening', 'the streets are safe enough', 'you can meet bad people', 'people often behave uncivilly', 'green areas are frequented by bad people' (Bonaiuto, Fornara & Bonnes 2003).

Three ideas from environmental psychology are of importance here; the notions of personal space and territory and the idea that safety acts as a dissatisfier (see Gifford 1987). First, the notion of personal space, which refers to an area with invisible boundaries surrounding a person's body into which intruders may not come. In Gifford's words, it is the distance component of interpersonal relations, an indicator of and integral part of the growth, maintenance and decline of interpersonal relationships. Appropriate distances, i.e. not too far away and certainly not too close, are associated with neutral or positive affect, but too-lose and too-far arrangements lead to negative affect. 'Fear of crime' in this view is the invasion of one's personal space, for example when a stranger is approaching a person and asking for money.

The second notion concerns territory. According to Gifford (1987), territoriality refers to the:

> pattern of behaviour and attitudes held by an individual or group that is based on perceived, attempted, or actual control of a definable physical space, object or idea and may involve habitual occupation, defence, personalization, and marking of it. (p. 137)

Different types of territory are defined by territorialities, for example varying in degrees of privacy and the affiliation or accessibility allowed by each type. One's own home is an example of one's primary territory. A primary territory is owned by a person or group, functions at a permanently basis, is controlled and central to daily live. A secondary territory has moderate significance, for which control is less essential, which is more likely to change; secondary territories rotate or are shared with strangers. Public territory are areas open to anyone in good standing with the community, they are open to everybody unless one is excluded (Gifford 1987). In this perspective, 'fear of crime' is the infringement of one's territory; whether it is an invasion, a violation, i.e. a temporary incursion into someone's territory, or mere contamination, i.e. leaving something behind.

The third idea from environmental psychology is the notion that safety acts as a dissatisfier. In environmental assessment, that focuses mainly on individuals' evaluation and descriptions of the quality of the ambient environment, dissatisfiers and satisfiers can be distinguished.[237] A satisfier means that the presence of it has a positive effect, whereas its absence does not really matter. A dissatisfier means that the presence is normal, it is a condition, and does not heighten satisfaction; this in contrast to the situation in which the dissatisfier is absent, which has a negative effect. In other words, in this perspective safety is considered a dissatisfier. Other satisfiers cannot compensate for the absence of the dissatisfier safety. Since safety cannot be entirely guaranteed, this means that 'fear of crime' is the logical result of the absence of total safety.

8.3.3.3   Fear of crime as part of city life

'Fear of crime' is, from the beginning, usually related to larger (inner-) cities and urban life (e.g. Bannister & Fyfe 2001; Flango 1979; Merry 1981; Silverman & Della-Giustina 2001). Hale (1996: 84) suggests that 'fear of crime' is maybe even better characterised as 'insecurity with modern living', a

---

[237] This comes from Herzberg's studies on job satisfaction as function of two types of conditions (hygiene or dissatisfier and motivator or satisfier attributes).

'perception of disorder' or as 'urban unease'. Neill (2001) introduces his analysis of the role that fear plays in promotional and marketing strategies of three major cities (Belfast, Berlin and Detroit) as follows:

> Here, the fears which lurked in the streets of the Dickensian city pale in comparison to the crime generated amidst the stark inequalities and urban horrors of cities in the developing world. (p. 815)

He suggests that fear "is an inescapable dimension of the modern urban experience", at least it is in the image of people and of (potential) visitors to the city (Neill 2001: 815). Stringer (1975b: 264) suggests that the city might be a source of stress, not because it is dirty or noisy, but because the physical environmental features and arrangements encourage activities and behaviour in which proximity between two persons is accidental and without any particular significance to these two persons. In other words, the city is indifferent (Stringer 1975b).

Occasionally, researchers have explicitly emphasised 'fear of crime' in rural areas (e.g. Cates, Dian & Schnepf 2003; Chakraborti & Garland 2003; Smith & Huff 1982; Yarwood & Edwards 1999). A recent article on women's 'fear of crime' in rural areas elaborates on the localised nature of fear and places 'fear of crime' and safety in the context of the 'rural idyll' (Little, Panelli & Kraack 2005; Yarwood 2001). The recurrent theme of the 'rural idyll' consists of strongly held beliefs about the rural community, society and landscape, which underpin the lives of those who live in the rural areas and that shape the expectations and understandings of those who do not live in these areas. Safety is a key component in this 'rural idyll', just like a belief in friendliness of rural people and in the honesty, genuineness, mutual trust and integrity of rural society. The rural social relations, i.e. the emotional bonds are thought to be nurturing, strong and endurable. This clearly is in contrast to the notion of the indifferent city, in which people live anonymously and accidentally run into each other (Stringer 1975b). It is the community that makes the countryside an ideal place for children to grow up (Matthews, Taylor, Sherwood, Tucker & Limb 2000; Valentine 1997). The whole 'rural idyll' circles around safety, as Little, Panelli and Kraack (2005) note:

> Central to the idyllic construction of community found in dominant understandings of rurality is the notion of safety. The harmonious, tight knit and authentic social relations ascribed to the rural community are strongly linked to feelings of security. The safety of the countryside is seen as partly a function of the scale and nature of social relations but also because of its separation from the city. Importantly, these comparisons between the 'safe' countryside and the 'dangerous' city are increasingly reflected in the representation of the urban as a threat to the rural. The safety of rural communities is at risk not from those who belong but from 'outsiders' from urban areas. (p. 154)

In contrast to the 'rural idyll', the city, the urban environment, is considered dangerous (see Davis 2003). This notion of urban crisis, deterioration and decay is reflected in for example television programs and movies (Heath & Petraitis 1987).

8.4   Meaning of fear

How many meanings can a concept, *in casu* 'fear of crime' have? 'Fear of crime' refers to a large variety in opinions, attitudes and concern with respect to crime, social norms and the violation of these norms. The meaning of 'fear of crime' is contingent and contextual, and as this chapter shows, highly dependent on the perspective one takes. In many studies 'fear of crime' means the fear for one's safety and the experience of safety, which is perceived to be threatened by an expected, perceived or encountered 'dangerous' other person. 'Fear of crime' then interacts with both the perception of risk, an estimation that an undesirable or dangerous event will occur and the subjective assessment of one's own ability to deal with the possible threat, the imminent danger. Stanko (1994) suggests most researchers would agree on the basic components of 'fear of crime', i.e. 'fear of crime' as representing a person's diffuse sense of danger about being physically harmed by criminal violence. 'Fear of crime' then is associated with a concern about being outside the home by oneself alone, in an urban area, and potentially vulnerable to personal harm (Stanko 1994). Yet, her work essentially argues that 'fear of crime' is much more than that, or at least it functions as something larger within present society, for example when she suggests that women's fear of crime is a reflection of our sexual integrity at risk (Stanko 1994). Ferraro (1995) theoretically and conceptually defines 'fear of crime' as an emotional response of dread or anxiety to crime or symbols that a person associates with crime, for which a recognition of a situation as at least *potentially* dangerous, real or imagined, is necessary.

So, how many meanings does 'fear of crime' have? All meanings of 'fear of crime' cannot be reduced to a concept with attributes according to the five different conceptual rules that De Klerk and Oostlander (1976) distinguish, who say the attributes within a concept can be affirmative, conjunctive, disjunctive, conditional and exclusively disjunctive. 'Fear of crime' much more reflects a concept with family meaning, since the meanings are dynamic but share some characteristics, i.e. family resemblance, among which are its uses (see Pawlowski 1980: 23-54). The previous chapters on the crime victim survey, criminal victimisation and risk have elaborated on the meaning of 'fear of crime'. One conclusion was that the concept 'fear of crime' derived its meaning from the items that were used from the beginning, which were items that resemble the items that had been and still are being used in public opinion polls. Since criminal victimisation and victimisation are interpreted in a variety of ways in this respect, the meaning of 'fear of crime', that is, how the concept usually is interpreted, is based on a particular interpretation of crime and victimisation and resembles many features with 'risk percpetion' as explored in a whole other discipline. Therefore, the notion of expressed fear and propositional fear is of importance. Table 8.1 summarises this chapter; the next chapter makes a change in focus and elaborates on *operationalisations* instead of *conceptualisations*.

Table 8.1. List of main assertions Chapter 8.

Topic	Explanation
Purpose	Demonstrate the many meanings of 'fear of crime', depending on perspective
Research questions	What are the conditions of a 'fear of crime' How can the concept 'fear of crime' be interpreted? What types of fear exist? To what extent has the notion of 'fear of crime' been dependent on its instrumental uses?
Main notions	Instrumental use of surveys provides fertile ground for 'fear of crime'; interest of the government in people's ideas 'Fear of crime' has two seemingly obvious basic conditions: fear and crime Rooted in its historical background: 'fear of crime' is a political symbol; dynamic interactions between people, public opinion, the press, politics and policy
	Prevention of vigilantism is used as argument not to ignore public's opinion (public's 'fear of crime') Other argument is that taking the public's opinion into account is essential in a democracy
	'Fear of crime' as political symbol and used as argument within specific political framework: A political framework typified as law and order, zero tolerance The democracy-at-work-thesis is used in this framework, but does not hold
	'Fear of crime' as psychological construct: all kinds of fear exist 'Fear of crime' as propositional attitude, as personality trait, as instrument of social control and as aspect of the quality of life Experiential fear (being afraid): suggests fear is an adaptive response to danger Propositional fear: 'fear of crime' comes down to a fear of strangers, an infringement of territory, part of city life
Conclusion	'Fear of crime' as political symbol: used as argument in favour of repressive, punitive measures 'Fear of crime' as psychological construct: propositional and expressed fear

9 Two strategies to improve measurement: continue & start over

As discussed in the introduction (chapter 1), this book focuses on both the conceptualisation and operationalisations of the so-called 'fear of crime'. In the previous chapters, three core concepts relating to 'fear of crime', i.e. victimisation, risk and fear, were unravelled. By now, it is clear that 'fear of crime' is much more complicated than just 'fear' of 'crime', at least as complicated as an elephant is. In the introductory chapter, the six-blind-men-and-the-elephant story was briefly described. The six blind men, each of them touching a different part of the elephant, drew six different conclusions about what an elephant is like. One man alone gives an incomplete description, and each description would be improved when the other parts of the elephant would have been touched as well. In other words, a complex phenomenon cannot be described or pictured when only one or two parts are studied in isolation, without reference to the context or to other possible conceptual elements. Also, there is not a single unique (re)presentation of a complex phenomenon, there is not one single possibility of numerically representing 'fear of crime', or just one and only operationalisation of 'fear of crime'. Questioning the operationalisation and measurement of 'fear of crime' is similar to the question: in what ways can an elephant be presented; what characteristics does the (re)presentation, i.e. the operationalisation and instrument, need in order for it to be referred to as 'elephant', or as 'fear of crime' .

Evidently, research on 'fear of crime' is lacking clear concepts, valid operationalisations and reliable measurement instruments. To a certain extent, research on 'fear of crime' so far has failed to produce a cumulative body of knowledge, which might be due to the failing relationship between the theoretical concept and its empirical realisation in the form of its measurement instrument. In the previous chapters, the focus has been on concepts (chapters 4-8). The next part of this book focuses on the advancement of measurement, while keeping the general objective of this research project in mind. This objective is to contribute both to clear conceptualisation and measurement in order to provide a better understanding of the phenomenon. More specifically, this and the next chapter report the development of more explicitly grounded operationalisations and propose reliable and more valid measurement instruments. In order to do so, two strategies have been employed to contribute to the development of appropriate measurement instruments. The first strategy *continues* with the indicators that have been used so far, which results in the proposal of an instrument that is based on an inventory of these indicators. This chapter builds upon the measurement instruments that have been used so far and attempts to improve these present instruments. The second strategy *starts all over* from scratch, which results in a proposed instrument that is different in format and content and is based on the semantic differential. This second strategy is central to chapter 10, which describes the development this other instrument. Both strategies have their own advantages and disadvantages, and these are discussed here first. Finally, chapter 11 discusses these two proposed measurement instruments in the light of the conceptual analyses and presents the main conclusions as well as some recommendations.

9.1   *Continue or start over: pros and cons*

So, the first strategy to contribute to the development of appropriate measurement instruments is to *continue* the work that has been done so far. This means that the indicators that have been used in research of the past decades are improved. Eventually, this results in the proposal of an instrument that is based on an inventory of these indicators. The second strategy to contribute to the development of an appropriate measurement instrument is to *start all over*, which eventually results in a proposed instrument that is – to a varying extent – both different in format and content. This newly developed instrument is based on the semantic differential (see chapter 10). The advantages and disadvantages of first 'continuing strategy' and second 'starting over strategy' are briefly outlined below.

9.1.1   Continue

9.1.1.1   Pros

A very important advantage of improving the items that are employed frequently is that it is still possible to make comparisons over time. All regular surveys, whether international, national or local, and their accompanying reports pay attention to trends, increases and decreases in 'fear of crime'. Examples of such notions of trends are easy to find in reports on the ICVS (Van Kesteren, Mayhew & Nieuwbeerta 2000), BCS (Allen, Dodd & Salisbury 2005: 8) and PMB (Projectbureau PolitieMonitor 2003a) or POLS Maas-De Waal 2004) and several other regular surveys. For example, Gallup Canada asks since 1970 on a familiar 'fear of crime' -question: "Is there any area around where you live, that is to say within a couple of kilometres, where you would be afraid to walk at night?". As can be seen in Figure 9.1, the percentage of respondents who answer affirmatively is fairly stable. This leads Roberts (2001: i) to conclude that "levels of fear have generally been consistent over the past few decades: 29% expressed fear of walking at night in 1970, and 27% 30 years later." Similarly, Stein (2001: 4) notes: "Since 1970, approximately one-third of those polled have responded that they would be afraid to walk at night in certain areas near where they live."

Besides this first advantage of continuing with the items that have been used for decades, another pro is essentially that it *has* indeed been used for decades. The Likert-type items are familiar and therefore appealing to the public, media, politicians, and so on. The results, usually in the form of descriptive statistics such as the percentage of respondents, who answer in a particular way, are easy to interpret. Press releases and messages in newspapers accordingly often refer to the percentage of respondents who feel unsafe, or the percentage that does feel safe. Increases and decreases in these percentages seem to be rather straightforward: more or less people feel safe. In addition, changes in the percentages are used as indicator of the effectiveness of particular policy measures. Overall then, the familiarity of the items is appealing to the public, the media, government and agencies, which can be seen as a point scored of the traditional items.

Next, improving the instruments that already exist, might turn out to be less expensive than starting all over and implementing a new measurement instrument. Also, improvement might work out better in practice than renewal. Not only because there is already a lot of experience with the traditional items, but also because many studies and surveys are available for more research to enhance the current instruments even further. However, this has hardly been done so far, and continuing with current, traditional items has, besides the advantages mentioned here, a few disadvantages as well.

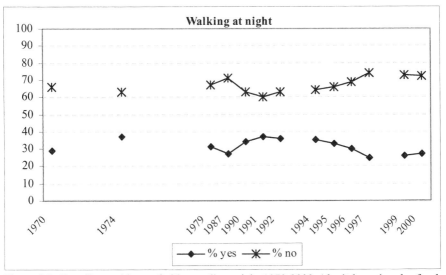

Figure 9.1. Canadian residents afraid to walk at night 1970-2000, 'don't know' and refusals are excluded. Adapted from Roberts (2001) and Stein (2001), original source of the data: Gallup Canada.

9.1.1.2   Cons

Some important drawbacks of continuing with currently used items, result from the historical roots of 'fear of crime', which is discussed extensively in chapters 5 and 8. The popularity of the crime victim survey has led to the problematisation as well as politicisation of 'fear of crime'. In the 1970s, not only crime was seen as a social problem, but 'fear of crime' itself became a problem as well and became a research subject in itself. Also, policy measures to decrease 'fear of crime' were taken and evaluated, frequently together with measures to prevent crime. Overall, 'fear of crime' is primarily related to crime statistics and surveys. Similar to these crime statistics, quantitative information on 'fear of crime' is pervasively instrumental. Descriptive statistics, whether derived from official institutions such as the police or courts, or originating from surveys, seem to be used to 'count & control' and to 'explain and tame'.

The very first crime victim surveys, as well as public opinion surveys on living conditions, often contained the familiar 'feeling safe alone after dark'-item, which became internationally known. Founded on public opinion polling, not so much on conceptual or theoretical considerations, which might explain part of the terminological chaos of related concepts and operationalisations (see chapter 2).

Thus, some disadvantages result from the historical background of 'fear of crime'. Firstly, the items are based on flawed assumptions and secondly, they are not thoroughly thought through conceptually. Crime and 'fear of crime' are historically intertwined, and 'fear of crime' appears to be self-evident, universal and necessary in the late 20th century. Apparently, this has made it almost impossible to look at 'fear of crime' as for instance, an attitude, or as a personality trait similar to neuroticism or trait anxiety. With such a connected history, it is no wonder that it is hard to think of 'fear of crime' as something that might not have to do with crime so much. Yet, this has hindered the understanding of 'fear of crime'.

Though continuing with traditionally used items seems to have the advantage of experience and familiarity, it is striking how research in this field has failed to produce a large body of knowledge, in accordance with the expenses involved. This might also be caused by the lack of specificity of the items, which is reflected by the lack of variance over time, as discussed before and which is reflected in the fairly stable picture of Figure 2.10 and Figure 2.11. Relatively little has been done to improve the reliability and validity of current instruments, let alone that more fundamental theoretical studies have been done, besides some interesting exceptions of recent date (e.g. Jackson 2004).

9.1.2   Start over: pros and cons

9.1.2.1   Pros

A new measurement instrument can benefit from the numerous surveys and studies that have been done so far. Thus, a more fundamental and thorough basis is provided for. Additionally, the instrument can be more conceptually (theoretically) embedded, which makes it possible to reveal new or other insights. Since such an instrument is work in progress, it might take some time to fully benefit from its development. Obviously, this is also one of the disadvantages of the starting-over strategy.

9.1.2.2   Cons

Thus, the new instrument is still work in progress: it has to be administered a couple of times before further analyses can be done in order to enhance the instrument. This might require an investment, and implementing the instrument may possibly cost more initially. Yet, the same can be said of the traditional items, which need to be improved as well. Another disadvantage is that comparisons over (past) time are not possible, which, together with the unfamiliarity of the items and their accompanying responses, is less appealing to the public, media and politics.

9.1.3 Two strategies: advantages and disadvantages

The two strategies that are employed to improve currently used measurement instruments clearly have their own advantages and disadvantages. The first strategy *continues* with the familiar Likert-type indicators that have been used so far, which makes comparisons over time possible. The current chapter employs this strategy and attempts to improve present instruments. The second strategy, described in chapter 10, *starts over*, which results in an instrument that is more thought through and is more conceptually embedded. The major advantages and disadvantages of both strategies are summarised in Table 9.1.

Table 9.1. List of main (dis)advantages two strategies.

Topic		Explanation
Background		Complexity of concepts, as shown in chapters on victimisation, risk and fear of crime
		Current operationalisations/ measurement instruments are flawed, which disables the production of a cumulative body of knowledge
		Two strategies can be employed; either continue and improve existing measurement instruments, or start all over and propose a newly developed one.
Continue	Pro	Comparisons over time still possible
		Familiarity of items is appealing to public, media, researchers, government, agencies
		Less costs implementing
		Improvement might work out better in practice than renewal
	Con	Based on flawed assumptions
		Not thoroughly thought through
		Lack of specificity, lack of variance
Start over	Pro	More conceptually (theoretically) embedded
		More thorough/fundamental basis
		Possibility of revealing new/other insights/understandings (nb gaps)
	Con	Still work in progress
		Comparisons over past time not possible
		Unfamiliarity of items is less appealing to public, media, researchers, government, agencies
		Possibly more costs implementing (investment)

9.1.3.1 *Methodological limitations of the improved measurement instruments*

Though the proposed measurement instruments, either based on a strategy of continuance or a fresh start, are definitely an improvement, they are not perfect. The main methodological limitations of the improved instruments such as described in this chapter and the next are briefly put forward here. Basically, the methodological aspects in the empirical work that call for attention are related to the samples of respondents and the use of self-report measures, which incorporates social desirability issues.

9.1.3.1.1   Respondents

A variety of datasets were used in this research project (see Appendix F), but the specific data that were collected in order to develop the proposed measurement instruments are based on both a student sample and an opportunity (snowball-) sample of older people. This means that the group of respondents is not nationally (let alone internationally) representative. Though such a representative sample would have been better, the current purposes are served well by the samples that were available. For example, compared to findings from national surveys, the sample showed less difference between male and female respondents. In other words, the choice of concepts for the instrument based on the semantic differential format is a cautious one. Furthermore, the results based on analysis of the two subsamples separately, i.e. the sample of students and of older people, showed similar structural features, as did random subsamples from the total sample and the two subsamples. In other words, the structure of the items that will described, is very stable across (random) subsamples, despite the sampling procedure and lack of representativeness.

9.1.3.1.2   Self-report

An obvious limitation relates to the use of self-reports, on which all the proposed measurement instruments rely; other methods to gather quantitative data regarding one's attitudes, perceptions, feelings or cognitions are simply not available.[238] This means that all criticism regarding self-report measures, response styles and –sets as well as (monosource) biases is relevant (see for example Alreck & Settle 1985; Robinson, Shaver & Wrightsman 1999; Tanur 1983). Krosnick (1999) describes two important sources of response sets, namely acquiescence and social desirability. Acquiescence is defined as "endorsement of an assertion made in a question, regardless of the content of the assertion" (Krosnick 1999: 39). In the different empirical studies that were conducted, the instruments employed item reversals, i.e. switching response alternatives from negative to positive and vice versa to minimalise acquiescence. In addition, a comparison is made between forced-choice questions instead of agree-disagree statements (e.g. Converse & Presser 1988). Another advantage of using item reversal, in which the questions do not have the same direction, is that in such a case acquiescence and social desirability do not confound (Hofstee et al. 1998).

In spite of the measures taken considering these flaws (based on especially Alreck & Settle 1985; Converse & Presser 1988; Jenkins & Dillman 1997), some issues remain problematic. For example, the indicators that are based on traditional instruments include elements in the items to describe a

---

[238] On a smaller scale and in an experimental (laboratory) setting, attitudes (and fear) are sometimes measured experimentally by examing physiological qualities and changes by means of for example magnetic resonance imaging, cardiovascular reactivity measures and event-related brain potentials (see Fazio & Olson 2003).

particular situation, like 'being alone in the street at night' or 'being alone at night in your home'. Respondents are invited to think about this situation and report their fear or feelings of (un)safety. However, for several respondents such a situation might be *unthinkable*, in the sense that it rarely occurs, for example because they avoid to end up in such a situation.[239] In many surveys the respondent who denies going out alone at night is asked the question 'how safe would you feel' instead of 'how safe do you feel' (e.g. Office for National Statistics 2004).

Another problem when using self-reports concerns social desirability related to gender differences; male and female respondents on average respond differently to questions about fear and unsafety, which can be partly due to social desirability effects. The social desirability bias refers to the tendency to present oneself in a socially accepted or preferable manner (Nunnally 1978). Differences in fear are, at least to a certain extent, dependent on differential socialisation. When 'fear of crime' and socialisation processes are entangled tightly, the question is even whether this social desirability effect is not *part* of the 'fear of crime' complex. The instrument based on the semantic differential format led to the general conclusion that women evaluate concepts more extremely than men do; 'bad things', such as rape, violence, unsafety and danger, are rated more negatively by women than men, while on the other hand, women rate concepts such as protection and safety more positively. The finding that women tend to report far more fear than men do is consistent in almost every Anglo-Saxon and Dutch study in this field. One approach is to regard this difference as valid and try to explain it; another approach is to consider the difference as a result of unintended measurement effects and thus *not* valid (Vanderveen 2002b). Exemplary of the first approach is Warr's (1984, 1985 and 1987) explanation of the difference that was discussed in chapter 6. He discriminates between offences that incorporate the probability of a personal confrontation with the perpetrator versus offences, which exclude such a confrontation. The offences, which might result in a personal confrontation, are associated with the possibility of assault and rape. In other words, rape is perceived to be a possible consequence of another offence that might involve personal interaction, like robbery or burglary; they are perceived to happen contemporaneously. According to Warr, women have a different 'complex of fear' (Warr 1985, 1987).

The second approach considers the difference to be a result of unintended measurement effects and thus *not* valid. These studies are mostly concerned with socialisation and gendered social desirability and argued that 'fear' or feeling unsafe is not a characteristic that is socially desirable for males and this will lead to underreporting (e.g. Goodey 1995). Thus, the difference that is found can (partly) be the result of *unintended* measurement effects and is

---

[239] Balkin (1979) already noted that (elderly) people avoid walking alone in the street at night precisely because of their 'fear of crime'. Several respondents who participated in the subway-study (chapter 9) said they do not travel alone at night, many of them say this is because of feelings of uneasiness and unsafety.

therefore not valid. Especially when using self-report surveys, which ask about socially sensitive issues like emotions or worries, social desirability bias might distort the information gained from these surveys (Jo 2000; Stöber & Wolfradt 2001). The possible presence of the social desirability bias suggests the necessity of further research to investigate which items are more susceptible to social desirability. For example, some studies have suggested that the gender difference on items concerning the perception of risk is rather small (e.g. Ferraro 1995; Vanderveen 2002b). However, this does not necessarily mean that social desirability is not an issue; again, the question remains whether this difference is valid or not.

In spite of these limitations, the proposed measurement instruments, either based on a strategy of continuance or a fresh start, are improvements when compared to the current state of affairs. Furthermore, the main limitations of the instruments that will be proposed are related to the use of self-report. All other instruments that apply self-report in the data collection, have similar limitations.

9.2   Continuation: inventory

The previous section discussed the pros and cons of improving present instruments. Next, the first strategy *continues* with the indicators that have been used so far, which results in the proposal of an instrument that is based on an inventory of these familiar indicators. The question what is being measured is more systematically analysed in a manner that is based on the ideas regarding content sampling and indicator analysis (Fiske 1971; Hox 1997; Lazarsfeld 1968, 1972a, 1993a). The topic tree in Figure 9.2 presents the outline of this chapter, which primarily is based on three different studies. The first study describes analyses and results of 250 interviews with people on subway stations in Rotterdam. The second study, which is related to the subway-study, administered a questionnaire that contained descriptions of situations, so-called vignettes, to a student sample. Both studies used three different types of techniques to analyse the data, namely factor analysis, hierarchical cluster analysis (HCA) and Multidimensional Scaling (MDS) both to enhance the interpretation of results and to avoid flawed results due to assumptions that are not met. Since these three techniques led to similar results and conclusions, only the MDS analyses and results are described in detail.

Following these two explorative studies and resulting from the previous work on the current state of affairs in chapter 2, an inventory and accompanying questionnaire were constructed. This inventory that consists of a large set of items, is used in several analyses as well. The main questions in this chapter that are addressed focus primarily on interitem-relations and the structure of the items. Attention is paid to the correspondence between items relating to 'feeling safe' and items relating to 'feeling at ease' and to items referring to night time and daytime. It becomes that clear that 'fear of crime' does not have so much to do with crime and that different operationalisations, all frequently used to measure the umbrella concept 'fear of crime' in fact measure different things.

This chapter concludes with the proposal of an instrument that is based on the inventory of the traditional indicators. Unfortunately, the validity of this instrument remains questionable.

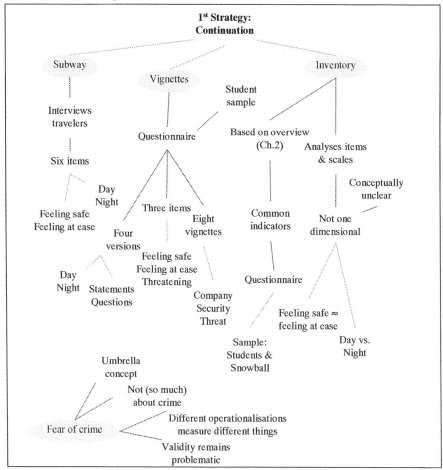

Figure 9.2. Topic tree of chapter 9.

9.3   Study I: Experiencing safety in the subway

This study intended to describe the experience of safety of people in the subway.[240] Moreover, it functioned as an exploration of several research questions on the measurement of feelings of (un)safety, the concept 'victimisation', gender differences regarding the nature of feelings of (un)safety and the influence of environmental cues. Here, only some of the results will be reported, since the question that is of primary interest here is: how are the items related, for example is 'feeling at ease' the same as 'feeling safe' and does the time adjunct 'at night' or 'by day' influence the response patterns?

---

[240] This study has been reported in Vanderveen (1998b, 1998c).

9.3.1   Method

9.3.1.1   Respondents

On six different stations of the subway in Rotterdam, people were asked to participate in a short interview regarding travelling with the subway. During weekdays, in the morning, afternoon and in the (late) evening, 250 interviews were collected. About 53% of the respondents were female, 42% male. The mean age was approximately 39 (SD = 19.8); the youngest respondent was 14 and the oldest 87 years old. A majority of the respondents (58%) travelled daily with the subway, a smaller group (24,8%) used the subway a few times a week. Ten percent of the respondents travelled a few times a month with the subway and 6.8% only a few times a year. Most respondents (33.6%) had finished primary or secondary vocational training; a smaller group (26%) had finished or was still in the last years of university or higher vocational training. About 18% had finished secondary school, and 10% of the respondents had only finished primary school.

9.3.1.2   Instrument

The interviewers[241] asked about personal details like age, education, usual time of travelling by subway, and travel frequency. Further, respondents were requested to indicate whether they themselves had experienced something annoying or unpleasant and whether they had seen something unpleasant happening to somebody else in the subway. These two questions were meant to inquire the direct and indirect victimisation of respondents without limiting the concept 'victimisation' to the offences in the scope of criminal law. The results were discussed in chapter 6 (see Figure 6.3 and Figure 6.4). Moreover, respondents were asked to indicate why they had felt unsafe or not at ease. Another question was about the reasons why respondents did feel safe or at ease. Respondents were also given the opportunity to mention a place or event at or near the station were they were being interviewed, which made them feel unsafe or safe. Of importance here are the items that have been used widely, or at least variations of them. These items attempt to measure feelings of safety, often referred to as 'fear of crime'.

Feelings of safety. Respondents were asked whether they occasionally had feelings of unsafety in the subway. [242] Furthermore, 6 items were used to measure the amount of feelings of unsafety and uneasiness, as listed in Table 9.2. Half of the items asked about these feelings in the daytime, the three others asked about feelings of unsafety or uneasiness in the night time. For example, an item consisted of the question: 'How often do you feel unsafe in the subway in the evening or at night'. The answers of the respondent of four items like this were encoded in categories ranging from 'always' (1), 'often', 'sometimes', 'hardly ever' to 'never' (5). Two items were encoded from 'very safe' to 'very

---

[241] The interviewers were students of the Erasmus University Rotterdam who participated in a course concerning safety. They received a brief training in interviewing.

[242] An important note is that respondents were told that the word 'subway' not only contains the tube itself, but also the station, platforms, and the halls leading to the platforms.

unsafe', since the items asked respondents 'how safe or unsafe do you feel when you are travelling alone by subway'. Another two items did not ask the respondent about 'feeling unsafe', but asked the respondent to say how often he or she did not feel at ease in the subway. When the six items were considered to constitute a scale together, Cronbach's alpha is sufficient ($\alpha = .76$). The scale has a possible range from 6 to 30; a person with a higher score feels safe, whereas a person with a lower score feels unsafe.

Table 9.2. Six items.

Variable	Description
Unsafday	How often do you feel unsafe in the subway during the day
Unsafnig	How often do you feel unsafe in the subway in the evening or at night
Easeday	How often do you not feel at ease in the subway during the day
Easenigh	How often do you not feel at ease in the subway in the evening or at night
Day	How safe or unsafe do you feel when you are travelling alone by subway during the day
Night	How safe or unsafe do you feel when you are travelling alone by subway in the evening or at night

9.3.1.3   Procedure

A structured interview schedule was used, consisting of quantitative and qualitative questions (Gorden 1980). The method of *field-coding* was employed, which is a technique that asks the respondent an open question and giving the respondent the freedom to decide what to answer. This answer however is encoded in the interview schedule. The interview schedule provides a complete list of possible answers and the interviewer marks the answer given by the respondent. Usually, the interviewer has to interpret the answer of the respondent. Therefore, the interviewer repeated the respondent's answer in terms of the list in the interview schedule. An example might clarify this procedure: The interviewer asks the respondent how often he or she travels on the subway. The respondent answers: "Only on Tuesday, Wednesday and Thursday, because I am going to night school then". The interviewer marks in the schedule the answer 'a few times a week' and says to the respondent: "So, you travel a few times a week on the subway". This procedure not only gives the possibility to verify the answer given by the respondent, but is also a way to show the respondent that the interviewer has been listening, is interested.

9.3.2   Analysis and results subway-items

The data on the seven items were screened with PRELIS (Jöreskog & Sörbom 1988a). From the whole sample (N=250), most respondents did not have any missing values, or just one (37) or two (28).[243] To increase the sample size, a multiple imputation procedure was applied (see Jöreskog 2001a), that used the responses on the other items to estimate the most likely response on the missing item. The distribution of data on six of the items is presented in Table

---

[243] Here, missing value refers also to the permitted response "don't know".

9.3.[244] The data on these six items were used in confirmatory factor analyses, which did not lead to proper solutions.[245]

Table 9.3. Univariate marginal distributions subway-items after imputation.

Variable	Frequency (%)				
	Always	Often	Sometimes	Hardly ever	Never
Unsafday	3 (1.2)	1 (0.4)	15 (6.0)	19 (7.6)	212 (84.8)
Unsafnig	6 (2.4)	17 (6.8)	46 (18.4)	4 (1.6)	177 (70.8)
Easeday	5 (2.0)	9 (3.6)	36 (14.4)	28 (11.2)	172 (68.8)
Easenigh	9 (3.6)	28 (11.2)	66 (26.4)	41 (16.4)	106 (42.4)
Day[246]	1 (0.4)	6 (2.4)	6 (2.4)	93 (37.2)	139 (55.6)
Night[247]	8 (3.2)	29 (11.6)	37 (14.8)	75 (30.0)	57 (22.8)

After that, descriptive statistics were used for explorative purposes.[248] Figure 9.3 represents the mean score on the six items regarding 'feelings of safety'. Some observations can be noted, for example the difference between daytime and night time, indicating that respondents, whether male or female, feel safer during the day. This finding is consistent with many other studies that use such an item. Also, at first sight, there seems to be a slight difference between *feeling unsafe* and *not feeling at ease*. Possibly, 'feeling at ease' encompasses more than 'feeling unsafe'. Another finding is that most respondents feel relatively safe, considering the mean score for every item, which varies from 3.51, the mean of female respondents on the item 'feeling at ease', to 4.9, the mean of the male respondents on the item 'feeling safe during the day'. A small majority of the female respondents (57.9%) and 81% of the men responded negatively to the question 'Do you once in a while feel unsafe in the subway'. About 42% of the women and only 19% of the men answered this

---

[244] On the dichotomous item, 77 respondents answered "yes" (30.8%) and the large majority, 173 respondents (69.2) answered "no".

[245] Confirmatory factor analysis was applied despite the violation of assumptions, which turned out to be problematic. This sample might not be large enough to estimate an asymptotic covariance matrix and the data is obviously not (multivariate) normally distributed. Boomsma & Hoogland (2001) have studied the consequences of small sample size and nonnormality with respect to the model estimates. Larger sample size, higher factor loadings and more indicators per factor lead to less nonconvergence and less improper solutions, and these three aspects may compensate for one another. Thus, when the number of indicators per factor, NI/NF, is two, a sample size of at least 400 is required, whereas when NI/NF = 3 or 4, a sample size of at least N=100 is required, and N > 200 is generally better. Moreover, they conclude that the Maximum Likelihood method (ML) of estimation works quite well under circumstances of nonnormality (Boomsma & Hoogland 2001). Therefore, confirmatory factor analysis was applied despite the violation of assumptions. Three models were tested, firstly a model within which all items represent one latent construct, secondly, a model that proposes two latent constructs, namely 'feeling safe' (4 items) and 'feeling at ease' (2 items). The third model consisted of two latent constructs as well, 'day' and 'night'. Both WLS and ML were used, but the results indicated improper solutions (i.e. negative errorvariances) and large fit statistics (both RMSEA and χ^2) or did not converge.

[246] Five respondents said they do not travel alone during the day (2.0%).

[247] Several respondents said they do not travel alone at night (N=44, 17.6%).

[248] Results presented here are based on imputed data. Original findings did not differ much from findings presented here; see Vanderveen (1998b, 1998c).

question affirmatively. Thus, most respondents do not 'feel unsafe'. This finding is in accordance with figures publicised by the company who operates the subway (VanOverbeeke 1993; RET 1996).

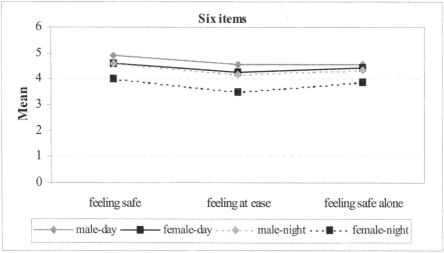

Figure 9.3. Feeling safe, at ease and feeling safe alone in the daytime and night time.

The interitemcorrelations, i.e. Pearson's correlation coefficients, are presented in Table 9.4.[249] Though all correlations are significant, they seem to be of a moderate magnitude (see Robinson, Shaver & Wrightsman 1999), which is reflected by Cronbach's alpha (α = .76). Cronbach's alpha is not a measure of item homogeneity or unidimensionality of a set of items (Boyle 1991; McDonald 1981; Schmitt 1996). Even when a scale is multidimensional, reliability might still be quite high (see Becker 2000; Shevlin et al. 2000; Streiner 2003). Thus, to be able to answer the question how the items are related, more analysis is needed. However, since structural equation modelling could not be used, three different types of analyses were done to investigate the structure of these six items. Besides a factor analysis, hierarchical cluster analysis (HCA) and Multidimensional Scaling (MDS) were applied as well, to enhance the interpretation of results and avoid flawed results due to assumptions that are not met. Since these three techniques led to similar results and conclusions, only the MDS analyses and results are described in detail and this section concludes with a summary of the results.

9.3.2.1   Multidimensional Scaling

Multidimensional Scaling (MDS) was applied, which was complemented by HCA and PCA to enable the interpretation of findings. The goal of MDS is to construct a map of locations of the items relative to each other (the distances) from data that specify how different the items are (dissimilarities)

---

[249] The nonparametric interitemcorrelations, namely Spearman's rho, based on the correlation between ranks, and Kendall's tau-b, were quite similar to the correlation coefficients presented in the Tableand were significant at the .01 level.

(see Coxon 1982). The items are moved around in such a way, that the result is a configuration that best approximates the dissimilarity data by transforming the raw data into disparities, which fit the distances in the configuration the best. This specific configuration has the maximum goodness-of-fit, or rather the minimal badness-of-fit that is usually reflected by the stress.[250] Next, the dissimilarities can be interpreted in terms of underlying dimensions.[251]

Table 9.4. Interitemcorrelations (pmcc) six items, N= 250.

Variable	Unsafday	Unsafnig	Easeday	Easenigh	Day
Unsafnig	.50**				
Easeday	.43**	.29**			
Easenigh	.31**	.58**	.57**		
Day	.16*	.20**	.37**	.17**	
Night	.17**	.43**	.20**	.53**	.34**

** correlation significant at .01 level; * significant at .05 level (2-tailed).

The six items were analysed by non-metric MDS (PROXSCAL).[252] The one-dimensional solution has a normalised raw stress of .056 and a Tucker's coefficient of congruence of .97. Thus, the six items can be represented by only one dimension, pictured as a horizontal line with the three items 'easeday' (-.67), 'unsafday' (-.56) and 'day' (-.46) clustered together on one side. The two items 'easenigh' (.29) and 'unsafnig' (.30) take a position somewhat in the middle, whereas the last item, 'night' (1.1) lies at the end of this dimension. The findings illustrate the similarity between 'at ease' and 'feeling safe' items. Large negative values on this sole dimension reflect feeling very safe and feeling at one's ease, and large positive values on this dimension reflect feeling unsafe.

Though the six items can be fitted on one dimension, a much better fit (less stress) is acquired when two dimensions are applied.[253] The normalised raw stress of this two-dimensional solution equals .001, which indicates an almost

---

[250] The higher the stress value, the worse is the fit of the reproduced distances in the configuration to the observed dissimilarities matrix. Although other related measures do exist, most of them amount to the computation of the sum of (squared) deviations of observed dissimilarity data from the reproduced distances (Coxon 1982; Kruskal & Wish 1978). Raw stress is the residual sum, and when normalised invariant under change of scale; a perfect stress is 0 and reflects a perfect monotone relationship between dissimilarities and distances (Kruskal 1964a, 1964b). Kruskal (1964a) states a stress of 2.5% is excellent and 5% is good, whereas a stress of 10% and 20% is fair and poor respectively.

[251] However, the orientation (the axes) might be arbitrary and therefore difficult to interpret. For example, the first axis might be the longest, the second the longest-but-one et cetera.

[252] The only assumptions of MDS are that the data are (dis)similarity data and measured in the same metric; no further distributional assumptions exist. However, the results are computed differently for the different measurement levels and thus might lead to different results. Ordinal or non-metric MDS is more problematic concerning the minimisation of the error and maximising the goodness-of-fit (Young 1981). Also, the data could be considered interval, since they are not mere rankings and possibly have enough answer categories. Therefore, both metric and non-metric MDS or rather PROXSCAL is applied (Meulman, Heiser & SPSS 1999). Both non-metric MDS and metric MDS were performed (see Kruskal & Wish 1978; Rabinowitz 1984). The metric and non-metric results are quite similar and therefore, only non-metric results are presented here.

[253] Though a third dimension in the configuration decreases stress, the decrease is too small to legitimate the less parsimonious solution. Non-metric MDS has a normalised raw stress of .0002, metric MDS of .0005.

perfect fit.[254] Though the number of coordinates is small, it appears that the x-axis distinguishes between the 'day' and 'night' items. The y-axis distinguishes the 'at ease' items, with positive value coordinates, from the 'unsafe'-items. However, this distinction is of lesser importance than the main notion that items referring to being 'at ease' and 'feeling safe' are rather similar. In the factor analyses, these items were not distinguished from one another. Similarly, findings from the HCA indicated on the one hand that the three 'day' items are different from the two items on 'feeling safe at night' and 'feeling at ease at night', while on the other hand the findings show the similarity between 'at ease' and 'feeling safe' items.

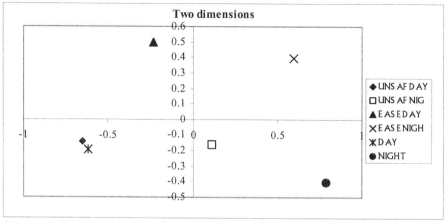

Figure 9.4. Two-dimensional configuration, non-metric PROXSCAL.

9.3.3 Brief discussion of results

This study was primarily intended to describe the experience of safety of people in the subway. Based on previous empirical studies, six familiar items were used to assess feelings of safety. Some items made reference to "feeling at ease" instead of "feeling safe". Cronbach's alpha of these six items together is sufficient, yet is not a measure of item homogeneity or unidimensionality. At first sight, descriptive statistics seem to point out a difference between *feeling unsafe* and *not feeling at ease*. Both factor analysis, hierarchical cluster analysis (HCA) and Multidimensional Scaling (MDS) were done to investigate the structure of these six items, enhance the interpretation of results and avoid flawed results due to assumptions that are not met. Only the results from MDS are reported here in detail.

All results from these three types of analyses show that though the items might be considered unidimensional, they appear to be less homogenous when looking at two-dimensional solutions. In general, the findings point out that the items referring to feeling 'at ease' and 'safe' are rather similar, whereas the format of the items (i.e. with reference to frequency or not) and especially

---

[254] In accordance with the stress, Tucker's coefficient of congruence is .9995.

the time adjunct ('day' or 'night') are of much more importance with respect to the structure of the six items.

9.4 Study II: Vignettes

The next study intended to describe the experience of safety of people when they think of themselves as being in the subway (see Vanderveen 1998b, 1998c). Again, the focus was on the exploration of several research questions like the measurement of the feelings of unsafety, the concept 'victimisation' , gender differences in the nature of feelings of unsafety and the influence of environmental cues. Here, some of the results of the study will be reported that focus primarily on the following three questions. First, do the three different types of items, i.e. the items on 'threat', 'feeling safe' and 'at ease' constitute three reliable scales of eight items each? Do the three different types of items, i.e. the items on 'threat', 'feeling safe' and 'at ease' represent one latent construct together or does each type represent one latent construct by itself? And third, does the format of the item, i.e. whether a question or a statement is used, influence the response?

9.4.1 Method

9.4.1.1 Respondents

The total sample (N= 232) consists of students of three different faculties of the Erasmus University Rotterdam participated in this study, following courses in law (N= 156), history of art (N= 25) and sociology (N= 51). Female respondents (65.9%) and male respondents (31.4%) had a mean age of 21.4 years (SD = 4.77); the youngest respondent was 18 and the oldest 60 years old. Since two to three returned questionnaires had a large number of missing values, most analyses were performed on a sample consisting of 229 or 230 respondents.

9.4.1.2 Instrument

Apart from some demographic questions, like age and sex, the questionnaire contained an item about the travel frequency of the respondent on the subway. Respondents were requested to indicate whether they themselves had experienced something annoying or unpleasant and whether they had seen something unpleasant happening to somebody else in the subway.[255]

Versions of vignettes. Each questionnaire contained eight descriptions of situations or vignettes. All vignettes were set at the subway platform and can best be described by using a mapping sentence. As presented in the mapping sentence in Figure 9.5, a version either presented situations during daytime or during the night, as well as three domain facets, namely 'company', 'security measure' and 'source of threat'. These three facets were varied in the descriptions of the situations, each having two elements, as can be seen in both

---

[255] In the questionnaire, the word 'subway' was described as containing the tube itself, but also the station, platforms, and the halls leading to the platforms. These general questions were similar to the questions that were used in the subway-study.

the mapping sentence (Figure 9.5) and Table 9.5. A possible structuple is: "Late at night, you're walking alone at the subway platform. There is a security officer present. A group of boys makes unpleasant remarks", which is vignette 1 in the night time questionnaire (see Table 9.5 and Table 9.6).[256]

A description belongs to the universe of 'vignettes on experience of safety'					
		Time		**Company**	
when it contains an	a1	by day	b1	alone	
indication of	a2	late at night	b2	with someone else	
		Security		**Threat**	
	c1	security officer	d1	group of boys make unpleasant remarks	
	c2	CCTV	d2	tramp lies on the ground	

Figure 9.5. Mapping sentence of vignettes.

After each vignette, three items followed that purported to measure 'fear of crime' or rather possible aspects of the experience of safety. These items were based on traditional items and were either in the form of a statement, or in the form of a question. In this manner, four versions of the questionnaire were created, differing in the time adjunct that was included and in item format (Table 9.6). The four different versions were randomly distributed and preliminary analysis showed no typical differences between the four groups of respondents.

Table 9.5. Vignettes and their structuples.

Vignette	Structuples	Company	Security	Threat
1	b1c1d1	alone	security officer	boys
2	b2c1d1	together	security officer	boys
3	b1c2d1	alone	CCTV	boys
4	b2c2d1	together	CCTV	boys
5	b1c1d2	alone	security officer	tramp
6	b2c1d2	together	security officer	tramp
7	b1c2d2	alone	CCTV	tramp
8	b2c2d2	together	CCTV	tramp

Items. Each participant read eight vignettes, descriptions of situations, and after each description, s/he responded to three items. Hence, each questionnaire contained (3x8) 24 items. In the statement-mode, responses ranged from '1' (absolutely disagree) to '5' (absolutely agree). The first item was formulated as "I find this situation threatening", the second item touched on the 'feeling safe'-operationalisation; "I feel safe in this situation" and the third item was "I feel at ease in this situation". The question-mode used the items "How threatening do

---

[256] The Dutch original was: "Je loopt 's avonds laat alleen op het metroperron. Er is een beveiligings-beambte aanwezig. Een groepje jongens maakt vervelende opmerkingen." A vignette in Dutch referring to a tramp or homeless person is for example: "Je loopt overdag alleen op het metroperron. Er is een beveiligingsbeambte aanwezig. Verderop ligt een zwerver." This can be translated as: "By daytime, you're walking alone at the subway platform. There is a security officer present. Further down lies a tramp".

you find this situation?" with responses ranging from '1' (not threatening at all) to '5' (very threatening). The second item asked: "How safe do you feel in this situation?" and responses ranged from '1' (very safe) to '5' (very unsafe) and the third item asked: "Do you feel at ease in this situation?" for which the responses ranged from '1' (yes, very at ease) to '5' (no, not at ease at all). Thus, for all types of items a higher score indicates more 'fear'.

Table 9.6. Four versions.

Time Format	Day	Night
questions	day1 (1) N=60	night1 (3) N=56
statements	day2 (2) N=54	night2 (4) N=62

9.4.1.3   Procedure

During a regular lecture of their course and after a brief introduction, the students were explained that they could participate by filling in a paper-and-pencil questionnaire. The questionnaires were returned during the break of the lecture.

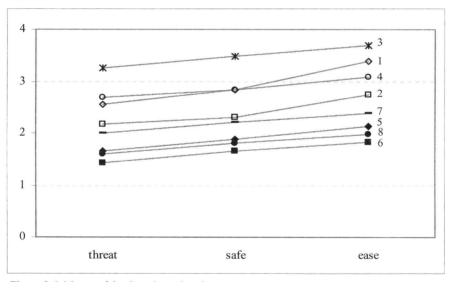

Figure 9.6. Means of the three items by vignette.

9.4.2   Analysis and results

9.4.2.1   Means

Figure 9.6 presents the means on the three item-types by the eight vignettes. Since a higher score indicates more 'fear', respondents have evaluated vignette 3 (alone, CCTV, group of boys) most negatively. The vignette (no.6) that appears to be the least threatening is the situation in which one is together with somebody else, while a security officer is present and a tramp lies on the ground.

9.4.2.2 Three reliable scales

Each student responded to eight vignettes by indicating the applicable answer on the three different types of items, i.e. the items on 'threat', 'feeling safe' and 'at ease'. This makes it possible to investigate whether three reliable scales can be constituted of eight items each. Table 9.7 presents Cronbach's alpha's for the whole sample, for each version and for each format. The reliabilities are high, although some variety exists as can be seen from the 'at ease' items in the fourth version (.74) and in the second version (.93). All reliabilities are high enough to state that the items on 'threat', 'feeling safe' and 'at ease' constitute three reliable scales. Whether these scales are one-dimensional and thus whether the items are homogeneous can be examined in further analysis.

Table 9.7. Reliability (Cronbach's α).[257] N= 229 or 230.

Sample	Threat (8)	Safe (8)	Ease (8)	Total (24)
Whole sample	.85	.87	.87	.94
day1 (1)	.89	.87	.88	.96
day2 (2)	.83	.89	.93	.95
night1 (3)	.85	.87	.88	.95
night2 (4)	.80	.78	.74	.90
questions (1+3)	.88	.88	.88	.96
statements (2+4)	.82	.84	.85	.93

9.4.2.3 Latent construct

As noted before, a high reliability does not necessarily mean internal homogeneity. The structure of the total 24 items and the three sets of eight items are studied by means of HCA, MDS and factor analysis, i.e. principal component analysis.[258] The question is whether the three different types of items, i.e. the items on 'threat', 'feeling safe' and 'at ease' represent one latent construct together or whether each type represents one latent construct by itself.[259]

Results from non-metric MDS (PROXSCAL) show that the items asking about threat, feeling safe and at ease can be presented on one dimension, but according to the stress, two dimensions fit the data slightly better.[260] The

---

[257] Standardised item alpha's are not presented because they are almost the same as Cronbach's alpha's.

[258] The sample size is too small to compute the asymptotic covariance matrix that is needed when performing ordinal structural equation modelling. Also, the covariance matrix of all the items is not positive definite, possibly due to the small sample size.

[259] All analyses reported here were also performed on the four subsamples, e.g. day1, as well as on two subsamples, e.g. the two versions using statements. Results are quite similar and the relevant conclusions are the same.

[260] The one-dimensional solution has a normalised raw stress of .013 and a Tucker's coefficient of congruence of .994; the two-dimensional solution has a normalised raw stress of .008 and a Tucker's coefficient of congruence of .997. Thus, stress is only decreased a little bit in the two-dimensional solution.

one-dimensional solution ranges from 'threat6' to 'ease3'. 'Threat6' refers to the threat-item on the structuple b2c1d2, thus the situation of walking with somebody, in the presence of a security officer while a tramp lies on the ground (see Table 9.5). The item 'ease3' refers to the ease-item of the b1c2d1-situation, thus referring to walking alone with CCTV present and a group of boys making unpleasant remarks. Overall, higher scores on this dimension mean that the situation is more negatively evaluated, i.e. more threatening, feeling less safe and not feeling at one's ease. Furthermore, the one-dimensional solution sharply distinguishes between the vignettes that incorporate the group of boys (nos.1, 2, 3 and 4) and vignettes that refer to the presence of a tramp (nos. 5, 6, 7 and 8). This is shown in Figure 9.7, which displays the magnitudes of the coordinates of the three types of items (threatening, feeling safe and at ease) for the eight different items. Evidently, the three types of items connected to the tramp-vignettes have negative coordinates on the one dimension, whereas the items of the boys-vignettes have positive coordinates. The figure also shows that the threat-item of vignette 6 ('threat6') has the most negative value and the ease-item of vignette 3 ('ease3') has the highest positive value.

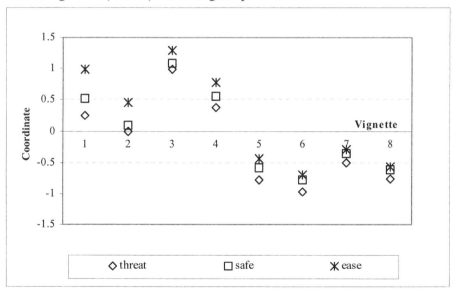

Figure 9.7. Coordinates of the three items by vignette; one-dimensional solution.

Though two dimensions decrease stress a little, this decrease might be too small to legitimate an extra dimension.[260] In the two-dimensional configuration, the horizontal axis clearly distinguishes between the twelve items connected with vignettes that note the 'tramp lying on the ground' (nos. 5, 6, 7 and 8), which have a negative value on this dimension, and the twelve items belonging to vignettes (nos. 1, 2, 3 and 4) that note the 'group of boys making unpleasant remarks'. This distinction is emphasised in Figure 9.8 and is similar to the one-dimensional findings. The items 'safe3' and 'ease3' have the highest, i.e. positive value, whereas 'threat6'and 'safe6' have the most negative values.[261] However, the vertical axis does not clearly discriminate between vignettes nor item-type, has a smaller range, and is more difficult to interpret. Therefore, the two sets of items, one set on the group of boys, the other on the tramp, were analysed by means of MDS separately as well.

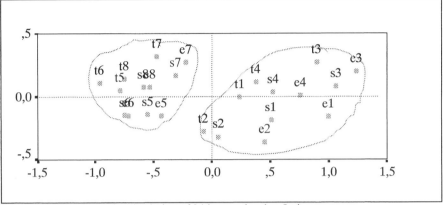

Figure 9.8. Two-dimensional solution of 24 items related to 8 vignettes.

The twelve items belonging to vignettes (nos. 1, 2, 3 and 4) that note the 'group of boys making unpleasant remarks' can best represented by two dimensions (Figure 9.9).[262] The two dimensions are difficult to interpret. It seems the horizontal dimension distinguishes between the third and second vignette most clearly, and these two vignettes differ with respect to one's company (alone or together) and the type of security that is present (CCTV or a security officer). The vertical axis does neither clearly discriminate between different vignettes nor types of items.

The twelve items belonging to vignettes (nos. 5, 6, 7 and 8) that note the 'tramp' can best represented by three dimensions.[263] Again, the dimensions are quite difficult to interpret, since they seem to distinguish between both type of item and vignette contents (Figure 9.10). It is helpful to check which items have the most extreme scores on a dimension. Three threat-items (t6, t8, t5) have the most negative scores on the first dimension, whereas safe and ease items have the most positive scores (e8, e5, s7, e7). The rest of the items, except for s6, do not have high scores on this dimension. In general, the first dimension seems to distinguish between threat-items, since three out of four have highly negative scores, and the safe and ease items, which have neutral or highly positive scores. Furthermore, all items of vignette 7 have positive coordinates on this first dimension. All the safe and ease items related to vignette 5, 6, and 8, score

---

[261] The x-values are: ease3 (1.24), safe3 (1.06), threat6 (-.96) and safe6 (-.78).

[262] The one-dimensional solution has a normalised raw stress of .052 and a Tucker's coefficient of congruence of .974; the two-dimensional solution has a normalised raw stress of .012 and a Tucker's coefficient of congruence of .994. The three-dimensional solution decreases stress (.002; .999) somewhat, but this small reduction does not seem to legitimate an additional dimension.

[263] The one-dimensional solution has a normalised raw stress of .17 and a Tucker's coefficient of congruence of .91; the two-dimensional solution has a normalised raw stress of .048 and a Tucker's coefficient of congruence of .976. The three-dimensional solution decreases stress further (.004; .998).

negatively on the second dimension. All threat-items as well as all items related to vignette 7 score positively on this dimension, which indicates again the difference between both type of item and contents of the vignettes. On the third dimension, the three items of vignette 8 have the most negative values, and the three items of vignette 5 have the most positive values. Overall, the three-dimensional configuration demonstrates both the different types of items and the different contents of the vignettes.

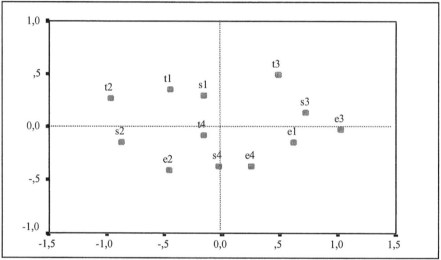

Figure 9.9. Two-dimensional solution of 12 items related to 4 vignettes referring to 'boys'.

Figure 9.10 clearly shows a pattern of the items relating to the type of vignette; one can draw a line easily through each set of items. Part of the figure accentuates these 'lines'. On the other hand, the order of the items on each of these four lines appears to follow a specific pattern as well; on the fictitious line is the order ease-safe-threat.

9.4.2.4   Three types of items

The PROXSCAL-procedure on the eight 'threat'-items demonstrate that these items are best represented by one dimension, on which the four items connected to vignettes referring to the 'group of boys' have positive values and the other four that refer to 'tramp' have negative values on this dimension. The 'safe'-items display the same pattern, as well as the 'at ease'-items. These latter eight items can also be placed in a two-dimensional space. Table 9.8 summarises the results from these PROXSCAL analyses.

The relevant findings from HCA indicate firstly that the differences between *vignettes* are more important than differences between the three types of items, since items are clustered (in later stages) with respect to the contents of the vignettes. However, a second notion derived from these results is that the 'safe' and 'at ease' items connected to a particular vignette are more similar than the 'at ease'-item and 'threat'-item of a vignette, whereas some 'threat' items are clustered together, e.g. threat5, threat6 and threat 8, which are all connected to vignettes that refer to 'tramp'. The factor analysis (PCA) of the dataset also indicates the importance of the contents of the vignettes, especially the difference between the threatening circumstance, i.e. 'group of boys' versus 'tramp', while on the other hand pointing out the similarity between the 'safe' and 'at ease' items. The results, which are not reported here in detail, clearly suggest the difference between tramp and boys vignettes on the one hand, and the distinction between the 'safe' and 'at ease' items versus 'threat'-items on the other hand.

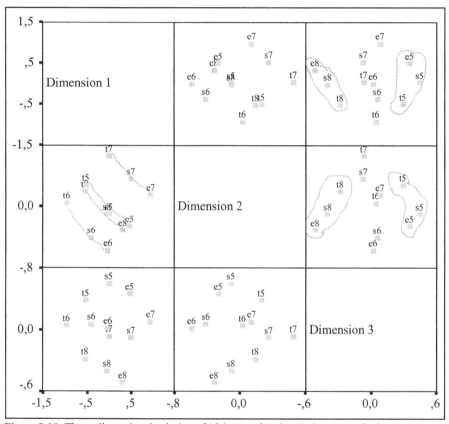

Figure 9.10. Three-dimensional solution of 12 items related to 4 vignettes referring to 'tramp'.

So, do the three different types of items, i.e. the items on 'threat', 'feeling safe' and 'at ease' represent one latent construct together? In a sense, they do, since the three different types end up in clusters or components with one another. The primary distinction appears to be resulting from the contents of the vignettes, specifically 'tramp' versus 'boys'. However, the results clearly suggest that the two types 'at ease' and 'safe' are more similar compared to 'threat'. Moreover, each type of item can be scaled well within a one-dimensional solution.

Table 9.8. Summary of findings non-metric PROXSCAL, different types of items.

No. of dimensions	Normalised raw stress	Tucker's coefficient of congruence
Threat		
One dimension	.0004	.9998
More dimensions	far more stress: worse fit	
Safe		
One dimension	.0004	.9998
More dimensions	far more stress: worse fit	
Ease		
One dimension	.0004	.9998
Two dimensions	.0002	.9999
More dimensions	far more stress: worse fit	

9.4.2.5   Format of items

Next, the question whether the format of the items influences the response, i.e. whether a question or a statement is used, is discussed. Based on the previous analyses, three scales were used, which are made up of the sum of the three types of items. Descriptive statistics were used for explorative purposes. Figure 9.11 represents the mean score on the three sumscales for each of the four versions of the questionnaire, a higher score means feeling not at ease, nor safe and finding the situation more threatening.

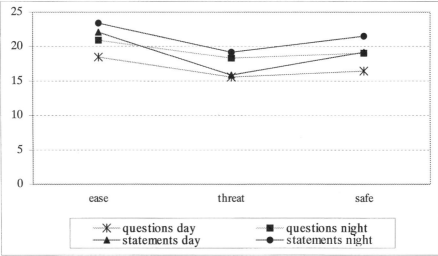

Figure 9.11. Means on three types of items by (2x2) sort of questionnaire.

From this figure, it can be seen that the night-versions yield higher responses than the day-versions and that the statement-format yields higher responses than the question-format. Simple t-tests show significant differences for sex on all three scales, confirming the frequent finding that men respond less 'fearfully'. Therefore, sex is used as covariate in a multivariate general linear model with a 2x2 factorial design of which the results are summarised in Table 9.9. The multivariate tests show that the factors 'time' and 'format' indeed have significant effects, but their interaction is not significant. A related model that specified interaction effects between the two factors and covariate 'sex' shows that these are not significant at all.

The magnitude of the time-effect, the format-effect and the sex-effect can be derived from the estimates of the effect size (eta-squared), which is an indication of the proportion of total variance of the dependent variable that is attributable to the particular factor or as the amount of overlap between the two groups. A common rule of thumb is that an effect size of .2 is small and all estimates are smaller than that (Cohen 1988), which is not to say that it is not important (cf. Chow 1988). For example, the effect size of the factor 'format' is larger than the effect size of the factor 'time'. Consequently, the question whether the format of the items influences the response, needs to be answered affirmatively. A questionnaire that employs statements will yield responses that indicate more feelings of uneasiness, unsafety and threat.

Table 9.9. Results of General Linear Model-analysis.

Effect	Dependent	df	F	Significance	Eta-squared
sex	multivariate	3	15.6	.000	.17
	ease	1	44.0	.000	.16
	threat	1	25.6	.000	.10
	safe	1	41.3	.000	.16
time	multivariate	3	8.1	.000	.10
	ease	1	7.2	.008	.03
	threat	1	23.0	.000	.10
	safe	1	14.1	.000	.06
format	multivariate	3	11.5	.000	.13
	ease	1	20.5	.000	.08
	threat	1	1.5	ns	.007
	safe	1	19.8	.000	.08
time x format	multivariate	3	1.2	ns	.02
	ease	1	1.2	ns	.005
	threat	1	.1	ns	.001
	safe	1	.3	ns	.001

9.4.3 Brief discussion of results

This vignette study used a mapping sentence to create eight descriptions of different situations, so-called vignettes. These situations differed regarding one's company, the type of security present, and the source of (possible) threat. Four questionnaires were made, varying on the time adjunct (night or day) and the format of the items. These items were based on traditional indicators and referred to 'feeling safe', 'feeling at ease' and 'threatening'. These three items followed after each of the eight vignettes. So, each participant responded to eight vignettes by indicating the applicable answer on the three different types of items, i.e. the items on 'threat', 'feeling safe' and 'at ease'.

Three questions were of primary interest here, firstly whether the three different types of items, i.e. the items on 'threat', 'feeling safe' and 'at ease' constitute three reliable scales of eight items each. All reliabilities appeared to be high enough to answer this question affirmatively; the items on 'threat', 'feeling safe' and 'at ease' constitute three reliable scales of eight items each. Since a high reliability does not necessarily mean internal homogeneity or one-dimensionality, the structure of the total 24 items and the three sets of eight items were studied by means of HCA, MDS and factor analysis (PCA). Thus, the second question that was investigated was whether the three different types of items, i.e. the items on 'threat', 'feeling safe' and 'at ease' represent one latent construct together or whether each type represents one latent construct by itself. When analysing all items, MDS made clear that though the 24 items asking about threat, feeling safe and at ease can in fact be presented on one dimension, stress is quite high. A two-dimensional solution has a better fit, in which the horizontal axis distinguishes between the twelve items connected with vignettes that note the 'tramp lying on the ground' (nos. 5, 6, 7 and 8), which have a negative value on this dimension, and the twelve items belonging to vignettes (nos. 1, 2, 3 and 4) that note the 'group of boys making unpleasant remarks'. Other findings from HCA and PCA in which all 24 items were analysed also indicate that the differences between *vignettes* regarding the source of (possible) threat might be more important than differences between the *three types of items*. The three different types end up in clusters or components with one another and the primary distinction is more related to the contents of the vignettes. For example, in PCA the different types of items end up in one factor related to the group of boys making remarks. Also, items are clustered with respect to contents of vignettes in a later stage, suggesting that the vignettes are more different from one another than the three item-types are. In spite of the importance of the vignettes, it became also clear that the 'safe' and 'at ease' items are more similar than the 'at ease' and 'threat' items. Thus, to some extent the three different types of items, i.e. the items on 'threat', 'feeling safe' and 'at ease' represent one latent construct together. Additionally, the 'at ease' and 'safe' items are rather similar compared to the 'threat' items. This is in line with some authors who have stated that 'feelings of safety' are rather vague and diffuse; these items on the extent to which somebody feels at one's ease might touch on the same vague affective construct.

Moreover, when analysing the three sets of eight items each separately, findings showed that each type of item could be scaled well within a one-dimensional solution. This means that the items on 'threat', 'feeling safe' and 'at ease' constitute three reliable and one-dimensional scales of eight items each.

The third question that was investigated focused on the *format* of the items. Since the item mode had been varied, the effect of the item format, i.e. whether a question or a statement is used, could be studied. It turned out that the effect size of the factor 'format' is even larger than the effect size of the factor 'time', though they are both quite small. However, this means that a questionnaire that employs statement will yield responses that indicate somewhat more feelings of uneasiness, unsafety and threat.

9.5   Study III: The inventory

The results of the overview of the various sources, i.e. survey questionnaires, raw data, articles, books and reports (see Table 2.2), served as the basis for a questionnaire. Many (variants of) the operationalisations and items described in the previous sections on the subway and vignette-study were included in the inventory, nonetheless some selections had to be made due to space and time limitations. Also, some less common items were given priority. Since the inventory results from the overview of the current state of affairs, items that have been criticised but are nonetheless frequently used, are included as well. In other words, this inventory is indeed the sheer continuation of past empirical research, since it includes all kinds of indicators that have been used so far. A questionnaire is constructed based on this inventory, which consequently consists of a large set of items.

9.5.1   Method

9.5.1.1   Respondents

One part of the sample consists of law students who followed a course in "psychology and law" (N= 149) at the faculty of law of the Erasmus University Rotterdam. Their mean age was 25 years (SD 5.9). Most of them (87.2%) were full-time students, who followed the course during the day. The other students participated in the same course in the evening. The course paid attention to empirical research and the questionnaire as well as its results were used to illustrate several aspects. Most of the students are female (72.5%). Subjects live with their parents (37.6%), together with their partner (22.1%), in a house with other students (18.8%) or alone (11.4%). We asked about the location of their high school as well; most of them went to school in a large city (30.9%), for example Rotterdam, or in a smaller town (46.3%) or village (16.1%).

The other part of the participants (N=105) consisted of older family members (M= 51.0; SD = 7.5) or acquaintances of the students. Students were asked to find somebody, preferably someone of an older generation like one's parent, who could fill in a questionnaire as well. Again, the majority (68%) is female. About 68% lives together with their partner. Our total sample thus consisted of 260 respondents, most of them (about 70%) female. The average age of our sample is about 36 years (M=35.8; SD=14.4).[264]

9.5.1.2   Instrument

The questionnaire consisted of different sections. Besides an introduction, indications how to fill in several parts and two general questions about both sex and date of birth, the questionnaire contained many scales of a study concerning the semantic differential as well, as will be discussed in

---

[264] In some analyses, fewer questionnaires were used (about 254). In these analyses, the seven questionnaires were excluded from the analysis performed here, due to the results of preliminary analysis. Missing value analysis indicated that respondents generally answered all items. The data were checked to identify possible response patterns and outliers.

chapter 10. Table 9.10 presents the most common operationalisations that were in fact included. These common operationalisations were discussed extensively in chapter 2, in which several examples of items, as used in former research, were given. The items included in the questionnaire have been copied from these previous studies and are therefore only briefly described here.

Table 9.10. Common operationalisations.

Label of operationalisation	Description of operationalisation
Perception of risk (RP)	Estimation of chance on victimisation of specific crime
Concern (CN)	Concern about becoming victim of specific crime
Feelings of safety (FS)	Feeling safe when walking alone at night
Behavioural constraints (BC)	Constraining own behaviour, taking precautionary measures
Relative perception of risk (Rel)	Chance on victimisation compared to others
Seriousness of consequences (Ser)	Estimation of consequences when becoming victim of crime
Afraid of victimisation (AF)	Being afraid of becoming victim of specific crime
Afraid of other's victimisation (AFO)	Being afraid that significant other becomes victim of crime

Feelings of safety. The basic item 'how safe do you feel when walking alone at night?' was used as a template to create five other items. A day and night-version of 'how safe do you feel walking alone in the street' and the same for 'how safe do you feel when walking with somebody in the street' were used in the questionnaire. Also, the item 'how safe do you feel when alone at home at night' was included in this set and format. Answers vary from 1 'very safe' to 7 'very unsafe'.

Concern about victimisation. The next four items are rather common in surveys as well and refer to the amount of concern about becoming a victim of a specific crime. The first two items asked 'how concerned or unconcerned are you about becoming harassed, threatened or abused, in this neighbourhood', specifying the time by adding 'by day' and 'by night'. The other two asked 'how concerned or unconcerned are you about getting burgled when you're not at home', again specifying the time by adding 'by day' and 'by night'. Answers range from 1 'very concerned' to 7 'very unconcerned'.

Relative risk perception. Three items asking about an estimation of the chance on becoming a victim of a crime compared to others were included. Instead of varying the type of criminal offence, the comparison was varied, that is 'do you think you have a bigger chance on becoming a victim of a crime than others in your neighbourhood/ in the city you live in/ in the Netherlands'. Answers range from 1 'a much bigger chance' to 7 'much less chance'.

Feeling at ease. Although not frequently used at all, the five items referring to feelings of safety were reformulated by using the phrase 'feeling at ease'. Based on the subway and vignette-study, these items were included: 'to what extent do you feel at ease when walking alone in the street at night/ being alone at home at night/ walking with company in the street at night/ walking alone in the street during the day/ walking with company in the street during the day'. Answers have a range from 1 'very much at ease' to 7 'not at ease at all'.

Seriousness of the consequences. Items were included on the estimation of the seriousness of the consequences when becoming a victim of burglary/ vandalism/ robbery/ maltreatment/ threat/ fight/ and sexual harassment.[265] The questions used the formulation 'how big do you think the seriousness of the consequences will be when you yourself will become a victim of....during this year?' Answers vary from 1 'very big' to 7 'very small'.

Objects of fear. Fourteen items asked about particular 'objects' of fear, touching on the degree of fearing certain situations, people or places. The formulation of the items have the format 'to what extent are you afraid in the subway/ alone in a car/ at a tram/bus stop at night/ in a badly lit street/ of youth hanging around/ when walking alone in the street at night/ of junkies/ of Dutchmen/ when alone at home at night/ of foreigners/ when walking with company in the street/ of men with tattoos/ of people who seem to be aggressive/ when walking alone in the street during the day'. Answers range from 1 'not afraid at all' to 7 'very afraid'.

Perception of risk. This refers to the estimation of the chance on becoming a victim of a specific crime. Items on the perception of risk of becoming a victim of burglary/ vandalism/ robbery/ maltreatment/ threat/ fight/ sexual harassment were included, using the template 'how big do you think the chance will be that you yourself will become a victim of....during this year? Answers range from 1 'very big' to 7 'very small'.

Fear of victimisation. These same offences were used in questions touching on the fear of victimisation, the degree of being afraid of becoming a victim of a specific crime. We used the format 'to what extent are you afraid of becoming a victim of burglary/ vandalism/ robbery/ maltreatment/ threat/ fight/ sexual harassment. Answer categories range from 1 'not afraid at all' to 7 'very afraid'.

Fear of other's victimisation. This refers to what has been called 'altruistic fear', the degree of being afraid that significant others (e.g. partner, children) will become a victim of a specific crime. Similar to the items on fear of personal victimisation, the items on fear that somebody else is victimised followed the format 'to what extent are you afraid that somebody you love will become a victim of burglary/ vandalism/ robbery/ maltreatment/ threat/ fight/ sexual harassment.[266] Again, answers vary from 1 'not afraid at all' to 7 'very afraid'.

Media portrayal. The last set of questions is more heterogeneous; these do not seem to attempt to make up a scale, reflecting a latent construct. Two questions referred to crime and violence as pictured in the media, namely: 'crime/violence is more serious/less serious/about as serious as the newspapers and television tell us'.

---

[265] Robbery has been the translation of the Dutch "diefstal op straat" (being robbed while on the street).

[266] This is the version of the questionnaire for the older generation. Students received a version in which 'somebody you love' was replaced by 'your friend', in Dutch 'je vriend of vriendin' which can be interpreted as 'boyfriend' or 'girlfriend' as well, but not necessarily so.

Comparison of neighbourhood. Another question was included as well: 'according to you, how dangerous or safe[267] is your neighbourhood, compared to others', with categories ranging from 1 'much more dangerous' to 7 'much safer'.

Increase or decrease in crime. Two items are related to the magnitude of crime, namely 'do you think crime in your neighbourhood has increased, decreased or stayed the same?' and its variant, replacing 'in your neighbourhood' with 'in the Netherlands'. Answer categories, analogous to the question, are 'increased', 'decreased' and 'stayed the same'.

Ringing doorbell. The item on the situation that a person is at home alone and hears a ringing doorbell ring is included, asking respondents whether s/he would open the door as usual, would not open the door at all, open the door only when it is somebody s/he knows or when the person at the door makes a reliable impression.

Constrained behaviour. Three items refer to the extent to which a person constrains his or her behaviour, two of them using categories from 1 'always' to 7 'never'. These are 'how often does it happen that you avoid certain areas in the place you live because you feel unsafe' and 'how often does it happen that you are on your guard (alert) when you're walking on the street'. The last question, 'to what extent do you adapt or restrict your behaviour because of reasons of safety', could be answered from 1 'a lot' to 5 'not at all'.

9.5.1.3   Procedure

Students followed a course focussing on empirical research in the field of psychology and law. Both the questionnaire and its results were used to illustrate several aspects. During a class, the questionnaire was introduced and students were briefly informed about purpose and contents of the study. Students were asked to fill in the questionnaire during class. The paper-and-pencil questionnaire included an extensive introduction and explanation. Examples were used to illustrate in what way a respondent could indicate an answer.

Also, students were asked to find somebody, preferably someone of an older generation like one's parent, who could fill in a questionnaire as well. This questionnaire was returned at another class, two weeks later. This questionnaire differed from the student-questionnaire only slightly. For example, the introduction and instructions used a different personal pronoun.[268] Regarding contents, there is a difference in the formulation of the items on the fear that somebody else becomes a victim. The students received a version that asked 'to what extent are you afraid that your friend will become a victim'[269] whereas the other version asked 'to what extent are you afraid that somebody you love will become a victim'.

---

[267] In Dutch: 'gevaarlijk' (dangerous) and 'ongevaarlijk' (not-dangerous).

[268] The students received a questionnaire, which used the Dutch pronoun 'je'. The other questionnaire addressed the participants more formally, using the pronoun 'U'.

[269] In Dutch the phrase 'je vriend of vriendin' was used, which *can* be interpreted as 'boyfriend' or 'girlfriend', but not necessarily so.

9.5.2 General analysis and results of the inventory

Many items in the inventory have been used as indicators in other publications; that is, they are presented as if they measure a (latent) concept. Factor analysis is used to learn more about the structure of this particular set of items and the meaning of the concepts, as measured by the inventory.[270] Factor analysis identifies a relatively small number of underlying factors or constructs (e.g. scales) which account for the correlations between the variables (i.c. items). Thus, it is possible to investigate whether items supposedly having a strong association (namely the items which tend to measure more or less the same) are actually explained by the same factor. The question studied here is: what is the relationship between all the items? For example, do items touching on concern about victimisation differ from items that refer to the likelihood of this victimisation?

9.5.2.1 Results of the factor analysis: general relationships

In this explorative analysis, a principal component analysis was used as well as a Varimax rotation to enhance interpretability. To determine how many factors should be included in the model, eigenvalues, factorloadings and the scree plot were studied.[271] In Table 9.11 you will find the results of the factor analyses after rotation. Only the variables having a factorloading of .6 or higher are printed.[272]

In general, the items that were supposed to measure about the same thing can in fact be described as linear functions of factors. The ten factors together explained 72.6% of the variance. The first two factors, which explained 13.6% and 9.1% of the variance, touch on the fear a person has that either a significant other or that s/he personally becomes victimised. The third factor (8.9%) includes all items about how serious the consequences will be when actually victimised. The fourth factor (8.4%) contains the items concerning the perception of risk, whereas the fifth factor (7.2%) contains items on the diffuse feelings of safety at night, but also the items that touch on a more general feeling of being at ease at night. Four items on concern about victimisation make up the sixth factor (5.7%). The seventh factor (5.4%) contains three items 'feeling safe', and the three items on the chance on victimisation compared to others load high on the eight factor (5.3%). Also, the three items on behaviour make up the

---

[270] Though factor analysis requires an interval level of measurement and the current level of measurement is ordinal, an interval level is assumed here. This seems justified, since the results of a cluster analysis, which assumes an ordinal level are quite similar.

[271] The criterion that a factor (component) should have an eigenvalue of 1 or more was used. This means that every factor in the final solution has at least a variance of 1, since the eigenvalue expresses the variance of a factor. The scree plot offered a visual check for the number of factors. Also, the factor needs to be constituted of items, touching on the interpretation of the factors, with a factorloading of at least .6. In the general factor structure, an 11th factor with an eigenvalue of more than 1 appeared as well. However, since no item had a factorloading of more than .6, this factor is omitted.

[272] The following items have a factorloading which is less than .6, so they do not appear in the factor solution: fear of becoming a victim of burglary, perception of risk on becoming a victim of a fight and perception of risk on becoming a victim of sexual harassment. This last item loaded as the only item (.54) on the 11th factor.

9th factor (4.6%) and two items regarding "being at ease during the day" are the only items of the 10th factor (4.4%).

The general conclusion from these analyses is that most sets of items, that vary on a specific theme, like the fear of personal victimisation, are reflected by the factor structure as well. Thus, the fear of becoming a victim of crime can be distinguished from feeling unsafe and from the perception of risk. However, two departures from this general picture are very clear. First, the distinction between feelings of safety by night is distinguished from the feelings of safety by day. Additionally, another observation is that 'feeling safe' is *not* differentiated from 'being at ease'. These sets of items seem to touch on the same latent construct, although a distinction is made between these diffuse feelings of safety during the day and similar feelings at night.

Table 9.11. Results of explorative factor analysis.

General structure of the inventory for the whole sample	
1st Fear of victimisation of others	**13.6%**
Fear that other becomes victim of threat	.89
Fear that other becomes victim of physical abuse	.88
Fear that other becomes victim of robbery	.84
Fear that other becomes victim of vandalism	.82
Fear that other becomes victim of fight	.81
Fear that other becomes victim of sexual harassment	.81
Fear that other becomes victim of a burglary	.79
2nd Fear of personal victimisation	**9.1%**
Fear of becoming a victim of threat	.79
Fear of becoming a victim of physical abuse	.78
Fear of becoming a victim of sexual harassment	.75
Fear of becoming a victim of a fight	.72
Fear of becoming a victim of robbery	.72
3rd Seriousness of the consequences of victimisation	**8.9%**
Seriousness of consequences when victim of violence	.90
Seriousness of consequences when victim of physical abuse	.88
Seriousness of consequences when victim of threat	.86
Seriousness of consequences when victim of sexual harassment	.80
Seriousness of consequences when victim of sexual assault	.77
Seriousness of consequences when victim of burglary	.61
4th Perception of risk on victimisation	**8.4%**
Perception of risk on becoming victim of vandalism	.76
Perception of risk on becoming victim of physical abuse	.75
Perception of risk on becoming victim of threat	.75
Perception of risk on becoming victim of burglary	.75
Perception of risk on becoming victim of theft	.68
5th Feelings of safety at night	**7.2%**
Feeling safe when alone in street at night	.76
Being at ease when alone in street at night	.74
Feeling safe when alone at home at night	.67
Being at ease when alone at home at night	.62
Being at ease when together in street at night	.60

Table 9.11 – continued.

General structure of the inventory for the whole sample	
6th Concern about victimisation	**5.7%**
Concern about getting harassed, threatened, abused by day	.78
Concern about burglary when not at home during the day	.75
Concern about burglary when not at home at night	.69
Concern about getting harassed, threatened, abused at night	.69
7th Feelings of safety during the day	**5.4%**
Feeling safe when together in street during daytime	.84
Feeling safe when alone in street during daytime	.81
Feeling safe when together in street at night	.71
8th Relative perception of risk	**5.3%**
Chance on victimisation than somebody else in city	.87
Chance on victimisation than somebody else in neighbourhood	.85
Chance on victimisation than somebody else in Netherlands	.81
9th Behavioural constraints	**4.6%**
Adjust or constrain behaviour	.82
Being alert in the street	.82
Avoidance of certain places	.64
10th Being at ease during the day	**4.4%**
Being at ease when together in street during daytime	.83
Being at ease when alone in street during daytime	.80

This became more evident in another explorative factor analysis (see Vanderveen 2000) of the same sample, except twenty respondents who were excluded because of extreme responses, in which comparable results were found. Yet, some differences appear as well. For example, the items on 'feeling safe' and 'at ease' clustered together in two factors; the distinguishing feature appeared not to be that either people feel safe or at ease, but rather how they generally feel at night or during the day. Here, this is only reflected by the fifth factor that shows a similar pattern, since it is made up of both items on 'feeling safe' and 'at ease', with a common characteristic namely 'at night'. Another difference is that the items on the perception of risk were separated into two factors; one factor touched on the perception of risk on becoming a victim of a criminal event that implies a physical confrontation with the perpetrator. The items on the perception of risk on becoming a victim of a crime that implies a certain loss, destruction or damage of property and other material objects loaded high on the ninth factor.

This general factor structure has been replicated in a cluster analysis, using the same sample. Moreover, Rietveld administered the inventory to students in Amsterdam and applied cluster analysis, which revealed a very similar pattern (Rietveld 2000). Also, though some differences do emerge, this global picture of the factor analytical structure is approximately the same for men and women. Thus, about the same underlying factors or constructs (e.g. scales) account for the correlations between the items. However, the results of the male sub sample were more difficult to interpret and showed a few negative loadings and two uninterpretable remaining factors (see Vanderveen 2000).

9.5.3   Analysis and results three-factor solution

9.5.3.1   Retaining three factors

As a next step, the inventory was used in a factor analysis in which only three factors were extracted.[273] This was done to explore whether the analytical difference between the affective, cognitive and conative modality is represented by the empirical data. Scales measuring aspects of the same modality (e.g. affect) are assumed to have a common basis, and should end up in the same factor when a (restricted) factor analysis is done. The total sample was used in a similar procedure as the previous ones, with the exception of the restriction of the number of factors. The three factors together explained only 45.5% of the variance (see Table 9.12). Many items were excluded from the final solution, since they had a loading less than .6. For example, all the items on the perception of risk, relative risk and the items that purport to measure behavioural constraints are excluded from the final results. Also, all except one item referring to concern were not included in one of the three factors.[274]

Table 9.12. Three-factor solution.

Three factors in the structure of the inventory	
1st Fear of victimisation	**19.6%**
Fear that other becomes victim of vandalism	.85
Fear that other becomes victim of burglary	.85
Fear that other becomes victim of robbery	.84
Fear that other becomes victim of threat	.84
Fear that other becomes victim of physical abuse	.80
Fear that other becomes victim of a fight	.77
Fear that other becomes victim of sexual harassment	.69
Fear of becoming a victim of burglary	.68
Fear of becoming a victim of vandalism	.72
Fear of becoming a victim of robbery	.62
2nd Feelings of safety	**16.8%**
Being at ease when together in street at night	.70
Being at ease when alone in street at night	.70
Feeling safe when together in street at night	.64
Feeling safe when alone at home at night	.63
Feeling safe when alone in street during daytime	.62
Being at ease when alone at home at night	.61
Feeling safe when alone in street at night	.60
3rd Seriousness of the consequences	**9.2%**
Seriousness of consequences when victim of violence	.90
Seriousness of consequences when victim of physical abuse	.86
Seriousness of consequences when victim of threat	.83
Seriousness of consequences when victim of sexual harassment	.81
Seriousness of consequences when victim of sexual assault	.77

---

[273] Instead of the criterion that all factors are retained that have an eigenvalue of at least 1.

[274] Other items not included: seriousness consequences burglary, being at ease when home alone at night, being at ease when together in street during the day.

The three factors do not represent the three modalities. The first factor (19.6%) holds rather specific affective items, relating to fear of a concrete victimisation experience. The second factor (16.8%) touches on vague affective states, embracing items on feelings of safety and being at ease. Finally, the last factor (9.2%) comprises items on an estimation of the impact of victimisation that touch more on a cognitive modality. Again, this factor solution shows that fear of criminal victimisation is different from feelings of safety.

9.5.4 Discussion of general results

The inventory, embracing several common operationalisations, was used in factor analysis and cluster analysis to examine the general structure as well as differences between men and women and to examine whether the analytical distinction between the cognitive, affective and conative modality was represented by the data.

Probably the most important conclusions (see Table 9.13), derived from the results are that most sets of items do not have the same latent factor, they are not similar to one another; the fear of other's victimisation is different from the fear of personal victimisation, which are both different from concern about victimisation and from general feelings of safety. On the contrary, these general feelings of safety consist of items on feeling safe and being at ease, whereas these feelings during the day have something different in common than these diffuse feelings by night.

Table 9.13. Relevant conclusions.

Conclusions: factor analytical structure of inventory
Clear
Fear victimisation others $\neq$ fear personal victimisation
Fear victimisation (others $\vee$ personal) $\neq$ perception of risk $\neq$ feelings of safety $\neq$ concern about victimisation $\neq$ seriousness consequences $\neq$ behavioural constraints
Perception of risk $\neq$ perceived relative risk
Less clear
Perception of physical risk $\neq$ perception of material risk
(Being at ease during day $\cong$ feelings of safety during day) $\neq$ (Being at ease at night $\cong$ feelings of safety at night)

From the restricted factor analysis, it becomes clear that three factors do not represent the three modalities. Many items were omitted since they did not meet the criteria. Nonetheless, the difference is shown once again between rather specific affective items, relating to fear of a concrete victimisation experience, items on vague or diffuse affective states, embracing items on feelings of safety and being at ease, and finally items on the estimation of the impact of victimisation. A major disadvantage is the small number of behavioural items, which might have led to the result that no behavioural factor was found in this last analysis. Considering the results of the previous analyses, in which the behavioural items were among the last factors and explaining little variance, this is not very likely to be a major drawback.

The plausible conclusion from this exploratory research is that the distinction between different aspects or operationalisations makes sense.[275] The underlying structure of several items generally seems to be in accordance with the intended structure. That is, the different 'scales' appeared clearly in the results of the factor analysis. In the next section, these 'scales', their structure and relationships with one another are examined more closely, resulting in the proposal of an instrument.

9.6   Deriving an instrument from the inventory

From the previous part, it is clear that the distinction between different aspects or operationalisations makes sense, at least empirically. Overall, the different 'scales' appeared clearly in the results of the factor analysis. Some basic statistics for these scales, which for current purposes incorporate all relevant items, are presented in Table 9.14.[276] The results from factor and cluster analysis suggest that the 'feeling safe' items and 'at ease' items belong together, distinguishing between items with a reference to night or day. Thus, two more scales were constructed that incorporate these items, named *okd* and *okn*. Here, a *higher mean* on a scale means *more* of the aspect or supposedly latent construct that is being measured. Thus, a higher mean on for example *fs* (feelings of safety) and *eas* (feeling at ease) indicates feeling *more* safe and feeling *more* at ease, whereas a higher score on *cn* (concern), *rp* (perception of risk), *af* (afraid of victimisation) means *more* concern, *more* perceived risk and being *more* afraid of victimisation. The mean value of each respondent on every scale was calculated by dividing the values on several scales by the number of items (M/I in Table 9.14). A reliability analysis was included as well. According to the simple criterion that holds that an alpha of .65 is the lower limit, all reliabilities are sufficient.

The various operationalisations are obviously different. In other words, the operationalisations and/or indicators that have been used to measure the umbrella-concept 'fear of crime' are not comparable, since they measure different things. Not surprisingly, since the conclusion from the conceptual analysis of the three core concepts relating to 'fear of crime', i.e. victimisation, risk and fear, was that 'fear of crime' is much more complicated than just 'fear' of 'crime'. When administering a survey that includes items such as the 'feeling safe'– items that were included here, the results cannot be compared to findings derived from a survey that included items on the perception of risk, or items on concern about victimisation or items that ask how afraid the respondent is to become a victim of a specific crime. In accordance with the story of the elephant, when only one part is touched, it is not possible to draw any conclusions regarding the whole. The analysis of the inventory shows that a complex phenomenon cannot be described or pictured when only one or two

---

[275] More confirmatory factor analyses are required to study the replicability and exclude the possibility of capitalisation on chance in this analysis. Since this questionnaire has already been administered to other samples, more analyses will become possible in the near future.

[276] In spite the fact that not all items were equally important, e.g. some loaded much higher than others on a factor, and some were excluded from the final factor solution.

parts are studied. The correlation coefficients in Table 9.15 show that the different operationalisations do seem to touch on related aspects. This is in line with the notion that there is not one single possibility of numerically representing 'fear of crime', or just one and only operationalisation of 'fear of crime'.

Table 9.14. Basic statistics and reliability; listwise valid N = 238.

	Scale	N	Items	M	M/I	SD	α[277]
rp	Perception of risk	257	7	22.6	3.2	8.7	.86
cn	Concern	260	4	11.8	3.0	6.0	.85
fs	Feelings of safety	259	5	26.9	5.4	6.1	.82
bc	Behavioural constraints	259	3	12.0	4.0	4.7	.74
rel	Relative perception of risk	260	3	8.1	2.7	4.1	.84
ser	Seriousness of consequences	259	6	33.9	5.7	7.6	.89
eas	Being at ease	256	5	27.1	5.4	6.3	.83
af	Being afraid of victimisation	258	7	23.3	3.3	10.1	.92
afo	Being afraid of victimisation of others	256	7	27.6	3.9	11.6	.96
okd	Safe & at ease (ok) day	260	4	24.4	6.1	4.5	.82
okn	Safe & at ease (ok) night	256	6	29.6	4.9	8.0	.86

Table 9.15. Correlations (pmcc), N=250.

Var.	rp	cn	fs	bc	rel	ser	eas	af	afo	okd	okn
rp	1										
cn	.60**	1									
fs	-.45**	-.41**	1								
bc	.26**	.31**	-.27**	1							
rel	.32**	.24**	-.14**	.27**	1						
ser	.17**	.18**	-.13**	ns	ns	1					
eas	-.50**	-.41**	.68**	-.27**	-.18**	-.17**	1				
af	.56**	.55**	-.47**	.37**	.27**	.25**	-.50**	1			
afo	.45**	.51**	-.38**	.22**	.21**	.30**	-.38**	.67**	1		
okd	-.39**	-.32**	.77**	-.15**	ns	ns	.74**	-.37**	-.31**	1	
okn	-.51**	-.44**	.86**	-.33**	-.22**	-.22**	.88**	-.54**	-.41**	.60**	1

** correlation significant at .01 level; * significant at .05 level (2-tailed); ns= not significant.

Unfortunately, the question remains what exactly is being measured by an operationalisation. What does an operationalisation and instrument need in order for it to be referred to as 'fear of crime'. Is it really necessary that items explicitly refer to crimes or victimisation? If the answer is yes, than clearly something is wrong with the widely and most frequently used item on 'feeling safe alone after dark'. Due to the historical background and development of 'fear of crime' and its indicators, it seems to be impossible to think of 'fear of crime' as something that might have not so much to do with crime per se. Yet, when 'feeling safe' (the most frequently applied indicator of 'fear of crime')

---

[277] Standardised item alpha is not different or .01 higher and therefore not presented here.

correlates highly with and is structurally rather similar to 'feeling at ease', while on the other hand is different from concern about victimisation, being afraid to become a victim of a specific crime, it is difficult to insist on the idea that 'fear of crime' is about crime.

9.6.1 Proposal of improved instrument based on traditional instruments

Here, not a theory-driven approach has been applied, in which a concept is translated into an operationalisation, which points to the observable indicator. Rather, the questionnaire construction is based on a data-driven or empirical entry approach that operationally defines a (theoretical) concepts (see Broers 1994). In other words, the item(s) or questionnaires are used as research instruments to define the concepts. Such a data-driven approach does not so much emphasise the theoretical power, but rather focuses on psychometric appropriateness. In other words, the development of a theoretical model is not the main goal.

Table 9.16. Summary of (second part of) chapter 9: continuation.

Measurement based on traditional way: continuation strategy	
Subway	Similarity between 'at ease' and 'feeling safe' items
	Distinction between day and night items
	Format (reference to frequency or not) of items important
Vignettes	Three different item-types: similarity between 'at ease' and 'feeling safe' items
	Contents of vignettes of more importance than type of item
	Three reliable and unidimensional scales
	Format (question or statement) of items important
Inventory	Based on overview and inventory of traditional operationalisations
	Data-driven approach
	Different operationalisations of 'fear of crime' measure different things
	Similarity between 'at ease' and 'feeling safe' items
	Several reliable scales possible, validity is unclear
	Fear of crime is umbrella concept without conceptual clarity
	Fear of crime not fear of *crime*
	Improved instrument based on data-driven approach and common criteria: Appendix G.

A large pool of items was collected. These items have been widely used in large samples and were used in smaller samples in this current research project. Moreover, this questionnaire has already been administered to other samples, for example to a large representative sample of the population of Amsterdam (Flight 2003).[278] On that basis, this pool of items can be refined, taking face validity into account. The items that do not perform well according to common criteria, concentrating on the item-total correlations and high factor loadings on the same factor, are excluded. These criteria are based on the idea of contiguity, which states that items that are more similar conceptually will be

---

[278] This questionnaire was used in other samples as well (Rietveld1 and Rietveld2 in Appendix F).

more similar empirically (Brown 1985). When taking the current findings as well as these common criteria into account, an improved measurement instrument can be derived from the inventory, which is presented in Dutch in Appendix G. Table 9.16 summarises the second part of this chapter; Table 9.1 focuses on the first part.

10 Starting over: portraying safety, risk and crime

The previous chapter attempted to improve currently used measurement instruments by *continuing* with the indicators that have been used so far, which resulted in an instrument that is based on an inventory of these familiar indicators. Also, the two strategies were discussed. A strategy of continuing or *starting all over* and thus to propose a newly developed instrument, which is somewhat different in format and content. Another measurement instrument can benefit from the numerous surveys and studies that have been done so far and can be more conceptually (theoretically) embedded, which makes it possible to reveal new or other insights. However, the instrument is still work in progress; consequently it might take some time to fully benefit from its development. Another disadvantage, already described in chapter 9, is that comparisons over (past) time are not possible, which, together with the unfamiliarity of the items and their accompanying responses, is less appealing to the public, media and politics. In brief, the choice whether to continue and thus improve the indicators that have been used so far, or whether to take a chance and start the use of the new instrument, can essentially be considered a choice between items that are comparable with items from the past time (comparability) or items with a higher validity (quality). The applications and examples of the instrument at the end of this chapter will make this clearer.

The topic tree in Figure 10.1 represents the outline of this chapter. The main purpose of this chapter is to describe the construction of a measurement instrument and to present it. Though a couple of applications of this instrument are suggested and illustrated with relevant examples, clearly more research is required before the instrument can be applied in the field. This will be briefly discussed at the end of this chapter, together with some possible future applications of the instrument. First, the background of the semantic differential is sketched, which provides the format that is utilised in the measurement instrument. The semantic differential can be used to investigate the meaning of objects, concepts, words, or phenomena and can supply an attitude scale, both of which are of interest here. After that, the construction of the instrument that uses the semantic differential format is described, which includes the choice of twenty concepts that are appraised as well as the choice of seventeen adjectives or attributes on which the concepts are rated. All concepts and items make up a large item bank, all of which have been administered by means of a questionnaire. The data are then used in further analyses. These analyses function on the one hand as examples of applications, on the other hand as scale construction. The examples of possible applications focus primarily on the concepts, by grouping methods and comparing the profiles of meaning. Other analyses aid the construction of an instrument that measures the directionality and intensity of the attitudinal response towards (the experience of) safety. These analyses mainly compare the (more familiar) Likert-type scales from the previous chapter with a selection of the semantic differential items. Also, groups that differ on two socio-demographic variables, i.e. sex and age, are contrasted with one another as well. These types of comparison are generally considered to be checks of the validity of an operationalisation.

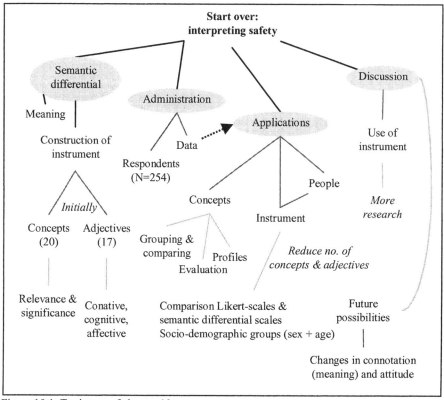

Figure 10.1. Topic tree of chapter 10.

10.1 Starting over: measuring meaning, imaging safety

In order to develop an instrument that will give an indication of people's experience of safety, the instrument needs to fulfil some practical requirements. First, the instrument should be feasible to conduct in similar events that historically had utilised the indicators as described in chapter 2. Thus, it should be possible to administer the instrument to large groups of people at one sitting. Also, different options regarding the procedure and method should be kept open; enabling a paper-and-pencil procedure as well as computer assisted or telephone interviews in principle.

Besides these practical conditions, other requirements concern the reliability and validity of the operationalisation, and therefore the concept or phenomenon of interest. Previous chapters showed the blurred boundaries between fear of crime, the perception of risk, worry, fear of victimisation and so on. Employing a strategy based on a grounded theory approach enabled the grouping of several concepts into higher order categories, which in turn were compared and grouped in a similar procedure in even more abstract categories.

In this manner, this eventually resulted in three core categories or concepts that appear to be central to 'fear of crime'. The three core concepts (criminal) victimisation, risk (perception) and fear derive their meaning by and in the context of the discursive frameworks in which they play the leading part. The meaning of concepts is conveyed by language, and can be gathered from discourses, using the notion of schemas; (intersubjectively shared) simplifications that are used to make sense of social reality. Yet, the meaning of concepts can be looked at in a more quantitative manner as well, which will be explained in the next section.

10.1.1 Semantic differential

All considerations together led eventually to the format of the semantic differential, developed originally by Osgood. Osgood and others developed the idea that *meaning* can be measured (e.g. Osgood, Suci & Tannenbaum 1978; Snider & Osgood 1969). They state that a combination of associational and scaling procedures provided the most adequate measurement of the (connotative) meaning of a concept or term (Osgood 1969a). The connotative meaning embraces the attributes that define the concept as well as the non-defining associates of the concept, in other words, what is suggested by the concept. Empirically, their essential point on the meaning of concepts is that these concepts (or objects, terms) can be distinguished or differentiated from each other along three dimensions, namely the dimension evaluation E (good-bad), potency P (strong-weak) and activity A (active-passive) as third factor (e.g. Osgood & Suci 1969; Osgood, Suci & Tannenbaum 1978).[279] This general theory of meaning or rather, the method that is derived from it, is usually referred to as the semantic differential. The semantic differential makes it first of all possible to describe the meaning of a concept as a location in a three-dimensional space. Also, the semantic differential can be used to rate the meaning of any concept or object on those three dimensions and thus compare the ratings of one concept with ratings of another concept.[280]

The semantic differential is based on both associational and scaling procedures; that is, respondents are not asked the questions directly or explicitly

---

[279] Usually, the pair of adjectives good – bad loads highly on the Evaluation-dimension, the Potency-dimension is defined by strong – weak and the Activity factor by active – passive. These three dimensions intuitively make sense in the present research project, since a person or something (e.g. a dog, a storm) is judged firstly as good or bad (i.e. being a threat or representing a danger), next whether this person or phenomenon is strong or stronger than the person him/herself. Finally, the question remains whether the bad, strong person or phenomenon apparently is making a move towards the person. Clearly, somebody who is judged as bad, strong and active evokes different reactions than somebody who is judged as good, weak and passive.

[280] However, denotatively distinct concepts, like 'hero' and 'success' might be connotatively indiscriminable (Osgood, Suci & Tannenbaum 1978). That is, concepts may have the same profiles according to the three dimensions E, P and A, and thus may occupy the same region of the semantic space and yet be denotatively distinct. Accordingly, Brown (1969) criticises the semantic differential for not being clear about philosophical problems of meaning. He especially focuses on the mixture of meaning that is being measured; although Osgood et al. claim it is the *connotative* meaning that is being measured, not the denotative meaning, Brown argues it is a mixture. Here, the denotation of a concept refers to the population of objects, which may be so designated.

as is done in most research in the field of 'fear of crime'. Rather, subjects are asked to assess the meaning of a concept, which is based more on association. In that sense, a plausible assumption is that responses on semantic differential items might be less influenced by typical social desirability issues than responses to straight and explicit questions such as "how safe or unsafe do you feel when you're at home alone at night".[281]

The amenities of the semantic differential are more comprehensible when the possible applications are clear. First of all, the Evaluation-dimension or the evaluative factor resembles attitude scores. The semantic differential might be used to select adjective pairs for the construction of an attitude scale correspondingly (Brinton 1969). A semantic differential scale measures both the *directionality* of a reaction or response (e.g. good versus bad) and the *intensity* (slight through extreme) (Heise 1970). In other words, an important application of the semantic differential is its use as an instrument to measure attitude.[282] The second application is relevant in the light of the research questions of this project, that are concerned with the meaning of concepts such as 'crime' and 'risk' to common people, how for example the concept 'safety' is linked to concepts as security, danger, and vulnerability. In this research project, concepts like *fear, feelings of unsafety* and *risk* play a major role. Since these concepts are not only used by the researcher, but are incorporated in every-day-language, in articles in newspapers or in surveys of the police, it is relevant to investigate how people 'see' these entities. The research question for the semantic differential study is how aspects of the experience of safety are perceived; how safety is interpreted. Are different concepts indeed perceived differently? How do concepts relate to one another? For example, are risk and danger the same? How are these concepts pictured? The semantic differential can enable a better understanding in the meaning of one particular concept by itself, providing an *image* or portrait of the sole concept, and the connection between a certain concept and others.

10.1.2 The meaning(s) of a concept (again)

Chapter 4 already argued that the meaning(s) of a concept is or are conveyed by language (symbols, signs) used by individuals or for example by the mass media, narratives, and institutions. This, in turn, continuously shapes or constructs the context in which we again perceive, interpret and give meaning to our everyday lives. Following Shore (1991, 1996), meanings are "twice born"; meanings are considered products of both individual cognition and of the social and cultural context. That is, external publicly available instituted (conventional)

---

[281] Response-set effects can be minimised by changing place of favourable and unfavourable adjectives (see Verberk, Scheepers & Felling 1995).

[282] In fact, instruments adopting a semantic differential format have been applied in a wide variety of studies. For example, the study of Leunes, Bourgeois & Grajales (1996) used a 25-item semantic differential scale arranged on a 7-point continuum to assess attitudes and attitude change regarding 'juvenile delinquent', 'state correctional facility for juvenile delinquents', and 'treatment staff for juvenile delinquents'. According to the researchers, the changes in attitudes result from a talk by violent juvenile offenders from a local correctional facility and a tour sponsored by the correctional facility that had provided the speakers.

models (cultural schemas) are internalised and reconstructed as personal models and hence govern human activity, while on the other hand these cultural schemas are derived from such activity (Shore 1991).[283] The meaning of a concept as a product of the social and cultural context resembles the basic ideas of a social construction approach to a great extent. Such an approach has been adopted in the chapters on the concepts of victimisation, risk and fear of crime, in which the language employed by individuals or the media have been examined. In these previous chapters, different *schemas* were discussed, like the schema on the ideal victim. According to Shore (1996), cultural models, which are part of cultural knowledge, are cognitive schemas that are intersubjectively shared by a cultural group. He distinguishes such cultural schemas and *intersubjective* meaning from personal mental models, idiosyncratic schemas that are constructed individually and contain personal associations with words and one's own personal history and that encompass *subjective* meaning (Shore 1991).[284]

The instrument, of which the construction is described in this chapter, is a way to gain sense of the general interpersonally shared meaning of concepts, while on the other hand personal mental models, e.g. typical personal associations with words, can be identified as well. In other words, the instrument that adopts a semantic differential format might enable the empirical study of both cultural knowledge as well as personal knowledge.

10.2 Construction of the instrument (semantic differential format)

When using the semantic differential, several words reflecting (part of) the entity or concept are necessary, as well as adjectives or attributes, which are more or less adequate to assess the meaning of the entity. Alreck and Settle (1985) describe the semantic differential as a method to learn the image of an entity (concept) in the minds of the public. This concept is rated by letting individuals judge attributes and adjectives to evaluate the concept or topic being rated. Therefore two sets should be compiled when designing the specific semantic differential. First, a particular set of concepts that reflects the phenomenon of interest. Second, a set of adjectives that is most adequate to assess the concepts. The selection of both sets, the set of concepts and the set of adjectives, is discussed below.

---

[283] Shore (1991: 10) describes *institutionalisation* as "the creation of novel responses to situations and the objectification of these creations as external institutions, characterised by stable intersubjective significance". In this context, 'fear of crime' is a perfect example of such institutionalisation, as already argued in chapter 4, since it has become self-evident and necessary in research and policy.

[284] Though cultural models or schemas are interindividually shared, this is not to say that these schemas are all exactly the same; Shore (1996) suggests that the models are socially distributed and thus that different perspectives within models may exist. A common schema does not preclude the considerable variation in how individuals use or apply the schema in practice (Shore 1991: 18). For example, while ordinary people might share a schema on 'visiting a restaurant', such schemas may be different to a certain extent for men and women, parents (or their children) and non-parents. The cultural models are not only ways in which people make meaning of their experiences and of the world, they mainly function as salience-enhancing templates.

10.2.1 Which concepts?

What is the relationship between fear, crime and safety? Does the risk of victimisation mean the same as danger? Based on the review of the literature (see chapter 2) and chapters 6, 7 and 8, on criminal victimisation, risk and its perception and 'fear of crime' respectively, twenty concepts were selected which were to be used in the initial semantic differential-type instrument. All these concepts are related to the experience and interpretation of safety. Some of these are directly linked with crime (like *rape* or *violence*), others are not (e.g. *natural disaster*), but most of the entities to be used in the semantic differential are not explicitly related to crime or criminal behaviours, but might be within a certain frame of reference; for example *danger* and *risk*. In this paragraph, the initial selection of these twenty concepts will be discussed briefly. As previously noted, they were chosen on the basis of the review and the the conceptual analyses. Moreover, because of methodological reasons, some concepts were included because of their apparent positive connotation, like *precautions*, *protection*, *safety* and *defensibility*.

Table 10.1 shows the concepts that were included to be rated, Appendix H lists the concepts in Dutch.

10.2.1.1 Fear

Since *fear of crime* is made up of the two concepts *fear* and *crime*, both of them were included. In the past decades, in which *fear of crime* as a concept has grown in popularity and familiarity, the component of *fear* has been unquestioned and has not been problematised at all. Following Gordon (1980) and Davis (1987), three basic types of fear were distinguished in chapter 8. *Experiental fear* refers to the experience or (emotional) state of fear and is marked by physiological characteristics like sweating and a rapid heartbeat. In other words, *experiental fear* is *being afraid*. *Propositional fear*, which means fearing that something is or will be the case, is called relational since it is related to that 'something'. The third type of fear that was distinguished is also relational and was called *reactive fear*. *Reactive fear* means being afraid of or frightened by something, it is fear as a result of something (Davis 1987). By including the concept *fear* in the semantic differential, it is possible to gain more insight what *fear* means to the respondents.

10.2.1.2 Crime, rape and violence

The conceptual analysis of (criminal) victimisation points to the concepts *crime*, *rape* and *violence*. Obviously, *crime* is included in the selection of concepts because it is considered to be the chief object of fear when considering *fear of crime*. Apparently, when talking about 'fear of crime', there are a few types of crime that are thought of or feared the most, such as robbery or other incidents involving a (violent) personal confrontation with the offender (see chapter 6). The popular image of crime in the context of 'fear of crime' in the Western world concentrates especially on (random) *violence* that might occur in the public sphere. For women, not only violent personal confrontations with an offender appear to be saillant, but the mere possibility of sexual violence when encountering the offender seems to be of even more importance. Therefore, the concept *rape* is included as well.

Since the selection of concepts to be judged contains *crime, violence* as well as *rape*, it will be possible to examine empirically whether these concepts are evaluated differently, or not. For example, when the concept *crime* is judged similarly to the concept *violence*, this would provide an indication that to people, these concepts are connotatively indiscriminable. A similar comparison can be made regarding *violence* and *rape*.

10.2.1.3 Precautions, protection, defensibility and vulnerability

In order to discourage respondents to give consistently moderate answers or oppositely, to give extreme answers, some concepts were included because of their apparent positive connotation, like *precautions, protection*, and *defensibility*. These three concepts are presumably of importance for the perception of risk, 'fear of crime' or the experience of safety as well. Chapter 7 on the concept 'risk' described the importance of precautionary and protective measures in relation to exposure, the risk on victimisation and the fear-victimisation paradox. Also, one's life style or routine activities are interrelated with precautions and protection. Furthermore, the analyses of risk and victimisation led to the inclusion of *defensibility* and *vulnerability* as well. Both concepts refer to the subjective assessment of one's own capabilities to hold one's own, and being able to cope with the situation without getting things out of hands. In the case of a real or imaginary personal confrontation with an offender, this implicates a comparison of one's own physical capabilities compared with the physical capabilities of the offender. Moreover, many respondents in different empirical studies brought up the perceptions or feelings of defensibility and vulnerability as well (e.g. Hollander 2001; Yeoh & Yeow 1997).

10.2.1.4 Risk and danger

The meaning of the concept *risk* has changed, influenced by the development of probability theory and statistics (see chapters 5 and 7). In the modern Western world, risk is no longer a neutral term for calculating probabilities, rather, it signifies *danger* and is associated with hazards or undesirable outcomes. For example, the risk of various kinds of death can be calculated in an 'objective' way, based on empirical evidence. Chance has become a pattern; a hazard is not an unpredictable danger anymore, but a calculable risk.

Knowledge of *risk* is used to control *danger*, thus, danger can be located and quarantined, controlled, mapped and managed. The discourse on *risk* suggests the concept *risk* is negatively evaluated, in other words, *risk* has a definite negative connotation, which would come to light empirically when the concept is judged and its profile compared with danger. Chapter 7 argued that in current Western discourse on risk, risk is not a neutral term for calculating probabilities, rather, it signifies danger and is associated with hazards. When the proposed instrument is administered, a comparison between the connotative meaning of *risk* and *danger* will become possible. Drawing a comparison between these two concepts and the concepts safety, unsafety and insecurity might be of interest as well.

10.2.1.5 Safety, unsafety and insecurity

So, risks can be calculated. Dangers are located and quarantined in reassuringly predictable circumstances and reliably produce *safety* and *security*. The modern cosmologies as Freedgood (2000) calls them, are strategies that provide large-scale consolation and reassurance. The aim is to increase safety and to reduce danger and insecurity. The hope is always for ever-greater security and a safe paradise, whereas risk is a violation of that paradise.

The concepts *safety*, *unsafety* and *insecurity* are central to theoretical elaborations of risk and the so-called risk society.[285] Yet, they appear to be meaningful regarding fear of criminal victimisation as well (see chapter 6 in particular). People refer to safe and dangerous places, or safe and dangerous people. Everyday narratives reflect ideas on appropriate behaviour, the crimes that should be feared, or when and where a place is dangerous and ideas on who is dangerous and who is safe. Concern or fear for one's safety is one of the most important warning mechanisms of every living being (see also chapter 8).

An important note is that in some languages, among which the Dutch language, a single word refers to the English words 'safety' and 'security'. For example, the words *veiligheid* (Dutch), *sécurité* (French) and *seguridad* (Spanish) can be used to indicate *safety* as well as *security*.[286] The current instrument has been constructed in Dutch; the words 'veiligheid' (safety/security), 'onveiligheid' (unsafety/ insecurity) and 'onzekerheid' (insecurity) were included.

10.2.1.6 Accident and natural disaster

When elaborating on risk, the rationale why some misfortunes have become classified specifically as *accidents* in the late twentieth century received attention as well. *Accident* is used in every day life in two rather different ways; firstly, to refer to certain kinds of outcome, e.g. as synonym for injury or damage. Secondly, *accident* is used as a moral term, pointing to a causal sequence and a lack of cause, to an unmotivated and unpredictable event, which happened without culpability or blame. Yet, sometimes it is said that people did (not) deserve the accident and an accident is not necessarily unambiguously unpredictable, since it is said that the "accident was waiting to happen". Again,

---

[285] Note that the original wording in Dutch; 'onzekerheid' was translated here as insecurity, though 'uncertainty' is a good translation as well. 'Safety' and 'unsafety' are the translations of 'veiligheid' en 'onveiligheid' respectively. See Appendix H.

[286] Van Zuijlen (2004) describes the etymological and historical roots of the Dutch words *veiligheid* and *zekerheid* by analysing the meaning of the Latin *securitas* and the legal theoretical implications of the changes in the meaning of *securitas* and *veiligheid*. After the Middle Ages, *securitas* refers both to the protection of a citizen's life and property from other citizens within the state, and to the protection of the whole nation against other nations. Van Zuijlen (2004) argues the first meaning refers to domestic safety ('binnenlandse veiligheid'), which seems to resemble public safety. The second meaning refers to 'buitenlandse veiligheid' (foreign security), which resembles homeland security.

similar to risk, in the late 20th century the random accident has become a predictable and thus preventable accident.

While *accidents* can happen with regard to traffic, industry, health care, labour, and so on, clearly, a *natural disaster* is firstly related to the forces of nature, like a flood or earthquake. The work that has been done on the perception of risk in the context of industry and technology makes reference to such natural disasters as well. Chapter 7 on risk described some relevant cross-disciplinary themes and findings from several disciplines, especially from the work of Sjöberg, Slovic and others on perceived risk. Many of the findings can presumably be generalised to the criminological field. In order to compare crime as a hazard with a common hazard used in these studies, *natural disaster* was included in the list of concepts as well.

10.2.1.7   Fault and inattention

Just as *accident* might be used as a moral term that implicates a certain causal sequence, which happened without culpability or blame, *victimisation* is subject of similar attribution processes correspondingly. As discussed in the chapter on victimisation (chapter 6), attributions of 'deservedness' and culpability are of importance and are also present in notions of the 'ideal victim', the convincing victim or the culturally approved victim. The key question is whether or not, and to what degree, the victimisation has been the victim's own *fault*. Specific characteristics of the victim (and offender), like sex and sexual orientation, as well as the context in which the victimisation occurs, influences how the victimisation is interpreted. These characteristics influence notions of deservedness, since blame and responsibility are attributed to both victim and perpetrator, i.e. when a victim is regarded 'undeserved' or 'innocent' in contrast with a 'deserving' or 'just' victim. The behaviour of a victim is relevant as well; has the victim been on his or her guard, has s/he been aware of the environment, and has s/he paid attention to suspicious events and people. On the contrary, *inattention* is not part of being street smart and decreases the ability to act in the case of danger. *Inattention* is also of importance in the context of accidents, especially concerning the assignation of blame and the attribution of responsibility. Chapter 7 described moral outrage and the newsworthiness of an incident and studies indicate the importance of outrage and the possibility of blaming somebody for a story to take off in the media. *Inattention* is linked with blame and responsibility.

10.2.1.8   Concern, social concern and concern about others

Besides the term *fear of crime*, *concern* is another concept that has been widely used (see the overview in chapter 2). Van der Wurff (1990) for example states that the fear that is connected to a specific type of crime (e.g. robbery or rape) differs from the more abstract concern about crime. When a person is more involved, s/he thinks for example about personally becoming a victim of crime, whereas one could also be worried in general. Also, Ferraro (1995) discriminates between 'concern about crime to self' and 'fear for self-victimisation'. In general, fear, worry or concern about victimisation often occur in studies that employ surveys and interviews and the terms are frequently exchanged. Sometimes respondents are asked how worried or concerned they are about becoming a victim of certain types of crime. Also, less specific concerns are sometimes adopted, like concern about crime in the community, or worry about decline and deterioration. Therefore, in the current list of concepts, both *concern* and *social concern* were included.[287]

Concern about others refers to the fear or worry that a significant other, like one's child or spouse, might be harmed. This fear for others has been called 'altruistic fear' and was already present in a survey in 1969 (Harris 1969 Urban Crime Survey, no. 1935, see Appendix F). The Dutch PMB, the periodic survey commissioned by the police corps and by the Ministries of Justice and the Interior, asks respondents with children younger than fifteen whether they ever forbid their children to go some place, because they think it's not safe.

10.2.1.9 Twenty concepts

The twenty concepts that were included to be rated are listed in Table 10.1. Sometimes an English synonym is given between brackets, to make the concepts used clearer, since the concepts originally were in Dutch (Appendix H). The concepts were chosen because of their frequent use and significance in the discourses on risk, victimisation and fear of crime. The concepts are thought to reflect several aspects of the experience of safety accordingly, the primary concept of interest here.

Table 10.1 summarises the motivation to include them and the primary chapter(s) in which the concept can be found. In the next part, the selection of the adjectives will be described in more detail.

Table 10.1. Selected concepts.

Concept	Motive	Chapter
Accident	Link with research on risk perception; accident, like victimisation, as moral term; attribution of responsibility and blame	7 (risk)
Concern (worry)	Frequent use in surveys concerning both 'fear of crime' and risk perception; conceptually related to fear	2 (overview) 8 (fear of crime)
Concern about others	Use in surveys concerning 'fear of crime'; so-called altruistic fear	2 (overview) 8 (fear of crime)
Crime	Supposedly bounds 'fear of crime'; chief object of fear when considering 'fear of crime'; relationship with popular images of crime (violence)	2 (overview) 6 (victimisation) 8 (fear of crime)
Danger	ık with research on risk perception; frequent use and significance in discursive frameworks	6 (victimisation) 7 (risk)
Defensibility	Positive connotation; used as explanation in discussion on gender differences regarding 'fear of crime'; related to 'shadow of sexual assault'	2 (overview)

---

[287] Note that the original wording in Dutch; 'maatschappelijke onrust' and 'bezorgdheid' are translated here as social concern and concern (worry). See Appendix H.

Table 10.1 – continued.

Concept	Motive	Chapter
Fault (guilt)	Link with research on risk perception; attributions of blame; important element within schema of ideal victim	6 (victimisation) 7 (risk)
Fear (anxiety)	1questioned component of 'fear of crime'; frequent use and significance in discursive frameworks	2 (overview) 6 (victimisation) 7 (risk) 8 (fear of crime)
Inattention (carelessness)	Link with research on risk perception; attributions of blame; important element within schema of ideal victim and element of moral outrage	6 (victimisation) 7 (risk)
Insecurity	Frequent use and significance in discursive frameworks; conceptual relationship with unsafety; link with research on risk perception	7 (risk) 8 (fear of crime)
Natural disaster	Link with research on risk perception	7 (risk)
Precautions	Positive connotation; link with research on risk perception; important as for attributions of blame (schema of ideal victim, moral outrage)	6 (victimisation) 7 (risk)
Protection (security)	Positive connotation; link with research on risk perception; important as for attributions of blame (schema of ideal victim, moral outrage)	6 (victimisation) 7 (risk)
Rape	1portance of 'shadow of sexual assault' for women; sexual violence used as explanation fear-victimisation paradox	6 (victimisation)
Risk	Link with research on risk perception; victimisation risk calculated by means of statistics; important concept in fear-victimisation paradox debate; perception of risk also used as operationalisation; differentiation between perception of victimisation risk and fear of criminal victimisation; frequent use and significance in discursive frameworks	2 (overview) 6 (victimisation) 7 (risk)
Safety	Positive connotation; frequent use and significance in discursive frameworks; conceptual relationship with unsafety and insecurity; used in operationalisations	2 (overview) 6 (victimisation) 7 (risk) 8 (fear of crime)
Social concern	Used in discursive frameworks; linked with moral outrage (risk perception research); political context of 'fear of crime'	6 (victimisation) 7 (risk) 8 (fear of crime)
Unsafety	Frequent use and significance in discursive frameworks; conceptual relationship with safety and insecurity; used in operationalisations	2 (overview) 6 (victimisation) 7 (risk) 8 (fear of crime)
Violence	Popular image of crime in the context of 'fear of crime'; violent personal confrontations with an offender	2 (overview) 6 (victimisation)
Vulnerability	Used as explanation in discussion on gender differences regarding 'fear of crime'; related to 'shadow of sexual assault'	2 (overview) 6 (victimisation)

10.2.2 Which adjectives?

10.2.2.1 Initial selection

In chapter 2, three modalities have been distinguished, namely a cognitive, conative and affective modality of the concept 'fear of crime', analogous to the conceptual framework of Fishbein and Ajzen (1975). These three modalities guided the decisions which adjectives would be used and which not. Publications of Osgood and others (in particular Osgood, Suci & Tannenbaum 1978; Snider & Osgood 1969) suggest several adjectives that were used in this study; other pairs of adjectives were derived from other empirical studies on the experience of safety. The attributes or adjectives used in the semantic differential need to be more or less bipolar; i.e. good versus bad. Also, Alreck and Settle (1985) advise that in the instrument, half of the items puts the more positive adjectives first, the other half puts the more negative adjectives first. Furthermore, they suggest placing these items in random order in the semantic differential scale. These suggestions were taken into consideration in the procedure that was followed in the current study. The set of attributes that were used initially can be found in Table 10.2; Appendix H lists the adjectives or attributes in Dutch.

Table 10.2. The pairs of adjectives or attributes.

Conative	Cognitive	Affective
Fast – slow	Desirable – undesirable	Sad – happy
Quiet – busy	Risky – riskless	Friendly – unfriendly
Flee – seek	Dangerous – harmless	Afraid – at ease
Avoid – provoke	Good – bad	Pleasant – unpleasant
Steer – let go	Predictable – unpredictable	Nice – nasty
Active – passive	Benign – malign	

10.3 Initial administration

The semantic differential scales were included in the questionnaire that has been described in chapter 9, which focused on the continuation-strategy.

10.3.1 Method

10.3.1.1 Respondents

Part of the participants are law students who followed a course in "psychology and law" (N=149) at the faculty of law of the Erasmus University Rotterdam. Their mean age was 25 years (SD 5.9). Most of them (87.2%) were full-time students, who followed the course during the day. The other students participated in the same course in the evening. The course paid attention to empirical research and the questionnaire as well as its results were used to illustrate several aspects. Most of the students are female (72.5%). The other part of the participants (N=105) consisted of older family members (M= 51.0; SD = 7.5) or acquaintances of the students. Students were asked to find somebody, preferably someone of an older generation like one's parent, who could fill in a questionnaire as well. Again, the majority (68%) is female. More details can be found in chapter 9. Our total sample thus consisted of 254 respondents, most of them (about 70%) female. The average age of our sample is about 36 years (M=35.8; SD=14.4).[288]

Table 10.3. Concepts and versions.

Version 1	Version 2
Fear	Fear
Unsafety	Unsafety
Risk	Protection
Insecurity	Danger
Accident	Violence
Fault	Inattention
Crime	Concern
Precautions	Safety
Natural disaster	Concern about others
Social concern	Rape
Vulnerability	Defensibility

10.3.1.2 Instrument

The questionnaire consisted of different sections. Besides an introduction, indications how to fill in the various parts and two general questions about both sex and date of birth, the questionnaire contained many items on for example concern about becoming a victim of a specific crime and the perception of risk (see chapter 9), as well as two sections that applied the semantic differential. Since we needed our respondents to judge the entities on many adjectives, we decided to make two versions of the semantic differential.[289] Table 10.3 shows the concepts that were included in the two versions; both versions included the concepts *fear* and *unsafety*. Since every respondent rated eleven concepts on seventeen pairs of adjectives, so per respondent 187 scored items were collected. As recommended by Alreck and Settle (1985), positive and negative items were randomly placed at the left side. The semantic differential took the form of a 7-point scale, without the use of labels, as is pictured in the example in Figure 10.2:

	Concept	
X	|........|........|........|........|........|........|........|........|	-X
-Y	|........|........|........|........|........|........|........|........|	Y

Figure 10.2. Format of semantic differential as used in current study.

---

[288] Though 261 questionnaires were returned, we only used 254. Seven questionnaires were excluded from the analysis performed here, due to the results of preliminary analysis. Missing value analysis indicated that respondents generally answered all items. The data were checked to identify possible response patterns and outliers.

[289] The semantic differential can take several forms, like a 5- or 7-point scale, and can differ in the degree and type of labelling. However, these characteristics were not varied; the two versions that were administered only differed in the concepts they included.

10.3.1.3 Procedure

Students followed a course focussing on empirical research in the field of psychology and law. Both the questionnaire and its results were used to illustrate several aspects. During a class, the questionnaire was introduced and students were briefly informed about purpose and contents of the study. Students were asked to fill in the questionnaire during class. The paper-and-pencil questionnaire included an extensive introduction and explanation. Examples were used to illustrate in what way a respondent could indicate an answer. Also, students were asked to find somebody, preferably someone of an older generation like one's parent, who could fill in a questionnaire as well. This questionnaire was returned at another class, two weeks later. This questionnaire differed from the student-questionnaire only slightly. For example, the introduction and instructions used a different personal pronoun.[290]

10.3.1.4 Data

The data were recoded,[291] in order that all pairs of adjectives with a negative connotation (like 'malign') are on the left side of the semantic differential. Thus, a higher score means that the concept is rated more positively. The dataset resulting from these actions can be analysed for several purposes, depending on the focus of interest (see Table 10.4). In this paper, the focus is both on the concepts and on the respondents and a couple of applications are discussed accordingly. The next section describes the preliminary analyses of the adjectives that have, among other things, resulted in a smaller set of adjectives that were used in subsequent analyses.

Table 10.4. Different options of data analysis.

Analysing → Interest in ↓	Respondents	Adjectives	Concepts
Scores	Do respondents differ in their answers?	How do the scores on the adjectives vary?	Which concepts are rated more positive?
Clusters	Can the respondents be clustered?	Which adjectives 'belong together'?	Which concepts are perceived as more equal?
Instrument	How do respondents perceive the concepts?	Which are important in the judgement of concepts?	Which concepts are most important or representative?

10.3.2 Preliminary analyses of the adjectives

Each respondent rated eleven concepts on seventeen pairs of adjectives, so per respondent 187 scored items were collected. For some purposes, a smaller dataset that represents the whole dataset is more practical. In a few analyses, a selection of adjectives has been used instead of the whole set of (seventeen)

---

[290] The students received a questionnaire, which used the Dutch pronoun 'je'. The other questionnaire addressed the participants more formally, using the pronoun 'U'.
[291] Recoded were: nasty-nice; malign-benign; seek-flee; unpredictable-predictable; quiet-busy.

adjectives. This selection of adjectives is based on preliminary analyses that are briefly described below.

10.3.2.1 Selection of adjectives: factor analyses

First, we did a factor analysis for every concept and checked how many times an adjective appeared in the factor solution, with the criterion of an eigenvalue of 1 and factorloadings >.6 (Table 10.5). Two things are important to note; first, some adjectives appear more frequently than others in the final solution and the general correspondence which adjectives are prevailing, is striking. See for example the pair sad-happy, this pair is for nineteen concepts of importance, whereas dangerous-harmless only appears in the final solution with a factorloading greater than .6 of ten concepts. A second note is that the adjectives differ in their allocation: friendly – unfriendly is part of the 1st factor in eighteen cases, but risky – riskless only one time.

Table 10.5. Selecting adjectives.

Adjectives in the final solution, loading >.6	No restrictions on number of factors[292]				
	1st factor	2nd factor	3rd factor	4th factor	Total
Nice – nasty	15	2	0	0	17
Pleasant – unpleasant	18	0	0	0	18
Desirable – undesirable	16	0	1	0	17
Sad – happy	18	1	0	0	19
Afraid – at ease	7	2	0	0	9
Friendly – unfriendly	18	1	0	0	19
Benign – malign	11	3	0	0	14
Risky – riskless	1	6	3	2	13
Steer – let go	0	2	7	7	17
Good – bad	18	0	0	0	18
Dangerous – harmless	4	4	1	0	10
Predictable – unpredictable	0	3	6	5	17
Quiet – busy	0	4	6	2	17
Active – passive	0	5	7	3	17
Fast – slow	0	5	2	7	17
Flee – seek	8	2	2	1	14
Avoid – provoke	9	2	2	2	14

The decisions which adjectives would be used in the further analyses were based on the initial factor analyses, of which the results are not extensively described here. In general, the frequencies with which the pairs of adjectives pop up in the 1st factor and other factors as well as the factorloadings were used to make a selection. In other words, and more specifically, the first criterion is a high factorloading on the first factor. The pairs friendly – unfriendly, pleasant – unpleasant, good – bad are the three best performing

---

[292] When putting constraints on the factor analytical model, i.e. restricting the number of factors to three, results do not show a surprisingly different picture, with some minor exceptions (see Table A.11.2). The analyses will proceed with the factor analytical results without the restriction.

pairs. When looking at the second, third and fourth factor, risky – riskless, active – passive, fast – slow, steer – let go and predictable – unpredictable come forward, since the factorloadings of these adjectives prevail repeatedly in the second, third and fourth factor; a second selection criterion. Thus, the set of adjectives (attributes) that will be used in some of the subsequent analyses is presented in Table 10.6.

Table 10.6. Selected set of adjectives.

Set of adjectives
Friendly – unfriendly
Pleasant – unpleasant
Good – bad
Risky – riskless
Active – passive
Fast – slow
Steer – let go
Predictable – unpredictable

10.3.2.2 Subsequent analyses of the adjectives

All adjectives as well as the selection presented in Table 10.6, were used in further exploratory analyses. Hierarchical Cluster Analysis (HCA) was used to detect meaningful clusters underlying all as well as the selection of adjectives. These analyses are not described in detail here. In short, the selection of the adjectives showed two clusters of relative homogeneity. The first cluster, containing friendly – unfriendly, good – bad and pleasant – unpleasant, could be called an evaluative-affective cluster. The second distinct cluster comprises the pairs active – passive, fast – slow and steer – let go. The pairs risky – riskless and predictable – unpredictable were less typically part of one of the clusters.

A similar analysis of all adjectives might be helpful to see which clusters are formed when all adjectives instead of only a selection are used and might function as a control for the selection that has been made. Thus, to see how predictable – unpredictable and the other pairs relate to one another, a HCA was conducted once again, this time using all seventeen pairs of adjectives instead of the selection. When looking at the results, an initial set of five clusters can be identified.

The first cluster consists of the adjectives nice – nasty, (un)pleasant, (un)desirable, sad – happy, good – bad, (un)friendly and, though less convincingly, benign – malign. These adjectives clearly are evaluative or affective by nature and equal the Evaluation-dimension E that has been found frequently. The second cluster holds risky – riskless, harmless – dangerous and afraid – at ease, all three pairs involving *threat*, and in that sense evaluative as well. Besides evaluative, it seems this cluster is related to Osgood's Potency dimension as well, though this dimension is usually defined by the pair strong-weak. The third cluster is made up of only two pairs, namely (un)predictable and quiet – busy. By itself, this cluster seems difficult to interpret. Three pairs, all indicating some sort of dynamics or activity, are in the fourth cluster; fast – slow, active – passive and steer – let go. Only two pairs again, avoid – provoke and flee – seek form the fifth cluster. Both of these pairs seem to be touching on (in)escapability. In the next stages, the initial first two clusters are combined, making up an evaluative-affective cluster. Also, the third and fourth are combined, touching on dynamics. The two pairs (un)predictable and quiet – busy fit in this interpretation of this cluster. The results of this analysis suggest that the adjectives form three relatively homogenous clusters, one of them evaluative-affective, the next cluster touching on dynamics (potency) and the last one involving (in)escapability or actions (activity).

Obviously, the eight pairs that were selected do not and cannot mirror all adjectives. The general picture however is satisfactory, especially when keeping the necessity of parsimony in mind. The eight pairs of adjectives are proposed here as a set that can be used in research that is primarily focused on differences and similarities between the connotative meaning of concepts. In further analyses, both this selected set as well as all adjectives are used to analyse the different concepts. These analyses, which are described in the next sections, support the conclusion that the eight pairs of adjectives can be used instead of all pairs, as far as the comparison of concepts is concerned.

10.4 Possible applications: concepts and people

The data gathered by the instrument based on twenty concepts and seventeen adjectives can be used for several research questions and purposes. For example, an attitude scale can be derived from this kind of semantic differential data (see Brinton 1961; Heise 1970; Taylor 1971). Also, the semantic differential can be used to examine the differences among various groups, like men and women or victims and non-victims, in the meaning of one concept (Osgood, Suci & Tannenbaum 1978). Osgood (1969b) employed the semantic differential in a comparative study of different countries. When comparing the meaning of concepts in different cultures, both similarities as well as differences arise. Americans, Belgians and Finns who rated the concepts 'crime', 'danger' and 'fear', showed similar profiles, namely E-, P+ and A+ (in other words: bad -strong - active). The profile, based on Japanese responses, shows a different pattern, bad -weak - passive (E-, P-, A-). Note that all these groups rated the evaluation-dimension as negative (Osgood 1969b). Differences among individuals regarding the meaning of one sole concept can be studied as well, for example respondents varying on a scale that purports to measure the perception of risk. Finally, the semantic differential can be used to examine the differences among different concepts for the same group or individual (Osgood, Suci & Tannenbaum 1978).

This last possibility, i.e. examining the differences among different concepts for the same group, is elaborated on below. Some other possibilities are explored here as well, focusing on the one hand on concepts and on the other hand on people, or respondents. But first, the focus is on the variation between the concepts themselves; the semantic differential data are used to examine the differences among the different concepts. The concepts can be grouped by means of MDS (multidimensional scaling) and HCA (hierarchical cluster analysis), and their profiles can be compared. After that, the focus is on people; i.e. the variation between respondents. In addition, a short instrument that can be used to assess the intensity and direction of one's attitude, or evaluative and affective responses, towards the experience of safety is presented.

10.4.1 Concepts

Not every possible application or example will be described or elaborated on here; yet, the purpose is to give an overview of the different possibilities of analysing the data that are gathered by means of the semantic differential instrument. The examples mostly go back to issues that have been discussed in the previous chapters. In this section in which the focus is on the variation between the concepts themselves, the semantic differential data are used to examine the differences among the various concepts. First, the concepts are grouped by means of MDS, HCA and PCA (principal component analysis), in order to examine (dis)similarities between concepts. The conclusion from these analyses is that the concepts differ on two dimensions of which the first and most important is clearly evaluative. The second dimension has to do with attribution of responsibility, with careless versus careful behaviour. Furthermore, the concepts can be classified in three clusters, the first two with a negative connotation, i.e. *threat* and *emotion*, the third cluster with a positive connotation.

Second, the ranking of concepts stemming from the scores on the evaluative or affective dimension (E) is presented, which gives a clear picture of the negative or positive connotation of concepts. Third, the concepts' profiles can be compared, using all adjective pairs in a comparison of two to four concepts of interest. Also, the profiles of concepts from different groups of people can be compared. Here, the profiles of the four concepts, safety and unsafety, and danger and protection for both men and women are offered as an example.

10.4.1.1 Grouping the concepts

How are the various concepts perceived? Is security the same as safety, danger the same as risk? What is their meaning? Are some concepts more similar to others? How can the concepts be interpreted in relation to shared similarities? To answer these questions, HCA, MDS (Multidimensional Scaling) as well as factor analysis can be applied. Whereas HCA and MDS use dissimilarity data, MDS iteratively arranges the concepts in a space with a particular number of dimensions. In other words, the originally observed dissimilarities are reproduced or re-arranged into distances in a configuration, which enables the interpretation of the dissimilarities in terms of underlying dimensions.

10.4.1.1.1 Results from MDS

The data resulting from the semantic differential can be used in MDS procedures. Here, only the two-dimensional configurations will be discussed. Following Norusis (1993), the analyses will be done on both the interval and ordinal level.[293] Also, not only the data derived from the selection of adjectives will be used as the raw dataset, but also the data based on all adjectives. This is done to see whether the selection performs almost as all adjectives do. In brief, four analyses were done, to examine the question whether the configurations are any different and how the concepts are plotted. The results of the MDS analyses are summarised in Table 10.7. As you can see, all four configurations have a low stress and a high RSQ, indicating a high goodness-of-fit for all adjectives as well as the selection of adjectives.[294]

Table 10.7. Summary MDS-results two-dimensional configuration.

| Adjectives | Indicators of fit | Measurement level | |
		Ordinal	Interval
All	No. of iterations	8	4
	Stress (RSQ)	0.031 (0.997)	0.152 (0.937)
Selection	No. of iterations	7	4
	Stress (RSQ)	0.076 (0.981)	0.154 (0.928)

The results of the analysis done with the original data based on all adjectives and considering the data as ordinal, i.e. nonmetric MDS, are presented here. The plot of the configuration is presented in Figure 10.3.[295] Firstly, two groups of concepts can be observed; one in the (upper) left, holding 'safety', the other in the lower right, with concepts like 'crime' and 'danger'. The horizontal axis, the first dimension, appears to reflect *evaluation*, ranging from *good* (safety, precautions, protection) to *bad* (violence, crime, rape). The vertical (2nd) dimension is less easily to interpret. Fault, inattention, crime and

---

[293] A basic question is whether these data should be considered on the interval or ordinal level. The ordinal level will lead to nonmetric MDS, which is more problematic concerning the minimisation of the error and maximising the goodness-of-fit (Young 1981). When the data is considered to be on the interval level, different results are acquired than when the data is assumed to be ordinal since different representation functions will be utilised. On the one hand, the data could be considered ordinal, since we do not exactly know whether the intervals of the answer categories of the semantic differential are the same. On the other hand, the data could be considered interval, since the data are not mere rankings and have enough answer categories. Also, the data being analysed is not the data as reported by respondents, but has been computed by employing all judgements of all respondents on the adjectives.

[294] The goodness-of-fit, which indicates how well a specific configuration reproduces the dissimilarity data, is usually reflected by the stress. The smaller the stress value, the better is the fit of the reproduced distances in the configuration to the observed dissimilarities matrix. Another indicator of the goodness-of-fit of the configuration is RSQ, which is interpreted as the proportion of variance of the disparities (the scaled or transformed data) that is accounted for by the distances D in the configuration. In other words, RSQ is the squared correlation between the distances D in the MDS configuration and the transformed data T. Next to the stress and RSQ, scatterplots of linear fit, which plot the disparities and the distances, scatterplots of non-linear fit and plots of transformation, which present the raw dissimilarity data horizontally and the transformed data, the disparities, vertically, were checked.

[295] The scatterplot of linear fit showed little scatter, only some for small disparities. This is an artefact of the procedure used, in which squared distances instead of the distances are being fit to the data. The scatterplot of non-linear fit showed the same methodological artefact. The plot of transformation appeared more or less linear and smooth, without any horizontal steps. This suggests not only that the transformation is pretty continuous, but also that a metric analysis could be appropriate, which was done in next analyses.

insecurity all have to do with blame, purpose, an (evil) intention or a lack of responsibility, whereas concern and concern for others clearly refer to empathy and involvement. Yet, the position of violence and rape are conflicting with this interpretation, which is why the other techniques (HCA and PCA) have been applied as well.[296]

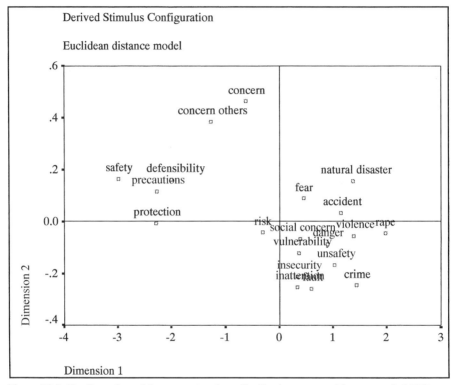

Figure 10.3. Configuration of the concepts when all adjectives are used in nonmetric MDS.

In the analyses in which the *selection* of adjectives was used in both metric and nonmetric MDS, the fit was expected to be worse, since a selection is usually doing less well than the whole. Yet, both configurations were accompanied by a rather low stress and high RSQ (see Table 10.7). Like the configuration discussed above, the other three configurations show a similar horizontal axis. This first dimension reflects *evaluation*, ranging from *good* (safety, precautions, protection) to *bad* (violence, crime, rape). The plot of the configuration resulting from the nonmetric MDS that applied only the eight selected adjective pairs is presented in Figure 10.4. The horizontal dimension is

---

[296] The other configurations, two resulting from the metric MDS that analysed all adjectives, are slightly different (results available on request). The appearance of the configurations is heavily influenced by the orientation and scale of the axes; the distances between the various concepts are quite the same. In other words, the same concepts cluster together, like 'inattention' and 'fault' or 'crime' and 'rape'. Most importantly, the horizontal axis is similar in all four configurations.

similar to the 1st dimension in the configuration in Figure 10.3, the second dimension has a different scale and has a different orientation.

Interestingly, in this configuration, the 'bad things that can happen to a person', such as natural disaster, accident and crime, are all in the lower right quadrant. This is clearly in contrast with the upper left group of concepts, i.e. defensibility, protection and precautions, which all refer to 'good things that you can do (or influence) yourself'. Hypothesising that the second dimension would reflect the attribution of responsibility and blame to oneself, it becomes clearer that insecurity, fault and inattention are gathering. Like the previously described configuration, the second dimension possibly has to do with someone's own role, influence and involvement, and consequently, someone's blame and deservedness. Supposedly, the concepts insecurity, fault and inattention are perceived as influenceable by somebody in person. In contrast, natural disaster and accident, and apparently concern for others, concern and risk too, are perceived as something that happens without the controlling influence or manipulation of a person him/herself. When the second dimension is interpreted this way, it appears that *rape* has the most neutral position on this dimension, more so than violence and crime.

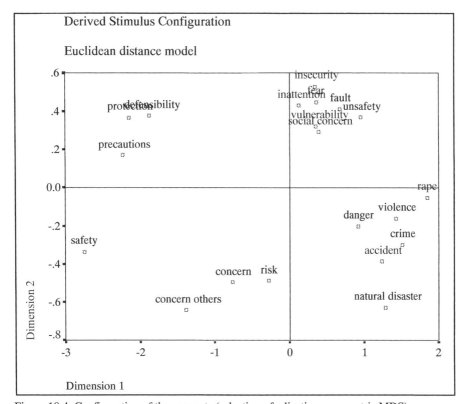

Figure 10.4. Configuration of the concepts (selection of adjectives; nonmetric MDS).

10.4.1.1.2   Results from HCA

Next, Hierarchical Cluster Analysis (HCA) was used to detect meaningful clusters underlying the concepts, in a different way than MDS does. The two techniques together complement each other and give more information, which enables interpretation, than the mere results of only one technique. The proximity matrix that consists of dissimilarity or distance data is the same as in the MDS analyses and can be based both on the selection of adjectives as well as on the entire set. Therefore, two analyses were performed, which could be considered as another check of the selection of adjectives.

Table 10.8. Two- factor solution; results from analysis of all adjectives.

Two factors underlying the concepts	92%
1st Evaluation (bad-good)	66.5%
Vulnerability	.96
Fear	.94
Social concern	.94
Danger	.94
Crime	.93
Accident	.92
Unsafety	.92
Insecurity	.92
Fault	.92
Violence	.92
Natural disaster	.89
Rape	.87
Inattention	.86
Risk	.86
Concern	.62
Safety	-.71
Protection	-.57
Defensibility	-.47
Precautions	-.43
2nd Attribution of responsibility or: (bad) luck / carelessness - careful	25.5%
Concern others	.94
Defensibility	.84
Precautions	.83
Protection	.77
Safety	.66
Concern	.60
Rape	-.45
Natural disaster	-.38

As mentioned previously, a large coefficient in cluster analysis means that the clusters being merged are very dissimilar; the squared Euclidian distance is quite large. On the other hand, a small coefficient means that fairly homogeneous clusters are being combined. The dendogram and agglomeration schedule of the HCA using only the selected adjectives and all concepts suggest three main clusters of relative homogeneity. One cluster, containing crime, violence, unsafety, accident, natural disaster, danger and rape has to do with *threat*. Another cluster, holding fault, social concern, fear, insecurity, vulnerability and inattention touches on *emotion*. The third cluster, with precautions, protection, defensibility, safety and concern others is mainly focused on *control*. A fourth small cluster contains only two concepts, namely risk and concern.

The results of the HCA using the entire set of adjectives show a rather similar picture; three main clusters appear. Again, the first cluster, which is holding for example natural disaster, danger and crime, looks like the cluster *threat* of the previous analysis. Also, the second main cluster, with concepts like vulnerability and fear, resembles what has been called the *emotion*-cluster. Similarly, a third cluster touches on *control*, e.g. protection and precautions. The smallest cluster (concern and concern others) appears to be not as stable as the other three; it is possible a fourth cluster exists, which touches on a dimension the other three exclude. However, it seems that the concepts belonging to such a hypothetical cluster, were not included in the semantic differential.[297]

10.4.1.1.3 Factor analysis

Besides HCA and MDS, a factor analysis was done to get more insight in the structure of the concepts. A principal component analysis was performed with a Varimax rotation to enhance interpretability. The eigenvalues, factorloadings and the scree plot showed that only two factors should be extracted; which together explained 92% of the variance (Table 10.8). After a Varimax rotation was done, the concepts could be plotted in a two-dimensional space (see the component plot in Figure 10.5). The factors can best be interpreted by their polar extremes; thus the first factor represents *evaluation*, with negative values reflecting 'good', whereas 'bad' or unpleasant things (e.g. vulnerability, fear, danger) have highly positive values. This factor alone already explains 66.5% of the variance, which is a clear indication of its importance. The second factor, rather similar to the second dimension in the MDS configurations, seems to touch on someone's own active role, intention and involvement; on the one hand the things that 'happen', because of (bad) luck or because of careless stupidity (e.g. inattention, fault) and on the other hand deliberate involvement and carefulness.[298] Somehow, this dimension is related to the attribution of responsibility and blame; on the one hand it is related to careless behaviour and 'stupid mistakes', on the other hand it refers to caring and careful behaviour.

---

[297] To check the stability of the clusters, other analyses were done that used random samples. The results confirmed the results reported here.

[298] Again, random samples were used as well in order to check the stability of the factor solution. These other analyses confirmed the results. Furthermore, factor analyses were performed in which the concepts concern and risk were excluded respectively, to check whether a one-dimensional factor solution would be adequate. This appeared *not* to be the case.

10.4.1.1.4 Interpretation of concepts: results from MDS, HCA and PCA

The different MDS procedures clearly lead to configurations in which the first dimension is alike; this dimension reflects *evaluation*, ranging from *good* (safety, precautions, protection) to *bad* (violence, crime, rape). The second dimension seems to touch on attribution of responsibility, someone's own role, influence and involvement, and consequently, someone's blame and deservedness. The results from the factor analysis can be interpreted similarly; the first dimension, which by itself explains 66.5% of the variance, represents *evaluation*. The second factor refers to attribution of responsibility; it differentiates between the things that 'happen', because of (bad) luck or because of carelessness from deliberate involvement and carefulness.

The HCA procedures show that three main clusters of relative homogeneity appear to be most saillant; Table 10.9 summarises them.[299] The first two clusters consist of concepts with a more negative connotation, such as crime, violence, fault and inattention. The third cluster, which is named *control* here, consists of the concepts with a clear positive connotation. A possible, less stable, fourth small cluster incorporates 'concern' and depending on the specific analysis that is employed, 'risk' and 'concern others'. Though this fourth small cluster appears to be not as stable as the other three; it might touch on a dimension the other three groups of concepts exclude. The findings from MDS and the factor analyses suggest that the second dimension possibly refers to two different abstract facets as well; relating both to the attribution of cause and to the attribution of responsibility. Things can happen because of (bad) luck, or because of somebody's own behaviour and on the other hand, responsibility is attributed to a person or to a metaphysical entity such as fate.

Table 10.9. Three groups of concepts.

Threat	Emotion	Control
Crime	Fault	Precautions
Violence	Social concern	Protection
Unsafety	Fear	Defensibility
Accident	Insecurity	Safety
Natural disaster	Vulnerability	Concern others
Danger	Inattention	
Rape		

These results from MDS, HCA and PCA show general (dis)similarities between the twenty concepts. All the concepts are related to the experience or interpretation of safety and have been chosen on the basis of the review of the literature and measurement instruments and arise from the conceptual analysis of the three key concepts within the 'fear of crime' discursive framework, i.e. victimisation, risk and 'fear of crime' itself. Assuming that the twenty concepts

---

[299] Besides checking the stability of the clusters by using random samples in the HCA procedures, which confirmed the results, another check was performed by doing MDS-procedures in which a three-dimensional space was used; these results were confirmatory as well.

together cover the various and possibly different aspects of the experience of safety, the examination of the (dis)similarities between the concepts gives more insight in the meaning of (the experience of) safety. Two aspects are of major importance, evaluation (bad things) and attribution (why is it happening and/or who is to blame). Also, the findings support the idea that the experience of safety is firstly about threat and the perception thereof, i.e. the dangerous or bad things, the various emotions concerning this threat, including notions of guilt and responsibility, and about dealing with the threat, which refers to responsibility as well. Though this might not come as a surprise, and is in accordance with the previous conceptual analyses, these results provide an empirical argument for the idea that 'fear of crime' is not at all (only) about crime and criminal statistics.

In this section the variation between concepts has been of primary concern; in the next section, the focus is still on the concepts themselves. Since evaluation appears to be of essential importance, the concepts are compared on this aspect only. This is possible when making use of the semantic differential data once again.

10.4.1.2 Evaluation of concepts

The semantic differential is a method to measure the meaning of a concept for an individual. Concepts (or objects, terms) can be distinguished or differentiated from each other along three dimensions, namely the dimension evaluation E (good – bad), potency P (strong – weak) and activity A (active – passive) as third factor (e.g. Osgood & Suci 1969; Osgood, Suci & Tannenbaum 1978). These three dimensions essentially reflect three elements of an attitude, of which the first and foremost element is the respondent's evaluation (E) of the concept. This evaluative dimension, which is very similar to favorable – unfavorable of a Likert-type attitude scale, is the most consistent and important one found in research that uses semantic differential scales, and can be used as the chief indicator of a person's attitude towards the concept.[300] The current instrument based on a semantic differential format can be treated as a series of attitude scales, since respondents rated the given concepts (e.g. crime, rape, violence) on several 7-point bipolar scales (e.g. good – bad, nice – nasty). The scores on the bipolar scales belonging to the evaluative or affective dimension (E) reflect the evaluative component of an attitude. Thus, based on the previously described analyses of the adjectives, the scores on the pairs nice – nasty, pleasant – unpleasant, desirable – undesirable, sad – happy, friendly – unfriendly and good – bad can be summed up.

---

[300] For some purposes, the other two dimensions, namely the respondent's notion of the potency or power (P) of the concept and the respondent's notion of the activity (A) of the concept, can provide additional information.

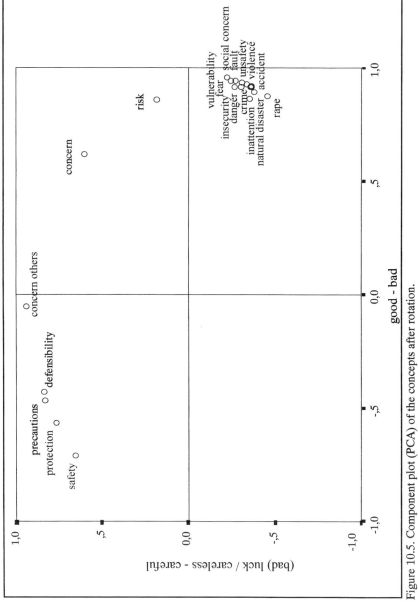

Figure 10.5. Component plot (PCA) of the concepts after rotation.

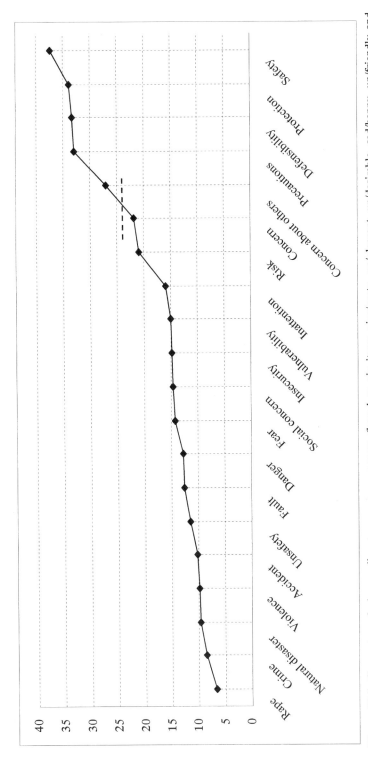

Figure 10.6. Concepts ranked according to average sumscore (based on six items nice/nasty, un/pleasant, un/desirable, sad/happy, un/friendly and good/bad).

Table 10.10. Basic statistics and reliability; all have six items (nice/nasty, un/pleasant, un/desirable, sad/happy, un/friendly and good/bad).

Name	Sum 6 items of	N	M	M/I	SD	α^{301}
e_accide	Accident	123	10.1	1.7	4.6	.88
e_concer	Concern	137	21.9	3.7	8.0	.91
e_concot	Concern about others	137	27.1	4.5	7.6	.89
e_crime	Crime	119	8.5	1.4	4.1	.91
e_danger	Danger	135	12.7	2.1	6.2	.91
e_defens	Defensibility	136	33.3	5.6	6.9	.89
e_fault	Fault	121	12.6	2.1	5.4	.86
e_fear	Fear	257	14.3	2.4	6.0	.85
e_inatte	Inattention	135	15.9	2.7	6.2	.89
e_insecu	Insecurity	122	14.8	2.5	5.2	.84
e_disast	Natural disaster	121	9.7	1.6	4.8	.88
e_precau	Precautions	122	33.0	5.5	7.7	.89
e_protec	Protection	135	33.9	5.7	6.1	.84
e_rape	Rape	136	6.7	1.1	2.4	.79
e_risk	Risk	123	20.9	3.5	6.9	.93
e_safety	Safety	136	37.4	6.2	5.2	.92
e_soconc	Social concern	120	14.7	2.5	6.2	.90
e_unsaf	Unsafety	258	11.5	1.9	4.9	.85
e_violen	Violence	135	9.8	1.6	4.8	.86
e_vulner	Vulnerability	118	15.0	2.5	6.2	.89

When focusing on respondents, the particular sumscore indicates the respondent's position on the main dimension of attitude, namely *evaluation*, toward the concept being rated. However, the variation between respondents will be of later concern. Here, the focus is on the concepts, therefore the average sumscore per concept and the variation between concepts on these evaluation sumscores are of interest. This sumscore can vary from 6 to 42, since six diferent 7-point bipolar scales were used. Table 10.10 presents the basic statistics and the reliability of the sum of the six pairs; a higher sumscore means a more positive attitude and a lower sumscore indicates a more negative attitude. The mean sumscores range from 6.7 for *rape* to 37.4 for *safety*. This means that *rape* is evaluated most negatively; in other words, respondents have the most negative attitude towards *rape*. This is clearly in contrast with the concept *safety*, which is evaluated most positively; meaning that respondents have the most positive attitude towards *safety*.

Figure 10.6 presents the order of the concepts according to the sumscore of the six items with a clear evaluative character. A respondent who would have rated all concepts as 'neutral' on every of the six scales, would have a sumscore of 24. Therefore, and considering the high reliabilities of all sumscores, a score of 24 can be considered a cut-off point (see the small dashed line in Figure 10.6). In other words, concepts having a lower score than 24

---

[301] Standardised item alpha is .82. The other reliabilities are Cronbach's alpha's; they did not differ from the accompanying standardised item alpha's.

evoke negative responses, while concepts having a higher score than 24 are positively evaluated. Most concepts, as expected, were evaluated negatively, though the intensity varies greatly.[302] The concept *rape* clearly stands out as the most negative one.[303] Another striking finding is the relative neutrality, or at least the lack of clear negativity, of *risk*. This will be elaborated on below. Similarly, *concern* and *concern about others* are neither evaluated (very) positively, nor (very) negatively.

10.4.1.3 Profiles of concepts

Next to the grouping of concepts, the specific profiles of particular concepts can be visually examined with respect to one another as well.[304] This is another application of the instrument that applies a semantic differential format. Such a profile is merely a visual presentation of the average scores of a concept on several adjective pairs. The profile of fear will be described with respect to the three dimensions that have been found in studies on the semantic differential. After that, safety and unsafety are compared, answering the question whether safety and unsafety are indeed polar opposites or whether safety might be encompassing more than just the absence of unsafety. Three other examples of profiles are presented, one example incorporates risk and danger; the next involves crime, accident and natural disaster. The comparison touches on the question whether crime can be considered a hazard, which is done in some empirical studies within the field of risk perception. The last example of profiles draws a parallel between crime, violence and rape. Before entirely turning to the variation between respondents instead of concepts, the profiles of different groups, i.e. men and women, are compared.

10.4.1.3.1 Fear

In previous research on cross-cultural differences and similarities regarding the meaning of concepts, Americans, Belgians and Finns rated the concepts 'crime', 'danger' and 'fear', which showed similar profiles, namely E-, P+ and A+ (in other words: bad – strong – active) (Osgood 1969b). Our sample evaluates fear negatively as well. Fear is judged as unfriendly, malign, undesirable, nasty, bad and unpleasant.[305] Osgood's Potency dimension is usually defined by the pair strong – weak, which was not included in our list of

---

[302] Table 10.1 presents concepts and the reasons why they were included. Defensibility, precautions, protection (security) and safety were used, among other reasons, because of their apparent positive connotation.

[303] The differences, tested by means of a paired samples t-test, between violence and rape, ($t(133) = 8.51$, $p < .000$) and crime and natural disaster ($t(118) = -3.38$, $p < .001$) are significant. The differences between the other concepts could not be tested, since the concepts were not included in the same version of the questionnaire and thus other groups of respondent rated them.

[304] These profiles were made in Harvard Graphics 98. Alreck & Settle (1985) suggest that such a profile is less difficult to interpret when all positives are placed on one side, and the negative counterparts on the other. Also, reordering the items on the basis of the mean might facilitate the recognition of patterns and comparisons among items. These suggestions were taken into account when appropriate.

[305] These six adjectives end up in the first factor when factor analysis is performed, with loadings from .77 to .67. This first factor explains 28.2 % of the variance; together the adjectives make up a reliable scale (Cronbach's alpha = .87).

adjectives. The second factor of adjectives comprised fast – slow, afraid – at ease, seek – flee and provoke – avoid, which is not a typical potency dimension.[306] The third factor consisted of the items active – passive, steer – let go and predictable – unpredictable, but did not have sufficient reliability to make up a scale (Cronbach's alpha = .36). In other words, unfortunately the scales P and A that Osgood and others found so many times were not replicated here. Most importantly, the respondents clearly see fear as something that is negative that should be avoided (see Figure 10.7).

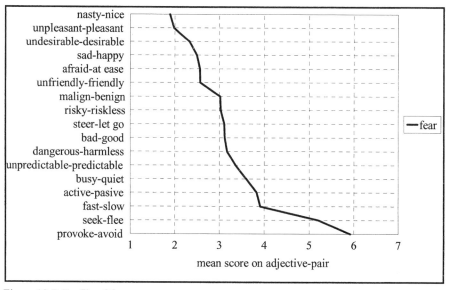

Figure 10.7. Profile of fear.

10.4.1.3.2 Is safety the opposite of unsafety ?

Figure 10.8 presents the profiles of the concepts unsafety (onveiligheid) and safety (veiligheid). Two thinner lines indicate the profiles of danger (gevaar) and insecurity (onzekerheid). Is safety the opposite of unsafety? If the concept 'safety' would be the exact opposite of 'unsafety', both profiles would be mirror images, when placing the mirror in the middle (average score 4). In general this seems to be the case, though some adjectives seem to be performing slightly differently, a t-test showed that the distances to the middle of the scale is not significantly different.[307] In other words, safety and unsafety are indeed perceived as polar opposites.

Does unsafety mean about the same as danger and as insecurity? Obviously, the three concepts danger, unsafety and insecurity seem to be related; they somewhat cluster together in contrast to 'safety'. Paired samples t-

---

[306] These four items (Cronbach's alpha .70) loaded from .72 till .51.
[307] T-tests that tested the differences between the distances of each adjective to the neutral value 4 indicated that these distances were indeed not significantly different. Thus, safety and unsafety are polar opposites.

tests indicate that unsafety and danger differ only significantly on the adjectives fast – slow, predictable – unpredictable and quiet – busy. Danger is perceived as faster and busier and more unpredictable than unsafety. Furthermore, the average sumscores on the six evaluative items are different; respondents have a *less* negative attitude towards *danger* (M = 12.7) than towards *unsafety* (M = 11.5).[308] Overall, the general picture is that danger and unsafety are almost, but not entirely, the same. Especially the difference on the attitudinal scale, based on the six evaluative items, is of interest.

The concepts unsafety and insecurity differ significantly on this attitudinal scale; unsafety is evaluated more negatively. These concepts differ on these evaluative items and the other adjective pairs, but they are perceived as approximately equal in reference to fast – slow, sad – happy, predictable – unpredictable, steer – let go and quiet – busy. Overall, insecurity is rated less extreme than unsafety.

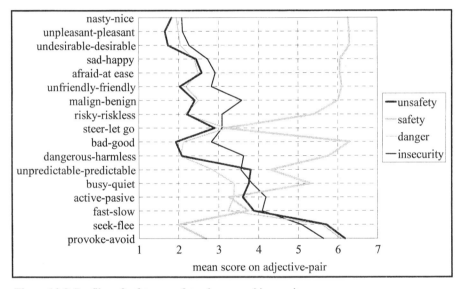

Figure 10.8. Profiles of safety, unsafety, danger and insecurity.

10.4.1.3.3 Does risk signify danger?

Chapter 7 argued that in current Western discourse on risk, risk is not a neutral term for calculating probabilities; above all it signifies danger. When this is true, the profiles of the concepts risk and danger should be about the same. The data from the instrument enables a comparison between the connotative meaning of *risk* and *danger*. The profiles of risk and danger are presented in Figure 10.9. These profiles are obviously not the same; except for some pairs of

---

[308] As previously described, the sumscore is based on the pairs nice/nasty, un/pleasant, un/desirable, sad/happy, un/friendly and good/bad. A higher sumscore means a more positive (or less negative) attitude.

adjectives, risk does *not* mean the same as danger. Danger is much more negatively evaluated than risk.[309]

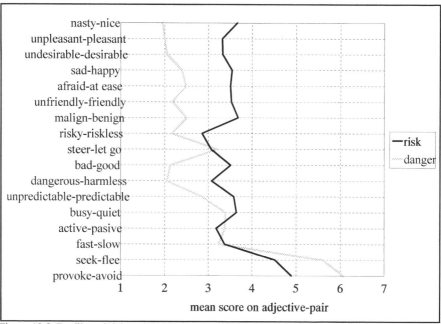

Figure 10.9. Profiles of risk and danger.

10.4.1.3.4 Is crime just another hazard?

In some studies on risk perception, crime is considered as a hazard, together with for example a power plant or thunderstorm. The current dataset enables the comparison between *crime, accident* and *natural disaster*. Figure 10.10 shows that these three concepts are connotatively rather similar. Paired samples t-tests indicate that *crime* and *accident* differ significantly on most items, except for the adjectives provoke – avoid, sad – happy and quiet – busy. Crime and natural disaster are more similar; only seven pairs of adjectives out of the seventeen are significantly different.[310] In particular, crime is perceived as faster, worse, unfriendlier, more malign, whereas natural disaster is considered unpredictable and slightly more dangerous. Furthermore, the sumscore on the

---

[309] Risk and danger were not included in the same version of the questionnaire. Therefore, paired samples t-tests are not possible. The two subsamples that received the two different versions did not differ on socio-demographic variables nor in general response patterns. Therefore, another procedure was applied. The average scores on each adjective pair were calculated for the two concepts. After that, the differences between these averages were used in a one-sample t-test, that tested whether these differences were significantly different from zero. When both concepts would have been scored exactly the same, the differences between the (seventeen) average values would all be zero. A one-sample t-test would then turn out not to be significant. Risk and danger were subjected to this procedure and the results indicate that risk and danger are not the same, since the set significantly differs from zero ($t(16) = -2.99$, $p = .009$).

[310] These pairs are fast – slow, bad – good, friendly – unfriendly, predictable – unpredictable, benign – malign, dangerous – harmless and steer – let go.

six evaluative items differs significantly, indicating that crime is perceived more negatively than natural disaster is. Though crime might not be just another hazard, these findings confirm the idea that crime is a specific hazard. Accident and natural disaster appear to be even more similar to one another; the evaluation-sumscore does not differ significantly, only five items do.[311]

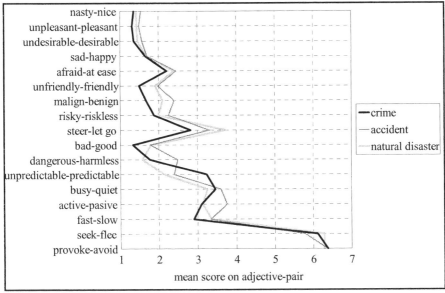

Figure 10.10. Profiles of crime, accident and natural disaster.

10.4.1.3.5 Crime, violence and rape

Crime, violence and *rape* were included in the list of concepts. Thus, it is possible to examine empirically whether these concepts are evaluated and perceived differently, or not. For example, when the concept *crime* is judged similarly as the concept *violence*, this would provide an indication that to people, these concepts are connotatively indiscriminable. A similar comparison can be made regarding *violence* and *rape*. From the figure, it is clear that the three concepts have similar profiles. Crime has been included in another version of the questionnaire than rape and violence have; a paired samples t-test could not be performed. Another analysis can roughly indicate whether crime and violence, and crime and rape, are connotatively the same (see note 280) The average scores on each of the seventeen adjective pair were calculated and the differences between these averages were used in a one-sample t-test, that tested whether these differences were significantly different from zero. In other words, the average score on nasty – nice of violence was subtracted from the average score on nasty – nice of crime. When both concepts would have been scored exactly the same, the differences between the (seventeen) average values would be zero. A one sample t-test would then turn out not to be significant. This is in

---

[311] These items are seek – flee, benign – malign, dangerous – harmless, active – passive and steer – let go.

fact the case when crime and rape are analysed this way, which roughly indicates that crime and rape do not differ significantly. The same holds for crime and violence, though less convincingly.[312] This procedure shows that violence and rape differ significantly ($t(16) = -2.16$, $p < .05$), which implicates that crime is rather similar to rape, crime and violence are also quite the same, but violence and rape are distinct.[313]

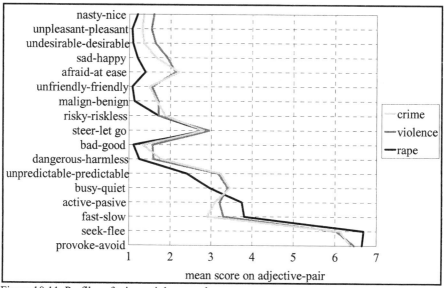

Figure 10.11. Profiles of crime, violence and rape.

Interestingly, when these analyses are done for male and female respondents separately, some differences arise. For males, crime and violence, violence and rape, but not crime and rape are significantly different from one another. In contrast, these three comparisons turn out to be non-significant for the female sub sample. These findings suggest that while men discriminate between violence, rape and crime, women do not. The female respondents perceive crime, rape and violence as connotatively equal.[314] The next section will elaborate on these gender differences.

10.4.1.3.6 Comparing the profiles of different groups: gender differences

Obviously, people evaluate distinct concepts differently. Besides variation among the concepts, people vary too. However, before completely focusing on the variation between respondents instead of concepts, some examples of the profiles of different groups, i.e. men and women, are presented

---

[312] Crime and rape ($t(16) = 1.3$, $p =.21$); crime and violence ($t(16) = -2.06$, $p =.056$).

[313] Since rape and violence are in the same version and the same respondents rate both, a paired samples t-test is possible. The results confirm the conclusion; only three pairs of adjectives are not significantly different. These are provoke – avoid, risky – riskless and steer – let go.

[314] This conclusion is based on the one-sample t-test. The paired-samples t-test that could be performed for rape and violence shows that men perceive these two concepts as significantly different on a large number of items, but to a lesser extent than women.

here. Four concepts were chosen to present here, since they are quite representative for the general picture. The profiles of these four concepts, safety and unsafety, and danger and protection, are portrayed in Figure 10.12 and Figure 10.13 respectively.

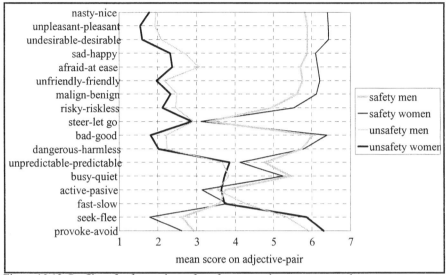

Figure 10.12. Profiles of safety and unsafety, for men and women separately.

In general, women appear to evaluate concepts more extreme than men do. That is, 'bad things', such as rape, violence, unsafety and danger, are rated more negatively than men do. On the other hand, women more than men rate concepts such as protection and safety more positively. This is demonstrated in the figures (Figure 10.12 and Figure 10.13) as well. The significant difference between the male and female sub sample does not hold for every concept; for example, both men and women evaluate crime negatively and no significant difference arises from the analyses on the evaluation sumscore. Furthermore, not all adjective pairs show significant differences. The concept safety for instance shows significant as well as insignificant differences.[315] That is men and women perceive safety on some adjective pairs unequally (e.g. on risky – riskless, predictable – unpredictable, malign – benign), while on others the two subsamples have made comparable judgments (e.g. on fast – slow, provoke – avoid, dangerous – harmless). A more parsimonious attitude scale, an instrument that measures the directionality and intensity of the attitudinal response towards (the experience of) safety, could be helpful when comparisons are drawn between socio-demographic groups. The construction of such an instrument is described in the next section. The analyses on the differences between the male and female sub sample are used as criterion. Other analyses that functioned as criteria concentrate on the (more familiar) Likert-type scales from the previous

---

[315] Differences were tested by means of paired-samples t-test, of which the detailed results not described here.

chapter and on differences regarding another socio-demographic variable, namely age. The general procedure is that groups, whether the groups are based on the age and sex or on the scores on the Likert-scales, are contrasted with one another. These types of comparison are generally considered to be checks of the validity of an operationalisation.

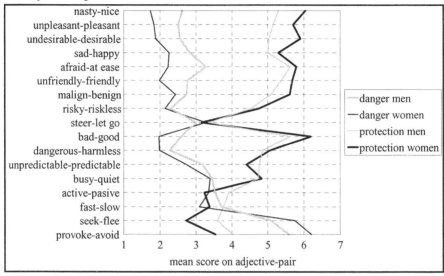

Figure 10.13. Profiles of danger and protection, for men and women separately.

10.4.2 People

10.4.2.1 An attitude scale from the semantic differential instrument

Since the evaluation-dimension or the evaluative factor from the semantic differential resembles attitude scores, the semantic differential can be used to construct an attitude scale (Brinton 1969), of which the scores reflect both the *directionality* of a response (e.g. good versus bad) and the *intensity* (slight through extreme) (Heise 1970). Respondents have rated the given concepts (e.g. crime, rape, violence) on several 7-point bipolar scales (e.g. good – bad, nice – nasty) and these ratings can be considered as a series of attitude scales. For each concept, the sum of the scores on the pairs nice – nasty, pleasant – unpleasant, desirable – undesirable, sad – happy, friendly – unfriendly and good – bad is an indication of the respondent's position on the main dimension of attitude, namely *evaluation*, toward the concept being rated. When necessary, these six items can be reduced to a set of three items. As described previously, initial factor analyses showed that friendly – unfriendly, pleasant – unpleasant, good – bad are the three best performing pairs.[316] Here, analyses were performed with all six pairs.

---

[316] Both the frequencies with which the pairs of adjectives pop up in the 1st factor and other factors as well as the factorloadings were used as criteria; these three pairs have the highest factorloading on the first factor.

Obviously, for a measurement instrument it would not be practical nor useful when it is too long. Besides the number of adjectives or attributes, the number of concepts needs to be reduced as well. Five questions provide the 'hints' whether to keep a concept *in* or leave a concept *out*. Three questions basically come down to comparing the Likert-type scales with the semantic differential scales, the other two questions are related to comparisons between socio-demographic groups. Table 10.11 summarises these five questions, which eventually results in a smaller list of concepts. This list consists of the concepts danger, fear, inattention, rape, safety, unsafety and violence. The next passages discuss this reduction process in more detail.

10.4.2.1.1 *Comparing Likert-type scales with semantic differential scales*

A common method to examine the validity of an operationalisation, is to compare different operationalisations of the same construct to one another. The current dataset enables the comparison between the scores on the Likert-type scales and the scores on the evaluative semantic differential scales on the twenty concepts.[317] The two sets of scales, i.e. the scores on the evaluative semantic differential scales and the scores on the Likert-scales, were compared in three different ways, the results of which are only briefly described here. Appendix I discusses the comparisons and the results more extensively. The first comparison makes use of the correlations between the sum scores of the two sets of scales. Two other ways make use of only two third of the sample, since the whole group of respondents is divided in three according to the scores on either the Likert-scales or the semantic differential scales. Only the lowest third and highest third scores on the Likert-scales are used to test the difference of the means on the semantic differential scales. In addition, the lowest third and highest third scores on the semantic differential scales are used to test the difference of the means on the Likert- scales.[318] These two ways of comparing the two sets of scales provide a basic argument for the decision which concepts to choose for the final instrument with a semantic differential format.

First, the correlations with the familiar Likert-type scales were examined, and the number of correlations of these scales per concept was taken into account. The correlations between the Likert-type scales and the sumscores of the six evaluation-items were calculated for the whole sample, and the male and female sub sample (see Appendix I). The number of significant correlations between the Likert-type scales and the semantic differential scales has been added up, which provided a first hint of which concept to include and which not

---

[317] Chapter 9 discussed the inventory; an informal meta-analysis of the Anglo-Saxon and Dutch literature which led to a number of operationalisations. These operationalisations were then used to construct a questionnaire, which has been administered to four samples (see Inventory, Rietveld1, Rietveld2 and Flight 2002 in Appendix F). The structure of the inventory was analysed, making use of simple correlations, factor and cluster analysis. Since one of these samples received a questionnaire, which included the inventory as well as the semantic differential scales, it is possible to examine the relationship between the semantic differential data and the data derived from the more traditional inventory items.
[318] Note that a low sumscore on a semantic differential scale indicates a more negative attitude or evaluation, and a higher sumscore indicates a more positive attitude.

(see Table 10.11). As you can see in Table 10.11, the sum scores of the concepts danger, fear, inattention, rape, safety and unsafety have four or more significant correlations with the Likert-type scales. For example, the sum score of the evaluative items of the concept *safety* (e_safety) correlates significantly with four Likert-type scales (see Appendix I).

For the next comparison, the lowest third and highest third scores on the semantic differential scales are used to test the difference of the means on the Likert-scales. In other words, the group of respondents was divided in three groups of the same number of respondents and recoded, thus constructing three groups with the lowest, middle and the highest scores on each evaluative sum score. Only the lowest third and highest third scores on the semantic differential scales were applied to test the difference of the means on the semantic differential scales, using simple t-tests. The number of significant differences between the means were added up, which provided a second hint of which concept to include and which not (Table 10.11). The groups that score the lowest and the highest on the concepts danger, inattention, rape, and unsafety show four or more significant differences between the means on the Likert-type scales. Groupings based on the other concepts show less or no significant differences. For example, the respondents with the lowest scores, i.e. a more negative attitude, on the evaluative items of *precautions* (e_precautions) do not differ significantly on any of the Likert-type scales with the group of respondents that have the highest scores, i.e. a positive attitude, on *e_precautions*. This in contrast to the two groups that have the lowest and highest scores for *danger*; these two groups have significantly different means on seven Likert-type scales, among which are the indices to measure *seriousness of the consequences*, *feeling at ease* and *being afraid* (Appendix I).

Similar to the previous comparison, the whole group of respondents was divided into three groups of the same number of respondents and recoded, thus constructing three groups with the lowest, middle and the highest scores on each Likert-type scale. The means on the semantic differential scales of the two groups, i.e. the lowest third and highest third scores on the Likert-scales, were tested. Again, the number of means that was significantly different from one another is presented in Table 10.11, giving a third hint of which concepts to keep in and which to leave out. As you can see, when the grouping is based on the Likert-type scales, nine concepts show at least four significant differences between the means on the semantic differential scales. For example, the respondents who score low on the four Likert-type indices feeling *safe and at ease during the night, seriousness of the consequences, feeling at ease* and *being afraid* have a mean on e_rape that significantly differs from those who have a high score on the four Likert-type scales (see Appendix I).

Table 10.11. Five questions that guide the decision whether to keep a concept in, or leave a concept out. All scales have six evaluative items.[319]

Name	Concept	1. Correlations Likert-type scales				2. Differences means Likert-type scales		3. Differences means sem. dif. scales		4. Differences means ♂-♀		5. Differences means young-old		Score
		All	M	F	Hint	2 groups	Hint	2 groups	Hint		Hint	2 groups	Hint	In or out?
e_accide	Accident	2	0	0	X	1	X	1	X	No	X	Yes	✓	Out
e_concer	Concern	0	0	0	X	0	X	0	X	No	X	No	X	Out
e_concot	Concern about others	0	0	0	X	0	X	0	X	No	X	Yes	✓	Out
e_crime	Crime	2	1	1	X	0	X	1	X	No	X	Yes	✓	Out
e_danger	Danger	7	5	2	✓	7	✓	5	✓	Yes	✓	No	X	In
e_defens	Defensibility	0	1	0	X	1	X	0	X	No	X	No	X	Out
e_fault	Fault	3	1	3	?	1	X	5	✓	No	X	Yes	✓	Out
e_fear	Fear	5	2	3	✓	3	?	7	✓	Yes	✓	Yes	✓	In
e_inatte	Inattention	8	0	6	✓	6	✓	8	✓	Yes	✓	No	X	In
e_insecu	Insecurity	1	1	0	X	0	X	0	X	No	X	No	X	Out
e_disast	Natural disaster	1	1	1	X	1	X	2	X	No	X	Yes	✓	Out
e_precau	Precautions	0	0	0	?	0	X	2	X	No	X	No	X	Out
e_protec	Protection	3	1	0	✓	3	?	6	✓	Yes	✓	No	X	Out
e_rape	Rape	4	1	1	✓	4	✓	3	?	Yes	✓	No	X	In
e_risk	Risk	2	0	1	X	2	X	2	X	No	X	Yes	✓	Out
e_safety	Safety	4	0	3	✓	2	X	5	✓	Yes	✓	No	X	In
e_soconc	Social concern	2	1	0	x	2	X	4	✓	No	X	No	X	Out
e_unsaf	Unsafety	8	1	7	✓	8	✓	8	✓	Yes	✓	Yes	✓	In
e_violen	Violence	3	1	1	?	2	X	4	✓	Yes	✓	No	X	In
e_vulner	Vulnerability	1	4	1	?	1	X	1	X	No	X	No	X	Out

Note that X means not adequate; ✓ adequate; ? unsure or possibly adequate.

[319] The five questions refer to the following: the first question concerns the number of correlations with familiar Likert-type scales, the second the number of significant differences between the means on Likert-scales when grouping is based on the scores on the semantic differential scales, the third the number of significant differences between the means on the semantic differential scales when grouping is based on Likert-scores, the fourth question asks whether the means between the male and female subsamples are significantly different, and the final question concerns the differences between the means of the youngest and oldest third of respondents.

10.4.2.1.2 Comparing socio-demographic groups: sex and age

The three ways of comparing the Likert-type scales with the semantic differential scales that were briefly described, provided three 'hints' for the reduction process. The two other questions that can help in the decision whether to keep a concept *in* or leave a concept *out* are related to comparisons between socio-demographic groups. Most notably and extensively discussed in for example the chapter on victimisation, is the difference between men and women regarding issues of safety and crime. Therefore, the concepts that do discriminate between sexes are filtered. Only the concepts danger, fear, inattention, protection, rape, safety, unsafety and violence show a significant t-test for the equality of means and discriminate between the sexes (see Table 10.12).

The difference between age groups is considered less important. Simple t-tests were conducted to test whether the means of the youngest third respondents on the semantic differential scales were significantly different from the means of the oldest third respondents. The results indicate that the younger and older respondents differ on eight concepts, namely accident, concern about others, crime, fault, fear, natural disaster, risk, and unsafety.

Table 10.12. Basic statistics for male and female respondents; six *evaluative* semantic differential items of all twenty concepts.

Name	Concept	Males			Females			t-test for equality of means	
		N	M	SD	N	M	SD	t	df
e_accide	Accident	40	10.5	5.1	78	9.8	4.4	ns	
e_concer	Concern	34	20.8	8.0	101	22.9	8.1	ns	
e_concot	Concern about others	34	26.8	7.6	101	27.1	7.6	ns	
e_crime	Crime	40	9.0	4.8	74	8.3	3.8	ns	
e_danger	Danger	34	15.9	7.5	99	11.7	5.4	3.52**	131
e_defens	Defensibility	34	33.5	6.2	100	33.2	7.1	ns	
e_fault	Fault	40	12.7	5.5	76	12.7	5.4	ns	
e_fear	Fear	72	16.4	7.0	180	13.5	5.4	3.42*	250
e_inatte	Inattention	34	17.9	6.4	99	15.2	6.0	2.27*	131
e_insecu	Insecurity	40	15.0	5.8	77	14.8	4.9	ns	
e_disast	Natural disaster	40	10.8	5.5	76	9.0	4.4	ns	
e_precau	Precautions	40	32.0	8.5	77	33.5	7.4	ns	
e_protec	Protection	34	31.5	6.8	99	34.8	5.7	-2.75*	131
e_rape	Rape	34	7.7	3.4	100	6.4	1.9	2.89*	132
e_risk	Risk	40	22.1	6.6	78	20.4	6.8	ns	
e_safety	Safety	34	35.3	5.8	100	38.0	4.8	-2.74*	132
e_soconc	Social concern	40	16.2	6.6	75	14.1	5.9	ns	
e_unsaf	Unsafety	74	13.1	5.2	79	10.9	4.6	3.28**	251
e_violen	Violence	34	12.6	6.5	99	8.7	3.5	4.40*	131
e_vulner	Vulnerability	39	15.1	6.2	74	15.2	6.2	ns	

** significant at .01 level; * significant at .05 level (2-tailed); ns= not significant.

10.4.2.1.3 A reduced scale

The five questions that provided the 'hints' to decide whether to keep a concept in, or leave a concept out have led to a reduced list of concepts. The first three questions basically come down to three different ways of comparing the Likert-type scales with the semantic differential scales, which corresponds with procedures that examine the validity of operationalisations. First, the number of significant correlations between the Likert-type scales and the semantic differential scales were added up. Second, the lowest third and highest third scoring respondents on the Likert-type scales were used to test the difference of the means on the semantic differential scales. The number of significant differences between the means of the two groups was considered as second hint. The third hint consisted of the number of significant differences between the means on the Likert- scales, where the two groups were the lowest third and highest third scoring respondents on the semantic differential scales. The other two questions that provided the 'hints' whether to keep a concept in, or leave a concept out, were related to comparisons between the sexes and between the youngest and oldest third respondents. Table 10.11 summarises these five questions or hints, which have resulted in a list of seven concepts, namely *danger, fear, inattention, rape, safety, unsafety* and *violence*. Each of the concepts that are included in the (reduced) scale is rated on the generally best performing pairs friendly – unfriendly, pleasant – unpleasant and good – bad. This means that seven concepts actually make up 21 items, which is considered too many.

These seven concepts can be further reduced to a smaller number, not so much based on quantitative criteria but rather guided by matters of relevance and current interests. The scale that is finally proposed incorporates the concepts *danger, unsafety* and *violence*. The concept *inattention* by itself is considered less relevant here. Also, safety has been excluded because it is apparently perceived as the opposite of unsafety, which is also reflected by the relatively high correlation between the two ($r = -.57$; see Table 10.13). The remaining five concepts (danger, unsafety, violence, rape, fear) can make up several scales, the reliabilities and percentage explained variance are presented in Table 10.14. The results show that when rape is included, this has a decreasing effect on the reliability; therefore, rape has been left out as well. The reliabilities of the possible combinations also indicate that an instrument containing four concepts and thus twelve items, since every concept is linked to the three items friendly – unfriendly, pleasant – unpleasant and good – bad, is not necessary at all.

Table 10.13. Correlations between six *evaluative* semantic differential items of all twenty concepts.

Name	accide	concer	concot	crime	danger	defens	fault	fear	inatte	insecu	disast	precau	protec	rape	risk	safety	soconc	unsaf	violen	vulner
accide	1																			
concer	X	1																		
concot	X	.50**	1																	
crime	.57**	X	X	1																
danger	X	ns	ns	X	1															
defens	X	ns	.21*	X	ns	1														
fault	.61**	X	X	.52**	X	X	1													
fear	.42**	ns	ns	.41**	.68**	ns	.40**	1												
inatte	X	ns	ns	X	.27**	-.21*	X	.36**	1											
insecu	.35**	X	X	.27**	X	X	.38**	.35**	X	1										
disast	.70**	X	X	.66**	X	X	.51**	.44**	X	.34**	1									
precau	-.31**	X	X	-.29**	X	X	-.30**	-.22*	X	-.27**	-.39**	1								
protec	X	ns	X	X	-.40**	.21*	X	-.21*	-.26**	X	X	X	1							
rape	X	.27**	X	X	.20*	ns	X	.41**	.25**	X	X	X	ns	1						
risk	.26**	X	X	ns	X	X	.29**	.37**	X	.21*	.22*	ns	X	X	1					
safety	X	ns	.18*	X	-.47**	.35**	X	-.35**	-.42**	X	X	ns	.42**	ns	X	1				
soconc	.29**	X	X	.33**	X	X	.31**	.25**	X	.35**	.38**	-.20*	X	X	.47**	X	1			
unsaf	.44**	ns	-.20*	.42**	.57**	-.20*	.46**	.56**	.53**	.29**	.43**	-.20*	-.38**	.20*	.33**	-.57**	.32**	1		
violen	X	ns	ns	X	.44**	ns	X	.44**	.34**	X	X	X	-.26**	.39**	X	-.30**	X	.48**	1	
vulner	.46**	X	X	.40**	X	X	.34**	.37**	X	.45**	.44**	ns	X	X	.21*	X	.41**	.41**	X	1

X: no correlation can be calculated, since the concepts are part of the two different versions of the questionnaire. N varies from 117–136 and N=255 for correlation fear – unsafety.

* correlation significant at .01 level; * significant at .05 level (2-tailed); ns=not significant.

Table 10.14. Possible scales.

Label	Concepts	Reliability	Explained variance (single factor)
	12 items		
Duvr	Danger unsafety violence rape	.85	38.6%
Fuvr	Fear unsafety violence rape	.80	33,5%
Fuvd	fear unsafety violence danger	.87	43.4%
Fdvr	fear danger violence rape	.84	39.2%
Furd	fear unsafety rape danger	.84	39.4%
	9 items		
Duv	Danger unsafety violence	.87	49.1%
Dur	danger unsafety rape	.82	42,1%
Dvr	Danger violence rape	.79	41.0%
Uvr	Unsafety violence rape	.79	37.6%
Fuv	Fear unsafety violence	.81	42.6%
Fur	fear unsafety rape	.73	35.1%
Fvr	Fear violence rape	.77	41.7%
Fud	fear unsafety danger	.86	48.7%
Fvd	fear violence danger	.85	46.7%
Fdr	Fear danger rape	.82	45.7%
	6 items		
Du	Danger unsafety	.86	58.7%
Dv	Danger violence	.81	52.5%
Dr	Danger rape	.76	53.2%
Df	Danger fear	.84	58.1%
Fv	Fear violence	.76	47.6%
Fr	Fear rape	.74	56.6%
Fu	Fear unsafety	.77	49.1%
Uv	Unsafety violence	.84	55.4%
Ur	Unsafety rape	.69	42.0%
Vr	Violence rape	.69	47.5%

Note that the number of factors has been restricted to one. When a criterion of eigenvalue > 1 is applied, results generally indicate that three items for each concept makes up one factor.

All possible scales that are listed in Table 10.14 differentiate (highly) significantly between male and female respondents. A procedure similar to a procedure described earlier shows that none of the possible scales discriminate significantly between the lowest third and highest third scores on the 'feeling okay during the day' (okd) Likert-type scale nor on the concern (cn) Likert-scale. All possible scales demonstrate a significant difference between the means when the grouping is based on okn ('feeling okay at night'), seriousness of the consequences (ser), feeling at ease (eas) and afraid that a loved one becomes a victim (afo), the latter except for the six-item scale referring to fear and violence (fv). The difference between the means of the lowest third and highest third scores on being afraid (af), feeling safe (fs) and perception of risk (rp) show mixed results. Out of all six-item scales, only *du* and *dv* have a significant difference between the means of the lowest scoring group and the highest scoring group on *af, fs* and *rp*. From the four remaining nine-item scales, i.e. *duv*, *fud*, *fuv* and *fvd*, only the first two show significant differences between the means of the lowest scoring group and the highest scoring group on *af* and *rp*. Since an explicit connection with (a type of) crime, the scale that is finally proposed incorporates the concepts *danger, unsafety* and *violence*.[320] This measurement instrument (in Dutch) can be found in appendix J, together with the basic statistics for the whole sample, and for the male and female subsamples. In brief, the instrument contains nine items; each one of the three concepts danger, unsafety and violence is rated on three pairs of adjectives, namely friendly – unfriendly, pleasant – unpleasant and good – bad. The correlations (Table 10.15) between the main Likert-type scales and *duv*, *du* and *dv* show that an instrument based on six items might perform sufficiently.

Table 10.15. Correlations between Likert-type scales and duv, dv and du; N varies from 132 to 135.

Label	okd	okn	ser	eas	af	afo	cn	fs	rp
duv	ns	.39**	-.28**	.37**	-.29**	-.30**	ns	.23**	-.24**
du	ns	.38**	-.27**	.36**	-.30**	-.31**	ns	.23**	-.25**
dv	ns	.36**	-.29**	.31**	-.29**	-.28**	ns	.23**	-.24**

** correlation significant at .01 level; * significant at .05 level (2-tailed); ns= not significant.

10.5 Portraying safety

This chapter proposed a newly developed instrument, which is somewhat different in format and content. The instrument is based on an extensive review of the literature and has a semantic differential format. Though the instrument is work in progress, I think the instrument is more conceptually embedded and makes it possible to reveal new or other insights. Some possible applications were shown and revealed for example that 'risk' is not at all similar to 'danger'.

The semantic differential format can be used to investigate the meaning of concepts such as crime, danger and safety. The findings and examples of applications show that some concepts are perceived more alike than others (in a two-dimensional space). Also, the concepts can be clustered, e.g. in three main groups, touching on emotion, threat and control. Though a couple of applications of this instrument are suggested and illustrated with relevant examples, clearly more research is required before the instrument can be applied in the field.

A probably practical application is the use of the proposed attitude scale. For the latter use, the set of twenty concepts and seventeen adjectives has been reduced, leading to a smaller set of items that measures the directionality and intensity of the attitudinal response. Table 10.16 summarises this chapter. Two brief methodological difficulties regarding the use of the semantic differential in the attitudinal scale are noted here. First, the pair steer – let go

---

[320] Such a scale also incorporates both *du* and *dv*, two scales that perform very well. Future research can provide additional support for a further reduction of the three-concepts-nine-items-scale that is proposed here.

highlights the problem that a pair of adjectives or attributes can have several meanings. It seems that this pair might have two meanings; on the one hand, steer – let go can be interpreted as 'can X be steered', in which X is the concept that is appraised; on the other hand 'should X be steered', 'is it desirable that X is steered'. Thus, 'steer' (or 'let go') is both an attribute of the concept itself, and a desired action related to X. Another methodological difficulty is the midpoint on the scale. The midpoint of the scale might reflect both attitude ambivalence (mixed feelings) and non-attitude (neutral) (see Krosnick & Fabrigar 1997; McCroskey, Prichard & Arnold 1967; Nemeth & Endicott 1976). Again, further research is needed to check for example whether the order of the pairs and the concepts has an independent effect on the responses given.

Table 10.16. List of main assertions Chapter 10.

Measurement based on semantic differential format: start over- strategy	
Format	Semantic differential format: measuring meaning and deriving attitude scale
	Initial choice of concepts: based on extensive analysis of literature
	Initial choice of adjectives: cognitive, affective, conative and based on convention
Selection of adjectives	Eight pairs were selected; these perform quite well and show similar findings to the whole set of adjectives
Selection of attitudinal adjectives	Six pairs were selected (nice/nasty, un/pleasant, un/desirable, sad/happy, un/friendly and good/bad); can be reduced to three (un/friendly, un/pleasant, good/bad)
Selection of concepts for attitude scale	Danger, unsafety and violence are included; the choice of which is based on comparison with Likert-type scales and discriminatory qualities
Attitudinal scale	Nine items; each one of the three concepts danger, unsafety and violence is rated on three pairs of adjectives, namely un/friendly, un/pleasant, and good/bad
	Improved instrument

11 Interpreting fear, crime, risk and safety

Two main issues, i.e. the conceptualisation and operationalisation of 'fear of crime' have been of interest. The story of the six blind men who encounter an elephant is a good metaphor for this project indeed, since analogous to the elephant so-called 'fear of crime' is a complex phenomenon that consists of different parts. Overall, this study has shown that the traditional umbrella concept 'fear of crime' is used as a term that actually embraces all kinds of attitudinal knowledge regarding disapproved or unwanted behaviour, crime and (perceived) safety. This traditional 'fear of crime' consists of at least five different (sub)constructs, of which the improved measurement instruments will be reviewed below. By now, it is definitely clear that such a complex phenomenon as the traditional 'fear of crime' apparently is, cannot be described or pictured by referring to only one or two parts, without any explicit reference.

The term 'fear of crime' itself suggests something different than the several intertwined global and diffuse phenomena it actually embraces. The problems involved have been pointed out extensively and the inevitability of its meaning and measurement has been criticised (see chapter 4). In other words, this book and the studies that were described in it are essentially problematising and intend to destabilise the current *status quo*. My line of reasoning argues that the way in which 'fear of crime' is currently understood has no inherent necessity at all.

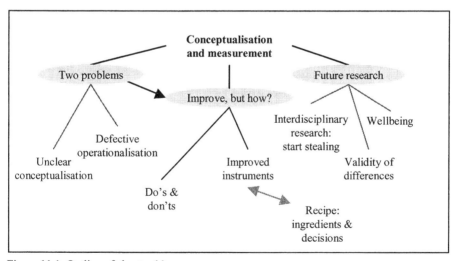

Figure 11.1. Outline of chapter 11.

In this book, the several prevailing usages have been analysed, which showed that some of the disputes that exist in this field are of the blind-men-and-the-elephant kind, with the debating parties disagreeing on the implicit referents of the terms they use. This book has made these implicit referents more explicit and essentially pleads for the complexity of the traditional 'fear of crime', which has resulted in two approaches of measurement; a traditional approach and a novel approach. In other words, this research project does not only criticise the current state of affairs, but gives better alternatives for the status quo as well. This concluding chapter, of which the outline is pictured in Figure 11.1, circles around the two approaches and the measurement instruments derived from it in particular.

First, the two basic problems that have been of primary interest are recalled; the conceptualisation and measurement of 'fear of crime'. Once the problematic and failing conceptualisation and operationalisation are established, the subsequent section offers advice and guidelines on how 'fear of crime' is to be measured in the form of general "do's" and "don'ts". This is followed by a concise review of the measurement instruments that have been developed and which are listed in Table 11.1. Appendix G provides concrete examples of the instruments based on traditional instruments and Appendix J offers a concrete example of the instrument with the semantic differential format. Table 11.2 supplies the recipe for the valid and reliable measurement of 'fear of crime', which covers both the ingredients that need to be included and the decisions that have to be made during the process.

11.1 Two basic problems: concept and measurement

This project and in particular the overview in chapter 2 shows that 'fear of crime' has two problematic features, concerning the flawed conceptualisation and operationalisation. While it is generally acknowledged that all measurement instruments need minimum levels of validity and reliability, it turns out that the familiarity of these criteria has not been a guarantee for research of high quality; seemingly obvious and well-known qualities of research turn out to be not so common after all, which is why the measurement instruments were improved and developed in the first place.

11.1.1 Unclear conceptualisation

'Fear of crime' is a diffuse term that embraces all kinds of (sub)concepts. These (sub)concepts as well as their interrelations appear to be inconsistent, unclear and therefore not very fruitful. Sometimes a concept is used as an explanation of a phenomenon; other times it is an aspect of the same phenomenon, as in the case of 'perception of risk' and 'fear of crime'. Despite common practice, it is definitely necessary to distinguish between different (sub)concepts, because the concept and the measuring instrument used influence the reported 'fear of crime'. In other words, one part of 'fear of crime' or one part of the elephant does not necessarily tell us everything there is to know about the whole. A small trunk or a small perception of risk does not mean that the whole elephant or the whole 'fear of crime' is small, neither empirically nor conceptually.

This project has taken 'fear of crime' as its central core. Chapter 6 on the many meanings of criminal victimisation and chapter 7 on risk have shown that 'fear of crime' encompasses so much more than just plain 'fear' of 'crime'. The fear for one's safety and the experience of safety, which is perceived to be threatened by an expected, perceived or encountered 'dangerous' other person, is connected with attributions of responsibility, guilt and blame. Therefore, 'fear of crime' exceeds fear and exceeds crime likewise. The umbrella concept 'fear of crime' actually embraces all kinds of attitudinal knowledge regarding crime and (perceived) safety or the perceived threat to one's own safety or the safety of a loved one because of the potential danger from others.

11.1.2 Defective operationalisation

In the introductory chapter, the operationalisation and measurement of 'fear of crime' was said to be similar to the question: in what ways can an elephant be presented; what characteristics does the (re)presentation, i.e. the operationalisation and instrument, need in order for it to be referred to as 'elephant'. Chapter 2 and 3 discussed the ways in which 'fear of crime', or parts thereof traditionally have been measured and exemplary traditional indicators were described. Findings from the literature as well as the conclusions derived from own data argue that the measurement of 'fear of crime' is certainly not the same as the measurement of a part thereof, i.e. as the measurement of a (sub)concept. Furthermore, the practice of using only one item is problematic, as well as other current habits of measurement in this field. The overall conclusion then is that the current habits of measurement are definitely not the most appropriate ones, especially when reliability and (construct) validity are concerned.

11.2 Improved conceptualisation and operationalisation

Once the problematic and failing conceptualisation and operationalisation have been established, the next question is how these flaws can be resolved. Explicating the concept of interest and the reliable and valid measurement thereof is a necessary condition without which it is neither possible to fruitfully discuss let alone criticise 'fear of crime' as social construct, the political uses of 'fear of crime' and its accompanying statistics, nor to influence 'fear of crime' that leads some people to adapt and constrain their behaviour by means of policy, or to measure the effectiveness of these kind of interventions.

When something like 'fear of crime' in fact is being measured, preference should be given to the most proper indicators available, within the context of the amount of time and money that the whole procedure may cost. Evidently, it is better to measure aspects of 'fear of crime' more properly in a smaller sample than using only one item (e.g. "how safe do you feel walking alone at night") in a huge regionally representative sample. If 'fear of crime' plays a role in present society *and* is considered relevant for society and the government, the way knowledge about it is acquired deserves a great deal of attention. So far, relatively little effort has been made to improve the survey contents, i.e. the instruments or items that supposedly measure 'fear of crime' till now. The way in which knowledge on 'fear of crime' is acquired or 'fear of crime' is measured, needs and deserves improvement. Therefore, it is about time that a beginning is made with the implementation of the improved measurement instruments that were developed and are reviewed here.

Why is the term 'fear of crime' still used in this last chapter? Shouldn't the label 'fear of crime' be abandoned? On the one hand, one could consider to get rid of the term 'fear of crime', since the label itself denotes something that is only a very small part of the whole range of phenomena involved. It is not so much 'crime' that is of concern, but much more the potential of danger, the possibility of a violent confrontation with the offender in person. Narrowing down 'fear of crime' to the fear of victimisation of legally sanctioned behaviour neglects too much. Though the common approaches to the concept 'fear of crime' with respect to the crime-part has the longest history, these common interpretations are not accurate and lack validity. This has been extensively discussed in section 6.6. The interpretation of events and its consequences are of importance, even in the case of legally defined criminal victimisation. This interpretation is grounded in attributions of deservedness, responsibility or culpability to the victim, which reflect the schemas of the ideal types of victim and perpetrator (see section 4.3, section 6.4 and 6.5, Table 6.2). These schemas provide the information on appropriate behaviour, attributions of deservedness, responsibility or culpability and feelings. Since this variety of phenomena is not reflected by the term 'fear of crime', it would be best to abandon it.

On the other hand, the use of the term 'fear of crime' can be continued, on a couple of conditions. The reasons for *not* abandoning the term are mainly practical; a body of research and literature incorporate the term and apparently the term is appealing to all kinds of professionals; it is evidently appealing to researchers, the public, politicians and the media. The requirements that should be met in order to use the term least improperly or most appropriately are outlined below.

11.3 Measuring 'fear of crime': guidelines

This section suggests what researchers in practice should do and should not do; advices and guidelines that are all based on the studies as described in this book. They contain the requirements that should be met in order to use the term most appropriately. First, general advice is given on "do's" and "don'ts", followed by specific "do's" and "don'ts", depending on the measurement strategy that is preferred (traditional or novel). A summary of the improved traditional instruments and the novel instruments are listed in Table 11.1. Appendix G provides concrete examples of the instruments based on traditional instruments and Appendix J offers a concrete example of the instrument with the semantic differential format. Table 11.2 supplies the recipe for the valid and reliable measurement of 'fear of crime', which covers both the ingredients that need to be included and the decisions that have to be made during the process.

11.3.1 What to do and what not to do in general

This section offers general advice when measuring 'fear of crime'. This research project has shown that there is not one clear, uniform, let alone simple, conceptual model of 'fear of crime'. The analysis, in which the social-political nature of core concepts was taken into account, has above all problematised the simple, familiar, traditional 'fear of crime'. To put it simply: there is not one 'fear of crime'. The extensive analysis of three core concepts that appear to be central to 'fear of crime' argues for such a problematisation as well. 'Fear of crime' is an umbrella label that actually embraces several distinct constructs. The measurement of only one of these constructs (by means of a set of items) does not equal the measurement of another construct, nor does it equal the measurement of the whole concept. The researcher has to *choose* between the different constructs and *select* the construct or constructs of interest, while bearing in mind that it is better to measure one construct reliably than a bunch of constructs unreliably. The chosen construct(s) needs to be explicitly specified. The researcher should consider the constructs that have been chosen thoroughly, since the measurement of one aspect of 'fear of crime' does not say that much about other aspects. That is, conclusions derived from a study on only one part in isolation, like 'feelings of safety in the street' or 'the perception of risk of becoming a victim' should not be generalised to the whole phenomenon like 'fear of crime'. Even when a (sub)concept such as the 'fear of becoming a victim' related to a range of crimes or events is measured extensively and reliably, the findings cannot be extended to other concepts. No attempt should be made to generalise the findings to other (sub)concepts. In practice, this means that reference should be made for example to the 'feelings of safety' or 'the fear that an intimate other will become a victim of crime', and not to 'fear of crime'. Apart from being specific and being explicit about the construct or constructs s/he has chosen to measure, these constructs should *not* be mixed up or used interchangeably with other constructs.

Once the construct or constructs of interest have been selected, the instrument, i.e. a series of items that measures a particular construct, needs to be chosen. The series should consist of a set of at least three items to enhance reliability. Above all, studies on 'fear of crime' or the experience of and attitudes on safety, crime and risk should not attempt to measure the (sub)concept of interest with only one item. Using only one item seriously challenges both reliability and validity. A complex phenomenon deserves more than just one item, such a phenomenon simply cannot be described or pictured when only one part is studied by measuring this sole part by only one item. The common practice of using only one item as indicator of 'fear of crime' needs to be ended.

Two measurement strategies are proposed here. The first is based on the traditional indicators of 'fear of crime' and leads to the five most important (sub)constructs, namely the fear of others' victimisation, the fear of victimisation, the seriousness of the consequences of victimisation, the perception of risk on victimisation and feelings of safety at night. Other constructs, such as behavioural constraints, are not recommended here. Using the improved Likert-type instruments of these five constructs has the advantage of continuation, practicality and comparability. Besides that, the items are appealing and have, in that sense, face validity. The second measurement strategy proposed here is novel and touches on one's attitude regarding crime and safety. These novel instruments take a semantic differential format. These

new instruments are firmly embedded in the literature and empirical research on
'fear of crime' and the perception of risk. The instrument that measures one's
attitude is connected with the concepts derived from these fields of research and
has been created in conformance with generally accepted tests of validity.

11.3.2 Improved instruments: concepts and their measurement

Despite their limitations, that are in part the well-known flaws of all
research on perceptions, attitudes and so forth, the proposed measurement
instruments, either based on a strategy of continuance or a fresh start, are
certainly preferred over the common traditional indicators. Table 11.1 lists the
five distinct (sub)constructs that need to be distinguished when one wants to
continue with an instrument that is most comparable with traditional items.
These most important constructs, based on an approach of continuance and on
traditional indicators are the:
- fear of others' victimisation
- fear of victimisation
- seriousness of the consequences of victimisation
- perception of risk on victimisation
- feelings of safety at night.

Table 11.1. Summary of improved measurement instruments.

Construct of interest	Complete instrument
Improved (traditional)	See Appendix G
Fear of others' victimisation	Fear that other becomes victim of threat, physical abuse, robbery, vandalism, a fight, sexual harassment, a burglary
Fear of victimisation	Fear of becoming a victim of threat, physical abuse, robbery, a fight, sexual harassment, burglary
Seriousness of consequences of victimisation	Seriousness of consequences when victim of violence, physical abuse, threat, sexual harassment, sexual assault, burglary
Perception of risk on victimisation	Perception of risk on becoming victim of vandalism, physical abuse, threat, burglary, robbery
Feeling safe at night	Feeling safe when alone in street at night Being at ease when alone in street at night Feeling safe when alone at home at night Being at ease when alone at home at night Being at ease when together in street at night
Novel	See Appendix J
Meaning of concepts	Friendly – unfriendly; pleasant – unpleasant; good – bad; risky – riskless; active – passive; fast – slow; steer – let go; predictable – unpredictable (per concept)
Evaluation of concepts	Nice – nasty, pleasant– unpleasant, desirable – undesirable, sad – happy, friendly – unfriendly and good – bad (per concept)
Attitude towards (un)safety; 'fear of crime'	Danger, unsafety and violence are rated on three pairs of adjectives each, namely friendly – unfriendly, pleasant – unpleasant and good – bad

In accordance with the general advice on "do's" and "don'ts" described earlier, choose one or more of the improved traditional constructs and verbalise these constructs explicitly. When using two or more series of items, for example when interested in both the fear of victimisation and the perception of risk on victimisation, apply a similar number (preferably at least five) of answer categories to both sets. Also, make the range of answer categories symmetric; e.g. from "entirely disagree" to "entirely agree". When indeed measuring more than one construct, it is recommended to use similar references to particular offences. That is, when measuring both the fear of personal victimisation and the perception of risk of becoming a victim of a specific type of crime, the crimes, like assault, burglary and so forth, that are referred to are preferably the same. When a short instrument, for example in a large-scale survey is preferred over more depth and quality, e.g. in experimental settings or when good data quality is required, the complete instrument can be reduced to a series of at least three items. Appendix G provides some concrete examples of the improved instruments based on traditional instruments and an approach of continuance.

Table 11.1 also lists the instrument that can be used when one wants to make a fresh start and use the validated measurement instrument that employs a semantic differential format. When one is primarily interested in the comparison between concepts, the selection of eight pairs of adjectives performs well. When one's main concern is to measure the attitude towards safety and crime, as another operationalisation of an aspect of 'fear of crime', the instrument that consists of three concepts that are rated on three pairs of adjectives each is recommended. Appendix J offers a concrete example of the latter instrument with the semantic differential format. In summary; the novel approach leads to three different kinds of instruments that can be used for varying purposes:
- portraits of concepts; comparing the meaning of concepts
- evaluation of concepts; comparing concepts on the evaluative/affective dimension (E)
- attitude measurement; attitude towards (un)safety

Table 11.2. Recipe for the valid en reliable measurement of 'fear of crime'.

Step		Options & alternatives	Possible decision outcome
1	Choose purpose & interest	Comparability over time Familiarity of instruments	Traditional instruments based on strategy of continuance
		Conceptual embeddedness Attitude measurement Comparison of 'meaning' or portraying concepts	Novel instruments based on strategy of starting over
2	Acknowledge that 'fear of crime' is multidimensional, which necessitates choices	No alternatives; choices are required	

Table 11.2 – continued.

3	Choose construct(s) of interest	Traditional	Fear of others' victimisation Fear of victimisation Seriousness of consequences of victimisation Perception of risk on victimisation Feeling safe at night
		Novel	Meaning of concepts Attitude towards (un)safety
4	Denote the selected construct(s) explicitly	No alternatives; make a choice and give reasons for the decision made	
5	Choose the measurement instrument that fits the chosen construct(s) See Appendix G and Appendix J	**Based on traditional indicators; use at least 3 items (Table 11.1) per construct:** Fear of others' victimisation Fear of victimisation Seriousness of consequences of victimisation Perception of risk on victimisation Feeling safe at night	- Use at least 3 items per construct of interest - Match the target crimes - Choose format: statements or questions - Apply a similar number of answer categories and at least five - Make the range of answer categories symmetric
		Based on novel approach (see (Table 11.1): Meaning of concepts: 8 items per concept and # concepts	A number of relevant concepts Items: friendly – unfriendly; pleasant – unpleasant; good – bad; risky – riskless; active – passive; fast – slow; steer – let go; predictable – unpredictable
		Attitude towards (un)safety: 9 items	Concepts danger, unsafety and violence rated on 3 items (pairs of adjectives) each; friendly/unfriendly, pleasant/unpleasant, good/ bad
		Evaluation of concepts: at least 3 bipolar scales of evaluative or affective dimension (E) per concept; # concepts	A number of relevant concepts At least 3 items per concept from: nice/nasty, pleasant/unpleasant, desirable/undesirable, sad/happy, friendly/unfriendly and good/bad
6	Report findings and DO NOT overgeneralize	No alternatives; report findings derived from the instrument that fitted the construct(s) of interest best. Be specific and explicit. Do not mix up the investigated construct with (the) other constructs or use them interchangeably. Do not generalize findings to other constructs.	

The different instruments are summarised in Table 11.1, but there are many more decisions to make, which is evident in the description of the do's and don't' s as well. The possibilities, instruments and choices to be made are concisely summarised in Table 11.2. Table 11.2 provides the recipe that, when followed, gives the best results. Six steps need to be taken, and three steps involve important decisions that have to be made, explicated and reasons should be advanced for and against the chosen outcome. As noted previously, further research is needed, especially as far as the novel instruments are concerned. Though these instruments are more conceptually embedded and make it possible to reveal new or other insights, it is still work in progress. Further research should focus on the multidimensional nature of 'fear of crime' and the interrelationships between the concepts in different populations. The different instruments, traditional as well as novel, are summarised in Table 11.1, and the possibilities, instruments and choices to be made are concisely summarised in Table 11.2, which provides a sort of recipe of measuring reliably and validly. Appendices G and J offer concrete examples. These concrete and practical guidelines and suggestions make future research that employs these improved instruments actually possible. After all, as the old proverb says, "the proof of the pudding is in the eating." The next paragraph offers some suggestions for future research, in which the improved measurement instruments might be fruitfully applied. When taking the findings from the current research project into account, future studies cannot ignore the necessity of making choices and cannot use the label 'fear of crime' when it is not specified properly.

11.4 Suggestions for future research

11.4.1 Start stealing

Based on the current research project, some suggestions for future research are put forward here. First, since other disciplines besides the criminological one are concerned with the experience and interpretation of fear, risk and (un)safety, with perceptions of threat and the fear for one's safety it is worthwhile to investigate, in Osgood's (1998) words, what can be stolen from our friends. As discussed in the first chapter, he argues for incorporating more than a single field of research within a particular discipline in his essay "Interdisciplinary Integration: Building Criminology by Stealing from Our Friends". He suggests that academic thievery should be made a regular practice by keeping our eyes on sister disciplines to see what ideas would be useful to take for ourselves. The research fields that are most attractive to steal from, according to the findings of the current research project, are social cognitive psychology and the field of risk perception. Worthwhile to steal from is the work in the field of just world beliefs and trust in (governmental) institutions as well (see Furnham 2003).

11.4.2 Validity of gender differences

Although most items in surveys are supposed to measure a more or less abstract concept, such as aspects of the experience of safety or 'fear of crime', it might unintentionally measure some other qualities as well. Subsequently, though the gender difference is expected to represent an actual difference, it might also be a difference on social desirability. The question why a gender difference does exist still remains. Do men have less information on actual hazards, or do they feel stronger to cope with a potential threat? Do the sexes differ in a sort of threshold on the perception of hazards relating to the personal experience of safety, which functions as a basis underneath? Does a universal feeling of vulnerability among women exist and is this feeling amplified by the actual crime rate?

When differences between groups do not reflect actual differences on the construct, this calls for attention and for research that investigates which items are more susceptible to social desirability than others. Such studies might give some insight regarding the comparability of countries (or actually different cultures) with respect to socially favourable characteristics. Elsewhere, I showed a consistency in the proportions of men and women who say they are avoiding places or feel unsafe (Vanderveen 2002b). The larger the proportion of women who say so, the larger the proportion of men is as well. It seems interesting whether this consistency mirrors the possible risks, dangers, societal unrest and threats in a society, which could be investigated using data from the ICVS and results from other studies (e.g. Van Wilsem 2001). This is linked with possible research on the standard of living and wellbeing.

11.4.3 Standard of living & wellbeing

The findings from Vanderveen (2002b) also point to a regional distinction; on the whole, countries from the same region flock together. Anglo-Saxon and Western-European, as some Asian countries, showed smaller proportions of persons avoiding places and feeling unsafe, as well as a bigger proportion of respondents thinking a break-in is not likely to happen. Eastern-European, Latin American and African countries presented a more negative portrait (Vanderveen 2002b). This could mean that certain continental or rather societal differences might roughly be associated with the experience of safety. It could be hypothesised that on an aggregated level, the experience of safety is connected with the standard of living of a population. On the other hand, it could perhaps signify a correlation between the experience of safety and the actual risks and dangers (or social unrest) in the society, or the general perception of these breaches.

11.5 Conclusion

This book essentially problematises traditional research on 'fear of crime'. The problematic and failing conceptualisation and operationalisation have been shown and suggestions for improvement have been put forward. The thesis demonstrated complexity of 'fear of crime'; 'fear of crime' encompasses much more than just plain 'fear' of 'crime'. The fear for one's safety and the experience of safety, which is perceived to be threatened by an expected, perceived or encountered 'dangerous' other person, is connected with attributions of responsibility, guilt and blame. Therefore, 'fear of crime' exceeds fear and exceeds crime likewise. However, this research project does not only criticise the current state of affairs, but gives better alternatives for the status quo as well. The complexity of the umbrella concept has resulted in two approaches of measurement, one that is based on traditional indicators and survey items, the other firmly embedded in the literature, connected with the concepts that are of importance and the instrument has been empirically validated.

The newly developed instruments that are presented here can be fruitful in practice; especially when the call for investment in quality and depth of the data is heard. This also means that we might want to contain ourselves in employing excessively technically advanced statistical modelling methods, especially when the data are of the poor quality regarding the content. In other words, more of the same kind of research we were already doing does not have priority; new avenues of research have. This research projects and the improved measurement instruments can contribute to that. Following Osgood (1998) in his plead for interdisciplinary research, new questions lead to data that are to be collected that would otherwise not have been collected, which will generate findings about new topics, leading to genuinely new knowledge, and not only, or just, refinement of current knowledge.

Appendices

Appendix A. Glossary of acronyms and abbreviatons
Appendix B. Bibliographic databanks
Appendix C. Example of extensive review
Appendix D. Questions used when reviewing
Appendix E. Comparing one item with three items together
Appendix F. Datasets
Appendix G. Improved instruments (traditional)
Appendix H. English and Dutch equivalents
Appendix I. Constructing instrument (semantic differential format)
Appendix J. Final instrument (semantic differential format)

Appendix A. Glossary of acronyms and abbreviatons

Table A.1 Abbreviations

Abbre-viation	English	Dutch[321]
ABS	Australian Bureau of Statistics	
BCS	British Crime Survey	
BJS	Bureau of Justice Statistics (USA)	
BNSW	Bibliography Dutch Social Sciences	Bibliografie Nederlandse Sociale Wetenschappen
CAPI	Computer assisted personal interview	
CASS	Centre for Applied Social Surveys	
CATI	Computer assisted telephone interview	
CBS	Netherlands Official Statistics	Centraal Bureau voor de Statistiek
CPTED	Crime Prevention Through Environmental Design	
CSS	Crime and Safety Survey	
ECHP	European Community Household Panel	
ERV	Legal Protection and Safety Survey	Enquête Rechtsbescherming en Veiligheid
ESM	Survey of Victims of Criminal Acts	Enquête Slachtoffers Misdrijven
GE	Health Survey	Gezondheidsenquête
GLIN	Grey Literature Netherlands	Grijze Literatuur in Nederland
GSS	General Social Survey	
ICBS	International Crimes against Business Survey	
ICPSR	Inter-university Consortium for Political and Social Research	
ICVS	International Crime Victimisation/ Victims Survey	
IPSA	International Political Science Abstracts	
IRSS	Institute for Research in Social Science	
IVAWS	International Violence against Women Survey	
JSTOR	Journal Storage	
MBI	Monitor of Companies and Institutions	Monitor Bedrijven en Instellingen
MTMM	Multi Trait Multi Method	
NACJD	National Archive of Criminal Justice Data	
NCC	Dutch Central Catalogue	Nederlandse Centrale Catalogus
NCS	National Crime Survey (1973-1992; USA)	
NCJRS	National Criminal Justice Reference Service (USA)	

---

[321] The Dutch equivalent is only specified when the abbreviation originally comes from a Dutch description.

Table A.1 - continued

Abbre-viation	English	Dutch
NCVS	National Crime Victimization Survey	
NDM	National Drug Monitor	Nationale Drug Monitor
NIJ	National Institute of Justice (USA)	
NIPO	Dutch Institute for Public Opinion and Market Research	Nederlands Instituut voor de Publieke Opinie en het Marktonderzoek
NSCR	Netherlands Institute for the Study Criminalty and Law Enforcement	Nederlands Studiecentrum Criminaliteit en Rechtshandhaving
NSO		Nationaal ScholierenOnderzoek
NIWI	Netherlands Institute for Scientific Information Services	Nederlands Instituut voor Wetenschappelijke Informatiediensten
NVAW	National Violence Against Women Survey	
PMB	Police Monitor of the Population	PolitieMonitor Bevolking
PMBI	Police Monitor of Companies and Institutions	PolitieMonitor Bedrijven en Instellingen
POLS	Permanent Study of Living Conditions/ Permanent Quality of Life Survey	Permanent Onderzoek Leefsituatie
REL	Law and Living Conditions	Recht en Leefsituatie
REM	Law and Environment	Recht en Milieu
REP	Law and Participation	Recht en Participatie
RIEM	Reporting of Policy of Integration of Ethnic Minorities	Rapportage Integratiebeleid Etnische Minderheden
SCI	Science Citation Index	
SSCI	Social Sciences Citation Index	
SCP	Social and Cultural Planning Office of the Netherlands	Sociaal Cultureel Planbureau
SEB	Victim Survey Companies	Slachtofferenquête bedrijven
SOSIG	Social Science Information Gateway	
SPVA	Survey Social position and use of welfare facilities of ethic minorities	Survey Positie en Voorzieningengebruik Allochtonen
SSRN	Social Science Research Network	
SWL	Social Scientific Literature	Sociaal Wetenschappelijke Literatuur-Databank
UN	United Nations	Verenigde Naties
UNCJIN	United Nations Crime and Justice Information Network	
UNICRI	United Nations Interregional Crime and Justice Research Institute	
WODC	Research and Documentation Centre of the Dutch Ministry of Justice	Wetenschappelijk Onderzoek- en DocumentatieCentrum
WoS	Web of Science	

Appendix B. Bibliographic databanks

Table B.1 Bibliographic databanks

Source	Brief description
BNSW	Bibliography of Dutch and Flemish publications in the social sciences; from 1978
Current contents	Databank of articles published in international journals; social and behavioural sciences; by Institute for Scientific Information (ISI)
Francis	Databank holding international publications; social sciences & humanities; by Institut de l'Information Scientifique et Technique du Centre National de la Recherche Scientifique (INIST-CNRS)
GLIN	Bibliographic of Dutch and Flemish grey literature; by National Library of the Netherlands (Koninklijke Bibliotheek)
Ingenta	Databank holding information about articles published in the USA; formerly known as UnCover
IPSA	Databank of articles published in international journals; political sciences; by International Political Science Association
JSTOR	Archive of fulltext journals; arts & sciences, general science, language & literature collections
Medline/ PubMed	Bibliographic databank covering international literature; medicine and life sciences; by National Library of Medicine
NCC	Databank contains bibliographic references of books and periodicals available in The Netherlands
PiCarta/ Online contents	Databank holding tables of contents of academic journals available in the Netherlands
PsycINFO	Databank of articles published in international journals; psychology and related disciplines; by American Psychological Association (APA)
Science Direct	Full-text journals that are published by Elsevier Science
Sociological Abstracts	Databank of international publications; sociology and related disciplines; formerly known as Sociofile; by Cambridge Scientific Abstracts
Swetswise	Databank of references and full-text; published in several international journals; by Swets Blackwell
SSRN	Databank of references and full-text reports and papers; international research institutes; social sciences, law
SWL	Bibliographic of Dutch and Flemish (grey) literature; by NIWI; till 2002
WoS (SCI + SSCI)	Databank of citations and articles published in international journals; social and behavioural sciences; by Institute for Scientific Information (ISI)
Wiley InterScience	Fulltext journals that are published by John Wiley & Sons; law, social sciences, medical and life sciences, statistics
Women's Resources International	International databank; women's studies, gender issues, feminism; by National Information Services Corporation (NISC)

Appendix C. Example of extensive review

Note that this article is a typical example of the problems concerning conceptualisation and operationalisation in research on 'fear of crime'.

Publication

Dull, T.R. & Wint, A.V.N. (1997). Criminal victimization and its effect on 'fear of crime' and justice attitudes. *Journal of Interpersonal Violence*, 12, 5, 748-758.

Why is the study done and for whom?

This publication is from the section "brief notes" from the "journal of interpersonal violence" and is written for an academic public. It does not mention any authorities that directed or supported the research project.

The publication does not explicitly state the objective (so it cannot be evaluated on the criteria of congruence and directiveness) of this study, but seems to be implied in the research questions that are explicitly stated. As derived from the introduction, the main goal of the study is to get an understanding of the effect of criminal victimisation on fear of crime/feelings of personal well-being or personal level of fear and attitudes toward criminal justice system/ sentencing punitiveness attitudes during the formative years of college education. The researchers seem to be focused on the description of the effect of criminal victimisation on attitudes; "the only adequate way to determine if individual's attitudes have changed is to measure that attitude over a period of time". The use of the different terms "fear of crime", "feelings of personal well-being", "personal level of fear", "these attitudes", "attitudes toward criminal justice system" and "sentencing punitiveness attitudes" confuses me (see discussion of concepts).

What type of knowledge and research (sub)questions?

They want to obtain descriptive and possibly some explanatory knowledge. The descriptive knowledge (on attitudes) is necessary to explain differences between students who have and have not been victimised and to explain attitude change because of the criminal victimisation.

The research questions or problems as presented in the introduction are: "what impact, then, does victimization, during these formative years, have on these attitudes? ... What effect does criminal victimization have on one's feelings of personal well-being or personal level of fear?" And also: "The issue for this research is what effect does criminal victimization have on sentencing punitiveness attitudes". Later, the research questions are formulated as: "two basic research questions that examine the relationship between criminal victimization of a college student cohort and its impact on their fear of crime and attitudes related to the justice system".

Which concepts, model, hypotheses?

Nothing is mentioned on conceptualisation and operationalisation. No (formal) theoretical model is presented; it is merely an exploration of "attitude change". No hypotheses are presented.

In what case a specific term is used, is not clear. Is 'fear of crime' an attitude? ("these attitudes"), what is the relationship between "feelings of personal well-being", "fear of crime" and "personal level of fear"? Are "fear of crime" and "criminal justice attitudes" substantively related? Are "criminal justice attitudes" made up of attitudes toward the police, "attitudes toward the courts" and their ability "to adequately sentence criminals"? Also, does "sentencing punitiveness" consist of two aspects, namely "courts are doing a good job in sentencing" and the "issue of the death penalty"?

The concepts are not theoretically embedded, besides maybe implicitly in the theory of attitudes. The terms are not consistently applied, do not seem to be completely measured and it is not at all clear how the different terms (or concepts) are related. When the findings are discussed, it seems that "fear of crime" is indeed considered to be an attitude (as is also expressed in the Tables that present the results). Moreover, "criminal justice attitudes" are denoted as "justice evaluations" as well. Also, "belief, fear, and attitudinal changes" are mentioned, to me it is not clear how these three terms relate to one another. Is fear an attitude or not? When belief is an aspect of an attitude, then why mention it separately? It seems that fear, feelings, belief, attitudes and evaluations are used synonymously.

How, who, what: data collection?

The operationalisation procedure receives little (or rather no) attention. It is not clear why is chosen for the particular operationalisations that were used. Probably, the researchers have taken operationalisations that had been used by others, but this is not discussed. Nothing is mentioned about whatever sort of validity.

The data are collected by means of a twicely mailed self-report questionnaire. The questionnaire was pretested. Nothing is mentioned about adaptations because of this pretesting. The first time, a random sample of thousand students at a large California university was "drawn from the entire population of the incoming freshman class", of which 557 returned usable questionnaires. Were any questionnaires returned that were not usable? These 557 students got the same questionnaire during their fourth (senior) year of college; of which 271 usable questionnaires were returned. The representativeness of these 271 students of the entire population is accounted for in a note. The procedure seems to be a very practical data collection method and can be very well in accordance with the research questions and purpose.

Since the researcher wanted to "explore the belief, fear, and attitudinal changes that took place during a 4-year academic period for both victimized and non-victimized subgroups of our sample" items are used to represent victimisation, measured by questions asking about victimisation during the past year of specified crimes (i.e. burglary, motor vehicle theft, theft, robbery, assault, rape, or vandalism). This is a rather common way of measuring victimisation in surveys. The typical (response) format is not presented. Presumably, questions were used.

Five items that measure "attitudes related to Fear of Crime" or "fear of crime" were used; these can be deduced from the tables and the discussion of the findings. The choices and decisions regarding the use of these particular items are not discussed. Four items specify the sort of crime; i.e. rape, assault, theft and vehicle theft. A fifth item is supposed to measure "general fear (fearful of all crimes)". In the table, this is probably denoted by the label "do not fear". The exact question and response format is not presented. Since more than one item is used, which is a plus, I do not understand why they have not tried to make a scale or why a reliability coefficient is not presented? Now, the question remains how the items relate to one another since they tend to measure the same thing.

Seven items to measure attitudes regarding "the Criminal Justice System" or "justice attitudes" are used. Again, the choices and decisions regarding the use of the particular items are not discussed. Consequently I have deduced them from the tables and discussion of the findings. Three items focus on the police ("changes in police attitudes"). One item probably asked if the respondent believed "that the police were effective in fighting crime", (later: "dealing with crime"), which is relating to "police crime-fighting effectiveness". The other items asked whether the respondent "believed that the police were courteous" and "believed that the police treat all people equally".

The "attitude concerning courts and sentencing" is measured by one item, I am not sure about the formulation since findings are discussed with different formulations; e.g. whether the respondent "believe the courts are not doing a good job", "believed they were sentencing properly" and "stated that the courts were doing a good job in sentencing". Three items that "look at sentencing punitiveness explored the issue of capital punishment", probably by asking respondents whether or not, or to what extent they are against the death penalty (in Table: "opposed") and whether or not, or to what extent they would favour the death penalty for murder and rape. How the items relate to one another (e.g. an exploratory factorial structure, interitem correlations) is not described.

Overall, I find the data collection procedure inventive, and the use of several items measuring one latent construct would have been promising, if it would have been more clearly expressed and more fruitfully applied.

How are data analysed?

The students "stating in both surveys that they had not been the victim of a crime were included in the non-victimized subgroup". Actually, four groups could have been made; firstly the group of students who were not victimised at all, secondly the ones who had been victimised the year prior to the first questionnaire and not the year prior to the second time, thirdly the ones who had not been victimised the year prior to the first questionnaire and were victimised the year prior to the second time and fourthly the students who were both victims during the year prior to the first questionnaire and during the year prior to the second questionnaire. Then, the attitude changes of these four groups could have been examined.

Although the measurement level of independent and dependent variables does get some attention ("either interval, dummy, or high ordinal levels of measurement") and the use of "interval-level statistics" is explicitly stated, no mention is made of possible violations of the assumptions implied by these "interval-level statistics". A paired-samples t-test procedure is used, which compares the means of two variables for one single group by computing the differences between values of the two variables for each case and tests whether the average differs from 0. This procedure assumes that the items, the paired differences are on the interval or ratio-level; that the paired observations are made under the same conditions and that the mean differences are normally distributed (see Norusis 1993). The assumptions could have been examined by analysing the paired differences and the residuals, using for example a normality test, boxplot, histogram or normal probability plot for the paired differences and the residuals.

The paired-sample t-test analyses were separately conducted for both the victimised sample and nonvictimised sample. Some basic descriptive statistics of the sample (e.g. sex, age) are given in a note, which also says that no significant demographic differences between victims and non-victims were found in crosstabulations. No frequency distributions of these samples on the items are given. I do not quite understand why this procedure has been chosen, besides because of reasons of simplicity. Why not use techniques like variance analysis, regression, general linear model analysis or structural equation modelling?

Findings, results, suggestions, explanations and interpretations are discussed all at once, but nicely separated for the "relationship between victimization and fear of crime" and the "relationship between victimization and justice attitudes". The results on "fear of crime" show that students who belonged to the group of victims have "significantly greater fear of becoming future victims of property crime" but "no significant change in their fear of personal crimes". Non-victims "showed a significant increase in their fear of assault". The authors explain, not very convincingly in my opinion, these findings by referring to two other studies. Also, they note a rather interesting hypothesis that non-victims may be –

> aware of acquaintances who have been assaulted. In addition, newspapers, TV, and other sources of crime news, which generally emphasize violent crimes, may be distorting their view of the world and making them more fearful of these types of crimes. Those who have been victims would have a more realistic view of the type of crime distribution and see property crime, and not personal crime, as a far more likely event to take place in their lives.

Results of the t-test are presented in two tables, separately for victims and non-victims. The tables present "freshmen means", "senior means", t-values (of the test of difference between these means) and two-tail probabilities, separately for victims and non-victims. No confidence intervals, variances or effect sizes are given, neither is mentioned how is dealt with missing values. Possibly, since only "usable questionnaires" were analysed, these questionnaires did not have any missing values.

Overall, I find this publication an example typical of many studies in which terms and concepts are messily applied and are not theoretically embedded. Choices and decisions are scarcely explicitly stated and I find the study as a whole, the results and its conclusions not convincing. Table C.1 presents an overview of the review questions & answers.

Table C.1 Review questions & answers article by Dull & Wint (1997).

Question & plausible answers	Explanation	Evaluation
Why?		
With what purpose? "understanding of/ description of relationship" to..?	Objective not explicitly stated but implied	Difficult to evaluate since not explicitly stated. See overall.
For whom? Scientific forum	Academic journal; no mention of authorities or organisations	
What?		
What type of knowledge?	Descriptive & explanatory Descriptive: explore relationship between variables examine relationship	Quite clear and directive
	Explanatory: effect of criminal victimisation influence of formative years of college education	
What subquestions?	Consequences of victimisation on attitudes; development of attitudes during college years; difference between groups: victims versus non-victims	
	Main question is "relationship between criminal victimization of a college student cohort and its impact on their fear of crime and attitudes related to the justice system"	Appears to be pretty clear at first sight.

Table C.1-continued

Which?		
Which concepts?	Victim Victimisation Fear Crime Fear of crime Feelings of personal well-being Personal level of fear Attitude (change) Criminal justice system Sentencing punitiveness attitudes	Confusing use of different terms; inconsistent. Different names for same concepts? Names for different concepts? Names for different aspects of same concepts? Theoretical embeddedness not clear. Nothing on conceptualisation, neither on operationalisation process.
Which theoretical model?	Absent Only an implied model; victimisation influences fear/ attitudes; college years influence/moderates/mediates Attitude differences victims/ non-victims	The study is merely descriptive; not clear what kind of ideas are behind on the one hand influence of victimisation, other hand college education. Is the focus on the difference between the groups (victims vs. non-victims) or within individual (attitude change over time)? And how are these inter-and intra-individual differences related?
How are concepts related?	Absent	Interrelatedness of concepts not clear Contents of concepts more or less implied; reader can derive them from descriptions of operationalisations/ indicators Concepts are not problematised, "common sense"-approach
Which?		
Which hypotheses?	Absent No explicit hypotheses; yet implied: victimisation influences attitudes college years influence attitudes	No explicit hypotheses, so these cannot be evaluated easily. However, they are implied, and these implied hypotheses are testable. Do authors use the term "exploration" to keep their and readers' expectations low or to justify themselves for possible criticism?
How?		
How are concepts operationalised?	Nothing on operationalisation procedure,	Since concepts are not circumscribed, not clear whether they are measured completely and adequately
How is validity established?	Nothing about validity	Not clear, since concepts are not specified

Table C.1-continued

How?		
How are data collected?	Self-administered questionnaire, mailed	Practical and common method
How is the procedure?	Students received questionnaire by mail	
When?	1st year of college: probably late 80s, early 90s? 4th year of college: probably 90s	
Where?	At home (because questionnaire was mailed)	
Who?		
Who are participants?	Cohort of students who return usable questionnaire	Congruent with research questions; good note on representativeness. Usable questionnaire?
How are subjects sampled?	Random sample of students of a Californian/ American university	Congruent with research questions
What?		
What is the nature of the data?	Quantitative survey data	
What instruments are used?	Questionnaire containing: Items on victimisation of burglary, motor vehicle theft, theft, robbery, assault, rape, or vandalism Five items on "attitudes related to Fear of Crime" or "fear of crime"; specifying rape, assault, theft and vehicle theft. Fifth item measures "general fear (fearful of all crimes)" Seven items on "justice attitudes", about police, "courts doing a good job" and death penalty Nothing on response format	Nothing on validity or reliability Items on victimisation rather common Why not the same crimes as asked in questions on victimisation? Pro: more items are used Why aren't the items used in a summative Likert-type scale? Why these items? Pro: Pro: more items are used Why aren't the items used in a summative Likert-type scale?
How is instrument developed?	Nothing on development of instrument	Pretested, but nothing about consequences of pretest
What is said about reliability and validity?	Nothing on reliability, neither on validity	

Table C.1-continued

How?		
How are data analysed?	Two groups: victims and non-victims	Why not four groups? Would have been more congruent with notion of effect. Because of too small sample, not enough respondents in each of four groups?
	Paired-samples t-test	Why this procedure? Because of "exploratory" nature? This test not most adequate one for examining research questions neither for (implied?) purpose chosen
		Why not general linear model analysis or structural equation modelling?
How is dealt with assumptions?	Assumption of measurement level is noted; but nothing on violations	Pro: stated explicitly Con: nothing is done with it
How are results presented?	Description of results; two tables with results of paired-samples t-test for victims and non- ictims	
Overall evaluation		
Could have been interesting and fruitful; but goal, theoretical ideas, concepts are messy and unclear. I'm afraid not much can be learned from it		

Appendix D. Questions used when reviewing

Table D.1 question: what (sub)questions

Question: what	Potential answers	Example
What subquestions?	Prevalence of	
	Harassment	Macmillan et al. (2000)
	Rape	Koss et al. (1987)
	Development of (time)	
	Crime	Maas (2002)
	Victims	Huys (2001)
	Difference between groups	
	Young & old	Fuentes & Cox (2000)
	Men & women	Carr (2001)
	Difference between areas	
	Urban & rural	Smith & Huff (1982)
	Neighbourhoods	Sampson & Groves (1989)
	International differences	
	Worldwide	Nieuwbeerta (2002)
	Developing countries	Zvekic & Del Frate (1995)
	Correlation/ related to	
	Media	Chiricos et al. (2000)
	Children	Veenema & Schroeder-Bruce (2002)
	Consequences of	
	War	Thabet et al. (2003)
	Partner abuse	Hathaway et al. (2000)
	Cause of	
	Fear of victimisation	Warr & Stafford (1983)
	Fear	Bamber (1979)
	Effect on	
	Women	Mesch (2000)
	Punitiveness	Sprott (1999)
	Construction of	
	Crime	Barak (1994)
	Fear	Yeoh & Yeow (1997)

Table D.2 question: which concepts

Question: which	Potential answers	Example
Which concepts?	Safety	Balkin (1979)
	Danger	Merry (1981)
	Victim	Hindelang, Gottfredson & Garofalo (1978)
	Victimisation	Westervelt (1998)
	Fear	Abdel-Khalek (1997)
	Angst	Scott (2000)
	Fear and anger	Ax (1953)
	Anxiety	Schmidt & Joiner (2002)
	Panic	Cox, Endler & Swinson (1991)
	Phobia	Mineka & Ohman (2002)
	Crime	Gaubatz (1995)
	Protection	Vacha & McLaughlin (2000)
	Precaution	Devlin (2000)
	Vigilance	Ingalls (1988)
	Violence	Beke, De Haan & Terlouw (2001)
	Violent crime	Franke (1994)
	Mental health	Kilpatrick et al. (1985)
	Physical health	Hathaway et al. (2000)
	Social support	Kaniasty & Norris (1992)
	Social cohesion	Maas-De Waal & Wittebrood (2002)
	Neighbourhood	Sirgy & Cornwell (2002)
	Risk attitude	Smidt (1992)
	Public opinion	Garofalo (1977)
	Law & Order	Danigelis & Cutler (1991)
	Altruistic fear	Warr & Ellison (2000)
	Fear of	
	crime	Van Koppen & De Vette (1990)
	victimisation	Singer et al. (1988)
	criminal victimisation	May (1999)
	sexual victimisation	Macmillan, Nierobisz & Welsh (2000)
	rape	Gordon & Riger (1978)
	sexual assault	Day (1999)
	personal security	Levine & Wachs (1986b)
	Feelings of	
	unsafety	Soetenhorst-De Savornin Lohman (1982)
	safety	Green, Gilbertson & Grimsley (2002)
	insecurity	Wiegman & Gutteling (1995)
	security	Bartal, Jacobson & Freund (1995)
	anxiety	Travis & Velasco (1994)
Question: which	**Potential answers**	**Example**
	Fear-victimisation paradox	Chadee (2000)
	men/women	Vanderveen (1999)
	elderly	Niederfranke & Greve (1996)
	Experience of	
	danger	Stanko (1990)
	safety	Vanderveen (2002b)
	violence	Kelly (1988)
	risk	Monaghan (2003)

Table D.2-continued

Question: which	Potential answers	Example
	Perception(s) of	
	security	Smoke (1996b)
	danger	Herzog & Chernick (2000)
	safety	Barker & Page (2002)
	violence	Carroll, Hebert & Roy (1999)
	risk	Warner (1981)
	rape	Shotland & Goodstein (1983)
	Risk	
	(ir)rational	Lee (1981)
	proneness	Fetchenhauer & Rohde (2002)
	estimate	Heimer (1988)
	assessment	Fox (1981)
	perceived	Chiricos, McEntire & Gertz (2001)

Table D.3 question: which model

Question: which	Potential answers	Example
Which theoretical model?	Empirically supported	Dowd, Sisson & Kern (1981)
	Formally tested	Shyu (1989)
Form & contents	Theoretical/ abstract	Douglas (1992)
	Crime → fear	Lewis & Maxfield (1980)
	Victimisation → fear	Denkers (1996)
	Imaginable victimisation → fear	Guo, Zhu & Chen (2001)
	Disorder → fear	Donnely (1988)
	Social structure → fear	Doeksen (1997)
	Socialisation → fear	Dillon, Wolf & Katz (1985)
How are concepts related?	Causally	Markowitz et al. (2001)
	Correlated	Gudjonsson (1984)
	Indirectly related	Van Dijk et al. (2000)
	Directly related	Thabet, Abed & Vostanis (2002)
Which hypotheses?	Various; see 'theoretical model'	

Appendix E. Comparing one item with three items together

Different manners of classifying the data all have in common that they illustrate the problem when only one item is applied. A crosstabulation is presented in Table E.1. One item has four substantive response categories, with the original labels "entirely safe", "fairly safe", "a bit insecure" and "very insecure". Three other items, namely feeling unsafe when at home alone, answering doorbell when it rings unexpectedly after 10pm, and avoiding scary places, have been summed here to construct a scale. All four items together were used in the NSCR-study as a scale, based on a factor analysis in which the four ended up together in one factor (Wittebrood & Ter Voert 1996: 523). A higher score on both the scale and the sole item indicates the respondent feels more unsafe.

Table E.1 Crosstabulation item and scale

Scale		"entirely safe"	"fairly safe"	"a bit insecure"	"very insecure"	Total
		Item: "Insecurity alone in neighborhood after dark"				
3	N	553	262	20	8	843
	%	19.2 %	9.1 %	0.7 %	0.3 %	29.2 %
4	N	165	332	68	6	571
	%	5.7 %	11.5 %	2.4 %	0.2 %	19.8 %
5	N	111	258	80	12	461
	%	3.9 %	8.9 %	2.8 %	0.4 %	16.0 %
6	N	44	224	95	19	382
	%	1.5 %	7.8 %	3.3 %	0.7 %	13.2 %
7	N	12	137	106	32	287
	%	0.4 %	4.8 %	3.7 %	1.1%	9.9 %
8	N	9	74	84	17	184
	%	0.3 %	2.6 %	2.9 %	0.6 %	6.4 %
9	N	3	22	56	14	95
	%	0.1 %	0.8 %	1.9 %	0.5 %	3.3 %
10	N	-	11	14	15	40
	%	-	0.4 %	0.5 %	0.5 %	1.4 %
11	N	-	4	1	11	16
	%	-	0.1 %	0.03 %	0.4 %	0.6 %
12	N	-	1	-	6	7
	%	-	0.03 %	-	0.2 %	0.2 %
Total	N	897	1325	524	140	2886
	%	31.1 %	45.9 %	18.2 %	4.9 %	100 %

When both the scale and the item would be dichotomised, differentiating between groups of respondents with "low fear" or who are "feeling safe" and those with "high fear" or who are "feeling unsafe" would lead to four groups such as is presented in Figure 2.14. Since the scale is made up of three items with an equal number of and similar answer categories, the scale that ranges from 3 to 12 can be dichotomised as well. The group of respondent that is denoted as "feeling safe" by both scale and item, together with the group of respondents that is denoted as "feeling unsafe" by both of them, makes up about 80% of all respondents. This means that about 20% of the respondents is not grouped correspondingly (see Table E.2). When a more refined grouping method is applied, for example by using all four categories of the item and dividing the scale in four categories as well, about half of the respondents is not grouped correspondingly when the two different operationalisations are used.

A third method uses quartiles. Firstly, when using the sole item, the second category of the Likert-type scale holds the third quartile. If the scale is used, 75% of the respondents have a score equal to or less than 6. The two groups that are definitely similarly categorised in "low fear" and "high fear" hold about 40% of the respondents. Also, about 8% is definitely *not* correspondingly classified. More than half of the respondents have chosen an answer that holds the 3rd quartile; how to group them is ambiguous. When deciding that half of these respondents will be assigned to the group with "low fear" and the other half to "high fear", grouped, about two third will be classified in a corresponding manner by both the item and scale. However, the remaining one third will be grouped differently. So, the classification of respondents into groups with "low fear" and "high fear" depends on the operationalisation that has been used.

Table E.2. Grouping respondents; N=2886; source of data: NSCR, Wittebrood, Michon & Ter Voert (1997); Wittebrood & Ter Voert (1997).

Grouping method sole item – scale	Groups	% in group	total % corresponding	total % (not) corresponding
dichotomous (2 x 2)	corresponding – safe	72.7 %	80.2 %	
	corresponding – unsafe	7.5 %		
	safe – unsafe	4.3 %		
	unsafe – safe	15.5 %		19.8 %
four groups (4 x 4)	corresponding – very safe	26.8 %	49.8 %	
	corresponding – safe	17.0 %		
	corresponding – very unsafe	0.9 %		
	corresponding – unsafe	5.1 %		
	not corresponding	50.2 %		50.2 %
3rd quartile (2 x 2)	corresponding – safe	28.7 %	41.1 %	
	corresponding – unsafe	12.3 %		
	not corresponding	7.6 %		7.6 %
	ambiguous (3rd quartile)	51.4 %	51.4 %	

Appendix F. Datasets

ID	Title	Source	Responsibility	Date (of collection)	Brief Summary Note	Methodology Notes	N	Universe	Reference
Secondary data: descriptives[322]									
BCS/ StatBase	British Crime Survey	StatBase; reports	Home Office, Research Development Statistics Directorate/ Office for National Statistics	'84 and '88, every two years; '92-'00, '01 and 2001/02	Beliefs about change in national and local crime rate over the previous two years; perceived risk referring to five offenses; incivilities; how much of a problem; impact of fear of crime on quality of life; worry about specific offences and feeling unsafe after dark (at home and walking alone on the streets)	Sweeps in 1982, 1984, 1988, 1992, 1994, 1996, 1998, 2000 and 2001; since 2001/02 annually Scotland & Northern Ireland now have own survey; interviews	Varies; in BCS 2001/02 about 30 thousand	Varying number of respondents, inhabitants of Britain; aged 16 or over	Hough & Mayhew (1983) Kershaw et al. (2000) Maguire & Kynch (2000) Mayhew & Hough (1988) Simmons & Dodd (2002)
CBS	ESM, ERV, POLS (REM & REP)	Statline; reports	Netherlands Official Statistics	ESM 1980 - 1992 ERV 1992-1996 POLS since 1997	Item on adapting behaviour: going out less often, avoiding places, not going away alone at night, not going out at night; 'afraid when at home alone'; preventive measures	Interviews (both CAPI and CATI); sample based on geographical categories and its inhabitants	Varies; relevant questions asked to about 5,000 persons	Non-institutiona-lised, registered inhabitants of Netherlands; aged 12 (or 15) or over	Beukenhorst et al. (1993) CBS (1998)
Gallup	Various; administered by the Gallup Organization	Bureau of Justice Statistics U.S.A; Source-book	Gallup Organization/ BJS, the Gallup Poll		Various surveys on public opinion; fear of walking alone, feeling unsafe at home at night, level of crime in area, level of crime in U.S., preventive measures because of concern over crime	Usually a telephone interview, randomly selected national sample, 18 years of age and older	Varies	Varying number of respondents, inhabitants of the U.S	Sourcebook of Criminal Justice Statistics 2000 Online
SCP	Culturele Verkenningen see: CBS				More or less crime in Netherlands, crime a real problem				CV 1991-2000; SCP (2000); Wittebrood (2001)

---

[322] No raw data from respondents, but descriptive statistics like counts, frequencies, percentages.

Secondary data: raw dataset

Harris

Harris1964	Harris 1964 Johnson's presidency survey, no. 1301	IRSS, Odum Institute; Louis Harris Data Center	Louis Harris & Associates	March, 1964	Survey, also on personal concerns, problems facing people, among which "juvenile delinquency and crime"	Random multi-stage cluster sampling, national cross-section sample of likely voters. Questionnaire, face-to-face interview.	1419	likely voters in USA
Harris1969	Harris 1969 Urban Crime Survey, no. 1935	IRSS, Odum Institute; Louis Harris Data Center, University of North Carolina	Louis Harris & Associates, for LIFE Magazine	May, 1969	Survey of residents in Baltimore, Maryland, USA. One of the 1st surveys to systematically investigate attitudes toward neighbourhood, reasons for increase in crime, perceptions of law and order, local police, neighbourhood safety, and 'fear of crime'. Some questions focus on methods of protection against crime and other crime prevention measures. Also item on 'ringing doorbell'	A questionnaire was used in a face-to-face interview with a cross-section sample of Baltimore residents 21 years of age and over.	1545	

Harris1975	Harris 1975 Housing and Health Care survey, no. 7588	IRSS, Odum Institute; Louis Harris Data Center, University of North Carolina	Louis Harris & Associates	1975	Survey on attitudes toward neighbourhood; asks about cost, size, location, neighbours, and safety. E.g. "want a place where there is not as much crime" as possible reason for wanting to move. Other items refer to: "safety from robberies and break-ins"; "safety of the house from break-ins"; "safety of the neighbourhood from crime"; "can feel safe from crime"	A questionnaire was used in a face-to-face interview with a cross-section sample of USA residents 18 years of age and over. A random multi-stage cluster sampling design was used.	1400	Population of the USA, 18 years and older	
Various									
GSS	General Social Survey	National Opinion Research Center (NORC); The Roper Center for Public Opinion Research (ICPSR)	NORC	1973-2000	Typical survey; items like "Spending too much, too little, or about the right amount on halting the rising crime rate/ solving the problems of the big cities/ dealing with drug addiction"; is there any area around here— that is, within a mile— where you would be afraid to walk alone at night; "how about at home at night— do you feel safe and secure, or not?"; items on victimisation and importance of crime issue.	Interviews (personal)	About 1500 till 1993 (annually), from 1994 on about 3000 (biannual)	English-speaking residents (18 years of age or over), living in non-institutional arrangements within the United States.	Altheide (1997); GSSDIRS, website on the General Social Survey Data and Information Retrieval System; DeFronzo (1979); Haynie (1998); Hill, Howell & Driver (1985); NORC (n.d.); Will & McGrath (1997)

	Name	Source	Fieldwork	Dates	Content	Sampling	N	Population	References
NCVS	National Crime Victimization Survey	BJS	U.S. Census Bureau for the U.S. Department of Justice, Bureau of Justice Statistics	Each year, ongoing from 1973	Victimisation of rape, sexual assault, robbery, assault, theft, household burglary, and motor vehicle theft; several items on fear of crime, preventive behaviours. Supplements are SCS and Police Public Contact Survey	Nationally representative sample; continuous survey of a representative sample of households in the United States, CATI	about 45,000 households and about 80,000 persons	U.S. residents age 12 or older	Skogan (1990b)
NNSP (IRSS 7901)	California Poll February 1979	IRSS Odum Institute	Field Institute, San Francisco, CA	February 10 - 19, 1979	Items on 'danger from crime' greater or less, more or less crime in neighbourhood, not going 'because thought it would be unsafe to go there'	Probability sample, face-to-face interviews Representative cross-section of the California adult population	983	Californian adults	
NSCR	Netherlands Survey on Criminality and Law Enforcement 1996	Personal contact with NSCR (Leiden, NL)	NSCR, fieldwork by Inter/View	Several periods in 1996	Nation-wide survey of Dutch citizens, questions about victimisation experiences, offending and norm deviant behaviour and perceptions of criminality and law enforcement. Questions on perceptions of neighbourhood, (incivilities), risk perception, 'fear of crime'	Using a step-by-step procedure for the selection of addresses based on the mail delivery register, a random sample was approached of 1) the Dutch population above the age of 15 and of 2) the Dutch population from 15 to 30. Face-to-face interviews based on CAPI as well as self-administered questionnaires were used.	1) N=1939 2) N=1012 Data used in this book: N=2951	Dutch residents, 15 years of age and over	Wittebrood & TerVoert (1997); Wittebrood, Michon & TerVoert (1997)
Rietveld1 + Rietveld2	Questionnaire Rietveld	Personal contact (Rietveld)	Rietveld, survey based on inventory Vanderveen	2000, 2002	Questionnaire administered contained inventory, state and trait anxiety - scales	Opportunity sample of students	317	Students of the University of Amsterdam, Netherlands	Rietveld (2000)

Code	Full name	Org	Source	Fielded	Content	Sample	N	Respondents	Reference
SCS	School Crime Supplement	BJS	U.S. Census Bureau for the U.S. Department of Justice, Bureau of Justice Statistics	Fielded with the 1995 and 1999 NCVS	Fear of harm and attack at school, avoidance of places at/going to or from school	Nationally representative sample of students	1995: 9.728 1999: 8.398	Students from 12 to 18 in the U.S., grades 6 through 12	Phillip Kaufman et al, Indicators of School Crime and Safety, 2001, NCES 2002-113/NCJ 190075 (Washington, DC: U.S. Departments of Education and Justice, 2001), pp. 77, 78. Table adapted by Sourcebook staff.
NIWI									
NIWI 1069	Meningen van de Nederlandse bevolking over criminaliteit 1985	NIWI, Steinmetz archive	WODC/ Ministry of Justice, fieldwork by NIPO	February 1985	Interviews with representative sample of Dutch population with main theme societal reactions against crime. Attitudes on crime, sanctions Actual and perceived risk of victimisation.	Random sample based on data from CBS on households. Respondent from a household is selected in such a way that the final sample is representative.	1697	Dutch residents, 18 years and older	Berghuis & Essers (1986) NIPO (1985)
NIWI 1071	Meningen van de Nederlandse bevolking over criminaliteit	NIWI, Steinmetz archive	WODC/ Ministry of Justice, fieldwork by NIPO	March 1990	Related to NIWI P1069 Interviews with representative sample of Dutch population, whether crime is a social problem, security measures, sanctions, victimisation.	NIPO-method; probably similar to P1069, thus sample based on household characteristics.	1025	Dutch residents, 18 years and older	Junger-Tas & Terlouw (1991a, 1991b)
NIWI 1127	Slachtofferschap en politiefunctioneren	NIWI, Steinmetz archive	Statistics & Research-department of city of Breda, Netherlands	Spring 1990, March & April 1992	Telephone interviews, questions about police, victimisation, thinking about becoming a victim of a specific crime, fear to become a victim at home alone, 'ringing doorbell', avoid places	Representative sample of population of Breda (corrected)	1990: 3000 1992: 2310	Residents of Breda, 15 years and older	Aarts & Berdowski (1992)

ID	Title	Repository	Author / Funding	Years	Description	Sample	Population	References
ICPSR 2371	Impact of Neighborhood Structure, Crime, and Physical Deterioration on Residents and Business Personnel in Minneapolis-St.Paul, 1970-1982	ICPSR	McPherson et al.; Minnesota Crime Prevention Center	1970-1982	Secondary analysis of ICPSR 8167; relevant items on neighbourhood, commitment to neighbourhood, fear of crime, perceived incivilities	870	Adult residents in the adjoining neighbourhood of commercial centers	Taylor (1995a, 1997a)
ICPSR 2352	Crime Changes in Baltimore, 1970-1994	ICPSR	Taylor et al. Funding from United States Department of Justice. National Institute of Justice.	1981-1982 and 1994	Study of relationships among crime rates, residents' attitudes, physical deterioration, and neighbourhood structure in selected urban Baltimore neighbourhoods. Observation of physical characteristics, use of space as well as interview/ survey (by telephone/ CATI) 66 neighbourhoods, blocks, households, individuals were sampled through multistage random sampling	1622 (1982) 704 (1994)	Residents of urban neighbour-hoods in Baltimore	Covington & Taylor (1991); Perkins & Taylor (1996); Taylor (1997a, 1997b, 1999); Taylor & Covington (1993); Quillian & Pager (2001); Robinson et al. (2003)
ICPSR 2566	Violence and Threats of Violence Against Women and Men in the United States, 1994-1996	NACJD; ICPSR	Tjaden & Thoennes, Center for Policy Research	1995-1996	NVAW, samples of both men and women. Relevant items in Section A, fear of violence, precautionary behaviour, whether personal safety for women had improved since the respondent was a child, or whether violent crime, domestic violence, sexual harassment, and sexual assault were more of a problem today, concern about personal safety and about being stalked, carry something to defend or to alert others. National stratified random sample, random-digit dialing; computer-assisted interviews	16000	All adults in American households with telephone, 18 years or older	Tjaden & Thoennes (1998a, 1998b, 1998c, 2000a, 2000b)

ID	Title	Source	Holder	Date	Description	Sampling	Sample size	Population	Reference
ICPSR 2800	Evaluation of Community Policing initiatives in Jefferson County, West Virginia, 1996-1997	Free Our Citizens of Unhealthy Substances Coalition (FOCUS)	ICPSR	January / February 1996 and 1997	Telephone interviews. Evaluation of community policing initiatives; six items on concern about specific crimes, for example rob or attack them, break into or vandalise their home, or try to sexually attack them/someone they cared about. Also items on crime in neighbourhood versus elsewhere, how personal safety had changed in neighbourhood and US, and respondent's activities.	Random sample of county residents, drawn from local telephone books, 30% response rate.	2x300=600	Residents of Jefferson County with telephone	McCoy (1997)
ICPSR 3098 (BSA)	British Social Attitudes Survey	National Centre for Social Research (formerly Social and Community Planning Research)	ICPSR; UK Data Archive	BSA since 1983	BSA is similar to the GSS from the National Opinion Research Center (NORC) in the United States; also about "fear of crime". Items "do you ever worry about the possibility that you or anyone who lives with you might be the victim of a crime", "is this a big worry, a bit of a worry or an occasional doubt", items that ask to compare how much crime there is in relation to rest of Britain, and compared with two years ago.	Part of continuing survey on social attitudes in Great Britain; interviews and self-completion questionnaire; randomly-selected adults,	3,633 in 1995	Adults (18 and over) living in private households in Great Britain	National Centre for Social Research (2003)
ICPSR 3212	Longitudinal Study of Violence Against Women: Victimization & Perpetration Among College Students in a State-Supported University in the USA, 1990-5	White, Smith, Humphrey; funding by US Departments	ICPSR	1990-1995	Concerned with various kinds of victimisation and perpetration; crime victim survey with main focus on sexual assault; sexual and physical violence and characteristics of the relationship between victim and perpetrator, course of the incident. Also indirect victimisation (whether respondent knew somebody).	Interviews (telephone and personal); mail-back questionnaires.	1580 females, 851 males	Undergraduate students in one university in the USA; considered representative of state colleges	Humphrey & White (2000); White & Smith (2001a, 2001b)

ICPSR 7682	Residential Neighborhood Crime Control Project: Hartford, Connecticut, 1973-1979	ICPSR	Fowler, funding by US Department of Justice, National Institute of Justice	Five surveys (in 1973, 1975, 1976, 1977 and 1979)	Surveys contain items on victimisation, fear of being victim of specific crime (house broken into, purse snatched, robbed/injured on street), perceived risk of becoming victim of target crime, feeling safe alone in neighbourhood day & night, crime up or down last year, perceptions of neighbours, about strangers in neighbourhood (acting suspicious).	Interviews (telephone and personal); stratified random area probability sampling, clustered area probability sampling, and systematic random sampling.	Varies	Residents (18 or older) of Hartford, Connecticut, living in the same housing unit for at least six months.	Fowler (1979, 1982)
ICPSR 7951	Characteristics of High and Low Crime Neighbor-hoods in Atlanta	ICPSR	Greenberg; funding by United States Department of Justice, National Institute of Justice.	1980	Several items on attitudes to neighbourhood, disorder/ incivilities, fear of crime (feeling unsafe and same five items as ICPSR 8167), avoidance (sidewalk, street corner, shopping area etc.) and protective measures. E.g. question: 'how worried are you about being held up on the street/ home broken into'. Also: indirect and direct victimisation; seeing suspicious people, strangers; crime increased or decreased.	Three pairs of adjacent neighbourhoods in Atlanta with distinctly different crime levels; stratified random sample of households within 6 neighbour-hoods; personal interviews	523	Adults from households in six neighbourhoods	Taylor & Hale (1986)

| ICPSR 7991 | CBS News/New York Times National Surveys | ICPSR | CBS News/New York Times | 1981 (relevant interview: June) | Part of continuing series of monthly surveys that solicit public opinion on the presidency and on various other political and social issues. Telephone interviews with respondents; relevant contents of interview: "Perceptions of crime and the criminal justice system" and "respondents' fears of being a victim of crime, perceptions of the seriousness of crime in the United States" | Stratified, random-digit dialing, initial screening interviews, respondent selection within households was designed to control for sex and the relative age composition of the household. When using specified weights, sample approximates U.S. Census figures for age, sex, race and education of U.S. adult population | - | U.S. adult population (with telephone) | Langworthy & Whitehead (1986) |

	Title		Author/Institution	Year	Description	Sampling	N	Population	References
ICPSR 8086	Citizen Participation and Community Crime Prevention	ICPSR	Lavrakas & Skogan; Center for Urban Affairs and Policy Research, Northwestern University	1979	How much of a problem is crime and safety in the neighbourhood, crime decreased/increased, avoid being outside alone at night/ walking near certain types of strangers/ carrying a lot of cash/ places specifically because of crime. Also: how often use a timer on indoor lights or a radio/ have a neighbour watch home and several other items on protective measures; feeling safe out alone in neighbourhood at night; items on likelihood and seriousness, robbery, fire in kitchen, attacked by stranger, develop heart trouble	Modified random-digit dialing	1803	Adults 18 years and older in the Chicago metropolitan area, in households with telephone	Riger & Lavrakas (1981) Skogan & Maxfield (1981)
ICPSR 8100	ABC News Poll of public opinion on crime	ICPSR	ABC News; carried out by Chilton Research Services	Dec-82	Part of a continuing series of monthly surveys that solicit public opinion on the presidency and on various other political and social issues. Relevant contents of interview: "Perceptions of crime and the criminal justice system" and "respondents' fears of being a victim of crime, perceptions of the seriousness of crime in the United States"	When using specified weights, sample approximates U.S. Census figures for age, sex, race and education of U.S. adult population	2,464	U.S. adult population	Langworthy & Whitehead (1986)

ID	Title	Archive	Author / Funding	Year	Items	Methodology	N	Sample	References
ICPSR 8167	Crime, Fear, and Control in Neighborhood Commercial Centers: Minneapolis and St. Paul, 1970-1982 (part 4: Resident Survey)	ICPSR	McPherson et al.; Minnesota Crime Prevention Center	1970 -1982	Relevant items on commitment to neighbourhood, various items on fear of crime, perceived incivilities	Random selection of adult residents in the surrounding neighbourhood, one survey per household, telephone survey. (also assessment of physical characteristics of of commercial centers)	870	Adult residents in the adjoining neighbourhood of commercial centers; all commercial and residential areas in Minneapolis and St. Paul, Minnesota	McPherson (1978)
ICPSR 9741	Testing Theories of Criminality and Victimization in Seattle, 1960-1990	ICPSR	Miethe, funding by National Science Foundation	1990	Items on crime and victimisation, i.e. burglaries, stolen property, physical assaults by strangers, vandalism, car thefts. Also questions on neighborhood, home, and security measures such as locks but also avoiding eye-to-eye contact with strangers, walking at a faster pace than usual. Also worry about physical attack, breaking into one's home and stealing property, incivilities.	Multistage clustered sampling of 600 selected city blocks and immediate neighbors on these blocks.	5.302	Households in Seattle with telephones in 1990, sampled from selected blocks	Bellair (2000); Miethe (1991), Wilcox, Quisenberry & Jones (2003); Rountree (1998); Rountree & Warner (1999)

Primary data

Subway	Author's project	Vanderveen, Erasmus University Rotterdam/OMV	1997	Face-to-face structured interview		250	Opportunity and stratified sample of travellers in subway of Rotterdam
Inventory+ semdif	Author's project	Vanderveen, Erasmus University Rotterdam/OMV	1999	Paper-and-pencil questionnaire administered	Opportunity and snowball sample of students (N=149) and their parents or other older family members (N=105)	254	Respondents
Vignette	Author's project	Vanderveen, Erasmus University Rotterdam/OMV	Nov-97	Paper-and-pencil questionnaire administered	Opportunity and stratified sample of students of courses in international law, History of Art and Sociology of Erasmus University Rotterdam (N=232), divided in two groups, using questions in one group (N=116) and statements in the other (N=116)	232	Students of main courses at Erasmus University
P&L	questionnaire P&L; Project of Staff of Section Psychology & Law	Section Psychology & Law, Erasmus University Rotterdam	November 1997/ beginning 1998.	Paper-and-pencil questionnaire administered	Opportunity sample of law students of the course 'Psychology and Law'; snowball sample: their parents or other older person	195	Law students of the course from Erasmus University; their parents or other older person

Appendix G. Improved instruments (traditional)

In this appendix, concrete examples of the instruments (the sets of items) are presented. The first four sets contain mostly similar target crimes. When a researcher wants to measure the different constructs, these target crimes are preferably similar. Furthermore, the researcher can choose between statements and questions; the example is in a question-format. In the Vignette-study (see section 9.4) the items that employed a statement-format yielded higher responses than items in the the question-format. With respect to the target crimes, it should be noted that the Dutch 'inbraak' can be translated both as 'burglary' and a 'break-in'. The Dutch 'diefstal op straat', which was taken from a survey, might be rephrased as 'beroving'. In the example below, only the extreme answer categories are presented; the researcher can choose whether to present all categories, i.e. not afraid at all, not afraid, not really afraid, neutral, a little afraid, afraid and very much afraid when using a question-format.

Fear of others' victimisation

An example of the instrument; i.e. the set of items, that measures the fear that a significant other becomes a victim is presented below. Another decision to make is on the significant other that is referred to; I used "partner" (spouse) in the older subsample and "friend" (in Dutch 'vriend of vriendin') in the student subsample. Another possibility is referring to "somebody you love".

English example
How afraid are you that your friend will become a victim of ....

	Not afraid at all						Very much afraid
.....threat?	O	O	O	O	O	O	O
.....physical abuse?	O	O	O	O	O	O	O
.....robbery?	O	O	O	O	O	O	O
.....vandalism?	O	O	O	O	O	O	O
....a fight?	O	O	O	O	O	O	O
....sexual harassment?	O	O	O	O	O	O	O
....a burglary?	O	O	O	O	O	O	O

Dutch example
In hoeverre ben je bang dat je (beste) vriend of vriendin slachtoffer wordt van....

	Helemaal niet bang						Zeer bang
.....bedreiging?	O	O	O	O	O	O	O
.....mishandeling?	O	O	O	O	O	O	O
.....diefstal op straat?	O	O	O	O	O	O	O
.....vandalisme?	O	O	O	O	O	O	O
....een vechtpartij?	O	O	O	O	O	O	O
....ongewenste intimiteiten?	O	O	O	O	O	O	O
....een inbraak?	O	O	O	O	O	O	O

Fear of victimisation

An example of the instrument; i.e. the set of items that measures the fear that a significant other becomes a victim is presented below. Please note that the target crime vandalism has not been included in this series of items (see section 9.5).

English example
How afraid are you that you will become a victim of ....

	Not afraid at all						Very much afraid
.....threat?	O	O	O	O	O	O	O
.....physical abuse?	O	O	O	O	O	O	O
.....robbery?	O	O	O	O	O	O	O
....a fight?	O	O	O	O	O	O	O
....sexual harassment?	O	O	O	O	O	O	O
....a burglary?	O	O	O	O	O	O	O

Dutch example
In hoeverre ben je bang dat je zelf slachtoffer wordt van ....

	Helemaal niet bang						Zeer bang
.....bedreiging?	O	O	O	O	O	O	O
.....mishandeling?	O	O	O	O	O	O	O
.....diefstal op straat?	O	O	O	O	O	O	O
....een vechtpartij?	O	O	O	O	O	O	O
....ongewenste intimiteiten?	O	O	O	O	O	O	O
....een inbraak?	O	O	O	O	O	O	O

Seriousness of consequences of victimisation

The inventory and the surveys that have actually been derived from this inventory did not refer to the same set of target crimes. The set of items that is presented here is based on the empirical analyses of the data from the inventory and these particular surveys, which means that the target crimes do not mirror the target crimes in the other three sets. The researcher should choose which target crimes s/he wants to include.

11.5.1.1 English example

How serious do you think the consequences will be when you happen to become
a victim of ....

	Very large						Very small
.....threat?	O	O	O	O	O	O	O
.....physical abuse?	O	O	O	O	O	O	O
.....violence?	O	O	O	O	O	O	O
....sexual assault?	O	O	O	O	O	O	O
....sexual harassment?	O	O	O	O	O	O	O
....a burglary?	O	O	O	O	O	O	O

Dutch example

Hoe groot denk je dat voor jou de nadelige gevolgen zijn, als jij zelf slachtoffer wordt van...

	Heel groot						Heel klein
.....bedreiging?	O	O	O	O	O	O	O
.....mishandeling?	O	O	O	O	O	O	O
.....een geweldsmisdrijf?	O	O	O	O	O	O	O
....een seksueel misdrijf?	O	O	O	O	O	O	O
....ongewenste ntimiteiten?	O	O	O	O	O	O	O
....een inbraak?	O	O	O	O	O	O	O

Perception of risk on victimisation

The same issues regarding the choice of target crimes apply. Besides
that, it might be worthwhile to experiment with the suggested time frame,
though 'the next year' is rather common.

English example

How likely do you think it is that in the next year you will become a victim of ....

	Very unlikely						Very likely
.....threat?	O	O	O	O	O	O	O
.....physical abuse?	O	O	O	O	O	O	O
.....robbery?	O	O	O	O	O	O	O
....vandalism?	O	O	O	O	O	O	O
....a burglary?	O	O	O	O	O	O	O

Dutch example

Hoe groot denk je dat de kans is om in de loop van dit jaar zelf slachtoffer te worden van...

	Heel groot						Heel klein
.....bedreiging?	O	O	O	O	O	O	O
.....mishandeling?	O	O	O	O	O	O	O
.....diefstal op straat?	O	O	O	O	O	O	O
....vandalisme?	O	O	O	O	O	O	O
....een inbraak?	O	O	O	O	O	O	O

Feeling safe at night

As noted previously, the researcher can choose between statements and questions. The English and Dutch example below are in a statement-format.

English example

	Entirely agree						Entirely disagree
I feel safe when I'm walking alone in the street at night	O	O	O	O	O	O	O
I am at ease when I'm alone at home at night	O	O	O	O	O	O	O
I'm at ease when I'm walking alone in the street at night	O	O	O	O	O	O	O
I feel safe when I'm alone at home at night	O	O	O	O	O	O	O
I am at ease when I'm walking together with somebody in the street at night	O	O	O	O	O	O	O

Dutch example

	Helemaal mee eens						Helemaal mee oneens
Ik voel me veilig als ik 's avonds alleen over straat loop	O	O	O	O	O	O	O
Ik voel me op mijn gemak als ik 's avonds alleen thuis ben	O	O	O	O	O	O	O
Ik voel me op mijn gemak als ik 's avonds alleen over straat loop	O	O	O	O	O	O	O
Ik voel me veilig als ik 's avonds alleen thuis ben	O	O	O	O	O	O	O
Ik voel me op mijn gemak als ik 's avonds met iemand over straat loop	O	O	O	O	O	O	O

Appendix H. English and Dutch equivalents

Table H.1 Concepts in Dutch and English

English equivalent	Concept in Dutch
Fear (anxiety)	Angst
Unsafety	Onveiligheid
Risk	Risico
Insecurity	Onzekerheid
Precautions	Voorzorgsmaatregelen
Accident	Ongeluk
Fault (guilt)	Schuld
Social concern	Maatschappelijke onrust
Vulnerability	Kwetsbaarheid
Crime	Criminaliteit
Natural disaster	Natuurramp
Safety	Veiligheid
Rape	Verkrachting
Concern about others	Bezorgdheid voor anderen
Defensibility	Weerbaarheid
Protection (security)	Beveiliging
Danger	Gevaar
Violence	Geweld
Inattention (carelessness)	Onoplettendheid
Concern (worry)	Bezorgdheid

Table H.2 Adjectives in Dutch and English

English equivalent	Adjective in Dutch
Conative	**Conatief**
Fast – slow	Snel – langzaam
Quiet – busy	Rustig – druk
Flee – seek	Vluchten – opzoeken
Avoid – provoke	Vermijden – uitlokken
Steer – let go	Sturen – laten gaan
Active – passive	Actief – passief
Cognitive	**Cognitief**
Desirable – undesirable	Gewenst – ongewenst
Risky – riskless	Risicovol – risicoloos
Dangerous – harmless	Gevaarlijk – ongevaarlijk
Good – bad	Goed – slecht
Predictable – unpredictable	Voorspelbaar – onvoorspelbaar
Benign – malign	Goedaardig – kwaadaardig
Affective	**Affectief**
Sad – happy	Verdrietig – blij
Friendly – unfriendly	Aardig – onaardig
Afraid – at ease	Bang – op gemak
Pleasant – unpleasant	Plezierig – onplezierig
Nice – nasty	Prettig – naar

Appendix I. Constructing instrument (semantic differential format)

The final instrument does not include all concepts. The number of concepts needs to be reduced, which was done by focusing on a number of issues. Initially, whether or not a significant difference exists between the means of the subgroups of males and females was taken into consideration. For that purpose, a t-test for the equality of the means has been conducted, which led to a smaller list of applicable concepts. In addition, the scores on the Likert-type scales (Likert-scales) and the scores on the evaluative semantic differential scales on seventeen concepts can be compared in a couple of ways, which are generally considered checks of validity. First, the correlations with the familiar Likert-types scales were examined, and the number of correlations of these scales per concept was taken into account. The correlations (see Table I.1) between the Likert-type scales and the sumscores of the six evaluation-items were calculated for the whole sample, and for the male and female subsample.

Two other ways of comparison make use of only two third of the sample, since the whole group of respondents is divided in three according to the scores on either the Likert-scales or the semantic differential scales. Only the lowest third and highest third scores on the Likert-scales are used to test the difference of the means on the semantic differential scales. Thus, the scores on each Likert-type scales were split in three groups of the same number of respondents and recoded, thus constructing three groups with the lowest, middle and the highest scores on each scale. The difference between the means of the lowest third and the highest third were tested, using simple t-tests (see Table I.2).In addition, the lowest third and highest third scores on the semantic differential scales are used to test the difference of the means on the Likert-scales (Table I.3). These two ways of comparing the two sets of scales provide a basic argument for the decision which concepts to choose for the final instrument with semantic differential format.

Table I.1. Correlations (pmcc) between familiar Likert-type scales and evaluation-items semantic differential; total sample, fe/male subsample

Variable		okd	okn	ser	eas	af	afo	cn	fs	bc	rel	rp
accide	Total	ns	ns	-.24**	ns	ns	ns	-.19*	ns	ns	ns	ns
	♂	ns	ns	ns	ns	ns	ns	ns	ns	ns	ns	ns
	♀	ns	ns	ns	ns	ns	ns	ns	ns	ns	ns	ns
concer	Total	ns	ns	ns	ns	ns	ns	ns	ns	ns	ns	ns
	♂	ns	ns	ns	ns	ns	ns	ns	ns	ns	ns	ns
	♀	ns	ns	ns	ns	ns	ns	ns	ns	ns	ns	ns
concot	Total	ns	ns	ns	ns	ns	ns	ns	ns	ns	ns	ns
	♂	ns	ns	ns	ns	ns	ns	ns	ns	ns	ns	ns
	♀	ns	ns	ns	ns	ns	ns	ns	ns	ns	ns	ns
crime	Total	ns	ns	-.22*	ns	ns	ns	-.21*	ns	ns	ns	ns
	♂	ns	ns	ns	ns	ns	ns	ns	ns	ns	-.39*	ns
	♀	ns	ns	-.37**	ns	ns	ns	ns	ns	ns	ns	ns
danger	Total	ns	.32**	-.30**	.26**	-.31**	-.32**	ns	.23**	ns	ns	-.24**
	♂	ns	.38*	-.40**	.39*	-.55**	ns	ns	ns	ns	ns	-.51**
	♀	ns	.21*	ns	ns	ns	-.35**	ns	ns	ns	ns	ns
defens	Total	ns	ns	ns	ns	ns	ns	ns	ns	ns	ns	ns
	♂	ns	ns	ns	ns	ns	ns	ns	.43*	ns	ns	ns
	♀	ns	ns	ns	ns	ns	ns	ns	ns	ns	ns	ns
fault	Total	ns	ns	-.21*	ns	ns	ns	-.27**	ns	ns	ns	-.19*
	♂	ns	ns	ns	ns	ns	ns	ns	ns	ns	-.46**	ns
	♀	ns	ns	-.30**	ns	ns	-.26*	-.28*	ns	ns	ns	ns
fear	Total	ns	.20**	-.27**	.17**	ns	-.15*	ns	ns	ns	ns	-.13*
	♂	ns	ns	-.29*	ns	ns	ns	ns	ns	ns	ns	-.30*
	♀	ns	.17*	-.17**	ns	ns	-.17*	ns	ns	ns	ns	ns
inatte	Total	ns	.32**	-.25**	.28**	-.24**	-.29**	-.22*	.20*	ns	ns	-.17*
	♂	ns	ns	ns	ns	ns	ns	ns	ns	ns	ns	ns
	♀	ns	.38**	-.35**	.34**	-.28**	-.36**	ns	.29**	ns	ns	ns
insecu	Total	ns	ns	ns	ns	ns	ns	ns	ns	ns	-.20*	ns
	♂	ns	ns	ns	ns	ns	ns	ns	ns	ns	-.43**	ns
	♀	ns	ns	ns	ns	ns	ns	ns	ns	ns	ns	ns
disast	Total	ns	ns	-.21*	ns	ns	ns	ns	ns	ns	ns	ns
	♂	ns	ns	ns	ns	ns	ns	ns	ns	ns	-.32*	ns
	♀	ns	ns	-.27*	ns	ns	ns	ns	ns	ns	ns	ns
precau	Total	ns	ns	ns	ns	ns	ns	ns	ns	ns	ns	ns
	♂	ns	ns	ns	ns	ns	ns	ns	ns	ns	ns	ns
	♀	ns	ns	ns	ns	ns	ns	ns	ns	ns	ns	ns
protec	Total	ns	-.29**	ns	-.19*	ns	ns	ns	-.25**	ns	ns	ns
	♂	ns	-.35*	ns	ns	ns	ns	ns	ns	ns	ns	ns
	♀	ns	ns	ns	ns	ns	ns	ns	ns	ns	ns	ns
rape	Total	ns	.23**	-.38**	.22*	ns	ns	ns	.17*	ns	ns	ns
	♂	ns	ns	-.50**	ns	ns	ns	ns	ns	ns	ns	ns
	♀	ns	ns	-.20*	ns	ns	ns	ns	ns	ns	ns	ns
risk	Total	ns	ns	ns	ns	ns	-.26**	-.20**	ns	ns	ns	ns
	♂	ns	ns	ns	ns	ns	ns	ns	ns	ns	ns	ns
	♀	ns	ns	ns	ns	ns	-.27*	ns	ns	ns	ns	ns

Table I.1 – continued.

Variable		okd	okn	ser	eas	af	afo	cn	fs	bc	rel	rp
safety	Total	ns	-.22**	.20*	ns	.18*	.22*	ns	ns	ns	ns	ns
	♂	ns	ns	ns	ns	ns	ns	ns	ns	ns	ns	ns
	♀	.17*	-.23*	ns	ns	ns	.28**	ns	ns	ns	ns	ns
soconc	Total	ns	ns	-.22*	ns	ns	ns	-.20*	ns	ns	ns	ns
	♂	ns	ns	ns	ns	ns	ns	ns	ns	ns	ns	-.37*
	♀	ns	ns	ns	ns	ns	ns	ns	ns	ns	ns	ns
unsaf	Total	ns	.27**	-.30**	.27**	-.23**	-.27**	-.18**	.17**	ns	ns	-.17**
	♂	ns	ns	-.35**	ns	ns	ns	ns	ns	ns	ns	ns
	♀	ns	.29**	-.20**	.25**	-.23**	-.34**	-.23**	.27**	ns	ns	ns
violen	Total	ns	.28**	-.23**	.27**	ns	ns	ns	ns	ns	ns	ns
	♂	.36*	ns	ns	ns	ns	ns	ns	ns	ns	ns	ns
	♀	ns	ns	-.21*	ns	ns	ns	ns	ns	ns	ns	ns
vulner	Total	ns	ns	-.23*	ns	ns	ns	ns	ns	ns	ns	ns
	♂	ns	ns	ns	ns	ns	ns	-.35*	-.36*	-.43**	-.39*	ns
	♀	ns	ns	-.24*	ns	ns	ns	ns	ns	ns	ns	ns

** correlation significant at .01 level; * significant at .05 level (2-tailed); ns= not significant.

Table I.2. T-test for equality of means; comparing two groups (lowest ⅓ and highest ⅓ scores on familiar Likert-type scales) on evaluation-items in semantic differential format

Means of	Grouping (lowest ⅓ and highest ⅓) based on scores of											
	okd	okn	ser	eas	af	afo	cn	fs	bc	rel	rp	LFT
accide	°	ns	+	ns	ns	ns	ns	ns	ns	ns	ns	+
concer	ns	ns	ns	ns	ns	ns	ns	ns	ns	ns	ns	ns
concot	ns	ns	ns	ns	ns	ns	ns	ns	ns	ns	ns	+
crime	ns	ns	°	ns	ns	ns	°	ns	ns	ns	ns	+
danger	ns	+	+	+	+	+	°	+	ns	ns	+	ns
defens	+	ns	ns	ns	ns	ns	ns	ns	ns	ns	ns	ns
fault	ns	ns	ns	ns	ns	ns	+	ns	ns	ns	ns	+
fear	ns	ns	+	+	ns	+	ns	ns	ns	ns	ns	+
inatte	ns	+	+	+	+	+	°	ns	ns	ns	ns	ns
insecu	ns	ns	ns	ns	ns	ns	ns	ns	ns	ns	ns	ns
disast	ns	ns	+	ns	ns	ns	ns	ns	ns	ns	ns	+
precau	ns	ns	ns	ns	ns	ns	ns	ns	ns	ns	ns	ns
protec	ns	+	ns	+	ns	ns	+	ns	ns	ns	ns	ns
rape	ns	+	+	+	ns	ns	+	ns	ns	ns	ns	ns
risk	ns	ns	ns	ns	ns	+	+	ns	°	ns	ns	+
safety	ns	°	°	+	ns	+	ns	ns	ns	ns	ns	ns
soconc	ns	ns	+	ns	ns	ns	+	ns	ns	ns	ns	ns
unsaf	ns	+	+	+	+	+	+	+	ns	ns	+	+
violen	ns	°	+	+	ns	ns	ns	ns	ns	ns	ns	ns
vulner	ns	ns	+	ns	ns	ns	ns	ns	ns	ns	ns	ns
No. of sign. t-tests	5	10	8	3	6	4	5					8

+ significant at .01 or .05 level; ° significant at .1 level (all 2-tailed); ns= not significant.

Table I.3. T-test for equality of means; comparing two groups (lowest ⅓ and highest ⅓ scores on evaluation-items semantic differential format) on familiar Likert-type scales

Grouping based on scores of	Means of											
	okd	okn	ser	eas	af	afo	cn	fs	bc	rel	rp	LFT
accide	ns	ns	+	ns	ns	ns	°	ns	ns	ns	ns	+
concer	ns	ns	ns	ns	ns	ns	ns	ns	ns	ns	ns	ns
concot	ns	ns	ns	ns	ns	ns	ns	ns	ns	ns	ns	+
crime	ns	ns	°	ns	ns	°	+	ns	ns	ns	ns	+
danger	ns	+	+	+	+	+	ns	ns	ns	ns	°	ns
defens	ns	ns	ns	ns	ns	ns	ns	ns	ns	ns	ns	ns
fault	ns	ns	+	ns	+	+	+	ns	ns	ns	+	+
fear	ns	+	+	+	+	+	+	ns	ns	ns	+	+
inatte	ns	+	+	+	+	+	+	+	ns	ns	+	+
insecu	ns	ns	ns	ns	°	ns	ns	ns	ns	ns	ns	ns
disast	ns	ns	+	ns	ns	ns	+	ns	ns	ns	ns	ns
precau	ns	ns	ns	ns	ns	ns	+	ns	ns	+	ns	ns
protec	ns	+	ns	+	+	+	°	+	ns	ns	+	ns
rape	ns	+	+	+	ns	ns	ns	ns	ns	ns	ns	ns
risk	ns	ns	ns	ns	ns	+	+	ns	ns	ns	ns	+
safety	ns	+	°	+	+	+	ns	+	ns	ns	°	ns
soconc	ns	ns	+	ns	ns	+	+	ns	ns	ns	+	°
unsaf	°	+	+	+	+	+	+	+	ns	ns	+	+
violen	ns	+	+	+	+	°	ns	ns	ns	ns	ns	+
vulner	ns	ns	+	ns	ns	ns	ns	ns	ns	ns	ns	ns
No. of sign. t-tests		8	11	8	8	9	9	4				6	9

+ significant at .01 or .05 level; ° significant at .1 level (all 2-tailed); ns= not significant.

Appendix J. Final instrument (semantic differential format)

Coincidentally, all three items in the original survey had the negative pole on the left, the positive pole on the right. To minimise response-effects, the three pairs of adjectives should vary, both the poles and ideally the order of the pairs as well. Future research should investigate whether the order of the pairs and the concepts has an independent effect on the responses given. A possible format of the instrument (in Dutch) is as follows:

Onveiligheid

slecht	.....	.....	.....	.....	.....	.....	.....		goed
aardig	.....	.....	.....	.....	.....	.....	.....		onaardig
onplezierig	.....	.....	.....	.....	.....	.....	.....		plezierig

Gevaar

aardig	.....	.....	.....	.....	.....	.....	.....		onaardig
onplezierig	.....	.....	.....	.....	.....	.....	.....		plezierig
goed	.....	.....	.....	.....	.....	.....	.....		slecht

Geweld

onaardig	.....	.....	.....	.....	.....	.....	.....		aardig
slecht	.....	.....	.....	.....	.....	.....	.....		goed
plezierig	.....	.....	.....	.....	.....	.....	.....		onplezierig

Table J.1 Basic statistics for total sample, and fe/male respondents; scale based on concepts danger , unsafety and violence.

Name	α	Possible range	Min.-max.	All			♂			♀		
				N	M	SD	N	M	SD	N	M	SD
duv (9)	.87	9 – 63	9 – 40	133	16.5	6.8	34	20.6	8.0	98	15.1	5.8
du (6)	.86	6 – 42	6 – 30	133	11.9	5.3	34	14.6	6.3	98	11.0	4.6
dv (6)	.81	6 – 42	6 – 28	135	11.0	4.8	34	13.9	5.9	99	9.9	4.0

References

A

Aarts, M., & Berdowski, S. (1992). *Slachtofferschap en politiefunctioneren* (No. 841). Breda: Council of Breda, Statistics & Research department.

Abdel-Khalek, A.M. (1997). A survey of fears associated with Iraqi agression among Kuwaiti children and adolescents: A factorial study 5.7 years after the Gulf War. *Psychological Reports, 81*, 247-255.

Abrams, D., Viki, G.T., Masser, B., & Bohner, G. (2003). Perceptions of stranger and acquaintance rape: The role of benevolent and hostile sexism in victim blame and rape proclivity. *Journal of Personality & Social Psychology,* January *84*(1), 111-125.

Acierno, R. (2000). *Screening Measures for Domestic Violence, Sexual Assault, and Physical Assault,* 2000. Retrieved from   http://www.nvaw.org/research/screening.shtml [25 July 2005]

Adam, B., Beck, U., & Loon, J. van (Eds.). (2000). *The Risk Society and Beyond: Critical Issues for Social Theory.* London; Thousand Oaks, CA: Sage.

Adam, B., & Loon, J. van (2000). Introduction: Repositioning risk: The challenge for social theory. In: B. Adam, U. Beck & J. van Loon (Eds.), *The Risk Society and Beyond: Critical Issues for Social Theory* (pp. 1-31). London; Thousand Oaks, CA: Sage.

Adams, J. (1995). *Risk.* London: UCL Press.

Adams, R.E., Rohe, W.M., & Arcury, T.A. (2005). Awareness of community-oriented policing and neighborhood perceptions in five small to midsize cities. *Journal of Criminal Justice, 33*(1), 43-54.

Adams, R.E., & Serpe, R.T. (2000). Social integration, fear of crime, and life satisfaction. *Sociological Perspectives, 43*(4), 605-629.

Adu-Mireku, S. (2002). Fear of crime among residents of three communities in Accra, Ghana. *International Journal of Comparative Sociology, 43*(2), 153-168.

Aharoni, Y. (1981). *The No-Risk Society.* Chatham, New Jersey: Chatham House Publishers.

Ajzen, I., & Fishbein, M. (1980). *Understanding Attitudes and Predicting Social Behavior.* Englewood Cliffs, NJ: Prentice-Hall.

Alexander, D. (2002). Nature's impartiality, man's inhumanity: Reflections on terrorism and world crisis in a context of historical disaster. *Disasters: The Journal of Disaster Studies and Management, 26*(1), 1-10.

Allen, J., Dodd, T., & Salisbury, H. (2005). *Crime in England and Wales: Quarterly Update to September 2004* (No. Statistical Bulletin 03/05). London: Home Office.

Allen, J., Livingstone, S., & Reiner, R. (1997). The changing generic location of crime in film: A content analysis of film synopses, 1945-1991. *Journal of Communication, 47*(4), 89-101.

Allport, F.H. (1937). Toward a science of public opinion. *Public Opinion Quarterly, 1*(1), 7-23.

Alreck, P.L., & Settle, R.B. (1985). *The Survey Research Handbook.* Homewood: Richard D. Irwin.

Altheide, D.L. (1997). The news media, the problem frame, and the production of fear. *Sociological Quarterly, 38*(4), 647-668.

Altheide, D.L. (2000). Tracking discourse and qualitative document analysis. *Poetics, 27*(4), 287-299.

Altheide, D.L. (2002). Children and the discourse of fear. *Symbolic Interaction, 25*(2), 229-250.

Altheide, D.L. (2003). Notes towards a politics of fear. *Journal for Crime, Conflict and the Media, 1*(1), 37-54.

Altheide, D.L., & Michalowski, R.S. (1999). Fear in the news: A discourse of control. *Sociological Quarterly, 40*(3), 475-504.

Aluja-Fabregat, A., & Torrubia-Beltri, R. (1998). Viewing of mass media violence, perception of violence, personality and academic achievement. *Personality and Individual Differences, 25*(5), 973-989.

Anderson, J.F., Grandison, T., & Dyson, L. (1996). Victims of random violence and the public health implication: A health care or criminal justice issue? *Journal of Criminal Justice, 24*(5), 379-391.

Andrews, F.M., & Withey, S.B. (1976). *Social Indicators of Well-being: Americans' Perceptions of Life Quality.* New York, NY: Plenum Press.

Aneshensel, C.S., & Sucoff, C.A. (1996). The neighborhood context of adolescent mental health. *Journal of Health and Social Behavior, 37*(4), 293-310.

d'Anjou, L.J.M. (2000). Strafrecht als product van moreel ondernemen: Over de criminalisering van stalking. *Justitiële verkenningen, 26*(5), 23-35.

Annells, M. (1996). Grounded theory method: Philosophical perspectives, paradigm of inquiry, and postmodernism. *Qualitative Health Research, 6*(3), 379-393.

Ashcroft, J. (2001). *Cyberstalking: A New Challenge for Law Enforcement: Report to Congress on Stalking and Domestic Violence* (NCJ 186157, pp. 1-16). Washington: DC: Department of Justice.

Asher, H.B. (1984). The research process. In: H.B. Asher, H.F. Weisberg, J.H. Kessel & W.P. Shively (Eds.), *Theory-Building and Data Analysis in the Social Sciences* (pp. 3-20). Knoxville: University of Tennessee Press.

Astor, R.A., Benbenishty, R., Zeira, A., & Vinokur, A. (2002). School climate, observed risky behaviors, and victimization as predictors of high school students' fear and judgments of school violence as a problem. *Health Education & Behavior, 29*(6), 716-736.

Atkinson, D., & Stewart, L. (1998). *Katsushika Hokusai (1760-1849): Life and Art of Katsushika Hokusai.* Retrieved from http://www.csuchico.edu/art/contrapposto/contrapposto99/pages/essays/themefloating/hohusaimnt.html [18 May 2005].

Atmore, C. (1999). Victims, backlash, and radical feminist theory (or, the morning after they stole feminism's fire). In: S. Lamb (Ed.), *New Versions of Victims: Feminists Struggle with the Concept* (pp. 183-211). New York: New York University Press.

Austin, D.M., Woolever, C., & Baba, Y. (1994). Crime and safety-related concerns in a small community. *American Journal of Criminal Justice, 19*, 79-97.

Ax, A. (1953). The psychological differentiation between fear and anger in humans. *Psychosomatic Medicine, 15*, 433-442.

Axelrod, R. (1973). Schema theory: An information processing model of perception and cognition. *The American Political Science Review, 67*(4), 1248-1266.

B

Baas, N.J. (1998). *Stalking: Slachtoffers, daders en maatregelen tegen deze vorm van belagen* (Onderzoeksnotities No. 1998/1). The Hague: Wetenschappelijk Onderzoek- en Documentatiecentrum.

Baba, Y., & Austin, D.M. (1989). Neighborhood environmental satisfaction, victimization, and social participation as determinants of perceived neighborhood safety. *Environment and Behavior, 21*, 763-780.

Baer, J., & Chambliss, W.J. (1997). Generating fear: The politics of crime reporting. *Crime, Law & Social Change, 27*, 87-107.

Bain, R. (1928). An attitude on attitude research. *American Journal of Sociology, 33*(6), 940-957.

Baker, M., Nienstedt, B., Everett, R.S., & McCleary, R. (1983). The impact of a crime wave: Perceptions, fear, and confidence in the police. *Law & Society Review, 17*(2), 319-335.

Balkin, S. (1979). Victimization rates, safety, and fear of crime. *Social Problems, 26*, 343-358.

Ball, T. (1984). From paradigms to research programs: Toward a post-Kuhnian political science. In: H.B. Asher, H.F. Weisberg, J.H. Kessel & W.P. Shively (Eds.), *Theory-Building and Data Analysis in the Social Sciences* (pp. 23-49). Knoxville: University of Tennessee Press.

Bamber, J.H. (1979). *The Fears of Adolescents* (Vol. 20). London: Academic Press.

Bankoff, G. (2001). Rendering the world unsafe: 'Vulnerability' as Western discourse. *Disasters: The Journal of Disaster Studies and Management, 25*(1), 19-36.

Bannister, J., & Fyfe, N. (2001). Fear and the city. *Urban Studies, 38*(5-6), 807-813.

Barak, G. (1994). *Media, Process, and the Social Construction of Crime: Studies in Newsmaking Criminology* (Vol. 1690.). New York: Garland Pub.

Barer, B.M., & Johnson, C.L. (2003). Problems and problem solving among aging White and Black Americans. *Journal of Aging Studies, 17*(3), 323-340.

Barker, H. (1998). *Newspapers, Politics, and Public Opinion in Late Eighteenth-century England*. Oxford: Clarendon Press.

Barker, M., & Page, S.J. (2002). Visitor safety in urban tourism environments: The case of Auckland, New Zealand. *Cities, 19*(4), 273-282.

Baron, S.W., & Hartnagel, T.F. (2002). Street youth and labor market strain. *Journal of Criminal Justice, 30*(6), 519-533.

Bartal, D., Jacobson, D., & Freund, T. (1995). Security feelings among Jewish settlers in the occupied territories: A study of communal and personal antecedents. *Journal of Conflict Resolution, 39*(2), 353-377.

Baty, K. (2003). *A Girl's Gotta Do What a Girl's Gotta Do: The Ultimate Guide to Living Safe and Smart*: Rodale Press.

Baumer, T.L. (1985). Testing a general model of fear of crime: Data from a national sample. *Journal of Research in Crime and Delinquency, 22*, 239-255.

Bazargan, M. (1994). The effects of health, environmental, and socio-psychological variables on fear of crime and its consequences among urban black elderly individuals. *International Journal of Aging & Human Development, 38*(2), 99-115.

Beach, H. (1990). Perceptions of risk, dilemmas of policy: Nuclear fallout in Swedish Lapland. *Social Science & Medicine, 30*(6), 729-738.

Beck, J., & Schouten, R. (2000). Workplace violence and psychiatric practice. *Bulletin of the Menninger Clinic*, 64 (61), 36-48.

Beck, U. (1992). *Risk Society: Towards a New Modernity*. London; Newbury Park, CA: Sage Publications.

Beck, U. (1998). Politics of risk society. In: J. Franklin (Ed.), *The Politics of Risk Society* (pp. 9-22). Malden, Mass.: Polity Press.

Beck, U. (1999). *World Risk Society*. Malden, Mass: Polity Press.

Beck, U. (2000). Risk society revisited: Theory, politics and research programmes. In: B. Adam, U. Beck & J. van Loon (Eds.), *The Risk Society and Beyond: Critical Issues for Social Theory* (pp. 211-229). London; Thousand Oaks, CA: Sage.

Becker, G. (2000). Coefficient alpha: Some terminological ambiguities and related misconceptions. *Psychological Reports, 86*(2), 365-372.

Becker, G.D. (1997). *The Gift of Fear: Survival Signals that Protect us from Violence* (1st ed.). Boston: Little Brown.

Becker, J. (2003). Opvattingen over het beleid. In: Sociaal en Cultureel Planbureau, *De sociale staat van Nederland 2003* (pp. 291-313). The Hague: Sociaal en Cultureel Planbureau.

Beckett, K. (1997). *Making Crime Pay: Law and Order in Contemporary American Politics*. New York: Oxford University Press.

Beckett, K., & Sasson, T. (2000). *The Politics of Injustice: Crime and Punishment in America*. Thousand Oaks, CA: Pine Forge.

Beirne, P. (1987). Adolphe Quetelet and the origins of positivist criminology. *American Journal of Sociology, 92*(5), 1140-1169.

Beke, B.M.W.A., Haan, W.J.M. de, & Terlouw, G.J. (2001). *Geweld op straat, daders, slachtoffers en getuigen over 'geweld op straat'*. The Hague: Wetenschappelijk Onderzoek- en Documentatiecentrum.

Bell, D.J. (1985). Domestic violence: Victimization, police intervention, and disposition. *Journal of Criminal Justice, 13*(6), 525-534.

Bellair, P.E. (2000). Informal surveillance and street crime: A complex relationship. *Criminology, 38*(1), 137-169.

Bemmelen, J.M. van (1958). *Criminologie: Leerboek der misdaadkunde* (4th ed.). Zwolle: Tjeenk Willink.

Bennett, T. (1991). The effectiveness of a police-initiated fear-reducing strategy. *British Journal of Criminology, 31*(1), 1-14.

Berger, P. L., & Luckmann, T. (1966). *The social construction of reality; a treatise in the sociology of knowledge* ([1st] ed.). Garden City: Doubleday.

Berghuis, A.C., Ministry of Justice & WODC (1985). Meningen van de Nederlandse bevolking over criminaliteit 1985. (Opinions of the Dutch population on criminality 1985). [datafile]. Amsterdam, Steinmetz-Archief P1069.

Berghuis, A.C., & Essers, J.J.A. (1986). Criminaliteitsbestrijding en publieke opinie. *Tijdschrift voor criminologie* (4), 159-178.

Berka, K. (1983). *Measurement: Its Concepts, Theories and Problems* (A. Riska, Trans. Vol. 72). Boston: D. Reidel Publishing Company.

Berns, N. (2001). Degendering the problem and gendering the blame: Political discourse on women and violence. *Gender and Society, 15*(2), 262-282.

Bernstein, P.L. (1998). *Against the Gods: The Remarkable Story of Risk*. New York: John Wiley & Sons.

Best, J. (1999). *Random Violence: How we Talk about New Crimes and New Victims*. Berkeley: University of California Press.

Best, J. (2001). *Damned Lies and Statistics: Untangling Numbers from the Media, Politicians, and Activists*. Berkeley, CA: University of California Press.

Beukenhorst, D.J. (1992). *Verschillen in slachtofferrisico van bevolkingsgroepen*. Voorburg: Centraal Bureau voor de Statistiek.

Beukenhorst, D.J., Huys, H.J.W.M., Oudhof, J., & Rooduijn, J. (1993). *De overgang van Enquete Slachtoffers Misdrijven naar Enquete Rechtsbescherming en Veiligheid* (Recht en Statistiek, no. 16). Voorburg: Centraal Bureau voor de Statistiek.

Bezembinder, T.G., & Roskam, E.E. (1976). Theorieen en modellen. In: J.A. Michon, E.G.J. Eijkman & L.F.W. DeKlerk (Eds.), *Handboek der psychonomie* (pp. 55-99). Deventer: Van Loghum Slaterus.

Bickerstaff, K. (2004). Risk perception research: socio-cultural perspectives on the public experience of air pollution. *Environment International, 30*(6), 827-840

Bilsky, W. (1993a). Blanks and open questions in survey research on fear of crime. In: W. Bilsky, C. Pfeiffer & P. Wetzels (Eds.), *Fear of Crime and Criminal Victimization* (pp. 9-19). Stuttgart: Enke.

Bilsky, W., & Wetzels, P. (1997). On the relationship between criminal victimization and fear of crime. *Psychology, Crime and Law, 3*, 309-318.

Blalock, H.M. (1961). Theory, measurement, and replication in the social sciences. *American Journal of Sociology, 66*(4), 342-347.

Blalock, H.M. (1968a). The measurement problem: A gap between the languages of theory and research. In: H.M. Blalock & A.B. Blalock (Eds.), *Methodology in Social Research* (pp. 5-27). New York: McGraw-Hill.

Blalock, H.M. (1968b). Theory building and causal inferences. In: H.M. Blalock & A.B. Blalock (Eds.), *Methodology in Social Research* (pp. 155-198). New York: McGraw-Hill.

Blalock, H.M. (1982). *Conceptualization and Measurement in the Social Sciences*. Beverly Hills: Sage Publications.

Blalock, H.M. (Ed.). (1974). *Measurement in the Social Sciences: Theories and Strategies*. London: Macmillan.

Block, R.L. (1971). Fear of crime and fear of the police. *Social Problems, 19*(1), 91.

Bochove, C. van (1999). Census, no census, virtual census. In: J.G.S.J. van Maarseveen, M.B.G. Gircour & R. Schreijnders (Eds.), *A Century Rounded up: Reflections on the History of the Central Bureau of Statistics in the Netherlands*. Voorburg: Statistics Netherlands (CBS).

Body Gendrot, S. (2001). The politics of urban crime. *Urban Studies, 38*(5), 915-928.

Boeije, H. (2002). A purposeful approach to the constant comparative method in the analysis of qualitative interviews. *Quality and Quantity, 36*(4), 391-409.

Boesjes-Hommes, R.W. (1974). *De geldige operationalisering van begrippen*. Meppel: Boom.

Bohner, G. (2001). Writing about rape: Use of the passive voice and other distancing text features as an expression of perceived responsibility of the victim. *British Journal of Social Psychology, 40*, 515-529.

Bohner, G., Reinhard, M. A., Rutz, S., Sturm, S., Kerschbaum, B., & Effler, D. (1998). Rape myths as neutralizing cognitions: Evidence for a causal impact of anti-victim attitudes on men's self-reported likelihood of raping. *European Journal of Social Psychology, 28*(2), 257-268.

Boholm, A. (1998). Comparative studies of risk perception: A review of twenty years of research. *Journal of Risk Research, 1*(2), 135-163.

Bonaiuto, M., Fornara, F., & Bonnes, M. (2003). Indexes of perceived residential environment quality and neighbourhood attachment in urban environments: A confirmation study on the city of Rome. *Landscape and Urban Planning, 65*(1-2), 41-52.

Boomsma, A. (1995a). De adequaatheid van covariantiestructuurmodellen: Een overzicht van maten en indexen. Paper Sociaal-Wetenschappelijke Sectie van de Vereniging voor Statistiek, Utrecht 21 maart 1995. Groningen: University of Groningen.

Boomsma, A. (1995b). Analyse van covariantiestructuren: De adequaatheid van het model 1. Groningen: University of Groningen.

Boomsma, A. (1996). Analyse van covariantiestructuren: Schattingsmethoden 2. Groningen: University of Groningen.

Boomsma, A., & Hoogland, J.J. (2001). The robustness of LISREL modeling revisited. In: R. Cudeck, S. du Toit & D. Sörbom (Eds.), *Structural Equation Models: Present and Future: A Festschrift in Honor of Karl Jöreskog* (pp. 139-168). Chicago: Scientific Software International.

Borg, I., & Staufenbiel, T. (1993). Facet theory and design for attitude measurement and its application. In: D. Krebs & P. Schmidt (Eds.), *New Directions in Attitude Measurement* (pp. 206-237). Berlin: Walter de Gruyter.

Borooah, V.K., & Carcach, C.A. (1997). Crime and fear: Evidence from Australia. *British Journal of Criminology, 37*(4), 635-657.

Borsboom, D., Mellenbergh, G.J., & van Heerden, J. (2003). The theoretical status of latent variables. *Psychological Review, April, 110*(2), 203-219.

Boudon, R. (1993). Introduction. In: R. Boudon (Ed.), *On Social Research and its Language* (pp. 1-29). Chicago: University of Chicago Press.

Box, S. (1975). *Deviance, Reality and Society* (2nd ed. 1981). London: Holt, Rinehart and Winston.

Box, S., Hale, C., & Andrews, G. (1988). Explaining fear of crime. *British Journal of Criminology, 28*(3), 340-356.

Boyle, G.J. (1991). Does item homogeneity indicate internal consistency or item redundancy in psychometric scales? *Personality and Individual Differences, 12*(3), 291-294.

Bramston, P., Pretty, G., & Chipuer, H. (2002). Unravelling subjective quality of life: An investigation of individual and community determinants. *Social Indicators Research, 59*(3), 261-274.

Brenot, J., Bonnefous, S., & Marris, C. (1998). Testing the cultural theory of risk in France. *Risk Analysis, 18*(6), 729-739.

Brinton, J.E. (1961). Deriving an attitude scale from semantic differential data. *Public Opinion Quarterly, 25*(2), 289-295.

Brinton, J.E. (1969). Deriving an attitude scale from semantic differential data. In: J.G. Snider & C.E. Osgood (Eds.), *Semantic Differential Technique: A Sourcebook* (pp. 467-473). Chicago: Aldine.

Britkov, V., & Sergeev, G. (1998). Risk management: Role of social factors in major industrial accidents. *Safety Science, 30*(1-2), 173-181.

Brodsky, A.E., O'Campo, P.J., & Aronson, R.E. (1999). PSOC in community context: Multi-level correlates of a measure of psychological sense of community in low-income, urban neighborhoods. *Journal of Community Psychology, 27*(6), 659-679.

Brody, L.R., Lovas, G.S., & Hay, D.H. (1995). Gender differences in anger and fear as a function of situational context. *Sex Roles, 32*(1/2), 47-78.

Broers, N. (1994). *Formalized Theory of Appraisive Judgments.* Catholic Universtiy Nijmegen, Nijmegen.

Brown Eve, S. (1985). Criminal victimization and fear of crime among the non-institutionalized elderly in the United States: A critique of the empirical research literature. *, 10*(1-4), 397-408.

Brown, J. (1985). An introduction to the uses of facet theory. In: D. Canter (Ed.), *Facet Theory: Approaches to Social Research* (pp. 17-57). New York: Springer-Verlag.

Brown, R.M. (1977). *Strain of Violence: Historical Studies of American Violence and Vigilantism.* New York: Oxford University Press.

Brown, R.W. (1969). Is a boulder sweet or sour? In: J.G. Snider & C.E. Osgood (Eds.), *Semantic Differential Technique: A Sourcebook* (pp. 85-88). Chicago: Aldine.

Browne, M.W., & Cudeck, R. (1992). Alternative ways of assessing model fit. *Sociological Methods & Research, 21*, 230-258.

Brownmiller, S. (1975). *Against our Will: Men, Women, and Rape.* New York: Simon and Schuster.

Bryman, A. (1984). The debate about quantitative and qualitative research: A question of method or epistemology? *British Journal of Sociology, 35*(1), 75-92.

Buck, W., Chatterton, M., & Paase, K. (1995). *Obscene, Threatening and other Troublesome Phone Calls to Women: Findings from the British Crime Survey.* (Research Findings No. 23). London: Home Office.

Budd, T., & Mattinson, J. (2000). *Stalking: Findings from the 1998 British Crime Survey* (Research Findings No. 129). London: Home Office.

Buikhuisen, W. (1975). *Geregistreerde en niet-geregistreerde kriminaliteit.* The Hague: Wetenschappelijk Onderzoek- en Documentatie Centrum, Ministerie van Jusititie.

Burger, E.J. (Ed.). (1993). *Risk.* Ann Arbor: University of Michigan Press.

Burger, T. (1987). *Max Weber's Theory of Concept Formation: History, Laws, and Ideal Types* (expanded ed.). Durham: Duke University Press.

Burke, R. (1998). The socio-political context of zero tolerance policing strategies. *Policing: An International Journal of Police Strategies and Management, 21*(4), 666-682.

Burns, R., & Crawford, C. (1999). School shootings, the media, and public fear: Ingredients for a moral panic. *Crime, Law & Social Change, 32*, 147-168.

Bursik, J., Robert J., & Grasmick, H.G. (1993). The use of multiple indicators to estimate crime trends in American cities. *Journal of Criminal Justice, 21*(5), 509-516.

Bursik, R.J. (2000). The systemic theory of neighbourhood crime rates. In: S.S. Simpson (Ed.), *Of Crime and Criminality: The Use of Theory in Everyday Life.* Thousand Oaks, CA: Pine Forge Press.

Bursik, R.J., & Grasmick, H.G. (1993). *Neighborhoods and Crime: Neighborhood Dynamics and the Fear of Crime.* New York: Lexington Books.

Burt, M.R. (1980). Cultural myths and supports of rape. *Journal of Personality and Social Psychology, 38*, 217-230.

Butts, R.E. (1966). Feyerabend and the pragmatic theory of observation. *Philosophy of Science, 33*(4), 383-394.

Buunk, B.P., & Mussweiler, T. (2001). New directions in social comparison research. *European Journal of Social Psychology, 31*(5), 467-475.

Buunk, B.P., Ybema, J.F., Gibbons, F.X., & Ipenburg, M. (2001). The affective consequences of social comparison as related to professional burnout and social comparison orientation. *European Journal of Social Psychology, 31*(4), 337-351.

Buunk, B.P., Zee, K. van der, & Yperen, N.W. van (2001). Neuroticism and social comparison orientation as moderators of affective responses to social comparison at work. *Journal of Personality, 69*(5), 745-763.

Byrd, T.L., & VanDerslice, J. (1996). Perception of Environmental Risk in Three El Paso Communities. Paper presented at the Proceedings of the HSRC/WERC Joint Conference on the Environment, May 1996.

C

Cabanac, M. (2002). What is emotion? *Behavioural Processes, 60*(2), 69-83.

Camerer, L., Louw, A., Shaw, M., Artz, L., & Scharf, W. (1998). *Crime in Cape Town.* Pretoria/Cape Town, South Africa: Institute for Security Studies.

Cameron, C. (1975). Accident proneness. *Accident Analysis & Prevention, 7*(1), 49-53.

Campbell, D.T., & Fiske, D.W. (1959). Convergent and discriminant validation by the multitrait-multimethod matrix. *Psychological Bulletin, 56*, 81-105.

Cannon, W.B. (1914). Recent studies of bodily effects of fear, rage, and pain. *The Journal of Philosophy, Psychology and Scientific Methods, 11*(6), 162-165.

Canter, D. (Ed.). (1985). *Facet Theory: Approaches to Social Research.* New York: Springer-Verlag.

Cantor, D., & Lynch, J.P. (2000). Self-report surveys as measures of crime and criminal victimization. In: D. Duffee (Ed.), *Criminal Justice 2000: Measurement and Analysis of Crime and Justice* (volume 4 ed.): U.S. Department of Justice, Office of Justice Programs, National Institute of Justice.

Carlson, J.M., & Williams, T. (1993). Perspectives on the seriousness of crimes. *Social Science Research, 22*(2), 190-207.

Carnap, R. (1936). Testability and meaning. *Philosophy of Science, 3*(4), 419-471.

Carnap, R. (1937). Testability and meaning: Continued. *Philosophy of Science, 4*(1), 1-40.

Carnap, R. (1968). The methodological character of theoretical concepts. In: H. Feigl & M. Scriven (Eds.), *The Foundations of Science and the Concepts of Psychology and Psychoanalysis* (6th printing ed., Vol. I, pp. 38-76). Minneapolis: University of Minnesota Press.

Carr, N. (2001). An exploratory study of gendered differences in young tourists perception of danger within London. *Tourism Management, 22*(5), 565-570.

Carrington, K., & Watson, P. (1996). Policing sexual violence: Feminism, criminal justice and governmentality. *International Journal of the Sociology of Law, 24*(3), 253-272.

Carroll, G.B., Hebert, D.M.C., & Roy, J.M. (1999). Youth action strategies in violence prevention. *Journal of Adolescent Health, 25*(1), 7-13.

Cassuto, J., & Tarnow, P. (2003). The discotheque fire in Gothenburg 1998: A tragedy among teenagers. *Burns, 29*(5), 405-416.

Castaneda, C. (2000). Child organ stealing stories: Risk, rumour and reproductive technologies. In: B. Adam, U. Beck & J. van Loon (Eds.), *The Risk Society and Beyond: Critical Issues for Social Theory* (pp. 136-154). Thousand Oaks, CA: Sage.

Cates, J., Dian, D., & GW, S. (2003). Use of protection motivation theory to assess fear of crime in rural areas. *Psychology Crime & Law, 9*(3), 225-236.

Cavender, G. (1981). 'Scared straight': Ideology and the media. *Journal of Criminal Justice, 9*(6), 431-439.

Cavender, G., Bond-Maupin, L., & Jurik, N.C. (1999). The construction of gender in reality crime TV. *Gender & Society, 13*(5), 643-663.

Centraal Bureau voor de Statistiek (CBS) (1991). *Profielen van slachtoffers van veel voorkomende criminaliteit* (Recht en Statistiek, no.12). Voorburg: Centraal Bureau voor de Statistiek.

Centraal Bureau voor de Statistiek (CBS) (1998). *Special Issue: Integration of Household Surveys: Design, Advantages and Methods.* Voorburg: CBS.

Centraal Bureau voor de Statistiek (CBS) (2002). *Permanent onderzoek leefsituatie.* Voorburg/Heerlen: Centraal Bureau voor de Statistiek.

Chadee, D. (2000). Fear of Crime, Safety and Community Integration: Another Fear-Safety Paradox? Paper presented at the annual meeting of the American Society of Criminology, San Francisco, CA, USA.

Chakraborti, N., & Garland, J. (2003). Under-researched and overlooked: An exploration of the attitudes of rural minority ethnic communities towards crime, community safety and the criminal justice system. *Journal of Ethnic and Migration Studies, 29*(3), 563-572.

Chalmers, A. (1997). *Wat heet wetenschap?* Meppel: Boom.

Chan, W., & Rigakos, G.S. (2002). Risk, crime and gender. *British Journal of Criminology, 42*(4), 743-761.

Chandola, T. (2001). The fear of crime and area differences in health. *Health & Place, 7*(2), 105-116.

Chapman, S., & Schofield, W.N. (1998). Lifesavers and Samaritans: Emergency use of cellular (mobile) phones in Australia. *Accident Analysis & Prevention, 30*(6), 815-819.

Chartier, J., & Gabler, S. (2001). *Risk Communication and Government: Theory and Application for the Canadian Food Inspection Agency:* Canadian Food Inspection Agency; Public and Regulatory Affairs Branch.

Chermak, S. (1998). Predicting crime story salience: The effects of crime, victim, and defendant characteristics. *Journal of Criminal Justice, 26*(1), 61-70.

Chevigny, P. (2003). The populism of fear: Politics of crime in the Americas. *Punishment and Society, 5*(1), 77-96.

Chilton, S., Covey, J., Hopkins, L., Jones-Lee, M., Loomes, G., Pidgeon, N., et al. (2002). Public perceptions of risk and preference-based values of safety. *Journal of Risk & Uncertainty* November, *25*(3), 211-232.

Chiricos, T., & Eschholz, S. (2002). The racial and ethnic typification of crime and the criminal typification of race and ethnicity in local television news. *Journal of Research in Crime and Delinquency, 39*(4), 400-420.

Chiricos, T., Eschholz, S., & Gertz, M. (1997). Crime, news and fear of crime: Toward an identification of audience effects. *Social Problems, 44*(3), 342-357.

Chiricos, T., McEntire, R., & Gertz, M. (2001). Perceived racial and ethnic composition of neighborhood and perceived risk of crime. *Social Problems, 48*(3), 322-340.

Chiricos, T., Padgett, K., & Gertz, M. (2000). Fear, TV news, and the reality of crime. *Criminology, 38*(3), 755-785.

Chow, S.L. (1988). Significance test or effect size? *Psychological Bulletin, 103*(1), 105-110.

Christie, N. (1986). The ideal victim. In: E.A. Fattah (Ed.), *From Crime Policy to Victim Policy: Reorienting the Justice System* (pp. 17-30). New York, NY: St. Martin's Press.

Citrin, J., & Muste, C. (1999). Trust in government. In: J.P. Robinson, P.R. Shaver & L.S. Wrightsman (Eds.), *Measures of Political Attitudes* (pp. 465-532). New York: Academic Press.

Clark, A. (1987). *Women's Silence, Men's Violence: Sexual Assault in England, 1770-1845.* London; New York: Pandora.

Clarke, J. (2001). The pleasures of crime: Interrogating the detective story. In: J. Muncie & E. McLaughlin (Eds.), *The Problem of Crime* (2nd ed., pp. 71-106). London; Thousand Oaks, CA: Sage; Open University.

Clarke, L., & Short, J.F., Jr. (1993). Social organization and risk: Some current controversies. *Annual Review of Sociology, 19*, 375-399.

Clemente, F., & Kleiman, M.B. (1976). Fear of crime among the aged. *The Gerontologist, 16*(3), 207-210.

Clemente, F., & Kleiman, M. B. (1977). Fear of Crime in the United States: A Multivariate Analysis. *Social Forces, 56*(2, Special Issue), 519-531.

Cleveland, W.S. (1993). *Visualizing Data.* Summit, NJ: Hobart Press.

Cobb, S. (1976). Support as a moderator of life stress. *Psychosomatic Medicine, 38*(5), 300-314.

Cohen, D.A., Farley, T.A., & Mason, K. (2003). Why is poverty unhealthy? Social and physical mediators. *Social Science & Medicine, 57*(9), 1631-1641.

Cohen, J. (1988). *Statistical Power Analysis for the Behavioral Sciences* (2nd ed.). New Jersey: Lawrence Erlbaum.

Cohen, L.E., & Felson, M. (1979). Social change and crime rate trends: A routine activities approach. *American Sociological Review, 44*(1), 588-608.

Cohen, L.E., Kaufman, R.L., & Gottfredson, M.R. (1985). Risk-based crime statistics: A forecasting comparison for burglary and auto theft. *Journal of Criminal Justice, 13*(5), 445-457.

Cohen, L.E., Kluegel, J.R., & Land, K.C. (1981). Social inequality and predatory criminal victimization: An exposition and test of a formal theory. *American Sociological Review, 46*(5), 505-524.

Cohl, H.A. (1997). *Are we Scaring ourselves to Death? How Pessimism, Paranoia, and a Misguided Media are Leading us toward Disaster* (1st St. Martin's Griffin ed.). New York: St. Martin's Griffin.

Connors, M.M. (1992). Risk perception, risk taking and risk management among intravenous drug users: Implications for AIDS prevention. *Social Science & Medicine, 34*(6), 591-601.

Converse, J.M., & Presser, S. (1988). *Survey Questions: Handcrafting the Standardized Questionnaire* (2nd ed.). London: Sage Publications.

Coogan, D. (2002). Public rhetoric and public safety at the Chicago Transit Authority: Three approaches to accident analysis. *Journal of Business and Technical Communication, 16*(3), 277-305.

Coote, A. (1998). Risk and public policy: Towards a high-trust democracy. In: J. Franklin (Ed.), *The Politics of Risk Society* (pp. 124-131). Malden, Mass.: Polity Press.

Correll, J., Park, B., Judd, C.M., & Wittenbrink, B. (2002). The police officer's dilemma: Using ethnicity to disambiguate potentially threatening individuals. *Journal of Personality & Social Psychology,* December, *83*(6), 1314-1329.

Costelloe, M.T., Chiricos, T., Burianek, J., Gertz, M., & Maier-Katkin, D. (2002). The social correlates of punitiveness toward criminals: A comparison of the Czech Republic and Florida. *Justice System Journal, 23*(2), 191-220.

Coston, C.T.M. (1993). Worries about crime: Rank-ordering survival concerns among urban transient females. *Deviant Behavior, 14*(4), 365-376.

Coston, C.T.M., & Finckenauer, J.O. (1993). Fear of crime among vulnerable populations: Homeless women. *Journal of Social Distress and the Homeless, 2*(1), 1-21.

Coulter, M.L., Runyan, D.K., Everson, M.D., Edelsohn, G.A., & King, N.M.P. (1985). Conflicting needs and interests of researchers and service providers in child sexual abuse cases. *Child Abuse & Neglect, 9*(4), 535-542.

Covello, V.T., Sandman, P.M., & Slovic, P. (1988). *Risk Communication, Risk Statistics, & Risk Comparisons: A Manual for Plant Managers.* Washington, DC: Chemical Manufacturers Association.

Covington, J., & Taylor, R.B. (1991). Fear of crime in urban residential neighborhoods: Implications of between-neighborhood and within-neighborhood sources for current models. *Sociological Quarterly, 32*(2), 231-249.

Cox, B.J., Endler, N.S., & Swinson, R.P. (1991). Clinical and nonclinical panic attacks: An empirical test of a panic-anxiety continuum. *Journal of Anxiety Disorders, 5*(1), 21-34.

Cox, D., Crossland, B., Darby, S.C., Forman, D., Fox, A.J., Gore, S.M., et al. (1992). Estimation of risk from observation on humans. In: Royal Society, *Risk: Analysis, Perception and Management* (pp. 67-87). London: The Royal Society.

Coxon, A.P.M. (1982). *The User's Guide to Multidimensional Scaling.* London: Heinemann Educational.

Cozijn, C., & Dijk, J.J.M. van (1976). *Onrustgevoelens in Nederland.* The Hague: Wetenschappelijk Onderzoek- en Documentatiecentrum, Ministerie van Justitie.

Craig, R., & Newcomb, H. (Ed.) (2003). *Courtroom Television: The Encyclopedia of Television.* Retrieved from http://www.museum.tv/archives/etv/C/htmlC/courtroomtel/courtroomtel.htm [July 18 2005]

Crank, J.P., Giacomazzi, A., & Heck, C. (2003). Fear of crime in a nonurban setting. *Journal of Criminal Justice, 31*(3), 249-263.

Criminal Justice Center's Survey Research Program (1998). *1998 Texas Crime Poll.* Retrieved from http://www.shsu.edu/~icc_drl/1998_TEXAS_CRIME_POLL.html [25 July 2005].

Crisp, B.R., & Barber, J.G. (1995). The effect of locus of control on the association between risk perception and sexual risk-taking. *Personality and Individual Differences, 19*(6), 841-845.

Croake, J.W., Myers, K.M., & Singh, A. (1987). Demographic features of adult fears. *International Journal of Social Psychiatry, 33*(4), 285-293.

Cronbach, L.J., & Meehl, P.E. (1968). Construct validity in psychological tests. In: H. Feigl & M. Scriven (Eds.), *The Foundations of Science and the Concepts of Psychology and Psychoanalysis* (6th ed., Vol. I, pp. 174-204). Minneapolis: University of Minnesota Press.

Crossland, B., Bennett, P.A., Ellis, A.F., Farmer, F.R., Gittus, J., Godfrey, P.S., et al. (1992). Estimating engineering risk. In: *Risk: Analysis, Perception and Management* (pp. 13-34). London: The Royal Society.

Cullen, M.J. (1975). *The Statistical Movement in Early Victorian Britain: The Foundations of Empirical Social Research.* Hassocks, Sussex: Harvester Press Limited.

Cummings, J. (1918). Statistical work of the federal government of the United States. In: J. Koren (Ed.), *The History of Statistics: Their Development and Progress in Many Countries: In Memoirs to Commemorate the Seventy Fifth Anniversary of the American Statistical Association* (pp. 573-689). New York: Macmillan.

Cummings, L.C. (1986). The political reality of artificial sweeteners. In: H.M. Sapolsky (Ed.), *Consuming Fears: The Politics of Product Risks* (pp. 116-140). New York: Basic Books.

Cvetkovich, G., Siegrist, M., Murray, R., & Tragesser, S. (2002). New information and social trust: Asymmetry and perseverance of attributions about hazard managers. *Risk Analysis, 22*(2), 359-367.

D

Dake, K., & Wildavsky, A. (1993). Theories of risk perception: Who fears what and why? In: E.J. Burger (Ed.), *Risk* (pp. 41-60). Ann Arbor: University of Michigan Press.

Danigelis, N.L., & Cutler, S.J. (1991). Cohort trends in attitudes about law and order: Who's leading the conservative wave? *Public Opinion Quarterly, 55*(1), 24-49.

Danylewich, P.H. (2001). *Fearless: The Complete Personal Safety Guide for Women.* Toronto: University of Toronto Press.

Danziger, K. (1997). The varieties of social construction. *Theory & Psychology, 7*(3), 399-416.

Darwin, C., & Ekman, P. (Eds.). (1998). *The Expression of the Emotions in Man and Animals.* London: Harper Collins.

Das, T.K., & Teng, B.S. (2004). The risk-based view of trust: A conceptual framework. *Journal of Business and Psychology, 19*(1), 85-116.

David, F.N. (1998). *Games, Gods, and Gambling: A History of Probability and Statistical Ideas.* Mineola, NY: Dover Publications.

David, K.B., Nias, B.A., & Phil, M. (1979). Desensitisation and media violence. *Journal of Psychosomatic Research, 23*(6), 363-367.

Davis, F.J. (1952). Crime news in Colorado newspapers. *American Journal of Sociology, 57*(4), 325-330.

Davis, M. (2003). Beyond blade runner: Urban control: The ecology of fear. In: E. McLaughlin, G. Hughes & J. Muncie (Eds.), *Criminological Perspectives: Essential Readings* (pp. 527-541). London: Sage.

Davis, R., Taylor, B., & Bench, S. (1995). Impact of sexual and nonsexual assault on secondary victims. *Violence and Victims, 10*(1), 73-84.

Davis, W.A. (1987). The varieties of fear. *Philosophical Studies, 51*(3), 287-310.

Day, K. (1995). Assault prevention as social control: Women and sexual assault prevention on urban college campuses. *Journal of Environmental Psychology, 15 (4)*, 261-281.

Day, K. (1999). Stranger in the night: Women's fear of sexual assault on urban college campuses. *Journal of Architecture & Planning Research, 16*(4), 289-312.

DeChano, L.M., & Butler, D.R. (2001). Analysis of public perception of debris flow hazard. *Disaster Prevention and Management, 10*(4), 261-269.

Decker, S.H. (1977). Official crime rates and victim surveys: An empirical comparison. *Journal of Criminal Justice, 5*(1), 47-54.

Decure, N. (1989). V.I. Warshawski, a 'lady with guts': Feminist crime fiction by Sara Paretsky. *Women's Studies International Forum, 12*(2), 227-238.

Decure, N. (1993). Pam Nilsen, 'Some kind of commie feminist': The four-dimensional detective of Barbara Wilson's crime fiction. *Women's Studies International Forum, 16*(2), 181-191.

Deflem, M. (1997). Surveillance and criminal statistics: Historical foundations of governmentality. In: A. Sarat & S. Silbey (Eds.), *Studies in Law, Politics and Society* (Vol. 17, pp. 149-184). Greenwich, CT: JAI Press.

DeFronzo, J. (1979). Fear of crime and handgun ownership. *Criminology, 17*(3), 331-339.

DelaRoche, R. (1996). Collective violence as social control. *Sociological Forum, 11*(1), 97-128.

Delbeke, L. (1976). Meetvariabelen- en methoden. In: J.A. Michon, E.G.J. Eijkman & L.F.W. DeKlerk (Eds.), *Handboek der psychonomie* (pp. 14-54). Deventer: Van Loghum Slaterus.

Denkers, A.J.M. (1996). *Psychological Reactions of Victims of Crime: The Influence of Pre-Crime, Crime, and Post-Crime Factors.* Vrije Universiteit, Amsterdam.

Denner, B. (1992). Research as a moral crusade. *American Psychologist, 47*(1), 81-82.

Derksen, W., Korsten, A.F.A., & Bertrand, A.F.M. (Eds.). (1988). *De praktijk van onderzoek: Problemen bij onderzoek van politiek, bestuur en beleid.* Groningen: Wolters-Noordhoff.

Dessens, J.A.G., & Jansen, W. (1987). *Operationaliseren: Traditie en kritiek.* State University Utrecht, Utrect.

Devlin, A.S. (2000). City behavior and precautionary measures. *Journal of Applied Social Psychology, 30*(10), 2158-2172.

Diener, E., & Suh, E. (1997). Measuring quality of life: Economic, social, and subjective indicators. *Social Indicators Research, 40*(1-2), 189-216.

Dijk, B. van, & Overbeeke, R. van (2002). *Veiligheids rapportage Amsterdam 2002.* Amsterdam: DSP-groep.

Dijk, J.J.M. van (1990). On the Uses of Local, National and International Crime Surveys. Paper presented at the International Trends in Crime: East Meets West, Bali.

Dijk, J.J.M. van (1994, 21-26 August 1994). Crime and Victim Surveys. Paper presented at the 8th International Symposium on Victimology, Adelaide, South Australia.

Dijk, J.J.M. van, & Kesteren, J. van (1996). The prevalence and perceived seriousness of victimization by crime: Some results of the International Crime Survey. *European Journal of Crime, Criminal Law and Criminal Justice, 4*(1), 48-70.

Dijk, J.J.M. van, & Mayhew, P. (1992). *Criminal Victimization in the Industrialized World: Key Findings of the 1989 and 1992 International Crime Surveys.* The Hague: Ministry of Justice, The Netherlands.

Dijk, J.J.M. van, Mayhew, P., & Killias, M. (1990). *Experiences of Crime across the World: Key Findings from the 1989 International Crime Survey.* Deventer: Kluwer.

Dijk, J.J.M. van, & Steinmetz, C.H.D. (1979). *De WODC-slachtofferenquetes 1974-1979* (Onderzoek en Beleid No. 13). The Hague: Ministry of Justice.

Dijk, T. van, Flight, S., & Oppenhuis, E. (2000). *Voor het beleid, achter de cijfers: De uitkomsten van de GSB-monitor veiligheid en leefbaarheid nader geanalyseerd.* Hilversum: Intomart.

Dillman, D.A. (1991). The design and administration of mail surveys. *Annual Review of Sociology, 17,* 225-249.

Dillman, D.A. (1999). *Mail and Internet Surveys: The Tailored Design Method.* New York: John Wiley Company.

Dillon, K.M., Wolf, E., & Katz, H. (1985). Sex roles, gender, and fear. *Journal of Psychology, 119*(4), 355-359.

Disch, W.B., Harlow, L.L., Campbell, J.F., & Dougan, T.R. (2000). Student functioning, concerns, and socio-personal well-being. *Social Indicators Research, 51*(1), 41-74.

Ditton, J., Farrall, S., Bannister, J., & Gilchrist, E. (1998). Measuring fear of crime. *Criminal Justice Matters, 31,* 10-12.

Ditton, J., Short, E., Phillips, S., Norris, C., & Armstrong, G. (1999). *The Effect of Closed Circuit Television Cameras on Recorded Crime Rates and Public Concern about Crime in Glasgow:* The Scottish Office Central Research Unit.

Dixon, T.L., & Linz, D. (2000). Race and the misrepresentation of victimization on local television news. *Communication Research, 27*(5), 547-573.

Dobash, R.E., & Dobash, R.P. (1988). Research as social action: The struggle for battered women. In: K. Yllö & M.L. Bograd (Eds.), *Feminist Perspectives on Wife Abuse* (pp. 51-74). Newbury Park: Sage Publications.

Doeksen, H. (1997). Reducing crime and the fear of crime by reclaiming New Zealand's suburban street. *Landscape and Urban Planning, 39*(2-3), 243-252.

Dominick, J. (1973). Crime and law enforcement on prime-time television. *Public Opinion Quarterly, 37,* 241-250.

Donnelly, P.G. (1988). Individual and neighborhood influences on fear of crime. *Sociological Focus, 22*(1), 69-85.

Donovan, P. (2002). Crime legends in a new medium: Fact, fiction and loss of authority. *Theoretical Criminology, 6*(2), 189-215.

Doob, A.N., & Macdonald, G.E. (1979). Television viewing and fear of victimization: Is the relationship causal? *Journal of Personality & Social Psychology, 37*(2), 170-179.

Douglas, M. (1986). *Risk Acceptability According to the Social Sciences*. London: Routledge and Kegan Paul.
Douglas, M. (1992). *Risk and Blame: Essays in Cultural Theory*. London; New York: Routledge.
Douglas, M. (1993). Risk as a forensic resource. In: E.J. Burger (Ed.), *Risk* (pp. 1-16). Ann Arbor: University of Michigan Press.
Douglas, M., & Wildavsky, A. (1983). *Risk and Culture: An Essay on the Selection of Technological and Environmental Dangers*. Berkeley: University of California Press.
Dowd, J.J., Sisson, R.P., & Kern, D.M. (1981). Socialization to violence among the aged. *Journal of Gerontology, 36*(3), 350-361.
Drottz-Sjöberg, B.-M. (1991). *Perception of Risk: Studies of Risk Attitudes, Perceptions and Definitions*. Stockholm: Center for Risk Research, Economic Research Institute, Stockholm School of Economics.
Drottz-Sjöberg, B.M., & Sjöberg, L. (1990). Risk perception and worries after the Chernobyl accident. *Journal of Environmental Psychology, 10*(2), 135-149.
Dugan, L. (1999). The effect of criminal victimization on a household's moving decision. *Criminology, 37*(4), 903-930.
Dull, R.T., & Wint, A.V.N. (1997). Criminal victimization and its effect on fear of crime and justice attitudes. *Journal of Interpersonal Violence, 12*(5), 748-758.
Duncan, O.D. (1984). *Notes on Social Measurement: Historical and Critical*. New York: Russel Sage Foundation.
Duncan, O.D. (2000). Gun use surveys: In numbers we trust? *Criminologist, 25*(1), 1-7.
Dupre, M.E., & Mackey, D.A. (2001). Crime in the public mind: Letters to the editor as a measure of crime salience. *Journal of Criminal Justice and Popular Culture, 8*(1), 1-24.
Durant, J. (1998). Once the men in white coats held the promise of a better future.... In: J. Franklin (Ed.), *The Politics of Risk Society* (pp. 70-75). Malden, Mass.: Polity Press.

E

Edwards, A.L. (1957). *Techniques of Attitude Scale Construction*. New York: Appleton-Century-Crofts.
Edwards, R. (1990). Connecting method and epistemology: A white woman interviewing black women. *Women's Studies International Forum, 13*(5), 477-490.
Eijken, A.W.M. (1994). *Criminaliteitsbeeld van Nederland: Aard, omvang, preventie, bestraffing en zorg voor slachtoffers van criminaliteit in de periode 1980-1993*. The Hague: Stafafdeling Informatievoorziening Directie Criminaliteitspreventie Ministerie van Justitie.
Elffers, H. (2000). Kijkt u maar! Ontleedt u maar! Onthult u maar! Kort verslag van een publieksenquete naar de aanvaardbaarheid van technologische hulpmiddelen in de opsporing. Paper presented at the Publieke presentatie Onderzoekschool Maatschappelijke Veiligheid, The Hague.
Ellaway, A., & Macintyre, S. (1998). Does housing tenure predict health in the UK because it exposes people to different levels of housing related hazards in the home or its surroundings? *Health & Place, 4*(2), 141-150.
Ellen, J.M., Adler, N., Gurvey, J.E., Dunlop, M.B.V., Millstein, S.G., & Tschann, J. (2002). Improving predictions of condom behavioral intentions with partner-specific measures of risk perception. *Journal of Applied Social Psychology, 32*(3), 648-663.
Ellickson, R.C. (1996). Controlling chronic misconduct in city spaces: Of panhandlers, skid rows, and public-space zoning. *Yale Law Journal, 105*(5), 1165.

Ellis, A., & Highsmith, D. (2000). About face: Comic books in library literature. *Serials Review, 26*(2), 21-43.

Emsly, C. (1999). The policing of crime in the nineteenth century. In: M. Lappalainen & P. Hirvonen (Eds.), *Crime and Control: In Europe from the Past to the Present* (pp. 144-164). Helsinki: Academy of Finland.

Ensink, B. (1987). Reactie op Junger & Van der Heijden 'Seksueel geweld: Van overdreven angst naar gerechtvaardigde woede' en weer terug? Een kritiek op de publikatie van Ensink en Van Buuren. *Tijdschrift voor criminologie, 29*(4), 100-101.

Ensink, B., & Buuren, E. van (1987). Seksueel geweld: van overdreven angst naar gerechtvaardigde woede. *Tijdschrift voor criminologie, 29*(2/3), 90-100.

Epperlein, T., & Nienstedt, B.C. (1989). Reexamining the use of seriousness weights in an index of crime. *Journal of Criminal Justice, 17*(5), 343-360.

Epstein, S., Lipson, A., Holstein, C., & Huh, E. (1992). Irrational reactions to negative outcomes: Evidence for two conceptual systems. *Journal of Personality and Social Psychology, 62*, 328-339.

Ericson, R.V. (1994). The division of expert knowledge in policing and security. *British Journal of Sociology, 45*(2), 149-175.

Ericson, R.V., Baranek, P.M., & Chan, J.B.L. (1991). *Representing Order: Crime, Law, and Justice in the News Media.* Milton Keynes: Open University Press.

Ericson, R.V., & Haggerty, K.D. (1997). *Policing the Risk Society.* Toronto; Buffalo: University of Toronto Press.

Ernst Eck, J., & Riccio, L.J. (1979). Relationship between reported crime rates and victimization survey results: An empirical and analytical study. *Journal of Criminal Justice, 7*(4), 293-308.

Erskine, H. (1974). The polls: Fear of violence and crime. *The Public Opinion Quarterly, 38*(1), 131-145.

Eschholz, S. (2002). Racial composition of television offenders and viewers' fear of crime. *Critical Criminology, 11*(1), 41-60.

Eschholz, S., Blackwell, B.S., Gertz, M., & Chiricos, T. (2002). Race and attitudes toward the police: Assessing the effects of watching 'reality' police programs. *Journal of Criminal Justice, 30*(4), 327-341.

Eschholz, S., & Bufkin, J. (2001). Crime in the movies: Investigating the efficacy of measures of both sex and gender for predicting victimization and offending in film. *Sociological Forum, 16*(4), 655-676.

Evans, D. (2001). Spatial analyses of crime. *Geography, 86*(Part 3), 211-223.

Evans, D.J., & Fletcher, M. (2000). Fear of crime: Testing alternative hypotheses. *Applied Geography, 20*(4), 395-411.

Evans, G.W., & Garling, T. (1991). Environment, cognition and action: The need for integration. In: T. Garling & G.W. Evans (Eds.), *Environment, Cognition, and Action: An Integrated Approach* (pp. 3-13). New York: Oxford University Press.

Eynde, J. van de, Veno, A., & Hart, A. (2003). They look good but don't work: A case study of global performance indicators in crime prevention. *Evaluation and Program Planning, 26*(3), 237-248.

F

Farge, A. (1995). *Subversive Words: Public Opinion in Eighteenth-century France.* University Park, Pa.: Pennsylvania State University Press.

Farrall, S., Bannister, J., Ditton, J., & Gilchrist, E. (1997). Questioning the measurement of the 'fear of crime': Findings from a major methodological study. *British Journal of Criminology, 37*(4), 658-679.

Farrall, S., & Gadd, D. (2004). Research note: The frequency of the fear of crime. *British Journal of Criminology, 44*(1), 127-132.

Fattah, E.A. (1993). Research on fear of crime: Some common conceptual and measurement problems. In: W. Bilsky, C. Pfeiffer & P. Wetzels (Eds.), *Fear of Crime and Criminal Victimization* (pp. 45-70). Stuttgart: Enke.

Felson, M. (2002). *Crime and Everyday Life* (3rd ed.). Thousand Oaks: Sage Publications.

Felson, R., & Messner, S. (1996). To kill or not to kill? Lethal outcomes in injurious attacks. *Criminology*, 34 (34), 519-545.

Felson, R.B., Messner, S.F., Hoskin, A.W., & Deane, G. (2002). Reasons for reporting and not reporting domestic violence to the police. *Criminology, 40*(3), 617-647.

Ferguson, S.D. (2000). *Researching the Public Opinion Environment: Theories and Methods.* Thousand Oaks, CA: Sage Publications.

Ferraro, K.F. (1995). *Fear of Crime: Interpreting Victimization Risk.* Albany: State University of New York Press.

Ferraro, K.F. (1996). Women's fear of victimization: Shadow of sexual assault? *Social Forces, 75*(2), 667-690.

Ferraro, K.F., & LaGrange, R. (1987). The measurement of fear of crime. *Sociological Inquiry, 57*, 70-101.

Ferraro, K.F., & LaGrange, R.L. (1988). Are older people afraid of crime? *Journal of Aging Studies, 2*(3), 277-287.

Festinger, L. (1954). A theory of social comparison processes. *Human Relations, 7*, 117-140.

Fetchenhauer, D., & Rohde, P.A. (2002). Evolutionary personality psychology and victimology: Sex differences in risk attitudes and short-term orientation and their relation to sex differences in victimizations. *Evolution & Human Behavior, 23*(4), 233-244.

Fetzer, J.H. (1991). Aspects of the theory of definition. In: J.H. Fetzer, D. Shatz & G.N. Schlesinger (Eds.), *Definitions and Definability: Philosophical Perspectives* (pp. 3-17). Dordrecht; Boston: Kluwer Academic Publishers.

Feyerabend, P.K. (1970). Against method: Outline of an anarchistic theory of knowledge. In: M. Radner & S. Winokur (Eds.), *Analyses of Theories and Methods of Physics and Psychology* (Vol. 4, pp. 17-130). Minneapolis: University of Minnesota Press.

Finkelhor, D., & Asdigian, N.L. (1996). Risk factors for youth victimization: Beyond a lifestyles-routine activities theory approach. *Violence and Victims, 11*(1), 3-20.

Fischer, A.H. (1991). *Emotion Scripts: A Study of the Social and Cognitive Facets of Emotions.* Leiden: DSWO Press.

Fischer, C.S. (1981). The public and private worlds of city life. *American Sociological Review, 46*(3), 306-316.

Fischhoff, B. (1995). Risk perception and communication unplugged: 20 Years of process. *Risk Analysis, 15*(2), 137-145.

Fischhoff, B., Gonzalez, R.M., Small, D.A., & Lerner, J.S. (2003). Judged terror risk and proximity to the World Trade Center. *Journal of Risk and Uncertainty, 26*(2-3), 137-151.

Fischhoff, B., Slovic, P., & Lichtenstein, S. (1982). Lay foibles and expert fables in judgments about risk. *American Statistician, 36*(3, Part 2: Proceedings of the Sixth Symposium on Statistics and the Environment), 240-255.

Fischhoff, B., Slovic, P., Lichtenstein, S., Read, S., & Combs, B. (1978). How safe is safe enough? A psychometric study of attitudes towards technological risks and benefits. *Policy Sciences, 9*, 127-152.

Fiselier, J.P.S. (1978). *Slachtoffers van delicten: Een onderzoek naar verborgen criminaliteit.* Utrecht: Ars Aequi Libri.

Fishbein, M., & Ajzen, I. (1975). *Belief, Attitude, Intention, and Behavior: An Introduction to Theory and Research.* Reading, Mass.: Addison-Wesley.

Fisher, B., & Nasar, J.L. (1995). Fear spots in relation to microlevel physical cues: Exploring the overlooked. *Journal of Research in Crime and Delinquency, 32*(2), 214-239.

Fisher, B.S., Cullen, F.T., & Turner, M.G. (2002). Being pursued: Stalking victimization in a national study of college women. *Criminology & Public Policy, 1*(2), 257-308.

Fiske, D.W. (1971). *Measuring the Concepts of Personality*. Chicago: Aldine.

Fiske, S.T., & Taylor, S.E. (1984). *Social Cognition*. Reading, Mass.: Addison-Wesley.

Flanagan, T.J. (1987). Change and influence in popular criminology: Public attributions of crime causation. *Journal of Criminal Justice, 15*(3), 231-243.

Flango, V.E. (1979). Urban governance and police expenditures. *Urban Systems, 4*(1), 53-63.

Flavin, J. (2001). Feminism for the mainstream criminologist: An invitation. *Journal of Criminal Justice, 29*(4), 271-285.

Flight, S. (2003). *Onveiligheidsgevoelens in Amsterdam: Kwantitatief onderzoek naar achtergronden van onveiligheidsgevoelens* (No. 03/62). Amsterdam: DSP-groep.

Fontaine, J.R.J., Poortinga, Y.H., Setiadi, B., & Markam, S.S. (2002). Cognitive structure of emotion terms in Indonesia and the Netherlands. *Cognition & Emotion, 16*(1), 61-86.

Forgas, J.P. (1980). Images of crime: A multidimensional analysis of individual differences in crime perception. *International Journal of Psychology, 15*(4), 287-299.

Forgas, J.P. (1981a). Affective and emotional influences on episode representations. In: J.P. Forgas (Ed.), *Social Cognition: Perspectives on Everyday Understanding* (Vol. 26., pp. 165-180). London; New York: Published in cooperation with European Association of Experimental Social Psychology by Academic Press.

Forgas, J.P. (1981b). *Social Cognition: Perspectives on Everyday Understanding*. London; New York: Published in cooperation with European Association of Experimental Social Psychology by Academic Press.

Forgas, J.P. (2000). *Feeling and Thinking: The Role of Affect in Social Cognition*. Cambridge; New York Paris: Cambridge University Press; Editions de la Maison des Sciences de lâ Homme.

Forgas, J.P. (2001). *Handbook of Affect and Social Cognition*. Mahwah, NJ: L.Erlbaum Associates.

Foucault, M. (1991). Governmentality. In: G. Burchell, C. Gordon & P. Miller (Eds.), *The Foucault Effect: Studies in Governmentality* (pp. 87-104). London: Harvester Wheatsheaf.

Fowler, F.J. (1979). Residential neighborhood crime control project: Hartford, Connecticut, 1973, 1975-1977, 1979 [Computer file]. Conducted by the Hartford Institute of Criminal and Social Justice. ICPSR ed. Ann Arbor, MI: Inter-university Consortium for Political and Social Research [producer and distributor], 1982.

Fowler, F.J., McCalla, M.E., & Mangione, T.W. (1979). *Reducing Residential Crime and Fear: The Hartford Neighborhood Crime Prevention Program: Executive Summary*. Washington, DC: U.S. Dept. of Justice; National Institute of Law Enforcement and Criminal Justice.

Fox, A.J. (1981). Mortality statistics and the assessment of risk. In: F. Warner (Ed.), *The Assessment and Perception of Risk* (pp. 65-75). London: The Royal Society.

Frank, R.H. (1988). *Passions within Reason: The Strategic Role of the Emotions*. New York: W. W. Norton & Company.

Franke, H. (1994). Violent crime in the Netherlands: A historical-sociological analysis. *Crime, Law and Social Change, 21*(1), 73-100.

Franken, R.E., Gibson, K.J., & Rowland, G.L. (1992). Sensation seeking and the tendency to view the world as threatening. *Personality and Individual Differences, 13*(1), 31-38.

Franklin, J. (Ed.). (1998a). *The Politics of Risk Society*. Malden, Mass.: Polity Press.

Franklin, J. (1998b). Introduction. In: J. Franklin (Ed.), *The Politics of Risk Society* (pp. 1-8). Malden, Mass.: Polity Press.

Freedgood, E. (2000). *Victorian Writing about Risk: Imagining a Safe England in a Dangerous World*. Cambridge, UK; New York: Cambridge University Press.

Frenken, J. (1997). Seksuele misdrijven en seksuele delinquenten. In: P.J. van Koppen, D.J. Hessing & H.F.M. Crombag (Eds.), *Het hart van de zaak* (pp. 177-219). Deventer: Gouda Quint.

Freudenburg, W.R. (1993). Risk and recreancy: Weber, the division of labor, and the rationality of risk perceptions. *Social Forces, 71*(4), 909-932.

Frewer, L.J., Miles, S., & Marsh, R. (2002). The media and genetically modified foods: Evidence in support of social amplification of risk. *Risk Analysis, 22*(4), 701-711.

Fried, C.S., & Reppucci, N.D. (2001). Criminal decision making: The development of adolescent judgment, criminal responsibility, and culpability. *Law and Human Behavior, 25*(1), 45-61.

Friedman, L.M. (1993). *Crime and Punishment in American History*. New York: BasicBooks.

Frijda, N.H. (1988). *De emoties: Een overzicht van onderzoek en theorie*. Amsterdam: Bakker.

Frijda, N.H., & Elshout, J.J. (1976). Probleemoplossen en denken. In: J.A. Michon, E.G.J. Eijkman & L.F.W. DeKlerk (Eds.), *Handboek der psychonomie* (pp. 413-446). Deventer: Van Loghum Slaterus.

Fuentes, K., & Cox, B. (2000). Assessment of anxiety in older adults: A community-based survey and comparison with younger adults. *Behaviour Research and Therapy, 38*(3), 297-309.

Funder, D.C. (1995). On the accuracy of personality judgment: A realistic approach. *Psychological Review, 102*(4), 652-670.

Funkhouser, G.R. (1973). The issues of the sixties: An exploratory study in the dynamics of public opinion. *Public Opinion Quarterly, 37*(1), 62-75.

Furedi, F. (1997). *Culture of Fear: Risk-taking and the Morality of Low Expectation*. London: Cassell.

G

Gabriel, U., & Greve, W. (2003). The psychology of fear of crime: Conceptual and methodological perspectives. *British Journal of Criminology, 43*(3), 600-614.

The Gallup Poll [Online]. Retrieved from http://www.gallup.com/poll/ [25 July 2005] Princeton, NJ: The Gallup Organization, Inc.

Gaquin, D. (1978). Measuring fear of crime: The national crime survey's attitude data. *Victimology, 3*(3), 314.

Gardner, C.B. (1995). *Passing by: Gender and Public Harassment*. Berkeley: University of California Press.

Gardner, J. (1994). Use of Official Statistics and Crime Survey Data in Determining Violence against Women. Paper presented at the 89th International Symposium on Victimology held in Adelaide, South Australia 21-12 August 1994.

Garfinkel, A. (1981). *Forms of Explanation: Rethinking the Questions in Social Theory*. New Haven: Yale University Press.

Garland, D. (2000). The culture of high crime societies: Some preconditions of recent 'law and order' policies. *British Journal of Criminology, 40*(3), 347-375.

Garland, D. (2001). *The Culture of Control: Crime and Social Order in Contemporary Society*. Oxford: Oxford University Press.

Garland, D. (2003). The rise of risk. In: R.V. Ericson & A. Doyle (Eds.), *Risk and Morality* (pp. 48-86). Toronto: University of Toronto Press.

Garofalo, J. (1977a). *The Police and Public Opinion: An Analysis of Victimization and Attitude Data from 13 American Cities*. Rockville, Md. Washington: U.S. Dept. of Justice Law Enforcement Assistance Administration National Criminal Justice Information and Statistics Service.

Garofalo, J. (1977b). *Public Opinion about Crime: The Attitudes of Victims and Nonvictims in Selected Cities*. Rockville, Md. Washington: U.S. Dept. of Justice Law Enforcement

Assistance Administration National Criminal Justice Information and Statistics Service.

Garofalo, J. (1979). Victimization and the fear of crime. *Journal of Research in Crime and Delinquency, 1*, 241-253.

Garofalo, J. (1981a). The fear of crime: Causes and consequences. *The Journal of Criminal Law & Criminology, 72*(2), 839.

Garofalo, J. (1981b). Crime and the mass media: A selective review of research. *Journal of Research in Crime and Delinquency, 18*(2), 319-350.

Garofalo, J. (1986). Lifestyles and victimization: An update. In: E.A. Fattah (Ed.), *From Crime Policy to Victim Policy: Reorienting the Justice System* (pp. 135-166). New York, NY: St. Martin's Press.

Garofalo, J., & Hindelang, M.J. (1977). *An Introduction to the National Crime Survey*. Washington: U.S. Dept. of Justice, Law Enforcement Assistance Administration, National Criminal Justice Information and Statistics Service.

Garofalo, J., & Laub, J. (1978). The fear of crime: Broadening our perspective. *Victimology, 3*, 242-253.

Gates, L.B., & Rohe, W. (1987). Fear and reactions to crime: A revised model. *Urban Affairs Quarterly, 22*, 425-453.

Gaubatz, K.T. (1995). *Crime in the Public Mind*. Ann Arbor: University of Michigan Press.

Gavey, N. (1999). 'I wasn't raped, but...': Revisiting definitional problems in sexual victimization. In: S. Lamb (Ed.), *New Versions of Victims: Feminists Struggle with the Concept* (pp. 57-81). New York: New York University Press.

Geary, D.C. (1995). Reflections of evolution and culture in children's cognition: Implications for mathematical development and instruction. *American Psychologist, 50*(1), 24-37.

Geary, D.C. (1996). The evolution of cognition and the social construction of knowledge. *American Psychologist, 51*(3), 265-266.

Gemeente Breda, Afdeling Statistiek en Onderzoek. Slachtofferschap en politiefunctioneren [P1127] [datafile]. Amsterdam, Steinmetz-Archief.

Gergen, K.J. (1985). The social constructivist movement in modern psychology. *American Psychologist, 40*, 266-275.

Gergen, K.J. (1997). The place of the psyche in a constructed world. *Theory & Psychology, 7*(6), 723-746.

Gerritsen, L., & De Jong-Gierveld, J. (1995). Validating the De Jong-Gierveld's loneliness measurement instrument: Young adults' concepts of loneliness investigated by means of the vignette technique. In: J.J. Hox & W. Jansen (Eds.), *Measurement Problems in Social and Behavioral Research* (SCO-rapport 381, pp. 89-113). Amsterdam: SCO-Kohnstamm Instituut voor Onderzoek van Opvoeding en Onderwijs.

Gettemy, C.F. (1918). The work of the several States of the United States in the field of statistics. In: J. Koren (Ed.), *The History of Statistics: Their Development and Progress in Many Countries: In Memoirs to Commemorate the Seventy Fifth Anniversary of the American Statistical Association* (pp. 690-739). New York: Macmillan.

Gibbs, J.J., Puzzanchera, C.M., Hanrahan, K.J., & Giever, D. (1998). The influence of personal safety and other environmental concerns on sense of control and emotional well-being. *Criminal Justice and Behavior, 25*(4), 403-425.

Gibson, C.L., Zhao, J.H., Lovrich, N.P., & Gaffney, M.J. (2002). Social integration, individual perceptions of collective efficacy, and fear of crime in three cities. *Justice Quarterly, 19*(3), 537-564.

Giddens, A. (1990). *The Consequences of Modernity*. Cambridge, UK, Oxford UK: Polity Press; Basil Blackwell.

Giddens, A. (1998). Risk society: The context of British politics. In: J. Franklin (Ed.), *The Politics of Risk Society* (pp. 23-34). Malden, Mass.: Polity Press.

Gifford, R. (1987). *Environmental Psychology: Principles and Practice*. Boston: Allyn and Bacon.

Gignilliat, R.L. (1977). Using the national crime survey files. *Urban Systems, 2*(4), 183-195.

Gilchrist, E., Bannister, J., Ditton, J., & Farrall, S. (1998). Women and the 'fear of crime': Challenging the accepted stereotype. *British Journal of Criminology, 38*(2), 283-298.

Gilliam, F.D., Jr., & Iyengar, S. (2000). Prime suspects: The influence of local television news on the viewing public. *American Journal of Political Science, 44*(3), 560-573.

Gilman, D. (1992). What's a theory to do... with seeing? Or some empirical considerations for observation and theory. *The British Journal for the Philosophy of Science, 43*(3), 287-309.

Girling, E., Loader, I., & Sparks, R. (1998). A telling tale: A case of vigilantism and its aftermath in an English town. *British Journal of Sociology, 49*(3), 474-490.

Glaser, B. (2002a). Conceptualization: On theory and theorizing using grounded theory. *International Journal of Qualitative Methods, 1*(2, Article 3).

Glaser, B.G. (2002b). Constructivist grounded theory? *Forum Qualitative Sozialforschung / Forum: Qualitative Social Research [On-line Journal], 3*(3).

Glaser, B.G., & Strauss, A.L. (1967). *The Discovery of Grounded Theory: Strategies for Qualitative Research*. Chicago: Aldine Pub. Co.

Glass, D.V. (1973). *The Development of Population Statistics: A Collective Reprint of Materials Concerning the History of Census Taking and Vital Registration in England and Wales*. Farnborough: Gregg International publishers.

Glassman, M. (1996). The argument for constructivism. *American Psychologist March, 51*(3), 264-265.

Glassner, B. (1999). *The Culture of Fear: Why Americans are Afraid of the Wrong Things*. New York: Basic Books.

Godfrey, B. (2003). Counting and accounting for the decline in non-lethal violence in England, Australia, and New Zealand, 1880-1920. *British Journal of Criminology, 43*(2), 340-353.

Gomme, I.M. (1986). Fear of crime among Canadians: A multi-variate analysis. *Journal of Criminal Justice, 14*(3), 249-258.

Goodey, J. (1995). Fear of crime: Children and gendered socialization. In: R.E. Dobash, R.P. Dobash & L. Noaks (Eds.), *Gender and Crime* (pp. 295-312). Cardiff: University of Wales Press.

Goodey, J. (1997). Boys don't cry: Masculinities, fear of crime and fearlessness. *British Journal of Criminology, 37*(3), 401-418.

Goodstein, L., & Shotland, R.L. (1980). The crime causes crime model: A critical review of the relationships between fear of crime, bystander surveillance, and changes in the crime rate. *Victimology, 5*(2), 133-151.

Gordon, M., & Heath, L. (1981). The news business, crime, and fear. In: D. Lewis (Ed.), *Reactions to Crime* (pp. 227-250). Thousand Oaks, CA: Sage.

Gordon, M.T., & Riger, S. (1978). The fear of rape project. *Victimology: An International Journal, 3*(3), 346.

Gordon, M.T., & Riger, S. (1989). *The Female Fear*. New York London: Free Press; Collier Macmillan.

Gordon, R.M. (1980). Fear. *The Philosophical Review, 89*(4), 560-578.

Gore, A. (2004). The politics of fear, *Social Research* (Vol. 71, pp. 779-798): New School for Social Research.

Gottfredson, M.R. (1984). *Victims of Crime: The Dimensions of Risk* (No. 81). London: Home Office Research and Planning Unit.

382 INTERPRETING FEAR, CRIME, RISK AND UNSAFETY

Gottfredson, M.R., & Hindelang, M.J. (1977). A consideration of telescoping and memory decay biases in victimization surveys. *Journal of Criminal Justice, 5*(3), 205-216.

Green, E., Hebron, S., & Woodward, D. (1987). Women, leisure and social control. In: J. Hanmer & M. Maynard (Eds.), *Women, Violence, and Social Control* (pp. 75-92). Atlantic Highlands, NJ: Humanities Press International.

Green, G., Gilbertson, J.M., & Grimsley, M.F.J. (2002). Fear of crime and health in residential tower blocks: A case study in Liverpool, UK. *European Journal of Public Health, 12*(1), 10-15.

Green, J. (1997). *Risk and Misfortune: A Social Construction of Accidents.* London: UCL Press.

Greenberg, S. (1980). Characteristics of high and low crime neighborhoods in Atlanta, 1980 [Computer file]. ICPSR ed. Ann Arbor, MI: Inter-university Consortium for Political and Social Research [producer and distributor], 1997.

Greenberg, M.S., & Beach, S.R. (2004). Property crime victims' decision to notify the police: Social, cognitive, and affective determinants. *Law and Human Behavior, 28*(2), 177-186.

Greenberg, M.S., & Ruback, R.B. (1984). Criminal victimization: Introduction and overview. *Journal of Social Issues, 40*(1), 1-8.

Greene, J.R., & Bynum, T.S. (1982). TV crooks: Implications of latent role models for theories of delinquency. *Journal of Criminal Justice, 10*(3), 177-190.

Greenwood, D.J., & Levin, M. (2000). Reconstructing the relationship between universities and society through action research. In: N.K. Denzin & Y.S. Lincoln (Eds.), *Handbook of Qualitative Research* (2nd ed., pp. 85-106). Thousand Oaks: Sage.

Greer, S. (1997). Nietzsche and social construction: Directions for a postmodern historiography. *Theory & Psychology, 7*(1), 83-100.

Grobe, D., & Douthitt, R. (1995). Consumer acceptance of recombinant bovine growth hormone: Interplay between beliefs and perceived risks. *Journal of Consumer Affairs, 29*(1).

Grobe, D., Douthitt, R., & Zepeda, L. (1999a). A model of consumers' risk perceptions toward recombinant bovine growth hormone (rhGH): The impact of risk characteristics. *Risk Analysis, 19*(4), 661-673.

Grobe, D., Douthitt, R., & Zepeda, L. (1999b). Consumer risk perception profiles regarding recombinant bovine growth hormone (rbGH). *Journal of Consumer Affairs, 33*(2), 254-275.

Groenhuijsen, M.S. (1998). Stalking: Strafrecht als interventierecht. *Delikt & delinkwent, 28*(6), 521-526.

Grogger, J., & Weatherford, M.S. (1995). Crime, policing and the perception of neighborhood safety. *Political Geography, 14*(6/7), 521-541.

Groot, A.D. de (1972). *Methodologie: Grondslagen van onderzoek en denken in de gedragswetenschappen* (7th ed.). The Hague: Mouton & Co.

Groot, A.D. de & Medendorp, F.L. (1986). *Term, begrip, theorie: Inleiding tot de signifische begripsanalyse.* Meppel: Boom.

Groves, R.M. (1987). Research on survey data quality. *Public Opinion Quarterly, 51*(part 2: Supplement: 50th Anniversary Issue), S156-S172.

Groves, R.M. (1990). Theories and methods of telephone surveys. *Annual Review of Sociology, 16*, 221-240.

Gudjonsson, G.H. (1984). Attribution of blame for criminal acts and its relationship with personality. *Personality and Individual Differences, 5*(1), 53-58.

Guo, Z.S., Zhu, J.J.H., & Chen, H.L. (2001). Mediated reality bites: Comparing direct and indirect experience as sources of perceptions across two communities in China. *International Journal of Public Opinion Research, 13*(4), 398-418.

Guttman, L. (1954). An outline of some new methodology for social research. *Public Opinion Quarterly, 18*(4), 395-404.

Guttman, L. (1959a). Introduction to facet design and analysis. *Acta Psychologica, 15*, 130-138.

Guttman, L. (1959b). A structural theory for intergroup beliefs and action. *American Sociological Review, 24*(3), 318-328.

Guttman, R., & Greenbaum, C.W. (1998). Facet theory: Its development and current status. *European Psychologist, 3*(1), 13-36.

H

Habel, U., & Schneider, F. (2001). Psychosocial intervention to help child and adolescent witnesses in court. *Psychotherapie Psychosomatik Medizinische Psychologie, 51*(3-4), 160-165.

Hacking, I. (1964). On the foundations of statistics. *British Journal for the Philosophy of Science, 15*(57), 1-26.

Hacking, I. (1967a). Possibility. *The Philosophical Review, 76*(2), 143-168.

Hacking, I. (1967b). Slightly more realistic personal probability. *Philosophy of Science, 34*(4), 311-325.

Hacking, I. (1971). Equipossibility theories of probability. *British Journal for the Philosophy of Science, 22*(4), 339-355.

Hacking, I. (1975a). All kinds of possibility. *Philosophical Review, 84*(3), 321-337.

Hacking, I. (1975b). *The Emergence of Probability: A Philosophical Study of Early Ideas about Probability, Induction and Statistical Inference.* London; New York: Cambridge University Press.

Hacking, I. (1983). Nineteenth-century cracks in the concept of determinism. *Journal of the History of Ideas, 44*(3), 455-476.

Hacking, I. (1988). Symposium papers, comments and an abstract: The sociology of knowledge about child abuse. *Nous, 22*(1, 1988 A.P.A. Central Division Meetings), 53-63.

Hacking, I. (1990). *The Taming of Chance.* Cambridge, UK; New York: Cambridge University Press.

Hacking, I. (1999a). *The Social Construction of What?* Cambridge: Harvard University Press.

Hacking, I. (1999b). The time frame problem: The law, social construction, and the sciences. *The Social Science Journal, 36*(4), 563-573.

Hacking, I. (2000). How inevitable are the results of successful science? *Philosophy of Science, 67*(3, Supplement), S58-S71.

Haggerty, K. (2001). Negotiated measures: The institutional micropolitics of official criminal justice statistics. *Studies in History and Philosophy of Science*, 32A (34), 705-722.

Hale, C. (1996). Fear of crime: A review of the literature. *International Review of Victimology, 4*, 79-150.

Hales, J., & Stratford, N. (1999). *1998 British Crime Survey: England and Wales: Technical Report* (No. SCPR P1720). London: SCPR.

Halfmann, J. (1999). Community and life-chances: Risk movements in the United States and Germany. *Environmental Values, 8*, 177-197.

Hall, D.M. (1998). The victims of stalking. In: J.R. Meloy (Ed.), *The Psychology of Stalking: Clinical and Forensic Perspectives* (pp. 113-137). San Diego: Academic Press.

Hamblin, R.L. (1974). Social attitudes: Magnitude measurement and theory. In: H.M. Blalock (Ed.), *Measurement in the Social Sciences: Theories and Strategies* (pp. 61-120). London: Macmillan.

Hamlin, J.E. (1988). Who's the victim? Women, control, and consciousness. *Women's Studies International Forum, 11*(3), 223-233.

Hampson, S.E., Severson, H.H., Burns, W.J., Slovic, P., & Fisher, K.J. (2001). Risk perception, personality factors and alcohol use among adolescents. *Personality and Individual Differences, 30*(1), 167-181.

Hancock, G.R., & Freeman, M.J. (2001). Power and sample size for the root mean square error of approximation test of not close fit in structural equation modeling. *Educational and Psychological Measurement, 61*(5), 741-759.

Hanmer, J., & Maynard, M. (Eds.). (1987). *Women, Violence, and Social Control.* Atlantic Highlands, NJ: Humanities Press International.

Hansen, E.B., & Breivik, G. (2001). Sensation seeking as a predictor of positive and negative risk behaviour among adolescents. *Personality and Individual Differences, 30*(4), 627-640.

Hanson, R.F., Smith, D.W., Kilpatrick, D.G., & Freedy, J.R. (2000). Crime-related fears and demographic diversity in Los Angeles County after the 1992 civil disturbances. *Journal of Community Psychology, 28*(6), 607-623.

Harcourt, B.E. (1998). Reflecting on the subject: A critique of the social influence conception of deterrence, the broken windows theory, and order-maintenance policing New York style. *Michigan Law Review, 97*(2), 291-389.

Harris, R. (1969). *The Fear of Crime.* New York: Praeger.

Hart, J. de, Maas-DeWaal, C., & Roes, T. (Eds.). (2002). *Zekere banden: sociale cohesie, leefbaarheid en veiligheid.* The Hague: Sociaal en Cultureel Planbureau.

Hartnagel, T.F. (1979). The perception and fear of crime: Implications for neighborhood cohesion, Social Activity, and Community Affect. *Social Forces, 58*(1), 176-193.

Hathaway, J.E., Mucci, L.A., Silverman, J.G., Brooks, D.R., Mathews, R., & Pavlos, C.A. (2000). Health status and health care use of Massachusetts women reporting partner abuse. *American Journal of Preventive Medicine, 19*(4), 302-307.

Havenaar, J.M., Wilde, E.J. de, Bout, J. van den, Drottz-Sjöberg, B.M., & Brink, W. van den (2003). Perception of risk and subjective health among victims of the Chernobyl disaster. *Social Science & Medicine, 56*(3), 569-572.

Hayes, M.V. (1992). On the epistemology of risk: Language, logic and social science. *Social Science & Medicine, 35*(4), 401-407.

Haynie, D.L. (1998). The gender gap in fear of crime, 1973-1994: A methodological approach. *Criminal Justice Review, 23*(1), 29-50.

Heath, H., & Cowley, S. (2004). Developing a grounded theory approach: A comparison of Glaser and Strauss. *International Journal of Nursing Studies, 41*(2), 141-150.

Heath, L. (1984). Impact of newspaper crime reports on fear of crime: Multimethodological investigation. *Journal of Personality and Social Psychology, 47*(2), 263-276.

Heath, L., & Gilbert, K. (1996). Mass media and fear of crime. *American Behavioral Scientist, 39*(4), 379-386.

Heath, L., Kavanagh, J., & Thompson, S.R. (2001). Perceived vulnerability and fear of crime: Why fear stays high when crime rates drop. *Journal of Offender Rehabilitation, 33*(2), 1-14.

Heath, L., & Petraitis, J. (1987). Television viewing and fear of crime: Where is the mean world? *Basic and Applied Social Psychology, 8,* 97-123.

Hedley, M. (2002). The geometry of gendered conflict in popular film: 1986–2000. *Sex Roles, 47*(5-6), 201-217.

Heimer, C.A. (1988). Social structure, psychology, and the estimation of risk. *Annual Review of Sociology, 14,* 491-519.

Heise, D.R. (1970). The semantic differential and attitude research. In: G.F. Summers (Ed.), *Attitude Measurement* (pp. 235-253). Chicago: Rand McNally.

Hemenway, D., Solnick, S.J., & Azrael, D.R. (1995). Firearms and community feelings of safety. *Journal of Criminal Law & Criminology, 86*(1), 121-132.

Hempel, C.G. (1952). *Fundamentals of Concept Formation in Empirical Science* (Vol. 2; no. 7). Chicago: University of Chicago Press.

Henderson, M.L., Cullen, F.T., Cao, L., Browning, S.L., & Kopache, R. (1997). The impact of race on perceptions of criminal injustice. *Journal of Criminal Justice, 25*(6), 447-462.

Hening, J., & Maxfield, M.G. (1978). Reducing fear of crime: Strategies for intervention. *Victimology, 3*(3), 297.

Herbert, S. (2001). Policing the contemporary city: Fixing broken windows or shoring up neo-liberalism? *Theoretical Criminology, 5*(4), 445-466.

Herbert, S. (2002). Illusion of order: The false promise of broken windows policing. *Theoretical Criminology, 6*(1), 103-106.

Herek, G.M., Gillis, J.R., & Cogan, J.C. (1999). Psychological sequelae of hate-crime victimization among lesbian, gay, and bisexual adults. *Journal of Consulting and Clinical Psychology, 67*(6), 945-951.

Herzog, T.R., & Chernick, K.K. (2000). Tranquility and danger in urban and natural settings. *Journal of Environmental Psychology, 20*(1), 29-39.

Hier, S.P. (2003). Risk and panic in late modernity: Implications of the converging sites of social anxiety. *British Journal of Sociology, 54*(1), 3-20.

Hightower, N.R. van., Gorton, J., & DeMoss, C.L. (2000). Predictive models of domestic violence and fear of intimate partners among migrant and seasonal farm worker women. *Journal of Family Violence, 15*(2), 137-154.

Hill, G.D., Howell, F.M., & Driver, E.T. (1985). Gender, fear, and protective handgun ownership. *Criminology, 23*(3), 541-552.

Hill, M.S., & Fischer, A.R. (2001). Does entitlement mediate the link between masculinity and rape-related variables? *Journal of Counseling Psychology,*January, *48*(1), 39-50.

Hindelang, M.J. (1974). The uniform crime reports revisited. *Journal of Criminal Justice, 2*(1), 1-17.

Hindelang, M.J., Gottfredson, M.R., & Garofalo, J. (1978). *Victims of Personal Crime: An Empirical Foundation for a Theory of Personal Victimization.* Cambridge, Mass.: Balinger.

Hintikka, J. (1991). Towards a general theory of identifiability. In: J.H. Fetzer, D. Shatz & G.N. Schlesinger (Eds.), *Definitions and Definability: Philosophical Perspectives* (pp. 161-183). Dordrecht: Kluwer Academic Publishers.

Hoffman, P.B., & Hardyman, P.L. (1986). Crime seriousness scales: Public perception and feedback to criminal justice policymakers. *Journal of Criminal Justice, 14*(5), 413-431.

Hollander, J.A. (2001). Vulnerability and dangerousness: The construction of gender through conversation about violence. *Gender & Society, 15*(1), 83-109.

Hollway, W., & Jefferson, T. (1997). The risk society in an age of anxiety: Situating fear of crime. *British Journal of Sociology, 48*(2), 255-266.

Holton, G. (1998). *The Scientific Imagination.* Cambridge, Mass.: Harvard University Press.

Horlick-Jones, T. (1998). Meaning and contextualisation in risk assessment. *Reliability Engineering & System Safety, 59*(1), 79-89.

Hough, J.M., & Mayhew, P. (1983). *The British Crime Survey: First Report.* London: Home Office Research and Statistics Department.

Hough, M. (1986). Victims of violent crime, findings from the British crime survey. In: E.A. Fattah (Ed.), *From Crime Policy to Victim Policy: Reorienting the Justice System* (pp. 117-132). New York, NY: St. Martin's Press.

Houts, S., & Kassab, C. (1997). Rotter's social learning theory and fear of crime: Differences by race and ethnicity. *Social Science Quarterly, 78*(1), 122-136.

Howard, G.S. (1991). Culture tales: A narrative approach to thinking, cross-cultural psychology, and psychotherapy. *American Psychologist,* March, *46*(3), 187-197.

Howard, J.A. (1984). The 'normal' victim: The effects of gender stereotypes on reactions to victims. *Social Psychology Quarterly, 47*(3), 270-281.

Hox, J.J. (1997). From theoretical concept to survey question. In: L. Lyberg, P. Biemer, M. Collins, E. DeLeeuw, C. Dippo, N. Schwarz & D. Trewin (Eds.), *Survey Measurement and Process Quality* (pp. 47-69). New York: John Wiley & Sons.

Hox, J.J., & Jansen, W. (Eds.). (1995). *Measurement Problems in Social and Behavioral Research* (SCO-rapport 381). Amsterdam: SCO-Kohnstamm Instituut voor Onderzoek van Opvoeding en Onderwijs.

Hox, J.J., & Jong-Gierveld, J. de (Eds.). (1990). *Operationalization and Research Strategy.* Amsterdam: Swets & Zeitlinger.

Hox, J.J., Mellenbergh, G.J., & Swanborn, P.G. (Eds.). (1995). *Facet Theory: Analysis and Design.* Zeist: SETOS.

Hox, J.J.C.M. (1986). *Het gebruik van hulptheorieën bij operationalisering: Een studie rond het begrip subjectief welbevinden.* Proefschrift Universiteit van Amsterdam, Amsterdam.

Hu, L., & Bentler, P.M. (1999). Cutoff criteria for fit indexes in covariance structure analysis: Conventional criteria versus new alternatives. *Structural Equation Modeling, 6*(1), 1-55.

Huff, D. (1969). *How to Lie with Statistics* (10th ed.). London: Lowe & Brydone.

Hughes, P.P., Marshall, D., & Sherrill, C. (2003). Multidimensional analysis of fear and confidence of university women relating to crimes and dangerous situations. *Journal of Interpersonal Violence, 18*(1), 33-49.

Huls, F.W.M., Schreuders, M.M., Horst-Van Breukelen, M.H. ter, & Tulder, F.P. van (2001). *Criminaliteit en rechtshandhaving 2000: Ontwikkelingen en samenhangen.* The Hague: Wetenschappelijk Onderzoek- en Documentatiecentrum/ Centraal Bureau voor de Statstiek.

Humphrey, J.A., & White, J.W. (2000). Women's vulnerability to sexual assault from adolescence to young adulthood. *Journal of Adolescent Health, 27*(6), 419-424.

Hunter, A., & Baumer, T.L. (1982). Street traffic, social integration, and fear of crime. *Sociological Inquiry, 52*, 123-131.

Hurwitz, J., & Smithey, S. (1998). Gender differences on crime and punishment. *Political Research Quarterly, 51*(1), 89-115.

Huys, H.W.J.M. (1997). *Veel voorkomende criminaliteit: Kerncijfers 1980-1996.* Voorburg: Centraal Bureau voor de Statistiek.

Huys, H.W.J.M. (2001). Slachtoffers van criminaliteit. In: F.W.M. Huls, M.M. Schreuders, M.H. ter Horst-Van Breukelen & F.P. van Tulder (Eds.), *Criminaliteit en rechtshandhaving 2000: Ontwikkelingen en samenhangen* (pp. 73-201). The Hague: Wetenschappelijk Onderzoek- en Documentatiecentrum/ Centraal Bureau voor de Statistiek.

I

Illner, M. (1998). The changing quality of life in a post-communist country: The case of Czech Republic. *Social Indicators Research, 43*(1), 141-170.

Inciardi, J.A., & McBride, D.C. (1976). Victim survey research: Implications for criminal justice planning. *Journal of Criminal Justice, 4*(2), 147-151.

Ingalls, R.P. (1988). *Urban vigilantes in the New South: Tampa, 1882-1936.* Knoxville: University of Tennessee Press.

Inhorn, M.C., & Whittle, K.L. (2001). Feminism meets the 'new' epidemiologies: toward an appraisal of antifeminist biases in epidemiological research on women's health. *Social Science & Medicine, 53*(5), 553-567.

Innes, M., & Fielding, N. (2002). From community to communicative policing: 'Signal crimes' and the problem of public reassurance. *Sociological Research Online, 7*(2), U116-U131.

Ippolito, D.S., Walker, T.G., & Kolson, K.L. (1976). *Public Opinion and Responsible Democracy.* Englewood Cliffs, NJ: Prentice-Hall.

Irwin, A., Allan, S., & Welsh, I. (2000). Nuclear risks: Three problematics. In: B. Adam, U. Beck & J. van Loon (Eds.), *The Risk Society and Beyond: Critical Issues for Social Theory* (pp. 78-104). London; Thousand Oaks, CA: Sage.

J

Jackson, J. (2004). Experience and expression: Social and cultural significance in the fear of crime. *British Journal of Criminology, 44*(6), 946-966.

Jacoby, W.G. (1998). *Statistical Graphics for Visualizing Multivariate Data*. London: Sage.

James, W. (1997). The names of fear: Memory, history, and the ethnography of feeling among Uduk refugees. *Journal of the Royal Anthropological Institute, 3*(1), 115-131.

Janson, P., & Ryder, L.K. (1983). Crime and the elderly: The relationship between risk and fear. *The Gerontologist, 23*(2), 207-212.

Jasanoff, S. (1998). The political science of risk perception. *Reliability Engineering & System Safety, 59*(1), 91-99.

Jaycox, V.H. (1978). The elderly's fear of crime: Rational or irrational. *Victimology: An International Journal, 3*(3), 329.

Jeffords, C.R. (1983). The situational relationship between age and the fear of crime. *International Journal of Aging & Human Development, 17*(2), 103-111.

Jenkins, C.R., & Dillman, D.A. (1997). Towards a theory of self-administered questionnaire design. In: L. Lyberg, P. Biemer, M. Collins, E. DeLeeuw, C. Dippo, N. Schwarz & D. Trewin (Eds.), *Survey Measurement and Process Quality* (pp. 165-196). New York: John Wiley & Sons.

Jenkins, P. (1989). Serial murder in the United States 1900-1940: A historical perspective. *Journal of Criminal Justice, 17*(5), 377-392.

Jenni, K., & Loewenstein, G. (1997). Explaining the identifiable victim effect. *Journal of Risk and Uncertainty, 14*(3), 235-257.

Jensen, G.F., & Brownfield, D. (1986). Gender, lifestyles, and victimization: Beyond routine activity. *Violence & Victims, 1*(2), 85-99.

Jimenez, J.A., & Abreu, J.M. (2003). Race and sex effects on attitudinal perceptions of acquaintance rape. *Journal of Counseling Psychology, 50*(2), 252-256.

Joffe, H. (1999). *Risk and 'the Other'*. Cambridge, UK; New York, NY: Cambridge University Press.

Johnson, B.B., & Covello, V.T. (Eds.). (1987). *The Social and Cultural Construction of Risk: Essays on Risk Selection and Perception*. Dordrecht; Boston Norwell: D. Reidel; Kluwer Academic Publishers.

Johnson, B.B., & Slovic, P. (1995). Presenting uncertainty in health risk assessment: Initial studies of its effects on risk perception and trust. *Risk Analysis, 15 (4)*, 485-494.

Johnson, C.Y., Bowker, J.M., & Cordell, H.K. (2001). Outdoor recreation constraints: An examination of race, gender, and rural dwelling. *Southern Rural Sociology, 17*, 111-133.

Johnson, H., & Sacco, V.F. (1995). Researching violence against women: Statistics-Canada national survey. *Canadian Journal of Criminology: Revue Canadienne de Criminologie, 37*(3), 281-304.

Johnson, I., & Sigler, R. (2000). Forced sexual intercourse among intimates. *Journal of Family Violence, 15* (11), 95-108.

Johnson-Dalzine, P., Dalzine, L., & Martin-Stanley, C. (1996). Fear of criminal violence and the African American elderly: Assessment of a crime prevention strategy. *Journal of Negro Education, 65*(4, Educating Children in a Violent Society, Part II: A Focus on Family and Community Violence), 462-469.

Johnston, D.M., Bebbington, M.S., Lai, C.-D., Houghton, B.F., & Paton, D. (1999). Volcanic hazard perceptions: Comparative shifts in knowledge and risk. *Disaster Prevention and Management, 8*(2), 118-126.

Johnston, L. (1996). What is vigilantism? *The British Journal of Criminology, Delinquency and Deviant Social Behaviour, 36*(2), 220-236.

Johnston, L. (2001). Crime, fear and civil policing, *Urban Studies* (Vol. 38, pp. 959-976): The Editors of Urban Studies.

Jonah, B.A. (1986). Accident risk and risk-taking behaviour among young drivers. *Accident Analysis & Prevention, 18*(4), 255-271.

Jones, C.O. (1984). Doing before knowing: Concept development in political research. In: H.B. Asher, H.F. Weisberg, J.H. Kessel & W.P. Shively (Eds.), *Theory-Building and Data Analysis in the Social Sciences* (pp. 51-64). Knoxville: University of Tennessee Press.

Jones, E.T. (1976). The press as metropolitan monitor. *Public Opinion Quarterly, 40*(2), 239-244.

Jones, K., & Duncan, C. (1995). Individuals and their ecologies: Analysing the geography of chronic illness within a multilevel modelling framework. *Health & Place, 1*(1), 27-40.

Jones, L. (2002). Adolescent understandings of political violence and psychological well-being: A qualitative study from Bosnia Herzegovina. *Social Science & Medicine, 55*(8), 1351-1371.

Jones, W.B. (1978). Theory-ladenness and theory comparison (in observation and theory). *PSA: Proceedings of the Biennial Meeting of the Philosophy of Science Association, Volume One: Contributed Papers*, 83-92.

Jong-Gierveld, J. de (1984). *Eenzaamheid: Een meersporig onderzoek.* Deventer: Van Loghum Slaterus.

Jöreskog, K.G. (2001a). *Analysis of Ordinal Variables I: Preliminary Analysis*

Jöreskog, K.G. (2001b). *Analysis of Ordinal Variables 2: Cross-sectional Data*

Jöreskog, K.G., & Sörbom, D. (1988a). *PRELIS: A program for multivariate data screening and data summarization: A preprocessor for LISREL.* (Version 2nd ed. ; 2.51). Chicago, Illinois: Scientific Software, Inc.

Jöreskog, K.G., & Sörbom, D. (1988b). *LISREL 7: A Guide to the Program and Applications.* Chicago, Illinois: SPSS.

Jöreskog, K.G., & Sörbom, D. (1993). *LISREL 8: User's Reference Guide.* Chicago, Illinois: Scientific Software International.

Junger, M., & Heijden, P.G.M. van der (1987a). 'Seksueel geweld: Van overdreven angst naar gerechtvaardigde woede' en weer terug? Een kritiek op de publikatie van Ensink en Van Buuren. *Tijdschrift voor criminologie, 29*(4), 92-99.

Junger, M., & Heijden, P.G.M. van der (1987b). Naschrift. *Tijdschrift voor criminologie, 29*(4), 102-103.

Junger-Tas, J., & Terlouw, G.J. (1991a). Het Nederlands publiek en het criminaliteitsprobleem. *Delikt & delinkwent, 21*(3), 256-267.

Junger-Tas, J., & Terlouw, G.J. (1991b). Het Nederlands publiek en het criminaliteitsprobleem (II). *Delikt & delinkwent, 21*(4), 345-362.

Junger-Tas, J., & Zee-Nefkens, A.A. van der (1978). *Publiek en politie: Ervaringen, houdingen en wensen.* The Hague: Wetenschappelijk Onderzoek- en Documentatiecentrum; Ministerie van Justitie.

K

Kamphuis, J., & Emmelkamp, P. (2001). Traumatic distress among support-seeking female victims of stalking. *American Journal of Psychiatry, 158*(5), 795-798.

Kanan, J., & Pruitt, M. (2002). Modeling fear of crime and perceived victimization risk: The (in)significance of neighborhood integration. *Sociological Inquiry, 72* (74), 527-548.

Kania, R.R.E. (1998). TV Crime and Real Crime: The Impact of Prime-Time Viewing. Paper presented at the Annual Meeting of the American Society of Criminology, Wahington, DC.

Kaniasty, K., & Norris, F.H. (1992). Social support and victims of crime: Matching event, support, and outcome. *American Journal of Community Psychology, 20*(2), 211-241.

Kappas, A. (2002). The science of emotion as a multidisciplinary research paradigm. *Behavioural Processes, 60*(2), 85-98.

Kasperson, R.E., Renn, O., Slovic, P., Brown, H.S., Emel, J., Goble, R., et al. (1988). Social amplification of risk: A conceptual framework. *Risk Analysis, 8*, 177-187.

Katajala, K. (1999). Swedish Treason legislation and peasant unrest. In: M. Lappalainen & P. Hirvonen (Eds.), *Crime and Control: In Europe from the Past to the Present* (pp. 8-61). Helsinki: Academy of Finland.

Katz, J. (1987). What makes crime 'news'? *Media, Culture and Society, 9*, 47-75.

Katz, J. (2003). Metropolitan crime myths. In: D. Halle (Ed.), *New York and Los Angeles: Politics, Society and Culture*. Chicago: University of Chicago Press.

Kawachi, I., Kennedy, B.P., & Wilkinson, R.G. (1999). Crime: Social disorganization and relative deprivation. *Social Science & Medicine, 48*(6), 719-731.

Keane, C. (1998). Evaluating the influence of fear of crime as an environmental mobility restrictor on women's routine activities. *Environment and Behavior, 30*(1), 60-74.

Kearon, T., & Leach, R. (2000). Invasion of the 'body snatchers': Burglary reconsidered. *Theoretical Criminology, 4*(4), 451-472.

Keat, R., & Urry, J. (1975). *Social Theory as Science*. London: Routledge & Kegan Paul.

Kelaher, M., & Ross, M.W. (1992). Sources of bias in perception of HIV risk by injecting drug-users. *Psychological Reports, 70*(3), 771-774.

Kelling, G.L., & Coles, C.M. (1997). *Fixing Broken Windows: Restoring Order and Reducing Crime in our Communities*. New York: Simon & Schuster.

Kelly, K.D., & DeKeseredy, W.S. (1994). Women's fear of crime and abuse in college and university dating relationships. *Violence and Victims, 9*(1), 17-30.

Kelly, L. (1987). The continuum of sexual violence. In: J. Hanmer & M. Maynard (Eds.), *Women, Violence, and Social Control* (pp. 46-60). Atlantic Highlands, NJ: Humanities Press International.

Kelly, L. (1988). How women define their experiences of violence. In: K. Yllö & M. Bograd (Eds.), *Feminist Perspectives on Wife Abuse* (pp. 114-132). London: Sage.

Kempe, G.T. (1967). *Inleiding tot de criminologie*. Haarlem: Bohn.

Kempe, G.T., & Vermaat, J. (1939). *Criminaliteit in Drenthe* (Vol. III). Utrecht: Dekker & Van de Vegt.

Kennamer, J.D. (1992). Public opinion, the press, and public policy: An introduction. In: J.D. Kennamer (Ed.), *Public Opinion, the Press, and Public Policy* (pp. 1-17). Westport, Conn.: Praeger.

Kennedy, L.W., & Silverman, R.A. (1984). Significant others and fear of crime among the elderly. *International Journal of Aging & Human Development, 20*(4), 241-256.

Kershaw, C., Budd, T., Kinshott, G., Mattinson, J., Mayhew, P., & Myhill, A. (2000). *The 2000 British Crime Survey England and Wales* (Statistical Bulletin). London: Home Office.

Kesteren, J. van, Mayhew, P., & Nieuwbeerta, P. (2000). *Criminal Victimisation in Seventeen Industrialised Countries: Key Findings from the 2000 International Crime Victimisation Survey* (Vol. 187). The Hague: WODC.

Killias, M. (1990). Vulnerability: Towards a better understanding of a key variable in the genesis of fear of crime. *Violence and Victims, 5*(2), 97-108.

Killias, M., & Clerici, C. (2000). Different measures of vulnerability in their relation to different dimensions of fear and crime.

Kilpatrick, D.G., Best, C.L., Veronen, L.J., Amick, A.E., Villeponteaux, L.A., & Ruff, G.A. (1985). Mental health correlates of criminal victimization: A random community survey. *Journal of Counseling and Clinical Psychology, 53*(6), 866-873.

Kirkpatrick, C. (1936). Assumptions and methods in attitude measurements. *American Sociological Review, 1*(1), 75-88.

Kleck, G. (1996). Crime, culture conflict and the sources of support for gun control: A multilevel application of the general social surveys. *American Behavioral Scientist, 39*(4), 387-404.

Klerk, L.F.W. de, & Oostlander, A.M. (1976). Het leren van concepten en beoordelingsregels. In: J.A. Michon, E.G.J. Eijkman & L.F.W. DeKlerk (Eds.), *Handboek der psychonomie* (pp. 388-412). Deventer: Van Loghum Slaterus.

Knight, P. (2001). ILOVEYOU: Viruses, paranoia and the environment of risk. In: J. Parish & M. Parker (Eds.), *The Age of Anxiety: Conspiracy Theory and the Human Sciences* (pp. 17-30). Oxford: Blackwell.

Koomen, W., Visser, M., & Stapel, D.A. (2000). The credibility of newspapers and fear of crime. *Journal of Applied Social Psychology, 30*(5), 921-934.

Koppen, P.J. van, & Vette, R.C.M. de. (1997). Vrees voor criminaliteit als ingebeelde ziekte. In: K. Wittebrood, J.A. Michon & M.J. ter Voert (Eds.), *Nederlanders over criminaliteit en rechtshandhaving* (pp. 45-54). Deventer: Gouda Quint.

Koren, J. (Ed.). (1918). *The History of Statistics: Their Development and Progress in Many Countries: In Memoirs to Commemorate the Seventy Fifth Anniversary of the American Statistical Association.* New York: Macmillan.

Koskela, H., & Pain, R. (2000). Revisiting fear and place: Women's fear of attack and the built environment. *Geoforum, 31*(2), 269-280.

Koski, D.D. (2002). Jury decisionmaking in rape trials: A review & empirical assessment. *Criminal Law Bulletin, 38*(1), 21-159.

Koss, M.P. (1985). The hidden rape victim: Personality, attitudinal, and situational characteristics. *Psychology of Women Quarterly, 9*(2), 193.

Koss, M.P., Gidycz, C.A., & Wisniewski, N. (1987). The scope of rape: Incidence and prevalence of sexual aggression and victimization in a national sample of higher education students. *Journal of Consulting and Clinical Psychology, 55*(162-170).

Koss, M.P., Goodman, L.A., Browne, A., Fitzgerald, L.F., Keita, G.P., & Russo, N.F. (1994). *No Safe Haven: Male Violence against Women at Home, at Work, and in the Community.* Washington, DC: American Psychological Association.

Krause, N. (1991). Stress and isolation from close ties in later life. *Journal of Gerontology, 46*(4), S183-S194.

Krause, N. (1996). Neighborhood deterioration and self-rated health in later life. *Psychology & Aging, 11*(2), 342-352.

Krosnick, J.A., & Abelson, R.P. (1997). The case for measuring attitude strength. In: L. Lyberg, P. Biemer, M. Collins, E. DeLeeuw, C. Dippo, N. Schwarz & D. Trewin (Eds.), *Survey Measurement and Process Quality* (pp. 177-203). New York: John Wiley & Sons.

Krosnick, J.A., & Fabrigar, l. R. (1997). Designing rating scales for effective measurement in surveys. In: L. Lyberg, P. Biemer, M. Collins, E. DeLeeuw, C. Dippo, N. Schwarz & D. Trewin (Eds.), *Survey Measurement and Process Quality* (pp. 141-164). New York: John Wiley & Sons.

Kruskal, J.B. (1964a). Multidimensional scaling by optimizing goodness of fit to a nonmetric hypothesis. *Psychometrika, 29*, 1-27.

Kruskal, J.B. (1964b). Nonmetric multidimensional scaling: A numerical method. *Psychometrika, 29*, 115-129.

Kruskal, J.B., & Wish, M. (1978). *Multidimensional Scaling.* London: Sage.

Kuhn, T. (1996). *The Structure of Scientific Revolutions* (3rd ed.). Chicago: University of Chicago Press.

Kunda, Z. (1999). *Social Cognition: Making Sense of People.* Cambridge, Mass.: MIT Press.

Kury, H., & Smartt, U. (2002). Prisoner-on-prisoner violence: Victimization of young offenders in prison: Some German findings. *Criminal Justice, 2*(4), 411-437.

Kuttschreuter, M. (1990). De berichtgeving in de massamedia en angst voor criminaliteit. In: F.W. Winkel & A. van der Wurff (Eds.), *Angst voor Criminaliteit* (pp. 200-213). Amsterdam: Swets & Zeitlinger.

Kuttschreuter, M., & Wiegman, O. (1996). Voorlichting over criminaliteit: Het effect van een tell-the-truth-campagne. *Tijdschrift voor communicatiewetenschap, 24*(2), 181-194.

Kuttschreuter, M., & Wiegman, O. (1997). Crime communication at information meetings. *British Journal of Criminology, 37*(1), 46-62.

Kuttschreuter, M., & Wiegman, O. (1998). Crime prevention and the attitude toward the criminal justice system: The effects of a multimedia campaign. *Journal of Criminal Justice, 26*(6), 441-452.

Kwan, Y.K., Chiu, L.L., Ip, W.C., & Kwan, P. (2002). Perceived crime seriousness: Consensus and disparity. *Journal of Criminal Justice, 30*(6), 623-632.

Kwan, Y.K., Ip, W.C., & Kwan, P. (2000). A crime index with Thurstone's scaling of crime severity. *Journal of Criminal Justice, 28*(3), 237-244.

L

LaGrange, R.L., Ferraro, K.F., & Supancic, M. (1992). Perceived risk and fear of crime: Role of social and physical incivilities. *Journal of Research in Crime and Delinquency, 29*(3), 311-334.

Lamb, S. (1999a). Introduction. In: S. Lamb (Ed.), *New Versions of Victims: Feminists Struggle with the Concept* (pp. 1-12). New York: New York University Press.

Lamb, S. (1999b). Constructing the victim: Popular images and lasting labels. In: S. Lamb (Ed.), *New Versions of Victims: Feminists Struggle with the Concept* (pp. 108-138). New York: New York University Press.

Lane, J. (2002). Fear of gang crime: A qualitative examination of the four perspectives. *Journal of Research in Crime and Delinquency, 39*(4), 437-471.

Lane, J., & Meeker, J. (2000). Subcultural diversity and the fear of crime and gangs. *Crime and Delinquency, 46* (44), 497-521.

Lane, J., & Meeker, J.W. (2003). Ethnicity, information sources, and fear of crime. *Deviant Behavior, 24*(1), 1-26.

Langford, I.H., Marris, C., McDonald, A.L., Goldstein, H., Rasbash, J., & O'Riordan, T. (1999). Simultaneous analysis of individual and aggregate responses in psychometric data using multilevel modeling. *Risk Analysis, 19*(4), 675-683.

Langworthy, R.H., & Whitehead, J.T. (1986). Liberalism and fear as explanations of punitiveness. *Criminology, 24*(3), 575-591.

Lash, S. (2000). Risk culture. In: B. Adam, U. Beck & J. van Loon (Eds.), *The Risk Society and Beyond: Critical Issues for Social Theory* (pp. 47-62). London; Thousand Oaks, CA: Sage.

Laudan, L. (1997). *Danger Ahead: The Risks You Really Face on Life's Highway.* New York: J. Wiley & Sons.

Lauer, R.H., & Lauer, J.C. (2004). Violence. In: R.H. Lauer & J.C. Lauer (Eds.), *Social Problems and the Quality of Life* (pp. 120-148). Boston, MA: McGraw-Hill Higher Education.

Lavrakas, P.J. (1982). Fear of crime and behavioral restrictions in urban and suburban neighborhoods. *Population and Environment, 5*(4), 242-264.

Lavrakas, P.J., & Skogan, W.G. (1997). Citizen participation and community crime prevention, 1979: Chicago Metropolitan Area Survey [Computer file]. Conducted by Northwestern University, Center for Urban Affairs and Policy Research. 2nd ICPSR ed. Ann Arbor, MI: Inter-university Consortium for Political and Social Research [producer and distributor], 1997.

Lawton, M.P., & Yaffe, S. (1980). Victimization and fear of crime in elderly public housing tenants. *Journal of Gerontology, 35*(5), 768-779.

Lazarsfeld, P.F. (1959/1972a). Problems in methodology. In: P.F. Lazarsfeld, A.K. Pasanella & M. Rosenberg (Eds.), *Continuities in the Language of Social Research* (pp. 17-24). New York: The Free Press.

Lazarsfeld, P.F. (1968). Evidence and inference in social research. In: M. Brodbeck (Ed.), *Readings in the Philosophy of the Social Sciences* (pp. 608-634). New York: Macmillan.

Lazarsfeld, P.F. (1972b). *Qualitative Analysis: Historical and Critical Essays*. Boston: Allyn and Bacon.

Lazarsfeld, P.F. (1972c). Notes on the history of concept formation. In: P.F. Lazarsfeld (Ed.), *Qualitative Analysis: Historical and Critical Essays* (pp. 5-52). Boston: Allyn and Bacon.

Lazarsfeld, P.F. (1972d). Some principles of classification in social research. In: P.F. Lazarsfeld (Ed.), *Qualitative Analysis: Historical and Critical Essays* (pp. 225-240). Boston: Allyn and Bacon.

Lazarsfeld, P.F. (1993a). The relevance of methodology. In: R. Boudon (Ed.), *On Social Research and its Language* (pp. 236-254). Chicago: University of Chicago Press.

Lazarsfeld, P.F. (1993b). Classifying and building typologies. In: R. Boudon (Ed.), *On Social Research and its Language* (pp. 158-171). Chicago: University of Chicago Press.

Lazarsfeld, P.F., & Barton, A.H. (1968). Qualitative measurement in the social sciences: Classification, typologies, and indices. In: D. Lerner & H. Lasswell (Eds.), *The Policy Sciences* (pp. 155-192). Stanford: Stanford University Press.

Lazarus, R.S. (1984). On the primacy of cognition. *American Psychologist, 39*(2), 124-129.

Lazarus, R.S. (1991). Cognition and motivation in emotion. *American Psychologist, 46*(4), 352-367.

Leahey, T.H. (1991). *A History of Modern Psychology*. Englewood Cliffs: Prentice Hall.

Leather, P., Beale, D., Lawrence, C., & Dickson, R. (1997). Effects of exposure to occupational violence and the mediating impact of fear. *Work and Stress, 11*(4), 329-340.

Lee, M. (1999). The fear of crime and self-governance: Towards a genealogy. *Australian & New Zealand Journal of Criminology, 32*(3), 227-246.

Lee, M. (2001). The genesis of 'fear of crime'. *Theoretical Criminology, 5*(4), 467-485.

Lee, M.R. (2000). Community cohesion and violent predatory victimization: A theoretical extension and cross-national test of opportunity theory. *Social Forces, 79*(2), 683-706.

Lee, T.R. (1981). The public's perception of risk and the question of irrationality. In: F. Warner (Ed.), *The Assessment and Perception of Risk* (pp. 5-16). London: The Royal Society.

Leger, J.-P. (1991). Trends and causes of fatalities in South African mines. *Safety Science, 14*(3-4), 169-185.

Lerner, J.S., Gonzalez, R.M., Small, D.A., & Fischhoff, B. (2003). Effects of fear and anger on perceived risks of terrorism: A national field experiment. *Psychological Science, 14*(2), 144-150.

Lerner, J.S., & Keltner, D. (2000). Beyond valence: Toward a model of emotion-specific influences on judgement and choice. *Cognition & Emotion, 14*(4), 473-493.

Lerner, J.S., & Keltner, D. (2001). Fear, anger, and risk. *Journal of Personality & Social Psychology, 81*(1), 146-159.

Leunes, A., Bourgeois, A., & Grajales, R. (1996). The effects of two types of exposure on attitudes toward aspects of juvenile delinquency. *The Journal of Social Psychology, 136 (6)*, 699-708.

Levant, R.F. (1996). The new psychology of men. *Professional Psychology: Research and Practice, 27*(3), 259-265.

Levine, J.M. (1986). Hearts and minds: The politics of diet and heart disease. In: H.M. Sapolsky (Ed.), *Consuming Fears: The Politics of Product Risks* (pp. 40-79). New York: Basic Books.

Levine, N., & Wachs, M. (1986b). Bus crime in Los Angeles: II :Victims and public impact. *Transportation Research Part A: General, 20*(4), 285-293.

Levy, S. (1985). Lawful roles of facets in social theories. In: D. Canter (Ed.), *Facet Theory: Approaches to Social Research* (pp. 59-96). New York: Springer-Verlag.

Lewis, D.A., & Maxfield, M.G. (1980). Fear in the neighbourhoods: An investigation of the impact of crime. *Journal of Research and Delinquency, 17*, 160-189.

Lewis, D.A., & Salem, G. (1986). *Fear of Crime: Incivility and the Production of a Social Problem*. New Brunswick: Transaction Books.

Lianos, M., & Douglas, M. (2000). Dangerization and the end of deviance: The institutional environment. *British Journal of Criminology, 40*(2), 261-278.

Liebrucks, A. (2001). The concept of social construction. *Theory & Psychology, 11*(3), 363-391.

Likert, R. (1968). The sample interview survey as a tool of research and policy formation. In: D. Lerner & H. Lasswell (Eds.), *The Policy Sciences* (pp. 233-251). Stanford: Stanford University Press.

Linares, L.O., Heeren, T., Bronfman, E., Zuckerman, B., Augustyn, M., & Tronick, E. (2001). A mediational model for the impact of exposure to community violence on early child behavior problems. *Child Development, 72*(2), 639-652.

Lindquist, J.H., & Duke, J.M. (1982). The elderly victim at risk: Explaining the fear-victimization paradox. *Criminology, 20*, 115-126.

Lindström, M., Merlo, J., & Östergren, P.-O. (2003). Social capital and sense of insecurity in the neighbourhood: A population-based multilevel analysis in Malmo, Sweden. *Social Science & Medicine, 56*(5), 1111-1120.

Lira, L.R., & Andradepalos, P. (1993). Fear of victimization in Mexico. *Journal of Community & Applied Social Psychology, 3*(1), 41-51.

Liska, A.E., & Baccaglini, W. (1990). Feeling safe by comparison: Crime in the newspapers. *Social Problems, 37*, 360-374.

Liska, A.E., & Bellair, P.E. (1995). Violent-crime rates and racial composition: Covergence over time. *American Journal of Sociology, 101*(3), 578-610.

Liska, A.E., Sanchirico, A., & Reed, M.D. (1988). Fear of crime and constrained behavior specifying and estimating a reciprocal effects model. *Social Forces, 66*(3), 827-837.

Liska, A.E., & Warner, B. (1991). Functions of crime: A paradoxical process. *American Journal of Sociology, 96*, 1441-1464.

Little, C.B., & Sheffield, C.P. (1983). Frontiers and criminal justice: English private prosecution societies and American vigilantism in the eighteenth and nineteenth centuries. *American Sociological Review, 48*(6), 796-808.

Little, J., Panelli, R., & Kraack, A. (2005). Women's fear of crime: A rural perspective. *Journal of Rural Studies, 21*(2), 151-163.

Loewenstein, G.F., Weber, E.U., Hsee, C.K., & Welch, N. (2001). Risk as feelings. *Psychological Bulletin, 127*(2), 267-286.

Lonsway, K.A., & Fitzgerald, L.F. (1995). Attitudinal antecedents of rape myth acceptance: A theoretical and empirical reexamination. *Journal of Personality and Social Psychology, 68*(4), 704-711.

Loon, J. van (2000). Virtual risks in an age of cybernetic reproduction. In: B. Adam, U. Beck & J. van Loon (Eds.), *The Risk Society and Beyond: Critical Issues for Social Theory* (pp. 165-182). London; Thousand Oaks, CA: Sage.

Lós, M. (2002). Post-communist fear of crime and the commercialization of security. *Theoretical Criminology, 6*(2), 165-188.

Lowry, D.T., Nio, T.C.J., & Leitner, D.W. (2003). Setting the public fear agenda: A longitudinal analysis of network TV crime reporting, public perceptions of crime, and FBI crime statistics. *Journal of Communication, 53*(1), 61-73.

Luger, B. (1989). Misdaad tussen feit en fictie. In: S. Faber, S. van Ruller, C. Fijnaut, J. van der Linden, H.J. Franke, H.A. Diederiks, C.G.T.M. Leonards, R.M. Dekker, G. Hekma, W.C. de Vlaming & B. Luger (Eds.), *Criminaliteit in de negentiende eeuw* (pp. 141-149). Hilversum: Verloren/ Historische Vereniging Holland.

Luhmann, N. (1993). *Risk: A Sociological Theory.* New York: A. de Gruyter.

Lupton, D., & Tulloch, J. (1999). Theorizing fear of crime: Beyond the rational/irrational opposition. *British Journal of Sociology, 50*(3), 507-523.

Lupton, D., & Tulloch, J. (2002). 'Risk is part of your life': Risk epistemologies among a group of Australians. *Sociology, 36*(2), 317-334.

Luxenburg, J., Cullen, F.T., Langworthy, R.H., & Kopache, R. (1994). Firearms and fido: Ownership of injurious means of protection. *Journal of Criminal Justice, 22*(2), 159-170.

Luymes, D. (1997). The fortification of suburbia: Investigating the rise of enclave communities. *Landscape and Urban Planning, 39*(2-3), 187-203.

Lyberg, L., Biemer, P., Collins, M., DeLeeuw, E., Dippo, C., Schwarz, N., et al. (Eds.). (1997). *Survey Measurement and Process Quality.* New York: John Wiley & Sons.

Lynch, M.J., & Krzycki, L.A. (1998). Popular culture as an ideological mask: Mass-produced popular culture and the remaking of criminal justice-related imagery. *Journal of Criminal Justice, 26*(4), 321-336.

M

Maarseveen, J.G.S.J. van, Gircour, M.B.G., & Schreijnders, R. (Eds.). (1999). *A Century Rounded up: Reflections on the History of the Central Bureau of Statistics in the Netherlands.* Voorburg: Statistics Netherlands (CBS).

Maas-De Waal, C. (2002a). Justitie en strafrechtspleging. In: Sociaal en Cultureel Planbureau, *Sociaal en cultureel rapport 2002: De kwaliteit van de quartaire sector* (pp. 629-692). The Hague: Sociaal en Cultureel Planbureau.

Maas-De Waal, C. (2002b). Veiligheid, ontwikkelingen en stand van zaken. In: J. de Hart, C. Maas-DeWaal & T. Roes (Eds.), *Zekere banden: Sociale cohesie, leefbaarheid en veiligheid* (pp. 245-278). The Hague: Sociaal en Cultureel Planbureau.

Maas-De Waal, C. (2004). Veiligheid, politie en justitie. In: Sociaal en Cultureel Planbureau, *In het zicht van de toekomst: Sociaal en cultureel rapport 2004* (pp. 457-497). The Hague: Sociaal en Cultureel Planbureau.

Maas-De Waal, C., & Wittebrood, K. (2002). Sociale cohesie, fysieke buurtkenmerken en onveiligheid in de grotere steden. In: J. de Hart, C. Maas-DeWaal & T. Roes (Eds.), *Zekere banden: sociale cohesie, leefbaarheid en veiligheid* (pp. 279-315). The Hague: Sociaal en Cultureel Planbureau.

Macdonell, W.R. (1902). On criminal anthropometry and the identification of criminals. *Biometrika, 1*(2), 177-227.

MacKenzie, D.A. (1981). *Statistics in Britain, 1865-1930: The Social Construction of Scientific Knowledge.* Edinburgh [Midlothian]: Edinburgh University Press.

Macmillan, R., Nierobisz, A., & Welsh, S. (2000). Experiencing the streets: Harassment and perceptions of safety among women. *Journal of Research in Crime & Delinquency, 37*(3), 306-322.

Madden, M.E. (1995). Perceived vulnerability and control of martial arts and physical-fitness students. *Perceptual and Motor Skills, 80*(3), 899-910.

Madriz, E. (1997a). *Nothing Bad Happens to Good Girls: Fear of Crime in Women's Lives.* Berkeley: University of California Press.

Madriz, E.I. (1997b). Images of criminals and victims: A study on women's fear and social control. *Gender & Society, 11*(3), 342-356.

Maguire, K., & A.L.Pastore (Eds.). (n.d.). *Sourcebook of Criminal Justice Statistics* [Online]. Available: http://www.albany.edu/sourcebook/ [Retrieved 25 July 2005].

Maguire, M., & Kynch, J. (2000). *Public Perceptions and Victims' Experiences of Victim Support: Findings from the 1998 British Crime Survey.* London: Home Office Research, Development and Statistics Directorate.

Malesky, A., & Keim, J. (2001). Mental health professionals' perspectives on sex offender registry web sites. *Sexual Abuse: A Journal of Research and Treatment, 13*(1), 53-63.

Maltz, M.D. (1975). Crime statistics: A mathematical perspective. *Journal of Criminal Justice, 3*(3), 177-194.

Manning, P.K. (2001). Theorizing policing: The drama and myth of crime control in the NYPD. *Theoretical Criminology, 5*(3), 315-344.

Marenin, O. (1997). Victimization surveys and the accuracy and reliability of official crime data in developing countries. *Journal of Criminal Justice, 25*(6), 463-475.

Margolis, H. (1996). *Dealing with Risk: Why the Public and the Experts Disagree on Environmental Issues.* Chicago, IL: University of Chicago Press.

Marion, N. (1997). Symbolic policies in Clinton's crime control agenda. *Buffalo Criminal Law Review, 1*, 67-108.

Markowitz, F.E., Bellair, P.E., Liska, A.E., & Liu, J.H. (2001). Extending social disorganization theory: Modeling the relationships between cohesion, disorder, and fear. *Criminology, 39*(2), 293-320.

Marris, C., Langford, I.H., & O'Riordan, T. (1998). A quantitative test of the cultural theory of risk perceptions: Comparison with the psychometric paradigm. *Risk Analysis, 18*(5), 635-647.

Marris, C., Langford, I. H., Saunderson, T., & O'Riordan, T. (1997). Exploring the "psychometric paradigm": Comparisons between aggregate and individual analyses. *Risk Analysis, 17*(3), 303-312.

Marris, C., O'Riordan, T., & Langford, I. (1996). Risk Perceptions and Cultural Biases in Norfolk. Paper presented at the The 1996 Annual Meeting of the Society for Risk Analysis-Europe.

Marsh, H.L. (1991). A comparative analysis of crime coverage in newspapers in the United States and other countries from 1960-1989: A review of the literature. *Journal of Criminal Justice, 19*(1), 67-79.

Marsh, H.W., Hau, K.T., Balla, J.R., & Grayson, D. (1998). Is more ever too much? The number of indicators per factor in confirmatory factor analysis. *Multivariate Behavioral Research, 33*(2), 181-220.

Marshall, B.L. (1995). Communication as politics: Feminist print media in English Canada. *Women's Studies International Forum, 18*(4), 463-474.

Martinez, M.L., Black, M., & Starr, R.H. (2002). Factorial structure of the perceived neighborhood scale (PNS): A test of longitudinal invariance. *Journal of Community Psychology, 30*(1), 23-44.

Maruna, S., Matravers, A., & King, A. (2004). Disowning our shadow: a psychoanalytic approach to understanding punitive public attitudes. *Deviant Behavior, 25*(3), 277-299.

Massey, C.R., & McKean, J. (1985). The social ecology of homicide: A modified lifestyle/routine activities perspective. *Journal of Criminal Justice, 13*(5), 417-428.

Mastro, D.E., & Robinson, A.L. (2000). Cops and crooks: images of minorities on primetime television. *Journal of Criminal Justice, 28*(5), 385-396.

Matei, S., Ball-Rokeach, S.J., & Qiu, J.L. (2001). Fear and misperception of Los Angeles urban space: A spatial-statistical study of communication-shaped mental maps. *Communication Research, 28*(4), 429-463.

Matthews, H., Taylor, M., Sherwood, K., Tucker, F., & Limb, M. (2000). Growing-up in the countryside: Children and the rural idyll. *Journal of Rural Studies, 16*(2), 141-153.

Maxfield, M.G., & Great Britain. Home Office. Research and Planning Unit. (1984). *Fear of Crime in England and Wales*. London: Her Majesty's Stationery Office.

May, D.C. (1999). Scared kids, unattached kids, or peer pressure: Why do students carry firearms to school? *Youth & Society, 31*(1), 100-127.

May, H. (1999). Who killed whom? Victimization and culpability in the social construction of murder. *British Journal of Sociology, 50*(3), 489-506.

Mayhew, P., & Dijk, J.J.M. van (1997). *Criminal Victimisation in Eleven Industrialised Countries: Key findings from the 1996 International Crime Victims Survey*. The Hague: Wetenschappelijk Onderzoek- en Documentatiecentrum.

Mayhew, P., & Hough, M. (1988). The British crime survey: Origins and impact. In: M. Maguire & J. Pointing (Eds.), *Victims of Crime: A New Deal?* (pp. 156-163). Milton Keynes: Open University Press.

McComas, K.A. (2003). Public meetings and risk amplification: A longitudinal study. *Risk Analysis, 23*(6), 1257-1270.

McCorkle, R.C. (1992). Personal precautions to violence in prison. *Criminal Justice and Behavior, 19*(2), 160-173.

McCormick, T.C. (1945). Simple percentage analysis of attitude questionnaires. *American Journal of Sociology, 50*(5), 390-395.

McCoy, D.C. (1997). Evaluation of community policing initiatives in Jefferson County, West Virginia, 1996-1997 [Computer file]. ICPSR version. Charles Town, WV: Focus (Free Our Citizens of Unhealthy Substances) [producer], 1997. Ann Arbor, MI: Inter-university Consortium for Political and Social Research [distributor], 2000.

McCoy, H.V., Wooldredge, J.D., Cullen, F.T., Dubeck, P.J., & Browning, S.L. (1996). Lifestyles of the old and not so fearful: Life situation and older persons' fear of crime. *Journal of Criminal Justice, 24*(3), 191-206.

McCroskey, J.C., Prichard, S.V.O., & Arnold, W.E. (1967). Attitude intensity and the neutral point on semantic differential scales. *Public Opinion Quarterly, 31*(4, The Historical Study of Public Opinion), 642-645.

McDonald, R.P. (1981). The dimensionality of tests and items. *British Journal of Mathematical & Statistical Psychology, 34*(1), 100-117.

McDonell, G. (1997). Scientific and everyday knowledge: Trust and the politics of environmental initiatives. *Social Studies of Science, 27*(6), 819-863.

McDowall, D., & Loftin, C. (1983). Collective security and the demand for legal handguns. *American Journal of Sociology, 88*(6), 1146-1161.

McEwan, S.L., de Man, A.F., & Simpson-Housley, P. (2002). Ego-identity achievement and perception of risk in intimacy in survivors of stranger and acquaintance rape. *Sex Roles, 47*(5-6), 281-287.

McGrath, R.D. (1984). *Gunfighters, Highwaymen & Vigilantes: Violence on the Frontier*. Berkeley, CA: University of California Press.

McKenna, F.P. (1983). Accident proneness: A conceptual analysis. *Accident Analysis & Prevention, 15*(1), 65-71.

McKenna, F.P. (1993). It won't happen to me: Unrealistic optimism or illusion of control? *British Journal of Psychology, 84*, 39-50.

McNeill, S. (1987). Flashing: Its effect on women. In: J. Hanmer & M. Maynard (Eds.), *Women, Violence, and Social Control* (pp. 93-109). Atlantic Highlands, NJ: Humanities Press International.

McPherson, M. (1978). Realities and perceptions of crime at the neighborhood level. *Victimology, 3*(3/4), 319-328.

McPherson, M., Silloway, G. & Frey, D. (1983). Crime, fear, and control in neighborhood commercial centers: Minneapolis and St. Paul, 1970-1982 [Computer file]. 2nd ICPSR version. Minneapolis, MN: Minnesota Crime Prevention Center, Inc. [producer], 1983. Ann Arbor, MI: Inter-university Consortium for Political and Social Research [distributor], 1998.

Mearns, K., & Flin, R. (1995). Risk perception and attitudes to safety by personnel in the offshore oil and gas industry: A review. *Journal of Loss Prevention in the Process Industries, 8*(5), 299-305.

Melossi, D. (2000). Changing representations of the criminal. *British Journal of Criminology, 40*(2), 296-320.

Meloy, J.R. (Ed.). (1998). *The Psychology of Stalking: Clinical and Forensic Perspectives.* San Diego: Academic Press.

Melville, M.B., & Brinton Lykes, M. (1992). Guatemalan Indian children and the sociocultural effects of government-sponsored terrorisms. *Social Science & Medicine, 34*(5), 533-548.

Menard, S., & Covey, H.C. (1988). UCR and NCS: Comparisons over space and time. *Journal of Criminal Justice, 16*(5), 371-384.

Merry, S.E. (1981). *Urban Danger: Life in a Neighborhood of Strangers.* Philadelphia: Temple University Press.

Mesch, G.S. (2000a). Perceptions of risk, lifestyle activities, and fear of crime. *Deviant Behavior, 21*(1), 47-62.

Mesch, G.S. (2000b). Women's fear of crime: The role of fear for the well-being of significant others. *Violence and Victims, 15*(3), 323-336.

Meulman, J.J., Heiser, W.J., & SPSS. (1999). *SPSS Categories 10.0.* Chicago: SPSS.

Michalos, A., & Zumbo, B. (2000). Criminal victimization and the quality of life. *Social Indicators Research*, 50 (53), 245-295.

Michalos, A.C. (2003). Policing services and the quality of life. *Social Indicators Research, 61*(1), 1-18.

Michalos, A.C. (2004). Social indicators research and health-related quality of life research. *Social Indicators Research, 65*(1), 27-72.

Michalos, A.C., Hubley, A.M., Zumbo, B.D., & Hemingway, D. (2001). Health and other aspects of the quality of life of older people. *Social Indicators Research, 54*(3), 239-274.

Michinov, E., & Michinov, N. (2001). The similarity hypothesis: A test of the moderating role of social comparison orientation. *European Journal of Social Psychology, 31*(5), 549-555.

Miethe, T.D. (1991). Testing theories of criminality and victimization in Seattle, 1960-1990 [Computer file]. 2nd ICPSR version. Blacksburg, VA: Virginia Polytechnic Institute producer], 1991. Ann Arbor, MI: Inter-university Consortium for Political and Social Research [distributor], 1998.

Miethe, T.D., & Meier, R.F. (1990). Opportunity, choice, and criminal victimization: A test of a theoretical model. *Journal of Research in Crime and Delinquency, 27*(3), 243-266.

Miethe, T.D., & Meier, R.F. (1994). *Crime and its Social Context: Toward an Integrated Theory of Offenders, Victims, and Situations.* Albany, NY: State University of New York Press.

Miethe, T.D., Stafford, M.C., & Long, J.S. (1987). Social differentiation in criminal victimization: A test of routine activities/lifestyle theories. *American Sociological Review, 52*(2), 184-194.

Milburn, M.A., Mather, R., & Conrad, S.D. (2000). The effects of viewing R-rated movie scenes that objectify women on perceptions of date rape. *Sex Roles, 43*(9-10), 645-664.

Miller, J. (2002). The strengths and limits of 'doing gender' for understanding street crime. *Theoretical Criminology, 6*(4), 433-460.

Miller, W.B. (1973). Ideology and criminal justice policy: Some current issues. *Journal of Criminal Law and Criminology, 64*, 141-162.

Mineka, S., & Ohman, A. (2002). Born to fear: Non-associative vs associative factors in the etiology of phobias. *Behaviour Research and Therapy, 40*(2), 173-184.

Ministerie van Binnenlandse Zaken en Koninkrijksrelaties (BZK) (2004). *Jaarverslag Nederlandse Politie 2003* (Criminaliteit en openbare orde (Politie) No. Bijlage bij kamerstuk 28824, no. 22). The Hague: Ministerie van Binnenlandse Zaken en Koninkrijksrelaties.

Mirrlees-Black, C., & Allen, J. (1998). *Concern about Crime: Findings from the 1998 British Crime Survey* (Home Office Research Findings No. 83). London: Home Office.

Mohler, B. (2002). Exposure to violence and fear of violence in adolescents: A comparison between Swiss and US adolescents. *Acta Psychiatrica Scandinavica, 105*, 155.

Monaghan, L. (2003). Danger on the doors: Bodily risk in a demonised occupation. *Health, Risk & Society, 5*(1), 11-31.

Monahan, J. (1982). The case for prediction in the modified desert model of criminal sentencing. *International Journal of Law and Psychiatry, 5*, 103-113.

Morris, M.W., & Peng, K. (1994). Culture and cause: American and Chinese attributions for social and physical events. *Journal of Personality and Social Psychology, 67*(6), 949-971.

Morris, R.M. (2001). 'Lies, damned lies and criminal statistics': Reinterpreting the criminal statistics in England and Wales. *Crime, Histoire & Sociétés, 5*(1), 111-127.

Morry, M.M., & Winkler, E. (2001). Student acceptance and expectation of sexual assault. *Canadian Journal of Behavioural Science, 33*(3), 188-192.

Moscarello, R. (1991). Posttraumatic stress disorder after sexual assault: Its psychodynamics and treatment. *The Journal of the American Academy of Psychoanalysis, 19*(2), 235-253.

Moulton, J. (1983). A paradigm of philosophy: The adversary method. In: S. Harding & M.B. Hintikka (Eds.), *Discovering Reality: Feminist Perspectives on Epistemology, Metaphysics, Methodology, and Philosophy of Science* (Vol. 161, pp. 149-164). Dordrecht: Reidel.

Mourato, S., Saynor, B., & Hart, D. (2004). Greening London's black cabs: A study of driver's preferences for fuel cell taxis. *Energy Policy, 32*(5), 685-695.

Mulvey, A. (2002). Gender, economic context, perceptions of safety, and quality of life: A case study of Lowell, Massachusetts (USA), 1982-96. *American Journal of Community Psychology, 30*(5), 655-679.

Muris, P., Luermans, J., Merckelbach, H., & Mayer, B. (2000). 'Danger is lurking everywhere': The relation between anxiety and threat perception abnormalities in normal children. *Journal of Behavior Therapy and Experimental Psychiatry, 31*(2), 123-136.

Murray, D., Schwartz, J., & Lichter, S.R. (2001). *It Ain't Necessarily So: How Media Make and Unmake the Scientific Picture of Reality.* Lanham: Rowman & Littlefield.

N

Nasar, J.L., Fisher, B., & Grannis, M. (1993). Proximate physical cues to fear of crime. *Landscape and Urban Planning, 26*(1-4), 161-178.

National Centre for Social Research. (2003). *British Social Attitudes Survey,2001* [computer file]. Colchester, Essex: UK Data Archive [distributor], 10 February 2003. SN: 4615.

National Opinion Research Center (n.d.). General social survey: GSS Publications, Bibliography. [Retrieved at 25 July 2005] from http://www.icpsr.umich.edu/GSS/index.html.

Neill, W.J.V. (2001). Marketing the urban experience: Reflections on the place of fear in the promotional strategies of Belfast, Detroit and Berlin., *Urban Studies* (Vol. 38, pp. 815-828): The Editors of Urban Studies.

Nemeth, C., & Endicott, J. (1976). The midpoint as an anchor: Another look at discrepancy of position and attitude change. *Sociometry, 39*(1), 11-18.

Newburn, T. (2002). Atlantic crossings: 'Policy transfer' and crime control in the USA and Britain. *Punishment and Society, 4*(2), 165-194.

Newman, G.R. (1990). Popular culture and criminal justice: A preliminary analysis. *Journal of Criminal Justice, 18*(3), 261-274.

Niederfranke, A., & Greve, W. (1996). Violence as threat in old age: Arguments for a social-science perspective. *Zeitschrift Fur Gerontologie und Geriatrie, 29*(3), 169-175.

Nieuwbeerta, P. (Ed.). (2002). *Crime Victimization in Comparative Perspective: Results from the International Crime Victims Survey 1989-2000*. The Hague: Boom.

Nikolic-Ristanovic, V. (1995). Fear of crime in Belgrade. *International Review of Victimology, 4*, 15-31.

NIPO (Nederlands Instituut voor de Publieke Opinie en het Marktonderzoek)(1985). *Onderzoek criminaliteit in Nederland: no. D-999: Kodeboek*. The Hague: NIPO.

Nitz, K., Peralta, L., Lee, R.E., & Muhawi, H.D. (1997). Perceived risk for STDs and HIV infection among sexually active adolescent girls. *Journal of Adolescent Health, 20*(2), 150.

Norris, F.H. (1997). Frequency and structure of precautionary behavior in the domains of hazard preparedness, crime prevention, vehicular safety, and health maintenance. *Health Psychology, 16*(6), 566-575.

Norris, F.H., & Kaniasty, K. (1992). A longitudinal study of the effects of various crime prevention strategies on criminal victimization, fear of crime, and psychological distress. *American Journal of Community Psychology, 20*(5), 625-648.

Norris, F.H., & Kaniasty, K. (1994). Psychological distress following criminal victimization in the general population: Cross-sectional, longitudinal, and prospective analyses. *Journal of Consulting and Clinical Psychology, 62*(1), 111-123.

Norusius, M.J. (1993). *SPSS for Windows: Base System User's Guide: Release 6.0*. Chicago: SPSS.

Nurius, P.S. (2000). Risk perception for acquaintance sexual aggression: A social-cognitive perspective. *Aggression and Violent Behavior, 5*(1), 63-78.

O

O'Connell, M. (1999). Is Irish public opinion towards crime distorted by media bias? *European Journal of Communication, 14*(2), 191-212.

Ohlemacher, T. (2001). Racketeering and restaurateurs in Germany: Perceived deficiencies in crime control and effects on confidence in democracy. *British Journal of Criminology, 42*(1), 60-76.

Öhman, A., & Soares, J.J.F. (1994). 'Unconscious anxiety': Phobic responses to masked stimuli. *Journal of Abnormal Psychology, 103*(2), 231-240.

Oliver, W.M. (2002). The pied piper of crime in America: An analysis of the presidents' and public's agenda on crime. *Criminal Justice Policy Review, 13*(2), 139-155.

Oliver, W.M. (2003). The power to persuade: Presidential influence over congress on crime control policy. *Criminal Justice Review, 28*(1), 113-132.

Olsen-Fulero, L., & Fulero, S.M. (1997). Commonsense rape judgments: An empathy-complexity theory of rape juror story making. *Psychology, Public Policy, & Law,* June/September, *3*(2-3), 402-427.

O'Muircheartaigh, C. (1997). Measurement error in surveys: A historical perspective. In: L. Lyberg, P. Biemer, M. Collins, E. DeLeeuw, C. Dippo, N. Schwarz & D. Trewin (Eds.), *Survey Measurement and Process Quality* (pp. 1-25). New York: John Wiley & Sons.

Oosterveld, P. (1996). *Questionnaire Design Methods*. Nijmegen: Berkhout.

Orth, U. (2002). Secondary victimization of crime victims by criminal proceeding. *Social Justice Research, 15*(4), 313-326.

Osborne, T., & Rose, N. (1999). Do the social sciences create phenomena? The example of public opinion research. *British Journal of Sociology, 50*(3), 367-396.

Osgood, C.E. (1969a). The nature and measurement of meaning. In: J.G. Snider & C.E. Osgood (Eds.), *Semantic Differential Technique: A Sourcebook* (pp. 3-41). Chicago: Aldine.

Osgood, C.E. (1969b). Semantic differential technique in the comparative study of cultures. In: J.G. Snider & C.E. Osgood (Eds.), *Semantic Differential Technique: A Sourcebook* (pp. 303-332). Chicago: Aldine.

Osgood, C.E., & Suci, G.J. (1969). Factor analysis of meaning. In: J.G. Snider & C.E. Osgood (Eds.), *Semantic Differential Technique: A Sourcebook* (pp. 42-55). Chicago: Aldine.

Osgood, C.E., Suci, G.J., & Tannenbaum, P.H. (1978). *The Measurement of Meaning* (4th ed.). Urbana: University of Illinois Press.

Osgood, D.W. (1998). Interdisciplinary integration: Building criminology by stealing from our friends. *The Criminologist, 23*(4).

Osterlind, S.J. (1983). *Test Item Bias* (Vol. 30). Beverly Hills: Sage Publications.

Oudenhoven, N. van, Pieper, I., & Engelfriet, T. (2001). *Jong in Den Haag 2001*. The Hague: ICDI (International Child Development Initiatives).

Outhwaite, W. (1983). *Concept Formation in Social Science*. London: Routledge & Kegan Paul.

Outhwaite, W. (1987). *New Philosophies of Social Science: Realism, Hermeneutics and Critical Theory*. London: Macmillan.

Overbeeke, R.V. (1993). *Metrobeheer (RET) eerste rapportage: Passagiers over de technische voorzieningen, observatie van alle stations*. Amsterdam: Van Dijk, Van Soomeren en partners.

P

Pacione, M. (2003). Urban environmental quality and human wellbeing: A social geographical perspective. *Landscape and Urban Planning, 65*(1-2), 19-30.

Pain, R. (1997). Whither women's fear? Perceptions of sexual violence in public and private space. *International Review of Victimology, 4*, 297-312.

Pain, R., Williams, S., & Hudson, B. (2000). Auditing Fear of Crime on North Tyneside: A Qualitative Approach. Paper presented at the British Criminology Conference: Selected Proceedings. Volume 3, Retrieved from: <http://www.lboro.ac.uk/departments/ss/bsc/bccsp/vol03/pain.html>

Palmer, C. (2003). Risk perception: Another look at the 'white male' effect. *Health, Risk & Society, 5*(1), 71-83.

Pantazis, C. (2000). 'Fear of crime', vulnerability and poverty: Evidence from the British crime survey. *British Journal of Criminology, 40*(3), 414-436.

Parish, J. (2001). The age of anxiety. In: J. Parish & M. Parker (Eds.), *The Age of Anxiety: Conspiracy Theory and the Human Sciences* (pp. 1-16). Oxford: Blackwell.

Parker, M. (2001). Human science as conspiracy theory. In: J. Parish & M. Parker (Eds.), *The Age of Anxiety: Conspiracy Theory and the Human Sciences* (pp. 191-207). Oxford: Blackwell.

Paulsen, D.J. (2002). Wrong side of the tracks: Exploring the role of newspaper coverage of homicide in socially constructing dangerous places. *Journal of Criminal Justice and Popular Culture, 9*(3), 113-127.

Pawlowski, T. (1980). *Concept Formation in the Humanities and the Social Sciences*. Dordrecht: Reidel Publishing Company.

Pearson, G. (1983). *Hooligan: A History of Respectable Fears*. London: Macmillan.

Pearson, K., & Pearson, E.S. (1978). *The History of Statistics in the 17th and 18th Centuries against the Changing Background of Intellectual, Scientific, and Religious Thought: Lectures by Karl Pearson given at University College, London, during the Academic Sessions, 1921-1933*. London: C. Griffin.

Peasley-Miklus, C., & Vrana, S.R. (2000). Effect of worrisome and relaxing thinking on fearful emotional processing. *Behaviour Research and Therapy, 38*(2), 129-144.

Peelo, M., & Soothill, K. (2000). The place of public narratives in reproducing social order. *Theoretical Criminology, 4*(2), 131-148.

Pelser, E., Louw, A., & Ntuli, S. (2000). *Poor Safety: Crime and Policing in South Africa's Rural Areas.* Pretoria/Cape Town, South Africa: Institute for Security Studies.

Perkins, D.D., Florin, P., Rich, R.C., Wandersman, A., & Chavis, D.M. (1990). Participation and the social and physical environment of residential blocks: Crime and community context. *American Journal of Community Psychology, 18*(1 (feb)), 83.

Perkins, D.D., Meeks, J.W., & Taylor, R.B. (1992). The physical-environment of street blocks and resident perceptions of crime and disorder: Implications for theory and measurement. *Journal of Environmental Psychology, 12*(1), 21-34.

Perkins, D.D., & Taylor, R.B. (1996). Ecological assessments of community disorder: Their relationship to fear of crime and theoretical implications. *American Journal of Community Psychology, 24*(1), 63-107.

Perloff, L.S., & Fetzer, B.K. (1986). Self-other judgments and perceived vulnerability to victimization. *Journal of Personality and Social Psychology, 50*, 502-510.

Perse, E.M., Ferguson, D.A., & McLeod, D.M. (1994). Cultivation in the newer media environment. *Communication Research, 21*(1), 79-104.

Petts, J., Horlick-Jones, T., & Murdock, G. (2001). *Social Amplification of Risk: The Media and the Public* (No. contract research report 329/2001). Norwich: Health and Safety Executive.

Phillips, L.M. (1999). Recasting consent: Agency and victimization in adult-teen relationships. In: S. Lamb (Ed.), *New Versions of Victims: Feminists Struggle with the Concept* (pp. 82-107). New York: New York University Press.

Phillips, L.M. (2000). *Flirting with Danger: Young Women's Reflections on Sexuality and Domination.* New York: New York University Press.

Phillips, T., & Smith, P. (2004). Emotional and behavioural responses to everyday incivility: Challenging the fear/avoidance paradigm. *Journal of Sociology, 40*(4), 378-400.

Pidgeon, N. (1998). Risk assessment, risk values and the social science programme: Why we do need risk perception research. *Reliability Engineering & System Safety, 59*(1), 5-15.

Pidgeon, N., Hood, C., Jones, D., Turner, B., & Gibson, R. (1992). Risk perception. In: Royal Society, *Risk: Analysis, Perception and Management* (pp. 89-134). London: The Royal Society.

Pierce, K.A., & Kirkpatrick, D.R. (1992). Do men lie on fear surveys. *Behaviour Research and Therapy, 30*(4), 415-418.

Pilisuk, M., Parks, S.H., & Hawkes, G. (1987). Public perception of technological risk. *The Social Science Journal, 24*(4), 403-413.

Pini, B. (2002). Focus groups, feminist research and farm women: Opportunities for empowerment in rural social research. *Journal of Rural Studies, 18*(3), 339-351.

Pligt, J. van der (1996). Risk perception and self-protective behavior. *European Psychologist, 1*(1), 34-43.

Politiemonitor, P. (2003a). *Ontwikkeling 2002-2003 politie (prestatie) monitor (bevolking).* The Hague; Hilversum: Projectbureau Politiemonitor (B&A Groep; Intomart).

Pollman, C. (1997). *Scenario zedenzaken en maatschappelijke onrust: Plan van aanpak rondom zedenzaken met (vermoedelijk) meerdere slachtoffers ter minimalisering van maatschappelijke onrust.* Amsterdam: GG&GD Politie Amsterdam Amstelland.

Popper, K. (1968). *The Logic of Scientific Discovery.* New York: Harper & Row.

Porter, T.M. (1996). *Trust in Numbers: The Pursuit of Objectivity in Science and Public Life.* Princeton, NJ: Princeton University Press.

Poulton, R., & Menzies, R.G. (2002). Non-associative fear acquisition: A review of the evidence from retrospective and longitudinal research. *Behaviour Research and Therapy, 40*(2), 127-149.

Price, P.C. (2001). A group size effect on personal risk judgments: Implications for unrealistic optimism. *Memory & Cognition, 29*(4), 578-586.

Pride, R.A. (2002). How critical events rather than performance trends shape public evaluations of the schools. *The Urban Review, 34*(2), 159-178.

Prior, L., Glasner, P., & McNally, R. (2000). Genotechnology: Three challenges to risk legitimation. In: B. Adam, U. Beck & J. van Loon (Eds.), *The Risk Society and Beyond: Critical Issues for Social Theory* (pp. 105-121). London; Thousand Oaks, CA: Sage.

Pritchard, D., & Hughes, K.D. (1997). Patterns of deviance in crime news. *Journal of Communication, 47*(3), 49-67.

Programmabureau Veilig (2002). *Veiligheidsindex Rotterdam voorjaar 2002: Rapportage bevolkingsenquête januari 2002 en feitelijke criminaliteitsgegevens en stadsgegevens over 2001.* Rotterdam: Programmabureau Veilig/ Gemeente Rotterdam.

Programmabureau Veilig (2004). *Veiligheidsindex Rotterdam 2004: Meting van de veiligheid in Rotterdam: Rapportage bevolkingsenquête januari-februari 2004 en feitelijke criminaliteitsgegevens en stadsgegevens over 2003.* Rotterdam: Programmabureau Veilig/ Gemeente Rotterdam.

Psillos, S. (2000). Rudolf Carnap's 'theoretical concepts in science'. *Studies in History and Philosophy of Science Part A, 31*(1), 151-172.

Putnam, H. (1962/1971). The analytic and the synthetic. In: H. Feigl & G. Maxwell (Eds.), *Scientific Explanation, Space, and Time* (3rd ed., Vol. III, pp. 358-397). Minneapolis: University of Minnesota Press.

Q

Quarantelli, E.L. (2001). Statistical and conceptual problems in the study of disasters. *Disaster Prevention and Management, 10*(5), 325-338.

Quillian, L., & Pager, D. (2001). Black neighbors, higher crime? The role of racial stereotypes in evaluations of neighborhood crime. *American Journal of Sociology, 107*(3), 717-767.

Quinn, B. A. (2002). Perspectives: Sexual harassment and masculinity the power and meaning of "girl watching". *Gender and Society, 16*(3), 386-403.

R

Rabinowitz, G.B. (1984). An introduction to nonmetric multidimensional scaling. In: H.B. Asher, H.F. Weisberg, J.H. Kessel & W.P. Shively (Eds.), *Theory-Building and Data Analysis in the Social Sciences* (pp. 391-438). Knoxville: University of Tennessee Press.

Rafter, N. (2000). *Shots in the Mirror: Crime, Films, and Society.* New York: Oxford University Press.

Rafter, N.H. (2001). American criminal trial films. *Journal of Law & Society, 28*(1), 9-24.

Ramasubramanian, S., & Oliver, M.B. (2003). Portrayals of sexual violence in popular Hindi films, 1997–99. *Sex Roles, 48*(7-8), 327-336.

Rantala, V. (1991). Definitions and definability. In: J.H. Fetzer, D. Shatz & G.N. Schlesinger (Eds.), *Definitions and Definability: Philosophical Perspectives* (pp. 135-159). Dordrecht: Kluwer Academic Publishers.

Rawlinson, P. (1998). Mafia, media and myth: Representations of Russian organised crime. *Howard Journal of Criminal Justice, 37*(4), 346-358.

Raykov, T. (1998). On the use of confirmatory factor analysis in personality research. *Personality and Individual Differences, 24*(2), 291-293.

Reddy, S.G. (1996). Claims to expert knowledge and the subversion of democracy: The triumph of risk over uncertainty. *Economy and Society, 25*(2), 222-254.

Renn, O. (1998). The role of risk perception for risk management. *Reliability Engineering & System Safety, 59*(1), 49-62.

Renn, O. (2004). Perception of risks. *Toxicology Letters, 149*, 405-413.

Renn, O., & Rohrmann, B. (2000). Cross-cultural risk perception: State and challenges. In: O. Renn & B. Rohrmann (Eds.), *Cross-cultural Risk Perception: A Survey of Empirical Studies* (Vol. 13, pp. 211-233). Dordrecht: Kluwer.

Renneberg, B., Chambless, D.L., & Gracely, E.J. (1992). Prevalence of SCID-diagnosed personality disorders in agoraphobic outpatients. *Journal of Anxiety Disorders, 6*(2), 111-118.

Riad, J.K., Norris, F.H., & Ruback, R.B. (1999). Predicting evacuation in two major disasters: Risk perception, social influence, and access to resources. *Journal of Applied Social Psychology, 29*(5), 918-934.

Richardson, D., & May, H. (1999). Deserving victims? Sexual status and the social construction of violence. *Sociological Review, 47*(2), 308-331.

Rietveld, M. (2000). *Angst voor criminaliteit en bekendheid met de woonplaats.* University of Amsterdam, Amsterdam.

Rigakos, G.S., & Hadden, R.W. (2001). Crime, capitalism and the 'risk society': Towards the same olde modernity? *Theoretical Criminology, 5*(1), 61-84.

Riger, S., & Gordon, M.T. (1981). The fear of rape: A study in social control. *Journal of Social Issues, 37*(4), 71-92.

Riger, S., Gordon, M.T., & LeBailly, R. (1978). Women's fear of crime: From blaming to restricting the victim. *Victimology, 3*(3/4), 274-284.

Riger, S., Gordon, M.T., & LeBailly, R.K. (1982). Coping with urban crime: Women's use of precautionary behaviours. *American Journal of Community Psychology, 10*, 381-390.

Riger, S., & Lavrakas, P.J. (1981). Community ties: Patterns of attachment and social interaction in urban neighborhoods. *American Journal of Community Psychology, 9*. 55-66.

Riger, S., LeBailly, R.K., & Gordon, M.T. (1981). Community ties and urbanites' fear of crime: An ecological investigation. *American Journal of Community Psychology, 9*(6), 653-665.

Risse, T., & Wiener, A. (1999). 'Something rotten' and the social construction of social constructivism: A comment on comments. *Journal of European Public Policy, 6*(5), 775-782.

Roberts, J.V. (2001). *Fear of Crime and Attitudes to Criminal Justice in Canada: A Review of Recent Trends: Report for the Ministry of the Solicitor General Canada.* Ottawa, Ontario: Department of Criminology; University of Ottawa.

Roberts, J.V., & Mohr, R.M. (1994). *Confronting Sexual Assault: A Decade of Legal and Social Change.* Toronto: University of Toronto Press.

Robertshaw, R., Louw, A., & Mtani, A. (2001). *Crime in Dar es Salaam: Results of a City Victim Survey.* Nairobi: United Nations Centre for Human Settlements, International Centre for the Prevention of Crime (Montreal), Institute for Security Studies (Pretoria).

Robertshaw, R., Louw, A., Shaw, M., Mashiyane, M., & Brettell, S. (2001). *Reducing Crime in Durban: A Victim Survey and Safer City Strategy.* Pretoria/Cape Town, South Africa: Institute for Security Studies.

Robinson, J.B., Lawton, B.A., Taylor, R.B., & Perkins, D.D. (2003). Multilevel longitudinal impacts of incivilities: Fear of crime, expected safety, and block satisfaction. *Journal of Quantitative Criminology, 19*(3), 237-274.

Robinson, J.P., Shaver, P.R., & Wrightsman, L.S. (1999). Scale selection and evaluation. In: J.P. Robinson, P.R. Shaver & L.S. Wrightsman (Eds.), *Measures of Political Attitudes* (pp. 1-36). New York: Academic Press.

Robinson, L.N. (1933). History of criminal statistics. *Journal of Criminal Law and Criminology, 24,* 125-139.

Rock, P. (1998). Murderers, victims and 'survivors': The social construction of deviance. *British Journal of Criminology, 38*(2), 185-200.

Rodgers, S., & Thorson, E. (2001). The reporting of crime and violence in the Los Angeles Times: Is there a public health perspective? *Journal of Health Communication, 6*(2), 169-182.

Rohe, W.M., & Burby, R.J. (1988). Fear of crime in public-housing. *Environment and Behavior, 20*(6), 700-720.

Rohlman, J.E. (2001). Attributions of cause for vehicular accidents: Effects of participants' sex, information level, and instructions to identify with the actor. *Psychological Reports, 88*(1), 3-16.

Roiphe, K. (1994). *The Morning After: Sex, Fear, and Feminism.* London: Hamish Hamilton.

Romer, D., Jamieson, K.H., & Aday, S. (2003). Television news and the cultivation of fear of crime. *Journal of Communication, 53*(1), 88-104.

Römkens, R., & Dijkstra, S. (1996). *Het omstreden slachtoffer: Geweld van vrouwen en mannen.* Baarn: Ambo.

Ropeik, D., & Gray, G. (2002). *Risk: A Practical Guide for Deciding What's Really Safe and What's Really Dangerous in the World Around You*: Mariner Books.

Rosen, D.A. (2001). Acoma v. Laguna and the transition from Spanish colonial law to American civil procedure in New Mexico. *Law and History Review, 19*(3), 513-546.

Rosen, J.B., & Schulkin, J. (1998). From normal fear to pathological anxiety. *Psychological Review, 105*(2), 325-350.

Ross, C.E. (2000). Neighborhood disadvantage and adult depression. *Journal of Health & Social Behavior, 41*(2), 177-187.

Ross, C.E., & Jang, S.J. (2000). Neighborhood disorder, fear, and mistrust: The buffering role of social ties with neighbors. *American Journal of Community Psychology, 28*(4), 401-420.

Ross, C.E., & Mirowsky, J. (1999). Disorder and decay: The concept and measurement of perceived neighborhood disorder. *Urban Affairs Review, 34*(3), 412-432.

Ross, C.E., & Mirowsky, J. (2001). Neighborhood disadvantage, disorder, and health. *Journal of Health and Social Behavior, 42*(3), 258-276.

Ross, C.E., Reynolds, J.R., & Geis, K.J. (2000). The contingent meaning of neighborhood stability for residents' psychological well-being. *American Sociological Review, 65*(4), 581-597.

Rossi, P.H., Wright, J.D., & Anderson, A.B. (Eds.). (1983). *Handbook of Survey Research.* New York: Academic Press.

Roth, R. (2002). Guns, gun culture, and homicide: The relationship between firearms, the uses of firearms, and interpersonal violence. *The William and Mary Quarterly: A Magazine of Early American History, 59*(1), 223-240.

Rotterdamse Electrische Trammaatschappij (RET) (1996). *Publieksonderzoek 1996: Sociale veiligheid en service RET.* Rotterdam.

Rowe, G., & Wright, G. (2001). Differences in expert and lay judgments of risk: Myth or reality? *Risk Analysis, 21*(2), 341-356.

Rowland, S. (2001). *From Agatha Christie to Ruth Rendell: British Women Writers in Detective and Crime Fiction.* New York: Palgrave.

Royal Society (1992). *Risk: Analysis, Perception and Management.* London: The Royal Society.

Rozeboom, W.W. (1962/1971). The factual content of theoretical concepts. In: H. Feigl & G. Maxwell (Eds.), *Scientific Explanation, Space, and Time* (3rd ed., Vol. III, pp. 273-357). Minneapolis: University of Minnesota Press.

Rychlak, J.F. (1993). A suggested principle of complementarity for psychology: In theory, not method. *American Psychologist, 48*(9), 933-942.

S

Salas, L., & Surette, R. (1984). The historical roots and development of criminological statistics. *Journal of Criminal Justice, 12*(5), 457-465.

Sampson, R.J. (1988). Local friendship ties and community attachment in mass society: A multilevel systemic model. *American Sociological Review, 53*(5), 766-779.

Sampson, R.J. (1991). Linking the micro- and macrolevel dimensions of community social organization. *Social Forces, 70*(1), 43-64.

Sampson, R.J., & Groves, W.B. (1989). Community structure and crime: Testing social disorganzation theory. *American Journal of Sociology, 94*, 774-802.

Sampson, R.J., & Lauritsen, J.L. (1990). Deviant lifestyles, proximity to crime, and the offender-victim link in personal violence. *Journal of Research in Crime and Delinquency, 27*(2), 110-139.

Sampson, R.J., Morenoff, J.D., & Gannon-Rowley, T. (2002). Assessing 'neighborhood effects': Social processes and new directions in research. *Annual Review of Sociology, 28*, 443-478.

Sampson, R.J., & Raudenbush, S.W. (1999). Systematic social observation of public spaces: A new look at disorder in urban neighborhoods. *American Journal of Sociology, 105*(3), 603-651.

Sampson, R.J., Raudenbush, S.W., & Earls, F. (1997). Neighbourhoods and violent crime: A multilevel study of collective efficacy. *Science, 277*, 918-924.

Sanders, B., & Moore, D. (1999). Childhood maltreatment and date rape. *Journal of Interpersonal Violence*, 14 (12), 115-124.

Sanders, L.M. (1999). Democratic politics and survey research. *Philosophy of the Social Sciences, 29*(2), 248-280.

Sandman, P.M. (1994). Mass media and environmental risk: Seven principles. *Risk: Health, Safety & Environment, 5*.

Sankey, H. (2000). The language of science: Meaning variance and theory comparison. *Language Sciences, 22*(2), 117-136.

Sapolsky, H.M. (Ed.). (1986a). *Consuming Fears: The Politics of Product Risks*. New York: Basic Books.

Sapolsky, H.M. (1986b). The changing politics of cigarette smoking. In: H.M. Sapolsky (Ed.), *Consuming Fears: The Politics of Product Risks* (pp. 19-39). New York: Basic Books.

Sapolsky, H.M. (1986c). The politics of product controversies. In: H.M. Sapolsky (Ed.), *Consuming Fears: The Politics of Product Risks* (pp. 182-202). New York: Basic Books.

Sapolsky, H.M. (1993). The politics of risk. In: E.J. Burger (Ed.), *Risk* (pp. 83-96). Ann Arbor: University of Michigan Press.

Sargent, R.M. (1997). The social construction of scientific evidence. *Journal of Constructivist Psychology, 10*(1), 75-96.

Sarno, C., Hough, M., & Bulos, M. (1999). *Developing a Picture of CCTV in Southwark Town Centres: Final Report*. London: Criminal Policy Research Unit, South Bank University.

Saunders, R. (1998). The legal perspective on stalking. In: J.R. Meloy (Ed.), *The Psychology of Stalking: Clinical and Forensic Perspectives* (pp. 25-49). San Diego: Academic Press.

Saunders, R., & Wheeler, T. (1991). *Handbook of Safety Management*. London: Pitman.

Sauvageau, J. (1999). Sokal and Bricmont's criticism of relativism in the humanities and its relevance to criminology. *Theoretical Criminology, 3*(1), 53-70.

Saxe, J.G., & Galdone, P. (1963). *The Blind Men and the Elephant*. New York: Whittlesey House.

Schachter, S., & Singer, J.E. (1962). Cognitive, social and physiological determinants of emotional state. *Psychological Review, 69*, 379-399.

Scheingold, S.A. (1984). *The Politics of Law and Order: Street Crime and Public Policy*. New York: Longman.

Scherpenzeel, A.C. (1995). *A Question of Quality: Evaluating Survey Questions by Multitrait-Multimethod Studies*. Unpublished Phd, University of Amsterdam, Amsterdam.

Scherpenzeel, A.C., & Saris, W.E. (1997). The validity and reliability of survey questions; a meta-analysis of MTMM Studies. *Sociological Methods and Research, 25*(3), 347-383.

Schlesinger, P., Tumber, H., & Murdock, G. (1991). The Media Politics of Crime and Criminal Justice. *British Journal of Sociology, 42*(3), 397-420.

Schmidt, N.B., & Joiner, T.E. (2002). Structure of the anxiety sensitivity index psychometrics and factor structure in a community sample. *Journal of Anxiety Disorders, 16*(1), 33-49.

Schmitt, N. (1996). Uses and abuses of coefficient alpha. *Psychological Assessment, 8*(4), 350-353.

Schubart, R. (1995). From desire to deconstruction: Horror films and audience reactions. In: D. KiddHewitt & R. Osborne (Eds.), *Crime and the Media: The Post-modern Spectacle* (pp. 219-242). London: Pluto.

Schuman, H., & Kalton, G. (1985). Survey methods. In: G. Lindzey & E. Aronson (Eds.), *Handbook of Social Psychology* (3rd ed., Vol. I, pp. 635-697). New York: Random House.

Schuman, H., & Presser, S. (1981). *Questions and Answers in Attitude Surveys: Experiments on Question Form, Wording, and Context*. New York: Academic Press.

Schwarz, N. (1997). Questionnaire design: The rocky road from concepts to answers. In: L. Lyberg, P. Biemer, M. Collins, E. DeLeeuw, C. Dippo, N. Schwarz & D. Trewin (Eds.), *Survey Measurement and Process Quality* (pp. 29-45). New York: John Wiley & Sons.

Scott, A. (2000). Risk society or Angst society? Two views of risk, consciousness and community. In: B. Adam, U. Beck & J. van Loon (Eds.), *The Risk Society and Beyond: Critical Issues for Social Theory* (pp. 33-46). London; Thousand Oaks, CA: Sage.

Scutt, J.A. (1986). Going backwards: Law 'reform' and women bashing. *Women's Studies International Forum, 9*(1), 49-55.

Scutt, J.A. (1992). The incredible woman: A recurring character in criminal law. *Women's Studies International Forum, 15*(4), 441-460.

Seccombe, K., James, D., & Walters, K.B. (1998). 'They think you ain't much of nothing': The social construction of the welfare mother. *Journal of Marriage and the Family, 60*(4), 849-865.

Segal, M.J. (1986). The politics of salt: The sodium-hypertension issue. In: H.M. Sapolsky (Ed.), *Consuming Fears: The Politics of Product Risks* (pp. 80-115). New York: Basic Books.

Semin, G.R., & Smith, E.R. (2002). Interfaces of social psychology with situated and embodied cognition. *Cognitive Systems Research, 3*(3), 385-396.

Shalhoub-Kevorkian, N. (1999). Towards a cultural definition of rape: Dilemmas in dealing with rape victims in Palestinian society. *Women's Studies International Forum, 22*(2), 157-173.

Shaluf, I.M., Ahmadun, F.l.-r., & Said, A.M. (2003). A review of disaster and crisis. *Disaster Prevention and Management, 12*(1), 24-32.

Shaw, M., & Louw, A. (1998). *Environmental Design for Safer Communities: Preventing Crime in South Africa's Cities and Towns*. Pretoria/Cape Town, South Africa: Institute for Security Studies.

Sheffield, C.J. (1993). The invisible intruder: Women's experiences of obscene phone calls. In: P.B. Bart & E.G. Moran (Eds.), *Violence Against Women: The Bloody Footprints* (pp. 73-78). Newbury Park: Sage Publications.

Sheley, J.F., & Ashkins, C.D. (1981). Crime, crime news, and crime views. *Public Opinion Quarterly, 45*(4), 492-506.

Sherman, L.W. (2000). Criminologie en criminalisering: Provocatie en de wetenschap van strafrechtelijke sancties. *Justitiële verkenningen, 26*(5), 58-74.

Shevlin, M., Miles, J.N.V., Davies, M.N.O., & Walker, S. (2000). Coefficient alpha: A useful indicator of reliability? *Personality and Individual Differences, 28*(2), 229-237.

Shore, B. (1991). Twice-born, once conceived: Meaning construction and cultural cognition. *American Anthropologist, 93*(1), 9-27.

Shore, B. (1996). *Culture in Mind: Cognition, Culture, and the Problem of Meaning*. New York: Oxford University Press.

Shotland, R.L., & Goodstein, L. (1983). Just because she doesn't want to doesn't mean it's rape: An experimentally based causal model of the perception of rape in a dating situation. *Social Psychology Quarterly, 46*(3), 220-232.

Shye, S. (1998). Modern facet theory: content design and measurement in behavioral research. *European Journal of Psychological Assessment, 14*(2).

Shyu, S.L. (1989). *Fear of Crime: A Structural Equation Modeling Approach*. Wayne State University, Detroit.

Siegrist, M., & Cvetkovich, G. (2000). Perception of hazards: The role of social trust and knowledge. *Risk Analysis, 20*(5), 713-719.

Siegrist, M., Earle, T.C., & Gutscher, H. (2003). Test of a trust and confidence model in the applied context of electromagnetic field (EMF) risks. *Risk Analysis, 23*(4), 195-203.

Silverman, E.B., & Della-Giustina, J.A. (2001). Urban policing and the fear of crime. *Urban Studies, 38*(5-6), 941-957.

Simmons, J. (2002). *Crime in England and Wales 2001/2002* (Home Office Statistical Bulletin 7/02). London: Home Office; Patterns of Crime Group in the Research Development and Statistics Directorate.

Simon, T., Crosby, A., & Dahlberg, L. (1999). Students who carry weapons to high school: Comparison with other weapon-carriers. *Journal of Adolescent Health*, 24 (25), 340-348.

Sims, B., Hooper, M., & Peterson, S.A. (2002). Determinants of citizens' attitudes toward police: Results of the Harrisburg citizen survey: 1999. *Policing: An International Journal of Police Strategies & Management, 25*(3), 457-471.

Singer, J.L., Singer, D.G., Desmond, R., Hirsch, B., & Nicol, A. (1988). Family mediation and children's cognition, aggression, and comprehension of television: A longitudinal study. *Journal of Applied Developmental Psychology, 9*(3), 329-347.

Sirgy, M.J., & Cornwell, T. (2001). Further validation of the Sirgy et al.'s measure of community quality of life. *Social Indicators Research, 56*(2), 125-143.

Sirgy, M.J., & Cornwell, T. (2002). How neighborhood features affect quality of life. *Social Indicators Research, 59*(1), 79-114.

Sjöberg, L. (Ed.). (1987). *Risk and Society: Studies of Risk Generation and Reactions to Risk* (Vol. 3). London: Allen & Unwin.

Sjöberg, L. (1998a). Risk perception: Experts and the public. *European Psychologist March, 3*(1), 1-12.

Sjöberg, L. (1998b). World views, political attitudes and risk perception. *Risk: Health, Safety & Environment, 9*, 137-152.

Sjöberg, L. (1999). Risk perception in Western Europe. *Ambio, 28*(6), 543-549.

Sjöberg, L. (2000a). Factors in risk perception. *Risk Analysis, 20*(1), 1-11.

Sjöberg, L. (2000b). The methodology of risk perception research. *Quality & Quantity November, 34*(4), 407-418. Sjöberg, L. (2001a). Political decisions and public risk perception. *Reliability Engineering & System Safety, 72*(2), 115-123.

Sjöberg, L. (2001b). Limits of knowledge and the limited importance of trust. *Risk Analysis, 21*(1), 189-198.

Sjöberg, L. (2002a). The allegedly simple structure of experts' risk perception: An urban legend in risk research. *Science Technology & Human Values, 27*(4), 443-459.

Sjöberg, L. (2002b). Are received risk perception models alive and well? *Risk Analysis, 22*(4), 665-669.

Sjöberg, L. (2003). Attitudes and risk perceptions of stakeholders in a nuclear waste siting issue. *Risk Analysis, 23*(4), 739-749.

Sjöberg, L., & Drottz-Sjöberg, B.M. (1991). Knowledge and risk perception among nuclear-power-plant employees. *Risk Analysis, 11*(4), 607-618.

Skogan, W.G. (1975). Measurement problems in official and survey crime rates. *Journal of Criminal Justice, 3*(1), 17-31.

Skogan, W.G. (Ed.). (1976). *Sample Surveys of the Victims of Crime*. Cambridge, Mass.: Ballinger.

Skogan, W.G. (1987). The impact of victimisation on fear. *Crime and Delinquency, 33*, 135-154.

Skogan, W.G. (1990a). *Disorder and Decline: Crime and the Spiral of Decay in American Neighborhoods*. New York: Free Press.

Skogan, W.G. (1990b). A Review: The national crime survey redesign. *Public Opinion Quarterly, 54*(2), 256-272.

Skogan, W.G. (1993). The various meanings of fear. In: W. Bilsky, C. Pfeiffer & P. Wetzels (Eds.), *Fear of Crime and Criminal Victimization* (pp. 131-140). Stuttgart: Enke.

Skogan, W.G. (1999). Measuring what matters: Crime, disorder, and fear. In: R.H. Langworthy (Ed.), *Proceedings From the Policing Research Institute Meetings* (pp. 37-88). Washington, DC.

Skogan, W.G., & Klecka, W.R. (1977). *The Fear of Crime* (SETUPS: supplementary empirical teaching units in political science). Washington, DC: American political science association.

Skogan, W.G., & Maxfield, M.G. (1981). *Coping with Crime: Individual and Neighbourhood Reactions*. London: Sage Publications.

Skolbekken, J.-A. (1995). The risk epidemic in medical journals. *Social Science & Medicine, 40*(3), 291-305.

Slanger, E., & Rudestam, K.E. (1997). Motivation and disinhibition in high risk sports: Sensation seeking and self-efficacy. *Journal of Research in Personality, 31*(3), 355-374.

Sloman, S.A. (1996). The empirical case for two systems of reasoning. *Psychological Bulletin, 119*, 3-22.

Slovic, P. (1987). Perception of risk. *Science, 236*, 280-285.

Slovic, P. (1992). Public perceptions of risk. *Risk Management, 39*(3), 54.

Slovic, P. (1998). The risk game. *Reliability Engineering & System Safety, 59*(1), 73-77.

Slovic, P. (1999). Trust, emotion, sex, politics, and science: Surveying the risk-assessment battlefield (Reprinted from Environment, ethics, and behavior, pp. 277-313, 1997). *Risk Analysis, 19*(4), 689-701.

Slovic, P. (2000). *The Perception of Risk*. London; Sterling, VA: Earthscan Publications.

Slovic, P., Finucane, M.L., Peters, E., & MacGregor, D.G. (2004). Risk as analysis and risk as feelings: Some thoughts about affect, reason, risk, and rationality. *Risk Analysis, 24*(2), 311-322.

Slovic, P., Fischhoff, B., & Lichtenstein, S. (1978). Accident probabilities and seat belt usage: A psychological perspective. *Accident Analysis & Prevention, 10*(4), 281-285.

Slovic, P., Fischhoff, B., & Lichtenstein, S. (1979). Rating the risks. *Environment, 21*(3), 14-20, 36-39.

Slovic, P., Fischhoff, B., & Lichtenstein, S. (1980). Facts and fears: Understanding perceived risk. In: R.C. Schwing, J. Walther & A. Alberts (Eds.), *Societal Risk Assessment: How Safe is Safe Enough?* (pp. 181-216). New York: Plenum Press.

Slovic, P., Fischhoff, B., & Lichtenstein, S. (1981). Perceived risk: Psychological factors and social implications. In: F. Warner (Ed.), *The Assessment and Perception of Risk* (pp. 17-34). London: The Royal Society.

Slovic, P., Layman, M., & Flynn, J.H. (1991). Risk perception, trust, and nuclear waste: Lessons from Yucca Mountain. *Environment, 33*(3), 6-11.

Slovic, P., Lichtenstein, S., & Fischhoff, B. (1984). Modeling the societal impact of fatal accidents. *Management Science, 30*(4, Risk Analysis), 464-474.

Small, D.A., & Loewenstein, G. (2003). Helping *a* victim or helping *the* victim: Altruism and identifiability. *Journal of Risk and Uncertainty, 26*(1), 5-16.

Smidts, A. (1992). *Risk Attitude, Strength of Preference and Intrinsic Risk Attitude: A Multiple Measurement Approach* (Management Report Series no. 125). Rotterdam: Rotterdam School of Management; Erasmus University.

Smith, S. J. (1984). Crime and the Structure of Social Relations. *Transactions of the Institute of British Geographers, 9*(4), 427-442.

Smith, B.L., & Huff, C.R. (1982). Crime in the country: The vulnerability and victimization of rural citizens. *Journal of Criminal Justice, 10*(4), 271-282.

Smith, D.A., & Jarjoura, G.R. (1989). Household characteristics, neighborhood composition and victimization risk. *Social Forces, 68*(2), 621-640.

Smith, E.R., & DeCoster, J. (2000). Dual process models in social and cognitive psychology: Conceptual integration and links to underlying memory systems. *Personality and Social Psychology Review, 4*(2), 108-131.

Smith, L.N., & Hill, G.D. (1991a). Perceptions of crime seriousness and fear of crime. *Sociological Focus, 24*(4), 315-327.

Smith, L.N., & Hill, G.D. (1991b). Victimization and fear of crime. *Criminal Justice and Behavior, 18*(2), 217-239.

Smith, M.D. (1994). Enhancing the quality of survey data on violence against women: A feminist approach. *Gender and Society, 8*(1), 109-127.

Smith, S.L., & Wilson, B.J. (2000). Children's reactions to a television news story: The impact of video footage and proximity of the crime. *Communication Research, 27*(5), 641-673.

Smith, W.R., & Torstensson, M. (1997). Gender differences in risk perception and neutralizing fear of crime: Toward resolving the paradoxes. *British Journal of Criminology, 37*(4), 608-634.

Smoke, R. (1996b). The research design of this study. In: R. Smoke (Ed.), *Perceptions of Security: Public Opinion and Expert Assessments in Europe's New Democracies* (pp. 18-30). New York: Manchester University Press.

Snider, J.G., & Osgood, C.E. (Eds.). (1969). *Semantic Differential Technique: A Sourcebook.* Chicago: Aldine.

Sociaal en Cultureel Planbureau (SCP) (2000). Justitie en strafrechtspleging. In: *Sociaal en cultureel rapport 2000, Nederland in Europa* (pp. 551-595). The Hague: Sociaal en Cultureel Planbureau.

Soetenhorst-De Savornin Lohman, J. (1982). Gevoelens van onveiligheid: Wat kan de overheid eraan doen? *Beleid & Maatschappij, 6*, 156-162.

Sokal, A., & Bricmont, J. (1999). *Intellectueel Bedrog: Postmodernisme, wetenschap en antiwetenschap.* Antwerpen; Breda: EPO; De Geus.

Sooman, A., & Macintyre, S. (1995). Health and perceptions of the local environment in socially contrasting neighbourhoods in Glasgow. *Health & Place, 1*(1), 15-26.

Sorell, T. (1990). Hobbes's persuasive civil science. *The Philosophical Quarterly, 40*(160), 342-351.

Sorensen, R. (1991). Vagueness and the desiderata for definition. In: J.H. Fetzer, D. Shatz & G.N. Schlesinger (Eds.), *Definitions and Definability: Philosophical Perspectives* (pp. 71-109). Dordrecht: Kluwer Academic Publishers.

Sorenson, S.B., Manz, J.G., & Berk, R.A. (1998). News media coverage and the epidemiology of homicide. *American Journal of Public Health, 88*(10), 1510-1514.

Sourcebook of Criminal Justice Statistics (2000). Table 2.86 (p. 161). High school seniors reporting that they worry about selected social problems, United States, 1988-2000. Retrieved from: URL: http://www.albany.edu/sourcebook/ [25 July 2005].

Sparks, R. (1992). *Television and the Drama of Crime: Moral Tales and the Place of Crime in Public Life*. Buckingham, UK; Philadelphia: Open University Press.

Spector, M. (1966a). Theory and observation (I). *The British Journal for the Philosophy of Science, 17*(1), 1-20.

Spector, M. (1966b). Theory and observation (II). *The British Journal for the Philosophy of Science, 17*(2), 89-104.

Sprague, J. (1997). Holy men and big guns: The can[n]on in social theory. *Gender and Society, 11*(1), 88-107.

Sprott, J.B. (1999). Are members of the public tough on crime? The dimensions of public 'punitiveness'. *Journal of Criminal Justice, 27*(5), 467-474.

Stafford, M.C., & Galle, O.R. (1984). Victimization rates, exposure to risk, and fear of crime. *Criminology, 22*, 173-185.

Stallings, R.A. (1994). Hindsight, organizational routines and media risk coverage. *Risk: Health, Safety & Environment, 5*, 271.

Stanko, E. (1987). Typical violence, normal precaution: Men, women and interpersonal violence in England, Wales, Scotland and the USA. In: J. Hanmer & M. Maynard (Eds.), *Women, Violence, and Social Control* (pp. 122-134). Atlantic Highlands, NJ: Humanities Press International.

Stanko, E. (1999). Identities and criminal violence: Observations on law's recognition of vulnerable victims in England and Wales. *Studies in Law Politics and Society,* (Vol 19, OL 19, pp. 99-119).

Stanko, E.A. (1985). *Intimate Intrusions: Women's Experience of Male Violence*. London: Routledge & Kegan Paul.

Stanko, E.A. (1988a). Hidden violence against women. In: M. Maguire & J. Pointing (Eds.), *Victims of Crime: A New Deal?* (pp. 40-46). Milton Keynes: Open University Press.

Stanko, E.A. (1988b). Fear of crime and the myth of the safe home. In: K. Ylló & M. Bograd (Eds.), *Feminist Perspectives on Wife Abuse* (pp. 75-88). London: Sage.

Stanko, E.A. (1990). *Everyday Violence: How Women and Men Experience Sexual and Physical Danger*. London; Winchester, Mass.: Pandora; Unwin Hyman.

Stanko, E.A. (1993). Ordinary fear: Women, violence, and personal safety. In: P.B. Bart & E.G. Moran (Eds.), *Violence against Women: The Bloody Footprints* (pp. 155-164). Newbury Park: Sage Publications.

Stanko, E.A. (1994, 21-26 August 1994). The Commercialism of Women's Fear of Crime. Paper presented at the 8th International Symposium on Victimology, Adelaide, South Australia.

Stanko, E.A. (1995). Women, crime, and fear. *The Annals of the AAPS, 539*, 46-58.

Stapleton, C.D. (1997). Basic Concepts and Procedures of Confirmatory Factor analysis. Paper presented at annual meeting of the Southwest Educational Research Association. Austin.

Statline/ StatWeb 3.0 [online] (CBS 2002). Tijdreeksen Mens en Maatschappij; Rechtsbescherming en Veiligheid; 1982-heden. Voorburg/Heerlen: Centraal Bureau voor de Statistiek, 2002. Retrieved from: URL: http://statline.cbs.nl/.

Stein, K. (2001). *Public Perceptions of Crime and Justice in Canada: A Review of opinion Polls* (No. RR2001-1e). Ottawa, Ontario: Research and Statistics Division; Department of Justice Canada.

Stern, P.C., & Kalof, L. (1996). *Evaluating Social Science Research* (2nd ed.). New York: Oxford University Press.

Stevens, J. (1996). *Applied Multivariate Statistics for the Social Sciences.* Mahwah, NJ: Lawrence Erlbaum Associates.

Stevens, L. (2002). *Strafrecht en seksualiteit: De misdrijven inzake aanranding van de eerbaarheid, verkrachting, ontucht, prostitutie, seksreclame, zedenschennis en overspel.* Antwerpen: Intersentia.

Stigler, S.M. (1986). *The History of Statistics: The Measurement of Uncertainty before 1900.* Cambridge, Mass.: Belknap Press of Harvard University Press.

Stigler, S.M. (1999). *Statistics on the Table: The History of Statistical Concepts and Methods.* Cambridge, Mass.: Harvard University Press.

StJohn, C., & Healdmoore, T. (1995). Fear of Black Strangers. *Social Science Research, 24*(3), 262-280.

Strauss, A.L., & Corbin, J.M. (1990). *Basics of Qualitative Research: Grounded Theory Procedures and Techniques.* Newbury Park, CA: Sage.

Strauss, A., & Corbin, J. (1994). Grounded theory methodology: An overview. In: N.K. Denzin & Y.S. Lincoln (Eds.), *Handbook of Qualitative Research* (pp. 273-285). Thousand Oaks: Sage.

Streiner, D.L. (2003). Starting at the beginning: An introduction to coefficient alpha and internal consistency. *Journal of Personality Assessment, 80*(1), 99-103.

Stringer, P. (1975b). Living in the city. In: D. Canter & P. Stringer (Eds.), *Environmental Interaction: Psychological Approaches to our Physical Surroundings* (pp. 253-279). London: Surrey University Press.

Stylianou, S. (2003). Measuring crime seriousness perceptions: What have we learned and what else do we want to know. *Journal of Criminal Justice, 31*(1), 37-56.

Sunstein, C. (1997). Bad deaths. *Journal of Risk and Uncertainty, 14*(3), 259-282.

Sunstein, C.R. (2003). Terrorism and probability neglect. *Journal of Risk & Uncertainty, 26*(2-3), 121-136.

Surette, R. (1989). Media trials. *Journal of Criminal Justice, 17*(4), 293-308.

Surette, R. (2001). Public information officers: The civilianization of a criminal justice profession. *Journal of Criminal Justice, 29*(2), 107-117.

Surette, R., & Otto, C. (2002). A test of a crime and justice infotainment measure. *Journal of Criminal Justice, 30*(5), 443-453.

Surette, R., & Richard, A. (1995). Public information officers: A descriptive study of crime news gatekeepers. *Journal of Criminal Justice, 23*(4), 325-336.

Svenson, O., Fischhoff, B., & MacGregor, D. (1985). Perceived driving safety and seatbelt usage. *Accident Analysis & Prevention, 17*(2), 119-133.

T

Tansey, J. (2004a). Risk as politics, culture as power. *Journal of Risk Research, 7*(1), 17-32.

Tansey, J. (2004b). 'If all you have is a hammer': A response to Sjöberg. *Journal of Risk Research, 7*(3), 361-363.

Tanur, J.M. (1983). Methods for large-scale surveys and experiments. *Sociological Methodology, 14*, 1-71.

Taylor, H. (1998a). Rationing crime: The political economy of criminal statistics since the 1850s. *Economic History Review, 51*(3), 569-590.

Taylor, H. (1998b). The politics of the rising crime statistics of England and Wales, 1914-1960. *Crime, History and Societies, 2*(1), 5-28.

Taylor, H.F. (1971). Semantic differential factor scores as measures of attitude and perceived attitude. *Journal of Social Psychology, 83*(2), 229-234.

Taylor, I. (1995). Private homes and public others: An analysis of talk about crime in suburban South Manchester in the mid-1990s. *British Journal of Criminology, 35*(2), 263-285.

Taylor, R.B. (1995a). Impact of neighborhood structure, crime, and physical deterioration on residents and business personnel in Minneapolis-St.Paul, 1970-1982 [Computer file]. ICPSR version. Philadelphia, PA: Temple University [producer], 1995. Ann Arbor, MI: Inter-university Consortium for Political and Social Research [distributor], 1998.

Taylor, R.B. (1995b). *Responses to Disorder: Relative Impacts of Neighborhood Structure, Crime, and Physical Deterioration on Residents and Business Personnel.* Philadelphia: Department of Criminal Justice; Temple University.

Taylor, R.B. (1996a). Impacts of specific incivilities on responses to crime and local commitment, 1979-1994: [Atlanta, Baltimore, Chicago, Minneapolis-St.Paul, and Seattle] [Computer file]. ICPSR version. Philadelphia, PA: Temple University [producer], 1996. Ann Arbor, MI: Inter-university Consortium for Political and Social Research [distributor], 1998.

Taylor, R.B. (1996b). Neighborhood responses to disorder and local attachments: The systemic model of attachment, social disorganization, and neighborhood use value. *Sociological Forum, 11*(1), 41-74.

Taylor, R.B. (1997a). Social order and disorder of street blocks and neighborhoods: Ecology, microecology, and the systemic model of social disorganization. *Journal of Research in Crime and Delinquency, 34*(1), 113-155.

Taylor, R.B. (1997b). *Crime, Grime, Fear, and Decline: A Longitudinal Look (Final Report).* Washington, DC: United States Department of Justice; National Institute of Justice.

Taylor, R.B. (1999). *Crime, Grime, Fear, and Decline: A Longitudinal Look.* [Washington, DC]: U.S. Dept. of Justice Office of Justice Programs, National Institute of Justice.

Taylor, R.B., & Covington, J. (1993). Community structural change and fear of crime. *Social Problems, 40*(3), 374-397.

Taylor, R.B., & Hale, M. (1986). Testing alternative models of fear of crime. *Journal of Criminal Law & Criminology, 77*(1), 151-189.

Taylor, R.B., & Harrell, A.V. (1996). *Physical Environment and Crime* (NIJ Research Report). Washington: U.S. Department of Justice; Office of Justice Programs; National Institute of Justice.

Taylor, R.B., & Shumaker, S.A. (1990). Local crime as a natural hazard: Implications for understanding the relationship between disorder and fear of crime. *American Journal of Community Psychology, 18*(5), 619-641.

Taylor, S.E. (1989). *Positive Illusions: Creative Self-deception and the Healthy Mind.* New York: Basic Books.

Thabet, A.A., Abed, Y., & Vostanis, P. (2002). Emotional problems in Palestinian children living in a war zone: A cross-sectional study. *Lancet, 359*(9320), 1801-1804.

Thomas, C.J., & Bromley, R.D.F. (1996). Safety and shopping: Peripherality and shopper anxiety in the city centre. *Environment and Planning C-Government and Policy, 14*(4), 469-488.

Thomas, C.J., & Bromley, R.D.F. (2000). City-centre revitalisation: Problems of fragmentation and fear in the evening and night-time city. *Urban Studies, 37*(8), 1403-1429.

Thompson, B. (1990). Alphamax: A program that maximizes coefficient alpha by selective item deletion. *Educational and Psychological Measurement, 50*(3), 585-589.

Thompson, R.S., Rivara, F.P., Thompson, D.C., Barlow, W.E., Sugg, N.K., Maiuro, R.D., et al. (2000). Identification and management of domestic violence: A randomized trial. *American Journal of Preventive Medicine, 19*(4), 253-263.

Thornton, B., Gibbons, F.X., & Gerrard, M. (2002). Risk perception and prototype perception: Independent processes predicting risk behavior. *Personality and Social Psychology Bulletin, 28*(7), 986-999.

Thurstone, L.L. (1928). Attitudes can be measured. *American Journal of Sociology, 33*(4), 529-554.

Tipples, J., Young, A.W., Quinlan, P., Broks, P., & Ellis, A.W. (2002). Searching for threat. *Quarterly Journal of Experimental Psychology, 55*(3/August 01), 1007-1026.

Tipton, L. (1992). Reporting on the public mind. In: J.D. Kennamer (Ed.), *Public Opinion, the Press, and Public Policy* (pp. 131-144). Westport, Conn.: Praeger.

Tjaden, P., & Thoennes, N. (1998a). *Prevalence, Incidence, and Consequences of Violence Against Women: Findings From the National Violence Against Women Survey: Research in Brief* (No. NCJ 172837). Washington, DC: United States Department of Justice, National Institute of Justice.

Tjaden, P., & Thoennes, N. (1998b). *Stalking in America: Findings From the National Violence Against Women Survey* (Research in Brief No. 169592). Washington, DC: Department of Justice.

Tjaden, P., & Thoennes, N. (1998c). Violence and threats of violence against women and men in the United States, 1994-1996 [Computer file]. ICPSR version. Denver, CO: Center for Policy Research [producer], 1998. Ann Arbor, MI: Inter-university Consortium for Political and Social Research [distributor], 1999.

Tjaden, P., & Thoennes, N. (2000a). *Extent, Nature, and Consequences of Intimate Partner Violence: Findings From the National Violence Against Women Survey, Research Report* (No. NCJ 181867). Washington, DC: United States Department of Justice, National Institute of Justice.

Tjaden, P., & Thoennes, N. (2000b). *Full Report of the Prevalence, Incidence, and Consequences of Violence Against Women: Findings From the National Violence Against Women Survey* (No. NCJ 183781). Washington, DC: United States Department of Justice, National Institute of Justice.

Tweede Kamer/ Staten Generaal. (1997). *Algemene politieke beschouwingen naar aanleiding van de Miljoenennota voor het jaar 1998*. Handelingen 1997-1998, no. 1, Tweede Kamer, pp. 10-99.

Toseland, R.W. (1982). Fear of crime: Who is most vulnerable? *Journal of Criminal Justice, 10*(3), 199-209.

Travis, R., & Velasco, S.C. (1994). Social structure and psychological distress among blacks and whites in America. *The Social Science Journal, 31*(2), 197-207.

Tufte, E.R. (1983). *The visual display of quantitative information*. Cheshire, Conn.: Graphics Press.

Türksever, A.N.E., & Atalik, G. (2001). Possibilities and limitations for the measurement of the quality of life in urban areas. *Social Indicators Research, 53*(2), 163-187.

Turner, S.P., & Factor, R.A. (1984). *Max Weber and the Dispute over Reason and Value: A Study in Philosophy, Ethics, and Politics*. London: Routledge & Kegan Paul.

U

Ulleberg, P., & Rundmo, T. (2003). Personality, attitudes and risk perception as predictors of risky driving behaviour among young drivers. *Safety Science, 41*(5), 427-443.

Upshaw, H.S. (1968). Attitude measurement. In: H.M. Blalock & A.B. Blalock (Eds.), *Methodology in Social Research* (pp. 60-111). New York: McGraw-Hill.

U.S. Bureau of the Census (1997). Historical statistics of the United States on CD-ROM: Colonial Times to 1970: Bicentennial Edition. Edited by Susan B. Carter, Scott Sigmund Gartner, Michael R. Haines, Alan L. Olmstead, Richard Sutch, and Gavin Wright (Ed.), Electronic edition edited by Susan B.Carter, et al. [machine-readable data file]. New York: Cambridge University Press.

U.S. Dept. of Justice, Bureau of Justice Statistics (1998). Criminal victimization and perceptions of community safety in 12 United States cities [Computer file]. ICPSR version. U.S. Dept. of Commerce, Bureau of the Census [producer], 1999. Ann Arbor, MI: Inter-university Consortium for Political and Social Research [distributor], 1999.

V

Vacha, E.F., & McLaughlin, T.F. (2000). The impact of poverty, fear of crime, and crime victimization on keeping firearms for protection and unsafe gun-storage practices: A review and analysis with policy recommendations. *Urban Education, 35*(4), 496-510.
Valentine, G. (1997). A safe place to grow up? Parenting, perceptions of children's safety and the rural idyll. *Journal of Rural Studies, 13*(2), 137-148.
Vanderveen, G. (1999). Felle ruzies en nuchtere discussies. *Tijdschrift voor Criminologie, 41*(2), 208-211.
Vanderveen, G.N.G. (1998a). The Influence of Risk Perception on Behavior and on Fear of Victimization: Primary and Secondary Risk. Paper presented at the 50th Annual Meeting of the American Society of Criminology; Crime, Justice and Public Policy: Examining Our Past and Envisioning Our Future, Washington, DC.
Vanderveen, G.N.G. (1998b). *De beleving van veiligheid in de metro: Een beschrijving.* Rotterdam: Erasmus University Rotterdam.
Vanderveen, G.N.G. (1998c). Feelings of Unsafety: Social and Physical Characteristics of the Subway in Rotterdam. Paper presented at the Western Association of Sociology & Anthropology, Vancouver, B.C., Canada.
Vanderveen, G.N.G. (1999). Stoere mannen, bange vrouwen? *Tijdschrift voor criminologie, 41*(1), 2-20.
Vanderveen, G.N.G. (2000). Reliable and Valid Fear: Measuring the Experience of Unsafety. Paper presented at the American Society of Criminology, San Francisco.
Vanderveen, G.N.G. (2001). Nederland vroeger veiliger? De veranderde beleving van onveiligheid. *Justitiële verkenningen, 27*(1), 34-48.
Vanderveen, G.N.G. (2002a). Beleving van veiligheid in de buurt: Relaties tussen persoon, buurt en samenleving. *Tijdschrift voor veiligheid en veiligheidszorg, 1*(1), 32-46.
Vanderveen, G.N.G. (2002b). Experiencing safety: Proposing a novel approach to scout differences between men and women in many countries. In: P. Nieuwbeerta (Ed.), *Crime Victimization in Comparative Perspective: Results from the International Crime Victims Survey 1989-2000* (pp. 335-351). The Hague: Boom.
Vanderveen, G.N.G. (2002c, May 30-June 1). Regarding Riskism: On the Primary Importance of Public Opinion on Safety and Security: On the Politics of Attitudinal Knowledge about Crime, Fear and Safety. Paper presented at the Law and Society Conference, Vancouver, British Columbia, Canada.
Vanderveen, G.N.G. (2004). Meten van veiligheid. In: E.R. Muller (Ed.), *Veiligheid* (pp. 71-123). The Hague: Kluwer.
Vanderveen, G.N.G., & Elffers, H. (2001). The Public Claims a Safe Society: Responses in Court. Paper presented at the European Association of Psychology and Law, Lissabon, Portugal.
Veenema, T.G., & Schroeder-Bruce, K. (2002). The aftermath of violence: Children, disaster, and posttraumatic stress disorder. *Journal of Pediatric Health Care, 16*(5), 235-244.
Verberk, G., Scheepers, P., & Felling, A. (1995). The Likert and the semantic differential technique applied to ethnocentric attitudes: A methodological comparison. In: J.J. Hox & W. Jansen (Eds.), *Measurement Problems in Social and Behavioral Research* (SCO-rapport 381, pp. 115-137). Amsterdam: SCO-Kohnstamm Instituut voor Onderzoek van Opvoeding en Onderwijs.

REFERENCES   415

Verrijn Stuart, C.A. (1918). The history and development of statistics in the Netherlands. In: J. Koren (Ed.), *The History of Statistics: Their Development and Progress in Many Countries: In Memoirs to Commemorate the Seventy Fifth Anniversary of the American Statistical Association* (pp. 429-444). New York: Macmillan.
Verschuren, P.J.M. (1994). *De probleemstelling van een onderzoek* (5th ed.). Utrecht: Het Spectrum.
Vijver, F. van der (1998). Introduction: Facet theory. *European Journal of Psychological Assessment, 14*(2).
Vijver, K. van der (1994). Politie en onveiligheidsgevoelens. *Tijdschrift voor ciminologie*(4), 316-329.
Viki, G.T., & Abrams, D. (2002). But she was unfaithful: Benevolent sexism and reactions to rape victims who violate traditional gender role expectations. *Sex Roles, 47*(5-6), 289-293.
Viklund, M.J. (2003). Trust and risk perception in Western Europe: A cross-national study. *Risk Analysis, 23*(4), 727-738.
Viscusi, W., Hakes, J., & Carlin, A. (1997). Measures of mortality risks. *Journal of Risk and Uncertainty, 14*(3), 213-233.
Vitelli, R., & Endler, N.S. (1993). Psychological determinants of fear of crime: A comparison of general and situational prediction models. *Personality and Individual Differences, 14*(1), 77-85.
Vlis, J.H. van der, & Heemstra, E.R. (1989). *Geschiedenis van kansrekening en statistiek.* Rijswijk, Netherlands: Pandata.
Vogel, B.L., & Meeker, J.W. (2001). Perceptions of crime seriousness in eight African-American communities: The influence of individual, environmental, and crime-based factors. *Justice Quarterly, 18*(2), 301-321.
Vogel, R.E., & Himelein, M.J. (1995). Dating and sexual victimization: An analysis of risk factors among precollege women. *Journal of Criminal Justice, 23*(2), 153-162.
Vrij, A., & Winkel, F.W. (1990). Misdaadverslaggeving en angst voor criminaliteit: De inhoud van de boodschap als informatiekenmerk. In: F.W. Winkel & A. van der Wurff (Eds.), *Angst voor criminaliteit* (pp. 221-235). Amsterdam: Swets & Zeitlinger.
Vrijling, J.K., Hengel, W. van, & Houben, R.J. (1998). Acceptable risk as a basis for design. *Reliability Engineering & System Safety, 59*(1), 141-150.

W

Wachs, E. (1988). *Crime-victim Stories: New York City's Urban Folklore.* Bloomington, IN: Indiana University Press.
Wåhlberg, A.E.A. (2001). The theoretical features of some current approaches to risk perception. *Journal of Risk Research, 4*(3), 237-250.
Wakefield, S., & Elliott, S.J. (2000). Environmental risk perception and well-being: Effects of the landfill siting process in two southern Ontario communities. *Social Science & Medicine, 50*(7-8), 1139-1154.
Walker, L.E., & Meloy, J.R. (1998). Stalking and domestic violence. In: J.R. Meloy (Ed.), *The Psychology of Stalking: Clinical and Forensic Perspectives* (pp. 139-161). San Diego: Academic Press.
Walker, M.A. (1994). Measuring concern about crime: Some interracial comparisons. *British Journal of Criminology, 34*(3), 366-378.
Walklate, S. (1995). Women as 'knowers' and the 'fear of crime' debate. In: S. Walklate *Gender and Crime* (pp. 55-79). Englewood Cliffs, NJ: Prentice-Hall.
Walklate, S. (1997). Risk and criminal victimization: A modernist dilemma? *British Journal of Criminology, 37*(1), 35-45.
Walklate, S. (1998a). Crime and community: Fear or trust? *British Journal of Sociology, 49*(4), 550-569.

Walklate, S.L. (1998b). Excavating the fear of crime: Fear, anxiety or trust? *Theoretical Criminology*, *2*(4), 403-418.

Walsh, J. (1996). *True Odds: How Risk Affects your Everyday Life* (1st ed.). Santa Monica, CA: Merritt.

Walsh, W.F., & Donovan, E.J. (1989). Private security and community policing: Evaluation and comment. *Journal of Criminal Justice, 17*(3), 187-197.

Wandersman, A., & Nation, M. (1998). Urban neighborhoods and mental health: Psychological contributions to understanding toxicity, resilience, and interventions. *American Psychologist, 53*(6), 647-656.

Warner, F. (1992). Introduction. In: Royal Society, *Risk: Analysis, Perception and Management* (pp. 1-12). London: The Royal Society.

Warner, F. (Ed.). (1981). *The Assessment and Perception of Risk: A Royal Society Discussion.* London: The Royal Society.

Warr, M. (1980). The accuracy of public beliefs about crime. *Social Forces, 59*(2), 456-470.

Warr, M. (1982). The accuracy of public beliefs about crime: Further evidence. *Criminology, 20*(2), 185-204.

Warr, M. (1984). Fear of victimization: Why are women and the elderly more afraid? *Social Science Quarterly, 65*, 681-702.

Warr, M. (1985). Fear of rape among urban women. *Social Problems, 32*(3), 238-250.

Warr, M. (1987). Fear of victimization and sensitivity to risk. *Journal of Quantitative Criminology, 3*(1), 29-46.

Warr, M. (1989). What is the perceived seriousness of crimes? *Criminology, 27*, 795-821.

Warr, M. (1990). Dangerous situations: Social context and fear of victimization. *Social Forces, 68*(3), 891-907.

Warr, M. (1992). Altruistic fear of victimization in households. *Social Science Quarterly, 73*(4), 723-736.

Warr, M., & Ellison, C.G. (2000). Rethinking social reactions to crime: Personal and altruistic fear in family households. *American Journal of Sociology, 106*(3), 551-578.

Warr, M., & Stafford, M. (1983). Fear of victimization: A look at the proximate causes. *Social Forces, 61*(4), 1033-1043.

Weber, M. (1949). *The Methodology of the Social Sciences.* New York: The Free Press.

Weiner, S.L. (1986). Tampons and toxic shock syndrome: Consumer protection or public confusion? In: H.M. Sapolsky (Ed.), *Consuming Fears: The Politics of Product Risks* (pp. 141-158). New York: Basic Books.

Weinrath, M. (1999). Violent victimization and fear of crime among Canadian Aboriginals. *Journal of Offender Rehabilitation, 30*(1-2), 107-120.

Weinrath, M., & Gartrell, J. (1996). Victimization and fear of crime. *Violence and Victims, 11*(3), 187-197.

Weinstein, N., & Klein, W. (1996). Unrealistic optimism: Present and future. *Journal of Social and Clinical Psychology, 15*(1), 1-8.

Weinstein, N.D. (1980). Unrealistic optimism about future life events. *Journal of Personality & Social Psychology, 39*(5), 806-820.

Weinstein, N.D. (1989). Effects of personal experience on self-protective behavior. *Psychological Bulletin, 105*(1), 31-50.

Weisz, M.G., & Earls, C.M. (1995). The effects of exposure to filmed sexual violence on attitudes toward rape. *Journal of Interpersonal Violence, 10*(1), 71-84.

Wesely, J.K., & Gaarder, E. (2004). The gendered 'nature' of the urban Ootdoors: Women negotiating fear of violence. *Gender and Society, 18*(5), 645-664.

Westervelt, S.D. (1998). *Shifting the Blame: How Victimization Became a Criminal Defense.* London: Rutgers University Press.

White, J.W., & Smith, P.H. (2001). *Developmental Antecedents of Violence Against Women: A Longitudinal Perspective* (No. NCJ 187775). Washington, DC: United States Department of Justice. National Institute of Justice.

White, J.W., & Smith, P.H, & Humphrey, J.A. (2001). Longitudinal study of violence against women: Victimization and perpetration among college students in a state-supported university in the United States, 1990-1995 [Computer file]. ICPSR version. Greensboro, NC: The University of North Carolina at Greensboro [producer], 2001. Ann Arbor, MI: Inter-university Consortium for Political and Social Research [distributor], 2002.

Wiegman, O., & Gutteling, J.M. (1995). Risk appraisal and risk communication: Some empirical data from the Netherlands reviewed. *Basic and Applied Social Psychology, 16*(1-2), 227-249.

Wilcox, P., Quisenberry, N., & Jones, S. (2003). The built environment and community crime risk interpretation. *Journal of Research in Crime and Delinquency, 40*(3), 322-345.

Wilcox Rountree, P. (1998). A reexamination of the crime-fear linkage. *Journal of Research in Crime and Delinquency, 35*(3), 341-372.

Wilcox Rountree, P., & Land, K.C. (1996a). Burglary victimization, perceptions of crime risk, and routine activities: A multilevel analysis across Seattle neighborhoods and census tracts. *Journal of Research in Crime and Delinquency, 33*(2), 147-180.

Wilcox Rountree, P., & Land, K.C. (1996b). Perceived risk versus fear of crime: Empirical evidence of conceptually distinct reactions in survey data. *Social Forces, 74*(4), 1353-1376.

Wilcox Rountree, P., & Warner, B. (1999). Social ties and crime: Is the relationship gendered? *Criminology,* 37 (34), 789-813.

Wildavsky, A., & Dake, K. (1990). Theories of risk perception: Who fears what and why. *Daedalus, 119*(4), 41-60.

Wiles, P., Simmons, J., & Pease, K. (2003). Crime victimization: Its extent and communication. *Journal of the Royal Statistical Society: Series A (Statistics in Society)* (Vol. 166, pp. 247-252): Blackwell.

Wilkins, L. (1980). Crime-police and criminal statistics. *British Journal of Criminology, 20*(4), 19-27.

Williams, B.L., Brown, S., Greenberg, M., & Kahn, M.A. (1999). Risk perception in context: The Savannah River Site Stakeholder Study. *Risk Analysis, 19*(6), 1019-1035.

Williams, J.S., Singh, B.K., & Singh, B.B. (1994). Urban youth, fear of crime, and resulting defensive actions. *Adolescence, 29*(114), 323-330.

Williams, P., & Dickinson, J. (1993). Fear of crime: Read all about it: The relationship between newspaper crime reporting and fear of crime. *British Journal of Criminology, 33*(1), 33-56.

Wilsem, J.A. van (1997). Slachtofferschap en onveiligheidsgevoelens. In: K. Wittebrood, J.A. Michon & M.J. ter Voert (Eds.), *Nederlanders over criminaliteit en rechtshandhaving* (pp. 55-66). Deventer: Gouda Quint.

Wilsem, J.A. van (2004). Crime victimization in cross-national perspective: An analysis of rates of theft, violence and vandalism across 27 countries. *European Journal of Criminology*(1), 89-109.

Wilson, J.Q., & Kelling, G.L. (1982). Broken windows. *The Atlantic Monthly,* February, 46-52.

Wilton, R.D. (1998). The constitution of difference: Space and psyche in landscapes of exclusion. *Geoforum, 29*(2), 173-185.

Wiltz, C.J. (1982). Fear of crime, criminal victimization and elderly blacks. *Phylon, 43*(4), 283-294.

Winkel, F.W. (1998). Fear of crime and criminal victimization: Testing a theory of psychological incapacitation of the 'stressor' based on downward comparison processes. *British Journal of Criminology, 38*(3), 473-484.

Winkel, F.W., & Steenstra, S. (1987). Voorlichting over seksueel geweld: Een instrument tot beinvloeding van aangiftebeslissingen. *Tijdschrift voor criminologie, 29*(2/3), 109-127.

Wise, S., & Stanley, L. (1987). *Georgie Porgie: Sexual Harassment in Everyday Life.* London; New York: Pandora.

Wittebrood, K. (2001). Criminaliteit. In: Sociaal en CP & T. Roes (Eds.), *De sociale staat van Nederland 2001* (pp. 169-193). The Hague: Sociaal en Cultureel Planbureau.

Wittebrood, K., Michon, J.A., & Voert, M.J. ter (Eds.). (1997). *Nederlanders over criminaliteit en rechtshandhaving.* Deventer: Gouda Quint.

Wittebrood, K., & Nieuwbeerta, P. (2000). Criminal victimization during one's life course: The effects of previous victimization and patterns of routine activities. *Journal of Research in Crime and Delinquency, 37*(1), 91-122.

Wittebrood, K., & Voert, M.J. ter (1997). *Netherlands Survey on Criminality and Law Enforcement 1996* (Technical Report). Leiden: NISCALE.

Wittmann, W.W. (1988). Multivariate reliability theory: Principles of symmetry and successful validation strategies. In: J.R. Nesselroade & R.B. Cattell (Eds.), *Handbook of Multivariate Experimental Psychology* (2nd ed., pp. 505-560). New York: Plenum Press.

WODC (Wetenschappelijk Onderzoek- en Documentatiecentrum) (1999). *Zinloos geweld.* The Hague: Wetenschappelijk Onderzoek- en Documentatiecentrum.

Wohl, A.S. (1983). *Endangered Lives: Public Health in Victorian Britain.* London: J.M. Dent.

Woollacott, M. (1998b). Risky business, Safety. In: J. Franklin (Ed.), *The Politics of Risk Society* (pp. 47-49). Malden, Mass.: Polity Press.

Wordfocus. (n.d.). *The Blind Men and the Elephant: by John Godfrey Saxe.* Retrieved from: http://www.wordfocus.com/word-act-blindmen.html [18 May 2005]

Wöstmann, M., & Bunt, H. van de (1987). Verbalisering van politieoptreden bij vrouwenmishandeling. *Tijdschrift voor criminologie, 29*(2/3), 155-167.

Wright, G. (2002). Game theory, game theorists, university students, role-playing and forecasting ability. *International Journal of Forecasting, 18*, 383-387.

Wright, G., Bolger, F., & Rowe, G. (2002). An empirical test of the relative validity of expert and lay judgments of risk. *Risk Analysis, 22*(6), 1107-1122.

Wright, J.P., Cullen, F.T., & Blankenship, M.B. (1995). The social construction of corporate violence: Media coverage of the imperial food-products fire. *Crime & Delinquency, 41*(1), 20-36.

Wurff, A. van der (1990). Angst voor criminaliteit: Een begripsbepaling. In: F.W. Winkel & A. van der Wurff (Eds.), *Angst voor Criminaliteit.* Amsterdam: Swets & Zeitlinger.

Wurff, A.W.I.M. van der (1992). *Aard en achtergronden van onveiligheidsgevoelens in de woonomgeving.* University of Amsterdam, Amsterdam.

Y

Yanchar, S.C., & Slife, B.D. (1997). Pursuing unity in a fragmented psychology: Problems and prospects. *Review of General Psychology, 1*(3), 235-255.

Yanich, D. (2001). Location, location, location: Urban and suburban crime on local TV news. *Journal of Urban Affairs, 23*(3&4), 221-241.

Yarwood, R. (2001). Crime and policing in the British countryside: Some agendas for contemporary geographical research. *Sociologia Ruralis, 41*(2).

Yarwood, R., & Edwards, B. (1999). Voluntary action in rural areas: The case of neighbourhood watch. *Journal of Rural Studies, 11*(4), 447-459.

Yeoh, B.S.A., & Yeow, P.L. (1997). Where women fear to tread: Images of danger and the effects of fear of crime in Singapore. *GeoJournal, 43*(3), 273-286.

Yiend, J., & Mathews, A. (2001). Anxiety and attention to threatening pictures. *Quarterly Journal of Experimental Psychology, 54A*(3), 665-681.

Young, F.W. (1981). Quantitative analysis of qualitative data. *Psychometrika, 46*, 357-388.

Z

Zani, B., Cicognani, E., & Albanesi, C. (2001). Adolescents' sense of community and feeling of unsafety in the urban environment. *Journal of Community & Applied Social Psychology, 11*(6), 475-489.

Zaret, D. (2000). *Origins of Democratic Culture: Printing, Petitions, and the Public Sphere in Early-modern England.* Princeton, New Jersey: Princeton University Press.

Zee, K.I. van der, Bakker, A.B., & Buunk, B.P. (2001). Burnout and reactions to social comparison information among volunteer caregivers. *Anxiety Stress and Coping, 14*(4), 391-410.

Zeller, R.A., & Carmines, E.G. (1980). *Measurement in the Social Sciences: The Link between Theory and Data.* Cambridge: Cambridge University Press.

Zhang, L., Welte, J.W., & Wieczorek, W.F. (2001). Deviant lifestyle and crime victimization. *Journal of Criminal Justice, 29*(2), 133-143.

Ziegler, R., & Mitchell, D.B. (2003). Aging and fear of crime: An experimental approach to an apparent paradox. *Experimental Aging Research, 29*(2), 173-187.

Zion, R.J. (1978). Reducing crime and fear of crime in downtown Cleveland. *Victimology: An International Journal, 3*(3), 341.

Zuijlen, R.W. van (2004). Veiligheid als begrip: Fundering van de rechtsorde. In: E.R. Muller (Ed.), *Veiligheid: Studies over inhoud, organisatie en maatregelen* (pp. 7-24). Alphen aan den Rijn: Kluwer.

Zvekic, U., & Del Frate, A.A. (1995). Criminal victimization in the developing world. *Journal of Criminal Justice, 23*(6), 573.

Samenvatting

Deze samenvatting geeft een beknopt overzicht van dit boek dat het resultaat is van mijn promotieonderzoek naar de conceptualisering ('wat is het') en operationalisering ('hoe meet je het') van het concept onveiligheidsbeleving, in de Engelstalige literatuur aangeduid met de term *fear of crime*. Een meer gedetailleerde synopsis per hoofdstuk vindt u in de *topic tree* die een overzicht geeft van de onderwerpen en de tabel met belangrijkste conclusies aan het eind van elk hoofdstuk.

De belangrijkste doelstellingen van het onderzoek waarvan verslag is gedaan zijn:
- Het geven van een overzicht van de studies die gedaan zijn op dit gebied en de huidige stand van zaken met betrekking tot de conceptualisering en operationalisering evalueren.
- Het verbinden van dit onderzoeksterrein met de disciplines die vanuit een ander perspectief dit concept en aspecten daarvan bestuderen.
- Het ontwikkelen van een conceptueel-analytisch kader, gebaseerd op een interdisciplinaire analyse waarin de sociaal-politieke achtergrond en context van de kernbegrippen in aanmerking wordt genomen.
- Het ontwikkelen van duidelijker onderlegde operationalisaties en uiteindelijk meer betrouwbare en valide meetinstrumenten.

Dit boek geeft dan ook een overzicht van de historische ontwikkeling van het concept, waarbij ik zowel inga op de sociaal-politieke achtergrond, de betekenis(sen), alsmede de diverse manieren van meten. Hiervoor heb ik de uitgebreide literatuur, waaronder de grijze literatuur, surveys en databestanden in kaart gebracht (hoofdstuk 2). Uit dit overzicht en de secundaire analyses van enkele representatieve databestanden blijkt dat de huidige stand van zaken met betrekking tot de conceptualisering en operationalisering van *fear of crime* voor verbetering vatbaar is (hoofdstuk 3). Het concept is overduidelijk meerdimensionaal, bestaat uit meerdere aspecten en het meten van één enkel aspect is niet hetzelfde als het meten van meerdere aspecten.

In hoofdstuk 4 tot en met hoofdstuk 8 is het conceptueel-analytisch kader geschetst. De betekenis van *fear of crime* is bestudeerd door de (historische) ontwikkeling van het concept te analyseren, zoals die gereflecteerd wordt in taal van individuen, media, anekdotes, politieke stukken en beleidsmaatregelen. Drie concepten zijn daarbij relevant: slachtofferschap (van criminaliteit), risico (en de perceptie daarvan) en angst (voor criminaliteit). De opkomst van statistieken en de slachtofferenquête, die bijna altijd een instrumentele en/of politieke rol hebben vervuld en nog steeds vervullen voor de diverse overheden, zijn noodzakelijke voorwaarden geweest voor het ontstaan van het begrip; voordat de eerste slachtofferenquête werd afgenomen, bestond het begrip nog niet. De vragen die in de eerste (Amerikaanse) slachtofferenquêtes zijn gesteld, zijn tot op heden gekopieerd en gebruikt in vele landen. Deze items, oorspronkelijk bedoeld als publieke opinievragen, zijn later gebruikt als meetinstrument voor het meer abstracte theoretische concept *fear of crime*. In het licht van de slachtofferenquêtes en de instrumentele rol daarvan, verwijst *fear of crime* naar de problematische gevolgen van criminaliteit in het dagelijks leven van mensen.

Wanneer het voor de betekenis van *fear of crime* relevante *crime* en vooral slachtofferschap is ontward, blijkt dat er meerdere interpretaties van de betekenis van *fear of crime* zijn, afhankelijk van de betekenis die men toekent aan *crime* en 'slachtofferschap'. De gebruikelijkste interpretaties zijn het oudst, simpelst en populairst, ook al zijn ze minder valide dan de meer geavanceerde interpretaties (zie tabel 6.3 en 6.4). *Fear of crime* heeft niet zozeer te maken met criminaliteit *an sich*, maar vooral met de veelvoorkomende en gender-gerelateerde stereotype beelden van daders en slachtoffers, de daaraan gekoppelde attributie van schuld en verantwoordelijkheid en de denkbare mogelijkheid dat iemand zelf of een geliefde ooit overkomt wat het stereotype slachtoffer overkomen is.

Voor een verder begrip van de betekenis van *fear of crime* is risico en de perceptie daarvan relevant, en daarmee andere disciplines die focussen op gepercipieerde risico's van bijvoorbeeld kernenergie en gentechnologie. Analoog aan onderzoek naar *fear of crime* keren twee thema's regelmatig terug in studies naar gepercipieerde risico's: ten eerste de discrepantie tussen de 'werkelijke' risico's en de 'overdreven' of 'irrationele' angst en ten tweede de breuk met het verleden: er is nu meer/het is nu anders. Ook resultaten van empirisch onderzoek naar risicoperceptie tonen diverse analogieën met de resultaten van *fear of crime*-studies. *Fear of crime* en risicoperceptie lijken grotendeels te overlappen. Hoewel *fear of crime* en risicoperceptie beide instrumenteel van karakter zijn, is de politieke symboliek van *fear of crime* veel meer uitgesproken. *Fear of crime* (onveiligheidsbeleving) wordt te pas en te onpas gebruikt als argument voor repressieve en punitieve maatregelen. *Fear of crime* kent vele betekenissen, waarbij het politieke symbool onderscheiden kan worden van het psychologische construct. Angst (voor criminaliteit), de *fear*-component in *fear of crime*, slaat niet zozeer op *experiential fear*, de 'echte' beleving van angst, maar op *propositional fear*. Onveiligheidsbeleving of *fear of crime* is propositioneel van aard en refereert aan de aanwezigheid van vreemden, inbreuk van het eigen domein en de stad.

Het conceptueel-analytisch kader heeft als achtergrond gediend voor de ontwikkelde operationalisaties. Twee strategieën hebben geleid tot meer betrouwbare en valide meetinstrumenten die in dit boek gepresenteerd worden. De eerste strategie bouwt voort op bestaande indicatoren en verbetert deze tot vijf meetinstrumenten voor de belangrijkste aspecten, met alle voor- en nadelen van dien (hoofdstuk 9). De tweede strategie gebruikt een semantische differentiaal-format waarbij mensen gevraagd wordt begrippen te beoordelen op een reeks attributen of adjectieven. Na validering levert dit een nieuw meetinstrument op, dat het mogelijk maakt zowel betekenis (propositioneel) en evaluatie van begrippen, alsook de attitude te meten (hoofdstuk 10). Het recept voor valide en betrouwbare meting en richtlijnen die helpen bij de beslissing wanneer welk instrument te gebruiken, zijn te vinden in hoofdstuk 11.

Index

Accident....51, 99, 147n, **152-154**, 157, 172, 175, 177, 179-181, 187n 272-273, *274*, 296-297

Affective modality *see also* evaluation....40, 48, **53-57**, 259, 276, 281

Age....231, 265, 304

Altruistic fear *see also* concern about others....**54-55, 123-124**, 199, 253, 259, 274, 352

Assault *see* violence, sexual assault

Attitude scales....265, 289, 295, 299, **300-309**

Attitudes....4, 13, **18-19**, 35, 40n, 41, 95, 102, 169, 179, 202, 230n, 289-290

Attribution (of blame, of responsibility)....110, 114-115, 125-126, 127n, 138-140, 143, 147, 155, 170, 177, 179, **181-185**, 187, 189, 289, 314

Behavioural modality.... *see* conative modality

Blame (culpability, deservedness) *see also* attribution....113-115, 134, 177, 180, **182-184**, 273, 287

Broken-windows-thesis....14, **43**, 206, 211-212

Cognitive modality....40, **48-52**, *276*

Community decline model....13-16, 42

Conative modality....**40,** 48, 57-58, **276**

Concepts, classification....30n, **38-41**, 87, 92, **270-275**, 282-300

Concepts, meaning of....65, 86, **91-94, 212-213, 222, 265-269**, 281

Conceptualisation....5, 7, **28-30,** 40, 53-54, 59n, **60-61**, 83, **86-88**, 92, 95-223, 328

Concern (about victimisation, crime)....9-10, 53-54, 72, **78-81**, 101, 169, 178, 192, 202, 208-209, 216, 222, 252, 259, 273-274, **208-209**, 255, 293

Concern about others *see also* altruistic fear....62, 273-274, 293

Crime....Infra, 9-10, 41, 134, 143, 146, 175-182, 199, 208-209, 270, 281, 296-298

Crime-causes-fear model....14-15, **41-43**, 109, 123

Crime stories....113, 115-117, 124, **129-133,** 135-136, 139-141, 182-183, 204, 217

Crime trends....**48-50,** 99, 128n, 254

Criminal statistics....**95-101, 104-107**, 133, 157, 159, 162, 169, 199-200, 203, 227

Criminology....4, 35n, 60n, 88n, 105, 147, 153, 162, 184, *192*

Danger....10, 74, 119, 130, 151, 153, 155, 161, 166-167, 169-171, 174-175, 270-272, *274*, 281, **294-296**, 300, 302, 205, 218, 222, 308

Dark number....96, 101-106, 157

Defensibility....216, 218, 270-271, *274*

Democracy....170, **202-203**

Democracy-at-work-thesis....202, **206-207**, 210

Differential sensitivity to risk *see also* gender differences....120

Discontinuity (of risk)....164-165, 190, *193*

Emotions....4, **18**, 40-41, 199, 214, **218-**219, 232, 287, 282, 292

Essential characteristics of role & event schema ideal victim....127, **138-142, 182**, 273

Evaluation *see also* attitudes....18, 40, 214, 267n, 281-284, 287-289, 300

Experiental fear....215-216, 218, 270

Fault (guilt)....273, *275*

Fear (anxiety)....64, 93, 118-119, 124, 126, 165, 172, 192, 194, 199, **213-223**, 230n, 242, 253, 268, 270, 275, 277, 281, 293, 305

Fear of crime....infra, 4-5, 12, **17-18**, 39-41, 60, 86, 93, 106, 112, 116, 118, 120, 142-143, 146, 176-177, 188-193, **197-224**, 260, 270, 288-289, 311-314

Fear-victimisation paradox....7, 42, 64, 109, 143, 156-160, 162, 164, *193*, 199, 214

Feeling-safe-item....45, *46*, **55-57, 62-64,** *67*, 78, 96, *101*, 102, 104-106, 199, 226, 228, 231-233, 240-250, 252, 260-261, 302, 307, 355

Films (movies)....127-128, **135-137**, 139, 222

Gender differences....44, 54, 64-65, **115-119**, 136, 139, 142, 144, 159, 188, 217, 231-232, 240, **298-300**, 304, 307, **319-320**

Grounded theory....5, 17, 23, 34-35, 85, 225, 266

Hazard....9-10, 148-152, 155, 161, 163, 165, 168, 171, **174-190**, 218, 271, 273, **296-297**

Ideal victim....110, 114-115, 117, 126-127, 129-130, 136-137, **138-142**, 178, 180-183, 186, 189, 217, 273

Images (of crime, of victims)....92, 115, **124-141**, 144, 180-182, 191

Imaginable victimisation....41-43, 92, 110, 120, **124**, 138, *143*, 182, 185

Inattention (carelessness)....273

Indirect victimisation....41n, 42, 92, 121, **123-124**, *143*, 156, 164, 211, 234

Insecurity....168-169, 209, 211, 272, *275*, 295, 305

Interdisciplinary research....3-6, 90, 147-148, 160, 164, 166, 188, *319*

Involvement....**39-40**

(Ir)rationality of risk perception....7, **160-165**, *193*

Likert-(type)scales....59, 226, 229, 265, 289, 299-308

Literature review....**23-38**, 83, 335-337, 340-351

Measurement instruments....5, 17, *26,* 59-61, 64-65, 69, 82, **225-319**, 352-361

Media (including newspapers)....8-9, 19, 91, 115n, 117, 124-125, 127-129, 137-138, 162-164, 191, 199, **203**, 253

Natural disaster....155, 270, 272-273, *275*, 293n, 296-297

Newsworthiness *see* media
Operationalisation....2-3, 21, 26, 28, **30-61**, *67*, 74, 83, 86n, 87n, 191, 225, 251-252, 259-262, 266, 313-314, 317n, 328
Outrage (outrage factors)....164, 178-179, 181-186, 193
Perceived risk....7-8, 40, 48, **52**, 60-62, **75-77**, 120, 142, 147, 155, 160-165, 171, 174-179, 180-181, **190-195**, 252-253, 255-256, 258, 266-267, 273, 281, 307, 354
Perceptually contemporaneous offences....120
Police....78, 100-103, 183-184, 204-205, 209-210
Politics....8-9, 88, 97-100, 103n, 105, 152, 169-170, 199-212
Precautions....57-59, 114, 158-159, 270-271, *275*, 302
Prevention....103, 154, **156-160**, 187n
Property crime (burglary, theft, etc.).... 51-53, 59, 61, 72, 75-81, 110, 112, 114, 126, 128, 144, 199, 208
Propositional fear....215, **219-221**, 270
Protection *see also* security....36n, 58, 144, 159, 270-271, *275*, 299-300
Psychology....4, 7, 11, 35n, 60-61, 100, 139, 147, 155, *192*, 193, 213-221
Public opinion...19, 100-103, 160-, 190, **199-205**, 228
Rape *see also* sexual assault....43, 53, 59, 89-90, 113, **115-120**, 130, 134, 136, **139-141**, 183, 186, 231, 270-271, *275*, 285, 292-293, **297-298**, 305
Reactive fear....215, **270**
Reliability....26, **31**, 62, 64-65, 82, 96, 228, *261*, 266
Responsibility *see also* attribution....114-115, 139-141, 155, 183-184, 288
Risk, *see also* perceived risk....9-10, 40, 60, 75n, 92-93, 142, **147-195**, 258, 268, 270-273, *275*, 293, **295-296**
Risk management....17, 60n, 147n, 150-159, 166-167
Risk society....152, 154, 162, 165-167, **169-171**, 184, *193*, 272
Routine activities of lifestyle theory 157-158, 160n
Safety *see also* feeling-safe item....12, 46, 78, 114, 125, 153, 157, 169-174, 202, 206, 208-209, 218-220, 234-240, 252, 255-259, 270, 272, 275, 277, 292, **294-295**, 302, 305, **308-309**
Schema, *see also* Images....91, 119, **139-143**, 181, 267, 269
Secondary victimisation *see* indirect victimisation
Security....*59*, 144, 153, 159, 219, 272

Semantic differential format....21, 61, 226, 230, **265-309, 357, 361**
Semantic differential inventory....**251-262, 276-304**
Seriousness of the consequences (of crime)....**50-52**, 76, 111, 120, 126n, 144, 159, 191, 252, 255, 302, 353
Sexual assault....45, 75-77, 79, 113, 117-119, *143*
Sexual violence....89, 111-113, 115-119, 136, 138, 142, 157
Shopping area study....**71-74**
Social comparison....124-127, *143*
Social concern *see also* concern, crime....215, 219, 273-275
Social construction 8, 86, **88-90**, 113, 149, 153, 198, 214n
Social control....15, 71, 97, 118n, 131, 208, **217-**
Social disorganisation....13-16, 43, 71, 133
Social structure....13-15, 41, 43-44
Socialisation....41, 43-46, 65, 116, 231
Sociology....4, 147, 179, 100, *192*
Stalking....**111-112**, 118, 158n
Statistical analyses....**69-84**, 235-239, 242-249, 255-259, 278-289, 338-339, 358-360
Street smarts....36n, 130-131, 155, 183, 217
Subway study....44n, 120-122, 231n, **232-240**
Surveys *see also* victim surveys....19, 37, **32, 95-100**, 226
Systemic crime model....13-16, 42
Television *see also* media....124, 127-128, **134-135**, 139, 222
Terrorism/terrorist attack....**189**, 206, 213
Threat....74-78, 119, 122, 149, 155, 171, 174, *178*, 218, 240-250, 280, 282, 287
Trust....132, 148, 161, 169-174, 183-184, 191
Unsafety *see also* safety....201, 234-240, 268, 272, **294-295**, 299, 305, 308
Urban (city) life vs. rural idyll....
Urban myths/urban legends (including metropolitan crime myth)....91, **129-133**, 139
Validity....26, **31**, 47, **64-65**, 83, 228, 266
Victim surveys *see also* surveys....37, 48-52, 96-106, 113, 143-144, 198-199, 226-
Victimisation....42, 45, 75-77, 92-93, 156-157, **100-104, 109-146**, 234, 253, 255-256, 259, 353-354
Victimology....4, 153, *192*
Vigilantism (*eigenrichting*)....8, 103, **202-203**, 213
Vignette study....121-123, 232, **240-250**
Violence....12, 51, 59, 75, 79-80, 112-114, 119, 122, 127-129, 134-138, 143, 144, 157, 171, 174, 202, 211, 218, 222, 270-271, *275*, 293n, **297-298**, 305, 308
Vulnerability....43, 126-127, 136, 168, 216, 271, *275*
Women *see also* gender differences....44-45, 64, 90, 111, 114, 116-120, 131-136, 138, 140, 142, 157-159, 173, 213, 217, 231, 299-300
Zero tolerance....14n, 43n, 200, 206-212